Clarendon Law Series

Edited by
PAUL CRAIG

CLARENDON LAW SERIES

Discrimination Law (3rd edition)
SANDRA FREDMAN

The United Kingdom Constitution: An
Introduction
NW BARBER

War
ANDREW CLAPHAM

Land Law (3rd edition)
ELIZABETH COOKE

Competition Law and Antitrust
DAVID J GERBER

Introduction to Company Law (3rd edition)
PAUL DAVIES

The Conflict of Laws (4th edition)
ADRIAN BRIGGS

Bentham and the Common Law Tradition
(2nd edition)
GERALD POSTEMA

Law and Values in the European Union
STEPHEN WEATHERILL

Personal Property Law (4th edition)
MICHAEL BRIDGE

The Idea of Arbitration
JAN PAULSSON

The Anthropology of Law
FERNANDA PIRIE

Law and Gender
JOANNE CONAGHAN

The Concept of Law (3rd edition)
HLA HART
With a Postscript edited by
Penelope A Bulloch and Joseph Raz
With an Introduction and Notes by
Leslie Green

Administrative Law (5th edition)
PETER CANE

An Introduction to the Law of Trusts
(3rd edition)
SIMON GARDNER

Natural Law and Natural Rights (2nd edition)
JOHN FINNIS

Employment Law (2nd edition)
HUGH COLLINS

International Law
VAUGHAN LOWE

Civil Liberties
CONOR GEARTY

Intellectual Property
MICHAEL SPENCE

Policies and Perceptions of Insurance Law in
the Twenty-First Century (2nd edition)
MALCOLM CLARKE

Philosophy of Private Law
WILLIAM LUCY

Law in Modern Society
DENIS GALLIGAN

An Introduction to Tort Law (2nd edition)
TONY WEIR

Equity (2nd edition)
SARAH WORTHINGTON

Atiyah's Introduction to the Law of Contract
(6th edition)
STEPHEN A SMITH AND PS ATIYAH

Unjust Enrichment (2nd edition)
PETER BIRKS

An Introduction to Family Law (2nd edition)
GILLIAN DOUGLAS

Criminal Justice
LUCIA ZEDNER

Contract Theory
STEPHEN A SMITH

Discrimination Law

Third Edition

SANDRA FREDMAN

Professor of the Laws of the British Commonwealth and the USA,
University of Oxford

Professorial Fellow, Pembroke College, Oxford
FBA, KC (Hon)

OXFORD
UNIVERSITY PRESS

OXFORD
UNIVERSITY PRESS

Great Clarendon Street, Oxford, OX2 6DP,
United Kingdom

Oxford University Press is a department of the University of Oxford.
It furthers the University's objective of excellence in research, scholarship,
and education by publishing worldwide. Oxford is a registered trade mark of
Oxford University Press in the UK and in certain other countries

First Edition published in 2002
Second Edition published in 2011
Third Edition published in 2022

Impression: 1

Published in the United States of America by Oxford University Press
198 Madison Avenue, New York, NY 10016, United States of America

British Library Cataloguing in Publication Data

Data available

Library of Congress Control Number: 2022945195

ISBN 978–0–19–885408–1 (hbk.)
ISBN 978–0–19–885927–7 (pbk.)

DOI: 10.1093/oso/9780198854081.001.0001

Printed and bound by
CPI Group (UK) Ltd, Croydon, CR0 4YY

This book is dedicated to my children, Jem, Kim, and Dan, to my husband Alan, and to my parents, Naomi and Mike.

Preface to the Third Edition

In the decade since the second edition of this book, we have witnessed graver challenges to the principle of equality than we could have imagined, denting the ideal of progress which imbued earlier editions. The global Covid-19 pandemic exposed and deepened existing inequalities, patterned along familiar lines of gender, race, disability, poverty, age, and regional differences. In the meanwhile, climate change has become an unavoidable reality. Not surprisingly, those who are already disadvantaged are most intensely affected.

This comes together with a significant weakening of the legal commitment to redressing inequality. In the US, the new right-wing majority of the Supreme Court puts many of the gains to substantive equality in the jurisprudence of the US in peril. At the same time, the UK's withdrawal from the EU removed the scaffolding for the right to equality which the EU had provided for many decades. Although the Equality Act 2010 remains intact for the meanwhile, political commitment to the Human Rights Act is fragile. In South Africa, the constitutional promise of equality is no more than a mirage, with South Africa showing the biggest inequality in income distribution worldwide in 2020.

There have been some positive signs. Courts in several jurisdictions, including Canada, India, and South Africa, have recognized and affirmed substantive equality. In 2015, the world committed itself to 'Transforming the World: The 2030 Agenda for Sustainable Development', setting out an ambitious plan of action which includes reducing inequality within and among countries and achieving gender equality and empowering all women and girls. Yet, as 2030 grows ever closer, the hope of achieving these ambitions is receding.

These setbacks make the quest for the right to equality more important than ever. This book uses the comparative method to cast light on the major issues in equality in several jurisdictions. As in previous editions, the aim is to contribute to the search for equality, not by providing the answers but by articulating the questions. Drawing together the major themes confronting courts and policymakers in the UK, EU, USA, Canada, South Africa, India, and under the European Convention on Human Rights, the book seeks to sharpen our understanding of our own jurisdiction, and suggests alternative means of accomplishing stated aims. Courts and lawmakers face similar challenges across all these jurisdictions, and there is increasing cross-pollination of legal concepts. At the same time, equality must be understood within a specific legal, social, and political context. The aim is therefore to find a conception of equality which is both generalizable and context sensitive. This edition deepens and extends the analysis of these historical and social factors in each jurisdiction in relation to the main grounds of discrimination. Also crucial is to examine not just the conceptual apparatus of equality law, but how to make the right to equality effective. This edition expands the analysis of models of enforcement, including strategic litigation and proactive measures.

I owe heartfelt thanks to a great many people for their help and support in writing the third edition. Special thanks go to Meghan Campbell, who is always ready to comment on my drafts; my research assistants, Rishika Sahgal and Aradhana Cherupara Vadekkethil; my doctoral students for the many challenging and passionate discussions we have in our research group; and my faculty colleagues and graduate law students for their input and interest in our courses in comparative equality and human rights law. The loss of Bob Hepple is still keenly felt, but his friendship and support over many years continue to sustain me. I would also like to thank OUP, and especially Arokia Anthuvan Rani, for their help in steering what has been a longer process than I had expected.

Ultimately, my deepest appreciation is to my husband and my children, who have grown to adulthood in the past decade. In this complicated and challenging world, their commitment and passion not only for justice and equality, but also for care and empathy, are my greatest inspiration.

Sandra Fredman
Oxford, October 2022

Preface to the Second Edition

In the ten years since this book first came out, much has changed and much has stayed the same. Increasingly sophisticated legal tools have emerged for addressing inequality; yet true equality remains elusive. Indeed, by paying more attention to inequalities, we are more aware of their scale. On the one hand, the legal landscape in the UK has been altered dramatically by the Equality Act 2010, which draws together the confusing plethora of anti-discrimination legislation which had grown piece-meal over the years. On the other hand, the social landscape is being ravaged by cuts to public services, making gains in the equality field appear increasingly fragile. Simultaneously, the legitimacy of human rights is being challenged in some political quarters.

As in the first edition, this book aims to contribute to the search for equality, not by providing answers, but by articulating the questions. The second edition deepens and extends the use of comparative law, drawing particularly on equality law in the USA, Canada, South Africa, and India. European Union law is also of central importance, as is that of the European Convention on Human Rights. Similar questions are asked across all these jurisdictions, and there is increasing cross-pollination of legal concepts. Comparative law sharpens our understanding of our own jurisdiction, enriches the debate as to the purposes of equality law, and suggests alternative means of accomplishing stated aims. At the same time, comparative law carries with it important challenges: equality must always be understood within the specific legal, social, and political context of a particular jurisdiction. The aim is therefore to find a conception of equality which is both generalizable and context sensitive.

I owe very special thanks to a great many people for their help and support in writing the second edition. Special thanks go to Bob Hepple, as ever, for his friendship and support over many years, to Paul Craig, as editor of the Clarendon series and colleague, and to my two research assistants, Natasa Mavronicola and Aaron Rathmell, for their sterling background research. I remain indebted too to the former editor of the series, the late Peter Birks, whose warmth, friendship, and unstinting support remain as vivid in memory as in life. As ever, I have benefited enormously from ongoing discussions with my students, both graduate and under-graduate, and with colleagues in Oxford, in India, in South Africa, and all over the world. I would also like to thank my publishers, OUP, and particularly Gwen Booth, Natasha Knight, Emma Hawes, and Joy Ruskin-Tompkins.

As ever, my deepest appreciation remains for my husband Alan, my children, Jem, Kim, and Dan, my mother Naomi, and my late father Mike. It is from them that I draw inspiration, energy, and hope for a future with fewer inequalities. I dedicate this book to them, with love beyond words.

Oxford
March 2011

Preface to the First Edition

Despite the widespread belief in equality, we live in a world which is marred by deep inequalities. As a white South African Jewish woman, an immigrant and member of an ethnic minority, I personally have experienced discrimination in many guises. I have been both a victim and, involuntarily, one of the perpetrator class. Growing up in a society twisted by the systematic racism of apartheid, with the scars of the Holocaust still fresh, and in a deeply sexist world, I discovered both the central value, and the elusiveness of equality. This book aims to contribute to the search for equality, not by providing answers, but by articulating the questions. It introduces the reader to the controversies we confront as soon as we try to translate our ideal of equality into legal form, and, more difficult still, into social and political reality. The book does not attempt to provide a single solution, but points to a range of possible responses, drawing on the experience of different jurisdictions, and locating the issues firmly within their appropriate historical and political frame. It is to be hoped that the reader will come away both with renewed faith in the ideal of equality, and with a heightened sensitivity to the problems to be faced.

There are a great many people to whom I owe very special thanks for their help and support in writing this book. My thanks are especially due to Peter Birks, as editor and colleague, who has been unstinting in his support for the project and the outcome. My special thanks too to Bob Hepple, not only for his detailed comments on this book, but also for the friendship and inspiration he has provided over many years. I could not have written this book without the formative input of Chris McCrudden, Mark Freedland, and Paul Davies, who have always been immensely generous in sharing their thoughts and ideas. I have also benefited enormously from ongoing discussions with many students and colleagues from all over the world. My two research assistants, Christopher Stothers and Suzanne Lambert, gave invaluable assistance in putting the final touches to the manuscript. I owe too a particular debt to the Arts and Humanities Research Board for their assistance in funding this project.

I dedicate this work to my husband Alan, to my children, Jem, Kim, and Dan, and to the hope that the world of their adulthood will be one with fewer inequalities than that of their childhood. I dedicate this book too to my mother, Naomi Fredman, and to my late father, Mike Fredman, whose courage in facing illness and death have added a deep poignancy to the process of writing it.

Sandra Fredman
September 2001

Contents

Table of Cases

Table of Legislation and Statutory Materials

1

Equality

Concepts and Controversies

... to labour in the face of the majestic equality of the law, which
forbids the rich as well as the poor to sleep under bridges, to beg
in the streets, and to steal bread.

Anatole France (1897)[1]

We hold these truths to be sacred and undeniable, that all men
are created equal and independent, that from that equal creation
they derive rights inherent and inalienable, among which are the
preservation of life, and liberty, and the pursuit of happiness.

Thomas Jefferson (c 1775)[2]

Equality as an ideal shines brightly in the galaxy of liberal aspirations. Nor is
it just an ideal. Attempts to capture it in legal form are numerous and often
grand: all human rights documents, both international and domestic, include an equality guarantee, and this is bolstered in many jurisdictions with
statutory provisions. This suggests that we all have an intuitive grasp of the
meaning of the right to equality and what it entails. Yet the more closely we
examine it, the more its meaning shifts. Is the right to equality captured by
the familiar aphorism that likes should be treated alike? This appears both
morally irrefutable and straightforward. But the initial logic fades as soon
as we begin to ask further questions. When can we say that one person is so
'like' another that they should be treated alike? For centuries, it was openly
asserted that women were not 'like' men and therefore deserved fewer rights,
and this remains true in some countries in the world. The same apparent

---

[1] A France, *Le Lys rouge* (Calmann-Lévy 1927) 106.
[2] "'Rough Draft' of the American Declaration of Independence' in JP Boyd (ed), *Papers of
Thomas Jefferson*, vol 1 (Princeton UP 1950) 423.

Discrimination Law. Third Edition. Sandra Fredman, Oxford University Press. © Sandra Fredman 2022.
DOI: 10.1093/oso/9780198854081.003.0001

logic has been used to deny rights to slaves, Black people,[3] indigenous people, marginalized ethnicities, linguistic, religious, and other minorities, as well as to people on account of their age, disability, sexual orientation, gender identity, sex characteristics, and migration status.

And even if we can agree on whether two individuals are relevantly alike, we may still have doubts as to whether they should always be treated alike. Experience has shown that equal treatment can, in practice, perpetuate inequalities. As Anatole France graphically depicts in the earlier quotation, a law which appears equal on its face bears far more heavily on the poor than the rich. A rule which requires a high level of formal education as a precondition for employment will, although applied equally to all, have the effect of excluding many who have suffered educational disadvantage, often a residue of racial discrimination or slavery. A rule which requires full-time working as a prerequisite for training, a pension, or promotion opportunities will operate to exclude many of those with primary responsibility for children, the vast majority of whom are still women. A rule which requires all employees or pupils to dress according to Christian traditions and take religious holidays according to the Christian calendar will perpetuate the exclusion of religious minorities.

How, then, do we explain how equal treatment can, in effect, lead to inequality, while unequal treatment might be necessary in order to achieve equality? The apparent paradox can be understood if we accept that the right to equality can be formulated in different ways, depending on which underlying conception of equality is chosen. Equality of treatment is predicated on the principle that justice inheres in consistency; hence, likes should be treated alike. But this, in turn, is based on a purely abstract view of justice, which does not take into account existing distributions of wealth and power. Consistency in treatment of two individuals who appear alike but in fact differ in terms of access to power, opportunities, material benefits, or physical attributes

---

[3] This book acknowledges that the terminology used to describe people subjected to discrimination is sensitive and contested. In the different jurisdictions covered here (UK, Europe, India, South Africa, Canada, and the US), outgroups, or groups that are 'othered' in their own societies or globally, prefer to refer to themselves in different and sometimes opposing ways. This can also change, reflecting changes in social forces and perceptions. Acknowledging these complexities, I have chosen to use 'Black people', 'marginalized ethnicities', and 'indigenous people', following the approach of the UN Special Rapporteur on the right to health, Tlaleng Mofokeng, in her report to the United Nations on sexual and reproductive health rights on 16 July 2021 (A/76/172) <https://undocs.org/A/76/172> accessed 31 May 2022. The reference to 'gender identity, gender expression and sex characteristics' follows her report on gender-based violence submitted to the UN on 14 April 2022 (A/HRC/50/28) <www.ohchr.org/en/documents/thematic-reports/ahrc5 028-violence-and-its-impact-right-health-report-special-rapporteur> accessed 31 May 2022.

results in unequal outcomes. The whole project of determining whether two individuals are relevantly alike is laden with unspoken value judgements. An alternative conception of equality, therefore, is based on a more substantive view of justice, which concentrates on correcting maldistribution. Such a principle would lead to a focus on equality of results, requiring unequal treatment if necessary to achieve an equal impact. Alternatively, the focus could lie on facilitating personal self-fulfilment, by equalizing opportunities. A notion of equality which stresses equal opportunities is consistent with inequality of treatment *and* inequality of results. Unequal treatment might be necessary to equalize the opportunities of all individuals, but once opportunities are equal, different choices and capacities might lead to inequality of results. A different approach might be to derive the right to equality from other values, such as dignity or autonomy.

The choice between different conceptions of equality is not one of logic but of values or policy. The right to equality could aim to achieve the redistributive goal of alleviating disadvantage, the liberal goal of treating all with equal concern and respect, the neoliberal goal of market or contractual equality, and the political goal of access to decision-making processes. It is striking that despite the widespread adherence to the ideal of equality, there is so little agreement on its meaning and aims.

Also complex is the relationship between equality and difference. It is an easy step to assume that 'difference' means inequality and inequality is synonymous with inferiority. This assumes a conceptual framework based on a set of dichotomies: reason and emotion, soul and body, good and bad, equal and different. In this schema, deriving from Aristotle, the second part of the pair is inferior to the first. Difference is characterized as the negative partner, legitimating detrimental treatment of those who are different. Yet in a plural society, difference and diversity should be regarded as positive attributes. Equality, far from suppressing difference, should accommodate and even celebrate it. Nor is difference necessarily an all-or-nothing concept. As Young argues:

> To say that there are differences among groups does not imply that there are not overlapping experiences, or that two groups have nothing in common. The assumption that real differences in affinity, culture, or privilege imply oppositional categorisation must be challenged. Different groups are always similar in some respects, and always potentially share some attributes, experiences and goals.[4]

---

[4] IM Young, *Justice and the Politics of Difference* (Princeton UP 1990) 171.

The previous discussion has assumed that equality is the prime value in society. But equality may well conflict with other basic social values, such as liberty from State interference, including freedom of speech and thought. How, then, do we decide which takes priority? Should individuals be able to assert their right to freedom of speech in order to protect their right to make racist comments? Or to produce pornographic material which degrades and stigmatizes women? On a different scale are the conflicts between equality and utilitarian or economic goals. Should the right to equality be defeasible on the grounds that its achievement is too costly, either for the State or for private individuals?

For lawmakers, facing the task of translating abstract notions into law, these questions are particularly complex. Legal formulations of equality must be coherent and comprehensible; and, equally importantly, they must contain mechanisms for making equality effective. But traditional enforcement and compliance mechanisms are often inappropriate in the equality context. Civil rights are normally enforceable in adversarial proceedings initiated by one party to the dispute and carrying a financial remedy. Yet a right to equality might be an empty promise if it requires each individual victim of discrimination to conduct proceedings against a particular defendant, particularly if the defendant is their employer, the factual and legal issues are complex, and the remedy limited to compensation. A wholehearted commitment to the right to equality might well require far more imaginative legal structures, including not just prohibitions of discriminatory behaviour or practices, but positive duties to promote equality. Indeed, closer attention to the causes of inequalities in society point to the need to institute broader social programmes, such as the provision of targeted training and childcare, the modification of working hours, and the alteration of premises to accommodate disability. Even so, at the end of the day, we may have to acknowledge the limits of traditional legal provisions and processes in bringing about social change.

The aim of this chapter is to examine in more detail some of these basic controversies. Chapters 2 and 3, recognizing that the right to equality is ultimately highly sensitive in the society in which it operates, briefly sketch the historical, social, and legal context in which the right to equality operates in five jurisdictions: the UK, Canada, the US, India, and South Africa. These jurisdictions are chosen because they have some important similarities, such as their common law roots, the influence of colonialism in setting patterns of inequality, and the use of English as at least one of the legal languages. Courts in these jurisdictions tend to pay attention to each other in making their decisions, as well as setting trends in constitutional law in other countries and internationally. On the other hand, there are important differences. They include a lower middle income country (India), an upper middle income country (South Africa), and high income countries (UK, US, and Canada); and straddle the Global South and the Global North. In addition, their constitutional texts and institutional structures differ, and, while some of the social challenges they face overlap, others are specific to their own context. For all these reasons, they constitute fruitful jurisdictions for comparative research. The EU is also covered because of its very powerful influence over the development of discrimination law in the UK. The comparative perspective runs through the remainder of the book. Chapter 2 concentrates on the historical, social, and legal context in which the right to equality developed in relation to gender, race, and religion and Chapter 3 does the same for sexual orientation, gender identity, disability, and age. Chapter 4 examines the scope of discrimination law. Who is protected and who is bound? Chapter 5 assesses the main legal tools used in discrimination law, particularly direct and indirect discrimination, or disparate treatment and disparate impact. Chapter 6 examines the challenges posed to these concepts in four particularly difficult areas: pregnancy and parenting; equal pay; sexual harassment; and reasonable accommodation. Chapter 7 focuses on one of the most contested aspects of discrimination law; namely, affirmative action or reverse discrimination, and Chapter 8 asks how we can refashion remedies to make equality laws effective.

I THE PRINCIPLE OF EQUALITY

(i) Background and Development

Equality as an ideal is a relatively modern construct. Classical and mediaeval societies were not founded on a principle of equality. Instead, society was ordered in hierarchical form, with entitlements and duties determined by birth or status rather than by virtue of an individual's inherent worth as a human being. Indeed, thinkers from Aristotle to Aquinas found no difficulty in justifying the subordination of women and slaves on the grounds of their inherent inferiority, their lack of rationality, and their need for supervision and guidance from free male householders.

It was only with the advent of mercantile capitalism and the loosening bonds of feudalism that equality began to emerge as an organizing social principle. Greater economic freedom of individuals to pursue a trade within a free market was accompanied by greater political freedom as Parliament gained power from the monarchy. It was in this hothouse climate of change and expectation that liberal ideology blossomed. John Locke, writing in 1690, captured the spirit of the age in his well-known aphorism: 'Men [are] by Nature all free, equal and independent.'[5] Politically, this meant increasing challenges to the authority of the monarch. Its economic manifestation was in the principle of freedom of contract. Freedom of contract was premised on the notion of equal parties, an abstract contractual equality which was oblivious to market reality.

Yet, even then, the promise of equality was ambiguous and exclusive. Indeed, a glance at the legal framework in the centuries following Locke reveals a landscape pockmarked with inequalities. Numerous groups, including women, slaves, religious and marginalized ethnic minorities, Black people,[6] Roma people and Travellers, and the unpropertied classes were excluded from the promise of liberal equality. Exclusion was achieved by the apparently logical argument that the basic rights to liberty and equality only inhered in individuals by virtue of their rationality. The concept of rationality could then be easily manipulated in an exclusive way. Women, slaves, and people who were subjected to colonial domination were characterized as irrational, emotional, or 'primitive' and therefore not entitled to the equal rights due to rational beings.[7] Thus, the newly ascendant equality principle coexisted with continued and unchallenged relations of domination. Slavery was not outlawed; colonialism flourished and women were denied basic rights such as the franchise, property ownership, and rights over their own children.[8] Locke himself saw no inconsistency between his lofty proclamation of equality and his description of the family as 'a Master . . . with all these subordinate Relations of Wife, Children, Servants and Slaves.'[9]

Nevertheless, the ideology of equality and freedom gave feminists and other disadvantaged groups the necessary vocabulary to argue for the emancipation of all. 'If all men are born free, why are women born slaves?' asked Mary Astell in 1700.[10] It was as a focus for political activism, rather than as a

---

[5] John Locke, *Two Treatises of Government* (P Laslett ed, CUP 1988), 'The Second Treatise', para 95.
[6] See n 3.
[7] S Fredman, *Women and the Law* (Clarendon Press 1997) ch 1.
[8] See Fredman (n 7) chs 1 and 2.
[9] Locke (n 5) 'Second Treatise', para 86.
[10] M Astell, 'Reflections upon Marriage' in M Astell and B Hill, *The First English Feminist* (Gower 1986).

legal concept, that equality began to emerge as a real force for combating sex discrimination and racism. But since the groups claiming equality inevitably lacked political power, progress was painfully slow. Three main phases in the development of a legal principle of equality can be discerned. The first required the dismantling of formal legal impediments. Women's subordination within marriage, and their exclusion from the suffrage and property rights, survived well beyond the liberal embrace of equality. It was only during the twentieth century that these legal impediments were slowly and grudgingly removed. The same was true for slavery, colonialism, and apartheid. For LGBTQI+ people, equality before the law was even slower in coming, with the criminalization of homosexuality and prohibitions on same-sex marriage extending well into the twenty-first century in some countries. While great strides were made in the availability of effective means of contraception for women, reproductive rights were and remain deeply contested, particularly in relation to women's rights to control their own bodies by means of safe and legal abortion.

However, although equality before the law is a major achievement, it soon became clear that it was far from sufficient to achieve genuine equality. Women, Black people, people from marginalized minorities,[11] LGBTQI+ people, persons with disabilities,[12] and others were still lawfully discriminated against in the labour market, in housing, in social security, and on the streets. There were no legal impediments to the continuing practices of paying women on separate and lower scales than men doing the same work; subjecting Black people and people from marginalized minorities to prejudice and exclusion; or treating people with disabilities as objects of charity or as if they did not exist. A new impetus was needed, in the form of legal prohibitions on discrimination by both public and private actors. This heralded the second stage, that of anti-discrimination legislation, which was capable of binding private actors and of reaching beyond equality before the law to individual acts of prejudice and, even further, to structural barriers. Such legislation has been achieved in most (but not all) of the jurisdictions considered here, and it continues to be developed in both coverage and depth. But this too, on its own, has not proved sufficient to dislodge the

---

[11] See n 3.

[12] The phrase 'persons with disabilities' is used here to reflect its use in the Convention on the Rights of Persons with Disabilities. However, as will be seen in Chapter 3, 'disability' is itself a social construct, and the phrase 'people with differing abilities' might be preferable. Many people prefer 'disabled people' to reflect the fact they are disabled by society.

tenacious patterns of discrimination and inequality which continue to pattern our societies.

Attention has therefore turned to investigating the possibilities of a new generation of equality laws which address the structural causes of discrimination and inequality. In some jurisdictions, this third phase has taken the form of permitting preference to be given to disadvantaged groups in employment or education.[13] Other models require 'mainstreaming' or incorporation of equality considerations into public authorities' decision making. Alternatively, public bodies might be required to consider the impact of laws and policies on protected groups and modify them to mitigate such consequences. This recognizes that it is not sufficient to rely on individual claims of discrimination against identified perpetrators. Instead, duties to take proactive steps to eliminate unlawful discrimination and promote equality of opportunity might be imposed on bodies which are in a position to bring about change.

Initial optimism about such proactive measures has, however, been dampened by a decade of austerity policies, in which severe budgetary restrictions hollowed out the commitment to reducing inequalities in society. Instead, the decade following the banking crisis in 2008 was marked by dramatic increases in inequality in many countries, both in the Global North and the Global South. There remains a deep reluctance to accept that the right to equality, like all other rights, is not confined to a negative duty—to refrain from discriminating—but necessarily includes positive duties on the State and powerful private parties to promote and fulfil the right to equality for all.[14]

It is against this background that we can begin to dissect the meaning of the right to equality. In Section (ii), I consider different notions of equality more closely, considering, first, formal equality or equality as consistency, and then turning to different types of substantive equality, including equality of results, equality of opportunity, and dignity (Sections (iii), (iv), and (v)). Section (vi) draws these insights together, to develop a four-dimensional understanding of the right to equality which is used as an analytic tool in the remainder of the book. In the final section, I consider two important competitors with equality; namely, liberty and market concerns.

---

[13] See further Chapter 7.
[14] S Fredman, *Human Rights Transformed: Positive Rights and Positive Duties* (OUP 2008).

(ii) Treating Likes Alike

The Aristotelian principle that likes should be treated alike continues to form the basis of our ideas about equality. Its enduring strength lies in its resonance with our instinctive idea that fairness requires consistent treatment. The State should not arbitrarily differentiate between individuals: hence, everyone should be equal before the law. This principle has therefore played a crucial role in dismantling express legal prohibitions in relation to particular identity groups. The power of this conception also lies in its invocation of the key liberal commitment to a notion of 'individual merit'. On this view, the guiding principle of fair treatment is that each individual should be treated according to their merits.

However, equality in this sense raises at least four sets of problems. The first concerns the threshold question of when two individuals are relevantly alike. Not every distinction is discriminatory; governments and individuals classify people into groups for a wide variety of reasons and many of them are legitimate. It is quite legitimate to distinguish between high-income and low-income groups for taxation reasons. Similarly, it is legitimate to distinguish between people with families and those without families in the allocation of socially funded housing or housing benefits. On the other hand, as we have seen, for many years it was thought to be legitimate to distinguish women from men and Black people, people from marginalized minorities, or indigenous people from white people.[15] What sort of distinctions, therefore, should be outlawed by the law as illegitimate and unacceptable? One of the biggest leaps in twentieth-century struggles for equality has been the recognition that characteristics based on race, gender, colour,[16] or ethnic origin should not, in themselves, constitute relevant differences justifying inferior treatment. In other areas, such as sexual orientation, this recognition has still not been fully achieved. This question is explored further in Chapter 3.

The second difficulty is that equality in this sense is merely a relative principle. It requires only that two similarly situated individuals be treated alike. In other words, fairness is a matter of consistency. There is no substantive underpinning—as long as two similarly situated people are treated the same,

---

[15] See n 3.

[16] This terminology reflects that in relevant statutes and international conventions (see UK Equality Act 2010, s 9(1)(a); South African Constitution, s 9; Canadian Charter of Rights and Freedoms, s 15; International Convention on the Elimination of All Forms of Racial Discrimination, Art 1; ICCPR, Art 2(1); ICESCR, Art 2(2)), which all refer to 'colour' in the list of protected characteristics.

there is no difference in principle between treating them equally badly and treating them equally well. For example, equal pay laws are of no benefit to a low paid woman if the only similarly situated male comparator is equally badly paid. The effect of this principle can be seen in a UK Supreme Court case[17] in which a woman who had undergone gender reassignment claimed that she had been discriminated against because officials responsible for unemployment benefit could deduce from the configuration of the database that she had very likely changed her gender. This was because a special procedure was needed to access the records of vulnerable customers. The UK Supreme Court held that since all vulnerable customers were subject to the same procedure, transgender customers were not treated less favourably on the grounds of their transgender status.[18] Thus, discrimination could not be established. Similarly, in a South African case, the South African Constitutional Court (SACC) held that a provision making sex work a criminal offence did not breach the right to gender equality because all sex workers were criminalized, whether they were women or men.[19] In both these cases, the equal treatment principle was held to be fulfilled on the basis that the two groups were equally badly treated.

Even more problematically, the absence of a substantive underpinning means that a claim of equal treatment can be met by removing a benefit from the relatively privileged group (levelling down). In a famous US case, the city of Jackson in Mississippi was ordered to desegregate its four 'whites only' swimming pools together with the single 'Blacks only' pool. Instead, it decided to close down all its public swimming pools.[20] It was held that identical treatment had been applied to both white people and Black people and that, therefore, there was no breach of the equality guarantee. The same approach was taken nearly eighty years later in *Sessions v Morales-Santana*.[21] The case concerned the right to transmit citizenship to children born abroad where only one parent was a US citizen. To transmit citizenship, the rule required unwed US-citizen fathers to have been present in the US for at least ten years before the child's birth. For an unwed US-citizen mother, this period was reduced to only one year. This distinction was challenged by the applicant, whose father, a US citizen, had been resident in the US for just short of ten years. Finding that the distinction between mothers and fathers breached the

---

[17] *R (C) v Secretary of State for Work and Pensions* [2017] UKSC 72.
[18] ibid [41].
[19] *S v Jordan* (CCT31/01) [2002] ZACC 22, 2002 (6) SA 642, 2002 (11) BCLR 1117 (SACC).
[20] *Palmer v Thompson* 403 US 217, 91 S Ct 1940 (1971).
[21] *Sessions v Morales-Santana* 137 S Ct 1678 (2017) (US Sup Ct).

right to the equal protection of the law, the US Supreme Court set out two remedial alternatives: to extend favourable treatment to the excluded class or withdraw favourable treatment from the favoured class. The Court opted for the latter. The ten-year requirement was held to apply to both mothers and fathers. The result was that the sex-based distinction was removed. But the claimant was no better off. Even more problematically, all those who relied on their mothers' citizenship were far worse off.

A similar response was seen in the UK in relation to legislation giving the authorities the power to detain non-UK nationals indefinitely without trial if they were suspected of international terrorism.[22] The House of Lords struck down the legislation on the grounds, inter alia, that it applied only to non-UK nationals and not to UK nationals who might also be suspected of international terrorism. The government speedily enacted legislation[23] which gave it power to issue orders curtailing the liberty (again without trial) of any individual suspected of involvement in terrorism-related activity, whether they were UK or foreign nationals. Equality as consistency was satisfied by intruding equally on the liberty of all.[24]

Levelling down has played a similar role in relation to equalizing pension ages between men and women. In many jurisdictions, including the UK, there has been a long-standing practice of setting a lower pension age of 60 for women as against 65 for men. Although older women remain among the poorest groups in Europe, increasing unemployment for male workers above 50 has meant that access to pension rights at an earlier age is of growing importance to men. Differential pension ages were contested as discriminatory against men in a claim upheld by the Court of Justice of the European Union (CJEU).[25] However, pension funds—claiming that the cost would be exorbitant—reacted by instituting policies to raise women's pension age to that of men over time. This strategy was initially upheld in further litigation before the CJEU.[26] The result was that poor women were worse off and poor men were no better off.[27]

The third drawback of equality as consistency is the need to find a comparator. Inconsistent treatment can only be demonstrated by finding a

---

[22] *A v Secretary of State for the Home Office* [2004] UKHL 56 (HL), Anti-Terrorism, Crime and Security Act 2001, s 23.

[23] Prevention of Terrorism Act 2005.

[24] S Fredman, 'From Deference to Democracy: The Role of Equality under the Human Rights Act 1998' (2006) 122 LQR 53, 53.

[25] *Barber v Guardian Royal Exchange Assurance Group* [1990] IRLR 240 (ECJ).

[26] Case C-408/92 *Smith v Avdel Systems Ltd* [1994] ECR I-4435 (ECJ).

[27] S Fredman, 'The Poverty of Equality: Pensions and the ECJ' (1996) 25 ILJ 91.

similarly situated person who does not share the characteristic in question (such as race or gender) and who has been treated more favourably than the complainant. The underlying assumption is that once these characteristics are disregarded, individuals can be treated entirely on their merit. This, in turn, assumes that individuals can be considered in the abstract, apart from their colour,[28] religion, ethnic origins, gender, or other such characteristic. Yet an individual's social, economic, and political situation is still heavily determined by these very characteristics. Even more fundamentally, each individual is constituted partly by group affinities,[29] whether it be her sense of identity, history, affinity with others, mode of reasoning, or expression of feelings. This is true of both the subject of discrimination and the comparator. Thus, the basic premise that there exists a 'universal individual' is deeply deceptive. Instead, the apparently abstract comparator is clothed with the attributes of the dominant gender, culture, religion, ethnicity, or sexuality. It is not a coincidence that when we talk of ethnicity we generally refer to ethnic minorities, rather than ethnic majorities, attributing a 'normality' to the dominant culture rather than its own ethnic specificity.

The result of the assumption of a 'universal individual' is therefore to create powerful conformist pressures. In the feminist literature, this has been dubbed the 'male norm'. Equality as consistency requires an answer to the question: 'Equal to whom?' The answer is, inevitably, 'equal to a man'. In the powerful words of Catharine MacKinnon:

> Concealed is the substantive way in which man has become the measure of all things. Under the sameness standard, women are measured according to our correspondence with man. . . . Gender neutrality is thus simply the male standard.[30]

The problem has been particularly acute in respect of pregnancy rights. On a strict view of equality as consistency, there is simply no appropriate male comparator and therefore no equality right arises. This difficulty was initially overcome by the unsatisfactory mechanism of comparing the treatment received by a pregnant woman with that of an ill man. It was only when courts in various jurisdictions could move beyond the idea of equality as consistency, and therefore beyond the need for a male comparator, that real progress

---

[28] See n 16.
[29] Young (n 4) 45.
[30] C MacKinnon, *Feminism Unmodified* (Harvard UP 1987) 34.

could be made.[31] But this problem continues to dog discrimination legislation. US legislation stills requires a comparison to be drawn between a pregnant woman and a person 'not so affected but similar in their ability or inability to work'.[32] The difficulty is not confined to pregnancy. In the area of equal pay, job segregation means that a low paid woman will frequently be unable to find a male comparator doing equivalent work in her establishment. A nursery nurse, a cleaner, or a secretary is likely to find herself in an all-female workforce; or in an establishment where the only men are in managerial positions and therefore not useful comparators.[33]

The assimilationist tendency has also been problematic in the context of religion and ethnicity. This is demonstrated in cases concerning religious dress at work, where prevailing assumptions of neutrality simply mirror the dominant culture's customs and habits. The result has been particularly exclusionary of women who wear the hijab as an aspect of their religion and culture. In the CJEU case of *Achbita*,[34] for example, the applicant's employer had a rule prohibiting workers from wearing visible signs of their political, philosophical, or religious beliefs in the workplace and Ms Achbita had subsequently been dismissed for wearing her hijab to work.[35] The CJEU held that the rule should be regarded as 'treating all workers of the undertaking in the same way by requiring them, in a general and undifferentiated way, *inter alia*, to dress neutrally, which precluded the wearing of such signs. Where such a rule was not applied differently to one worker as compared to any other, it had to be concluded that it did not introduce a difference of treatment that was directly based on religion or belief'.[36] This might mean that the only way to maintain religious practices which clash with majority expectations would be to resign. Parekh puts it starkly:

> The choice before the minorities is simple. If they wish to become part of and be treated like the rest of the community, they should think and live like the latter; if instead they insist on retaining their separate cultures, they should not complain if they are treated differently.[37]

---

[31] See further S Fredman, 'A Difference with Distinction: Pregnancy and Parenthood Reassessed' (1994) 110 LQR 106.

[32] Civil Rights Act 1964, s 701(k) inserted by the Pregnancy Discrimination Act of 1978.

[33] See further Fredman (n 7) 234 ff, Chapter 6 below.

[34] *Achbita v G4S Secure Solutions* [2017] 3 CMLR 21 (CJEU (Grand Chamber)).

[35] The court uses the term 'Islamic headscarf'.

[36] *Achbita* (n 34) 30–32.

[37] B Parekh, 'Integrating Minorities' in T Blackstone, B Parekh, and P Sanders (eds), *Race Relations in Britain* (Routledge 1998) 2.

The comparator requirement has proved almost insurmountable for claims of intersectionality. As Crenshaw has powerfully demonstrated, Black women become invisible in a legal structure which characterizes comparators along a single axis of either race or gender.[38] Crenshaw points to the US case of *Degraffenreid v General Motors*,[39] in which the plaintiffs claimed that General Motors' 'last hired-first fired' lay-off policies discriminated against them as Black women. The evidence showed that General Motors had hired no Black women prior to the Civil Rights Act 1964 and all the Black women hired after 1970 had lost their jobs during a subsequent recession under the seniority-based layoff. However, the single-axis framework of the legislation made it impossible to find an appropriate comparator to establish discrimination. The plaintiffs could not establish that they were less favourably treated on the grounds of their sex because General Motors had hired white women before 1964, and therefore they had sufficient seniority to survive the lay-off policy. Nor were they permitted to bring a race discrimination claim as Black women and were instead advised to consolidate their claim with a separate claim brought by Black male employees. As Crenshaw puts it, the court's refusal 'to acknowledge that Black women encounter combined race and sex discrimination implies that the boundaries of sex and race discrimination doctrine are defined respectively by white women's and Black men's experiences.'[40]

The fourth problematic aspect of equality as consistency is its treatment of difference. Only 'likes' qualify for equal treatment; there is no requirement that people be treated appropriately according to their difference. Pay structures frequently include gaps between women-only pay grades and male-dominated grades which are disproportionately large. Even if it is conceded that the work done is of less value (and, as we shall see in Chapter 6, job evaluation itself can include deep-seated assumptions which downgrade 'women's work'), there should be a requirement that women should be paid proportionately to the difference. This solution is not required, however, by the equality as consistency principle.[41] Nor does equality as consistency recognize the value of difference. Cultural and religious difference

---

[38] K Crenshaw, 'Demarginalising the Intersection of Race and Sex' (1989) University of Chicago Legal Forum 139.
[39] *DeGraffenreid v General Motors Assembly Division* 413 F Supp 142 (1976) (US District Ct).
[40] Crenshaw (n 38) 142–43.
[41] See Chapter 5.

might require positive measures which value difference in order to achieve genuine equality. Conversely, formal equality assumes that the aim is identical treatment. Yet, as we have seen, where there is antecedent inequality, 'like' treatment may in practice entrench difference. Unequal treatment may be necessary to achieve genuine equality. As Sen has argued: 'Equal consideration for all may demand very unequal treatment in favour of the disadvantaged.'[42]

Finally, equality as consistency is intensely individualist. Of course, the major contribution of equality has been its insistence that an individual be treated according to their own qualities or merits and not on the basis of negative stereotypes attributed to them because of their race, gender, or other protected characteristic. However, in rejecting the negative effects of taking group-based characteristics into account, the principle of formal equality has assumed that all aspects of group membership should be disregarded. Yet cultural, religious, and ethnic group membership is an important aspect of an individual's identity. Diverse individual identities may be enriching and desired. This demonstrates that the problem is not the diversity of characteristics but the detrimental treatment attached to it. The aim should not be to eliminate difference but to prohibit the detriment attached to such difference, preferably by adjusting existing norms to accommodate difference.

An equally problematic aspect of this individualism is the emphasis on individual fault as the only legitimate basis for imposing liability on a respondent. The correlative of treating a person only on the basis of their 'merit' is the principle that an individual should only be liable for damage for which they are responsible. This, in turn, means that only a respondent who can be proved to have treated the complainant less favourably on the grounds of a protected characteristic can be held liable for compensation. Yet discrimination extends far beyond individual acts of prejudice. Such prejudices are frequently embedded in the structure of society, and cannot be attributed clearly to any one person.

While formal equality or equality of treatment has a role to play, particularly in eradicating personal prejudice, it is clear from the previous discussion that other, more demanding, understandings of the right to equality are required. It is to these that we now turn.

---

[42]   A Sen, *Inequality Re-examined* (OUP 1992).

(iii) Equality of Results

The weaknesses of the principle that likes should be treated alike in addressing the complexity of discrimination and inequality have led to alternative conceptions. One of the most powerful has been to shift from a focus on equal treatment to one concerned with outcomes or results. On this view, the equality principle goes beyond a demand for consistent treatment of likes and requires, instead, that the results be equal. The strength of this notion of equality lies in its recognition that apparently identical treatment can in practice reinforce inequality because of past or ongoing discrimination. If there has been race discrimination in the provision of education for African American children,[43] a requirement of literacy as a precondition for voting rights will, although applied equally to all, in effect exclude a significant proportion of African American people. Similarly, given that many women have their children in their early twenties, an upper age limit of 28 for entry into the civil service, although applied to both men and women, will in effect exclude more women than men.[44] This description shows, too, that the aim of equality of results is different from that of equality as consistency. Equality of results is primarily concerned with achieving a fairer distribution of benefits; while formal equality is based on a notion of procedural fairness stemming from consistent treatment.[45]

However, a closer look at the notion of equality of results demonstrates some worrying ambiguities. Results or impact can be used in at least three different ways. The first focuses on the impact on the individual. Has the apparently equal treatment had a detrimental impact on this individual because of her race, sex, or other irrelevant characteristic? On this version, the aim is not to achieve equality of results but to obtain a remedy for the individual. Take, for example, the case of the school in the UK which prohibited the wearing of head coverings.[46] The result was to exclude an observant Sikh boy. The removal of the rule meant that the boy was no longer barred and the discriminatory impact on him was remedied. The dismantling of this particular obstacle would not, however, lead to a proportionate representation of Sikhs at the school.

---

[43] *Brown v Board of Education* 347 US 483 (1954) (US Sup Ct).
[44] *Price v Civil Service Commission* [1978] ICR 27 (EAT).
[45] John Gardner, 'Liberals and Unlawful Discrimination' (1989) 9 OJLS 1.
[46] *Mandla v Lee* [1983] 2 AC 548 (HL).

The second way in which equality of results is used focuses not on the results for the individual, but for the group. However, its aim is diagnostic, demonstrating the existence of obstacles to entry rather than prescribing an outcome pattern. Underlying this approach is the presumption that in a non-discriminatory environment a fair spread of members of different sexes, races, or religions would be found in any particular body, be it a workforce, an educational establishment, or a decision-making body. The absence of one group, or its concentration in less lucrative or important areas, is taken as a sign that discrimination is probably taking place. But this is only a presumption. If no exclusionary criterion or obstacle can be proved, then it is assumed that the maldistribution is due to other factors, such as workers' personal preferences. Alternatively, if there is such a criterion but it can be justified by the needs of the job, the presumption of discrimination is displaced. For example, a glance at the statistics shows that there are very few women airline pilots. This inequality of results raises a presumption of discrimination. If it can be shown that women are excluded because it is believed that they will not make good pilots, then the inequality of results has been diagnostic of discrimination. But if it is shown that they are excluded because there are not enough well-trained women, then it could be argued that, despite the inequality of results, there is no discrimination. This suggests that too little attention is being paid to the need to adapt existing structures to ensure that well-trained women pilots are indeed available.

The third and strongest meaning of 'equality of results' requires an equal outcome, for example that the spread of women, Black people, indigenous people, or people from marginalized identities[47] in a workforce category or university should reflect their proportions in the workforce or the population as a whole. There is no need for proof of an intervening 'discriminatory' factor to trigger action: the mere fact of under-representation is discriminatory. This notion of equality of results becomes controversial when it goes beyond the removal of exclusionary criteria and requires the achievement of an equal outcome by preferential treatment of the under-represented group. The reconciliation of preferential treatment or 'reverse' discrimination with the principle of equality is considered in detail in Chapter 7. But equality of results need not be achieved through openly preferential treatment; it could be achieved through encouragement, training, and other such measures.

---

[47] See n 3.

Equality of results is a strategically straightforward goal, since results appear to be relatively easily quantifiable. Many programmes and policies therefore focus on monitoring outcomes. However, this can be misleading. As Joshua Greenstein puts it: 'The choice of measurement is not value-neutral, but indicative of an implicit judgement about what type of inequality we should care about.'[48] Methodologies which might appear technical in fact reflect particular value choices as to the meaning and importance of inequality, as well as relations of power and influence. The well-known economist Thomas Piketty made this transparent when he explained his choice of measures on the basis of the political message he wanted to send; namely, a 'visceral understanding of social inequality'.[49]

Different types of measurement can lead to radically different conclusions as to whether inequality has increased. Greenstein gives a helpful example: if A earns $10 and B earns $100, and both experience a 20 per cent increase in their income, then both experience the same relative increase in their income, but the absolute difference between their income increases from $90 to $108. Both are reasonable measures, but the first, based on the percentage increase, registers no increase in inequality while the second, based on absolute figures, reveals a widening of inequality. This could be generalized to measuring two countries' per capita GDP. India has experienced consistently higher growth rates in per capita GDP than the US. But after twenty years of rapid growth, the absolute gap in per capita income between India and the US has actually grown.[50]

The principle of equality of results is therefore more challenging than at first appears. What 'results' matter and what does 'equality' mean in that context? It is tempting to focus entirely on goods or benefits, whether jobs, places at schools or universities, or, more radically, income. However, while distributive justice is one concern of anti-discrimination law, it is not the only one. Power differentials are the engine of ongoing inequality, yet are difficult to measure. The same is true for stigma, stereotyping, and prejudice. A further central concern of the right to equality—equal political participation—is also not easily captured by a focus on results. Increasing the numbers of under-represented groups on representative bodies is clearly an important goal. But democratically elected representatives are not expected to mirror

---

[48] J Greenstein, 'Narratives of Global Convergence and the Power of Choosing a Measure' (2020) 48 Oxford Development Studies 100, 111.

[49] T Piketty, *Capital in the Twenty-First Century* (Harvard UP 2013) 266–67.

[50] Greenstein (n 48) 103.

exactly the interests of the identity group to which they belong. Nor are the interests of an identity group necessarily homogeneous or easily identifiable. A more sophisticated theory is necessary to explain the application of distributive justice to political representation. A focus on results might therefore not capture the full range of harms caused by discrimination.

Even if we are clear as to which results we should focus on, we still need to determine what equality of results should entail. Should the results reflect the spread of all the identity groups in the population as a whole? This may be relatively easy to envisage in relation to gender or race. We might plausibly aim to achieve a balanced workforce or student body, with parity between women and men in all grades. But are we aiming to achieve a workforce, educational institution, or representative body which exactly reflects the population in relation to age, disability, religion or belief, sexual orientation, gender minorities, and other protected groups? And how do we factor in intersectional discrimination? As several jurisdictions have discovered, a simple focus on equality of results does not assist us in determining how we count representation of white women as against Black men, men from marginalized ethnicities, or indigenous men,[51] and where we position groups with intersectional identities, such as older women, women with disabilities, gay women, or women with all these characteristics.

It is not obvious that equality of results resolves the levelling-down problem. It is perfectly plausible to achieve equality of results by equalizing everyone at a lower level. One way forward is to follow Parfit's 'prioritarian' approach. On this view, the focus is on the worse off. In any scenario, the gains for the worse off are given greater value than the gains for anyone else. As Parfit frames it, this is not an egalitarian claim: 'We do not think it in itself bad, or unjust, that some people are worse off than others. . . . Egalitarians are concerned with relativities: with how each person's level compares with the level of other people. On the Priority View, we are concerned only with people's absolute levels.'[52] He concludes that this approach makes equality redundant. What matters are people's absolute entitlements rather than their entitlements relative to others. However, absolute entitlements tend to settle at the minimum and do nothing to redress disparities above the minimum. It is here that equality continues to play a role. A clear example is the difference between the right to minimum pay, which is an absolute entitlement, and the

---

[51] See n 3.
[52] D Parfit, 'Equality and Priority' (1997) 10 Ratio 202, 214.

right to equal pay for equal work for men and women, which is centrally and rightly concerned with disparities.

While the right to equality should be concerned with improving the position of the most disadvantaged, it should also aim to reduce the gap between the more disadvantaged and the less disadvantaged. The importance of both these aims can be seen by examining the Sustainable Development Goals (SDGs) Agenda, which commits the world to achieving an ambitious set of goals by 2030.[53] Equality is a central theme: SDG 5 commits the world to achieving gender equality and SDG 10 to reducing inequality within and between countries. Measuring the achievement of these goals is predominantly results-based, using 'indicators' to measure progress towards specific targets. However, as Fukuda-Parr argues, it was decided to quantify progress towards reducing inequality by measuring the income growth of the bottom 40 per cent of the population, without paying attention to how that compares with the top of the scale. This means that the focus is on social inclusion and removing poverty. While this is important, it does not address extreme inequalities between the top and the bottom of the distribution. As she puts it: 'The broader perspectives of extreme inequality search for deep rooted causes and seek solutions in institutions, particularly in economic institutions in areas such as taxation, investment and trade. Extreme inequality refers to the situation of the top percentiles, as well as the bottom. The narrower social inclusion perspectives are also informed by search for root causes, but focus on discrimination against particular groups such as by gender and age. These policy agendas challenge the economic interests of powerful actors less directly.'[54]

There is a deeper problem with equality of results. This is that altering outcomes need not necessitate any fundamental re-examination of the structures that perpetuate discrimination. A change in gender composition of a grade or sector, while to some extent positive, might reflect only an increasingly successful assimilationist policy. Women who achieve these positions might have done so by conforming to 'male' working patterns, contracting out their childcare obligations to other women, who remain as underpaid and undervalued as ever. Similarly, the increase in the number of women doing certain types of jobs might coincide with a decrease in the pay or status

---

[53] United Nations, 'Transforming our World: The 2030 Agenda for Sustainable Development' <https://sustainabledevelopment.un.org/post2015/transformingourworld>   accessed   19 April 2020.

[54] S Fukuda-Parr, 'Keeping out Extreme Inequality from the SDG Agenda—The Politics of Indicators' (2019) 10 Global Policy 61, 67.

of the job in question. Members of ethnic minorities who achieve these positions may be those who had assimilated, whether voluntarily or because of an absence of available options, in terms of dress, religious observance, or language. In the US, school desegregation, while appearing to achieve racial integration, in fact frequently replicated racial hierarchies within schools, as reflected in the fact that the racial achievement gap persists even in racially mixed, middle-class schools.[55] Quantifiable change might only partially reflect qualitative change.

As this discussion has shown, equality of results, while providing a welcome antidote to equality of treatment, can be seen to be at best a partial framework for situating anti-discrimination law. The right to equality should go beyond an exclusive focus on distributive harms. Attention should also be paid to stigma and stereotyping, the lack of a genuine voice in the political system, and institutional or structural inequalities.

(iv) Equality of Opportunity

An increasingly popular alternative to both equality as consistency and equality of results is the notion of equality of opportunity. This notion steers a middle ground between formal equality and equality of results. Proponents of this view recognize that equal treatment against a background of past and structural discrimination can perpetuate disadvantage. Using the graphic metaphor of competitors in a race, it is argued that true equality cannot be achieved if individuals begin the race from different starting points. However, according to this approach, to focus entirely on equality of results is to go too far in subordinating the right to individual treatment to a utilitarian emphasis on outcomes. Once individuals enjoy equality of opportunity, the problem of institutional discrimination has been overcome, and fairness demands that they be treated on the basis of their individual qualities, without regard to gender, race, or other protected characteristic. This model therefore specifically rejects policies which aim to correct imbalances in the workforce by quotas or targets, the aim of which is one of equality of outcome. Instead, an equal opportunities approach aims to equalize the starting point rather than the end result. Once all have equal opportunities, they should be judged on individual merit.

---

[55] M Minow, *In Brown's Wake* (OUP 2010) 26.

However, the metaphor of equal starting points is deceptively simple. What measures are required to ensure that individuals are genuinely able to compete equally? Williams distinguishes between a procedural and a substantive sense of equal opportunities. On a procedural view, equality of opportunity requires the removal of obstacles to the advancement of disadvantaged groups, such as women or minorities, but does not guarantee that this will lead to greater substantive fairness in the result.[56] For example, the abolition of word-of-mouth recruitment or non-job-related selection criteria removes procedural obstacles and so opens up more opportunities. But this does not guarantee that more women or minorities will, in fact, be in a position to take advantage of those opportunities. Those who lack the requisite qualifications as a result of past discrimination will still be unable to meet job-related criteria; women with childcare responsibilities will still not find it easier to take on paid work. In the famous words of US President Lyndon Johnson, it is 'not enough to open the gates of opportunity. All our citizens must have the ability to walk through those gates.'[57]

A substantive sense of equality of opportunity, by contrast, requires measures to be taken to ensure that persons from all sections of society have a genuinely equal chance of satisfying the criteria for access to a particular social good.[58] This requires positive measures, such as education and training, and family-friendly measures. It may go even further, and challenge the criteria for access, since the existing criteria of merit may themselves reflect and reinforce existing patterns of disadvantage. For example, criteria which stress a continuous work history would reflect a view that experience out of the paid labour force is of little value to a future job. Women who have left the paid workforce to bring up children would thereby be subject to detriment. As Hepple argues, one is not supplying genuine equality of opportunity if one applies an unchallenged criterion of merit to people who have been deprived of the opportunity to acquire 'merit'.[59]

In practice, equality of opportunity is rarely used in its substantive sense when framing equality laws. Equality of opportunity, like equality

---

[56] B Williams, 'The Idea of Equality' in P Laslett and WG Runciman (eds), *Philosophy, Politics and Society Second Series* (Blackwell 1965) 110 and see J Waldron in S Guest and A Milne (eds), *Equality and Discrimination* (F Steiner Verlag 1985) 97.

[57] Lyndon B Johnson, Address at Howard University (4 June 1965) cited in A Thernstrom, 'Voting Rights, Another Affirmative Action Mess' (1996) 43 UCLA L Rev 2031 fn 22.

[58] Williams (n 56) 125–26.

[59] B Hepple, 'Discrimination and Equality of Opportunity—Northern Irish Lessons' (1990) 10 OJLS 408, 411.

of results, therefore remains at most a partial basis for grounding anti-discrimination laws.

(v) Dignity

The limitations of formal equality have led courts, policymakers, and theorists to search for a more substantive core to the notion of equality. The foremost candidate has been the notion of dignity. The primacy of individual dignity and worth as a foundation for equality rights has been clearly articulated in a number of jurisdictions, whether in constitutions, legislation, or by courts. Particularly vocal in this regard has been the Supreme Court of Canada which has located dignity at the centre of the equality principle:

> Equality means that our society cannot tolerate legislative distinctions that treat certain people as second-class citizens, that demean them, that treat them as less capable for no good reason, or that otherwise offend fundamental human dignity.[60]

In other jurisdictions, dignity is a central pillar of the constitutional text itself. This is particularly true in South Africa. Addressing directly the history of humiliation and degradation to which the previous apartheid regime was dedicated, section 1 of the Constitution states that, amongst other things, the new South African State is founded on the values of 'human dignity, the achievement of equality, and the advancement of human rights and freedoms'. The general limitation clause in the South African Constitution also states emphatically that a right entrenched by the Constitution can only be limited to the extent that the limitation is 'reasonable and justifiable in an open and democratic society based on human dignity, autonomy and freedom'.[61] Every court, when interpreting human rights, must do so in a way that promotes the values of human dignity, equality, and freedom.[62] In one of the first equality cases to be decided, the SACC declared:

> At the heart of the prohibition of unfair discrimination lies a recognition that the purpose of our new constitutional and democratic order is the establishment of a society in which all human beings will be accorded equal dignity and respect

---

[60] *Law v Canada* [1999] 1 SCR 497, para 51 (Can Sup Ct).
[61] South African Constitution, s 36(1).
[62] ibid s 39(1) and (2).

regardless of their membership of particular groups. The achievement of such a society in the context of our deeply inegalitarian past will not be easy, but that that is the goal of the Constitution should not be forgotten or overlooked.[63]

Similarly, the German Basic Law, also strongly influenced by recent history, provides in its first and absolutely entrenched article, that human dignity is unassailable and that it is the duty of all State authorities to respect and protect it.[64] In the EU Charter of Fundamental Rights,[65] dignity plays a similarly central role. Not only is dignity mentioned in the preamble. In addition, the Charter includes a specific right to dignity, stating in Article 1 that 'Human dignity is inviolable. It must be respected and promoted.'

Certainly, there is much that makes dignity an intuitively appealing concept. Most importantly, dignity replaces rationality as a trigger for the equality right. As we have seen, linking equality to rationality has been used to deny access to the equality right; in particular to women, who were portrayed as lacking the prerequisite rationality. The crucial advance represented by substituting dignity for rationality is that dignity is seen to be inherent in the humanity of all people. In the well-known words of Immanuel Kant, a 'human being . . . is exalted above any price; for as a person, he is not to be valued merely as a means to the ends of others or even to his own ends, but as an end in itself, that is, he possesses a dignity (an absolute inner worth) by which he exacts respect for himself from all other rational beings in the world . . . and [can] value himself on a footing of equality with them'.[66] The value attached to individuals simply by virtue of their humanity logically connotes that all are entitled to equal concern and respect. As the German Federal Constitutional Court put it: 'Since all persons are entitled to human dignity and freedom and to that extent are equal, the principle of equal treatment is an obvious postulate for free democracy.'[67]

There are also several concrete ways in which the dignity value influences the development of the equality principle. First, dignity creates a substantive underpinning for the right to equality. This makes it impossible to argue that

---

[63]   *President of the Republic of South Africa v Hugo* (CCT 11/96) (18 April 1997), 1997 (4) SA 1 (CC), para 41.

[64]   Basic Law for the Federal Republic of Germany (Grundgesetz, GG), Art 1(1).

[65]   Charter of Fundamental Rights of the European Union [2012] OJ C326/391.

[66]   I Kant, 'Groundwork of the Metaphysics of Morals' in M Gregor and A Wood (eds), *Practical Philosophy: The Cambridge Edition of the Works of Immanuel Kant 1724–1904* (CUP 1996) 85 (436).

[67]   *Communist Party*, 5 BVerfGE 85 (1956). (I am indebted to Mr Justice LWH Ackermann for drawing my attention to this quote.)

the right to equality is satisfied by 'equally bad' treatment or by removing a benefit from the advantaged group and thereby 'levelling down'. Equality based on dignity must enhance rather than diminish the status of individuals. For example, when the SACC struck down the law criminalizing sodomy,[68] the fact that equality was underpinned by dignity was central. As Sachs J emphasized, the decision was not based on a comparison between the treatment of heterosexual couples and homosexual couples. Instead, the breach of the right to equality lay in the deep and fundamental assault on the dignity of gay men. More recently, this has been integrated into US jurisprudence. In the case of *Obergefell v Hodges*,[69] the US Supreme Court upheld the right of same-sex couples to marry by applying both the liberty and the equality elements of the Fourteenth Amendment in tandem, linked through the value of dignity. As Kennedy J concluded, the petitioners 'ask for equal dignity in the eyes of the law. The Constitution grants them that right.'[70] Similarly, the concept of equal dignity has been central to the reasoning of the Supreme Court of India in a series of recent cases striking down the criminalization of homosexuality,[71] affirming the equal rights of persons with disabilities,[72] ending discriminatory provisions on adultery,[73] and prohibiting the exclusion of menstruating women from the Sabarimala Hindu temple.[74]

The second way in which dignity influences equality relates to the coverage of equality laws. In many human rights documents, the list of groups who are protected against unlawful discrimination may be expanded by the courts. Drawing on the concept of dignity allows such expansion to take place in a principled manner. For example, the Canadian Supreme Court has held that the decision as to whether the equality guarantee in the Canadian Charter of Rights prevents discrimination on a ground not specifically enumerated should be decided by considering the primary mission of the equality guarantee. This mission, according to L'Heureux-Dubé J, is 'the promotion of a society in which all are secure in the knowledge that they are recognized

---

[68] *National Coalition for Gay and Lesbian Equality v Minister of Justice* 1998 (12) BCLR 1517, 121 (SACC).

[69] *Obergefell v Hodges* 2015 WL 1041665 (US Sup Ct).

[70] ibid.

[71] *Navtej Singh Johar v Union of India* (2018) 10 SCC 1, paras 139, 144, 147, 367–69, 459, 462, 482, 601, 640.2.7, 640.2.10 (Indian Sup Ct).

[72] *Jeeja Ghosh v Union of India* 2016 SCC OnLine SC 510, paras 37–39 (Indian Sup Ct).

[73] *Joseph Shine v Union of India* 2018 SCC OnLine SC 1676, paras 1, 48, 107, 114, 124, 190–92, 202, 209, 210, 213 (Indian Sup Ct).

[74] *Indian Young Lawyers Association v State of Kerala* 2018 SCC OnLine SC 1690, paras 201, 214, 215, 219, 220, 221, 285, 301, 357, 422.2 (Indian Sup Ct).

at law as human beings equally deserving of concern, respect and consideration.[75] On this view, a person or group has been discriminated against when a legislative distinction makes them feel that they are less worthy of recognition or value as human beings, as members of society.[76] Similarly, the question of whether differentiation on a ground not specified in the South African Constitution amounts to discrimination is answered by considering whether the differentiation is based on attributes or characteristics which objectively have the potential to impair the fundamental dignity of persons as human beings.[77]

Dignity has also been valuable in underscoring the role of the right to equality in the context of sexual harassment. In a crucial breakthrough, EU law framed the prohibition of sexual harassment in terms of the violation of dignity, thereby transcending the problematic need to demonstrate that a similarly situated comparator might have been treated more favourably. Harassment is defined as unwanted conduct which has the purpose or effect of violating the dignity of another person, or creating an intimidating, hostile, degrading, humiliating, or offensive environment.[78] Dignity has played a similar role in the EU Charter of Fundamental Rights, particularly in relation to age discrimination. Under Article 35 of the EU Charter: 'The Union recognises and respects the rights of the elderly to lead a life in dignity and independence and to participate in social and cultural life.'

Dignity clearly has a central role to play in relation to equality. Indeed, there has been a temptation to regard equality as reducible to dignity. However, dignity also has its difficulties.[79] As a start, the concept itself is open to different interpretations, and even opposite results.[80] This can be seen in one of the first decisions on equality of the SACC, the *Hugo* case.[81] The case concerned the pardon issued by President Mandela to all women prisoners who were mothers of young children. The pardon was challenged

[75] *Andrews v Law Society of British Columbia* [1989] 1 SCR 143, 171.
[76] *Egan v Canada* [1995] 2 SCR 513, 545 (para 39); *Vriend v Alberta* [1998] 1 SCR 493, 156 DLR (4th) 385, [1998] 4 BHRC 140, 185 (para 182).
[77] *Harksen v Lane NO & Others* [1997] ZACC 12 (SACC).
[78] Employment Act 2010, s 26; European Parliament and Council Directive 2006/54/EC, Art 2(1)(c) and (2)(a); for the similarly worded definition of racial harassment, see Council Directive 2000/43/EC, Art 2(3). See also Chapter 4.
[79] See S Fredman, *Comparative Human Rights Law* (OUP 2018) 32–37.
[80] See D Feldman, 'Human Dignity as a Legal Value' [1999] PL (Winter) 682; C McCrudden, 'Human Dignity and Judicial Interpretation of Human Rights' [2008] EJIL 655.
[81] *President of the Republic of South Africa v Hugo* (CCT 11/96) [1997] ZACC 4 (SACC).

by a male prisoner, the sole carer of his young children, on the basis that it discriminated on grounds of gender. The court rejected the claim. According to Goldstone J, 'The Presidential Act might have denied fathers an opportunity it afforded mothers, but it could not be said to have fundamentally impaired their rights of dignity or sense of equal worth.'[82] By contrast, for Kriegler J it was the assumption that women are the primary child carers which constituted an assault on their dignity. As he put it in his dissent:

> One of the ways in which one accords equal dignity and respect to persons is by seeking to protect the basic choices they make about their own identities. Reliance on the generalisation that women are the primary care givers is harmful in its tendency to cramp and stunt the efforts of both men and women to form their identities freely . . .[83]

Dignity can also operate to deny the right to equality to those that society regards as 'immoral', such as sex workers.[84] In *S v Jordan*, the SACC upheld a law which criminalized both sex workers and their customers. The Court found neither an infringement of dignity nor unfair discrimination. Ngcobo J giving the majority judgment stated: 'The stigma that attaches to prostitutes attaches to them not by virtue of their gender, but by virtue of the conduct they engage in. . . . By engaging in commercial sex work, prostitutes knowingly accept the risk of lowering their standing in the eyes of the community, thus undermining their status and becoming vulnerable.'[85]

Secondly, there is a risk that dignity comes to be regarded as an independent element in discrimination law, requiring a claimant to prove not just that she has been disadvantaged, but that this signifies lack of respect of her as a person. This danger was floridly demonstrated in the Supreme Court of Canada, in which the Court held that proof of disadvantage on the grounds of an enumerated characteristic would not in itself be discriminatory if the claimant could not prove in addition that this disadvantage signified that society regarded her as being of less value than others.[86] Thus, in *Gosselin*[87] welfare beneficiaries under thirty received significantly lower benefit than those

---

[82] ibid para 47.
[83] ibid para 80.
[84] I am grateful to Monica Arango Olaya for sharing this insight.
[85] *S v Jordan* (CCT31/01) (n 19) para 16.
[86] *Law v Canada* (n 60); *Gosselin v Quebec* 2002 SCC 84 (Can Sup Ct).
[87] *Gosselin v Quebec* ibid.

over thirty unless they participated in a designated work activity or education programme. In practice, there was a considerable shortfall in places available. As a result, many young people, including the claimant, experienced real poverty. She claimed that this constituted age discrimination, in breach of the equality guarantee in section 15(1) of the Canadian Charter. However, the majority held that 'the provision of different initial amounts of monetary support to each of the two groups does not indicate that one group's dignity was prized above the other's'.[88] It therefore rejected her claim. In a remarkably similar response, in the House of Lords in the UK case of *Reynolds*, Lord Rodgers stated:

> There is no doubt that the relevant regulations, endorsed by Parliament, deliberately gave less to those under 25. But this was not because the policymakers were treating people under 25 years of age as less valuable members of society.[89]

This problem has now been recognized by the Canadian Court. In an important case in 2010, *R v Kapp*,[90] it acknowledged that:

> several difficulties have arisen from the attempt . . . to employ human dignity as a legal test. There can be no doubt that human dignity is an essential value underlying the s. 15 equality guarantee. In fact, the protection of all of the rights guaranteed by the Charter has as its lodestar the promotion of human dignity. . . . But as critics have pointed out, human dignity is an abstract and subjective notion that . . . has . . . proven to be an additional burden on equality claimants, rather than the philosophical enhancement it was intended to be.[91]

These difficulties can be avoided by regarding dignity as an aspect of the right to equality rather than attempting to reduce the right to equality to a single notion of dignity. Dignity should also be further specified, to capture the key elements of stigma and stereotyping, rather than remaining a vague and malleable conception. This is elaborated later.

---

[88] ibid para 61 (McLachlin J).
[89] [2005] UKHL 37 [45].
[90] *R v Kapp* 2008 SCC 41 (Can Sup Ct).
[91] ibid paras 21, 22.

(vi) Substantive Equality: A Four-Dimensional Concept

It is clear, therefore, that substantive equality resists capture by a single principle, whether it be equality of results, equality of opportunity, or dignity. Rather, it should be seen as a multi-dimensional principle, incorporating the strengths of other conceptions and ameliorating their weaknesses. Most importantly, such a conception should overcome the flaws in the conception of the right to equality as like treatment. This means that it should move beyond an approach which regards the problem as simply the classification of a person according to race, gender, or other protected ground. Instead, it should be concerned with the disadvantage attached to such a classification. The first dimension of substantive equality should therefore aim to redress disadvantage, breaking the cycle of disadvantage associated with outgroups. This is a deliberately asymmetric approach. Measures, such as affirmative action, which use classification to address disadvantage, are not regarded as a breach of equality but a means to achieve it. Nor is it possible to achieve substantive equality by treating everyone equally badly or by levelling down: neither of these would redress disadvantage.

The move from an 'anti-classification' approach to one that focuses on disadvantage is not, however, sufficient to capture all the dimensions of the right to substantive equality. Disadvantage is created and perpetuated by stigma, stereotyping, prejudice, and violence, whether of racial inferiority, of women as primarily responsible for childcare, or as sexualized objects, of persons with disabilities as objects of charity, or LGBTQI+ people as violating the laws of God or nature. This is the second dimension. It speaks to the importance of promoting dignity and worth, but avoids the malleability of an open-ended conception of dignity by giving it specific content as stigma, stereotyping, prejudice, and violence.

The right to substantive equality should also address political and social exclusion. Those who have little voice in political or social decision making are those who paradigmatically need the protection of the right to equality. This is the third dimension. Finally, substantive equality needs to go beyond addressing many individual acts of prejudice. It should recognize that inequality inheres in the structures and institutions of society, which are patterned on the dominant norm and sustained by dominant powers. Nor should it exact conformity as the price of inclusion but should recognize difference as a facet of equality. Substantive equality should therefore require structures to be transformed and difference accommodated. This is the fourth dimension. These dimensions require simultaneous attention rather than falling into any type of lexical priority. In Alexy's terms, all four require optimization to the extent legally and factually possible.[92] As we will see later, all of these dimensions have strong resonance in the jurisprudence on the right to substantive equality from the jurisdictions considered here.

One of the benefits of a multi-dimensional approach to substantive equality is that it allows us to address the interaction between different facets of inequality. Philosophers and political scientists tend to focus on distributive inequality,[93] while discrimination lawyers see the right to equality as primarily concerned with countering prejudice and stereotyping, regarding distributive inequalities as the domain of policymakers. The interaction between these two aspects of the right to equality is, however, rarely examined;[94] nor is their interaction with participation and structural obstacles to equality. These interactions are not always harmonious. Indeed, they may conflict. But instead of excluding one or the other facet wholly from the right to equality, the four-dimensional framework requires them to be considered together. Where there is the potential for these facets to pull in opposite directions, the aim is find a way in which all the dimensions can be optimized,[95] rather than suggesting that substantive equality pursue one of the aims at the cost of obliterating the others. The four-dimensional approach is therefore not a definition as such, but an analytic framework which can be used to assess and assist in modifying policies and practices to better achieve substantive equality. Drawing attention to all the dimensions and insisting on resolving conflicts and building complementarities can move us positively towards ensuring that laws, policies, or programmes can be formulated in ways which further the right to substantive equality.

Each of these, together with the challenges they represent, is outlined later. For ease of reference, the grounds of discrimination are referred to as 'status' or 'protected characteristics'. These generally refer to gender, race, disability, sexual orientation, religion and belief, age, and nationality, but, as will be seen in Chapter 3, could encompass a range of other types of status. Because an asymmetric approach is advocated, however, it may not be that all status groups are the target of intervention. Only those which suffer disadvantage,

---

[92] R Alexy, *A Theory of Constitutional Rights* (OUP 2004).

[93] Joseph Raz, 'On the Value of Distributional Equality' in Stephen De Wijze, Matthew H Kramer, and Ian Carter (eds), *Hillel Steiner and the Anatomy of Justice: Themes and Challenges* (Routledge 2009).

[94] S Fredman, 'Redistribution and Recognition: Reconciling Inequalities' (2007) 23 South African J Human Rights 214.

[95] Alexy (n 92).

stigma, or exclusion may be in issue. These are sometimes referred to as 'outgroups'.

(a) Redressing disadvantage: the redistributive dimension

A key contribution of the notion of substantive equality as compared to the principle that likes should be treated alike is the recognition that it is not the use of race, gender, or other status in making decisions or allocating resources that needs to be addressed, but the detrimental consequences attached to such classifications. Substantive equality therefore focuses on the group which has suffered disadvantage: women rather than men, Black people, people from marginalized minorities, or indigenous people[96] rather than white people, persons with disabilities rather than those regarded as able-bodied, or LGBTQI+ people, rather than cisgender people and heterosexuals. Indeed, disadvantage is disproportionately concentrated among these groups. Women, Black people, people from marginalized minorities, indigenous people, and persons with disabilities tend to be amongst the lowest earners, to experience the highest rates of unemployment, and to predominate among those living in poverty or social exclusion. The first aim of the right to substantive equality should therefore be to correct the cycle of disadvantage experienced because of status or other protected characteristic.

Targeting disadvantage rather than aiming at race- or gender-neutrality has several advantages. As a start, it makes it impossible to argue that equally bad treatment fulfils the right to equality. For example, in a US case involving racial segregation of prisoners,[97] the prison authority argued that this should not be regarded as discriminatory because all races were 'equally segregated'. The US Supreme Court emphatically rejected the argument that equality could be satisfied by 'neutrality' of this sort: 'It is axiomatic that racial classifications do not become legitimate on the assumption that all persons suffer them in equal degree.'[98]

Equally importantly, targeting disadvantage removes the possibility of a levelling-down option. The importance of this can be seen in the progress in the European Court of Justice from accepting a levelling down option to requiring one that levels up. As we saw, the option of levelling down in relation to pension ages was initially accepted. Substantive equality, by contrast, would require the benefit to be extended to the disadvantaged group. This

---

[96] See n 3.
[97] *Johnson v California* 125 S Ct 1141 (2005) (US Sup Ct).
[98] Citing *Powers v Ohio* 499 US 400, 410 (1991).

approach has now been adopted by the Court of Justice. Where discrimination has been established, it has held, 'observance of the principle of equality can be ensured only by granting to persons within the disadvantaged category the same advantages as those enjoyed by persons within the favoured category. Disadvantaged persons must therefore be placed in the same position as persons enjoying the advantage concerned.'[99]

The asymmetry of this dimension also makes it possible to reconcile affirmative action with the right to equality. Although apparently breaching the principle of equal treatment, affirmative action in reality advances substantive equality by taking steps to redress the disadvantage. In addition, it allows us to show the links between distributive inequalities, which have traditionally been regarded as the terrain of the welfare state or socio-economic rights, and discrimination law. This dimension therefore captures the strengths of the understanding of substantive equality as equality of results, while avoiding some of its ambiguities.

However, focusing on disadvantage also carries with it some important challenges. The most important is to specify the nature of the disadvantage. Disadvantage is most easily understood in the context of redistribution of resources and benefits, addressing under-representation in jobs, underpayment for work of equal value, or limitations on access to credit, property, or similar resources. However, disadvantage should encompass more than maldistribution of resources. It also needs to take on board the constraints which power structures impose on individuals because of their status. Young argues forcefully that the distributive paradigm—which defines social justice as the morally proper distribution of social benefits and burdens among society's members[100]—has been given a distorted significance in theories of justice. Because it focuses on the allocation of material goods, the distributive paradigm ignores social structures such as decision-making power, the division of labour and culture, or the symbolic meanings attached to people, actions, and things. Power itself, in her view, is not appropriately defined as a distributive benefit, because this makes power appear to be a possession rather than a relationship. Instead, she argues, the focus should be on domination, or structures which exclude people from participating in determining their actions.[101] For example, women's disadvantage cannot be characterized

---

[99] Case C-406/15 *Milkova v Izpalnitelen direktor na Agentsiata za privatizatsia i sledprivatizatsionen control* [2017] 3 WLUK 236 (CJEU), para 65.
[100] Young (n 4) 16.
[101] ibid.

solely in terms of income poverty, but is centrally related to imbalances of power within and outside the family.[102] As Chant notes, household income may bear no relation to women's poverty because women may not be able to access it.[103] Women who are trapped in the private sphere will suffer disadvantage in this sense even if they live in affluent households. The same is true for power structures which create and perpetuate discrimination against Black people, people from marginalized minorities, indigenous people,[104] people with disabilities, poor people, and other disadvantaged groups. It is for this reason that this dimension, the need to redress disadvantage both materially and of power, must interact closely with the need to enhance voice and participation and bring about structural change.

Disadvantage can also be understood as a deprivation of genuine opportunities to pursue one's own valued choices. This draws on the insights of the 'capabilities' theory developed by Amartya Sen[105] and Martha Nussbaum.[106] Starting from the premise that each individual should be able to be and do what she values, this theory stresses the importance of considering the extent to which people are actually able to exercise their choices, rather than simply having the formal right to do so. It may not be feasible for a person to achieve the goals she values due to social, economic, or physical constraints, as well as due to political interference.[107] 'What people can achieve is influenced by economic opportunities, political liberties, social powers and the enabling conditions of good health, basic education, and the encouragement and cultivation of initiatives.'[108] Thus, it is not enough to treat everyone equally, since the same treatment of individuals with very different constraints can replicate disadvantage.

The capabilities approach incorporates aspects of the concept of equality of opportunity in that it emphasizes the importance of providing opportunities not available to outgroups because of their status. But it goes further in placing the emphasis not just on the existence of opportunities, but their feasibility. The capabilities approach also has similarities with the concept of equality of results, in that it highlights the ways in which the same treatment

---

[102] S Chant, 'The "Feminisation of Poverty" and the "Feminisation" of Anti-Poverty Programmes: Room for Revision?' (2008) 43 J Development Studies 165.

[103] S Chant, 'Rethinking the Feminisation of Poverty' (2006) 7 J Development and Capabilities 201.

[104] See n 3.

[105] A Sen, *Development as Freedom* (OUP 1999).

[106] M Nussbaum, *Women and Human Development* (CUP 2000).

[107] ibid 90–91.

[108] Sen (n 105) 5.

for different people can lead to widely varying results depending on their different capabilities. However, it is also richer in that it incorporates individual autonomy and the differing needs of differently situated individuals. It is also more difficult to measure.

The first dimension of equality therefore aims to redress disadvantage by removing obstacles to genuine choice. However, this is not the only way in which disadvantage should be understood. Choice itself can be problematic, since people often adapt their choices to their limited circumstances. Moreover, there are clearly circumstances in which the concern is not solely to increase the range of feasible options but to address the disadvantage attached to the circumstances a person actually finds herself in, even if she has chosen to be there. For example, the terms and conditions of work for part-time workers need to be improved, even if women have chosen to do such work.

Disadvantage needs, therefore, to refer both to material disadvantage, including differences in capabilities or feasible options, and power differentials. At the same time, the conception of disadvantage used here is integrally related to the issues highlighted in the other three dimensions; namely, stigma and stereotyping, lack of voice and participation, and structural barriers. Redressing disadvantage should not only be about minimum entitlements but also relative disadvantage, particularly between the best and the worst off. In this sense, it needs to be allied with structural change, the fourth dimension. Similarly, under-representation in decision making, while crucially related to power, is better dealt with as an aspect of the participative dimension of equality. The need to value individuals regardless of capabilities or choice is better dealt with under the second dimension, to which we now turn.

(b) Addressing stigma, stereotyping, prejudice, and violence: the recognition dimension

The focus on redressing disadvantage has been a key step forward for substantive equality. However, we should not be tempted to reduce the right to substantive equality wholly to correcting disadvantage. Even in its most expansive sense, disadvantage does not cover all the wrongs associated with inequality. Stigma, stereotyping, humiliation, and violence on grounds of gender, race, disability, sexual orientation, or other status remain at the core of discrimination, and can be experienced regardless of relative disadvantage. The second main aim of substantive equality should therefore be to address stigma, stereotyping, prejudice, and violence.

This is the dimension of equality which speaks to our basic humanity. The right to equality attaches to all individuals, not because of their merit, their rationality, their citizenship, or their membership of any particular group, but because of their humanity. Individuals should not be humiliated or degraded through racism, sexism, or other status-based prejudice. This draws on the intuition that human dignity lies at heart of the right to equality. However, specific content is given to this intuition by focusing on the harms of stigma, stereotyping, prejudice, and violence, rather than relying on a vague and easily manipulated definition of dignity.

This conception of the right to substantive equality also departs from the individualism for which dignity is often criticized. Rather than regarding each person as an isolated individual to whom dignity is attached, it roots the right to equality in relationships. In particular, it exposes the ways in which relationships, especially relationships of power and subordination, can be the vehicle for denigration and stereotyping. In this sense, this dimension is usefully understood through the concept of 'recognition', originally formulated by Hegel and powerfully developed by Nancy Fraser.[109] Recognition refers to the central importance of interpersonal affirmation to our sense of who we are. On this view, identity is shaped through the ways in which others recognize us, and we recognize others. Misrecognition or recognition inequalities arise through denigration, humiliation, and failure to value individuals. In a similar vein, the German Federal Constitutional Court has stressed that dignity does not connote 'an isolated sovereign individual; [but instead] . . . a relationship between individual and community in the sense of a person's dependence on and commitment to the community, without infringing on a person's individual value'.[110]

The acknowledgement that individuals cannot be abstracted from the society in which they live also means that substantive equality is capable of addressing race and gender as social constructs. Rather than regarding sex merely as a biological given, or race as a physiological truth, the ways in which society constructs these concepts through popular stereotypes and prejudices should be factored into the analysis. A similar approach can be

[109] N Fraser and A Honneth, *Redistribution or Recognition* (Verso 2003); S Fredman, 'Redistribution and Recognition: Reconciling Inequalities' (2007) 23 South African J Human Rights 214; S Liebenberg, 'Needs, Rights and Transformation: Adjudicating Social Rights', Center for Human Rights and Global Justice Working Paper, Economic and Social Rights Series; J Fudge, 'The Canadian Charter of Rights: Recognition, Redistribution, and the Imperialism of the Courts' in T Campbell, KD Ewing, and A Tomkins (eds), *Sceptical Essays on Human Rights* (OUP 2001).
[110] BVerfGE 4, 7, 15 (1954).

taken to disability: using the recognition dimension of substantive equality, it is possible to address the social implications of disability rather than focusing wholly on the impairment. Underlying these social constructs is invariably a relationship of power and subordination, perpetuated and legitimated through stereotypes and stigma.

It is also for this reason that violence is included on the same axis as stigma, stereotyping, and prejudice for the purposes of this dimension. Racist violence, sexual violence, homophobic violence, and other violence against protected groups is not simply constituted by individual acts of violence against other individuals, which are in any case prohibited by the criminal law. Such violence is fuelled and perpetuated by deep-seated stereotypes and stigmatic 'othering'. This is underscored by the Convention on the Elimination of Discrimination against Women (CEDAW), which requires States to adopt and implement measures to 'eradicate prejudices, stereotypes and practices that are the root causes of gender-based violence against women'.[111] Its operation can be seen in the judgment of the European Court of Human Rights in *Opuz v Turkey*.[112] In this case, the authorities repeatedly failed to provide protection to the applicant and her mother despite sustained and appalling violence by her husband, leading ultimately to her mother's death at his hands. The Court emphasized the ways in which stigma, stereotyping, and prejudice against women led the authorities to refuse to recognize the victims as worthy of State protection and to the passive or active condoning of perpetrators' actions. Importantly, the Court situated the particular hardship of the individual applicant in the context of wider patterns of gender-based violence in Turkey. The women most at risk, Kurdish women with no independent source of income and little education, were already some of the most disadvantaged in Turkey. This aggravated and reinforced the stereotypical view of women as being in a subordinate position to men and therefore worthy of less protection. Similarly, the police's dismissive attitude towards the victims' complaints against their husbands or other male perpetrators was part of a generalized refusal to recognize the unacceptability of such violence, whether in the private or public sphere.

This dimension of the right to substantive equality resonates with the jurisprudence of courts in several jurisdictions. Stigma and stereotyping were

---

[111] CEDAW, Arts 2(f) and 5(a); General Recommendation No 35 on gender-based violence against women (CEDAW/C/GC/35).

[112] *Opuz v Turkey* (2010) 50 EHRR 28 (ECtHR). See further A. Timmer, 'Toward an Anti-Stereotyping Approach for the European Court of Human Rights' (2011) 11 Human Rights Law Review.

central to *Brown v Board of Education*,[113] the path-breaking US Supreme Court decision that segregating schools on grounds of race breached the equality guarantee in the US Constitution. The US Supreme Court posed the question thus: 'Does segregation of children in public schools solely on the basis of race, even though the physical facilities and other "tangible" factors may be equal, deprive the children of the minority group of equal educational opportunities?'[114] The answer was unequivocally in the affirmative. And the reason given was strikingly resonant of recognition issues: 'To separate them from others of similar age and qualifications solely because of their race generates a feeling of inferiority as to their status in the community that may affect their hearts and minds in a way unlikely ever to be undone.'[115]

Similarly, after a century in which the statute books 'gradually became laden with gross, stereotyped distinctions between the sexes', the US Supreme Court in the seminal case of *Frontiero v Richardson* recognized that rationalizing the 'long and unfortunate history of sex discrimination by an attitude of "romantic paternalism" . . . in practical effect put women, not on a pedestal, but in a cage.'[116] Since then, the Court has seen stereotyping, or 'overbroad generalizations about the different talents, capacities or preferences of males and females'[117] as inherently suspect.[118] Importantly, this has not been limited to assumption that women are innately inferior, but extended to gendered roles of both women and men. Thus, the Court has held both that women should be admitted to the top-ranking military academy in Virginia and that men should be admitted to a State-supported professional nursing school in Mississippi.[119] Most recently, it has been applied to gendered expectations in relation to parenting, both within and outside marriage. Thus, in *Sessions v Morales Santana*,[120] the Court rejected not only the assumption that women are necessarily best equipped to care for children, but also the 'obsolescing' view that '"unwed fathers [are] invariably less qualified and entitled than mothers" to take responsibility for non-marital children'. This does not mean that women cannot invoke a 'compensatory purpose' to justify a women-only exemption where it intentionally and directly assists women who have been disproportionately burdened. Thus, because women 'have

---

[113] *Brown v Board of Education* 347 US 483 (1954) (US Sup Ct).
[114] ibid 493.
[115] ibid 494.
[116] *Frontiero v Richardson* 411 US 677, 684–85 (1973) (US Sup Ct).
[117] *US v Virginia* 518 US 515, 533 (1996) (US Sup Ct).
[118] *Sessions v Morales-Santana* (n 21) 1692.
[119] *US v Virginia; Mississippi University for Women v Hogan* 458 US 718 (1982) (US Sup Ct).
[120] *Sessions v Morales-Santana* (n 21).

been unfairly hindered from earning as much as men',[121] the Court upheld a statute which allowed women to eliminate more low-earning years than men with the same earning history for the purposes of computing social security retirement benefits.[122]

The role of stereotyping has also been central to recent developments by the Indian Supreme Court, which have moved beyond the understanding of 'sex' as a classification to one that encompasses assumptions about stereotypical gender roles. Thus, in *Joseph Shine*, the Supreme Court of India struck down a provision of the Indian Penal Code relating to adultery in part because, as the Court stated, the provision was 'premised upon sexual stereotypes that view women as being passive and devoid of sexual agency'.[123] Similarly, in the first decision in the long-running litigation to strike down the criminal prohibition of sodomy in India, the Delhi High Court held that discrimination 'on the basis of sexual orientation is grounded in stereotypical judgments and generalization about the conduct of either sex'.[124] This approach was resoundingly endorsed by Chandrachud J when the Supreme Court finally struck down the criminal prohibition. As he put it: 'A discrimination will not survive constitutional scrutiny when it is grounded in and perpetuates stereotypes about a class constituted by the grounds prohibited in Article 15(1). . . . If certain characteristics grounded in stereotypes, are to be associated with entire classes of people constituted as groups by any of the grounds prohibited in Article 15(1), that cannot establish permissible reason to discriminate'.[125]

At the same time, it is crucial to situate stigma, stereotyping, prejudice, and violence as only one dimension of the right to substantive equality, which must interact with redressing disadvantage, facilitating voice and participation and transforming or modifying underlying structures. This enables us to see that, unlike in the cases of *Gosselin* and *Reynolds* discussed earlier, a measure that causes socio-economic disadvantage on the basis of a protected characteristic could itself be stigmatic and based on stereotypes. This was highlighted in the South African case of *Khosa*,[126] which concerned a legislative measure which confined the right to child benefit and old-age pensions

---

[121] *Califano v Webster* 430 US 313, 318 (1977) (US Sup Ct).
[122] ibid.
[123] *Joseph Shine* (n 73) para 23.
[124] *Naz Foundation v Government of NCT of Delhi*, WP(C) No 7455/2001, 2 July 2009 (High Ct of Delhi).
[125] *Navtej Singh Johar v Union of India* (n 71) para 41.
[126] *Khosa and Mahlaule v Minister for Social Development* 2004 (6) BCLR 569 (SACC).

to South African citizens, to the exclusion of permanent residents. In striking down this measure as a breach of equality, Mokgoro J emphasized that the consequences of exclusion were not only socio-economic. In addition, the exclusion of permanent residents had a strong stigmatizing effect, creating the impression that non-citizens were inferior to citizens and less worthy of social assistance. Permanent residents were in effect 'relegated to the margins of society and deprived of what may be essential to enable them to enjoy other rights vested in them under the Constitution.'[127]

By contrast, in *Brown v Board of Education*,[128] despite the welcome focus on stigma, the US Supreme Court was blinkered by its lack of attention to the other dimensions, which would have highlighted the interrelationship between poverty and race and its multiplier effect for African American pupils. It is well known that, in reality, the facilities available to African American learners were inevitably inferior. Had the court paid attention to the first dimension of substantive equality, namely redressing disadvantage, this would have been obvious. Nor did the case pay sufficient attention to the need for underlying structural change. As Minow puts it: 'Because of *Brown*, schools stopped explicitly assigning students to schools that separate them by race, but parents and communities can produce similar results indirectly through housing patterns, district lines, and even some forms of school choice.'[129] As the aftermath of *Brown* demonstrates, simply addressing recognition harms without paying serious attention to redressing disadvantage and structural change, such as improving the quality of educational provision, is unlikely to achieve substantive equality.

(c) Facilitating participation, social inclusion, and political voice: the participative dimension

The third dimension of substantive equality relates to participation. When past discrimination has blocked the avenues for political participation by particular minorities, equality laws are needed both to compensate for this absence of political voice and to open up the channels for greater participation in the future. Indeed, one of the key contributions of the US Supreme Court has been its recognition of the role of equality in compensating for absence of political power. Thus, in one of the most famous footnotes in history, the US Supreme Court stated that judicial intervention under the

---

[127] ibid para 77.
[128] *Brown v Board of Education* (n 113).
[129] Minow (n 55) 8.

equality guarantee was particularly necessary because of the way in which 'prejudice against discrete and insular minorities . . . tends seriously to curtail the operation of those political processes ordinarily to be relied upon to protect minorities'.[130] Building on this approach, John Hart Ely has developed his 'representation–reinforcing' theory of judicial review in relation to groups 'to whose needs and wishes elected officials have no apparent interest in attending'.[131] Similarly, the Supreme Court of Canada in *Andrews v Law Society*[132] held that the equality guarantee should extend to non-citizens for the very reason that, lacking in political power, they were vulnerable to having their interests overlooked and their rights to equal concern and respect violated.

Participation, the third dimension, is an important complement to the first dimension, redressing disadvantage. The need for greater representativeness in political decision making is not the same as that in relation to jobs or university places. Participation is not so much about the need to distribute benefits as the need to ensure that the perspectives of 'outgroups' (or groups that are persistently 'othered' and marginalized by dominant groups) are heard and taken seriously. Participation is not, however, confined to political participation. Participation also refers to the importance of community in the life of individuals. Rather than the universal, abstract individual of formal equality, substantive equality recognizes that individuals are essentially social. To be fully human includes the ability to participate on equal terms in the community and society more generally. The importance of participation is highlighted in different ways by different theorists. Thus, as we have seen, Young argues that the focus of theories of justice should be on structures which exclude people from participating in determining their actions.[133] For Young, therefore, social equality refers both to the distribution of social goods and to the full participation and inclusion of everyone in major social institutions.[134] Fraser puts particular emphasis on participation, regarding parity of participation as the normative core of her conception of justice, encompassing both redistribution and recognition without reducing either one to the other.[135] Collins, in searching for a justification for departing from the equal treatment principle, develops the concept of social inclusion as

---

[130] *United States v Carolene Products Company* 304 US 144, 152 fn 4 (Stone J) (1938).
[131] JH Ely, *Democracy and Distrust: A Theory of Judicial Review* (Harvard UP 1980) 46.
[132] *Andrews v Law Society (British Columbia)* [1989] 1 SCR 143.
[133] Young (n 4) 31–32.
[134] ibid 173.
[135] Fraser and Honneth (n 109) 36–37.

central to his notion of substantive equality. Like Young and Fraser, Collins's conception includes but goes beyond distribution of material goods.

> Although . . . social inclusion shares with equality a concern with the distributive allocations to groups and individuals in a society, its more fundamental objective is the outcome of social cohesion. Social inclusion is a theory of how society can be integrated and harmonious. At its simplest, the theory is that if everyone participates fully in society, they are less likely to become alienated from the community and will conform to its social rules and laws.[136]

He sees the goal of social inclusion as having the potential to provide a vital ingredient in a more coherent account of the aims of anti-discrimination law. A further alternative characterization is that of solidarity, a value which is also expressed in the EU Charter of Fundamental Rights. Barnard argues that solidarity requires not just the removal of obstacles to participation, but also active measures to integrate individuals into society.[137]

The aim of facilitating participation in equality law plays out in several practical ways. For old people, for example, the ability to participate in the life of the community is a central demand. To achieve equal participation requires attention to be paid to such issues as sufficiency of transport, accessibility of community activities, and possibilities of voluntary work. This dimension also has implications for the public–private divide, requiring equal participation in both family and public life for both men and women. For persons with disabilities, the principle of meaningful participation in decision making about matters affecting their lives has been a key aspect of the demand for equality. The axiom 'Nothing about us without us', signals a demand for full recognition of persons with disabilities as subjects of all human rights.[138] Article 4(3) of the Convention on the Rights of People with Disabilities (CRPD) includes the obligation to 'closely consult and actively involve persons with disabilities, including children with disabilities, through their representative organizations' in decision-making processes concerning issues relating to persons with disabilities. Persons with disabilities and their

---

[136] H Collins, 'Discrimination, Equality and Social Inclusion' (2003) 66 MLR 16, 24.
[137] C Barnard in C Barnard, S Deakin, and G Morris (eds), *The Future of Labour Law: Liber Amicorum Sir Bob Hepple* (Hart Publishing 2004).
[138] Committee on the Rights of Persons with Disabilities, General Comment No 7 (2018).

representative organizations must also participate fully in monitoring the application of the Convention.[139]

(d) Accommodating difference and structural change: the transformative dimension

The transformative dimension constitutes an important step beyond the abstract individualism of the equal treatment principle, or 'anti-classification' approach. Under an anti-classification approach, gender, race, ethnicity, or other status are regarded as irrelevant. This presupposes that it is both desirable and possible to abstract an individual from these aspects of her identity and treat her entirely on 'merit'. By contrast, substantive equality recognizes that these characteristics can be valued aspects of an individual's identity. The problem is not so much difference per se, but the detriment which is attached to difference. The right to substantive equality should therefore aim to respect and accommodate difference, removing the detriment but not the difference itself.

The equal treatment principle assumes that the right to equality should only be concerned with specific acts of prejudice or unequal treatment directed against an individual by the State or another individual. However, as Young has argued, domination need not be attributable to the actions of any particular individual, but produces constraints which are the intended or unintended product of actions of many people.[140] Inequality inheres deeply in the structures of society, fuelled by imbalances of power. The fourth dimension of substantive equality therefore addresses the need for structural change. Crucially, it recognizes that conformity should not be a prerequisite for the right to equality. Existing social structures must be changed to accommodate difference, rather than requiring members of outgroups to conform to the dominant norm. Substantive equality is therefore potentially transformative. For example, working hours have always been patterned on the assumption that childcare takes place outside the labour market. Women who wish to participate in the paid labour market must conform to this paradigm, either by forgoing having children or leaving their children with family members or childcarers, who are most likely to be low-paid women. Substantive equality aims to change such institutions so that participative parenting is compatible with participation of all parents in the paid labour market. Similarly, the built environment must be adapted to accommodate

---

[139] CRPD, Art 33(3).
[140] Young (n 4) 31–32.

the needs of persons with disabilities, and dress codes and holidays must accommodate ethnic and religious minorities.

The transformative dimension grows out of and elaborates duties of accommodation in relation to religion and disability in the US, Canada, and the UK,[141] as well as experiments with mainstreaming and proactive duties. However, transformation goes further than accommodation. While duties of accommodation create exceptions or modify existing structures, a more thoroughgoing alternative to the conformist tendency of like treatment is to create a different norm. This possibility was graphically illustrated in a Canadian case, in which a woman forest firefighter was dismissed for narrowly failing to pass a fitness test based on an aerobic standard demonstrably based on male physiology. The Canadian Court of Appeals held that to apply a different standard for women would be creating reverse discrimination, unfairly discriminating against men. The Canadian Supreme Court reversed the decision. As McLachlin J put it: 'True equality requires that differences be accommodated . . . A different aerobic standard capable of identifying women who could perform the job safely and efficiently therefore does not necessarily imply discrimination against men.'[142]

As with the other facets of substantive equality, accommodating difference raises challenges. How much should employers or the State be expected to spend in order to accommodate difference? Duties of accommodation often include caveats, requiring only such action as is reasonable or practicable. In framing such caveats, however, it should be borne in mind that the question is not about how much to spend but who should bear the cost. It is misleading to argue that it is too costly to accommodate difference, since the cost is incurred in any event. The status quo, without legal intervention, requires the outgroup to bear the full cost: women bear the cost of childbearing and childcare; persons with disabilities bear the cost of disability, which are often socially imposed barriers; and ethnic minorities bear the cost of their own cultural or religious commitments. Whatever cost is not borne by employers or the State is left on the shoulders of those who are least able to bear it. At the same time, little notice is taken of the fact that society does bear the cost of the specific characteristics of dominant groups, be they male, able-bodied, or in the ethnic majority. Working time, the built environment,

---

[141] *US Airways v Barnett* 535 US 391 (2002) (US Sup Ct); *Multani v Commission scolaire Marguerite-Bourgeoys* 2006 SCC 6 (Can Sup Ct).

[142] *British Columbia (Public Service Employee Relations Commission) v BCGSEU* [1999] 3 SCR 3, para 81 (Can Sup Ct).

or religious or cultural holidays and dress already cater for the dominant groups. Substantive equality aims to redistribute these costs in ways which are fairer to all.

(e) Complementarities and conflicts

A major benefit of a multi-dimensional approach is that the dimensions can be used to buttress one another, so that the weaknesses of each alone can be countered. The combination of redressing disadvantage and addressing stigma is particularly salient. The multi-dimensional approach also flushes out potential conflicts between dimensions. Rather than rendering one aspect of the conflict invisible and therefore effectively permitting one to trump the other, the multi-dimensional approach requires synthesis and compromise. For example, measures to redress socio-economic disadvantage might themselves cause stigma and stereotyping. Social welfare rights, although aimed at redressing disadvantage, can be highly intrusive and demeaning, as well as being based on gender stereotypes, such as assuming a male breadwinner or that women are the primary childcarers. The demonizing of welfare recipients as lazy and scroungers in modern rhetoric is a further demonstration. Lister points to the ways in which Black people have been stereotyped and stigmatized through associating them with poverty and welfare dependency.[143] Similarly, Porter describes a 'disturbing pattern of scapegoating the poor' in Canada, where welfare recipients were seen in 'unremittingly negative terms by the economically secure'.[144] Thus, paying attention to both redressing disadvantage and the need to avoid stigma and stereotyping is essential to ensure that the design of social welfare rights is in tune with substantive equality. A similar point could be made about the design of affirmative action programmes which need to take care to avoid stigmatizing the beneficiaries.

A different kind of challenge is raised by the fourth dimension, the need to accommodate difference and achieve structural change. At what point is it unreasonable or even wrong to accommodate difference, or tolerate minority cultures? Many of these dilemmas arise in respect of religion. Should polygamy be accommodated? Should religious objections to equal

---

[143] R Lister, *Poverty* (Polity Press 2004). For a valuable discussion of the role of stigma, see I Solanke, *Discrimination as Stigma* (Bloomsbury 2017).

[144] Bruce Porter, 'Claiming Adjudicative Space: Social Rights, Equality and Citizenship' in Susan Boyd and others (eds), *Poverty: Rights, Social Citizenship and Legal Activism* (UBC Press 2007) 77.

rights for LGBTQI+ people or women be tolerated? Should burkas be permitted? Female genital mutilation? How does this compare with minority approaches to religious festivals, dietary laws, ritual slaughter of animals? Here again, resolution of these difficult dilemmas is facilitated by the multifaceted approach to equality. The transformative dimension must coexist with the second dimension, which addresses stigma, prejudice, stereotyping, and violence. Practices which compromise the basic dignity and humanity of individuals cannot be acceptable in order to accommodate difference. Sexism, racism, homophobia, and harmful practices would therefore not be capable of accommodation. There may, of course, be complex debates as to whether particular cultural or religious practices do breach the recognition dimension, particularly if their adherents believe they do not. However, the multi-dimensional structure gives a framework within which such debates can occur.

Participation also needs to confront questions about whose voice counts. Just because a woman, a Black person, a person from a marginalized minority, or an indigenous person[145] is in a position of power does not mean that the voice of excluded groups has been included. Internal stratifications, and especially intersectionality, need to be taken into account. Margaret Thatcher and Theresa May, both female prime ministers of the UK, were far from committed to ensuring poorer women, minority women, disabled women, lone mothers, or other women achieved substantive equality. The same is true for Justice Clarence Thomas who, despite being a Black member of the US Supreme Court, does not generally reflect the voice of Black people, and especially not Black women. Participation therefore needs to be allied with redressing disadvantage, addressing stigma and stereotyping, and structural change to facilitate genuine participation for those without a voice.

II COMPETING VALUES

Even when agreement is reached on a specific conception or set of conceptions of equality as a basis for a legislative formulation of equality, it is still necessary to consider whether and in what circumstances other, non-equality-based, values should trump equality concerns. Two related rivals of equality will be considered here: liberty and economic or market concerns.

---

[145] See n 3.

(i) Liberty, Freedom, and Autonomy

Possibly the most serious rival for priority with equality is liberty. Indeed, Isaiah Berlin in his famous work characterized liberty and equality as the two primary but frequently conflicting values.

> Both liberty and equality are among the primary goals pursued by human beings through many centuries; but total liberty for wolves is death to the lambs, total liberty of the powerful, the gifted is not compatible with the rights to a decent existence of the weak and the less gifted.[146]

Closer examination shows that just as equality can be interpreted in many differing ways, so can liberty. On one view, the essence of liberty is autonomy, or freedom from interference in individual choices. In its more specific, neoliberal sense, liberty is absence of State interference in the market. On a different view, freedom entails the ability to be and do what one values, requiring positive State action.[147] Correspondingly, the extent of conflict between equality and liberty depends in part on which conception of equality is chosen. A laissez-faire egalitarian might find no conflict between liberty and equality: individuals should be equally free from State interference in order to pursue their own goals, and their fate depends on their own abilities, initiative, and luck.[148] Dworkin argues for a stronger conception of equality, but formulates a principle of liberty which, far from conflicting with equality, is a crucial ingredient.[149]

It might be argued that autonomy is the central value inspiring equality. Such liberty-based approaches to discrimination law are increasingly popular among some recent theorists. Moreau argues that denial of freedom is the primary wrong in cases of discrimination. In particular, she asserts that we care about having valuable opportunities 'only because we care about being able to choose them ourselves and to choose how they fit into our lives . . . in a way that is insulated from pressures stemming from normatively extraneous features of us, such as our skin colour or our gender'.[150] Khaitan argues that 'the relevantly modest goal of discrimination law is to make us free in one

---

[146] I Berlin, *Four Essays on Liberty* (OUP 1969).
[147] Sen (n 105).
[148] ibid 131.
[149] ibid 122.
[150] S Moreau, 'In Defense of a Liberty-based Account of Discrimination' in D Hellman and S Moreau (eds), *Philosophical Foundations of Discrimination Law* (OUP 2013) 81.

respect—that our membership of a relatively disadvantaged group does not impede our pursuit of a good life'.[151]

However, while enhanced agency may be a positive consequence of the fulfilment of the right to substantive equality in all its dimensions, to regard equality as a derivative of autonomy can be problematic. In particular, this overstates the extent to which individuals genuinely have choices in their lives, or can shape their own perception and achievement of a good life. In particular, liberal theories of choice have periodically been used to defeat equality claims on the grounds that the claimant could have chosen to avoid the consequences of a policy or practice. For example, the SACC rejected a claim by a woman cohabitee for equal treatment with married women on the grounds that she could have chosen to get married.[152] Alternatively, the right to equality could be regarded as a prerequisite for genuine freedom. On this view, freedom of choice is constrained by discrimination and inequality of power within society. Freedom of contract in a market order belies deep inequalities of bargaining power, whether between workers and employers, consumers and corporations, or others. On this view, only with equality-based interventions can true freedom of choice be achieved. For example, unless childcare and parenting are shared within society, a woman's choice of paid work is heavily constrained by her childcare responsibilities. Sen's capabilities theory therefore emphasizes that genuine freedom of choice depends on the range of feasible alternatives available to people.[153]

Substantive equality has brought with it an acknowledgement that an individual should not be made to pay an unreasonable price for their choices. More fundamentally, autonomy or freedom of choice is not the only value to strive for. The right to equality for women or others in caring roles is not limited to providing a choice between caring and other preferred activities. The right to equality should aim to improve the conditions in which they provide care regardless of choice. Similarly, different identities should be valued regardless of whether or not they are chosen. Autonomy is therefore not considered as a separate dimension of the right to substantive equality within the four-dimensional approach.

Moreover, the practical experience of equality laws demonstrates a clear potential for conflict between liberty and equality. Courts have had to decide whether prohibitions on racist speech should be struck down as infringing

---

[151] T Khaitan, *A Theory of Discrimination Law* (OUP 2015) 120.

[152] *Volks v Robinson* [2005] ZACC 2 (SACC). But see now *Bwanya v Master of the High Court, Cape Town* [2021] ZACC 51 (South African Constitutional Court) paras 61–67.

[153] Sen (n 105).

freedom of speech or upheld as promoting racial equality. While the courts in the US have upheld the freedom of speech value, Canadian and South African courts have upheld the equality value.[154] Similarly, statutes restricting expenditure on political campaigns have been construed by the courts in some jurisdictions as unduly restricting liberty.[155] Yet the courts in other jurisdictions have construed similar expenditure limits as legitimately promoting equality by ensuring that the political voice of richer individuals does not drown out that of poorer people.[156] Particularly complex is the relationship of liberty to substantive equality based on socio-economic rights. Minimum wages and maximum hours laws could be struck down because they undermine individual freedom of contract or upheld because they promote substantive equality.[157]

(ii) Business- or Market-Oriented Concerns

The second major modern rival for priority with equality is that of business- or market-oriented concerns. In most jurisdictions, statutes and case law have specifically permitted individuals or States to defend incursions on equality on the grounds that this is justified as a pursuit of business needs or State macroeconomic policies. The question then concerns the weight to be given to each of these concerns. Should a policy or business interest displace equality simply because it is convenient or strategic, or must it be demonstrably necessary to achieve the business needs in question? The formulation and application of the justification test has been a central concern in numerous cases.

It is notable that little attention has been paid to why business needs should trump equality. One plausible justification is that of liberty itself: the liberty of employers or other powerful actors to pursue their own interests should not, on this view, be infringed. This view has been on the ascendant since the 1980s due to the political dominance of a neoliberal, laissez-faire ideology. The blatant preference for liberty over equality is often softened by the assertion that the good of the individual business will further the good of

---

[154] *RAV v City of St Paul, Minn* 505 US 377, 112 S Ct 2538 (1992); cf *R v Keegstra* (1996) 61 CCC (3d) 1 (Can Sup Ct).

[155] *Buckley v Valeo* 424 US 1 (1976); *Citizens United v Federal Election Commission* 130 S Ct 876 (2010) (US Sup Ct); *McCutcheon v Federal Election Commission* 134 S Ct 1434 (2014).

[156] *Bowman v UK* (1998) 26 EHRR 1.

[157] *Lochner v New York* 198 US 45, 25 S Ct 539 (1905).

all, even if it subordinates particular equality rights (eg the right of a woman to equal pay with a man doing work of equal value). In an attempt to counteract the power of this ideology, the more mellow final years of the twentieth century saw an attempt to create a convergence between the two notions. Far from detracting from market concerns, it was argued, equality laws are demonstrably capable of serving economic and particularly efficiency-based ends.[158] This was particularly true in the EU where fundamental rights justifications for equal opportunities between men and women were supported by labour market justifications. The result was that the impetus for gender equality was seen through an 'economic prism', which characterized the disadvantaged position of women in the labour market as a source of economic inefficiency, and therefore included sex equality within its strategy to achieve economic competitiveness.[159]

There was always the danger that instead of a genuine and mutually reinforcing coincidence of aims, the rhetoric of convergence would merely obscure the extent to which market concerns were stunting the growth of a truly rights-based equality principle. This was, indeed, exposed after the banking crisis in 2008, when austerity policies were imposed in several countries, signalling a severe cut-back on State spending on public services and social security. These policies have had a disproportionate impact on women, Black people, people from marginalized minorities or indigenous people,[160] people with disabilities, older people, and especially those in more than one of these groups. They were also accompanied by cuts in access to justice, such as legal aid, making it difficult to utilize anti-discrimination laws to counter these discriminatory effects. Courts in several jurisdictions were therefore asked to determine whether the State's appeal to the need for austerity in public spending was sufficient justification for the discriminatory effects of its policies.[161]

This puts the spotlight on how a balance is to be achieved between the right to equality and competing costs justification. When the court holds the balance between the equality value and that of market or business concerns, the weight given to the various values becomes crucial. A bias towards

---

[158] See S Deakin, 'Labour Law as Market Regulation' in P Davies and others (eds), *European Community Labour Law: Principles and Perspectives* (Clarendon Press 1996); S Deakin and F Wilkinson, 'Rights vs Efficiency?' (1994) 23 ILJ 289.

[159] See S Duncan, 'Obstacles to a Successful Equal Opportunities Policy in the EU' (1996) 3(4) European Journal of Women's Studies 399.

[160] See n 3.

[161] *R (MA) v Secretary of State for Work and Pensions* [2016] UKSC 58.

business needs would yield a test which allows mere convenience to justify an infringement on equality, whereas a greater (although not absolute) commitment to equality would require it to be limited only to the extent strictly necessary to achieve the stated aim. For example, if an employer wishes to justify paying female part-time workers less than male full-timers doing the same job, a lenient standard would allow them simply to assert that part-timers are less valuable, or that it is more profitable to pay them less. A strict standard would require the employer to prove that there was no less discriminatory alternative to achieving the stated aim of increased profits or creating a more productive workforce.[162] Most importantly, the costs to the workers themselves need to be factored in.

Faced with austerity justifications, courts in several jurisdictions have opted for the more lenient standard, at least in respect of State policies. Thus, the Supreme Court of Canada held that provincial legislation which had the intended effect of continuing to pay women hospital workers less than that paid to men for work of equal value was justifiable because of the need to address the fiscal crisis.[163] Although courts 'should look with strong scepticism at attempts to justify infringements of the [Canadian] Charter on the basis of budgetary constraints' the court nevertheless concluded that 'the courts cannot close their eyes to the periodic occurrence of financial emergencies when measures must be taken to juggle priorities to see a government through the crisis'.[164]

An even more lenient standard has been applied by the UK Supreme Court. In a series of cases, it has been held that policies with socio-economic implications which have a disproportionate impact on groups with protected characteristics will only be found to be unjustified if 'manifestly without reasonable foundation'.[165] Thus, in a case challenging benefit cuts which had a disproportionate impact on lone female-parent households, one of the government's stated aims was to make fiscal savings. Evidence showed that net savings were a miniscule proportion of the State's overall annual expenditure on welfare benefits for those of working age. At the same time, the impact on the vulnerable class was serious, reducing family income well below the poverty line, and having a long-term detrimental effect on children in such families.[166] Nevertheless, applying the 'manifestly without reasonable

---

[162] See further Chapter 4.
[163] *Newfoundland (Treasury Board) v NAPE* 2004 SCC 66 (Can Sup Ct).
[164] ibid para 72.
[165] *R (On the application of DA) v Secretary of State for Work and Pensions* [2019] UKSC 21 [65]. See also Chapter 3.
[166] ibid [34].

foundation' test, the majority of the court rejected the claim that the policy involved unjustifiable discrimination.[167] A stricter test would require the balance to be drawn very differently, most importantly by recognizing the cost to the affected families. As Lady Hale put it: 'Striking a fair balance would have set the very limited benefits to the public interest against the damage done to the family lives of young children and their lone parents if either their parents are forced to work outside the home in order to have enough for themselves and their children to live on or they are unable or unwilling to work outside the home and are thus forced to attempt to live on less than the state has decided that they need.'[168] Finding that the weight of the evidence showed that a fair balance had not been struck, she held that the regulations at issue involved unjustified discrimination against lone parents of children under the age of five, and against those children.

III CONCLUSION

This chapter has examined some of the major conceptual issues surrounding the equality principle. It has considered differing conceptions of the equality principle and proposed a four-dimensional solution, as well as sketching out possible limitations and complexities. The next chapter, recognizing that equality cannot be considered in the abstract but must be understood in its historical and political context, turns to a brief account of the development of the right to equality in the UK and EU, the US, India, South Africa, and Canada.

---

[167] ibid [88].
[168] ibid [156].

2

Social Context and Legal Developments

Gender, Race, and Religion

Anti-discrimination law is necessarily a response to particular manifestations of inequality, which are themselves deeply embedded in the historical and political context of a given society. Discrimination laws are only effective if they are moulded to deal with the types of inequalities which have developed in the society to which they refer. The legal framework has, in turn, developed and changed in response to a variety of influences, including political and social forces, and wider ranging human rights obligations. The result is a complex and interlocking set of factors, both legal and social, which continue to evolve in a dialectic fashion. This chapter and the following one aim to briefly trace the evolution of these factors in the jurisdictions examined here, focusing on the major groupings that form the context of modern anti-discrimination law. This chapter examines gender, race, ethnicity, and religion and belief, while Chapter 3 considers sexual orientation, gender identity, disability, and age.

I GENDER

(i) Challenges and Dilemmas: Sex, Gender, or Women?

As Simone de Beauvoir famously commented: 'One is not born, but rather becomes, a woman.'[1] How, then, should the quest for equality be understood? Is it about sex, gender, or women? International and national instruments generally refer to 'sex' as a ground of discrimination. Early feminists, however, began to draw a distinction between sex and gender 'with sex understood as a bodily or biological category and gender as the social meaning of sex'.[2] The use of gender is now widespread, including in official

---

[1] S de Beauvoir, *The Second Sex* (new edn, Vintage Digital 2014).
[2] N Lacey, *Unspeakable Subjects: Feminist Essays in Legal and Social Theory* (Hart Publishing 1998).

Discrimination Law. Third Edition. Sandra Fredman, Oxford University Press. © Sandra Fredman 2022.
DOI: 10.1093/oso/9780198854081.003.0002

documents. For example, in early 2020 the European Commission published its 'Gender Equality Strategy' for the period 2020–25.[3] Gender, it states, means 'the socially constructed roles, behaviours, activities and attributes that a given society considers appropriate for women and men'.[4] The South African Constitution refers to both 'sex' and 'gender'.[5] On the other hand, as its name suggests, the Convention on the Elimination of Discrimination against Women (CEDAW) deliberately foregrounds women. This, too, is not straightforward. As Simone de Beauvoir put it in her introduction to the *Second Sex*,[6] 'Biological and social sciences no longer believe that there are immutably determined entities that define given characteristics such as those of the woman, the Jew[ish person] or the Black [person] . . . If there is no such thing today as femininity, it is because there never was. Does the word "woman" then have no content?'[7] The answer, as she shows, is that in reality women have been subordinate to men throughout history. If we abolish the category 'woman', this might simply render invisible the many inequalities to which women are still subject, whether through express law, customary attributions, or structural barriers. On the other hand, binary distinctions risk ignoring the reality of gender fluidity. The very categories of sex, gender, men, and women, by insisting on rigid boundaries which cannot be traversed, threaten to erase the identity of gender fluid people, trans men and trans women.

Paradoxically, however, for trans women at least, there is a sense in which the category 'woman' must exist. Does this mean that the 'femininity' de Beauvoir and many subsequent feminists have so strenuously resisted is simultaneously an aspiration for trans women? Or is the problem not so much femininity as such but the negative connotations attached to it? Julia Serano argues powerfully from her own experience of transitioning that 'while biological gender differences are very real, most of the connotations, values and assumptions we associate with female and male biology are not'.[8] Her own experience of transitioning demonstrated to her that some attributes are clearly affected by hormones. However, socialization exaggerates these

[3] European Commission, 'A Union of Equality: Gender Equality Strategy 2020–2025', COM(2020) 152 final (Brussels, 5 March 2020).

[4] See also Council of Europe Convention on preventing and combating violence against women and domestic violence, Art 3(c).

[5] South African Constitution, s 9(3).

[6] de Beauvoir (n 1).

[7] ibid 23.

[8] J Serano, *Whipping Girl: A Transexual Woman on Sexism and the Scapegoating of Femininity* (Seal Press 2016) 76.

differences by attempting to discourage or erase the natural diversity in the way in which we experience the world. 'While embracing my own femaleness and femininity during my transition was personally empowering and rewarding, I nevertheless felt overwhelmed by all of the negative connotations and inferior meanings that other people began to project onto me.'[9]

It is in this spirit that this section examines the development of equality for women. Legal and social restrictions have been based on a classification of people into the categories of 'women' and 'men'. Just as assuming a 'race-blind'[10] or 'colour-blind'[11] world will not make race discrimination vanish, so abandoning the category of 'woman' will not itself erase women's subordination. At the same time, the gender ascriptions which continue to fuel this subordination need to be constantly contested. This means that 'woman' must always be inclusive of all those who identify as women, and of all the wide diversity of expressions, experiences, and social locations that women inhabit or which are ascribed to them. Nor does a recognition that inequality has for centuries been attached to women as women mean that there is an assumption of a gender binary world.

(ii) Historical Context

(a) From legal erasure to equality before the law

The development of equality for women in any real sense is disturbingly recent across the countries studied here.[12] Until well into the twentieth century in all the jurisdictions examined here, women were legally subordinate to men in a host of different ways. This was especially true of marriage. Under the common law, known as 'coverture', marriage constituted a legal obliteration of women's identity. 'The very being or legal existence of the wife is suspended during the marriage or at least incorporated and consolidated into that of the husband under whose wing, protection and cover she performs

---

[9] ibid 75.

[10] *Fisher v University of Texas at Austin* 136 S Ct 2198, 2236 (2016) (US Sup Ct).

[11] The term 'colour-blind' Constitution has been used by Justices of the US Supreme Court who argue that skin colour should never be a relevant factor in determining access to university or jobs, and therefore affirmative action in favour of disadvantaged groups should not be permitted (see Chapter 7). For a critique, see R Kennedy, 'Colorblind Constitutionalism' (2013) 82 Fordham L Rev 1.

[12] This section is drawn substantially from S Fredman, *Women and the Law* (Clarendon Press 1997) ch 2.

everything,'[13] wrote Blackstone in 1809. A married woman was a perpetual legal minor. Her husband had near-absolute control over her property as well as her person. She had no right to custody of their children and no right to testamentary freedom. Substantial levels of violence perpetrated against wives were condoned, initially explicitly through the husband's legal power of 'domestic chastisement' and later, tacitly, even when this power had come to be doubted. Nor was a married woman entitled to refuse consent to sexual intercourse with her husband. Indeed, it was not until the last decades of the twentieth century that rape in marriage was recognized as a crime.[14] Not surprisingly, John Stuart Mill described the law of marriage as 'the only legal bondage known to our law'.[15]

The colonial influence of England meant that similar patterns can be seen in the US, Canada, India, and South Africa where patriarchy was overlaid with racist and caste-based discrimination for Black women, indigenous women, lower caste women, and women from marginalized minorities.[16] In the US, the colonial laws of coverture applied well into the nineteenth century, with married women having no separate legal identity and therefore no rights to property ownership. The law of coverture lasted in several US States well into the twentieth century, with at least ten States limiting the capacity of married women to enter into contracts as recently as 1966.[17] As Justice Black put it in his dissenting opinion in *US v Yazell*, the law of coverture rests 'on the old common-law fiction that the husband and wife are one. This rule has worked out in reality to mean that though the husband and wife are one, the

---

[13] W Blackstone, *Commentaries on the Law of England* (15th edn, T Cadell & W Davies 1809) Book I, ch XV, 430.

[14] *R v R* [1991] 4 All ER 481 (HL). In Canada, Bill C-127 came into effect on 4 January 1983, making sexual assault against one's wife an offence. In the US, marital rape was made a crime in all fifty States between 1970 and 1993. In South Africa, marital rape was made a crime through the Prevention of Family Violence Act in 1993.

[15] JS Mill, *The Subjection of Women* (Wordsworth Classics 1996) 135.

[16] This book acknowledges that the terminology used to describe people subjected to discrimination is sensitive and contested. In the different jurisdictions covered here (UK, Europe, India, South Africa, Canada, and the US), outgroups, or groups that are 'othered' in their own societies or globally, prefer to refer to themselves in different and sometimes opposing ways, and this can change with changes in social forces and perceptions. Acknowledging these complexities, I have chosen to use 'Black people', 'marginalized ethnicities', and 'indigenous people', following the approach of the UN Special Rapporteur on the right to health, Tlaleng Mofokeng, in her report to the United Nations on sexual and reproductive health rights on 16 July 2021 (A/76/172) <https://undocs.org/A/76/172> accessed 31 May 2022. The reference to 'gender identity, gender expression and sex characteristics' follows her report on gender-based violence submitted to the UN on 14 April 2022 (A/HRC/50/28) <www.ohchr.org/en/documents/thematic-reports/ahrc5 028-violence-and-its-impact-right-health-report-special-rapporteur> accessed 31 May 2022.

[17] *United States v Yazell* 382 US 341 (1966) (US Sup Ct).

one is the husband.'[18] It was only in 1981 that the US Supreme Court struck down legislation giving the husband as 'head and master' of property owned jointly with his wife the right to unilaterally dispose of such property without his wife's consent.[19]

Similarly, Roman–Dutch law, which prevails in South Africa, included a doctrine of the marital power according to which a married woman was legally a minor under the guardianship of her husband. The marital power was only fully abolished for all civil marriages in 1993, but it remained in force for women in customary law marriages until as recently as 2000.[20] For Black women in South Africa, the confluence of racism, patriarchy, class, and colonialism has been particularly insidious. Legislation purporting to codify customary law relegated African women to the status of perpetual minors, creating matrimonial property systems which were in fact more reminiscent of the colonial law of coverture than the complex communal arrangements of property-holding among African people in pre-colonial times.[21] This multiple, intersecting disadvantage has still not been fully eradicated even in the formal legal system. As Goliath AJ put it in a recent case: 'During apartheid, the African woman was a particularly vulnerable figure in society and she suffered three-fold discrimination based on her race, her class and her gender. Reflecting upon the present, we must ask ourselves whether the African woman truly benefits from the full protection of the Constitution. Moreover, we must establish whether enough has been done to eradicate the discrimination and inequality that so many women face daily.'[22]

For Indian women, personal law systems based on religion have similarly overlaid patriarchy with colonial assumptions about women's secondary status. It was not until 2020, in *Joseph Shine*, that adultery laws were struck down as a breach of the right to equality. Justice Chandrachud acknowledged both the colonial foundations of the adultery laws in question[23] and the patriarchal notions they perpetuated, which assumed 'that the woman is but a chattel; the property of her husband'.[24] Marital rape is still not regarded as a crime in India. This is despite repeated calls to criminalize marital rape,

---

[18] ibid 361.

[19] *Kirchberg v Feenstra* 450 US 455 (1981) (US Sup Ct).

[20] Recognition of Customary Marriages Act 2000.

[21] *Rahube v Rahube* [2018] ZACC 22, para 28 (SACC). See also *Gumede (born Shange) v President of the Republic of South Africa and Others* (CCT 50/08) [2008] ZACC 23, 2009 (3) BCLR 243 (CC), 2009 (3) SA 152 (CC).

[22] *Rahube v Rahube* ibid para 2.

[23] *Joseph Shine v Union of India* (2019) 3 SCC 39, paras 138–40.

[24] ibid para 160.

most recently by the 2013 report of the Justice Verma Committee on reform of rape law.[25]

Muslim religious laws bring an added layer of complexity because of the intersecting axes of oppression faced by Muslim women in India, both on account of their gender and religious minority status. In 2017, triple *talaq*, the instant, irrevocable pronouncement of divorce by a Muslim man, was struck down as unconstitutional by the Indian Supreme Court.[26] The case was brought before the Court by a Muslim woman who had been divorced by her husband through triple *talaq*, and several Muslim women's organizations supported her case. They argued that the practice of triple *talaq* was both un-Islamic and a violation of the right to equality for Muslim women. Both arguments found favour with the majority of the Court. Similarly contentious has been the issue of maintenance for divorced Muslim women. In 1985, in the *Shah Bano* case, the Indian Supreme Court held that the general law on maintenance, 'enacted in order to provide a quick and summary remedy to a class of persons who are unable to maintain themselves' applied to Muslim women.[27] This was met with fierce criticism from a section of Muslims who considered this an interference with Muslim religious norms around provision of maintenance. Acceding to the criticism, the Indian Parliament enacted legislation requiring that there should be 'reasonable and fair provision and maintenance' to a divorced Muslim woman by her husband, limited to the *iddat* period prescribed under Muslim personal law.[28] The Act was criticized by women for being regressive, and was challenged for violating Articles 14 (right to equality) and 21 (right to life and personal liberty) of the Indian Constitution. It was contended that the Act discriminated against Muslim women by denying them a remedy available to all other women, and violated the right of divorced Muslim women to live a life of dignity. In *Danial Latifi*, the Supreme Court struck a fragile compromise. It upheld the validity of the Act by interpreting it to require the provision of maintenance equivalent to the general law on maintenance, although to be paid only in the *iddat* period.[29]

---

[25] Report of the Committee on Amendments to Criminal Law (23 January 2013) <https://prsindia.org/policy/report-summaries/justice-verma-committee-report-summary> accessed 25 July 2022.

[26] *Shayara Bano v Union of India* (2017) 9 SCC 1.

[27] *Mohd Ahmed Khan v Shah Bano Begum* (1985) 2 SCC 556, para 7.

[28] The Muslim Women (Protection of Rights in Divorce) Act 1986.

[29] *Danial Latifi v Union of India* (2001) 7 SCC 740, paras 28–33.

Nor was marriage the only source of women's inequality in all these jurisdictions. Until well into the twentieth century, women were barred from political participation. Women's continued subordination was reconciled with prevailing ideals of equality by characterizing women as irrational, temperamentally unsuited to political life, and by nature consigned to the home. Rejecting a proposal to extend the suffrage to women in 1892 in England, Asquith justified his position to Parliament by arguing that '[Women's] natural sphere is not the turmoil and dust of politics but the circle of social and domestic life.'[30] The refusal of nineteenth-century legislatures to accept women as equal citizens was supported by an intransigent judiciary.[31] In England, legislation granting women the municipal franchise in 1869[32] was immediately interpreted by the judges to exclude married women. On marriage, it was held, a woman's 'existence was merged with that of her husband', and therefore she could not vote.[33] Even when the right to vote at local level was established, judges moved quickly to hold that this did not include the right to stand for election. 'By the common law of England, women are not in general deemed capable of exercising public functions' and therefore only express words of a statute could change this.[34]

Political participation was similarly denied to women in the US. The Fifteenth Amendment, ratified in 1870, prohibited States from denying voting rights on the grounds of race. But sex was not mentioned, allowing States to deny women the right to vote with impunity. A similar pattern can be seen in Canada, where a statute of 1849 expressly enacted that no woman would be entitled to vote at any level for representatives in the legislative assembly of what was then the Province of Canada.[35] The same was true for pre-independence India and South Africa.

Within the workforce, women were similarly disadvantaged. Women have always participated in paid work. But it was assumed without question that women should be paid at a lower rate than men, even when they were engaged in identical work.[36] Again, this was justified by the well-worn myths that a woman's natural role was in the home; that she should depend on her husband for subsistence; that she did not have to support a family; or that

---

[30] Parl Deb (series 4) vol 3, col 1513 (27 April 1892).
[31] *Chorlton v Lings* (1868–69) LR 4 CP 374.
[32] Municipal Franchise Act 1869.
[33] *R v Harrald* [1872] LR VII QB 361.
[34] *De Souza v Cobden* [1891] 1 QB 687, 691 (CA).
[35] Statute of the Province of Canada 1849 (12 Vict c 27), s 46.
[36] See Fredman (n 12) 107 ff.

she was less productive than a man. Again, the courts in many jurisdictions were active proponents of such discrimination. When the English Borough Council of Poplar instituted equal pay for men and women on the lowest grade, the British House of Lords struck down the policy as irrational. In its view, the council had allowed itself to be guided by 'some eccentric principles of socialistic philanthropy, or by a feminist ambition to secure the equality of the sexes in the matter of wages in the world of labour'.[37]

As well as low pay for like work, job segregation was endemic. Women were formally excluded from important spheres of work, including medicine and law, until the late nineteenth century. In addition, women workers were often physically segregated from men, in separate rooms or floors; and possibilities for training or promotion were minimal. These patterns were often reinforced by trade unions, whose male membership perceived that equal pay for women would constitute a threat to the legitimacy of their demand for a 'family wage'; and that permitting women to compete for 'male' jobs might undercut their own position. It was only when trade unions came to the view that equal pay for women would in fact prevent cheap substitution of female labour that it was decided to support the campaign for equal pay.

The battle for juridical equality was a long and painful one. It was only in the late nineteenth century, and then at an excruciatingly slow pace, that these legal disabilities were gradually dismantled. In the UK, genuine progress towards formal equality in property rights between husband and wife was only clearly evident after 1882, a process which was not complete until 1935. Similarly, the father's absolute right to custody of the children was only fully reversed in 1925. Most glaring in its contradiction of liberalism's promise of equality was the refusal to extend political rights to women. Women were not permitted to vote in national elections until 1918 and, even then, a minimum voting age of thirty was imposed. True equality was not fully conceded until 1928, when the minimum voting age for men and women was equalized at twenty-one. However, women were still barred from the House of Lords, in which formal equality was not achieved until as recently as 1963.

In other jurisdictions, too, progress was halting and contested. In the US, it was not until 1920 that protracted struggles by women finally yielded the passage of the Nineteenth Amendment, which prohibits States from denying a person the right to vote based on their sex.[38] In India, women gained the

---

[37] *Roberts v Hopwood* [1925] AC 578, 591 (per Lord Atkinson) (HL).

[38] This required a majority in both the US House of Representatives and the US Senate, as well as ratification by three-quarters of States.

right to vote gradually during British rule, through the efforts of Indian suffragettes who strove for greater political participation of Indian women along with their struggle for Indian independence. Some progress was achieved by the 1919 Government of India Act, which gave Indian provincial legislatures the power to decide on the women's vote. In the 1930s, women became eligible to stand for elections to provincial legislatures. The 1935 Government of India Act gave the vote to selected groups of women: wives and widows of existing male voters or women with a literary qualification. It was only after independence in 1947 that Indian women gained universal franchise.

In Canada, most women were given the vote at the federal level in 1918 but with significant exclusions on racial grounds, as we will see later. Enfranchised women could stand for the House of Commons from 1919. However, appointment to the Senate continued to be barred, a position upheld in 1928 by the Supreme Court of Canada, which held that women were not 'qualified persons' for the purposes of the Act constituting the Senate (the British North America Act). The Court relied on an English decision dating back to 1868 as decisive authority for the view that, by the common law of England, women were legally incapable of holding public office:[39] 'Chiefly out of respect to women, and a sense of decorum, and not from their want of intellect, or their being for any other such reason unfit to take part in the government of the country, they have been excused from taking any share in this department of public affairs.'[40] It was the Privy Council in London that overturned this decision, holding that the word 'persons' in the British North America Act included members of either sex.[41] Importantly, the Privy Council held that decisions in England based on the common law disability of women to hold public office were inapplicable to the interpretation of the Act.

Everywhere, however, race, class, ethnicity, and caste were used to create divisions and ferment tensions between groups of women. The imposition of property ownership as a condition for eligibility to vote was one such divisive factor, tempting middle-class women to accept voting rights which excluded their working-class sisters. In England, arguments in the nineteenth century about the extension of the franchise to women were divided on class lines, particularly during the nineteenth century, when the extent to which

---

[39] *Re Meaning of the word 'Persons' in s 24 of British North America Act* [1928] SCR 276 (Can Sup Ct).

[40] *Chorlton v Lings* (n 31).

[41] *Edwards v Attorney-General for Canada* [1930] AC 124 (Privy Council).

working-class men were to be allowed to vote was still a matter of political controversy. Feminist groups were often divided over whether to insist on the franchise for all adults, regardless of property, or to press only for formal equality with men, thus limiting the suffrage to propertied women. Similarly, representatives of single women were prepared to advocate for the exclusion of married women from any proposed extension.[42] When the vote was finally gained, there were in fact no property requirements but, as we have seen, women under thirty were excluded from the vote until 1928.

Exclusion of Black women, indigenous women, and women from marginalized minorities[43] has been even more salient. In Canada, when the right to vote in federal elections was finally extended to women in 1918, exclusions based on race in the provinces were maintained.[44] Chinese, Japanese, and South Asian men and women were not included in the vote until after the Second World War and indigenous women and men were almost all excluded from the vote until 1960.[45] Nor has entitlement to vote signalled equality. Instead, enfranchisement has been used as an avenue for the assimilation of indigenous people, rather than one of emancipation. For indigenous women, in particular, the right to vote in federal elections until very recently entailed the loss of the rights and privileges of band members, such as the right to hold or inherit property on the reserve, to live or be buried there, or to access services. 'Gaining the vote can therefore be seen as a paternalistic and colonizing process, rather than one that signalled political liberation.'[46] The long-term effects of involuntary enfranchisement for women who married out have only partially been reversed.[47]

In the US, the Nineteenth Amendment, which prohibited the US or individual States from denying the right to vote on account of sex, did not differentiate on racial grounds. The eight million American voters who cast their votes for the first time in the presidential election of 1920 included many Black women. However, many others were prevented from voting by tactics such as poll taxes, literacy tests, discriminatory State voting laws, and intimidation. Native American women and men were also effectively barred from

---

[42] See further Fredman (n 12) 59–66.

[43] See n 16.

[44] Dominion Elections Act 1920. This covered Chinese, Japanese, and South Asians in British Columbia and Chinese in Saskatchewan. The Inuit and most First Nations were also excluded.

[45] The Canadian Encyclopaedia <www.thecanadianencyclopedia.ca/en/article/suffrage> accessed 21 September 2020.

[46] ibid   <www.thecanadianencyclopedia.ca/en/article/indigenous-women-and-the-franchise> accessed 21 September 2020.

[47] ibid.

voting in many States until 1962. It was only after many years of struggle that such tactics were barred by the Voting Rights Act of 1965,[48] a statute which has itself been subsequently diluted by judicial decisions.[49]

These divisions were even more acute in South Africa. White women were not given the vote until 1930, but the white women's suffrage movement was only successful in extracting this concession because the extra white votes diluted the importance of the few remaining Black voters in the Cape Province. As Hassim puts it: 'By their complicity in this political manoeuvre, white women placed their racial and class concerns above any solidarity between women.'[50] Black women and men only achieved full democratic participation after 1994.

(b) Equality through law: ambitions and illusions

Juridical equality was not, however, the end of the struggle. It was with deep disappointment that feminists and women's rights campaigners realized that lifting legal impediments was not sufficient to dislodge the deeply ingrained patterns of prejudice and disadvantage suffered by women. The radical shake-up of the First World War, when women were of necessity precipitated into male jobs, was not sufficient to dislodge these deep-seated patterns. After the war, in the UK pay differentials between men and women were institutionalized across the public and private sectors. In the civil service, women's pay was pegged at a maximum of 80 per cent of that of men; and statutory instruments prescribing pay in the police forces and teaching profession prescribed similar discrepancies for men and women doing the same work. Returning veterans were given priority for jobs and women were forced back into domestic work and other menial work by fierce polemical campaigns directed against women accused of taking men's jobs. An attempt to provide for equal pay in the teaching profession was vetoed by Churchill in 1944.

After the Second World War, women became a far more visible part of the workforce; helped by the increasing availability of contraception, falling family sizes, and rapidly advancing technology creating electrical appliances to assist with domestic work. But job segregation and pay disparities persisted. Women were still dismissed on marriage in many occupations until

---

[48] Martha S Jones, 'For Black women, the 19th Amendment didn't end their fight to vote' <www.nationalgeographic.com/history/2020/08/black-women-continued-fighting-for-vote-after-19th-amendment/> accessed 21 September 2020.

[49] *Shelby County v Holder* 133 S Ct 2612 (2013) (US Sup Ct). See further later in the chapter.

[50] S Hassim, '"A Conspiracy of Women": The Women's Movement in South Africa's Transition to Democracy' (2002) 69 Social Research 693, 705.

well into the postwar period; and the practice of paying women less than men for performing the same work was widespread and officially endorsed. For example, women civil servants were paid on separate and lower pay scales than men doing the same work until 1962.[51] Jobs were highly segregated with women clustered in low paid, low status 'women's work'.

Similar patterns can be seen in the other jurisdictions, again overlaid with race and caste discrimination. Although women were recruited into the labour force in large numbers in the US during the Second World War, they were expected to return to their role as homemakers once the war had ended, making space for returning war veterans. At its height, there were 18.2 million employed women in the workforce in the US during the Second World War, but this dropped to 15.8 million in 1947. After the war had ended, 3.5 million women had voluntarily, or involuntarily, left the labour force.[52] During the next decade, the ideology of woman as homemaker became increasingly influential. The average marriage age of women during the 1950s in the US dropped, and the birth rate climbed rapidly. Correspondingly, the proportion of women attending college plunged: from 47 per cent in 1920 to 35 per cent in 1958.[53] This was the period where US feminist writers, such as Betty Friedan, exposed the suffocation of the housewife role. 'It is more than a strange paradox that as all professions are finally open to women in America, "career woman" has become a dirty word; that as higher education becomes available to any woman with the capacity for it, education for women has become so suspect that more and more drop out of high school and college to marry and have babies, that as so many roles are theirs for the taking, women so insistently confine themselves to one role?'[54] Friedan called this the 'feminine mystique'. 'The feminists had only one model, one image, one vision of a full and free human being: man.'[55]

Friedan's exposure of the ideology of the 'Happy Housewife Heroine',[56] which in reality trapped women in suburban housekeeping and child-rearing, was a powerful stimulus for many women to pursue their potential outside the family. However, this important perception was itself trapped in the paradigm of the white middle-class woman; it was never true of the many women who had always had no option but to undertake paid work.

---

[51]   See Fredman (n 12) 134.
[52]   P Colman, *Rosie the Riveter* (Random House 1998).
[53]   B Friedan, *The Feminine Mystique* (Penguin 1963) 6.
[54]   ibid 49.
[55]   ibid 62.
[56]   ibid 21.

Moreover, while work can be liberating for those who can exit the home into a fulfilling profession, for Black, indigenous, marginalized ethnic,[57] and other working-class women, paid work frequently takes the form of the drudgery of cleaning, cooking, laundry, agricultural, or factory work.[58] Slavery did not distinguish between men and women in the infliction of drudgery, dirty, manual, or dangerous work.[59] Once liberated, African American women did not have the privilege of choosing to be stay-at-home mothers; instead, there is a long history of controlling their reproductive capacity. As Patricia Hill Collins puts it: 'If women are allegedly passive and fragile, then why are Black women treated as "mules" and assigned heavy cleaning chores? If good mothers are supposed to stay at home with the children, then why are US Black women on public assistance forced to find jobs and leave their children in day care?'[60] Moreover, racism against black men, profoundly shaped black women's role. 'Denying U.S. Black men a family wage meant that Black women continued working for pay. Motherhood as a privatized, female "occupation" never predominated in Black civil society because no social class foundation could be had to support it.'[61]

A similar pattern emerges in relation to Black women in South Africa and Dalit women in India. Under apartheid in South Africa, all Black workers were subject to highly oppressive laws restricting their movement and the kinds of jobs in which they could be employed.[62] Africans were not permitted to reside with their families in urban areas unless they fulfilled strict eligibility criteria.[63] Even then, they were required to live in segregated 'townships', characterized by poor housing and little or no infrastructure, such as electricity or running water. The remainder were consigned to the few small

---

[57] See n 16.

[58] P Collins, *Black Feminist Thought: Knowledge, Consciousness, and the Politics of Empowerment* (Routledge 2000) 58.

[59] ibid 50.

[60] ibid 11.

[61] ibid 53.

[62] See Population Registration Act 1950 (repealed 1991); Influx Control Act (preventing Black people from rural areas seeking work in cities, repealed 1986); Group Areas Act 1950 (preventing Black people from living in areas designated as 'white', which constituted 85 per cent of the country, repealed 1991); Industrial Conciliation Act 1956 (authorizing the reservation of jobs for different population groups, repealed 1981); Native Labour Relations Regulation Act 1953 (excluding Black workers from the definition of employee, preventing them from participating in collective bargaining and prohibiting strikes, repealed 1981); Labour Relations Amendment Act 1984 (further restricting the Black labour force).

[63] eg those who were born in the area, had worked legally for fifteen years, or had worked for the same employer in that area for ten years: Native Laws Amendment Act, Act No 54 of 1952, s 27.

rural areas 'reserved' for Africans, where the lack of employment fuelled the 'migrant labour' system which had emerged to provide labour in South Africa's gold and diamond mines. While migrant men lived in abysmal conditions in overcrowded, single-sex hostels close to their work, women were required to remain in the 'reserves' with their children. In addition to relentless poverty, these women, comprising about 80 per cent of African women, were subject to the authority of male chiefs, whose power was increasingly augmented during the 1950s and 1960s.[64]

For those women who had the right to reside in urban areas, opportunities for employment were largely limited to domestic work in white households. As Cock puts it, 'The situation of black and white women in South Africa presents a challenge to any oversimplified feminist notion of "sisterhood". That challenge is sharpest in the institution of domestic service where the wages paid and the hours of work exacted by white "madams" from their black "maids" suggests a measure of oppression of women by women.'[65] Restrictions on mobility, especially for migrant women, bound domestic workers very closely to their employers, in the knowledge that losing their job would consign them to the grinding poverty of the reserved areas. And yet domestic workers had no legal protection in relation to minimum wages, hours of work, or sickness or maternity protection and were vulnerable to instant dismissal. If they were not employed as domestic workers, Black[66] women workers congregated in the lowest paid and least secure jobs in agriculture and manufacturing, especially food, clothing, and textiles. As with their American counterparts, full-time motherhood was not a possibility for urban Black women, whose paltry income was essential for their own and their children's survival. At the same time, Cock points out, there was a rigid division of labour within the home, with cooking, cleaning, shopping, and childcare rigidly regarded as women's work. Men's involvement in family homework was virtually non-existent among the African working class.[67] On the other hand, there were very strong female mutual support networks which were crucial to the survival of women coping with the double burden of being mothers and workers.

---

[64] Bantu Authorities Act 1951.

[65] J Cock, 'Trapped Workers: Constraints and Contradictions Experienced by Black Women in Contemporary South Africa' (1987) 10 Women's Studies Int Forum 133, 133.

[66] In South Africa under apartheid, the term 'Black' was often used to denote all groups oppressed by apartheid: 'We are all oppressed by the same system'; Steve Biko, *I Write What I Like* (Oxford Heinemann 1987).

[67] ibid 136.

For Dalit women in India, their gender and lower caste status has intensified their oppression. Dalit people were treated as 'untouchables' and relegated to the most demeaning forms of labour, particularly manual scavenging—the degrading and dehumanizing caste-ordained practice of carrying human excreta.[68] This work was enforced through social ostracism and violence,[69] and included Dalit women who, unlike their higher caste counterparts, were not excluded from work outside their home. For Dalit women, the exploitative working conditions included gender-based violence, whether at work or in accessing work.[70] For some Dalit women, this exploitation was compounded by the *devadasi* system in southern India, and equivalent religious traditions elsewhere. Euphemistically labelled as the 'dedication' of Dalit women to temples, these women were then required to perform sex work for upper caste men.[71]

(c) First steps: equal pay legislation

In all these jurisdictions, then, equality before the law, where it had been achieved, was clearly not sufficient. Legislation was necessary to ban discrimination against women, both by private and public actors, especially in the workplace. In several jurisdictions, equal pay was the first issue to be given statutory attention. Women were routinely paid less than men although they were doing the same work. At the same time, widespread job segregation meant that women were consigned to traditionally female jobs such as care, cleaning, and catering. Because of the assumption that such jobs could be done unpaid in the home, pay for such work was significantly lower than traditionally male work such as refuse collection. As well as the principle of equal pay for like work, therefore, it was crucial to pay attention, too, to the principle of equal pay for work of equal value. Particularly foresighted, therefore, was the International Labour Organization (ILO) Equal Remuneration Convention (No 100) which as early as 1951 required Member States to provide equal pay for men and women for work of equal value.

---

[68] Jan Sahas Social Development Society and Fund for Gender Equality, United Nations Entity for Gender Equality and the Empowerment of Women, *Socio-Economic Status of Women Manual Scavengers—Baseline Study Report* (2014).

[69] Sukhadeo Thorat and Katherine S Newman, 'Caste and Economic Discrimination: Causes, Consequences and Remedies' (2007) 42(41) Economic and Political Weekly 4121.

[70] Jayshree P Mangubhai, *Human Rights as Practice: Dalit Women Securing Livelihood Entitlements in South India* (OUP 2014) 65.

[71] Anagha Tambe, 'Reading Devadasi Practice through Popular Marathi Literature' (2009) 44(17) Economic and Political Weekly 85; Janaki Nair, 'The Devadasi, Dharma and the State' (1994) 29(50) Economic and Political Weekly 3157.

Early statutory interventions at domestic level were, however, limited to requiring equal pay for like work. In Canada, most jurisdictions[72] had introduced such legislation by the end of the 1950s.[73] In the US, Congress enacted the Equal Pay Act in 1963 guaranteeing equal pay for the same work for women and men, while in the UK, the Equal Pay Act was enacted in 1970 but only came into force in 1975. In India, the importance of equal pay for men and women had been placed on the agenda in the Constitution itself in 1950. The Directive Principles of State Policy in the Indian Constitution require States to direct their policy towards securing equal pay for equal work for men and women.[74] While these are not enforceable in any court of law, the State is required to consider them in enacting laws. However, it was not until 1976 that legislation was brought into force. The Equal Remuneration Act 1976 requires employers to pay equal remuneration to men and women workers for the same work or work of a similar nature. Notably, as well as placing a duty on employers to provide equal remuneration to men and women workers for the same or similar work, it also prohibits discrimination in the recruitment of men and women.[75]

It was in this period, too, that the UK entered the EU,[76] which was to have a seminal influence on the future development of anti-discrimination legislation, until the UK left the EU in 2020. In one sense, this was a surprising source of women's rights. At its inception in 1957, the EU was conceived of primarily as creating a common market where competition was undistorted by domestic tariffs and restrictions. Protection of social rights was regarded as a matter for Member States rather than the Community. Nevertheless, France, which already had an equal pay law, successfully argued that it would be placed at an unfair competitive disadvantage if other Member States were permitted to pay women less for the same work. It was for this, primarily economic, reason that a right to equal pay for equal work for men and women was included in Article 119 of the Treaty of Rome.

In practice, however, Article 119 lay dormant until the mid-1970s, when it was ignited by a remarkable campaign by women at the European level. A test case brought on behalf of a Belgian air stewardess, Gabrielle Defrenne,

---

[72] Canada has fourteen jurisdictions with power to determine labour laws: one federal, ten provincial, and three territorial districts.

[73] P McDermott, 'Equal Pay in Canada' in F Eyraud (ed), *Equal Pay Protection in Industrialized Market Economies* (International Labour Office 1993) 43.

[74] Constitution of India, Art 39(d).

[75] Equal Remuneration Act, 1976 (India), ss 4 and 5.

[76] With effect from 1 January 1973.

led to the landmark decision of *Defrenne v Sabena*,[77] in which the European Court of Justice (ECJ) held that Article 119 was a source of rights which could be enforced in courts of the Member States even if there was no domestic legislation to that effect. Equally important, was the Court's assertion in *Defrenne* that the social aims of the EU were on a par with its economic aims. The Community, it stated, 'is not merely an economic union, but is at the same time intended . . . to ensure social progress and seek the constant improvement of the living and working conditions of their peoples'.[78] It was also at this time that the EU introduced legislation (known as directives) requiring not just equal pay for the same work, but also for work of equal value.[79] This, in turn, prompted the UK to widen the scope of the Equal Pay Act to include work of equal value. Article 119 (later Article 141) has been widened and deepened and appears as Article 157 in the most recent treaty—the Lisbon Treaty[80]—which came into force in December 2009. Equality between men and women is now expressly mentioned as one of the foundational values in EU law.[81] It is also a fundamental right under the EU Charter on Fundamental Rights.[82]

Because EU law is binding on all its Member States, the right to equal pay for work of equal value is applicable throughout most of Europe. In Canada, however, only three Canadian jurisdictions (the federal government in 1978, Quebec in 1976, and the Yukon territory) have introduced legislation providing for equal pay for work of equal value.[83] In the US, the issue of equal value or 'comparable worth', came to prominence in the late 1970s, when it became clear that wage disparities persisted despite the fact that, formally, women now had equal access to jobs. However, during the 1980s the federal government was hostile to the possibility of 'comparable worth' legislation. Only a small number of States have enacted such legislation, limited to public service employees.[84] In South Africa, it was not until 2014 that equal pay for work of equal value was included in the Employment Equity Act.[85]

---

[77]   Case 43/75 *Defrenne v Sabena* [1976] ECR 455 (ECJ).
[78]   ibid para 10.
[79]   Council Directive 75/117/EEC.
[80]   Treaty on the Functioning of the European Union (TFEU).
[81]   Treaty on European Union, Art 2.
[82]   Charter of Fundamental Rights of the European Union, Art 23.
[83]   McDermott (n 73) 44.
[84]   J Bellace, 'Equal Pay in the United States' in Eyraud (n 73) 159.
[85]   EEA, s 6(4).

(d) Next steps: prohibiting discrimination in work, education, and services

Equal pay legislation cannot, however, address discrimination against women in selection, promotion, or dismissal. Attention therefore quickly turned to broader legislation prohibiting discrimination at work. In the US, Title VII of the Civil Rights Act 1964 prohibited discrimination by employers on a number of grounds, including sex. Importantly, as will be seen in Chapter 5, this was interpreted by the US Supreme Court to include disparate impact, or indirect discrimination.[86] In the UK, the Equal Pay Act 1970 was complemented by the Sex Discrimination Act 1975 (SDA), which prohibited discrimination on the grounds of sex or marriage in employment more generally, including recruitment, promotion, and training. The SDA also made it unlawful to discriminate in education and the provision of services, incorporating, too, the concept of disparate impact in the form of a prohibition on indirect discrimination. At the EU level, provisions on gender equality have been deepened and expanded including a series of directives on equal treatment, social security, burden of proof, and other relevant areas. In 2010, Britain consolidated its complex array of anti-discrimination provisions into one statute, the Equality Act 2010, which remains in force today. In South Africa, the introduction of comprehensive legislation had to wait until after the end of apartheid. The Employment Equity Act deals with discrimination in employment, while the Promotion of Equality and Prevention of Unfair Discrimination Act addresses all other discrimination. In India, by contrast, comprehensive non-discrimination legislation is yet to be introduced.

In the UK, all this is set to change as a result of its departure from the EU in 2020. Withdrawal from the EU signified a return to parliamentary sovereignty unrestrained by any higher law. This means that there is no guarantee that current legislative protections of the right to equality will not be diluted by parliamentary majorities. The government has already severed all ties with the EU Charter of Fundamental Rights. Untangling UK law from EU law after fifty years of deep engagement is, however, complex. In the short term, existing EU law will remain part of domestic legislation until it is removed. This includes previous rulings of the European Court of Justice, which will be incorporated into domestic case law. However, judges in courts at all levels in the UK have been given the power to depart from these rulings.[87]

---

[86] *Griggs v Duke Power Co* 401 US 424 (1971) (US Sup Ct).
[87] European Union (Withdrawal) Act 2018.

Because EU law has played such a central part in the development of UK anti-discrimination law, and the ECJ has often given a broader interpretation to these provisions than the UK courts, this could well open the way for a dilution of equality rights in the UK domestic courts.

(iii) Current Inequalities

(a) Women and work

Anti-discrimination laws have not, however, eradicated the deep-seated inequalities between men and women. Indeed, the ILO reports that, globally, in the first two decades of the twenty-first century, gender gaps in relation to key labour market indicators did not narrow in any meaningful way.[88] While some express inequalities might have diminished, new and different manifestations have appeared. Women are entering the paid labour force in increasing numbers but they are not necessarily entering on equal terms.[89] This is because women's primary responsibility for childcare has remained unchanged. Women are now both homeworkers and breadwinners, constantly traversing the boundary between unpaid and paid work. This has partly been facilitated by the changing labour market, with a new emphasis on flexible working. Flexible working may seem the ideal forum for combining family responsibilities and paid work. However, the reason why employers tend to introduce flexible working is not to achieve 'family friendly' outcomes but to reduce labour costs by adjusting labour inputs to meet fluctuations in demand. The best opportunities for pay, training, promotion, job security, and employment-related benefits are still found in full-time working. The result is that women with young children tend to congregate in poorly paid, low status, part-time work, a pattern which has a lasting effect on their lifetime earnings. This is exacerbated in the countries, such as the UK, which have a culture of long working hours. The greater rewards open to men working long hours simply reinforce the gendered patterns of paid work and childcare.[90]

The equivalent of flexible working in developing countries such as India has been a return to home-based work. This gives women some opportunities

---

[88] ILO, 'A Quantum Leap for Gender Equality' (2019) <www.ilo.org/global/publications/books/WCMS_674831/lang--en/index.htm> accessed 2 October 2020.

[89] ibid.

[90] S Fredman, 'Women at Work: The Broken Promise of Flexicurity' (2004) 33 ILJ 299.

for income-generating work, especially where social norms place severe restrictions on mobility for women outside the home. However, home-based work is also fertile ground for exploitation, and is generally underpaid and undervalued. It allows employers to reduce their overhead costs in maintaining factory premises and paying salaries. Because workers are classified as self-employed, employers can avoid affording employment rights to home-based women workers. Employers are also exempt from health and safety regulation.[91]

These patterns are clearly evident from the statistics in all the countries considered here. In the UK, although the effect of the equal pay legislation which came into effect in 1975 was initially dramatic,[92] the momentum was quickly exhausted. Since 1980, the gender pay gap has been narrowing at a painfully slow pace.[93] For full-time employees, there has been very little change in the seven years from 2012, narrowing by a miserly 0.6 per cent to 8.9 per cent in 2019 for full-time employees[94] indeed, the differential has widened somewhat from 8.6 per cent in 2018.[95] Moreover, these figures understate the true extent of the pay gap. As a start, the figures exclude part-time employees. When part-time employees are included, the gender pay gap almost doubles, to 17.3 per cent in 2019, down by only 0.5 per cent since 2018.[96] This is because pay for part-time workers lags well behind that of full-time workers. In 2019, median hourly earnings of part-time employees were only £9.36, compared to £14.31 for full-time employees.[97] Yet the vast majority of part-time employees are women. In 2018, 41 per cent of women in employment were working part-time compared to only 13 per cent of men.[98] Moreover, the overall figure masks wide differences in the gender pay gap in respect of different types of jobs. Particularly notable is the increase

---

[91] D Dutta, 'No Work is Easy!: Notes from the Field on Unpaid Care Work for Women' in R Bhogal (ed), *Mind the Gap: The State of Employment in India* (Oxfam India 2019) 118.

[92] The average hourly pay of women in the UK rose from 61.8 per cent of that of men in 1970, to 74.2 per cent in 1977.

[93] Measured as the difference between average hourly earnings of men and women (excluding overtime) as a proportion of average hourly earnings of men (excluding overtime).

[94] Office for National Statistics (UK), 'Gender pay gap in the UK: 2019' (29 October 2019) <www.ons.gov.uk/employmentandlabourmarket/peopleinwork/earningsandworkinghours/bulletins/genderpaygapintheuk/2019> accessed 16 December 2019.

[95] Not a statistically significant increase.

[96] <https://blog.ons.gov.uk/2019/04/16/decoding-the-gender-pay-gap-how-a-bletchley-park-codebreaker-helped-explain-a-strange-paradox/> accessed 16 December 2019.

[97] <https://blog.ons.gov.uk/2019/04/16/decoding-the-gender-pay-gap-how-a-bletchley-park-codebreaker-helped-explain-a-strange-paradox/> accessed 16 December 2019.

[98] A Powell, 'Women and the Economy' (8 March 2019) House of Commons Briefing Paper No CBP06838, 3.

in the gender pay gap in the group of high-paying managers, professionals, and senior officials.[99] Indeed, the statistics show that the 10 per cent highest paid woman earns one-fifth less per hour than the 10 per cent highest paid man.[100] At the same time, women predominate amongst the lowest paid in the workforce. Over three-fifths of all jobs paid at the minimum wage in the UK are held by women.[101]

The causes of the pay gap and the corresponding pensions gap in the UK are complex. Occupational segregation is a major factor. Women are still concentrated in lower paying occupations, most of which are related to women's traditional roles in the family. Thus, in 2018 in the UK, women held 79 per cent of all jobs in the health and social work sector and 70 per cent of jobs in the education sector.[102] It is a sad reflection on our society that these jobs are poorly paid relative to their demands in terms of skill, effort, responsibility, and contribution to society. By contrast, women held only 14 per cent of jobs in construction, 23 per cent in transportation and storage, and 25 per cent of jobs in manufacturing.[103] Female-dominated work tends to be lower paid work. While a higher share of women than men are employed in the lowest paying occupations (27 per cent of female employees compared to 11 per cent of men in 2018), the reverse is true for high-paying occupations (19 per cent of female employees compared to 27 per cent of men).[104] Horizontal segregation into different jobs is also accompanied by vertical segregation, with women at the lower end of mixed occupations. Although around half of women in professional occupations in 2018 were employed as nurses, teachers, or other educational professionals, a higher share of men than women were working as managers, directors, or senior officials.[105]

But most important is the fact that women remain primarily responsible for childcare. Taking time out of the labour market, amassing less experience, limitations in respect of travel to work, and part-time work all extract a severe wage penalty. This is evident from the fact that the gender wage gap

---

[99] Office for National Statistics (n 94): here the pay gap, already large in 2018 (13.9 per cent) increased as much as 2 per cent to a disturbingly high figure of 15.9 per cent in 2019.

[100] ibid.

[101] Low Pay Commission, 'National Minimum Wage Report 2018', para 2.6: <https://assets. publishing.service.gov.uk/government/uploads/system/uploads/attachment_data/file/759 271/National_Minimum_Wage_-_Low_Pay_Commission_2018_Report.pdf> accessed 16 December 2019.

[102] Powell (n 98) 1.4.

[103] ibid.

[104] F McGuinness and D Pyper, 'The Gender Pay Gap' (November 2018) House of Commons Library Briefing Paper No 7068, 15.

[105] Powell (n 98) 1.5.

rises significantly once women begin to have children. Whereas men's wages continue to grow through their twenties and thirties, women's wages plateau. Thus, while there is a relatively small wage gap between men and women at the beginning of their working life, the gap gradually rises with the arrival of children, so that by the time the first child is aged twenty, women's hourly pay is approximately one-third of men's.[106] The effects of low pay, interrupted working lives, and job segregation stretch well beyond women's working lives. By retirement age, the pension gap is dramatic, with the median pension wealth of women in the UK standing at only one-third of that of men of the same age.[107] Many more women than men are heading towards retirement without any private pension savings, with as many as 1.2 million women in their fifties who will need to rely on the State pension to provide an income in their retirement.[108]

Gender in the UK, as in other countries, intersects with class, ethnic origin, and religion to produce an increasingly complex pattern. Women of all ethnicities earn substantially less than men. However, white women are not necessarily better off as far as pay is concerned than ethnic minority women. Indeed, statistics for the period 2002–14 show that ethnic minority women earned more than white British women, with marked pay advantages displayed by Indian, Chinese, British-born Black Caribbean, and British-born Black African women.[109] This was particularly large for Black African British women, whose mean hourly pay was 21 per cent more than white British women. For Pakistani and Bangladeshi women born in Britain, and female immigrants in the Black African and Black Caribbean group, pay levels were fairly similar to their white British counterparts. It is among Pakistani and Bangladeshi immigrant women that intersectional disadvantage is concentrated, lagging behind other women with a 12 per cent pay gap.

These figures, however, mask the fact that women of all ethnicities are working for extremely low pay. About 30 per cent of white British women were paid below the Living Wage, together with about one-third of Pakistani

---

[106] M Costa Dias, R Joyce, and F Parodi, *Wage Progression and the Gender Wage Gap: The Causal Impact of Hours of Work* (2018) IFS Briefing Note BN223, Institute for Fiscal Studies.

[107] Pensions Policy Institute, 'Understanding the Gender Pensions Gap' (July 2019), 5 <www.pensionspolicyinstitute.org.uk/media/3227/20190711-understanding-the-gender-pensions-gap.pdf> accessed 17 December 2019.

[108] ibid 1.

[109] Figures in this paragraph are taken from S Longhi and M Brynin, 'The Ethnicity Pay Gap' (2017) Equality and Human Rights Commission Research Report 108.

women, and as many as 40 per cent of Bangladeshi women.[110] Particularly striking are the large numbers of women of Pakistani or Bangladeshi origin who are not in the labour force. As many as 54.5 per cent of Pakistani women fell into this category in 2018, and 32.1 per cent are in this group because they are looking after the family or home.[111]

Women's disadvantage in the workforce is consistent throughout the EU. In 2017, the gender pay gap in the EU as a whole was as high as 16 per cent, a drop of only 0.6 per cent from 2014.[112] As in Britain, women's disadvantaged position in the labour market is closely related to the fact that women's primary responsibility for caring and unpaid work continues unabated. EU figures show that working women spend much more time in unpaid work than men, with working women spending an average of about twenty-two hours while men spend only nine hours on average. The gap is significantly smaller across the Nordic countries (six to eight hours) than in other countries such as Italy, Croatia, Slovenia, Austria, Malta, Greece, and Cyprus.[113] This is reflected, too, in the patterns of part-time working. Women throughout the EU predominate among part-time workers with as many as 30.8 per cent of employed women aged twenty to sixty-four working part-time in 2018 compared with 8.0 per cent for men.[114] Again, as in Britain, labour markets continue to be highly segregated. Women still cluster in women-only jobs or predominate in the low levels of mixed jobs. According to the EU Commission, about 30 per cent of the total gender pay gap across the EU is explained by the fact that women are over-represented in sectors such as care and education, which are relatively low-paying.[115] In some countries,[116] this is true even if on average women have a higher level of education than employed men.

---

[110] The Living Wage is set independently by the Living Wage Foundation and is based on the cost of living in the UK. Paying the Living Wage is voluntary. It is higher than the legally enforceable National Minimum Wage (now also confusingly called the Living Wage).

[111] Office for National Statistics, 'Ethnicity pay gaps in Great Britain: 2018' (2019) <www.ons. gov.uk/employmentandlabourmarket/peopleinwork/earningsandworkinghours/articles/ethnicitypaygapsingreatbritain/2018> accessed 25 July 2022.

[112] This figure represents the difference between average gross hourly earnings of males and females as a percentage of male gross earnings. The pay gap varies widely across the EU.

[113] Eurofound, *Striking a Balance: Reconciling Work and Life in the EU* (Publications Office of the European Union 2018).

[114] Eurostat Employment Statistics <https://ec.europa.eu/eurostat/statistics-explained/index.php/Employment_statistics#Rise_in_part-time_and_temporary_work> accessed 16 December 2019.

[115] European Commission, *2019 Report on Equality between Women and Men in the EU* (European Union 2019) 20.

[116] Portugal, Spain, Cyprus, Malta, Ireland, Estonia, Latvia, Finland, and Denmark: ibid 20.

Similar patterns are evident in other countries. In Canada, in 2018, female employees aged twenty-five to fifty-four still earned only 87 per cent of their male counterparts on average per hour.[117] Although this demonstrates a narrowing of the gap by 5.5 per cent since 1998, some of this reduction is due to periods of stagnant or decreasing wages among men, rather than a notable increase in women's wages.[118] For indigenous women, the gap is even wider. Figures from 2016 show that indigenous women working full-time earn on average only 65 per cent of non-indigenous men in Canada.[119] As in the UK and EU, there are two salient factors explaining these gaps. The first is women's over-representation among part-time workers, who have lower average wages than their full-time counterparts. The second is continuing job segregation. Men continued to dominate in the higher paid industries such as construction, manufacturing, mining, quarrying, and oil and gas extraction. In addition, male-dominated professional occupations offer far better employment opportunities and earnings than women-dominated occupations.[120] As in other countries, the 'motherhood penalty' in Canada is marked and lasting. Women in lower paid and precarious positions are in a particularly difficult position.[121] This is likely to be exacerbated by the Covid-19 pandemic. The labour-market impact of the economic shutdown in 2020 due to Covid-19 was particularly serious for lower wage workers in Canada, but especially for women. Employment recovery was the slowest for mothers with school-aged children.[122]

In the US, too, gender inequality persists. As in the UK, there was a striking improvement in the ratio of women's to men's earnings during the 1980s. Whereas women working full-time only earned 60 per cent at the median per hour compared to men in the 1970s, this figure leapt to 75 per cent in 1990. However, progress has slowed in recent decades and, on some indicators, stalled entirely.[123] By 2018, full-time women still earned only 83 per cent per hour of what men earned at the median. This can also be seen for annual rather than hourly earnings; women working full-time (at least thirty-five

---

[117] Statistics Canada, 'The Gender Wage Gap in Canada: 1998 to 2018' <www150.statcan.gc.ca/n1/pub/75-004-m/75-004-m2019004-eng.htm> accessed 2 October 2020.

[118] ibid.

[119] Canadian Women's Foundation, 'The Facts about the Gender Pay Gap in Canada' <https://canadianwomen.org/the-facts/the-gender-pay-gap/> accessed 25 July 2022.

[120] Statistics Canada (n 117).

[121] Canadian Women's Foundation (n 119).

[122] Statistics Canada, 'Labour Force Survey, June 2020' <www150.statcan.gc.ca/n1/daily-quotidien/200710/dq200710a-eng.htm> accessed 26 July 2022.

[123] Figures in this paragraph are taken from P England, A Levine, and E Mishel, 'Progress Toward Gender Equality in the United States has Slowed or Stalled' (2020) 117 PNAS 6990.

hours per week) earned a mere 58 per cent of their male counterparts at the median in the 1970s, a figure which jumped to 70 per cent during the 1980s. However, by 2018, this figure had only reached 81 per cent. This is despite the fact that in relation to educational attainment, women in the US are now ahead of men. Notably, because most American men and women work full-time, including part-time workers yields similar results. Particularly striking is the widening inequality between the top earners and those at the bottom of the distribution, a phenomenon much noted among male earners but also increasingly found between high-earning women and those with the lowest earnings.

As in other countries, a key factor driving these continued differences is the fact that women's increased role in the labour force has not been accompanied by a corresponding increase in men's role in family work.[124] This is fortified by segregation in choices of subjects in high school and university, fuelling occupational choices and entrenchment of the expectations of men and women undertaking gender-typical jobs. Such jobs continue to be undervalued relative to their skill requirements and working conditions.[125] As we have seen, however, legislation addressing unequal pay for jobs of comparable worth or equal value has never reached the statute books at the federal level.

For Black American women, the intersection of race and gender continues to shape their lives, but this has also now been further overlaid by class. As Collins puts it: 'All African-American women encounter the common theme of having our work and family experiences shaped by intersecting oppressions of race, gender, and class. But this commonality is experienced differently by working-class women . . . and by middle-class women.'[126] Equally importantly, the interjection of class differences has impacted on relationships between Black women. 'Large numbers of U.S. Black women in the working poor are employed as cooks, laundry workers, nursing home aides, and child-care workers. These women serve not only U.S. Whites, but more affluent U.S. Blacks, other people of colour, and recent immigrants. . . . [T]hese women can encounter Black middle-class teachers, nurses, bus drivers, and social workers who are as troublesome to them as White ones. Far too many Black single mothers living in inner-city neighbourhoods remain isolated and encounter middle-class Black women primarily as police officers,

---

[124] ibid 6994.
[125] ibid 6995.
[126] Collins (n 58) 66.

social workers, teachers, or on television. How will these working-class Black women, many of whom feel stuck in the working poor, view their more privileged sisters?'[127] The Black middle class remains fragile, less economically or politically secure than individuals in the white middle class. Indeed, Darity and others argue that the Black bourgeoisie should better be understood as a specific case of a 'subaltern middle class', which is the more affluent tier of a marginalized community.[128] But this, in turn, has not eliminated gender differentiation within the Black middle class itself. Although fewer Black men have positions in professional and managerial occupations than Black women, those who do are in higher paying, higher status jobs than Black women, who are concentrated in the lower paid, lower status echelons of professional and managerial positions.[129]

While in the US, the UK, and the EU there has been some, albeit slow, progress, for Indian women, the direction of travel has been in the opposite direction. Labour market participation has dropped, levels of unpaid work have climbed, and the gender pay gap remains as high as 34 per cent.[130] This is despite the unprecedented growth in India's GDP over recent decades.[131] Female workforce participation in rural areas is low, with 66.4 per cent of rural women out of the workforce, but in urban areas it is even lower, with as many as 78.6 per cent of urban women out of the labour force.[132] There has been remarkable progress in girls' enrolment in schools, with almost 70 per cent in secondary school. But this has not been sufficient to break through entrenched structural barriers. Continuing job segregation bars them from jobs fitting their qualifications, with the main sources of female work continuing to be found in semi- or unskilled work.[133] At the same time, as more girls go to school, more domestic work falls on older women. This is intensified with the increase in the number of nuclear families, meaning that there are fewer women relatives to share the housework.[134] Adolescent girls, unlike

---

[127] ibid 66–67.
[128] W Darity, F Addo, and I Smith, 'A Subaltern Middle Class: The Case of the Missing "Black Bourgeoisie" in America' (2020) 39 Contemporary Economic Policy.
[129] Collins (n 58) 65.
[130] 2011–12 figures.
[131] Indeed, although India experienced growth of as much as 8 per cent per annum in the first few years of the twenty-first century, a huge 77 per cent of the population remained poor and vulnerable (Mehrotra (n 141) 43).
[132] ILO, 'Care Work and Care Jobs: The Future of Decent Work' (2018).
[133] Dutta (n 91) 116.
[134] ibid 140.

boys, are therefore required to participate in unpaid work outside school hours.[135]

The decline in female labour force participation has been well documented. But this is only part of the picture. In fact, the withdrawal of women from the labour market has been accompanied by an increase in unpaid and unrecognized work.[136] Unpaid care work remains highly gendered, with women in urban areas spending 312 minutes a day on unpaid care work, as against only twenty-nine minutes spent by men.[137] Domestic work for their own use within the household takes women on average 297 minutes per day, with men spending a mere thirty-one minutes.[138] Time poverty is thus a serious but unmeasured aspect of women's continued inequality and, for the poorest women, this is extreme. Women have less time to sleep, eat, and drink, for personal hygiene, and for exercise and leisure than men.[139]

There is an even more fundamental problem, as Mondal and others demonstrate, which is that the definition of 'work' itself renders unpaid work invisible. Those engaged in domestic duties, free collection of goods (such as vegetables, firewood, or cattle feed), or sewing, tailoring, or weaving for household use, are classified as outside the labour force. Yet when these activities are outsourced for payment by households, they are considered to be 'work'. It is therefore clear that it is not so much that women's labour force participation has declined. It is that by only including paid work, the significant effort and energy expended by women in activities which are absolutely essential for both households and society are concealed.[140]

A large proportion of India's workers are still engaged in rural labour where, as Mehrotra puts it, employment relations 'are shaped by a political-economy of difference based on gender, caste and class'.[141] With men migrating and moving out of agriculture, Dalit women in particular are disproportionately concentrated in poorly paid and demeaning agricultural work.[142] Patriarchal norms confine women to the least paid agricultural tasks, such as weeding, while at the same time they carry the whole burden of those livelihood activities which do not have an immediate monetary value. These are frequently

[135] ibid 110.
[136] S Roy and P Mukhopadhyay, 'What Matters for Urban Women's Work' in Bhogal (n 91) 69.
[137] The corresponding figure for rural areas is 291 minutes for women and 32 minutes for men.
[138] ILO (n 132).
[139] Dutta (n 91) 107.
[140] B Mondal and others, 'Women Workers in India' (2018) CSE Working Papers 3, 6.
[141] I Mehrotra, 'Inequality and Rural Employment: Agrarian Distress and Dalit Women' in Bhogal (n 91) 47.
[142] ibid 48.

arduous, including collecting firewood and making and storing cow-dung cakes. Even more problematically, they are expected to provide unpaid labour to upper caste families, such as tending livestock and sweeping their courtyards.[143] For rural women, gender inequality is exacerbated by women's lack of access to land ownership. While 85 per cent of rural women in India are engaged in agriculture, only 13 per cent own land—a figure which is certainly even lower for Dalit women.[144] The equal right of women to property is unrealized due to the strength of social patriarchal norms, discriminatory State, personal, and customary laws, and a lack of implementation of equalizing laws such as the Hindu Succession Amendment Act 2005.[145] Mehrotra therefore argues that a key policy intervention should be to secure land rights for rural women.

Some reallocation of gender roles has been precipitated by MGNREGA, the rural employment scheme which in India takes the place of a proper social security net. However, although it provides work for women in traditionally male jobs, such as construction, these too are arduous and underpaid. Rural women are also increasingly being employed on public health programmes. However, these are on highly exploitative terms. Rural public health programmes rely on minimally trained rural women known as Accredited Social Health Activists (ASHAs) and auxiliary nurses and midwives (ANMs). Rather than being properly remunerated, these women are described as volunteers and receive honoraria which are well below minimum wages.[146] ASHAs have been particularly prominent during the Covid pandemic, where they have been tasked with tracing contacts of those who are infected, and ensuring that infected persons quarantine, as well as screening for fever, monitoring heart rates, and giving advice on Covid-19 precautions. In addition to their long hours for excruciatingly low levels of pay (£50 a month and sometimes even lower), they are exposed to multiple dangers to their own health and safety, and that of their families. Many have been infected and died from the virus, and violence against ASHA workers and their families has been widely reported.[147]

For urban women, there has been some improvement in women's access to professional and associate professional positions. But, apart from a very

---

[143] ibid 50.

[144] ibid 40.

[145] ibid 53.

[146] Mondal and others (n 140) 14.

[147] <https://news.sky.com/story/coronavirus-asha-healthcare-workers-in-india-share-their-stories-of-abuse-and-discrimination-12085390> accessed 4 October 2020.

small number of women accessing professions in the physical and engineering sciences, these have been largely in traditionally female-dominated activities in health and education.[148] Gender segregation in fact extends throughout the skills ladder, from highly skilled through semi-skilled to unskilled work. As well as severe job segregation, women are underpaid relative to similarly qualified men for similar jobs.[149] Even where men have entered traditionally female work, it is in relation to the relatively higher paid aspects. For example, commercial cleaning work in offices and hotels includes more men and is paid better than household-based domestic services usually performed by women.[150]

In South Africa, gender inequalities in the labour market are similarly intransigent, heavily overlaid by race. This is despite the fact that, at the legislative level, important progress has been made in relation to central issues such as reproductive rights, marriage, property and succession rights, employment equity in the workforce, non-discrimination laws, and protection against domestic violence. Instead, a report from Statistics SA in 2018 noted that over the previous decade there had been little change in women's labour market position. In fact, it had deteriorated in some respects.[151] As in other countries, the wage gap persists, with women earning on average approximately 30 per cent less than male workers.[152] And, again, as in the other countries previously discussed, job segregation is deeply entrenched. In 2018, only 32 per cent of managers in South Africa were women,[153] and the predominance of senior civil servants, such as general directors of government departments and chairs of national industries, were men. At the other end of the hierarchy, domestic work, where pay levels are abysmally low, is overwhelmingly Black and female, with only 3.0 per cent of domestic worker jobs occupied by men.[154]

At the same time, women continue to be more involved in unpaid work than men.[155] Reflecting patterns found throughout the world, South African women spend on average 2.2 hours more on unpaid housework and care

---

[148] Mondal and others (n 140) 10–11.

[149] Roy and Mukhopadhyay (n 136) 67.

[150] Mondal and others (n 140) 12.

[151] Statistics South Africa, 'How Do Women Fare in the South African Labour Market?' (1 August 2018) <www.statssa.gov.za/?p=11375> accessed 26 July 2022.

[152] Statistics South Africa, 'How Unequal is South Africa' (posted 4 February 2020; figures from 2015) <www.statssa.gov.za/?p=12930> accessed 26 July 2022.

[153] Statistics South Africa (n 151).

[154] ibid.

[155] ibid.

work per day than men, and this figure rises to about 3.3 hours if there is a child under seven in the household.[156] This is in part a reflection of the fact that as many as 43.1 per cent of children live with their mothers only, whereas a tiny 3.3 per cent live with their fathers only.[157] Children who do not live with a parent are often cared for by another female relative, generally a grandmother. This situation was intensified during the Covid pandemic.

A particular site of gendered inequality is within the informal workforce, in other words, in employment without adequate legal and social protection. Almost one-third of the South African workforce is in informal employment.[158] Although men and women are now evenly represented in informal employment, informal women workers earn only 69 per cent of men's income.[159] What is particularly striking is the extent to which gender hierarchies are repeated in this sector. As well as informal employers, the informal economy consists of own-account workers (self-employed workers who do not employ others), employees (workers in both the informal sector and the formal sector), and household and domestic workers. As we move down the hierarchy from employers to household and domestic workers, the proportion of women rises and with it the risk of poverty wages.[160] A mere 19 per cent of informal employers were women in 2018. By contrast, the vast majority of informal workers in private households are women, where earnings are unconscionably low (less than ZAR 20 per hour). Even where there are roughly even numbers of men and women in the categories of own-account workers and employees, there is a significant wage gap. As Rogan and Alfers show, this is a reflection of structural gender inequalities, already familiar to us from other jurisdictions, but heightened due to the precarity of these women's work situations. Childcare responsibilities are central: for example, women street hawkers might not be able to work at peak profitable times, such as early-morning rush hour, because that is a time their children need them most. Women without childcare support need to bring their children with them, making it difficult to give their full attention to their work, and exposing their children to risks. But there are also other gendered contributory

---

[156] E Rubiano-Matulevich and M Viollaz, 'Gender Differences in Time Use: Allocating Time Between the Market and the Household' (2019) World Bank Policy Research Working Paper 8981 <https://elibrary.worldbank.org/doi/abs/10.1596/1813-9450-8981> accessed 26 July 2022.

[157] D Casale and D Posel, 'Gender and the Early Effects of the COVID-19 Crisis in the Paid and Unpaid Economies in South Africa' (National Income Dynamics Study 2020).

[158] ILO, 'Global Wage Report 2018/19' (International Labour Office 2018).

[159] M Rogan and L Alfers, 'Gender Inequalities in the South African Informal Economy' (2019) 33 Agenda 91, 93.

[160] ibid 93.

factors. One is the violence that many women workers in the informal sector are exposed to. Another is the lack of proper urban infrastructure, such as sanitation, an absence which is particularly problematic for menstruating and pregnant women.[161]

(b) Violence

Economic disadvantage is not the only manifestation of continuing gender inequality in society. Violence, so well chronicled by John Stuart Mill two centuries ago, continues to stalk too many women's lives, whether in the home, at work, or in the street. As a recent report put it, 'violence against women has no boundaries, in terms of wealth, geography, race, religion, disability, age or sexual orientation'.[162] Violence against women manifests itself in many ways: it ranges from domestic abuse, rape, and sexual violence to female genital mutilation, forced and child marriage, and honour crimes, and includes human trafficking and sexual exploitation, sexual harassment, and prostitution. The figures paint a grim picture. In the UK, as many as one in four women will experience domestic abuse in her lifetime, and one in five will experience sexual assault.[163] Figures from England and Wales show little sign of abatement of the scourge of domestic abuse. In the year ending March 2019, an estimated 2.4 million adults in England and Wales experienced domestic abuse in the previous year, 1.6 million of whom were women and 786,000 were men.[164] These figures are much the same as those recorded in the previous year. Disturbingly, however, rape charges, prosecutions, and convictions in England and Wales are falling precipitously, even though allegations of rape to the police have increased substantially. Between 2016 and 2019, there was a 43 per cent rise in the number of rape allegations to the police. Yet the number of cases prosecuted by the Crown Prosecution Service (CPS) dropped by an astonishing 52 per cent.[165] In the meantime, honour crimes, forced and child marriage, and female genital mutilation continue

---

[161] ibid 99.

[162] Equality and Human Rights Commission, 'Breaking the Silence on Violence Against Women' (November 2009).

[163] Home Office, 'Violence Against Women and Girls and Male Position Factsheets' (7 March 2019)   <https://homeofficemedia.blog.gov.uk/2019/03/07/violence-against-women-and-girls-and-male-position-factsheets/> accessed 24 December 2019.

[164] Office for National Statistics, 'Domestic Abuse in England Wales Overview: November 2019' <www.ons.gov.uk/peoplepopulationandcommunity/crimeandjustice/bulletins/domesticabusein englandandwalesoverview/november2019> accessed 24 December 2019.

[165] HM Crown Prosecution Inspectorate (HMCPSI), 'Rape Inspection 2019' (17 December 2019) <www.justiceinspectorates.gov.uk/hmcpsi/inspections/rape-inspection-on-report-decem ber-2019/> accessed 24 December 2019.

to blight many women's lives. These patterns were intensified during the Covid pandemic, when severe public health restrictions on movement often trapped women and children with their abusers, leading to spikes in the levels of domestic violence and violence against women.

In India, this is particularly pronounced. In a survey conducted by Butta, as many as 41 per cent of men felt it was acceptable to beat a woman if she did not prepare a meal for the men in the family or failed to fetch water or wood for fuel. Even worse, as many as 54 per cent of those surveyed said that it was acceptable to beat a woman if she left the house without asking permission.[166] As many as 31 per cent of married women in India have experienced physical, sexual, or emotional violence at the hands of their spouse, with physical abuse being the most common.[167] Overall, India reported 4,05,861 cases of crimes against women in 2019, with the majority of cases registered under 'cruelty by husband or his relatives' (30.9 per cent).[168] An average eighty-seven rape cases were reported every day in 2019.[169] It should be noted that gender-based violence against women in India is widely acknowledged to be under-reported. Moreover, when disaggregating these figures by caste, we find that on average ten Dalit women were reported to have been raped each day in 2019,[170] and it has been found that less than 2 per cent of reported cases result in convictions.[171] In its concluding observations on India, the CEDAW Committee noted 'the escalation of caste-based violence, including rape, against [Dalit] women and girls, and the downplaying by key State officials of the grave criminal nature of sexual violence against [Dalit] women and girls'.[172] In October 2020, repeated incidents of rape and murder perpetrated against Dalit women and girls in the north Indian state of Uttar Pradesh, and especially the gang rape of a nineteen-year-old Dalit woman,

[166] Dutta (n 91) 115.

[167] Ministry of Health and Family Welfare, Government of India, and International Institute of Population Sciences, 'National Family Health Survey (NFHS-4) 2015–2016' (December 2017) <https://dhsprogram.com/pubs/pdf/FR339/FR339.pdf> accessed 26 July 2022.

[168] <https://scroll.in/latest/974499/up-had-most-cases-of-violence-against-women-in-2019-across-india-87-rapes-reported-per-day-ncrb> accessed 26 July 2022; National Crime Statistics Bureau, 'Crime in India 2019', vol I 'Statistics' <https://ncrb.gov.in/sites/default/files/CII%202019%20Volume%201.pdf> accessed 26 July 2022.

[169] ibid.

[170] A total of 3,486 rape cases were registered under the Scheduled Caste and Scheduled Tribe (Prevention of Atrocities) Act. National Crime Statistics Bureau (n 168).

[171] International Dalit Solidarity Network, 'Caste and Gender Justice' <https://idsn.org/wp-content/uploads/2019/06/Caste-and-Gender-Justice-Low-Res2.pdf> accessed 26 July 2022.

[172] CEDAW Concluding Observations, CEDAW/C/IND/CO/4-5 <http://tbinternet.ohchr.org/Treaties/CEDAW/Shared%20Documents/Ind/CEDAW_C_IND_CO_4-5_17678_E.doc> accessed 26 July 2022.

resulted in massive protests in India and abroad, demanding justice for Dalit women.[173]

As noted by the UN Special Rapporteur on violence against women, in South Africa 'there are no centralized statistics on incidents and types of violence against women beyond the mere recording of sexual offences under the Sexual Offences Act by the South African Police Service'.[174] Yet, it is widely acknowledged that 'violence against women and girls is widespread, at a high level, and normalized'.[175] In 2019–20, 53,293 incidents of sexual offences were recorded by the police.[176] These are likely to be a fraction of the real numbers. In September 2019, the South African government acknowledged that gender based violence was a 'national crisis' after protests erupted in the country in response to a growing number of femicides.[177] Women took to the streets wearing black and began a social media campaign with the hashtag #AmINext.[178] A woman is killed every three hours in South Africa[179] and more than 2,700 women were killed in 2019.[180]

In the US, 43.6 per cent of women (nearly 52.2 million) experienced some form of sexual violence in their lifetime.[181] Nearly one in six women (16.0 per cent, or 19.1 million) in the US had been the victims of stalking at some point in their lifetime, during which they felt very fearful or believed that they or someone close to them would be harmed or killed.[182] Over one in three (36.4 per cent, or 43.6 million) women had experienced contact

---

[173] <https://indianexpress.com/article/india/hathras-rape-case-protests-live-updates-congr ess-uttar-pradesh-police-yogi-adityanath-6703353/> accessed 26 July 2022.

[174] Report of the Special Rapporteur on Violence against Women, its Causes and Consequences on Her Mission to South Africa, A/HRC/32/42/Add.2 (18 November 2016) <https://digitallibr ary.un.org/record/861014?ln=en> accessed 26 July 2022.

[175] ibid.

[176] Southern African Police Service, 'Crime Statistics 2019/2020' <www.saps.gov.za/services/ crimestats.php> accessed 26 July 2022.

[177] <www.theguardian.com/world/2019/sep/06/south-africa-faces-national-crisis-of-viole nce-against-women-says-president> accessed 26 July 2022.

[178] Rosa Lyster, 'The Death of Uyinene Mrwetyana and the Rise of South Africa's "Am I Next?" Movement' The New Yorker (12 September 2019) <www.newyorker.com/news/news-desk/the- death-of-uyinene-mrwetyana-and-the-rise-of-south-africas-aminext-movement> accessed 26 July 2022.

[179] <www.aljazeera.com/gallery/2019/9/5/every-3-hours-a-woman-is-murdered-in-south- africa/> accessed 26 July 2022.

[180] <www.bbc.co.uk/news/av/world-africa-53096766> accessed 26 July 2022.

[181] SG Smith and others, 'The National Intimate Partner and Sexual Violence Survey (NISVS): 2015 Data Brief—Updated Release' (National Center for Injury Prevention and Control, Centers for Disease Control and Prevention 2018) <www.cdc.gov/violenceprevention/ pdf/2015data-brief508.pdf> accessed 26 July 2022.

[182] ibid.

sexual violence, physical violence, and/or stalking by an intimate partner during their lifetime.[183] Moreover, Black women face disproportionate rates of sexual violence.[184] The Black Lives Matter movement in 2020 brought increasing attention to police violence against Black people. Police violence against Black women is also extensive, as has been highlighted by the Say Her Name campaign. It is telling, in itself, that 'there is currently no accurate data collection on police killings nationwide, no readily available database compiling a complete list of Black women's lives lost at the hands of police, and no data collection on sexual or other forms of gender- and sexuality-based police violence'.[185] Yet numerous accounts exist of police violence against Black women in the US.

Intimate partner violence was the most common kind of violence experienced by women in Canada (45 per cent of all female victims aged fifteen to eighty-nine).[186] Violence against indigenous women is significantly higher. In 2017, indigenous women reported having experienced a violent crime at a rate 2.7 times higher than that reported by non-indigenous women (219 versus 81 incidents per 1,000 population).[187] In 2018, police-reported data showed that the homicide rate for indigenous women and girls was nearly seven times higher than amongst non-indigenous women and girls (4.54 versus 0.67 incidents per 100,000 population respectively).[188] Indigenous women are also more likely to have been sexually assaulted. In 2014, the self-reported sexual assault rate of indigenous females was more than three times higher than that of non-indigenous females (115 versus 35 incidents per 1,000 population).[189]

---

[183] ibid.

[184] National Center on Violence Against Women in the Black Community, 'Black Women and Sexual Assault' (2018) <https://ujimacommunity.org/wp-content/uploads/2018/12/Ujima-Womens-Violence-Stats-v7.4-1.pdf> accessed 26 July 2022.

[185] 2015 African American Policy Forum, Center for Intersectionality and Social Policy Studies, 'Say Her Name: Resisting Police Brutality against Black Women' (2015) <http://static1. squarespace.com/static/53f20d90e4b0b80451158d8c/t/560c068ee4b0af26f72741df/144362 8686535/AAPF_SMN_Brief_Full_singles-min.pdf> accessed 26 July 2022.

[186] Marta Burczycka, 'Statistics Canada. Section 2: Police-Reported Intimate Partner Violence in Canada, 2018' in Shana Conroy, Marta Burczycka, and Laura Savage, 'Family Violence in Canada: A Statistical Profile' (2019) 24 <www150.statcan.gc.ca/n1/en/pub/85-002-x/2019001/article/00018-eng.pdf?st=gsEzBpE5> accessed 26 July 2022.

[187] Tina Hotton Mahony, Joanna Jacob, and Heather Hobson, 'Women in Canada: A Gender-Based Statistical Report: Women and the Criminal Justice System' (Statistics Canada 2017).

[188] Joe Roy and Sharon Marcellus, 'Homicide in Canada, 2018' (Statistics Canada 2019).

[189] Samuel Perrault, 'Criminal Victimization in Canada, 2014' (Statistics Canada 2015).

II RACE, ETHNICITY, AND CASTE

(i) Challenges and Dilemmas

'The European Union rejects theories which attempt to determine the existence of separate human races. The use of the term "racial origin" in this Directive does not imply an acceptance of such theories.'[190]

The preamble to the EU Race Directive exemplifies a key paradox of race discrimination legislation. While racial oppression and subordination remain endemic, the concept of 'race' itself is highly problematic. Recent history is replete with insidious definitions of race to support laws imposing racial hierarchies, prohibiting marriage, removing land and voting rights, and decreeing genocide. In the US, racial subordination was institutionalized through widespread use of apparently biological definitions of race such as the 'one drop rule', epitomized in the Virginia Racial Integrity Act 1924. This Act stated that any person who had even one Black ancestor (or 'one drop' of Black blood) would be deemed to be what the legislation offensively called 'coloured' and therefore subject to highly oppressive racially based laws. In particular, racial classification was used to defend white supremacy and 'racial purity' by prohibiting marriage between white peoples and those defined as 'coloured'. The Virginia Act's prohibition on marriage was not overturned until *Loving v Virginia* in 1967.[191] A similar emphasis on 'racial purity' was used in Nazi Germany, where a Jewish person was defined as 'anyone who is descended from at least three grandparents who are racially full Jews'. To protect 'the purity of German blood', the Nuremberg laws of 1935 prohibited marriage between Jewish people and German citizens, deprived Jewish people of citizenship and the right to vote, forced them into ghettoes, and, ultimately, embarked on a chillingly systematic programme of extermination of the Jewish 'race'. In South Africa, racial classification was central to the apartheid regime's decades-long subordination of the majority Black population, with the Population Registration Act of 1950 basing its classification on 'appearance' including 'habits, education and speech, deportment and demeanour'.

Does eliminating racial discrimination therefore need to have a definition of race? The preamble to the Convention on the Elimination of Racial Discrimination (CERD) declares emphatically that 'any doctrine of

---

[190] EU Directive 2000/43, Preamble, para 6.
[191] *Loving v Virginia* 388 US 1 (1967) (US Sup Ct).

superiority based on racial differentiation is scientifically false, morally con-
demnable, socially unjust and dangerous, and that there is no justification for
racial discrimination, in theory or in practice, anywhere'. However, CERD
does not attempt to define 'race', beyond basing its prohibition on discrimination on a cluster of grounds including race, colour,[192] descent, or national
or ethnic origin. Similar clusters of grounds, rather than a direct definition of
race, are common in anti-discrimination provisions. In some jurisdictions,
such as the UK and Europe, race and ethnicity are regarded as particularly
closely related. The European Court of Human Rights has held that race is a
biological classification, whereas ethnicity reflects a shared history, culture, or
religion.[193] This definition of ethnicity is, however, deceptively simple, given
the many overlapping patterns of culture, history, and religion. Importantly,
it does not reflect relationships of domination and subordination and leaves
open the question of whether ethnicity is a matter of self-identification or
whether, as in the case of race, membership of an ethnic minority is imposed
by the dominant group.[194] Similarly, 'colour'[195] and 'race' are regarded as co-
extensive in some contexts, such as the US and South Africa, but not necessarily in Europe, where anti-Semitism and anti-Roma racism, Islamophobia,
and racism against indigenous people and marginalized minorities do not
map onto a white–Black dichotomy. Indeed, the EU Race Directive does not
even include colour[196] in its list of grounds of discrimination.

  A rejection of biological definitions of race, however, does not mean that
race and racial domination should disappear from view, whether under the
guise of racial neutrality or colour-blindness.[197] Ignoring the ongoing and
institutional role of race simply entrenches its role in legitimizing such hierarchies. As leading members of the Critical Race Studies movement put
it: 'Colour-blindness mobilizes a metaphor of visual impairment to embrace a simplistic and misleading affirmation of racial egalitarianism. Its emphasis on colour imagines racism to be an individualistic aversion to another

---

[192] This terminology reflects that used in international human rights law and relevant human
rights instruments in other jurisdictions (see UK EA 2010, s 9(1)(a); South African Constitution,
s 9; Canadian Charter, s 15; International Convention on the Elimination of All Forms of Racial
Discrimination, Art 1; ICCPR, Art 2(1); ICESCR, Art 2(2)), which all refer to 'colour' in the list
of protected characteristics.
[193] *Sejdić and Finci v Bosnia and Herzegovina* (Application nos 27996/06 and 34836/06), 22
December 2009 (ECtHR); *Mandla v Lee* [1983] 2 AC 548 (HL).
[194] *The Prosecutor v Jean-Paul Akayesu*, Case No ICTR-96-4-T (2 September
1998) (International Criminal Tribunal for Rwanda).
[195] See n 192.
[196] ibid.
[197] See n 11.

person's pigment rather than a systemic skewing of opportunities, resources and life chances along racial lines.'[198]

It is therefore increasingly recognized that race is itself a social construct, reflecting ideological attempts to legitimate domination, and heavily based on social and historical context. As Stuart Hall argues:

> 'Black' is essentially a politically and culturally constructed category, which cannot be grounded in a set of fixed transcultural or transcendental racial categories and which therefore has no guarantees in Nature. What this brings into play is the recognition of the immense diversity and differentiation of the historical and cultural experiences of black subjects.[199]

Racism is, therefore, not about objective characteristics but about relationships of domination and subordination, about hatred of the 'Other' in defence of 'Self', perpetrated and apparently legitimated through images of the 'Other' as inferior, abhorrent, even sub-human.

Because racism is based on a polarization of opposites—'we' and 'they', 'white' and 'Black', 'Self' and 'Other'—it also has the effect of assuming that there is a uniform, undifferentiated 'Other'. This has several consequences. First, racism is insensitive to diversity between groups. It is common to refer to 'ethnic minorities' as a homogeneous group, without noting the many differences between these groups. Moreover, the dominant group is considered 'normal' or natural, rather than one ethnicity among others. Secondly, the assumption of an undifferentiated 'Other' assumes that a group has a fixed essence, and that individuals can be wholly defined by their membership of their group. This, in turn, makes it easy to stereotype individuals, often linking their group identity to denigratory ascriptions. It also ignores the fact that many people have several different overlapping and intersecting sources of identity. Thirdly, such essentialism creates a rigid and static view of group identity, described from the outside. It ignores both the voices of those within the group and the constant, dynamic evolution of culture and ethnicity.

This complex picture of ethnic diversity and differential disadvantage prompts an equally sophisticated explanation. In the first energetic drive against racism, it was of fundamental importance to stress the unity of

---

[198] K Crenshaw and others, 'Introduction' in K Crenshaw and others (eds), *Seeing Race Again: Countering Colourblindness across the Disciplines* (University of California Press 2019) 4.

[199] S Hall, 'New Ethnicities' in J Donald and A Rattansi (eds), *Race Culture and Difference* (Open University 1992) 254.

oppressed peoples rather than their diversity. Thus 'Blackness' became a political epithet rather than a description of individual characteristics. Assertions
of differential ethnicity were thought to represent a strategy of 'divide and
rule'. However, where there is a diversity of cultural and socio-economic
experiences, some authors have been prompted to reconsider the strategic
value of an analysis based wholly on a Black–white dichotomy. Modood has
argued that such an analysis negates the specificity of different experiences of
oppression. South Asian Muslims, he argues, are victims of a distinctive kind
of racism, based on antithetical images of Islam. By contrast, Caribbeans
suffer from a different set of stereotypes. It is therefore more appropriate to
speak not of racism but of multiple racisms.[200] Moreover, contemporary racism cannot be understood simply as prejudice against individuals on the
grounds of their colour.[201] Besides 'colour-racism', Modood argues, there is a
developing set of 'cultural racisms', which 'use cultural difference to vilify or
demand cultural assimilation from groups who also suffer colour racism'.[202]

This recognition of the differential experience of oppression supports a
multi-dimensional understanding of equality. While socio-economic disadvantage might have reduced for some ethnic minorities, this does not mean
that the stigma, stereotyping, prejudice, and violence associated with racial
domination can be ignored. Moreover, equality should entail respect for and
celebration of difference, rather than requiring conformity as the price for
inclusion. As Parekh puts it, the demand for recognition goes 'far beyond the
familiar plea for toleration'. It goes further and demands respect for difference, not as a pathological deviation but 'as equally valid or worthy'.[203] Nor
should there be an assumption that the majority culture is 'right' or 'normal'.
Instead, the focus should be on the 'proper terms of the relationship between
different cultural communities'.[204]

Like race, the caste system in India is based on hierarchies of power and
subordination. The relationship between race and caste has been recognized
by CERD, which includes descent as a ground of discrimination. This has
been augmented by the CERD Committee in a General Recommendation

---

[200] R Bhavnani, *Black Women in the Labour Market: A Research Review* (EOC Research
Series 1994); T Modood, 'Ethnic Diversity and Disadvantage' in T Modood and others, *Ethnic
Minorities in Britain: Diversity and Disadvantage: The Fourth National Survey of Ethnic Minorities
in Britain* (Policy Studies Institute 1997) 353.
[201] See n 192.
[202] ibid 353.
[203] B Parekh, *Rethinking Multiculturalism* (Palgrave 2000) 13.
[204] ibid; see also B Parekh, *The Future of Multi-Ethnic Britain* (Profile Books 2000); W
Kymlicka, *Multicultural Citizenship* (OUP 1995).

issued in 2002, which reaffirmed that discrimination based on descent includes discrimination on grounds of caste.[205] Caste nevertheless has distinctive features which are considered in more detail later in the context of the development of equality law in India.

Although there are depressing similarities in the power structures patterned by racism in different jurisdictions, the evolution of equality law is fundamentally influenced by the specific social relations in each country. US equality law has been profoundly shaped by its history of slavery; Indian law by the heritage of colonialism, caste, and ethnicity; South Africa by the need to heal the wounds of apartheid; and Canada by its linguistic and First Nation minorities. Race discrimination law in Britain has been driven by its role in colonial domination followed by the deliberate encouragement of migration from former colonies to populate the workforce in the postwar period. A very brief flavour of these contexts is given below.

(ii)   Context: Historical, Legal, and Social

(a) The US

The American Declaration of Independence in 1776 asserted that: 'We hold these truths to be self-evident: that all men are created equal . . .'. These words would seem to 'embrace the whole human family'.[206] But they were not sufficient to displace an ideology which refused to acknowledge the basic humanity of enslaved people, or the vested interests which kept that ideology alive. 'It is too clear for dispute' stated the US Supreme Court in the infamous case of *Dred Scott*[207] in 1857, 'that the enslaved African race were not intended to be included [in the words of the Declaration] . . . The unhappy black race were separated from the white by indelible marks, and laws long before established, and were never thought of or spoken of except as property.'[208] Moreover, the Court held: 'the right of property in a slave is distinctly and expressly affirmed in the Constitution. . . . This is done in plain words—too plain to be misunderstood'.[209] The Court thereby endorsed a system which,

---

[205] Committee on the Elimination of Racial Discrimination, General Recommendation 29, 'Discrimination Based on Descent' (Sixty-first session, 2002).

[206] *Dred Scott v Sandford* 60 US 393, 411 (1857) (US Sup Ct).

[207] ibid.

[208] ibid.

[209] ibid 451–52.

by the middle of the nineteenth century, had enslaved four million African Americans.[210]

While the struggle against slavery, primarily by the African American people themselves, lasted throughout the nineteenth century,[211] it was only after the victory of the North in the Civil War of 1861–65 that progress could be made at the constitutional level. Three seminal amendments were ratified directly after the Civil War. The Thirteenth Amendment, adopted in 1865, outlawed slavery and prevented the imposition of any burdens or disabilities that constituted badges of slavery or servitude. The Fifteenth Amendment, adopted in 1870, provided equal suffrage to all adult male citizens: 'The right of citizens of the US to vote shall not be denied or abridged by the US or by any State on account of race, colour, or previous condition of servitude.' But by far the most important for our purposes was the Fourteenth Amendment, also adopted in 1870. As well as giving citizenship to all former slaves, it stated: 'All persons born or naturalized in the US, and subject to the jurisdiction thereof, are citizens of the US and of the States wherein they reside. No State shall make or enforce any law which shall abridge the privileges or immunities of citizens of the US, nor shall any State deprive any person of life, liberty or property, without due process of law; nor deny to any person the equal protection of the laws . . .'.

Despite the abolition of slavery and the constitutional guarantee of equality, blatant discrimination remained endemic throughout the US. African Americans were not permitted to vote in many States, and were consigned to separate and vastly inferior facilities. Nor was the Equal Protection Clause in the Fourteenth Amendment sufficiently robust to combat such inequality. In *Plessy v Ferguson*,[212] the Court refused to strike down a Louisiana statute, passed in 1890, providing for racially segregated railway carriages. The Court held that although the object of the Fourteenth Amendment 'was undoubtedly to enforce the absolute equality of the two races before the law, . . . it could not have been intended to abolish distinctions based upon colour, or to enforce social, as distinguished from political equality'.[213] The Court's assumption that enforced separation did not 'stamp' African Americans 'with a badge of inferiority' was forcefully rebutted by Harlan J. In a stinging dissent, he argued: 'Everyone knows that the statute in question

---

[210] I Berlin, *The Long Emancipation: The Demise of Slavery* (Harvard UP 2015).
[211] ibid 29 ff.
[212] *Plessy v Ferguson* 163 US 537 (1896) (US Sup Ct).
[213] ibid 544.

had its origin in the purpose, not so much to exclude white persons from railroad cars occupied by [B]lacks, as to exclude [Black] people from coaches occupied by or assigned to white persons. . . . No one would be so wanting in candour as to assert the contrary.'[214] *Plessy* not only endorsed but encouraged segregation laws, leading to a further proliferation of statutes requiring separate facilities across the range of social life. As Derrick Bell puts it, the purpose was 'not simply to exclude or separate but to subordinate those who, based on their colour and without regard to their accomplishments were presumed to be inferior to any white person no matter how low or ignorant'.[215]

It was not until well into the twentieth century that the majority of the Court began to echo the lone voice of Harlan J that 'such legislation, as that here in question, is inconsistent not only with that equality of rights which pertains to citizenship, National and State, but with the personal liberty enjoyed by everyone within the United States'.[216] Thus, in a seminal case concerning the internship of Japanese citizens during the Second World War, the Court held: 'Legal restrictions which curtail the civil rights of a single racial group are immediately suspect . . . Courts must subject them to the most rigid scrutiny.'[217] Although this in principle leaves open the possibility of justification of a racial classification, in practice the strict scrutiny test has almost invariably led to the Court striking down racial classifications operating to the detriment of African Americans.[218] In the famous case of *Brown v Board of Education* in 1954, the Court decisively rejected the 'separate but equal' doctrine. In a surprisingly brief but unequivocal judgment, the Court held that 'in the field of public education the doctrine of "separate but equal" has no place. Separate educational facilities are inherently unequal. Therefore, we hold that the plaintiffs . . . are, by reason of the segregation complained of, deprived of the equal protection of the laws guaranteed by the Fourteenth Amendment.'[219]

Brown is a ringing endorsement of the second dimension of substantive equality; namely, to address stigma, prejudice, stereotyping, and violence. 'To separate [African-American] children from others of similar age and qualifications solely because of their race generates a feeling of inferiority

---

[214] ibid 557.

[215] D Bell, *Silent Covenants* (OUP 2004) 12–13.

[216] *Plessy v Ferguson* (n 212) 555.

[217]   *Korematsu v United States* 323 US 214, 65 S Ct 193, 216 (1944) (US Sup Ct).

[218] See eg *McLaughlin v Florida* 379 US 184, 85 S Ct 283 (1964); *Loving v Virginia* 388 US 1, 87 S Ct 1817 (1967).

[219] *Brown v Board of Education* 347 US 483, 494 (1954) (US Sup Ct).

in their status in the community that may affect their hearts and minds in a way unlikely ever to be undone.'[220] However, the lack of attention to the other dimensions, which would have highlighted the interrelationship of poverty and race and its multiplier effect for Black pupils, had a lasting, limiting effect on the jurisprudence. It is well known that in reality the facilities available to Black learners were inevitably inferior, a product of a long and sordid history of discrimination and structural subordination. Had the Court paid attention to the first dimension of substantive equality—namely, to redress socio-economic disadvantage—this would have been obvious. Nor did the case pay sufficient attention to the role of voice and participation and the need for underlying structural change, the third or fourth dimensions of substantive equality. As Minow puts it: 'Because of *Brown*, schools stopped explicitly assigning students to schools that separate them by race, but parents and communities can produce similar results indirectly through housing patterns, district lines, and even some forms of school choice.'[221] The result has been increasing racial 'resegregation' in public schools in the US. In fact, schools are now more racially segregated than they were when the effort to achieve racial desegregation was at its height.[222] More worrying still, 'the vast majority of intensely segregated minority schools face conditions of concentrated poverty, which are powerfully related to unequal educational opportunity'.[223]

The failure of the constitutional equality guarantee to disrupt structural inequalities and the corresponding ideology of racial superiority led to widespread protest throughout the twentieth century. But it was not until 1964 that the constitutional promise of equality before the law was buttressed by federal anti-discrimination legislation, binding on private as well as public entities. In a crucial breakthrough in 1964, the Civil Rights Act was passed, banning discrimination on grounds of 'race, sex, color, religion, or national origin' in employment and other key areas. Title VII, the most important source of statutory protection in the US at the federal level, prohibits discrimination by employers (public or private) of fifteen or more employees,[224] as well as discrimination by private and public entities in access to public

---

[220] ibid.

[221] M Minow, *In Brown's Wake* (OUP 2010) 8.

[222] ibid 5.

[223] ibid 7.

[224] 42 USC § 2000e-2 (2006) and 42 USC § 2000e(b) (2006); amended in 1972 to prohibit employment discrimination by public as well as private employers (92 PS 261). The Equal Employment Opportunity Act of 1972 extended federal employment discrimination law to State employers.

accommodation (eg hotels, restaurants, and theatres).[225] Also important is Title IX, which prohibits discrimination by publicly funded educational institutions and by public entities that receive funds from federal government.[226] In addition, Title VI prohibits discrimination based on 'race, color, or national origin' in any 'program or activity' receiving 'federal financial assistance'.[227] This legislation is complemented by provisions for contract compliance, which were originally introduced by President Kennedy in 1961 and later embodied in Executive Order 11246 (1965). Contract compliance requires contractors of the federal government to increase the representation of racial minorities in their workforces as a condition for the award and the continuation of the contract.[228] Originally confined to race, these requirements have been extended to cover sex and religion.[229]

The Civil Rights Act 1964 was followed by the Voting Rights Act 1965, aimed at States and communities which suppressed minority voting through devices such as poll taxes, literacy tests, and drawing of constituency boundaries. In the words of Chief Justice Warren, the Voting Rights Act 'was designed to banish the blight of racial discrimination in voting, which has infected the electoral process in parts of our country for nearly a century'. The impact was immediate, with nearly 250,000 new Black voters registering by the end of that year. Initially, the Court supported these interventions as appropriate means for carrying out Congress's constitutional responsibilities. However, this support has drained away, especially in the early twenty-first century. As well as restrictive decisions on Title VII, which are discussed in later chapters, the Court has sharply clipped the wings of the Voting Rights Act. The battleground has been what is known as the 'pre-clearance' provision, intended to prevent reinstatement of discriminatory prohibitions. Under this provision, States with a history of racial discrimination in voting and lower minority voter participation were required to seek pre-clearance from the federal government for any changes in their voting laws. However, in 2013, the pre-clearance provision was struck down.[230] Although the majority acknowledged that, without doubt, voting discrimination still existed, it characterized the measure as an unwarranted interference by the federal government in State sovereignty. The majority relied, in particular, on gains

---

[225] 42 USC § 2000a(a)–(b) 2006. Sex is not included as a ground.
[226] 42 USC § 2000d (2006).
[227] Codified at 42 USC § 2000d (2010).
[228] Executive Order 10925.
[229] Executive Order 11246. See further Chapters 7 and 8.
[230] *Shelby County v Holder* (n 49).

made in voting rights, holding that the pre-clearance provision was no longer necessary. In her dissenting opinion, by contrast, Justice Ginsburg held that the improvements noted by the majority were precisely because of the pre-clearance regime. Striking down this provision, she stated, was 'like throwing away your umbrella in a rainstorm because you are not getting wet'.[231]

(b) Britain

Race relations in Britain have been similarly marked by deep-seated and institutionalized inequalities. However, the complex interaction of race, nationality, religion, and culture makes for a tangle of forces which do not yield to a straightforward narrative. While religious discord had been a feature of British history for many years, Britain came into the twentieth century with a fixed self-image as a homogeneous, white, Christian society. Even then, however, this was deceptive. There had always been small internal minorities, many of whom suffered prejudice and legal disabilities. Moreover, slavery was an accepted reality in eighteenth-century Britain. Men and women were sold openly at auctions and the use of slaves as domestic servants was fashionable and widespread. In 1770, there were between 14,000 and 20,000 slaves in London alone.[232] Slavery was not formally abolished in England and the colonies until 1833.

But the major factor shaping current patterns of ethnicity were the waves of migration to Britain from its ex-colonies in the postwar period.[233] The full political independence of Britain's colonies after the Second World War coincided with the urgent need for reconstruction of the battered British economy, which had lost many of its own workers in the war. Policies of active recruitment were instituted in many former colonies, particularly in the Caribbean, where systematic underdevelopment of the local economy had created a pool of desperate workers. In particular, faced with grinding poverty at home, people from the Caribbean flocked to the 'economic magnet, which lured so many of us to the Mother Country in the late forties and fifties'.[234] They were joined by increasing numbers of people from Africa, including significant numbers of East African Indians. Even greater numbers came from India after independence and the break-up of colonial India in

---

[231] ibid 2650.

[232] See B Hepple, *Race, Jobs and the Law in Britain* (2nd edn, Penguin Books 1970) 59–62.

[233] For a useful brief synopsis, see H Goulbourne, *Race Relations in Britain Since* 1945 (Macmillan Press 1998) ch 2.

[234] B Bryan, S Dadzie, and S Scafe, *The Heart of the Race: Black Women's Lives in Britain* (Virago 1985) 16.

1947. In addition, Ireland, starved of capital to develop its own domestic economy, remained a ready source of cheap labour for Britain.

However, life in the 'Mother Country' was far from a panacea for the new migrants.[235] Migrants were overwhelmingly in manual work, confined to a limited number of industries and often trapped in jobs below their level of qualification. Racial prejudice was widespread: there was an overt refusal by some employers to employ what were offensively called 'coloured' workers and employment opportunities were often available only in areas in which there were insufficient white workers to fill the posts. It was not uncommon for private landlords overtly to exclude Black people and members of marginalized ethnicities from private tenancies; mortgages were frequently only available on exorbitant terms; and very few migrants were in council housing. This left migrant families with little choice but to live in the worst available private rented housing in slum areas, with inevitably detrimental consequences for schooling and health. Disadvantage proved to be persistent: by 1974, minority groups were still disproportionately concentrated in semi-skilled and unskilled work and very few had succeeded in obtaining professional or managerial jobs, despite being qualified for those jobs.

Although there were no express legal prohibitions, as was the case for women, issues of race and colour[236] were dealt with by manipulating immigration rules. At first, citizenship rights were generous. In 1949, the colonial notion of the 'British subject' was replaced by the inclusive notion of 'citizen of the United Kingdom and Colonies'. This meant that postwar economic migrants arrived with immediate citizenship rights. However, by the early 1960s, the need for labour had abated and policymakers became more concerned with keeping jobs for local people. The response took the form of a rapid retreat from an inclusive notion of citizenship. Beginning with the Commonwealth Immigration Act 1962, immigration controls were progressively tightened. Although ostensibly neutral, these regulations were widely perceived as being primarily aimed at restricting the entry of Black people and those from South Asia. This, in turn, signalled a sea change in patterns of migration. Until 1961, there had been a constant ebb and flow of migration. Single men or women had come to Britain to work temporarily as migrant workers, retaining strong ties with their families and communities and often sending remittances back to their home country. Paradoxically, it was the policy of tightening up on immigration control which transformed

---

[235] The information in this section is taken from Modood and others (n 200) ch 10.
[236] See n 192.

temporary movements to and from home countries into a process of settlement. The announcement in 1961 of the Commonwealth Immigrants Act led to a rapid increase in migrants hoping to enter Britain before the ban came into force in 1962.[237] By 1981, the gate had clanged shut on new migration from the Caribbean and Indian sub-continent. Only families of men settled in Britain before 1973 were permitted to settle in Britain. In the meantime, the migrants of the 1960s have become the settled ethnic populations of the twenty-first century.

Without a constitutional equality guarantee, parliamentary intervention was needed to address race discrimination in postwar Britain. Prior to 1965, there was no legal protection against discrimination, racial or otherwise. Judge-made common law never recognized racial discrimination as a distinct legal wrong;[238] nor were judges prepared to declare race discrimination as contrary to public policy.[239] At the legislative level, considerable reluctance was similarly evident: the years from 1950 to 1965 saw the failure of at least ten attempts to persuade Parliament to legislate against race discrimination. The legislation that did finally emerge, in 1965 and 1968, was weak and ultimately ineffective.[240]

Renewed impetus for change led to the enactment of the Race Relations Act 1976 (RRA), which remained the central legislative source of protection against discrimination on grounds of race, colour,[241] nationality, and ethnic or national origins until the Equality Act (EA) 2010.[242] Following the model of the SDA, the RRA included both direct and indirect discrimination and covered employment, education, goods, facilities, and services available to the public. It differed from the SDA in that no division was drawn between pay and non-pay issues. Notably, it did not cover discrimination on the grounds of religion or belief. Only if a religious group could also be characterized as an ethnic minority would its members gain protection under the Act.[243]

Statutory prohibitions on individual acts of discrimination were not, as in other jurisdictions, sufficient on their own to address racism and racial inequality in Britain. These issues were forced to the surface by the case of

---

[237] H Ansari, *The Infidel Within: British Muslims since 1800* (C Hurst & Co 2004) 158.
[238] Hepple (n 232) 144.
[239] *Re Lysaght, Hill v Royal College of Surgeons* [1965] 3 WLR 391, 402.
[240] Hepple (n 232).
[241] See n 192.
[242] RRA 1976, s 3.
[243] *Mandla v Lee* [1983] 2 AC 548 (HL).

Stephen Lawrence, the victim of a racist assault and murder. Police failure to investigate the murder properly and to prosecute the perpetrators triggered allegations of racism. This, in turn, led to the establishment of what has been labelled a 'watershed' inquiry, led by Macpherson. The Report of the Inquiry[244] took a crucial step forward in recognizing that racism can extend beyond individual acts of prejudice to the institutional culture and organization of the police itself. Institutional racism was defined as the 'collective failure of an organisation to provide an appropriate and professional service to people because of their colour, culture, or ethnic origin. It can be seen or detected in process, attitudes and behaviour which amount to discrimination through unwitting prejudice, ignorance, thoughtlessness and racist stereotyping which disadvantage minority ethnic people.'[245] It persists because of an organizational failure to recognize and address its existence. Such 'institutional racism' was found to be endemic in the broader culture and structure of both the police and other agencies.[246]

The Macpherson Report prompted two significant extensions to the scope of the RRA in 2000. First, it became unlawful for public authorities to discriminate in any of their functions, not just employment, education, goods, facilities, and services.[247] Private bodies carrying out functions of a public nature were also included.[248] Secondly, and particularly innovative, was the introduction of a proactive duty. Rather than relying only on complaints of discrimination, the Act required public authorities to take the initiative in respect of eliminating unlawful discrimination, and promoting equality of opportunity and good race relations.[249] At the same time, the content of the duty was relatively mild. Authorities did not have to take steps to achieve these goals, but merely to 'have due regard' to the need to do so. This duty became the model for subsequent duties in relation to gender and disability, and was further extended in the EA 2010 to the other grounds of discrimination.[250]

At the EU level, while gender discrimination was part of the EU agenda from the beginning, race discrimination was surprisingly late in coming. It was not until the Treaty of Amsterdam in 1998 that the EU was given the competence to legislate on matters of, inter alia, racial or ethnic origin.[251]

---

[244] Home Office, 'Report of the Macpherson Inquiry' (Cmd 4262, 24 February 1999).
[245] ibid para 6.34.
[246] ibid para 6.34.
[247] RRA 1976, s 19B.
[248] ibid s 19B(2)(a).
[249] ibid s 71; now EA 2010, s 149.
[250] See Chapter 8.
[251] Treaty of Rome (Consolidated Version), Art 13.

This was quickly followed by the Race Directive.[252] The directive covers both direct and indirect discrimination as well as harassment. Particularly noteworthy is the scope of coverage of the directive. Whereas previous EU discrimination provisions had been confined to employment and vocational training, the Race Directive extends to social protection, including social security and healthcare, social advantages, education, and access to and supply of goods and services which are available to the public, including housing.[253] Notably, too, the directive specifies that the principle of equal treatment does not prevent a Member State from maintaining or adopting specific measures to prevent or compensate for disadvantages linked to racial or ethnic origin.[254] It also requires Member States to establish an equality body.[255]

Unlike the EA 2010 and the European Convention on Human Rights (ECHR), the Race Directive does not include nationality as a ground of discrimination. EU law already contains a strong principle of non-discrimination on grounds of nationality in respect of EU nationals. However, the situation of third country nationals is more complex. The directive itself states expressly that it does not cover difference of treatment based on nationality, and is without prejudice to provisions and conditions relating to the entry and residence of third country nationals and stateless persons and to any treatment which arises from their legal status.[256] Although third country nationals are protected against discrimination on grounds of race or ethnic origin, this prohibition does not cover differences of treatment based on nationality.[257]

Britain's ethnic diversity is no longer contestable.[258] However, equality remains illusory. Over two decades since the publication of the Macpherson Report, there is still deep concern at the continued evidence of systemic and institutional racism in policing and the criminal justice system. In 2017, figures showed that while making up 14 per cent of the population, Black people, people from marginalized minorities, and indigenous people constitute 25 per cent of prisoners. Even more worrying, over 40 per cent of young

---

[252] Council Directive 2000/43/EC.
[253] ibid Art 3(1)(e)–(h).
[254] ibid Art 5.
[255] ibid Art 13.
[256] ibid Art 3(2).
[257] ibid Preamble, para 13.
[258] In 2018, White British, constituted 79.5 per cent of the working population, Black African, Caribbean, or Black British (3.2 per cent), Indian (2.9 per cent), Pakistani and other ethnic groups (1.5 per cent), Bangladeshi and Chinese (less than 1 per cent each), and 'White Other', including those from the EU (7.9 per cent): Office for National Statistics, 'Ethnicity Pay Gaps in Great Britain: 2018' (2019).

people in custody were from Black, marginalized minorities, and indigenous backgrounds.[259] Particularly telling are statistics concerning the use of police powers to stop and search any person in a designated area without the need to establish that they have a 'reasonable suspicion' for doing so.[260] In 2018, Home Office statistics showed that Black people were forty times more likely to be stopped and searched under this power than white people.[261] This position was worsened during the Covid pandemic in 2020, during which police powers were expanded. Moreover, while there have been some attempts to increase representation of Black people, people from marginalized minorities, and indigenous people[262] in the police, in fact the number of Black police officers barely increased during the two decades following the Macpherson Report.[263]

Inequality extends right through the social structure. Figures from 2017 show that the poverty rate is twice as high for Black people, people from marginalized minorities, and indigenous people as for white groups. Black people, people from marginalized minorities, and indigenous people are twice as likely as white people to be living in an area of high deprivation, and despite increasing educational gains, these groups are more likely to be overqualified for the work they do, and experience high levels of underemployment as graduates.[264] Inequalities in health, housing, and employment were exacerbated by the Covid pandemic in 2020.

At the same time, differences between minority groups can be as striking as those between minority and majority groups. In 2018, the average hourly pay of all employees from the Indian ethnic group was £13.46, considerably higher than that for white employees (£11.87).[265] Indeed, between 2013

[259] D Lammy *The Lammy Review: An Independent Review into the Treatment of, and Outcomes for Black, Asian and Minority Ethnic Individuals in the Criminal Justice System* (2017) <www.gov.uk/government/publications/lammy-review-final-report> accessed 26 July 2022. See also n 16.

[260] Criminal Justice and Public Order Act 1990, s 60. The power must be authorized by an officer of or above the rank of inspector who believes that serious violence may take place in the designated area and that the exercise of the power could prevent such violence by recovering weapons from suspects.

[261] L Chapman, 'Section 60 Stop and Search: A Disproportionate and Ineffective Policing Tool' (2019) <www.bindmans.com/insight/blog/section-60-stop-and-search-a-disproportionate-and-ineffective-policing-tool> accessed 26 July 2022.

[262] See n 16.

[263] Criminal Justice Alliance, 'The Macpherson Report: Twenty One Years On' (June 2020) <http://criminaljusticealliance.org/twenty-one-years-after-macpherson-report-systemic-racism-in-policing-continues/> accessed 26 July 2022.

[264] Joseph Rowntree Foundation, 'Poverty and Ethnicity in the Labour Market' (2017) <www.jrf.org.uk/report/poverty-ethnicity-labour-market> accessed 26 July 2022.

[265] UK Government, 'Ethnicity Facts and Figures' (updated 15 September 2020) <www.ethnicity-facts-figures.service.gov.uk/work-pay-and-benefits/pay-and-income/average-hourly-pay/latest> accessed 15 September 2020.

and 2018, employees from the Indian ethnic group had the highest average hourly pay of all ethnic groups every year, while employees from the combined Pakistani and Bangladeshi ethnic group had the lowest hourly pay every year. Moreover, the gap between these two groups widened during that period. It is also crucial to recognize the extent to which the statistics obscure class divisions internal to groups. Some individuals in all these groups have succeeded, while others remain disadvantaged.

(c) India

Equality law in India has been heavily influenced by the Hindu caste structure which remains deeply engrained in Indian society. Also central has been the history of conflict between Muslims and Hindus, exacerbated by colonialism, and the creation of the State of Pakistan in 1947,[266] leaving a Muslim minority in India. Hindu society is characterized by a hierarchy of castes determined by birth. There are four main castes and those without caste, or outcastes.[267] This group are often known as 'Untouchables' because physical untouchability, and accompanying notions of pollution and impurity, are a central part of their subordination. In his determined campaign to integrate the 'Untouchables', Ghandi called them 'Harijan' or people of God; but members of this group in modern India prefer to be known as 'Dalits' or broken people. Dalits were oppressed for centuries. They were restricted to the most menial and degrading of tasks, such as manual scavenging or clearing human waste by hand. They were not permitted to draw water from common wells, own land, or keep cattle; and dominant castes would not accept food or water from them. They were often subject to violence and humiliation. As the chief architect of the Indian Constitution, Dr BR Ambedkar, himself a Dalit, put it: 'How can I call this land my own homeland and this religion my own wherein we are treated worse than cats and dogs, wherein we cannot get water to drink?'[268] Ambedkar was also acutely aware of the interaction between the stigmatic and degrading aspects of untouchability and the structures which sustained it. Untouchability, he wrote, was not merely a religious

---

[266] D Gilmartin, 'Partition, Pakistan, and South Asian History: In Search of a Narrative' (1998) 57 Journal of Asian Studies 1068.

[267] This paragraph and the following one rely heavily on Anup Surendranath, 'Sub-Classification of Scheduled Castes Before the Indian Supreme Court: The Case for a More Inclusive Approach' (D Phil thesis, Oxford University (2009)).

[268] B Ambedkar, *Dr Babasaheb Ambedkar: Writings and Speeches*, vol 17 (Government of Maharashtra 1979–2003) 53.

custom, but 'a system of unmitigated economic exploitation.'[269] All attempts to abolish untouchability had failed, he argued, because upper caste Hindus continued to benefit from the work of Dalits as sweepers, scavengers, and forced labour.

The abolition of untouchability became a central commitment of the Constitution of the newly independent India. Article 17 of the final Constitution, which came into effect in January 1950, specifically prohibits untouchability. Importantly, this provision binds both State and non-State actors, reflecting a recognition of the deep-seated social forces which continue to sustain it. In addition, the Indian Constitution contains a cluster of provisions pertaining to the right to equality more generally. The flagship provision, Article 14, derives directly from the Fourteenth Amendment of the US Constitution.[270] Thus, it states: 'The State shall not deny to any person equality before the law or the equal protection of the laws within the territory of India.' Article 14 has been held to form part of the basic structure of the Constitution. This means that it cannot be curtailed by constitutional amendment.[271] Unlike the US Constitution, however, the Indian Constitution goes beyond the requirement of equality before the law to a specific non-discrimination provision. Thus, Article 15(1) provides that the State shall not discriminate against any citizen 'on grounds only of religion, race, caste, sex, place of birth or any of them'. This is complemented by Article 16 which provides for equality of opportunity for all citizens in relation to employment or appointment to an office under the State and prohibits discrimination on the specified grounds in relation to State employment or office.

Importantly, too, the equality code of the Indian Constitution takes one step further than equality before the law and prohibitions on discrimination. It also sees a central role for positive measures to advance those who have been disadvantaged, particularly through 'reservations' or set-asides in public employment and education. Article 15 permits the State to make 'special provision for the advancement of any socially and educationally backward classes of citizens of the Scheduled Castes and the Scheduled Tribes',[272]

---

[269] B Ambedkar, *What Congress and Gandhi Have Done to the Untouchables* (Gautam Book Centre 2009 [1945]) 188–89 and see A Barua, 'Revisiting the Ghandi–Ambedkar Debates over Caste' (2018) 25 Journal of Human Values 25.

[270] I Jaising, 'Gender Justice and the Supreme Court' in B Kirpal and others (eds), *Supreme but not Infallible* (OUP 2000) 293.

[271] *Raghunath Rao v Union of India* AIR 1993 SC 1267, para 185.

[272] Constitution of India, Arts 341 and 342 provide that the President may specify by public notification who are deemed to be Scheduled Castes and Scheduled Tribes, and these are listed from time to time in statutory instruments. See the Constitution (Scheduled Castes) Order, [1950] 1 (CO 19).

specifically mentioning admission to educational institutions.[273] Article 16 also specifically permits the State to make provision for the 'reservation of appointments or posts in favour of any backward class of citizens which, in the opinion of the State, is not adequately represented in the services under the State'.[274] This has set the Indian equality guarantee on a very different trajectory from that of comparable jurisdictions. Rather than comprehensive anti-discrimination legislation, 'caste-based reservations in public employment and education have been India's primary vehicle for fulfilling its constitutional promise of an egalitarian society'.[275]

The caste-based structure in India is not the only form of social stratification which fuels inequalities. Constituting 13 per cent of the 1,406 million people in India, Muslims are, in the words of the Sachar Committee, 'seriously lagging behind in terms of most of the human development indicators'.[276] The Sachar Report, issued in 2006, found that Muslims are concentrated in the informal sector, where their position is particularly precarious and their access to social security is poor.[277] They face high levels of poverty, only slightly better than those of Scheduled Castes/Scheduled Tribes, particularly in urban areas.[278] Although there is considerable variation in their position in various parts of the country, the Muslim community as a whole exhibits deficits and deprivation in almost all dimensions of development.[279] This is particularly true of education, where the Sachar Report pointed to clear educational deprivation experienced by the Muslim community, a problem which is even more acute for girls.[280] To this is added their low participation in political spheres, reducing their opportunity to change their position through political processes.[281]

This lack of political voice has been especially problematic since the election in 2014 of the Hindu Nationalist Party, the Bharatiya Janata Party (BJP) led by Prime Minister Narendra Modi, and its re-election in 2019 after a campaign using explicitly anti-Muslim messages. The result has been an

---

[273] Constitution of India, Art 15(4) and (5).

[274] ibid Art 16(4).

[275] T Khaitan, 'Transcending Reservations: A Paradigm Shift in the Debate on Equality' (2008) 20(8) Economic and Political Weekly.

[276] R Sachar, 'Social, Economic and Educational Status of the Muslim Community of India', Prime Minister's High Level Committee (2006) 2 <www.minorityaffairs.gov.in/sites/default/files/sachar_comm.pdf> accessed 18 October 2020.

[277] ibid 106.

[278] ibid 161.

[279] ibid 237.

[280] ibid 243.

[281] ibid 241.

increase in anti-Muslim hostility across society and within political institutions. Particularly inflammatory was the Citizenship Amendment Act, enacted in 2019, which expressly excluded Muslims, Jewish people, atheists, and members of other faiths from the fast-tracking of citizenship for Hindu, Sikh, Jain, Parsi, and Christian migrants from Afghanistan, Bangladesh, and Pakistan. Potentially even more undermining was the recent exercise to update the National Register of Citizens, which was put in place in 1951 in the Indian State of Assam to determine whether residents were Indian citizens or migrants from neighbouring Bangladesh. About one-third of the State's thirty-two million residents are Muslims, and many were unable to provide the requisite documentation to prove their Indian citizenship. The result has been to place as many as 1.9 million people in Assam at risk of being stripped of their citizenship.[282] But the harshest and most unwarranted measures were taken in 2019 when the Modi government stripped India's only Muslim-majority State of its special constitutional autonomy. The residents of Jammu and Kashmir were subjected to emergency measures which removed many basic freedoms and thousands of people were detained, including prominent political figures. Mobile phone networks, internet services, and landline connectivity were all discontinued, restrictions of movement were imposed, and public gatherings banned.[283]

Despite the constitutional commitment to equality, caste and religion continue to play a central role in Indian society, with economic advantage concentrated in the upper castes.[284] Indeed, the rapid growth in GDP over the past three decades has brought with it increased inequality. Chancel and Piketty show that in 2015, as much as 21.3 per cent of national income was attributable to only 1 per cent of the population. In stark contrast, only 14.9 per cent of national income was attributable to the 397 million people in the

---

[282] 'Written Testimony of Lawyer Aman Wadud at the U.S. Commission on International Religious Freedom Hearing on Citizenship Laws and Religious Freedom Wednesday, March 4, 2020 2:30–4:00 PM', 3–4 <www.uscirf.gov/sites/default/files/Aman%20Wadud.pdf> accessed 3 June 2022. My thanks to Gautam Bhatia for pointing me to this source.

[283] S Zargar, *Between Rights and Risks: Life and Liberty in an Internet Dark Kashmir* (Digital Empowerment Foundation October 2020) <www.defindia.org/wp-content/uploads/2020/10/kashmir-longest-internet-shutdown.pdf> accessed 3 June 2022; Forum for Human Rights in Jammu and Kashmir, 'Two Years of Lockdown: Human Rights in Jammu and Kashmir' (August 2021) <https://indianculturalforum.in/2021/08/04/two-years-of-lockdown-human-rights-in-jammu-and-kashmir-2021/> accessed 3 June 2022.

[284] In 2019, Dalits constituted 20 per cent of the population, with Scheduled Tribes constituting 9 per cent. A further 41 per cent were classified as 'Other Backward Classes' (OBCs). Upper castes, although forming only 30 per cent of the population, constituted the major part of the affluent population (Statista 2020).

bottom 50 per cent of the population, down from 20.6 per cent in 2000. As Himanshu puts it: 'What is particularly worrying in India's case is that economic inequality is being added to a society that is already fractured along the lines of caste, religion, region and gender.'[285] Dalits, tribal groups, and Muslims are consistently disadvantaged, not just in access to wealth but also to basic services such as education, health, and nutrition.[286] This is exacerbated by the fact that job creation has been predominantly in the informal sector, or in precarious jobs within the formal sector. The result has been to normalize poor working conditions, inadequate pay, and no access to social security.[287] Even more worrying is the increasing divergence in assets held by disadvantaged groups such as Dalits, tribals, and Muslims as compared to affluent upper castes. The structure of the Indian economy, characterized by 'crony capitalism', has meant that the forward caste groups have been in the best position to seize the benefits of growth, enabling them to consolidate and improve their wealth positions.[288] Crony capitalism is defined as a system whereby wealth is gained not by success in the market, but through a nexus with government.[289] This growing divergence is also seen in other key indicators, such as health and education, in which State investment is poor and dwindling. Earlier commitments by the State to policies of inclusion have been replaced in recent decades by a strong ideology of privatization, opening up numerous possibilities for cronyism and preferential treatment of the rich at the cost of the poor. Such inequalities were exacerbated as a result of the Covid-19 pandemic, with India exhibiting extreme inequality in 2022.[290]

(d) South Africa

The South African Constitution must be understood in the context of the very recent history of apartheid, with its legally enforced, systematic, and wholesale racial subordination based on invidious racial classifications. Under apartheid, all people were classified into four groups—'White', 'African', 'Coloured', and 'Indian'[291]—and only those classified as 'White' enjoyed the

---

[285] <www.oxfam.org/en/india-extreme-inequality-numbers> accessed 26 July 2022.
[286] H Himanshu, 'Widening Gaps: India Inequality Report 2018' (Oxfam India), 11 <https://socialprotection-humanrights.org/resource/india-inequality-report-2018-widening-gaps/> accessed 15 October 2020.
[287] ibid 12.
[288] ibid 50.
[289] ibid 35.
[290] World Inequality Report 2022 <https://wir2022.wid.world/executive-summary/> accessed 1 June 2022.
[291] Population Registration Act No 30 of 1950.

full rights of citizenship. South Africans classified as 'African', 'Coloured', and 'Indian' were denied the right to vote, to own property in urban areas, and to move freely around the country. Strict social segregation was enforced, including requiring Black people[292] to live in townships on the periphery of white cities, prohibiting inter-racial marriage, segregating schools, and restricting Black participation in the labour market to largely unskilled work. White people owned the vast majority of land although they constituted a tiny proportion of the population, and Black families were deeply disrupted by the migrant labour system which banished Black women to rural 'homelands' while relying on Black men to work in the mines in urban areas. Black women were doubly and triply discriminated against, particularly in relation to the highly unequal personal laws of marriage, divorce, and property ownership. It was thus with the aim of making a clear break with history and healing the scars of the past that the Constitution of South Africa was framed.

After an extraordinarily participative constitution-building process, the final Constitution was signed into law in December 1996. As stated in the preamble, the Constitution was adopted to 'heal the divisions of the past and establish a society based on democratic values, social justice and fundamental human rights; lay the foundations for a democratic and open society in which government is based on the will of the people and every citizen is equally protected by law; improve the quality of life of all citizens and free the potential of each person; and build a united and democratic South Africa able to take its rightful place as a sovereign state in the family of nations.'

Equality permeates the Constitution. Both equality and dignity are part of its founding values. As stated in section 1, South Africa is founded on values which include 'human dignity, the achievement of equality and the advancement of human rights and freedoms; non-racialism and non-sexism; supremacy of the constitution and the rule of law; and universal adult suffrage'. The specific equality guarantee is found in section 9. Reflecting the direct influence of Canadian constitutional law, section 9(1) states: 'Everyone is equal before the law and has the right to equal protection and benefit of the law.' The remainder of section 9 fleshes out this concept. In a distinctive contribution, the concept of 'unfair' discrimination is included and, equally

[292] 'Black people' as used in this section include those classified as 'African', 'Indian', and 'Coloured' under the apartheid legislation. During apartheid, 'Black' was often used as a symbol of solidarity between all groups oppressed under the system, and as an antidote to the divide-and-rule policy of the Afrikaner Nationalist government. Some laws applied differentially to 'Indian' and 'Coloured' people—eg they were not consigned to rural homelands and 'Coloured' people were given labour preference in the Cape Province.

importantly, the provision is not confined to State action but proscribes un-fair discrimination by individuals against other individuals.[293] The South African Constitution also addresses distributive inequalities by expressly including socio-economic rights. Everyone has the right to have access to adequate housing, healthcare services, sufficient food and water, and social security.[294] In addition to the constitutional guarantee, the South African government has passed two major pieces of legislation on equality. The Employment Equity Act (EEA) applies to employment discrimination, while the Promotion of Equality and Prevention of Unfair Discrimination Act (Equality Act) applies outside employment.

The commitment to equality in the South African Constitution is not limited to prohibitions of individual acts of discrimination. In addition, there is an important and innovative emphasis on positive duties to advance pre-viously disadvantaged South Africans. The Constitution itself permits the State to take measures designed to advance those who are disadvantaged by unfair discrimination.[295] This is given specific context in the EEA, which requires designated employers to implement affirmative action measures to ensure the equitable representation of Black people, women, and people with disabilities in all occupational categories and levels of the workforce.[296] Even more novel has been the programme of Broad-Based Black Economic Empowerment (BBBEE). Given that the vast majority of the wealth in South Africa was owned by the white population, despite being a small minority, redistributive measures were regarded as essential. The BBBEE project was launched to advance the transformation of the economy and enhance the economic participation of Black South Africans.[297] Its aim is to increase Black representation in five domains: ownership, management control, skills development, enterprise and supplier development, and socio-economic de-velopment. Progress is measured according to a scorecard. For example, in mining, an entity is required to have 26 per cent Black ownership in order to be issued with mining rights.[298] Public procurement is also conditional on acceptable BBBEE scores.

[293] South African Constitution, s 9(3).

[294] ibid ss 26 and 27: the State is under a duty to take reasonable legislative and other meas-ures, within its available resources, to achieve the progressive realization of each of these rights.

[295] ibid s 9(2).

[296] Employment Equity Act 1998. Section 1 defines 'black people' as a 'generic term which means Africans, Coloureds and Indians'.

[297] Broad-Based Black Economic Empowerment Amendment Act, 2013 (Act No 46 of 2013). Section 1 states that '"Black people" is a generic term which means Africans, Coloureds and Indians' who are South African citizens.

[298] Mineral and Petroleum Resources Development Act 2002.

Although the background principle of redistribution is central to transformation in South Africa, it is not clear that the BBBEE project has been successful. In its 2020 report, the Commission on Broad Based Black Economic Empowerment, which is responsible for monitoring BBBEE, found that although there had been a slight increase in the ownership element of the BBBEE programme, there had been a general decline in the progress of companies in achieving targets for management control, skills development, enterprise and supplier development, and socio-economic development. Particularly concerning was the lack of representation of Black women and Black men at board level of entities listed on the Johannesburg Stock Exchange. The mismatch between the increase in Black ownership and the decline in management and control suggested that despite recorded Black ownership, Black people were not involved in the control and core operations of the entity. 'Economic transformation,' it concluded, 'remains too static for an inclusive economy and equal society to be achieved.'[299] Other research reveals deeper problems of corruption, fraud, mismanagement, and incompetence. Some argue that instead of its ideal of broad-based empowerment, BBBEE has led to the emergence of several powerful Black individuals who are able to manipulate procurement systems to give tenders to friends, peers, and relatives.[300] Indeed, in the first phase of BBBEE, 60 per cent of the empowerment deals amounting to R25.3 billion went to the companies of only two Black businessmen.[301] In any event, the tendering system favours those with substantial human and financial resources, making it impossible for those with limited funding to compete. There are also instances of 'fronting,' or schemes where Black people are signed up as fictitious shareholders to circumvent BBBEE requirements.[302]

Despite the far-reaching nature of the equality commitment in the Constitution and legislation, inequality in South Africa remains heavily racialized and gender biased. This is most conspicuous in the labour market. As well as being most likely to be unemployed, Black Africans earn the lowest wages when they are employed. Data from 2011 to 2015 show that the mean real earnings of white people in the labour market were more than three times

---

[299] B-BBEE Commission, *National Status and Trends on Broad-Based Black Economic Empowerment* (B-BBEE Commission 2020) 97. The term 'Black' here is used as defined in the statute: see n 292.

[300] E Shava, 'Black Economic Empowerment in South Africa: Challenges and Prospects' (2016) 8 Journal of Economics and Behavioural Studies 161, 168.

[301] A Fauconnier and B Mathur-Helm, 'Black Economic Empowerment in the South African Mining Industry' (2008) 39 South African J Business Management 1, 2.

[302] Shava (n 300) 167.

as high as for Black Africans. Although social grants for the bottom deciles have played an important role in reducing overall income inequality, South Africa is now one of the most unequal countries in the world.[303] Similar patterns can be seen when examining access to basic services and the ownership of assets. Asset inequality for Black Africans increased between 2009 and 2015. Since 1994, the government has attempted to address the deep inequalities created by apartheid in access to education, healthcare, and basic services (such as water, sanitation, refuse removal, and electricity). However, this has had varying levels of success. There have been notable improvements in school enrolment, although school outcomes for Black African learners remain some of the lowest in Africa. On the other hand, sharp inequalities in healthcare remain, with Black Africans having the lowest access to medical aid coverage. Although there have been some improvements in access to electricity, water, sanitation, and the internet, Black Africans tend to lag further behind other population groups. As we have seen, the intersection between race and gender has meant that Black African women are the most disadvantaged group. This has worsened as a result of the Covid-19 pandemic in 2020–21.

At the same time, class disparities continue to be highly racialized in South Africa. Successive governments since the end of apartheid, particularly under President Mbeki, have viewed the growth of a Black middle class as a major driver of change. The policy of Black Economic Empowerment quickly created a small group of Black capitalists.[304] The early post-apartheid period witnessed upward social mobility in both the public and private sectors, where affirmative action policies provided support for previously disadvantaged South Africans to enter the higher levels of the labour market. There was initially a large growth in this group with the Black middle class (measured on per capita household income) rising from 15.9 per cent in 1993 to 34.2 per cent in 2012.[305] However, the relatively poor performance of both the education system and the economy have made those gains difficult to sustain.[306] In the meantime, the poorest groups are overwhelmingly Black. At the other end of the spectrum, only one-fifth of the elite class is comprised

---

[303] Figures in this paragraph are taken from Statistics South Africa, 'Inequality Trends in South Africa' (2019) <www.statssa.gov.za/?p=12930> accessed 19 October 2020.

[304] For the definition of 'Black' in the BEE legislation, see n 292.

[305] R Burger and others, 'The Middle Class in Contemporary South Africa' (2014) Stellenbosch Economic Working Paper 11, 16.

[306] ibid 17.

of Black African-headed households, compared to white people who account for about 65 per cent.[307]

(e) Canada

Canadian equality law should be read against the backdrop of the colonization of the indigenous or First Nation peoples, the complex interaction between French and English linguistic groups, and the modern cosmopolitanism which has resulted from decades of immigration of ethnic groups from many parts of the world. Having negotiated the surrender of the preponderance of title of indigenous people, much governmental activity, both before and after the Canadian provinces became a federation in 1867, was premised on the paternalistic assumption that indigenous people were unable to defend their own interests and were consequently in need of guardianship.[308] Thus, according to the Supreme Court of Canada in a case decided in 1950, the 'Indian Act' was based on 'the accepted view that these [indigenous people] are, in effect, wards of the State, whose care and welfare are a political trust of the highest obligation'.[309] The guardianship ideology was, however, a smokescreen for subordination of the most intense kind. First Nations people, who were invidiously classified as 'Indians' under the 'Indian Act', were deprived of the right to vote in federal and provincial elections; and while men could vote in band elections, women were not permitted to vote in band elections until 1951. Band members residing outside the reserve only gained the right to vote in band elections as a result of a Supreme Court decision in 1999.[310] It was not until 1960 that all those classified as 'Indians' (now referred to as First Nations people), male and female, were permitted to vote in federal elections.[311] At the same time, the long-term aim was to assimilate them into the dominant culture.

Indigenous people continue to be among the most disadvantaged of Canadian society. In recent years, the indigenous population has begun to regenerate, growing by 45 per cent between 1996 and 2006 (compared with 8 per cent among the rest of the population) and surpassing one million in the 2006 census.[312] In 2016, about 1.67 million individuals in Canada

---

[307] Statistics South Africa (n 303).
[308] S Grammond, *Identity Captured by Law* (McGill-Queen's University Press 2009) 72–73.
[309] *St Anne's Shooting and Fishing Club v The King* [1950] SCR 211, 219.
[310] *Corbiere v Canada (Minister of Indian and Northern Affairs)* [1999] 2 SCR 203 (Can Sup Ct); see also Grammond (n 308) 103.
[311] Grammond ibid 74.
[312] Canadian Census 2006.

self-identified as indigenous people, corresponding to 4.9 per cent of the population. Amongst these, First Nations are the largest, followed by Métis, with the Inuit population being the smallest. The indigenous population of Canada is younger and growing faster, but they are more likely to be located in predominantly rural areas, and although their well-being has improved in recent decades, the pace of improvement lags behind other populations.[313]

A further source of complexity in the Canadian context has been the need to protect the Francophone minority. The choice of a federal system in 1867 was partly motivated by the desire to give the Francophone population control of the province of Quebec, where they formed a large majority. This was not, however, sufficient to protect the right of French-speaking Canadians elsewhere in Canada, nor of English-speaking Canadians in Quebec. Particularly controversial has been the need to secure the right to maintain the French language, for example through education.[314] At the same time, the Canadian population has become increasingly multicultural. 'Visible minorities', comprising mainly South Asian, Chinese, Black, Filipino, Arab, Latin American, Southeast Asian, West Asian, Korean, and Japanese, constituted more than one-fifth of the Canadian population in 2016.[315] Notably, more than one-quarter of young Canadians (aged fifteen to thirty-four) self-identified as a member of a diverse racial/ethnic group in 2016.[316] These groups have also faced racism and exclusion. In addition to measures subordinating indigenous people, many of the provinces included laws which were blatantly racist, discriminating against Chinese, Japanese, and other minorities.

Before the enactment of the Charter of Rights and Freedoms in 1982, Canadian courts failed signally to protect minorities from discrimination.[317] In a series of cases before the Supreme Court of Canada and the Privy Council (then the court of final resort), challenges to racist legislation

---

[313] OECD, 'Linking Indigenous Communities with Regional Development in Canada' (21 January 2020) <https://doi.org/10.1787/19909284>, see ch 2 'Profile of Indigenous Canada: Trends and Data Needs' <www.oecd-ilibrary.org/sites/e6cc8722-en/index.html?itemId=/content/component/e6cc8722-en> accessed 26 July 2022.

[314] Grammond (n 308) 153.

[315] Statistics Canada, 'Data Tables, 2016 Census Visible Minorities' <www12.statcan.gc.ca/census-recensement/2016/dp-pd/dt-td/Rp-eng.cfm?TABID=2&Lang=E&APATH=3&DETAIL=0&DIM=0&FL=A&FREE=0&GC=0&GID=1341679&GK=0&GRP=1&PID=110531&PRID=10&PTYPE=109445&S=0&SHOWALL=0&SUB=0&Temporal=2017&THEME=120&VID=0&VNAMEE=&VNAMEF=&D1=0&D2=0&D3=0&D4=0&D5=0&D6=0> accessed 26 July 2022.

[316] <www.catalyst.org/research/people-of-colour-in-canada/> accessed 26 July 2022.

[317] R Sharpe and K Roach, The Charter of Rights and Freedoms (3rd edn, Irwin Law 2005) 15.

were unsuccessful. This was somewhat counteracted in the postwar period by the enactment of human rights codes, aimed at providing legal protection against discrimination.[318] These provincial human rights codes played an important role in the struggle against racism, sexism, and other forms of discrimination in that period.[319] Much more disappointing was the Canadian Bill of Rights, which was enacted in the form of an ordinary Act of Parliament in 1960. Initially, it seemed that the Supreme Court of Canada would regard the Bill of Rights as quasi-constitutional in nature. In *R v Drybones*,[320] the Court struck down a provision in the 'Indian Act' which made it an offence for First Nations people to be intoxicated in any part of Canada outside the reserves—an offence which was considerably harsher than that which applied to others in the Northwest Territories. However, because it was an ordinary statute of Parliament and did not have constitutional status, judges in later cases did not regard it as giving them authority to invalidate duly enacted laws.[321] Moreover, the courts adopted a narrow and formal view of the right to equality in the Bill. In the case of *Lavell*,[322] a First Nations woman challenged the statutory provision depriving First Nations women of their status under the 'Indian Act' if they married non-First Nations men. The Court dismissed the application on the narrow and formal ground that the provision treated all women in her situation in the same way.

When the Charter of Human Rights and Freedoms was enacted in 1982, it deliberately invited judges to be more robust in the protection of human rights. In addition, the disappointing experience of the Canadian Bill of Rights meant that much effort was expended on drafting a stronger and more substantive equality guarantee in the form of section 15 of the Charter. Whereas the Canadian Bill of Rights referred only to the right to 'equality before the law and the protection of the law',[323] section 15 of the Charter states that 'every individual is equal before *and under* the law and *has the right to the equal protection and equal benefit of the law*' (emphasis added). Its addition of the right to equal protection echoed the formulation of the Fourteenth Amendment of the US Constitution[324] and the inclusion of 'equal benefit of the law' made it clear that it extended beyond a duty to refrain

---

[318] ibid.
[319] ibid 16.
[320] *R v Drybones* [1970] SCR 282 (Can Sup Ct).
[321] Sharpe and Roach (n 317) 17.
[322] *Canada (Attorney General) v Lavell* [1970] SCR 282 (Can Sup Ct).
[323] s 1(b).
[324] Sharpe and Roach (n 317) 310.

from discriminating to include a positive duty to redress and even eradicate poverty.[325] Indeed, it has been argued that 'with the broad wording and the addition of disability as a prohibited ground in section 15, Canada had adopted a unique protection of equality, considered more expansive than any in the world'.[326] Whether section 15 has lived up to this expectation remains controversial.

In addition to the Charter protection, there is a federal Human Rights Act and fourteen Human Rights Acts in different provinces. The most important human rights legislation at the federal level is the Canadian Human Rights Act[327] which came into force in 1978. The purpose of this Act is to 'to give effect, within the purview of matters coming within the legislative authority of Parliament, to the principle that all individuals should have an opportunity equal with other individuals to make for themselves the lives that they are able and wish to have and to have their needs accommodated, consistent with their duties and obligations as members of society, without being hindered in or prevented from doing so by discriminatory practices based on race, national or ethnic origin, colour, religion, age, sex, sexual orientation, marital status, family status, disability or conviction for an offence for which a pardon has been granted'.[328] The Act proscribes discrimination in employment and in the delivery of goods and services on any of these grounds, as well as on the grounds of pregnancy and childbirth, which are deemed to be discriminatory on grounds of sex. The Act applies to anyone working for either the federal government or a private company regulated by the federal government, as well as anyone who receives goods and services from any of those sectors. All federal government departments and Crown corporations, as well as private companies such as railroads, airlines, banks, telephone companies, and radio or TV stations, are bound by the Act. Each province has its own human rights law covering organizations not included under federal legislation, such as schools, retail shops, restaurants, factories, and the provincial governments themselves. This book does not deal with provincial legislation except in the context of decisions of the Canadian Supreme Court which have more general implications.

---

[325] B Porter, 'Expectations of Equality' (2006) 33 Supreme Court L Rev 2327.

[326] ibid 26.

[327] RSC, 1985, c H-6.

[328] Canadian Human Rights Act, s 2. Note that the statute uses the term 'colour', which is also widely used in international human rights law and relevant statutes in other jurisdictions (see UK EA 2010, s 9(1)(a); South African Constitution, s 9; Canadian Charter, s 15; International Convention on the Elimination of All Forms of Racial Discrimination, Art 1; ICCPR, Art 2(1); ICESCR, Art 2(2)), which all refer to 'colour' in the list of protected characteristics.

III RELIGION AND BELIEF

(i) Challenges and Dilemmas

Protection against discrimination on grounds of religion has been a core value of international human rights law since its inception. As Boyle and Sheen put it:

> from the Holocaust, the ultimate outworking of centuries of European intolerance against Jews, came a new idea, that of individual human rights, to be internationally defined and guaranteed to all persons everywhere in virtue of their humanity, without distinction as to race, sex, language or religion.[329]

At the same time, religious discrimination is a good deal more complex than other related grounds. On one hand, it bears strong similarities to, and is indeed closely allied with, other types of discrimination. Religious discrimination can be a form of racism at its most vicious, as witnessed by the atrocities committed by the Nazis against Jewish people in the Second World War in the name of pure racist ideology. In other contexts, religious discrimination constitutes a form of ethnic or cultural discrimination. Thus, as we have seen, Modood regards anti-Muslim prejudice in Europe as 'cultural racism'. Religious discrimination can also be closely linked to discrimination on grounds of political affiliation, as in Northern Ireland, where the tensions between Catholics and Protestants are rooted as much in communal identification, separate nationalisms, and political disagreement as in religion. Similarly, discrimination against Muslims in India meshes closely with political and nationalistic conflicts.

On the other hand, the relationship between religion and other grounds of discrimination is shifting and often conflicting. Religions find their source of authority in faith rather than reason and, in some cases, their allegiance is to God and a transcendental morality, rather than to the democratic legal system. This might make it difficult to find common ground either between one religion and another or between individual religions and a secular human rights regime.[330] Religions may also breed intolerance of other religions, and

---

[329] K Boyle and J Sheen (eds), *Freedom of Religion and Belief: A World Report* (Routledge 1997) 4.

[330] F Raday, 'Culture, Religion and Gender' [2003] 1(4) International J Constitutional Law 663, 669.

religious adherents might even discriminate against others of the same faith because they are less observant or have a different interpretation of religious doctrine. The discourse of 'self' and 'other', seen in racism, does not easily transplant onto religious discrimination.

Perhaps most problematic is the reliance on religious belief to justify other forms of discrimination. Particularly extreme was the use by the Afrikaner Nationalist Party of religious precepts to justify institutionalized racism in the apartheid State in South Africa. More common are attempts to defend sexism or homophobia on the grounds of religion. As will be seen, British and EU law has permitted priority to be given in specific circumstances to religious belief over the protection of others' rights, particularly those of women and LGBTQI+ people. Further complexities are added by the fact that it is not only religious belief but also the right not to believe that is usually protected by discrimination law. Other forms of belief are included, too. This raises the troublesome question of whether all kinds of belief should be equally protected.[331] Also complex is the relationship between religion, ethnicity, culture, and community. Some Muslims would object to an approach which conflated Islamic norms with ethnicity, regarding the former as fundamentally religious in nature and transcending ethnic demarcations.[332] On the other hand, both Jewish people and Sikhs have long been regarded as ethnic groups for the purposes of race discrimination law in Britain,[333] and many Jewish people regard themselves as both ethnic and religious.

(ii) Historical Context

(a) Britain

Religious discrimination has been part of the fabric of society in Britain in many different ways. Formal legal impediments have taken time to dismantle. Until the start of the twentieth century, institutionalized religious privilege in favour of the Church of England was matched by a mass of specific discriminatory laws against Jewish people, Catholics, and non-conformist Protestants.[334] Central to these legal disabilities was the requirement that

---

[331] L Vickers, *Religious Freedom, Religious Discrimination and the Workplace* (Hart Publishing 2008) and see further Chapter 3.
[332] Boyle and Sheen (n 329) 316.
[333] See Chapter 3.
[334] Acts of Uniformity from 1549 established the Church of England Prayer Book as the only legal form of worship.

every person taking public office (including Members of Parliament and university students) should swear allegiance to the monarch as Supreme Governor of the Church of England.[335] Failure to swear was treasonable. As well as excluding Jewish people and Muslims, this had the effect of barring Catholics from public office and Parliament. It was not until the Catholic Relief Act of 1829 that public life, including the right to sit in Parliament, was opened up to Catholics and the last of these limitations was not removed until 1871.

Jewish people, expelled from Britain in 1290, were only readmitted by Cromwell in 1656 because of the financial and political services which they could render to him. They were tolerated rather than welcomed and, although their community flourished, they continued to labour under severe legal disabilities. Like Catholics, they were barred from public life by the requirement to take the Christian oath in order to exercise central rights such as the right to vote, the right to stand for municipal election, and the right to be an MP. It was not until the mid-nineteenth century that these obstacles were gradually dismantled. Jewish people were permitted to become barristers in 1833 and to vote without having to take the Christian oath in 1835.[336] They were permitted to take municipal office in 1845, while a statute of 1846 gave them undisputed rights to own land. But attempts to open up Parliament to Jewish people by lifting the requirement to take the oath were defeated on multiple occasions,[337] and it was only in 1858 that the first Jewish MP could finally take his seat. In 1870, the University Test Act removed the obstacles in the way of Jewish people becoming university scholars or fellows.

Despite the legal restrictions, the settled Jewish community in Britain was not subject to the rabid anti-Semitism of many parts of Europe. This was, however, unsettled after 1881 when vicious pogroms against the Jewish population of Russia triggered an influx of Jewish refugees who, excluded from most of Europe, made their way to England. Between 1880 and 1914, between 150,000 and 200,000 Jewish people settled in Britain. Unlike their predecessors, who tended to be small traders, the vast majority of these immigrants entered the British workforce as workers in sweated industries.[338]

---

[335] Act of Supremacy 1559.

[336] In practice, some Jewish people had already been exercising the vote in boroughs where returning officers did not insist on the oath: Todd M Endelman, *The Jews of London 1656–2000* (University of California Press 2002) 103.

[337] D Cooper and D Herman, 'Jews and Other Uncertainties: Race, Faith and English Law' (1999) 19 Legal Studies 339, 345.

[338] Endelman (n 336) 132.

In these unsanitary and crowded workshops, Jewish workers were paid star-vation wages for working long hours producing cheap clothing, footwear, or furniture. For women, working conditions were particularly dire, with many of them working as homeworkers in dismal dwellings while at the same time looking after children and doing housework. Poverty-struck and often in ill health, these refugees inspired not sympathy but virulent anti-Semitism. Jewish people were blamed for their own plight and accused of undercutting local labour conditions.[339] It was only the enactment of effective factory le-gislation beginning in 1901, and the growth of Jewish trade unions, which led to the elimination of Jewish sweated labour.[340]

The Second World War signalled unparalleled horrors for the Jewish people of Europe. Although British Jewish people escaped the death and de-struction that swept over their continental Jewish communities, they could not avoid their repercussions.[341] Despite the defeat of the Nazis, fascism and anti-Semitism continued to plague the Jewish communities in the imme-diate postwar period.[342] However, in the decades after the war, anti-Semitism gradually declined, economic mobility accelerated, and the inner-city, Jewish working class all but disappeared.[343] As with other minorities, a major factor which contributed to increasing prosperity in this period was the opening up of educational possibilities. Quotas limiting Jewish entry to private schools receded from the scene in the 1980s and 1990s.[344] This coincided with the de-cline in social and economic discrimination against Jewish people.

The Jewish community is now one of the smallest religious minorities, numbering about 337,000 in 2018.[345] Although well established and rela-tively prosperous, the Jewish community has again found itself the subject of increasing anti-Semitism in recent decades. Indeed, in 2021 the Community Service Trust reported the highest total of anti-Semitic incidents since 2008.[346] In 2020, the Equality and Human Rights Commission published the

---

[339] Repealed 12 April 1920 by the Aliens Order 1920 under the Aliens Restriction (Amendment) Act 1919.

[340] Hepple (n 234) 68–69. Note that by 1939 a further 50,000 Jewish people sought refuge in the UK from the Nazis.

[341] Endelman (n 336) 183.

[342] ibid 232.

[343] ibid 229.

[344] ibid 242–43.

[345] Office for National Statistics, 'Muslim Population in the UK' (2 August 2018) <www.ons. gov.uk/aboutus/transparencyandgovernance/freedomofinformationfoi/muslimpopulationinth euk/> accessed 23 October 2020.

[346] CST, 'Anti-Semitic Incidents' (2021) <https://cst.org.uk/public/data/file/f/f/Incidents%20 Report%202021.pdf> accessed 26 July 2022.

results of its investigation into the Labour Party. The report identified serious failings in leadership and an inadequate process for handling anti-Semitism complaints across the Party.[347] It concluded that there were unlawful acts of harassment and discrimination for which the Labour Party was responsible. As well as evidence of political interference in the handling of complaints, the report found that a significant number of complaints of anti-Semitism were not investigated at all, especially in relation to social media. This meant, for example, that repeated sharing of anti-Semitic material escaped investigation because of a policy not to investigate complaints if the material was simply shared or retweeted without the sender adding a comment.[348]

Members of the Muslim population have similarly been subjected to religious discrimination in the UK. By 2018, there were 3.72 million Muslims living in Britain,[349] the fastest growing and largest minority religion. The 2011 census showed that nearly half of all Muslims had been born in the UK. Although Muslims have been in Britain for at least two centuries,[350] Muslims began to migrate to Britain in much larger numbers after the Second World War, and particularly during the 1960s. Most came from South Asia, but others came from parts of the Middle East, Africa, and Cyprus. As a result of this diversity in origin, culture, language, and even religious tradition, it is a mistake to regard British Muslims in the twenty-first century as ethnically or ideologically homogeneous.[351] Just over two-thirds are originally Asian, most of whom are of Pakistani origin but with significant numbers of Bangladeshi and Indian origin. However, there are also sizable numbers of Muslims within the Arab ethnic category, and increasing numbers of Muslims self-identify as 'Black African' or of 'other Black' origin.[352]

Discrimination on religious grounds against Muslims takes various forms. Most worrying are the stereotypical images of Muslims in the media. A recent report showed that nearly two-thirds of articles in the media in the last quarter of 2018 associated Muslims with negative behaviour, while one-third misrepresented or generalized about Muslims.[353] Of particular

---

[347] <www.equalityhumanrights.com/en/publication-download/investigation-antisemitism-labour-party> accessed 13 December 2020.

[348] ibid.

[349] Office for National Statistics (n 345).

[350] Ansari (n 238).

[351] ibid 2.

[352] Muslim Council of Britain, 'British Muslims in Numbers' (2015) <www.mcb.org.uk/wp-content/uploads/2015/02/MCBCensusReport_2015.pdf> accessed 26 July 2022.

[353] <https://mcb.org.uk/report/state-of-media-reporting-on-islam-and-muslims/> accessed 22 July 2022.

concern have been repeated complaints of Islamophobia within the ruling Conservative Party. Indeed, in 2019, the Muslim Council of Britain stated that Islamophobia was endemic and institutional within that party.[354] An internal inquiry into Islamophobia in the Conservative Party which reported in 2021 found that although anti-Muslim sentiment had been in evidence in local associations and by individuals, allegations of institutional racism were not borne out by the evidence.[355] The main reason given for this finding was that the processes for dealing with complaints relating to race, religion, or belief, or Islam, had not systematically or collectively let down any particular community or group. However, this focus on processes fails to capture the real import of institutional racism which is concerned with the wider culture of an institution. It was therefore not surprising that the findings were criticized by many, including a former chair of the Conservative Party.[356] The chair of the report himself acknowledged that there should be more than the adjustment of codes and procedures, but also adherence to the spirit of anti-discrimination principles by everyone in the party, particularly those in a position of responsibility.

There is also a sizeable Hindu population in England, numbering 817,000 (1.5 per cent of the population) at the census in 2011.[357] Hindu migration is relatively recent, dating from the postwar period: indeed, the 2001 census found that 63 per cent of Hindus were born outside the UK. Hindus from India began arriving in 1947 at the time of Indian independence and partition, while others were actively recruited by the British government to fill skills shortages.[358] A second group consists of East African Asians, expelled from Idi Amin's Uganda in the 1960s and 1970s. More recent immigrants have come as refugees from Sri Lanka's bitter civil war. The Hindu population in the UK is predominantly urban, with by far the largest numbers living in London. Hindus are more likely to be economically active than others

[354] <www.bbc.co.uk/news/election-2019-50561043> accessed 26 July 2022.
[355] 'Independent Investigation into Alleged Discrimination Citing Protected Characteristics within the Conservative and Unionist Party in England, Wales and Northern Ireland' (The Singh Investigation, 2021) <https://singhinvestigation.co.uk/wp-content/uploads/2021/05/Singh-Investigation-Report-for-download.pdf> accessed 26 July 2022.
[356] <www.theguardian.com/news/2021/may/25/tory-islamophobia-report-criticises-boris-johnson-over-burqa-remarks> accessed 26 July 2022.
[357] Office for National Statistics, 'Religion in England and Wales 2011' <www.ons.gov.uk/peoplepopulationandcommunity/culturalidentity/religion/articles/religioninenglandandwales2011/2012-12-11#religious-affiliation-across-the-english-regions-and-wales> accessed 26 July 2022.
[358] Statistics in this paragraph are taken from <https://religionmediacentre.org.uk/factsheets/hinduism-in-the-uk/> accessed 26 July 2022.

professing a major religion, possibly because Hindus are a relatively younger population in London. Over one-third of employed Hindus are in professional or senior managerial positions.[359] Their representation in top managerial and professional occupations increased by 5 per cent between 2001 and 2011, the largest increase in such representation among religious groups in England.[360]

Despite this increasing diversity, Britain remains culturally and politically primarily Christian. The Anglican Church of England retains its position as the established church in England, while the Presbyterian Church of Scotland performs the same role in Scotland. There are numerous formal links between State and Church. Most prominently, that twenty-five seats in the House of Lords are allocated to Church of England archbishops and bishops. The result is that religious minorities, while tolerated, have in practice had to find their place within the framework established by the culture and religion of Christianity. Christianity remains by far the biggest single religion. Up-to-date figures are not available, but the 2011 census showed that, despite falling numbers, 59.3 per cent or 33.2 million people identified as Christian in England and Wales.[361] A more recent survey of British social attitudes showed a steep decline in those identifying with Christianity, falling from 66 per cent in 1983 to 38 per cent in 2018, with 52 per cent of the public in 2018 stating that they did not regard themselves as belonging to any religion.[362] Nevertheless, Britain is far from a secular society. Major Christian holy days are public holidays and, because the English education system developed in partnership with the mainstream churches, a large proportion of State schools are maintained Church of England schools. In January 2019, as many as 26.1 per cent of all publicly funded mainstream primary schools in England were Church of England schools, with a further 10.3 per cent Roman Catholic or other Christian.[363] Moreover, a daily act of collective worship is mandatory in all State schools,[364] and statute provides that 'the required collective worship shall be wholly or mainly of a broadly Christian character'.[365] In addition, religious education is compulsory at all State schools and, although the syllabus can be decided locally, it must reflect the fact that 'the

---

[359] See ibid.
[360] ibid.
[361] Office for National Statistics (n 357).
[362] British Social Attitudes Survey (2018) <www.bsa.natcen.ac.uk/media/39293/1_bsa36_r eligion.pdf> accessed 26 July 2022.
[363] House of Commons Briefing Paper, 'Faith Schools in England' (20 December 2019).
[364] School Standards and Framework Act 1998, s 70.
[365] ibid sch 20 para 3(2).

religious traditions in Britain are in the main Christian whilst taking account of the teaching and practices of the other principal religions represented in Great Britain'.[366] Parents are, however, permitted to withdraw their children from religious education and from attendance at religious worship.[367]

This, in turn, has prompted minority religions to demand their own faith schools.[368] Only a handful of State-maintained faith schools are, however, associated with the minority religions. These are complemented by private faith schools, especially among the Muslim and Jewish communities. Faith schools in the maintained sector are permitted to give priority to applicants who are of the faith of the school, but they must follow the national curriculum.

(b) The US

Religious intolerance in England and Europe is usually credited with the establishment of an alternative North American territory in which all faiths were equally welcome.[369] The story of the Pilgrims arriving on the *Mayflower* in 1620 is emblematic of the self-image of the US as a new beginning for millions fleeing religious persecution to found a society in which all are free and equal in relation to faith. What is left out of this story is the people who already inhabited this land. The Pilgrim colony was set up on land belonging to the Wampanoag,[370] also known as the 'People of the First Light', who had lived in the area for at least 12,000 years. Indeed, one of the stated purposes of the London Company, formed in 1606 with the object of colonizing the eastern coast of North America, was to spread Christianity by converting the people living there and to counter the Catholic influence of rival colonizers, Spain and France.[371] The religious beliefs of Native Americans were regarded as superstition, and a pretext for seizing their land. Within half a century, the tribal population had been decimated, the lands colonized, and many sold off into slavery.[372] Religious discord between different groups of colonizers was

---

[366] Education Act 1996, s 375(3).
[367] School Standards and Framework Act 1998, s 71.
[368] ibid s 69(3); Religious Character of Schools (Designation Procedure) Regulations 1998 (SI 1998/2535).
[369] <www.smithsonianmag.com/history/americas-true-history-of-religious-tolerance-61312684/> accessed 26 July 2022.
[370] <https://mashpeewampanoagtribe-nsn.gov/culture> accessed 25 October 2020.
[371] <www.encyclopediavirginia.org/virginia_company_of_london#its1>;   <www.theusaonline.com/people/religion.htm>; <www.smithsonianmag.com/history/americas-true-history-of-religious-tolerance-61312684/> accessed 26 July 2022.
[372] <https://mashpeewampanoagtribe-nsn.gov/timeline> accessed 25 October 2020.

also endemic, especially between the Catholic French and Spanish and the English Protestants.

Such contestation, and the powerful desire not to replicate the English fusion of Church and State, led many States to include provisions in their constitutions providing for freedom of conscience and a separation of Church and State. Nevertheless, such a provision was absent from the original federal Constitution drawn up in 1787, and included only later in the form of the First Amendment, which provides that Congress should make no law respecting an establishment of religion or prohibiting its free exercise. This declaration of State abstention from religion allowed many religions to flourish. However, it did not signal the end of religious discrimination. Particularly oppressive have been laws and policies directed at assimilation of indigenous Americans. These included 'systematic attempts to stamp out Native American religious practices' aimed at 'reconstructing Native religions in conformity with dominant Protestant majority values in a myopic vision of what constitutes "civilized" religious behaviour'.[373] For example, indigenous American children were forcibly taken to Christian missionary schools where they were denied the rights to speak their language or practise their religion.[374] Such practices continued from the Civil War period all the way to the mid-twentieth century. It was not until 1973 that a series of laws were passed providing for the self-determination of indigenous Americans, culminating in the 1994 Native American Free Exercise of Religion Act. Among other things, this reversed a restrictive Supreme Court decision refusing to apply a religious exemption for users of peyote.[375]

Other religious groups, including Catholics and Jewish people, suffered religious discrimination well into the twentieth century. Particularly problematic was the Klu Klux Klan, which preached anti-minority, anti-Black, anti-Catholic, and anti-Semitic messages as an ideological justification for spreading violence, including beating, raping, and murdering. It was not until the 1950s and 1960s that anti-Jewish quotas on college admissions, discrimination against Jewish people in corporate hiring, and restrictive covenants on land purchase ended. In the meantime, anti-Muslim sentiment has been on the rise, especially since the attack on the World Trade Center in 2001. This was fuelled during the 2016 presidential campaign when Donald

---

[373] L Irwin, 'Freedom, Law, and Prophecy: A Brief History of Native American Religious Resistance' (1997) 21 American Indian Quarterly 36, 40.

[374] ibid 41.

[375] *Employment Division, Department of Human Resources of Oregon v Smith* 494 US 872 (1990) (US Sup Ct).

Trump issued a series of statements calling for a 'total and complete shutdown of Muslims entering the US' and stating that 'Islam hates us'. This was followed, once Trump came to power, by a proclamation imposing entry restrictions on nationals from eight, predominantly Muslim, countries which were regarded as potential security threats.[376] This proclamation, issued in 2017, was challenged under the First Amendment on the grounds that the stated concerns about national security were pretexts for discriminating against Muslims. The US Supreme Court rejected the claim, holding that immigration laws fell within a very broad executive discretionary power. This can be contrasted with the dissenting opinion of Justice Sotomayor, where she stated: 'The United States of America is a Nation built upon the promise of religious liberty. Our Founders honoured that core promise by embedding the principle of religious neutrality in the First Amendment. The Court's decision today fails to safeguard that fundamental principle. It leaves undisturbed a policy first advertised openly and unequivocally as a "total and complete shutdown of Muslims entering the United States" because the policy now masquerades behind a facade of national-security concerns. But this repackaging does little to cleanse Presidential Proclamation No. 9645 of the appearance of discrimination that the President's words have created. Based on the evidence in the record, a reasonable observer would conclude that the Proclamation was motivated by anti-Muslim animus.'[377]

Despite its secular Constitution, there remain strong religious currents in US society. The vast majority of Americans (83 per cent) identify as Christian. However, within this group is a great diversity of denominations, including many different Protestant groups as well as Catholicism and Eastern Orthodox. Christianity has been the inspiration of both highly conservative fundamentalists, opposing abortion and the teaching of evolution, and the Black civil rights movement in the 1960s. Judaism is the next largest religion totalling about 7.15 million in 2018,[378] while Islam is the fastest growing religion, reaching about 3.45 million in 2017, about 1.1 per cent of the population.[379]

---

[376] *Trump v Hawaii* 138 S Ct 2302 (2018) (US Sup Ct).

[377] ibid 2433.

[378] <www.jewishvirtuallibrary.org/jewish-population-in-the-united-states-nationally> accessed 26 October 2020.

[379] <www.pewresearch.org/fact-tank/2018/01/03/new-estimates-show-u-s-muslim-population-continues-to-grow/> accessed 26 July 2022.

(c) India

As we have seen, religion is a central factor in India's social and political life. India's population of 1.3 billion people is predominantly Hindu, constituting 79.8 per cent of the population in 2011.[380] The Muslim population are a significant minority, constituting 14.23 per cent of the total. Other religions, although a tiny percentage of the total population, nevertheless number in the millions. In 2011, there were 2.78 million Christians (2.3 per cent of the population) and 2.08 million Sikhs (1.72 per cent), with Buddhists, Jains, Jewish people, and other religions each constituting less than 1 per cent. More than 104 million members of Scheduled Tribes are officially classified as Hindu, although many practise indigenous religious beliefs and an estimated one-third have converted to Christianity.[381]

Discrimination against religious minorities has been fuelled in recent years by the ruling BJP, which subscribes to the ideology of Hindutva, aiming to turn India into a Hindu State, underpinned by Hinduism and Hindu values.[382] Under the BJP, there has been heightened enforcement of the rules against religious minorities, such as the prohibition on cow slaughter, restrictions on religious conversion, and cuts in foreign funding of civil society organizations on the grounds that they are regarded as detrimental to the national interest.[383] Both Muslim and Christian communities have been targeted on numerous occasions by Hindu nationalists for allegedly slaughtering cows or converting Hindus to Islam or Christianity.[384] The revocation of the semi-autonomous status of Jammu and Kashmir, which is a Muslim-majority State, has led to widespread restrictions on inhabitants of the State, human rights abuses, and detentions, including the closure of mosques. Sikhs have also reported harassment for wearing Sikh clothing, having unshorn hair, and carrying mandatory religious items, despite the express protection in Article 25 of the Constitution.[385] On the other hand, Tibetan Buddhists

---

[380] All the figures in this paragraph come from US Department of State Office of International Religious Freedom, 'Report for 2019' <www.state.gov/reports/2019-report-on-international-religious-freedom/india/> accessed 26 July 2022.

[381] See ibid.

[382] P Mehta, 'Hindu Nationalism: From Ethnic Identity to Authoritarian Repression' [2022] Studies in Indian Politics <https://doi.org/10.1177%2F23210230221082828> accessed 26 July 2022.

[383] Foreign (Contribution) Regulation Act 2010.

[384] US Department of State Office of International Religious Freedom (n 380); US Commission on International Religious Freedom, 'Annual Report 2017' <www.state.gov/reports/2017-report-on-international-religious-freedom/> accessed 26 July 2022.

[385] ibid.

living in India have been allowed to thrive, whereas in Tibet itself Buddhism remains extremely restricted.[386]

(d) South Africa

Historically, as in other countries, religion in South Africa was as much a weapon of oppression as a salve for the oppressed. The ruling National Party used the religious ideology of the Dutch Reformed Church to underpin its blatantly racist and systematically oppressive policies. On the other hand, schools and hospitals established by Christian missionaries were frequently important counterweights. In modern South Africa, religion nevertheless plays an important role. The population is overwhelmingly Christian, with over 80 per cent of South Africans following the Christian faith. Other major groups include Muslims, Hindus, Jewish people, and Buddhists.

(e) Canada

Canadian religious history is somewhat different. For over a century, running from 1841 to 1960, Canada was explicitly Christian. Although there was no official State Church, as in England, the mainstream churches formed what has been called a 'shadow establishment'. In broad terms, to be a (proper) Canadian, one had to be a (proper) Christian—in the same way that one had to be white or male.[387] This legitimated discrimination against non-Christian Canadians, such as Sikhs, Hindus, Buddhists, Muslims, and Jewish people, as well as minority Christian groups. Even more seriously, the equation of being Canadian with being Christian legitimated the dismissal of the spirituality and ways of life of indigenous people, and led to policies aimed at converting them. As in the US, conversion to Christianity had been a central element in the colonial strategy of domination of indigenous people since the sixteenth century. Christianity was equated with civilization, and conversion to Christianity was seen as a divinely ordained responsibility.[388]

By the nineteenth century, mission schools had become a key part of the policy of assimilation of First Nation people, with instruction in Christianity merging with assumptions of European racial and cultural superiority.[389] Even more problematic was the policy of instituting residential schools for

---

[386] See Additional Statement of Commissioner Tenzin Dorjee in ibid.

[387] D Seljak, 'Protecting Religious Freedom in a Multicultural Canada' (2012) 9 Diversity Magazine <www.ohrc.on.ca/en/book/export/html/8764> accessed 26 July 2022.

[388] *Report of the Royal Commission on Aboriginal Peoples* (1991) Part I, 165 <http://data2.archives.ca/e/e448/e011188230-01.pdf> accessed 29 October 2020.

[389] ibid 243.

children, as a way of fostering Christianity and 'countering the effects on young [First Nations Peoples] of exposure to the more traditional [First Nations] values of their parents'.[390] Well into the twentieth century, off-reserve residential schools were seen by successive governments as the key to the policy of forcible assimilation of indigenous people by removing children from their homes.[391] These schools expressly aimed to 'supplant the children's [indigenous] spirituality' with Christianity, which by then was also equated with becoming truly Canadian.[392] It was not until the 1970s that real commitment to establishing a more equal relationship between indigenous and non-indigenous people in Canada could be discerned.[393]

(iii) Legal Frameworks

Many Constitutions include a right to freedom of religion alongside a prohibition of discrimination on grounds of religion. Much of the jurisprudence centres on the freedom aspect of religion.[394] Equality rights are more likely to be asserted in the context of employment, education, or other horizontal relationships, where the powerful conformist tendencies of the dominant religion or secular culture might fail to accommodate religious differences.

This can be seen in the US, where Constitutional jurisprudence on religion is overwhelmingly focused on the First Amendment guarantees of freedom of religion and separation of Church and State, rather than the equality rights.[395] Non-discrimination is primarily adjudicated through Title VII of the Civil Rights Act, which prohibits most employers from discriminating on grounds of religion. Importantly, Title VII includes a requirement that employers demonstrate that they are unable to reasonably accommodate religious observance without undue hardship for their business. However, undue hardship has been interpreted liberally in favour of the employer.[396]

India's Constitution has a strong guarantee of freedom of religion; indeed, it was amended in 1976 'to spell out expressly the high ideals of [inter

---

[390] ibid 246.
[391] ibid 312.
[392] ibid 315.
[393] ibid 186.
[394] S Fredman, *Comparative Human Rights Law* (OUP 2018).
[395] See further ibid.
[396] *Ansonia Board of Education v Philbrook* 479 US 60 (1986) (US Sup Ct).

alia] secularism.[397] Religion is also one of the grounds expressly protected by Article 15(1) of the Constitution, which states that 'The State shall not discriminate against any citizen on grounds only of religion, race, caste, sex, place of birth or any of them.' Similarly, religion is one of the grounds explicitly protected against discrimination in relation to access to shops, public restaurants, hotels, places of public entertainment, or places or public places, as well as in relation to State employment.[398] Nevertheless, religion in India remains a source of social contestation as well as legal restrictions. A key concern is the fact that Buddhists, Jains, and Sikhs are legally classified as Hindus.[399] This means that they are subject to Hindu personal law, such as the Hindu Marriage Act. A further source of dispute arises from the prohibition of cow slaughter in Article 48 of the Constitution. Forbidding cow slaughter is a Hindu precept but conflicts with the religious practice of many Muslims, which includes the slaughter of a cow on Eid al-Adha. Laws criminalizing cow slaughter have also marginalized Muslims and Dalits who work in the leather or beef industry.

In Canada, since the 1960s, serious attempts have been made to address religious discrimination and intolerance, with a decided shift towards a more secular State. Freedom of conscience and religion is protected in the Canadian Charter,[400] and section 15 of the Charter prohibits discrimination on grounds of religion. The Canadian Multiculturalism Act 1988 asserted the commitment to a multicultural society, the right of all both to preserve and share their cultural heritage, and to participate fully and without discrimination in Canadian society. The Canadian Human Rights Act (1985),[401] the Employment Equity Act (1995), and the Canadian Labour Code all provide for non-discrimination on grounds inter alia of religion in relation to a wide area of Canadian life, including employment, provision of goods, facilities, or services, and pay. The duty of accommodation of religious practices by employers is well developed by the Canadian courts,[402] setting a higher bar for undue hardship defences than the US courts.

In South Africa, the equality guarantee in section 9 of the Constitution includes religion as a ground of discrimination, complementing the right to

---

[397] The Constitution (Forty-second Amendment) Act, 1976, Preamble, para 3 <www.india. gov.in/my-government/constitution-india/amendments/constitution-india-forty-second-amendment-act-1976> accessed 26 July 2022.

[398] Indian Constitution, Arts 15(2) and 16(2).

[399] ibid Art 25.

[400] s 2(a).

[401] Canadian Human Rights Act 1985, s 3(1).

[402] *Ontario Human Rights Commission v Simpsons-Sears Ltd* [1985] 2 SCR 53 (Can Sup Ct).

freedom of religion in section 15. This is replicated in both the EEA and the Equality Act, making it unlawful to discriminate on grounds of religion both at work and elsewhere. It is noteworthy that the Equality Act includes 'culture' as an enumerated ground. In the case of *Pillay*, the Constitutional Court for the first time sought to define the word 'culture', finding that a school's refusal to grant an exemption to allow a learner to wear a nose stud was unfair discrimination based on 'culture'. The Court held that while the outer bounds of the definition should remain open, the core meaning of 'culture' relates to groups defined by a combination of religion, language, geographical origin, and artistic tradition.[403]

The UK is the outlier. Religion was conspicuously lacking in British anti-discrimination law (outside Northern Ireland) until the end of the twentieth century. Although Northern Irish regulations covered religious discrimination, religion was deliberately omitted from the protection afforded by the RRA 1976. While Jewish people and Sikhs could bring themselves within the alternative statutory definition of 'ethnic origins',[404] Muslims could not. It was not until the incorporation of the European Convention on Human Rights into British law through the Human Rights Act 1998 (in force from 2000) that a right to freedom of religion and a right not to be discriminated against on grounds of religion first became law. In the employment field, this was buttressed by EU law, which from 2000 required Member States to legislate to prohibit discrimination on grounds of religion or belief.[405] This was implemented by regulations in 2003,[406] and fully incorporated into the EA 2010. Notably, there is an exception permitting different religions to require religious leaders, such as priests, imams, or rabbis, to be members of the relevant faith. Under both EU and UK law, employers may impose a requirement that a person be of a particular religion or belief, but only if, having regard to the religious ethos and the nature or context of the work, being of a particular religion or belief is an occupational requirement, and that applying such a requirement is a proportionate means of achieving a legitimate aim.[407]

---

[403] *MEC for Education: Kwazulu-Natal and Others v Pillay* (CCT 51/06) [2007] ZACC 21, 2008 (1) SA 474 (CC), 2008 (2) BCLR 99, para 50 (SACC).
[404] *Mandla v Lee* [1983] 2 AC 548 (HL).
[405] Council Directive 2000/78/EC.
[406] Employment Equality (Religion or Belief) Regulations 2003 (SI 2003/1660).
[407] EA 2010, sch 9 para 3.

IV CONCLUSION

This chapter has considered the social challenges facing discrimination law and critically assessed the corresponding legal responses in relation to gender, race, ethnicity and caste, and religion and belief in the five jurisdictions at issue here. Chapter 3 examines the same challenges and responses to sexual orientation, gender identity, disability, and age.

3

Social Context and Legal Developments

Sexual Orientation, Gender Identity, Disability, and Age

I INTRODUCTION

As stated in the previous chapter, anti-discrimination law is necessarily a response to the social and historical context in which it is embedded. Chapter 2
examined the evolution of the right to equality in relation to gender, race,
ethnicity and caste, and religion and belief. This chapter does the same for
sexual orientation, gender identity, disability, and age. For all of these, a key
first step has been to acknowledge the role of society in obscuring these identities and to recognize and conceptualize the rights-bearers as full participants in society. Equality laws must then be shaped to further the right to
equality on all four dimensions of substantive equality.

II SEXUAL ORIENTATION

Discrimination on grounds of sexual orientation is a particularly vicious denial of dignity and equality, since it strikes out against the sexual intimacy
at the very core of an individual's identity and well-being. The dimension of
inequality which is most pronounced is the recognition dimension; namely,
stigma, stereotyping, prejudice, and violence. However, this centrally im-
plicates the other axes. Harassment and bullying at school and at work can
have serious implications for progress in the workforce, leading to economic
disadvantage—the first dimension. The same is true for the participative dimension. LGBTQI+ people are generally small minorities on the political
scene, making it difficult for their voice to be heard through democratic processes. Moreover, rather than celebrating and accommodating difference, social structures require LGBTQI+ people to cover or hide their identity and
relationships, triggering the transformative dimension.[1] This itself leads to

---

[1] K Yoshino, 'The New Equal Protection' (2011) 124 Harv L Rev 747.

Discrimination Law. Third Edition. Sandra Fredman, Oxford University Press. © Sandra Fredman 2022.
DOI: 10.1093/oso/9780198854081.003.0003

social exclusion or marginalization. This is compounded for same-sex relationships. Failure to recognize LGBTQI+ relationships causes further recognition harms, particularly in relation to parenting rights, whether through
custody, adoption, or surrogacy. It also causes material disadvantage, including in relation to pensions, benefits, and housing.

Yet the criminalization of homosexuality has persisted in some jurisdictions well into the twenty-first century. It is only in the past few decades that
real strides towards equality have been taken. Even with this progress, the
basic right to equality before the law has still not been fully achieved. There
are three stages in the development towards equality in this context: first,
formal equality before the law in the form of decriminalization and removal
of actual legal impediments; secondly, protection against discrimination of
all kinds on the grounds of sexual orientation, including harassment and violence; and, thirdly, equal recognition of same-sex partnerships.

Even the first stage, formal equality before the law, has been slow in
coming. In Britain, same-sex sexual activity between men was decriminal-
ized in 1967, although only for sexual activity between two consenting men
in private. However, inequalities remained. The age of consent, which was
set at twenty-one (compared to sixteen for heterosexual or lesbian sexual
activity[2]), was not fully equalized until 2000.[3] It took a further three years
before the severe criminal prohibitions on homosexual behaviour in public
were removed.[4] However, progress towards equality has been far from consistent. The Conservative government in power from 1979 to 1997 carried its
hostility to homosexuality so far as to enact the notorious section 28 of the
Local Government Act 1988, which prohibited local authorities from intentionally promoting homosexuality or promoting the teaching of the 'accept-
ability of homosexuality as a pretended family relationship'. The provision
was not fully repealed until 2003.[5]

Canada tracked a similar path to that of Britain. Harsh criminal laws prohibiting sodomy and gross indecency led to arrests, intimidation, and persecution of gay men throughout the nineteenth century and well into the
twentieth. The sodomy and gross indecency laws were not amended until

---

[2] Sexual Offences Act 1956, s 12(1).
[3] Sexual Offences (Amendment) Act 2000; see also *Sutherland v UK* (Application no 25186/
94) (Commission Report, 1 July 1997). Note that it was reduced to eighteen in 1994: Sexual
Offences Act 1967, s 1 as amended by Criminal Justice and Public Order Act 1994.
[4] Sexual Offences Act 2003, sch 7 para 1. See generally R Wintemute, 'Sexual Orientation
Discrimination' in C McCrudden and G Chambers (eds), *Individual Rights and the Law in
Britain* (Clarendon Press 1994).
[5] Local Government Act 2003, sch 8(1) para 1.

1969 when an exception was made making such acts legal only between consenting adults of at least twenty-one years old and in private.[6] Homosexuality
remained a crime in many circumstances. Gay men and women were still
charged under the indecency laws, especially to intimidate an increasingly
assertive LGBTQI+ movement advocating equal rights. The offence of gross
indecency was not, however, repealed until 1987, and the age of consent was
only equalized at sixteen as late as 2019.[7]

In the US, India, and South Africa, achieving change was even more
painful and protracted, with LGBTQI+ people turning to the courts rather
than legislatures for reform. Courts were not initially forthcoming. In 1986,
by a majority of five to four, the US Supreme Court refused to invalidate
sodomy laws in twenty-five US States.[8] It was not until 2003, in the landmark
case of *Lawrence v Texas*,[9] that the Court reversed this approach, holding
that sodomy laws were invalid as a breach of the Fourteenth Amendment.[10]
In India, a landmark appeared to have been reached when the Delhi High
Court struck down the criminal provisions prohibiting sodomy[11] in *Naz
Foundation*.[12] However, this was overturned by the Supreme Court three
years later in *Koushal*.[13] It took four more years before the Court reversed
this position. In *Navtej Singh* in 2018, the Court resoundingly affirmed
LGBTQI+ rights and invalidated the sodomy provisions insofar as they
criminalized consensual homosexual acts.[14] In South Africa, although the
post-apartheid Constitution expressly (and uniquely at the time) mentioned
sexual orientation as a ground of discrimination, this did not in itself invalidate the sodomy rules. Instead, in the first step in a carefully constructed programme of strategic litigation, the National Coalition for Gay and Lesbian

---

[6]   Criminal Law Amendment Act 1968–69.

[7]   R Levy, 'The 1969 Amendment and the (De)criminalization of Homosexuality' in Historica
Canada (ed), *The Canadian Encyclopedia* (26 November 2019) <www.thecanadianencyclopedia.
ca/en/article/the-1969-amendment-and-the-de-criminalization-of-homosexuality> accessed 2
November 2020.

[8]   *Bowers v Hardwick* (1986) 478 US 186 (US Sup Ct).

[9]   *Lawrence v Texas* (2003) 123 S Ct 2472 (US Sup Ct).

[10]   See Chapter 4.

[11]   Vanita and Kidwai argue that prior to the British imposition of criminal liability for
sodomy, India's cultural heritage had always displayed a range of views on gender and sexuality
with many stories of same-sex love in Hindu sacred texts: R Vanita and S Kidwai (eds), *Same-
Sex Love in India* (Palgrave Macmillan 2000). See also <https://theconversation.com/indias-sod
omy-ban-now-ruled-illegal-was-a-british-colonial-legacy-103052> accessed 2 June 2022.

[12]   *Naz Foundation v Government of NCT of Delhi*, WP(C) No7455/2001, 2 July 2009 (High Ct
of Delhi).

[13]   *Suresh Kumar Koushal v Naz Foundation* (2014) 1 SCC 1 (Indian Sup Ct).

[14]   *Navtej Singh Johar v Union of India* (2018) 10 SCC 1 (Indian Sup Ct).

Equality approached the Constitutional Court to legalize homosexuality. The Court upheld the claim in a unanimous judgment in 1998.[15] Importantly, the case was decided squarely under the right to equality in section 9 of the Constitution.

The achievement of equality before the law in all these jurisdictions is not, as we have seen, sufficient. In addition, there is a need to include sexual orientation in anti-discrimination laws. Here, too, sexual orientation has lagged behind race and gender in most jurisdictions. South Africa stands out in having included sexual orientation expressly as a ground of discrimination in the Constitution.[16] This is mirrored in the two main anti-discrimination statutes.

In the UK, change was propelled by the EU. Until 2000, it was lawful both in UK and EU law to discriminate against individuals on grounds of their sexual orientation. However, under new powers given by the Treaty of Amsterdam, the EU Employment Directive was passed, requiring Member States to legislate to prohibit direct and indirect discrimination, as well as harassment, on grounds of sexual orientation.[17] Although the directive is limited in several respects, the CJEU has given a broad interpretation of its provisions in favour of LGBTQI+ claims. Thus, the preamble states that the directive is without prejudice to national laws on marital status and the benefits dependent thereon.[18] Nevertheless, the Court has held that a failure to accord the same employment-related benefits to same-sex partners as those given to opposite-sex spouses could be discriminatory.[19] Similarly, even though the scope of the directive is confined to matters which are largely employment-related, the CJEU has held that sport is subject to EU law to the extent that it constitutes an economic activity.[20] Thus, in the case of *ACCEPT*, a major shareholder in a football club stated publicly in the media that he would never accept a homosexual on the team. The CJEU held that such facts established a presumption that the club had discriminated on grounds of sexual orientation. Importantly in this case and in subsequent cases, the

---

[15] *National Coalition for Gay and Lesbian Equality v Minister of Justice* 1998 (12) BCLR 1517 (SACC).

[16] South African Constitution, s 9(3).

[17] EC Directive 2000/78.

[18] ibid Preamble, para 22.

[19] Case C-147/08 *Römer v Freie und Hansestadt Hamburg* [2013] 2 CMLR 11 (CJEU); Case C-267/06 *Maruko v Versorgungsanstalt der Deutschen Bühnen* [2008] 2 CMLR 32 (CJEU); Case C-267/12 *Hay v Crédit agricole mutuel de Charente-Maritime et des Deux-Sèvres* [2014] 2 CMLR 32 (CJEU).

[20] Case C-81/12 *Asociaţia ACCEPT v Consiliul Naţional pentru Combaterea Discriminării* [2013] 3 CMLR 26, para 45 (CJEU).

Court held that statements by employers to the effect that they would not wish to recruit or use the services of homosexuals could amount to discrimination on grounds of sexual orientation even though they were not made in the context of a particular recruitment policy and no individual victim was identified.[21]

The EU directive was implemented into UK law by regulations in 2003,[22] and this area is now governed by the EA 2010. The EA 2010 is broader than the directive in that discrimination on grounds of sexual orientation is now unlawful not only in relation to employment but also in the provision of services, public functions, the disposal of premises, and education.[23] However, this does not extend to protection against harassment in these non-employment-related spheres,[24] despite the fact that harassment on other grounds (eg gender, race, and disability) is unlawful in those contexts. Instead, a victim of homophobic harassment or bullying in contexts outside employment would have the more difficult task of proving direct discrimination.[25] Similarly problematic is the acceptance of religious discrimination on grounds of sexual orientation in specific circumstances. It is not unlawful to discriminate on grounds of sexual orientation where the employment is for the purposes of an organized religion and the employer applies a requirement related to sexual orientation in order to avoid conflicting with the strongly held religious convictions of a significant number of the religion's followers or to comply with the doctrines of the religion.[26] This exception has been interpreted relatively broadly by the UK Court of Appeal to refer to the teachings or beliefs of the religion, rather than to 'what might more narrowly be understood by "doctrine" within a specific religious community. . . . Whilst a court will not simply accept an assertion as to the doctrines of a religion, it equally cannot be expected to enter into theological debate to determine those doctrines for itself.'[27]

In Canada, the ECHR, the US, and India, the pathway to inclusion of sexual orientation as a ground for discrimination was, instead, through constitutional litigation. The Canadian Charter does not expressly mention

---

[21] ibid; Case C-507/18 *NH v Associazione Avvocatura per i diritti LGBTI* [2020] ICR 1124 (CJEU).
[22] Employment Equality (Sexual Orientation) Regulations 2003 (SI 2003/1661).
[23] EA 2010, s 202.
[24] ibid ss 29(8), 33(6).
[25] ibid s 212(5).
[26] ibid sch 9 para 2.
[27] *Pemberton v Inwood* [2018] EWCA Civ 564 [48] (UK Ct of Appeal) citing Judge Eady KC upheld at [62].

sexual orientation as one of those enumerated in its non-exhaustive list. However, in the important decision of *Egan v Canada*, the Supreme Court of Canada held that sexual orientation was an analogous ground. According to the majority, 'sexual orientation is a deeply personal characteristic that is either unchangeable or changeable only at unacceptable personal costs, and so falls within the ambit of section 15 protection as being analogous to the enumerated grounds'.[28] Similarly, under the ECHR, although sexual orientation is not mentioned as a ground of discrimination, it has been implied into the non-exhaustive list under Article 14. Moreover, not only has the ECtHR held that discrimination on grounds of sexual orientation is 'undoubtedly covered' by Article 14,[29] but that only very weighty reasons can justify any differentiation on this ground.[30] Indeed, distinctions based solely on sexual orientation are unacceptable.[31]

In the US, the absence of an enumerated list of grounds has meant that the question before the Court in Fourteenth Amendment cases has been not so much whether sexual orientation is an analogous ground, but what the standard of scrutiny should be. As will be seen in Chapter 4, the Court has refused to explicitly regard sexual orientation as a suspect ground, attracting strict scrutiny. Nevertheless, it has struck down some classifications based on sexual orientation on the grounds of rationality.[32] The contestation has been even more difficult in relation to civil rights legislation. Title VII of the Civil Rights Act prohibits discrimination in employment on the basis of a fixed list of grounds, which does not include sexual orientation. In a landmark decision in 2020, however, the US Supreme Court, by a narrow majority, held that 'sex' in Title VII includes sexual orientation.[33] The result is, for the first time, to prohibit employment discrimination on grounds of sexual orientation. In India, there is no comprehensive statute prohibiting discrimination nor a specific statute to that effect. The recognition in *Navtej Singh*[34] in 2018, however, of gender as encompassing gendered roles and therefore sexual orientation, potentially opens the way to clearer prohibitions on sexual-orientation discrimination.

---

[28] *Egan v Canada* [1995] 2 SCR 513 (Can Sup Ct). See further Chapter 4.

[29] *Salgueiro da Silva Mouta v Portugal* [2001] 31 EHRR 1055 (ECtHR).

[30] *EB v France* (2008) 47 EHRR 21 (ECtHR); *Smith and Grady v UK* (2000) 29 EHRR 493 (ECtHR).

[31] *Salgueiro da Silva Mouta v Portugal* (n 29); *EB v France* (n 30).

[32] *Romer v Evans* 517 US 620, 634, 116 S Ct 1620, 134 L Ed 2d 855 (1996) (US Sup Ct); *US v Windsor* 570 US 744 (2013) (US Sup Ct).

[33] *Bostock v Clayton County* 140 S Ct 1731 (2020) (US Sup Ct). See Chapter 4.

[34] *Navtej Singh Johar v Union of India* (n 14).

The third stage, recognition of the depth and permanence of same-sex relationships, has been even slower in coming. However, the twenty-first century has seen remarkable progress. Canada legalized same-sex marriage in 2005,[35] becoming only the fourth country in the world to do so, after the Netherlands (2000), Belgium (2003), and Spain (2005). In a preliminary reference to the Supreme Court of Canada, the proposed legislation legalizing same-sex marriage was upheld as consistent with the Charter. However, as in other jurisdictions, this was regarded as creating a potential conflict with religious freedom. Like several other jurisdictions, freedom of religion was given priority. Performance of marriage rites, the Court held, is a fundamental aspect of religious practice. Therefore, State compulsion of religious officials to perform same-sex marriages contrary to their religious beliefs would violate the guarantee of freedom of religion in section 2(1) of the Charter.[36]

In the UK, the impetus came originally from courts, which began to recognize same-sex partners as family members for the purposes of legislation entitling family members to inherit tenancy rights.[37] Following a parallel trajectory, the European Court of Human Rights (ECtHR) began incrementally to recognize same-sex family rights, tracking a growing consensus among contracting States.[38] Notably, the Court observed that 'the Convention is a living instrument, to be interpreted in the light of present-day conditions'.[39] Thus, the Court has gradually reversed its own case law[40] to hold in favour of granting parental rights,[41] the right to adopt a child,[42] and employment-related benefits for same-sex partners.[43] Similarly, the CJEU has held that the denial of employment-related benefits, such as a survivor's pension or a supplementary retirement pension, can be challenged as a breach of the directive if the benefit was available to opposite-sex spouses but not to same-sex partners.[44]

---

[35] Civil Marriage Act 2005.

[36] *Reference re Same-Sex Marriage* 2004 SCC 79 (Can Sup Ct).

[37] *Fitzpatrick v Sterling Housing* [1999] 2 WLR 1113 (HL), *Ghaidan v Godin-Mendoza* [2004] UKHL 30, [2004] 2 AC 557 (HL).

[38] *Salgueiro da Silva Mouta v Portugal* (n 29) (custody of children); *EB v France* (n 30) (adoption).

[39] ibid para 92.

[40] *Mata Estevez v Spain*, Reports of Judgments and Decisions 2001-VI, 311.

[41] *Salgueiro da Silva Mouta v Portugal* (n 29).

[42] ibid; *Fretté v France* (2004) 38 EHRR 21 (ECtHR).

[43] *PB and JS v Austria* (2012) 55 EHRR 31 (ECtHR); *Karner v Austria* (2004) 38 EHRR 24 (ECtHR).

[44] *Römer v Freie und Hansestadt Hamburg* (n 19); *Maruko v Versorgungsanstalt der Deutschen Bühnen* (n 19); *Hay v Crédit agricole mutuel de Charente-Maritime et des Deux-Sèvres* (n 19).

In 2004, a crucial breakthrough was achieved in the UK with the Civil Partnership Act 2004, which in many respects created an equivalent regime for same-sex partnerships as marriage.[45] However, the Act stopped short of affording same-sex couples the fundamental right to marriage itself. It was not until 2013 that the equal right to marry was finally achieved, with the government belatedly accepting that 'we should not prevent couples from marrying unless there are very good reasons—and loving someone of the same sex is not one of them'.[46]

As in Canada, this raised the question of how conflicting equalities can be managed. In particular, should it be permissible for religious people to argue that because of their religious convictions they can discriminate against women or LGBTQI+ people?[47] In balancing these conflicting demands, the UK, like Canada, has given priority to religion over other grounds of discrimination, albeit in a narrow range of circumstances. Where employment is for the purposes of an organized religion, the employer may require a person to be of a particular sex or not be a transsexual person. It is also permissible to apply a requirement that is related to a person's sexual orientation, or their marriage or civil partnership. In such a case, the employer must prove that the requirement is applied to comply with the doctrines of the religion or to avoid conflict with the strongly held religious convictions of a significant number of the religion's followers.[48] Similarly, while the Marriage (Same Sex Couples) Act 2013 enables same-sex couples to marry in civil ceremonies, it also states that no religious organization can be compelled to marry same-sex couples. The 2013 Act amends the EA 2010 to make it clear that it is not unlawful discrimination for a religious organization or representative to refuse to marry a same-sex couple. For a religious marriage ceremony of a same-sex couple to take place, the governing body of the religious organization must give explicit consent and the individual minister must also be willing to conduct the marriage. In addition, for the ceremony to take place in a place of worship, the latter needs to have been registered for such marriages.

This endorsement in Britain of the right to marry is nevertheless ahead of the ECtHR. Although robustly affirming the right of same-sex partners to an equivalent of marriage, such as civil partnership,[49] the ECtHR has confined

---

[45] Civil Partnership Act 2004, ss 71, 79, 75.

[46] Marriage (Same Sex Couples) Act: A factsheet.

[47] See S Fredman, 'Tolerating the Intolerant: Religious Freedom, Complicity and the Right to Equality' [2020] Oxford J Law and Religion 1.

[48] Employment Equality (Religion or Belief) Regulations 2003 (SI 2003/1660), sch 9 para 2.

[49] *Schalk v Austria* (2011) 53 EHRR 20 (ECtHR); *Vallianatos v Greece* (2014) 59 EHRR 12 (ECtHR).

the right to marry and found a family in Article 12 ECHR to the traditional marriage between persons of opposite sexes.[50] Reflecting its long-standing reluctance to enter into areas of political and social controversy, it has held that there is not sufficient consensus in Europe as a whole to warrant recognition of the right of same-sex couples to marry.

The South African Constitutional Court began to recognize same-sex relationships in a series of cases in which it endorsed the rights of same-sex partners to be treated in the same way as spouses for the purposes of immigration law,[51] survivors' pensions,[52] and adoption.[53] These culminated, in 2005, in the watershed decision of *Fourie*,[54] in which the Court struck down the prohibition on same-sex marriage. In a ringing endorsement of the rights to equality and dignity, Sachs J stated:

> Sections 9(1) and (3) cannot be read as merely protecting same-sex couples from punishment or stigmatisation. They also go beyond simply preserving a private space in which gay and lesbian couples may live together without interference from the state. Indeed, what the applicants in this matter seek is not the right to be left alone, but the right to be acknowledged as equals and to be embraced with dignity by the law. Their love that was once forced to be clandestine, may now dare openly to speak its name. . . . Accordingly, taking account of the decisions of this Court, and bearing in mind the symbolic and practical impact that exclusion from marriage has on same-sex couples, there can only be one answer to the question as to whether or not such couples are denied equal protection and subjected to unfair discrimination. Clearly, they are, and in no small degree. The effect has been wounding and the scars are evident in our society to this day.[55]

Recognition in the US courts has been far more grudging. It was nevertheless a momentous event when a sharply divided Supreme Court in *Obergefell v Hodges* decided that the fundamental right to marry should be available to everyone. According to Kennedy J: 'As the State itself makes marriage all the more precious by the significance it attaches to it, exclusion from that status

---

[50] *Hamalainen v Finland* (2015) 1 FCR 379 (ECtHR (Grand Chamber)).

[51] *National Coalition for Gay and Lesbian Equality and Others v Minister of Home Affairs and Others* 2000 (2) SA 1 (CC), 2000 (1) BCLR 39 (SACC).

[52] *Satchwell v President of the Republic of South Africa and Another* 2002 (6) SA 1 (CC), 2002 (9) BCLR 986 (SACC).

[53] *Du Toit and Another v Minister of Welfare and Population Development and Others (Lesbian and Gay Equality Project as amicus curiae)* 2002 (10) BCLR 1006, 2003 (2) SA 198 (CC) (SACC).

[54] *Minister of Home Affairs v Fourie* (CCT 60/04) [2005] ZACC 19, 2006 (3) BCLR 355 (CC), 2006 (1) SA 524 (CC) (SACC).

[55] ibid para 77.

has the effect of teaching that gays and lesbians are unequal in important respects. It demeans gays and lesbians for the State to lock them out of a central institution of the Nation's society. Same-sex couples, too, may aspire to the transcendent purposes of marriage and seek fulfilment in its highest meaning.'[56]

III GENDER IDENTITY

The presumption of a gender binary runs deep in social and legal institutions. The assignment at birth of the label male or female brings with it the assumption that the newborn child has certain fixed gendered attributes, which continue throughout their life trajectory, whether it relates to dress codes, emotional expectations, loving relationships, sports teams, public toilets, and even the grammar of he/she. Such binaries are reinforced when anti-discrimination laws require a comparison between men and women to establish discrimination. Importantly, feminists have exposed the ways in which society constructs gender, legitimating deep-seated patriarchal social and political structures. However, as Otto argues: 'While the advent of universal human rights law in 1945, with its core principles of equality and non-discrimination, made it possible to challenge the assumed hierarchy of gender (m>f), the understanding of sex/gender as dualistic (m/f) remained unquestioned.'[57] Queer theory, by contrast, challenges the notion of the binary itself. As Butler puts it: 'To assume that gender always and exclusively means the matrix of "masculine" and "feminine", is precisely to miss the critical point that the production of that coherent binary is contingent, that it comes at a cost, and that those permutations of gender which do not fit the binary are as much part of gender as its most normative instance.'[58] Nor is it appropriate, Butler argues, to replace the gender binary with a multiplicity of genders, provoking the question of how many genders there can be and how to count them.[59] In attempting to reproduce gender binaries, laws and practice have frequently damaged or rendered invisible those who do not readily conform.

---

[56] *Obergefell v Hodges* 2015 WL 1041665 (US Sup Ct). See further Chapter 4.
[57] D Otto, 'Queering Gender [Identity] in International Law' (2015) 33 Nordic J Human Rights 299, 302.
[58] J Butler, *Undoing Gender* (Routledge 2004) 42.
[59] ibid 43.

Any legal reform therefore needs to play close attention to the ways in which gender identity is characterized, and what criteria are imposed on individuals as a precondition for protection against discrimination. Several key questions arise. Are preconditions attached to a person's expression of their gender identity? Do they have to undergo surgery? Do they need a diagnosis of 'gender dysphoria'? Are they required to annul any existing marriage? Alternatively, are they permitted to self-identify, and if so for what purposes? Underlying these questions is the more fundamental question of whether deep-seated assumptions of gender binaries continue unquestioned or whether there is a recognition of the multiplicity of forms of gender identity and expression.

For many decades, transgender people were denied any legal identity in their preferred gender in the jurisdictions examined here.[60] As recently as 1970, in the highly influential case of *Corbett v Corbett*,[61] the UK High Court held that a person's sex was fixed at birth and could not be changed. A person born biologically male, it was held, could not contract a valid marriage as a woman despite having undergone surgery and having lived as a woman. Following *Corbett*, statutory provisions in the UK were enacted providing that a marriage is void unless the parties are male and female,[62] confining transgender persons to a double identity throughout their lives. This led to a series of cases before the ECtHR, arguing that this was a breach of the right to marry in Article 12 ECHR. Such cases initially received a hostile reception before the ECtHR.[63] However, in the seminal case of *Goodwin* in 2002,[64] the ECtHR reversed its previous jurisprudence. Although Article 12 refers in express terms to the right of a man and woman to marry, the Court held that gender should no longer be determined by purely biological criteria. 'The allocation of sex in national law to that registered at birth is a limitation impairing the very essence of the right to marry.'[65] Later cases have held that gender identification and name fall within the personal sphere protected by the right to respect for private life in Article 8 ECHR. 'Gender identity,' the Court held, 'is one of the most intimate private life matters of a person.'[66]

---

[60] In relation to India, see n 11.
[61] *Corbett v Corbett* [1970] 2 WLR 1306 (UK High Ct).
[62] Matrimonial Causes Act 1973, s 11(c) re-enacting s 1(c) of the Nullity of Marriage Act 1973.
[63] *Rees v United Kingdom* (1987) 9 EHRR 56; *Cossey v United Kingdom* (1991) 13 EHRR 622; *Sheffield and Horsham v United Kingdom* (1999) 27 EHRR 163; see also *X, Y and Z v UK* (Case no 75/1995/582/667, 30 March 1997).
[64] *Goodwin v UK* (2002) 35 EHRR 18.
[65] ibid para 101.
[66] *Van Kück v Germany* (2003) 37 EHRR 51, para 56 (ECtHR).

The Court has not, however, taken the further step of finding a violation of the ECHR if that would in effect permit same-sex marriage in jurisdictions where this is not yet allowed.[67] The Court's insistence on a wide margin of appreciation for States in relation to same-sex marriage has trumped its otherwise robust protection of transgender rights. The result has been to allow a State to compel a person to obtain a divorce from their existing spouse as a condition for achieving legal recognition of their gender change, even though the applicant wishes to remain married, if the result would be recognition of a same-sex marriage.[68]

The *Goodwin* case precipitated change in the UK. In *Bellinger v Bellinger*, the House of Lords declared that the requirement in the Matrimonial Causes Act 1973 that the parties be male and female as stated on their birth certificates was incompatible with the rights to private life and marriage in the Convention.[69] The case provided added impetus for legislation already proceeding through Parliament in the form of the Gender Recognition Act 2004. Under this Act, transgender persons can apply to a Gender Recognition Panel for a 'full gender recognition certificate' on the basis that they have or have had gender dysphoria, have lived in the acquired gender for at least two years, and intend to do so until death.[70] With a full gender recognition certificate, the person's gender becomes for all purposes the acquired gender. Most importantly, a person with such a certificate is able to marry someone of the opposite gender to their acquired gender. The Gender Recognition Act 2004 was groundbreaking in that it did not impose mandatory surgery or sterilization. On the other hand, the Act's requirement of a diagnosis of gender dysphoria can be stigmatic and exclusionary. The use of a medicalized procedure carries connotations of illness, which many trans individuals reject. It also requires engagement with medical services, an obstacle for those who find access to such services difficult.

In the meantime, widespread discrimination against transgender people in all areas of life began to be recognized as a breach of the right to equality. Momentum for change came initially from the courts, which have been willing to develop the meaning of 'sex' to encompass some forms of gender identity. This was the route taken by the ECJ in the seminal case of *P v S* in 1996.[71] If a person was dismissed on the grounds of gender reassignment,

---

[67] *Hamalainen v Finland* (n 50).
[68] ibid.
[69] *Bellinger v Bellinger* [2003] UKHL 21.
[70] Gender Recognition Act 2004, s 2(1).
[71] Case C-13/94 *P v S and Cornwall County Council* [1996] ECR I-2143.

the Court held, they were treated unfavourably compared to persons of the sex they were deemed to belong to before undergoing gender reassignment. Discrimination on the grounds of gender reassignment therefore fell within the EU prohibition of discrimination on grounds of sex.

Nearly twenty-five years later, the US Supreme Court took a similar path. In *RG & GR Harris Funeral Homes v EEOC*,[72] which was joined with *Bostock v Clayton*, the Court held that an employer who fires an individual merely for being gay or transgender violates Title VII, which makes it unlawful for an employer to discriminate on grounds, inter alia, of sex. The respondents had argued that the person had been dismissed on grounds of their transgender status not on grounds of their sex. Since transgender status was not mentioned in Title VII, Congress could not have intended to prohibit such discrimination and the dismissal was therefore lawful. Gorsuch J saw no merit in this position. As long as the discrimination was at least in part due to the sex of the person, other factors were irrelevant. Here the employer had intentionally relied in part on the individual employee's sex when deciding to discharge them. This was a violation on grounds of sex, in breach of the plain words of the statute.[73]

An even more emphatic position was taken by the Indian Supreme Court in 2013. In the case of *NALSA*,[74] the Court held that the right to non-discrimination on grounds of sex in Article 15 of the Indian Constitution included discrimination on the basis of stereotypical gender attributions attached to the sex of a person. 'Constitution makers, it can be gathered, gave emphasis to the fundamental right against sex discrimination so as to prevent the direct or indirect attitude to treat people differently, for the reason of not being in conformity with stereotypical generalizations of binary genders.'[75]

In some jurisdictions, legislative developments have followed the judicial lead. The EU directive on the principle of equal treatment between men and women in employment, known as the Recast Directive, now specifies in its preamble that it also applies to discrimination arising from gender reassignment.[76] Following the terminology used by the EU directive, the British EA 2010 includes 'gender reassignment' as a protected characteristic. Under the

[72] *RG & GR Harris Funeral Homes v EEOC* 140 S Ct 1731 (2020) (US Sup Ct); joined with *Bostock v Clayton County* (n 33).
[73] See further Chapter 4.
[74] *National Legal Services Authority (NALSA) v Union of India* (2014) 5 SCC 438 (Indian Sup Ct).
[75] ibid para 59.
[76] Directive 2006/54/EC (Recast Directive), Preamble, para (3).

Act, those undergoing gender assignment are fully protected against direct discrimination, indirect discrimination, harassment, and victimization, whether in employment, public functions, services, disposal of premises, or education.[77] The statute specifically provides that it is discriminatory to treat a person who is absent from work because he or she is undergoing the process of gender assignment less favourably than a person who is absent due to sickness or injury.[78] However, protection is not complete. As in sexual orientation, harassment in schools on grounds of gender reassignment is not specifically protected, leaving the applicant to claim under the direct discrimination provisions.[79] Moreover, freedom of religion takes priority over claims of discrimination on this ground. Clergymen, who are under a duty under the Marriage Act 1949 to marry anyone in their parish, are exempt from that duty where they reasonably believe that the gender of one of the parties is acquired under the Gender Recognition Act.[80] Similarly, such a refusal does not amount to unlawful discrimination.[81]

The provisions were widely welcomed. However, the scope of protection is inevitably narrowed by the continued reliance on 'gender reassignment'. This is despite the fact that the definition in the EA 2010 is broader than the definition under the Gender Recognition Act. 'Gender reassignment' under the EA 2010 applies to anyone who is 'proposing to undergo, is undergoing or has undergone a process (or part of a process) for the purpose of reassigning the person's sex by changing physiological or other attributes of sex'.[82] Importantly, it does not require an individual to undergo medical treatment to be protected. Moreover, unlike the Gender Recognition Act, the EA 2010 does not require a medical diagnosis or some official certification. For example, a person born physically female who lives as a man would be protected under the Act without the need to seek medical advice or medical intervention. A person who proposes to undergo gender assignment but then stops the process is similarly protected. Crucially, too, it protects children, again setting it apart from other legislation.

However, both the Gender Recognition Act and the EA 2010 retain the assumption of a gender binary, meaning that individuals who identify as non-binary remain invisible. This assumption was recently upheld by the UK

---

[77] Except in relation to harassment: see later.
[78] s 16.
[79] s 85(10).
[80] Marriage Act 1949, s 5B.
[81] EA 2010, sch 3 para 24.
[82] ibid, s 7(1).

Supreme Court when it rejected an application to require the UK passport to include the option of X, indicating an unspecified gender.[83] The court held that in the light of the unequivocal case law of the ECtHR, it could not be in dispute that the appellant's identification as non-binary is an aspect of private life within the meaning of Article 8 ECHR (respect for private life). However, given that this entailed imposing a positive obligation on the government to provide the appellant with an 'X' passport, a balance could be drawn between the importance of the interest at stake on the one hand, and the burden on the State on the other. It was here that the Supreme Court's inability to move beyond the legal erasure of non-binary persons became clear. According to Lord Reed: 'Notwithstanding the centrality of a non-gendered identification to the appellant's private life, it is difficult to accept that a particularly important facet of the appellant's existence or identity is at stake in the present proceedings. That is because it is only the designation of the appellant's gender in a passport which is in issue.'[84] On the other hand, particular importance was given to the considerations put forward by government as to the public interest, especially the need for government to have a coherent approach as to whether and if so in what circumstances gender categories beyond male and female should be recognized. The limitation on the claimant both to private life under Article 8 and to non-discrimination under Article 14 was therefore held to be objectively justified.

This contrasts with the Canadian approach. In 2017, legislation was passed adding references to 'gender identity or expression' to the list of prohibited grounds of discrimination.[85] This follows terminology in several provincial human rights laws in Canada. For example, the Ontario Human Rights Commission understands 'gender identity' as a person's internal experience of gender. Importantly, it refers to a person's sense not only of being a man or a woman but 'both, neither, or anywhere along the gender spectrum'. Gender expression refers to how a person expresses their gender in public, including behaviour, dress, voice, or chosen name and pronoun.[86]

In South Africa, the constitutional and statutory provisions, while not mentioning gender identity as such, are more open to being interpreted to incorporate protection for gender identity, in that they refer to both sex and

---

[83] R (On the application of Elan-Cane) v Secretary of State for the Home Department [2021] UKSC 56 (UK Sup Ct).

[84] ibid [57].

[85] Canadian Human Rights Act, s 3(1) as amended.

[86] Ontario Human Rights Commission, '3. Gender identity and gender expression', Policy on preventing discrimination because of gender identity and gender expression.

gender. The Equality Act has been relied on to protect a transgender person against discrimination based on their gender identity regardless of the fact that they have not officially transitioned or undergone medical treatment. The Equality Court in *September v Subramoney*[87] held that although transgender is not a listed ground in either the Constitution or the Equality Act, the profound impact on an individual's right to dignity and equality mean that the right to dignity includes the applicant's right to their gender identity.[88] The Court did, however, emphasize that this did not in any way challenge the underlying gender binary in South African law.[89] Indeed, legislation from 2003 only allows the sex description of a person to be altered in the birth register if their 'sexual characteristics have been altered by surgical or medical treatment or by evolvement through natural development resulting in gender reassignment'. Moreover, an application for alteration must be accompanied by a report prepared by a medical practitioner.[90] At the same time, both the Equality Act and the Alteration of Sex Description Act refer to intersex status, setting the South African provisions apart from others.

Perhaps the most profound understanding of the rights of transgender people has come from the Indian Supreme Court. In the case of *NALSA* in 2013,[91] members of the transgender community claimed a legal declaration of their gender identity other than the one assigned to them at birth. They argued that non-recognition of their gender identity violated the right to equality in Article 14 of the Constitution and the right to life in Article 21. In addition, members of the Hijra community and intersex community sought legal recognition of their status as a third gender. The Court noted the absence of suitable legislation in India dealing with the rights of members of the transgender community, despite the widespread discrimination, humiliation, and lack of access to services they faced. Importantly, it found that this was in breach of Article 14 of the Constitution, which states that the State shall not deny to 'any person' equality before the law or equal protection of the law. 'Article 14 does not restrict the word "person" and its application only to male or female. Hijras/transgender persons who are neither male/female fall within the expression "person" and, hence, entitled to legal protection of laws in all spheres of State activity, including employment, healthcare, education as well as equal civil and citizenship rights, as enjoyed

---

[87] *September v Subramoney* [2019] ZAEQC 4 (SA Equality Ct).
[88] ibid para 122.
[89] ibid para 159.
[90] Alteration of Sex Description and Sex Status Act No 49 of 2003, s 2.
[91] *NALSA* (n 74).

by any other citizen of this country.[92] As we have seen, the Court further held that the prohibition on discrimination on grounds of 'sex' in Articles 14 and 16 of the Constitution includes discrimination on grounds of gender identity.[93] Indeed, the Court went one step further than requiring protection against discrimination. The State, it held, was bound to take affirmative action under Article 16(4) of the Constitution to give transgender people due representation in public service.[94] The Court also went beyond other jurisdictions in its insistence on full recognition of gender non-binary and a third gender. 'Gender identity . . . the core of one's personal self, based on self-identification, not on surgical or medical procedure. Gender identity, in our view, is an integral part of sex and no citizen can be discriminated on the ground of gender identity, including those who identify as third gender.'[95]

Even so, there has been an important critique of the background assumption that transgender is itself a fixed category.[96] As Dutta puts it, 'the establishment of "transgender" as a trans/national term seeks to consolidate gender non-conforming people as stable and bounded "identities" and "populations".'[97] While it is crucial to enable individuals to have access to official identification, 'it may be necessary to destabilize the polarity between binary and nonbinary (or "third gender") identities—and more broadly to question the requirement of a singular, consistent identification in order to access rights and citizenship'.[98] Instead, Dutta and Roy propose that transgender should be used in the understanding of the multiple 'gendered identifications or practices enacted by a single body' so that 'to access the benefits or services provided by the category . . . one does not have to *identify* with any pre-given understanding of transgender'.[99]

Many of the more recent developments have drawn on the Yogyakarta Principles on the application of international human rights law in relation to sexual orientation and gender identity, adopted in 2006 by a distinguished group of human rights experts.[100] The Principles use the formulation of

---

[92] ibid para 54.
[93] ibid para 59.
[94] ibid para 60.
[95] ibid para 76.
[96] A Dutta, 'Contradictory Tendencies: The Supreme Court's NALSA Judgment on Transgender Recognition and Rights' (2014) 5 J Indian Law and Society 225.
[97] ibid 228.
[98] A Dutta and R Roy, 'Decolonizing Transgender in India' (2014) 1 Transgender Studies Quarterly 320, 334.
[99] ibid. With thanks to Almas Shaikh for pointing me to this literature.
[100] Yogyakarta Principles (March 2007) <http://yogyakartaprinciples.org/principles-en/about-the-yogyakarta-principles/> accessed 26 July 2022.

'gender identity' to refer to 'each person's deeply felt internal and individual experience of gender, which may or may not correspond with the sex assigned at birth, including the personal sense of the body (which may involve, if freely chosen, modification of bodily appearance or function by medical, surgical or other means) and other expressions of gender, including dress, speech and mannerisms'. The definition signals progress in that it does not treat gender identity as unique to transgender people, but as a characteristic that applies to everyone. It also moves away from defining gender identity as reliant on any particular bodily features, making it possible to acknowledge that women and men are only two of the possible gender identities.[101] However, Otto argues that by referring to a 'deeply felt internal and individual experience of gender', the definition reverts to an assumption of gender as fixed and innate, rather than socially constructed. As she puts it: 'The hard-won feminist understanding of gender [identity] as, in large part if not totally, socially constituted has disappeared in the context of promoting the rights of transgendered people'.[102] The definition was also criticized in that the framing around sexual orientation and gender identity excluded the rights of intersex people who have 'innate sex characteristics that do not fit medical norms for female or male bodies'.[103]

Ten years on, in an amendment to the Yogyakarta Principles,[104] the term 'gender expression' in the original understanding of gender identity is elaborated on to include a person's presentation of their gender through, inter alia, physical appearance, mannerisms, names, and personal references. It also notes that gender expression need not conform to a person's gender identity. In addition, the Principles add the term 'sex characteristics' to refer to a person's physical features relating to sex and affirm that the Principles apply equally to sex characteristics as a ground for protection against discrimination as they apply to sexual orientation, gender identity, and gender expression. The term 'sex characteristics' was preferred to 'intersex status' to follow through the commitment to universal applicability—everyone has sex characteristics but not everyone has intersex status.[105]

---

[101] Otto (n 57) 312.
[102] ibid 313.
[103] M Carpenter, 'Intersex Human Rights, Sexual Orientation, Gender Identity, Sex Characteristics and the Yogyakarta Principles plus 10' [2020] Culture, Health and Sexuality 1.
[104] The Yogyakarta Principles plus 10 (10 November 2017) <http://yogyakartaprinciples.org/principles-en/> accessed 26 July 2022.
[105] Carpenter (n 103).

Recognizing the exclusionary nature of regulation based on assumptions of a rigid gender binary opens up difficult questions in relation to safe spaces for women. Particularly controversial has been the question of whether it is lawful to exclude trans people from separate-sex and single-sex services. The British EA 2010 permits separate-sex services in certain circumstances; and this would usually mean that the service provider should treat transsexual people in the gender they present. However, the Act does permit discrimination on grounds of gender assignment in the provision of separate-sex services where this is a 'proportionate means of achieving a legitimate aim'.[106] In the statutory Code of Practice issued by the Equality and Human Rights Commission, it is stated that the denial of a service to a transsexual person should only occur in exceptional circumstances and on a case-by-case basis. The need of the transsexual person for the service, and the detriment to them if denied access, must be balanced against the detriment to other service users if the transsexual person is permitted access. Importantly, care should be taken to avoid making decisions based on ignorance or prejudice, and the provider must show that a less discriminatory way to achieve the objective was not available.[107] A similar approach is advised in relation to the denial of communal accommodation to a transsexual person, which is also permitted where the exclusion is a proportionate means of achieving a legitimate aim.[108]

Leaving the decision to service providers in this way may, however, prove problematic, given that frequently the decision to exclude transgender persons from accessing services in their preferred gender is fraught with prejudice and unwarranted stereotypes. This can be seen in the highly polarized debate in the US over access of transgender pupils and students to restrooms and toilets in their preferred gender. The Obama administration issued guidance to all schools in 2016, advising that in all schools transgender pupils should be permitted to access restrooms in their preferred gender. However, within months of taking office, President Trump rescinded the directive. This reversal of policy ran in parallel with litigation undertaken by Gavin Grimm against the refusal by his high school in Virginia to permit him to use

---

[106] EA 2010, sch 3, pt 7 para 28.

[107] Equality and Human Rights Commission, 'Services, Public Functions and Associations: Statutory Code of Practice' (2011) para 13.60 <www.gov.uk/government/publicati ons/equality-act-2010-draft-code-of-practice-on-services-public-functions-associations> accessed 26 July 2022.

[108] EA 2010, Sch 23, para 3; EHRC Code of Practice (n 107) paras 13.66–13.67.

the boys' bathroom. Gavin Grimm's birth-assigned sex was 'female' but his gender identity was male. From his first year in high school, he lived fully as a boy. The School Board, under pressure from some parents, adopted a policy under which students could only use restrooms matching their 'biological gender'. Grimm was required to use the bathroom in the nurse's office, some distance from his classrooms. Not only did this cause him to miss teaching time but he also experienced it as highly stigmatic, visibly branding him as different.

His long-running litigation, commenced in 2015, eventually reached the Federal Court of Appeals in 2020.[109] By a majority of two to one, the court held that the School Board's policy breached the Fourteenth Amendment. Relying on the 2020 decision in *Bostock* (see earlier),[110] it also found a breach of Title IX of the Education Amendments of 1972,[111] which prohibits discrimination on grounds of 'sex'. The court had no difficulty in rejecting the reasons given by the respondents for preventing transgender pupils from using bathrooms in their preferred gender, many of them repeating invidious prejudices against transgender people. Importantly, it held that there was no evidence to support the claim that allowing transgender students to access bathrooms in their preferred gender would 'open the door to predatory behaviour, particularly by male students pretending to be transgender in order to use the girls' bathroom'.[112] Indeed, trans-inclusive bathroom policies had been implemented in schools in many districts across the country and none of these negative consequences had occurred. In June 2021, the US Supreme Court declined certiorari, thus allowing the decision to stand.[113] In the meantime, the Biden administration has issued a notice of interpretation explaining that enforcement of Title IX's prohibition on discrimination on the basis of sex in education offered by a recipient of federal financial assistance[114] will include discrimination based on sexual orientation and gender identity.[115] This brings the interpretation of Title IX into line with *Bostock*.

---

[109] *Grimm v Gloucester County School Board* 972 F3d 586 (4th Cir, 2020) (US Federal Ct of Appeals); see also *Adams ex rel Kasper v Sch Bd of St John's Cnty* 968 F3d 1286 (11th Cir. 2020).

[110] *Bostock v Clayton County; RG & GR Harris Funeral Homes v EEOC* (n 72).

[111] 20 USC § 1681(a).

[112] *Grimm v Gloucester County School Board* (n 109) 599.

[113] *Gloucester County School Board v Grimm* 141 S Ct 2878 (2021) (US Sup Ct).

[114] Education Amendments of 1972, Title IX.

[115] <www2.ed.gov/about/offices/list/ocr/docs/202106-titleix-noi.pdf> accessed 22 July 2022.

IV DISABILITY

Disability differs from other types of discrimination in that it is a possibility which faces all members of society. The borderline between 'we' and 'they' is not only arbitrary but shifting. Nevertheless, able-bodied people tend to see disabled people as the 'Other', suppressing the knowledge, and the deep anxiety, that disability could come upon anyone at any time. People with disabilities have therefore always suffered from stigma, prejudice, and exclusion from society. The able-bodied norm is pervasive and exclusive: from public transport and pavements to working arrangements, to leisure and social facilities.

Until the last two decades of the twentieth century, disability was thought to be at most an issue for national assistance through social security or, in cases in which fault could be established, tort law. People with disabilities were depicted 'not as subjects with legal rights, but as objects of welfare, health and charity programs'.[116] Major international human rights documents did not even mention disability as one of the grounds to be protected against discrimination. This is still true both of the ECHR and the International Covenant on Civil and Political Rights.

The rights-based approach to disability only took root after 1980. Section 15 of the Canadian Charter was one of the first to include physical and mental disability expressly as an enumerated ground.[117] Importantly, too, section 15 includes disability as one of the grounds on which affirmative action is permitted.[118] Disability is also an enumerated ground under section 9 of the South African Constitution. This is reinforced by statute. Both the EEA and the Equality Act specify disability as an express ground of discrimination.[119] The EEA, moreover, includes disability as one of the three designated groups under the affirmative action provisions. These provisions require designated employers to implement affirmative action for people from designated groups, including preparing an employment equity plan.[120]

In jurisdictions in which disability is not expressly mentioned in an equal protection guarantee, courts have diverged sharply as to whether it should

---

[116] T Degener and G Quinn, 'A Survey of International Comparative and Regional Disability Law Reform' in Disability Rights Education and Defense Fund (ed), *From Principles to Practice: An International Disability Law and Policy Symposium* (Transnational Publishers 2000) 3.

[117] Disability is also mentioned in the Canadian Human Rights Act, s 3.

[118] See Chapter 5.

[119] EEA, s 6(1); Equality Act, s 9.

[120] Employment Equity Act 1998, Ch III.

be implied, and if so, how strictly disability-based classifications should be scrutinized. Under the ECHR, disability has been readily implied, with the ECtHR regarding both physical and mental disability as grounds for which particularly strict scrutiny should be applied.[121] However, the US Supreme Court has held that classifications based on disability should only be subject to rational-basis review under the Fourteenth Amendment.[122] On the other hand, disability is not mentioned in the fixed list of protected grounds under the Indian Constitution, and the Indian Supreme Court has not found a way to imply it.

In both the US and India, protection against disability discrimination has therefore been the sole task of legislation. The Americans with Disabilities Act 1990 prohibits discrimination in employment and requires access to public accommodations for persons with disabilities. The Individuals with Disability Education Act requires public schools to provide equal access to students with disabilities. In India, statutory protection was initially provided by legislation in 1995, the Persons with Disabilities Act 1995. This was amended and substantially overhauled in 2016 when the Rights of Persons with Disabilities Act 2016 was passed.

In the UK, early protection in the employment field took the form of quotas. The Disabled Persons (Employment) Act 1944 required employers of a substantial number of employees to employ a set quota of people registered as disabled, a quota which was enforced by criminal sanctions. However, compliance with the Act was negligible, partly because the conditions for registration as disabled were so severe as to exclude many genuinely disabled persons and partly because of a lack of proper enforcement. It was only in 1995, and after as many as sixteen unsuccessful attempts, that the Disability Discrimination Act finally reached the statute books. Disability legislation at the EU level was even more dilatory, with disability not included until the Employment Directive of 2000.

There is now widespread recognition, either in statute or in human rights instruments, of disability as a ground of discrimination. However, there remains considerable controversy as to how to formulate protection against discrimination in the context of disability. Central to the debate has been the conceptualization of disability itself. It has generally been assumed that the concept of disability points to the functional limitations of an individual.

---

[121] *Kiss v Hungary* (2013) 56 EHRR 38 (ECtHR); *Kiyutin v Russia* (2011) 53 EHRR 26 (ECtHR).
[122] *Cleburne v Cleburne Living Center* 473 US 432 (1985) (US Sup Ct).

This approach has come to be known as the 'medical model'. An alternative 'social model' recognizes the role of society in creating disabling barriers. Social institutions, attitudes, and the built environment are constructed for able-bodied persons. The problem consists not so much in functional limitations but in disabling barriers, whether attitudinal, physical, or political. A person is disabled by the prejudice, segregation, and exclusion that arise from disabling barriers rather than their body.[123] This means that the social distinction which attaches to impairment, and not the impairment itself, should be the focus of legal intervention.

The social model has signalled a paradigm shift, particularly in the self-perception of disabled persons, empowering them to assert their rights to social change rather than focusing on impairments. However, it has also been criticized for failing to reflect the personal experience of pain and restriction which can often come with impairment. As Shakespeare and Watson have argued, 'impairment is part of our daily personal experience, and cannot be ignored in our social theory or our political strategy. . . . We are not just disabled people, we are also people with impairments, and to pretend otherwise is to ignore a major part of our biographies.'[124] Impairment and disability are not dichotomous, but describe different aspects of a single experience. Others demonstrate the ways in which an exclusive focus on disabling social barriers may itself privilege certain, often more visible, impairments than others. Morris acknowledges that 'in making [the social model] argument we have sometimes colluded with the idea that the "typical" disabled person is a young man in a wheelchair who is fit, never ill, and whose only needs concern a physically accessible environment'. The risk of regressing into a medical model, which fuels exclusion and discrimination, has meant 'that we are forced into situations of denying the experience of our bodies, of trying to conform to the outside world's view of what it is to be a full human being'.[125] Instead, she argues, the experience of impairment needs to come back into the centre of disabled people's politics, making sure that what is needed as a result of illness, pain, and chronic conditions is properly addressed in health and support services.[126]

---

[123] J Morris, 'Impairment and Disability: Constructing an Ethics of Care Which Promotes Human Rights' (2001) 16 Hypatia: A Journal of Feminist Philosophy 1.

[124] T Shakespeare and N Watson, 'The Social Model of Disability: An Outdated Ideology?' in S Barnartt and B Altman (eds), Exploring *Theories and Expanding Methodologies: Where We Are and Where We Need to Go* (Research in Social Science and Disability), vol 2 (Emerald Group 2001) 23.

[125] Morris (n 123) 9–10.

[126] ibid.

A related area of contention is the way in which discrimination against people with disabilities is characterized. One approach is to draw on the understanding of race discrimination and regard people with disabilities as a minority group which requires legal and human rights intervention because of its lack of voice in the democratic political process.[127] Thus, in a striking parallel to the approach in early jurisprudence on race discrimination,[128] the Americans with Disabilities Act 1990[129] originally stated that individuals with disabilities were a 'discrete and insular minority' subjected to a history of purposeful unequal treatment, political powerlessness, and stereotypical assumptions.[130] The advantage of this analysis was to emphasize the political and social aspect of disability and to demonstrate its continuity with civil rights struggles. However, in practice, it led the US Supreme Court to interpret disability restrictively, excluding those who were not regarded as 'cluster[ing] among the politically powerless' nor as 'coalesc[ing] as historical victims of discrimination'.[131] To restore a broader definition of disability, the US legislation has now been amended to remove the references to persons with disabilities as a discrete and insular minority.[132] Indeed, given the diversity of people with disabilities, arguably disabled people do not form a discrete and insular group at all.

The 'minority group' analysis is also problematic in that it sets people with disabilities apart as different and distinct. Disability is characterized as fixed and dichotomous: either one has a disability or one does not.[133] Moreover, as Zola argues:

> Seeing people with a disability as 'different' with 'special' needs, wants and rights in this currently perceived world of finite resources, they are pitted against the needs, wants and rights of the rest of the population.[134]

---

[127] *United States v Carolene Products Co* 304 US 144, 152 fn 4 (1938).

[128] See Chapter 4.

[129] 104 Stat 327, 42 USC § 1210.

[130] ibid s 2(a)(7).

[131] *Sutton v United Air Lines* 527 US 471, 494 (1999) (US Sup Ct).

[132] Americans with Disabilities Act Amendments Act of 2008; USC Title 41, Ch 126, §§ 12101 ff.

[133] IK Zola, 'Towards the Necessary Universalizing of a Disability Policy' (1989) 67 The Millbank Quarterly 401; JE Bickenbach and others, 'Models of Disablement, Universalism and the International Classification of Impairments, Disabilities and Handicaps' (1999) 48 J Social Science and Medicine 1173, 1182.

[134] Zola ibid 406.

An alternative 'universalist view' suggests that rather than demarcating a discrete and insular minority, disability should be regarded as fluid and continuous. 'Disability is a normal aspect of life; all kinds of disabilities can happen to all types of people at all stages in their normal lifecycles.'[135] As Bickenbach puts it: 'Disability is not a human attribute that demarks one portion of humanity from another; it is an infinitely various but universal feature of the human condition. No human has a complete repertoire of abilities.'[136] Advocates of universalism call for a policy that 'respects difference and widens the range of the normal'. Designing the environment only for people within a narrow range of ability is seen to accord special privilege to those who happen to fall within that range.[137] 'Disability policy is therefore not policy for some minority group; it is policy for all.'[138]

Real progress towards capturing these important insights can be seen in the landmark UN Convention on the Rights of Persons with Disabilities, adopted in 2006. The Convention, which is fast becoming a benchmark for domestic legislation, manifests in a culmination of the development of a human rights approach to disability which incorporates the insights from the different approaches above.[139] Most importantly, it comprehensively and emphatically views persons with disabilities as subjects with rights rather than objects of charity, medical treatment, or social protection. It clearly foregrounds the insights of the social model, addressing the ways in which structural barriers and social conditions disable people, while at the same time continuing to recognize impairments. Thus Article 1 states: 'Persons with disabilities include those who have long-term physical, mental, intellectual or sensory impairments which in interaction with various barriers may hinder their full and effective participation in society on an equal basis with others.'

As well as a broad definition of disability, the Convention adopts an understanding of substantive equality which closely follows the multi-dimensional approach set out in Chapter 1. This, it will be recalled, identified four dimensions of equality: the redistributive dimension (redressing disadvantage), the recognition dimension (addressing stigma, prejudice, stereotyping, and

---

[135] UN Ad Hoc Committee on a Comprehensive and Integral International Convention on Protection and Promotion of the Rights and Dignity of Persons with Disabilities (New York, 2003), 'Issues and Emerging Trends Related to Advancement of Persons with Disabilities', Doc A/AC.265/2003/1, paras 9–10.

[136] Bickenbach and others (n 133) 1182.

[137] ibid 1183.

[138] ibid 1182.

[139] T Degener, 'Disability in a Human Rights Context' (2016) 5 Laws 35.

violence), the participative dimension, and the transformative dimension (accommodation of difference and structural change). Indeed, the four-dimensional model has been expressly adopted by the Committee on the Rights of People with Disabilities—the UN monitoring body for the CRPD—following submissions to the Committee by the author and colleagues.[140] Using the umbrella term of 'inclusive equality', the Committee explicitly sets out the four dimensions in CRPD General Comment No 6:

> Inclusive equality . . . embraces a substantive model of equality and extends and elaborates on the content of equality in: (a) a fair redistributive dimension to address socioeconomic disadvantages; (b) a recognition dimension to combat stigma, stereotyping, prejudice and violence and to recognize the dignity of human beings and their intersectionality; (c) a participative dimension to reaffirm the social nature of people as members of social groups and the full recognition of humanity through inclusion in society; and (d) an accommodating dimension to make space for difference as a matter of human dignity. The Convention is based on inclusive equality.[141]

Domestic legislation and constitutional protections were initially firmly anchored to a medical model of disability. But recognition of the CRPD model has gradually permeated both legislative frameworks and judicial interpretations. There have been three main areas in which such progress can be seen. The first is in the extent to which the role of disabling barriers has been integrated into the interpretation of disability. The second is in the extent to which stigma and stereotyping in relation to the perception of disability has been included in the reach of the notion of disability, so that the existence or absence of impairments becomes less important or irrelevant. The third is the requirement of reasonable accommodation. By imposing duties of reasonable accommodation, it is expressly recognized that instead of requiring conformity to the able-bodied norm, modification of the environment or of existing policies or practices is essential if people with disabilities are to have genuine equality of opportunity.

---

[140] Fredman and others, 'Achieving Transformative Equality for Persons with Disabilities: Submission to the CRPD Committee for General Comment No 6 on Article 5 of the UN Convention on the Rights of Persons with Disabilities' (Oxford Human Rights Hub 2017); Prof Dr Theresia Degener, 'Challenges of Disability Law', Keynote at the Berkeley Comparative Equality and Anti-Discrimination Law Study Group Annual Conference 2019.

[141] CRPD General Comment No 6 (2018) para 11.

In the UK, the definition of disability has always followed a decidedly medical model. The statutory definition of a disabled person refers to someone who has or had 'a physical or mental impairment and the impairment has a substantial and long-term adverse effect on [his or her] ability to carry out normal day to day activities'.[142] Much litigation has been expended on this definition and many claims have fallen at this barrier. On the other hand, in a strong affirmation of the social model, the legislation includes a duty to make reasonable adjustments to avoid the disadvantage caused to disabled people by practices, criteria, or provisions or physical features of the environment. This includes a requirement to take reasonable steps to provide auxiliary aids.[143] Moreover, it is asymmetric: from the very start, the legislation has acknowledged that differential treatment of people with disabilities was necessary to achieve equality.

At the EU level, the move from a medical to a social model, fully recognizing the disabling effects of the environment, has proved challenging. The initial approach of the ECJ tended towards the more static approach, marking disability as a separate category with rigid boundaries rather than a spectrum of capabilities responsive to the environment. In *Chacon Navós*, the Court saw its role as setting the appropriate boundary between sickness and disability.[144] In doing so, it regarded the concept of disability (which is not defined in the directive) as 'referring to a limitation which results in particular from physical, mental or psychological impairments and which hinders the participation of the person concerned in professional life'.[145] However, more recent cases have seen a greater sensitivity by the Court to the need to understand disability as an interaction with social and environmental factors, including disadvantage, stigma, and exclusion. Particularly important has been its acceptance of the more wide-ranging social approach of the CRPD, which was ratified by the EU in November 2009,[146] and therefore became part of the EU order. In the 2013 case of *Danmark*,[147] the Advocate General acknowledged that the definition in *Chacon* fell short of that in the CRPD in some respects, particularly in relation to its reference to the ways in which the hindrance to participation arises from various barriers in society.[148] The

[142] EA 2010, s 6(1).
[143] ibid s 20.
[144] Case C-13/05 *Chacón Navas v Eurest Colectividades SA* [2006] 3 CMLR 40 (CJEU (Grand Chamber)).
[145] ibid para 43.
[146] Decision 2010/48.
[147] Joined Cases C-335 and 337/11 *HK Danmark v Dansk Arbejdsgiverforening* [2013] 3 CMLR 21 (CJEU).
[148] ibid AG27.

definition in Article 1 CRPD was therefore accepted in its entirety by the Court, with only the added restriction to professional life and the workforce. Disability, it held, refers to 'a limitation which results in particular from physical, mental or psychological impairments which in interaction with various barriers may hinder the full and effective participation of the person concerned in professional life on an equal basis with other workers'.[149]

This meant, in turn, that the distinction between sickness and disability was less rigid: the scope of the directive was not restricted to disabilities that are congenital or result from accidents but could also apply to those caused by illness. Where an illness, whether curable or incurable, entails a long-term limitation which in interaction with various barriers hinders full and effective participation in professional life, it would constitute a disability.[150] Nor does a disability imply complete exclusion from work or professional life;[151] it could also cover a hindrance to the exercise of a professional activity, enabling a worker to work only part-time. A similar willingness by the Court to interpret the directive in the light of the CRPD led the Court to hold that reasonable accommodation might include an adjustment of working hours,[152] although account must be taken of the financial and other costs entailed, the resources of the undertaking, and the possibility of obtaining public funding or other assistance.[153] Equally importantly, absence from work because an employer failed to make the appropriate adjustments should not be treated the same as an absence from work through illness.[154]

The more substantive approach to the meaning of disability in *Danmark* was deepened and strengthened in *Kaltoft*, in December 2014, in which the Court of Justice demonstrated the applicability of this concept of disability to the situation of obesity.[155] Here the crucial point was not to attempt to classify obesity in the abstract as constituting a disability, but to ask 'if the obesity of the worker hindered his full and effective participation in professional life on an equal basis with other workers on account of reduced mobility or the onset, in that person, of medical conditions preventing him from carrying out his work or causing discomfort when carrying out his professional activity'.[156] Moreover, this conception of disability was independent of the

[149] ibid para 38.
[150] ibid para 41.
[151] ibid para 43.
[152] ibid para 56.
[153] ibid para 60.
[154] ibid para 68.
[155] Case C-354/13 *Fag og Arbejde (FOA), acting on behalf of Karsten Kaltoft v Kommunernes Landsforening (KL), acting on behalf of the Municipality of Billund* [2015] 2 CMLR 19 (CJEU).
[156] ibid para 60.

extent to which the individual concerned had contributed to her disability.[157] However, in concentrating on disadvantage in his physical ability to carry out the job, the Court omitted to consider the second dimension of substantive equality; namely, the stigma attached to obesity and its possible effect as an independent obstacle to his full participation in the workforce.

The Court now regularly refers to the CRPD definition in its jurisprudence on the meaning of disability. At the same time, the focus on disabling barriers can operate to obscure important impairments and the need for accommodation. For example, in Z, the Court upheld a refusal to extend the right to parental leave to the commissioning mother in a surrogacy arrangement. The applicant was unable to have children because she was born without a womb. The Court held that her inability to have a child did not constitute a hindrance to her professional activity. It was therefore not a disability for the purposes of the directive.[158]

In the US, the definition of disability in the Americans with Disabilities Act 1990 is similar to that of the UK in focusing on the effects of impairments on an individual's life activities. Thus, disability is defined as a 'physical or mental impairment that substantially limits one or more major life activities of an individual' or a 'record of impairment'. This definition was regarded as leaving sufficient flexibility to incorporate elements of a social model. It was, however, restrictively construed by the US Supreme Court. In particular, the Court held that if mitigating measures such as medication ameliorated the effects of the impairment on life activities, the person might not fall within the definition.[159] This led to an important set of amendments in the Americans with Disabilities Act Amendments Act of 2008 which required the definition to be interpreted, so far as possible, in favour of a broad coverage of individuals. It also specified that the determination of whether the impairment substantially limits a major life activity should not take into account the ameliorative effects of measures such as wheelchairs, medication, reasonable accommodations, or adaptive behaviour.[160]

An important contribution of the Americans with Disabilities Act is that the statute also protects individuals who are 'regarded as having an impairment'.[161] The 'regarded as' prong of the definition goes some way to incorporating the key dimension of combatting prejudices and stereotypes

---

[157] ibid para 56.
[158] Case C-363/ Z v A Goverment Department [2014] 3 CMLR 20 (ECJ).
[159] Sutton v United Air Lines (n 131).
[160] 42 USC § 1202, s 4(A)–(E).
[161] 42 USC § 1210, s 2(1)(A)–(C).

about persons with disabilities. A person can be protected under this prong on the basis of actual or perceived physical or mental impairments, regardless of whether this substantially limits a major life activity or is perceived to do so.

It is in relation to perception of disability that the Supreme Court of Canada has made its major contribution to this issue. In the case of *Mercier* in 2000,[162] Justice L'Heureux-Dubé, drawing directly on the work of Bickenbach and others, recognized the role of the social and political environment in determining whether an impairment becomes a disability. 'By placing the emphasis on human dignity, respect, and the right to equality rather than a simple biomedical condition,' she held, 'this approach recognizes that the attitudes of society and its members often contribute to the idea or perception of a [disability].'[163] A person may have no limitations in everyday activities other than those created by prejudice and stereotypes.'[164] Although preceding the CRPD, Justice L'Heureux-Dubé's judgment resonates with its central values. A disability, she held, 'may be the result of a physical limitation, an ailment, a social construct, a perceived limitation or a combination of all of these factors.'[165]

Indian legislation has been most directly influenced by the CRPD. Statutory protection was initially provided by the Persons with Disabilities Act 1995. However, this was based on a purely medical definition of disability, where disability was defined by reference to only seven listed conditions. A person with a disability was defined as a person suffering from not less than 40 per cent of any of the listed conditions certified by a medical authority. India's ratification of the CRPD, however, necessitated a change. The Rights of Persons with Disabilities Act 2016, which was brought in expressly to implement the CRPD, signalled a clear shift towards incorporating a social model. The definition, drawn from the very similarly worded formula in the CRPD, states that a person with a disability means a person 'with long-term physical, mental, intellectual or sensory impairment which, in interaction with barriers, hinders his full and effective participation in society equally with others'. In the words of Supreme Court Justice Chandrachud J, the 2016

---

[162] *Québec (Commission des droits de la personne et des droits de la jeunesse) v Montréal (City); Québec (Commission des droits de la personne et des droits de la jeunesse) v Boisbriand (City)* 2000 SCC 27 (Can Sup Ct).

[163] Quebec Charter of Human Rights and Freedoms, s 10 uses the word 'handicap'.

[164] *Quebec (Commission des droits de la personne et des droits de la jeunesse) v Montréal (City); Quebec (Commission des droits de la personne et des droits de la jeunesse) v Boisbriand (City)* [2000] 1 SCR 665, para 80 (Can Sup Ct).

[165] ibid para 79.

Act 'evidenc[es] a shift from a stigmatizing medical model of disability under the 1995 Act to a social model of disability which recognizes that it is the societal and physical constraint[s] that are at the heart of exclusion of persons with disabilities from full and effective participation in society'.[166]

The Act, which for the first time applies to both government and private establishments, includes the right not to be discriminated against on grounds of disability. This, however, is subject to a justification defence where an act or omission is a proportionate means of achieving a legitimate aim.[167] The Act also includes a duty of reasonable accommodation, defined as necessary and appropriate modifications. But, like other jurisdictions, this duty is limited to situations in which it does not impose a disproportionate or undue burden. Notably, too, the duty is not placed on establishments themselves but on State or central governments.[168]

The Indian legislation stands out from equivalent frameworks in other jurisdictions by its provision for reservations for persons with 'benchmark' disabilities. The 2016 Act requires employers to appoint persons with benchmark disabilities to no fewer than 4 per cent of identified posts.[169] It also provides for a 5 per cent reservation in both high schools and higher educational establishments.[170] Equally importantly, there is provision for a 5 per cent reservation for people with benchmark disabilities in the allotment of agricultural land and housing and in poverty-alleviation schemes, with appropriate priority accorded to women in both of these areas.[171] The definition of people with benchmark disabilities, however, looks very similar to the discarded medical model of the 1995 Act. To qualify for a reservation, a person must have at least 40 per cent of a disability specified in the schedule. This encouraged organizations to restrict other aspects of the 2016 Act, such as the duty of accommodation, to those with benchmark disabilities, thus threatening to undermine the advances towards a social model of disability in the 2016 Act. This was the view taken by the Union Public Service Commission (UPSC), the organization that conducts civil service examinations, when it refused to offer a candidate, who has a writing disorder, a scribe for his exam. This approach was roundly rejected by the Supreme Court in *Vikash Kumar* in 2021. The Court emphasized that the concept of a benchmark disability was

---

[166] *Vikash Kumar v UPSC* (2021) 5 SCC 370, para 36.
[167] Rights of Persons with Disabilities Act 2016, s 3(3).
[168] s 3(5).
[169] s 34.
[170] s 32.
[171] s 37.

specifically adopted in relation to the provisions for reservations. The restrictive definition should not be applied to the broader concept of disability as found in the Act. In particular, the duty of reasonable accommodation was held to apply to the wider concept of disability for the purposes of the legislation.[172]

V AGE

The issues raised by age discrimination differ in important respects from those discussed so far.[173] Since we have all been young and many of us will become old, the opposition between 'Self' and 'Other' prevalent in other types of discrimination is not as stark. Indeed, there is no clearly demarcated boundary between the group subject to discrimination and others. Some jurisdictions, such as the US in the Age Discrimination in Employment Act (ADEA), focus on a 'protected group' of people aged forty or over. Others, such as in the UK and EU legislation, refer to discrimination between any age groups. This means that there is no easily recognizable distinction between a dominant and subordinate group, a 'discrete and insular minority' defined by age. In fact, there may be patent conflicts of interest: the interests of younger workers may be compromised in order to cater for the interests of older workers and vice versa. Indeed, 'ageism' is often justified on the grounds that older people should in fairness be required to make space for younger people.

The notion that differentiation on the grounds of age might constitute unlawful discrimination is a relatively recent phenomenon. Age-based classifications abound in the law, and some, such as minimum age limits for voting or driving or legislation restricting children's ability to undertake paid work,[174] might be thought to be eminently justifiable. Conversely, it might be appropriate to give special treatment to elderly or young people, for example in relation to healthcare, subsidized transport, or training programmes. On the other hand, there remain significant areas of negative discrimination along all four dimensions of substantive equality. Both older and younger people face disadvantage on grounds of age, particularly in the workforce,

---

[172] *Vikash Kumar* (n 166) para 30.
[173] See further S Fredman, 'The Age of Equality' in S Fredman and S Spencer (eds), *Age as an Equality Issue* (Hart Publishing 2003).
[174] Council Directive 94/33/EC on the Protection of Young People at Work.

but also in relation to healthcare, education, and training or the provision of public services.[175] They can be subject to age-related stigma and stereotyping, marginalization and lack of voice, and structural discrimination. The relationship between positive and negative differentiation in this area can also become blurred. For example, programmes claiming to be for the 'good' of young people may in fact be detrimental.[176]

Older workers, in particular, suffer from some of the central hallmarks of discrimination. Stigma and stereotyping of older workers make it more difficult for them to retain their jobs or re-enter the labour market than younger workers. Stereotyping may be positive as well as negative: older staff may be regarded as more reliable or hard-working than younger employees; but both positive and negative perceptions contribute to employers 'age-typing' jobs.[177] Prejudice against older workers is most evident at the stage of recruitment but it also manifests in relation to training, development opportunities, and promotion. Many companies overtly restrict training opportunities on the grounds that older people are perceived to be more inflexible and not worth the investment of training resources. Older people are also very likely to suffer from indirect discrimination in the form of apparently neutral practices which in fact operate to exclude more older than younger people. This is particularly evident in respect of educational qualifications. Older workers tend to have fewer formal qualifications than younger workers.[178] Undue emphasis on formal qualifications rather than relevant experience or transferable skills disproportionately excludes older workers. As a result, once unemployed, workers over fifty remain unemployed for longer than other age groups. Younger people might also face discrimination in the workforce. In the UK, minimum wage legislation has consistently set lower levels for workers under the age of twenty-five.[179] In Canada, a scheme which required younger workers to undertake training as a condition for access to social security benefits was upheld by the Supreme Court of Canada.[180]

Nevertheless, the motivation for age discrimination legislation diverges in some important respects from the impetus driving race or gender equality laws. This is because the issue of age discrimination, in some jurisdictions at

---

[175] Fredman (n 173).
[176] *Gosselin v Quebec* 2002 SCC 84 (Can Sup Ct).
[177] D Smeaton and S Vegeris, 'Older People Inside and Outside the Labour Market: A Review', Research Report 22 (Equality and Human Rights Commission 2009) 16.
[178] Equality and Human Rights Commission, *How Fair is Britain?* (2010) Part II, 347.
[179] National Minimum Wage Act 1998.
[180] *Gosselin v Quebec* (n 176).

least, has been pushed to the fore by demography. In the Global North, such as in the EU, UK, Canada, and the US, populations are ageing rapidly, a result of the combined forces of lower fertility rates and increased longevity due to medical advances. By 2040, about one in five people in the US will be sixty-five or older, compared to about one in eight in 2000.[181] In the EU, the share of those over fifty-five years old will reach 40.6 per cent in 2050, up from just over one-third in 2019.[182] The implications for pension funds and age-related State benefits can be immense. This is exacerbated if older workers face barriers to remaining in employment even before they retire. In periods of recession and restructuring, older people have tended to be made redundant before younger people, and face higher barriers in attempting to return to the workforce or access retraining with the result that many people can spend decades in retirement. Prolonging labour force participation in both the US and the EU has therefore become a key labour market objective. In the UK, and the EU more widely,[183] age discrimination legislation was one of the measures put in place to achieve this end, together with a range of other policy initiatives. The demographic contrast with South Africa and India is stark. In South Africa, only 6.5 per cent of the Black population were sixty years and older in 2018, compared to almost 25 per cent of the white population. On the other hand, as many as 38 per cent of the total population were nineteen or younger.[184] In India in 2019, just over one-quarter of the population were under fifteen years old and only 6.38 per cent were over sixty-five.[185] In these countries, then, the demographic imperative is less urgent; instead, the pressing priority is the high level of youth unemployment.

This discussion has demonstrated that age discrimination legislation may have divergent purposes. The demographic impetus suggests that the focus should be on keeping older workers in the workforce which, in turn, points towards more instrumental aims and objectives of anti-discrimination legislation. Policy documents both at the EU and UK level regularly highlight the efficiency benefits of including older workers in the workforce. In particular,

---

[181] <www.urban.org/policy-centers/cross-center-initiatives/program-retirement-policy/projects/data-warehouse/what-future-holds/us-population-aging> accessed 9 December 2020.
[182] <https://ec.europa.eu/eurostat/statistics-explained/index.php?title=Ageing_Europe_-_statistics_on_population_developments#Older_people_.E2.80.94_population_overview> accessed 9 December 2020.
[183] Smeaton and Vegeris (n 177) 15.
[184] <www.statista.com/statistics/1116077/total-population-of-south-africa-by-age-group/> accessed 9 December 2020.
[185] <www.statista.com/statistics/271315/age-distribution-in-india/> accessed 9 December 2020.

it is argued that businesses benefit by avoiding the loss of expertise and experience resulting from prejudice and exclusion of older workers. US legislation similarly points to the higher incidence of the long-term unemployment of older workers relative to younger ones, with a consequent loss to productivity and potential.[186] This instrumental approach can be contrasted with an intrinsic view of the aims of anti-discrimination law. These emphasize the protection of individual dignity and the expansion of genuine choice for older or younger people. A further critical perspective on age discrimination legislation suggests that it has primarily benefited older white men who are not protected by other grounds of discrimination but are in fact relatively privileged in society.[187] It is, indeed, notable that age discrimination cases before the ECJ have far outnumbered cases on race discrimination, and that successful cases have predominantly been brought by white men, most of whom are older.[188] However, given the substantial discrimination in fact experienced by older women, younger and older ethnic minorities, and other intersectional groups, this may be a reflection of the cost and complexity of discrimination claims rather than the intrinsic bias of age discrimination protections in favour of more privileged individuals.

Indeed, there are important differences within the over-fifty age group, demonstrating the ways in which interlocking identities affect one another. At least 'two nations in early retirement' have been identified. One group has access to relatively good pensions and are able to retire to pursue other interests; a second group, frequently from lower social classes, have been compelled to leave work due to redundancy, poor skills, or bad health.[189] In addition, age and ethnicity frequently combine to intensify disadvantage. Women are particularly vulnerable to poverty in old age.[190] Interrupted work patterns due to child-bearing and childcare mean that women may be unable to sustain pension contributions and, if they do, the outcome might be lower.[191] For part-time workers, workers on job-shares, and precarious

---

[186] 29 USC 42 USC § 621: Congressional statement of findings and purpose.

[187] D Neumark, 'Age Discrimination Legislation in the United States' (2003) 21 Contemporary Economic Policy 297, 313.

[188] Case C-159/10 *Fuchs v Land Hessen* [2011] ECR I-6919 (CJEU); Joined Cases C-250 and 268/09 *Georgiev v Tehnicheski Universitet—Sofia, filial Plovdiv* [2011] 2 CMLR 179 (ECJ); Case C-341/09 *Petersen v Berufungsausschuss fur Zahnarzte fur den Bezirk Westfalen-Lippe* [2010] 2 CMLR 830 (ECJ); Case C-447/09 *Prigge v Deutsche Lufthansa AG* [2011] IRLR 1052 (ECJ); Case C-45/09 *Rosenbladt v Oellerking Gebäudereinigungsges mbH* [2011] 1 CMLR 1011 (ECJ); contrast Case C-143/16 *Abercrombie v Bordonaro* [2018] 1 CMLR 27 (CJEU).

[189] Smeaton and Vegeris (n 177) 17.

[190] ibid 39;J McLaughlin, 'Falling Between the Cracks: Discrimination Laws and Older Women' (2020) 34 Labour 215; S Fredman, *Women and the Law* (OUP 1997).

[191] McLaughlin (n 190); Fredman (n 190) ch 8.

workers, the vast majority of whom tend to be women, this has a lasting effect on their pension access in old age, a fact which has been recognized as indirect discrimination on grounds of gender by both the ECJ[192] and the Supreme Court of Canada.[193]

Although age is a relative newcomer in discrimination law, of all the jurisdictions examined here only India lacks either constitutional or statutory protection against age discrimination. Age is expressly mentioned as a ground of discrimination in both the Canadian Charter and the South African Constitution. The US Supreme Court has held that classifications based on age should only be subject to rational-basis review under the Fourteenth Amendment.[194] Nevertheless, age discrimination legislation in the form of the ADEA was introduced as early as 1967, soon after the Civil Rights Act barred discrimination on grounds of race and gender. Age was not regarded as a ground of discrimination in the EU until 2000, when it was included as a ground of discrimination together with sexual orientation, religion and belief, and disability in the 2000 Employment Directive.[195] It was considered sufficiently novel and complex for Member States to be given six years to bring age discrimination into force, so that domestic legislation making age a ground of discrimination was only enacted in 2006. Age is now incorporated into the EA 2010 as a ground of discrimination.

Several challenging issues remain across all these jurisdictions. The first is whether age discrimination legislation only protects older people or spans the whole age range. The US ADEA 1967 initially only protected those aged forty to sixty-five from age discrimination, but the upper age limit was extended to seventy years old in 1978. In 1986, the upper age limit was abolished altogether but the lower limit remains. Other jurisdictions see age as covering the full age range. This, however, brings in potential tensions between the needs of younger workers and those of older workers.

This also leads to the second challenge which has tended to dominate jurisprudence. This is the question of a mandatory retirement age, an issue which was taken for granted by earlier generations. On the one hand, setting a fixed age for retirement is a clear instance of age discrimination in that it automatically stereotypes older people as lacking in capacity. Regarding mandatory retirement as unfairly discriminatory also serves the instrumental aim of

---

[192] Case 1007/84 *Bilka-Kaufhaus* [1986] IRLR 317 (ECJ). See also *Fraser* (n 193).

[193] *Fraser v Canada (Attorney General)* 2020 SC 28 (Can Sup Ct).

[194] *Massachusetts Board of Retirement v Murgia* 427 US 307 (1976) (US Sup Ct).

[195] Council Directive 2000/78/EC establishing a General Framework for Equal Treatment in Employment and Occupation.

keeping older people in the workforce. On the other hand, abolishing mandatory retirement can introduce tensions between older and younger workers. Should older workers have to retire at a fixed age in order to make space for younger workers? Broadly speaking, the 'lump of labour' theory, which assumes that some have to exit the workforce for others to enter it, has been shown to be a fallacy. Nevertheless, there are positions which only fall vacant once the incumbent has left. Dignity-based justifications for abolishing mandatory retirement ages can also be turned on their head. It might be argued that individualized assessments based on the capacity of older people to do their jobs could be more demeaning than a simple blanket exit date. The objection to mandatory retirement is also based on a paradigm job to which many people do not have access. For those in heavy manual jobs, or working in highly stressful, precarious position for low rewards, the opportunity to retire might be a positive goal. All this is, of course, dependent on access to pensions or other social support. It is frequently precisely those in more precarious positions, particularly women, who might need to work beyond retirement age to access a pension.

In the US, the abolition of an upper limit on the age of the protected class brought with it the abolition of mandatory retirement ages. In South Africa, by contrast, the Labour Relations Act permits mandatory retirement by providing a defence to a claim of unfair age discrimination where the employee has reached 'the normal or agreed retirement age for persons in that capacity'.[196] The EU has taken a more nuanced position. Mandatory retirement is, in principle, discriminatory on grounds of age. However, it can be justified where it is a proportionate means of achieving a legitimate aim. Refreshing the workforce, or opening up opportunities for new or younger workers, is such an aim. In several cases, the Court has now held that if the number of posts available is limited, and incumbents tend to remain in post permanently with little or no turnover, a mandatory retirement age may be the only means of ensuring that young people have a fair opportunity to enter the profession in question.[197] This was held to be applicable to panel dentists,[198] university professors,[199] and prosecutors.[200] However, mandatory retirement is only a proportionate means of achieving this end if retiring workers have been able to amass a sufficient pension. Thus, in one of the earliest cases,

---

[196]   Labour Relations Act (Act 66 of 1995), s 187(2)(b).
[197]   *Fuchs v Land Hessen* (n 188) paras 58–59.
[198]   *Petersen v Berufungsausschuss fur Zahnarzte fur den Bezirk Westfalen-Lippe* (n 188) para 70.
[199]   *Georgiev v Tehnicheski Universitet—Sofia filial Plovdiv* (n 188).
[200]   *Fuchs v Land Hessen* (n 188) para 60.

Palacios de la Villa, the Court stated that compulsory retirement of workers at the age of sixty-five with the aim of encouraging recruitment would not unduly prejudice the legitimate claims of the workers concerned if they were entitled to a reasonable pension.[201] In *Fuchs*, the Court held that achieving an age-balanced workforce among prosecutors was a legitimate aim, and a mandatory retirement age was a proportionate means since retired prosecutors were eligible for pensions at approximately 72 per cent of their final salary.[202] Similarly, in *Georgiev*, the age limit applied to university professors at issue was five years higher than the pensionable age. The Court stressed that the measure could not be regarded as unduly prejudicing the legitimate claims of workers subject to compulsory retirement because the relevant legislation took account of the fact that the persons concerned were entitled to retirement pensions.[203]

VI CONCLUSION

Chapters 2 and 3 have shown the ways in which anti-discrimination laws have evolved as a response to manifestations of inequality deeply embedded in the historical and political context of a given society. Chapter 2 considered the social challenges facing discrimination law and critically assessed the corresponding legal responses in relation to gender, race, ethnicity and caste, and religion and belief in the five jurisdictions at issue here. Chapter 3 has focused, in particular, on sexual orientation, gender identity, disability, and age. The next chapter examines the scope of discrimination laws. Who is protected? Who is bound? And in what contexts? It is to these questions that we now turn.

---

[201] Case C-411/05 *Palacios de la Villa v Cortefiel Servicios SA* (2008) 1 CMLR 16, para 73 (CJEU); see also *Rosenbladt v Oellerking Gebäudereinigungsges mbH* (n 188) paras 73–76.
[202] *Fuchs v Land Hessen* (n 188) para 67.
[203] *Georgiev v Tehnicheski Universitet—Sofia filial Plovdiv* (n 188) para 54.

4

The Scope of Discrimination Law

Discrimination law poses a central dilemma. On the one hand, individuals should be judged according to their personal qualities. This basic tenet is contravened if the treatment accorded to individuals is based on their status, their group membership, or irrelevant physical characteristics. On the other hand, not every distinction is discriminatory. Governments classify people into groups for a wide variety of reasons and many of them are legitimate. In addition, there are many group characteristics that are a valued part of the identity of individuals. The challenge, therefore, is to frame laws that are sensitive enough to outlaw invidious distinctions while permitting, and even supporting, positive difference.

Which characteristics, then, ought to be protected against discrimination and why? Although there is now a general consensus that sex or gender and race should be within the list of grounds of discrimination, even these were only achieved after struggle and controversy. It is only relatively recently that other grounds, such as disability and sexual orientation, have been accepted as attracting special protection, and the inclusion of age in more recent years came as a surprise to some. But is there a unifying principle drawing all these together into a coherent whole and, if so, what is it? To what extent can the choice of grounds be explained by the underlying aims of equality? Section I of this chapter addresses these questions.

A related concern is the reach of equality law. Should discrimination on these grounds be unlawful in all walks of life or only in specific spheres, such as employment and education? Should both public and private actors be bound? Equality laws in many jurisdictions derive from a constitutional guarantee which may well bind only the State and not private actors. Only if legislation is specifically passed pursuant to such guarantees will private actors be bound. Section II of the chapter examines the reach of anti-discrimination law while Section III considers who is bound by such laws. The focus is on the UK, EU, ECHR, India, South Africa, the US, and Canada.

Discrimination Law. Third Edition. Sandra Fredman, Oxford University Press. © Sandra Fredman 2022.
DOI: 10.1093/oso/9780198854081.003.0004

I GROUNDS OF DISCRIMINATION

What sort of distinctions should be outlawed as illegitimate and unaccept-able? The answer to this question is heavily influenced by the political and social context in which discrimination law has developed. In the US, the de-velopment began with race. Expansion into other grounds has taken place primarily by way of extrapolation of principles developed for race. In the EU, by contrast, equality law began with nationality and gender. Race was not included until as recently as 2000, together with sexual orientation, dis-ability, age, and religion and belief.[1] The list of grounds in the European Convention on Human Rights (ECHR) reflects the immediate postwar con-text in which it was formulated. Hence, it expressly includes such character-istics as birth, political opinion, and property,[2] but not disability or sexual orientation. Similarly, the equality guarantee in the Indian Constitution re-sponds to the central role of caste in Indian society, but likewise makes no express mention of sexual orientation or disability. More modern equality guarantees range over new grounds, unforeseeable in earlier decades. The EU Charter of Fundamental Rights includes genetic features as one of four-teen listed grounds,[3] while the UK Equality Act (EA) 2010 includes gender reassignment and civil partnership amongst its list of eight grounds. The South African Constitution has a non-exhaustive list of seventeen grounds, including sex, gender, pregnancy, and marital status; as well as race, ethnic or social origin, colour,[4] religion, conscience, belief, culture, language, and birth. Sexual orientation, age, and disability feature in all three.[5] Even then, there are other contenders for a position in the magic circle of protection. Should HIV status be an independent ground? Should socio-economic dis-advantage or poverty?

Further complex questions quickly emerge. Is it enough for an individual to identify herself as having a particular identity or is it necessary to formu-late objective criteria? Trans people have fought for the right to self-identify,

---

[1] Council Directive 2000/43/EC of 29 June 2000 [2000] OJ L180/22; and Council Directive 2000/78/EC of 27 November 2000 [2000] OJ L303/16.

[2] ECHR, Art 14.

[3] Charter of Fundamental Rights of the European Union, Art 21.

[4] This terminology reflects that used in international human rights law and relevant human rights instruments in other jurisdictions (see British EA 2010, s 9(1)(a); South African Constitution, s 9; Canadian Charter, s 15; International Convention on the Elimination of All Forms of Racial Discrimination, Art 1; ICCPR, Art 2(1); ICESCR, Art 2(2)), which all refer to 'colour' in the list of protected characteristics.

[5] EU Charter, Art 21; EA 2010, s 4; Constitution of South Africa, s 9(3).

while many States insist on objective criteria. In other contexts, this might depend on whether identification brings with it persecution or benefits. Forced ascription of ethnicity has been the basis of racist oppression; while self-identification has been important in preventing States from denying rights of ethnic minorities to retain their culture or language. Also complex is the question of whether all grounds should be considered equally invidious. Are distinctions on the basis of some grounds more invidious than others? It will be seen that there is frequently an inverse relationship between the willingness of judges to extend categories of protection and the strictness with which such distinctions are scrutinized. And how should the law deal with those who belong to more than one specified group, such as Black women?

We could search for a unifying principle which explains existing grounds of discrimination and generates the answers to new questions. Or we could argue that the decision is simply a political one, reflecting the balance of opinion in society at a particular time. If there is no 'right answer' to this question, the real debate concerns which institution is most appropriate to make the decision: the courts or the legislature? On the one hand, the main reason for providing protection for particular groups is their political powerlessness. This suggests that the decision as to which groups should be protected should not lie with the majoritarian political process but the judiciary. On the other hand, judges may not have the legitimacy or competence to make value judgements of this sort. Alternatively, it could be argued that the decision should be taken at the international or regional level. This transcends the particular balance of power in any participating State. However, international human rights law, while binding at the international level, might have relatively little influence on the evolution of equality law or its interpretation at the national level.

In reality, the determination of protected grounds operates as a result of a creative tension between several different sources: political activism, constitutional instruments, statutes, judicial interpretation, and international or regional instruments. Judicial decisions might trigger legislative action. The CJEU, by extending sex discrimination protection to transgender persons, had an effect of this sort.[6] A similar dynamic might operate between supranational and national mechanisms. The EU and ECHR have exerted a key influence on the expansion of protected grounds of discrimination in the UK. This dynamic interaction between different sources goes some way towards

---

[6] Case C-13/94 *P v S and Cornwall County Council* [1996] ECR I-2143. See Chapter 3.

resolving the tension between the needs of minorities to be protected from majoritarianism and the democratic deficiencies of the judiciary.

More radical still is Iris Marion Young's challenge to the very assumption that groups are identified on the basis of apparently fixed attributes. Instead, she argues, a group is better described in terms of a sense of affinity between individuals and a social process of interaction. Moreover, groups intersect so that different groups share some common experiences and even have some common membership. This, in turn, entails a reconceptualization of the notion of difference itself. Instead of difference connoting 'absolute otherness', or deviance from a single norm, difference is about relationships between and within groups. This allows groups to define themselves rather than being subject to a devalued essence imposed from outside.[7] Thus, group membership is conceived of as having fluid boundaries, not dependent on a rigid definition of the group itself. This fluidity has proved difficult to capture in legal forms. At most, small steps have recently been taken in the direction of intersectional or cumulative discrimination affecting a person because she belongs to more than one group.

(i) Defining the Grounds: Three Models

There are three ways in which constitutional or legislative instruments formulate protected grounds of discrimination. The first is by means of an exhaustive list of grounds. Here the choice of ground is made wholly within the political, constitutional, or treaty-making process, with no discretion left to the judges. Grounds can be added or removed only legislatively or by amendment of the constitution or treaty. This 'fixed category' approach is found in both UK domestic and EU anti-discrimination legislation. A second model, at the other end of the spectrum, is to frame a broad, open-textured equality guarantee, stating simply that all persons are equal before the law, without specifying any particular grounds. This approach leaves it to judges to decide when a classification is prohibited under the constitution. It is epitomized by the US Constitution which simply states, in the Fourteenth Amendment, that no State may 'deny to any person within its jurisdiction the equal protection of the laws'.

---

[7] IM Young, *Justice and the Politics of Difference* (Princeton UP 1990) 168–72.

In between these two extremes is the third model, which specifies a list of grounds of discrimination but indicates that the list is not exhaustive, using the terms 'grounds such as', 'including', 'in particular', or 'other status'. This is the approach adopted in the ECHR, the EU Charter of Fundamental Rights, the Canadian Charter of Rights, and the South African Constitution. This approach gives judges some discretion to extend the list according to a set of judicially generated principles; but judicial discretion is shaped by the existence of enumerated grounds. In both the second and third models, courts tend to regard their role as one of determining not just whether to extend protection to a new ground but also how intensely such grounds should be scrutinized. As will be seen, expansion into a new ground is often tempered by a reduction in the intensity of scrutiny. In examining each of these models in this chapter, it is necessary to consider both the determination of grounds and the degree of scrutiny.

Some jurisdictions have a combination of models. Whereas the Fourteenth Amendment of the US Constitution is open-ended, Title VII of the Civil Rights Act 1964, which is at the centre of much of the seminal litigation, utilizes a closed list of grounds. The Indian Constitution has an open-ended equality provision in Article 14, which simply states that the State shall not deny equality before the law or equal protection of the laws to 'any person'. However, the non-discrimination provision in Article 15 uses a closed list, prohibiting discrimination 'on grounds only of religion, race, caste, sex, place of birth or any of them'. Similarly, section 9(1) of the South African Constitution includes a general equality guarantee, stating that: 'Everyone is equal before the law and has the right to equal protection and benefit of the law.' Section 9(3) complements this with a more specific prohibition of unfair discrimination using a non-exhaustive list of grounds. The interaction between these models within the same jurisdiction can be constructive, enhancing both, or give rise to tensions and potential contradictions.

Each model is examined here before turning to the difficult question of whether there is an underlying theoretical coherence. Are there unifying principles which allow us to understand and predict the emergence of grounds, or is this simply a result of the confluence of political, historical, and social factors?

(a) An exhaustive list: specifying the grounds

The first model utilizes an exhaustive set of grounds which cannot be extended by the judiciary, only through legislation or constitutional amendment. This does not, however, mean that courts have no role. Groups which are only marginally outside the delineated boundaries inevitably attempt to persuade courts to recharacterize recognized grounds in order to bring their members within the scope of protection. If sex is protected but not sexual orientation or transsexuality, then members of the latter groups will try to persuade the courts that they are being discriminated against on grounds of sex. If ethnic origin is protected but not religion, then religious groups will claim discrimination on grounds of ethnicity. This results in complex and anomalous distinctions. Such pressures on the boundaries of existing grounds have been endemic in British and EU law and, more recently, in India and Title VII litigation in the US. It is only when these pressures are powerful enough to generate change at the political level that such anomalies can be properly addressed. The result has been that incipient or marginalized groups seeking protection have been able to use both judicial and political means to achieve inclusion. These patterns have been particularly evident in the struggle for inclusion of pregnancy, sexual orientation, and gender identity as grounds of discrimination.

Success has, however, been variable. In some jurisdictions, change has been halting and limited to judicial interpretation. In others, judgments of the apex courts have closely tracked political developments, with the courts advancing the boundaries over some issues and legislative bodies taking the lead in relation to others. This can be seen in the UK and the EU where developments were closely intertwined until 2020 when the UK left the EU. In both jurisdictions, the protected grounds have gradually been expanded by the legislature to respond to a variety of legal and political pressures to incorporate excluded groups. The earliest UK statutes were concerned with gender and race discrimination, with the Sex Discrimination Act 1975 (SDA) covering sex and being married, while the Race Relations Act 1976 (RRA) covered discrimination on grounds of colour, race, nationality, or ethnic or national origins.[8] Discrimination on grounds of religion and political opinion, although prohibited in Northern Ireland, was deliberately excluded from protection in Great Britain.[9] In 1995, after sustained campaigning by disability rights groups, disability discrimination was made unlawful by the Disability Discrimination Act. From 2000, in response to developments in the EU (see later), provisions were enacted piecemeal to provide protection for age, religion and belief, and sexual orientation. The resulting tangle of legislative provision was finally reorganized and pulled together by the EA 2010. Notably,

---

[8] See n 4.
[9] RRA, s 3(1); SDA, ss 1–3; Fair Employment (Northern Ireland) Act 1989, s 49.

too, the opportunity was taken to include pregnancy as a separate ground. The grounds of discrimination, now known as 'protected characteristics', consist of age, disability, gender reassignment, race, religion or belief, sex, sexual orientation, as well as the extra grounds of marriage and civil partnership, and pregnancy and maternity.[10]

The coverage of EU law until the turn of the century had similarly grown in fits and starts. EU anti-discrimination law was initially shaped by the basic imperatives behind the formation of the European Community; namely, the creation of a common market in Europe. From the inception of the Community, therefore, equality as a principle was only relevant insofar as it was needed in the creation of a European-wide labour market.[11] In particular, free movement of labour required a legal prohibition of discrimination by one Member State against the nationals of other Member States. Outside nationality, there was only one area within traditional discrimination law that was considered relevant to the creation of a common market: pay discrimination between men and women. Member States that permitted lower wages for women than men doing the same work would, it was argued, enjoy a competitive advantage over those with equal pay laws.[12] The original treaty therefore created a right to equal pay for equal work for men and women, a right which was to grow into a powerful equality tool.[13] However, the elimination of race discrimination was simply not considered necessary to the project of creating a common market, and indeed raised awkward questions in relation to discrimination against non-EU nationals. As a result, the right not to be discriminated against on grounds of race was conspicuously absent, apart from several soft law initiatives.[14]

Such uneven coverage made it inevitable that excluded groups would attempt to bring themselves within established grounds. This, in turn, necessitated bright-line distinctions between different grounds of discrimination. In particular, the omission of sexual orientation and transsexuality led litigants to argue that discrimination on these grounds was a species of sex

---

[10] EA 2010, ss 4–12.

[11] See eg W Streeck, 'From Market Making to State Building' in S Leibfried and P Pierson (eds), *European Social Policy: Between Fragmentation and Integration* (Brookings Institution 1995) 397.

[12] International Labour Organization, 'Social Aspects of European Economic Co-operation' (1956) 74 International Labour Rev 107.

[13] Article 119 of the Treaty of Rome, which became Art 141 after the Treaty of Amsterdam, now Art 157 after the Treaty of Lisbon.

[14] See eg Joint Declaration on Fundamental Rights [1977] OJ C103/1; Action Plan on the Fight against Racism, COM(1998) 183 final (25 March 1998).

discrimination. The judicial response has been mixed and unpredictable. In the groundbreaking case of *P v S*,[15] the CJEU held that discrimination against transsexuals was a species of sex discrimination. To tolerate discrimination against a transsexual would be tantamount to a failure to respect the dignity and freedom to which they are entitled. More importantly still, the CJEU declared that the Equal Treatment Directive, which established the principle of equal treatment between men and women, was 'simply the expression, in the relevant field, of the principle of equality, which is one of the fundamental principles of Community law'.[16] However, the same court took a very different stance in relation to sexual orientation. In *Grant v South-West Trains Ltd*, it refused to hold that the prohibition of sex discrimination in the Equal Treatment Directive included a prohibition on sexual orientation discrimination.[17]

The impetus to remedy this jagged coverage came in 1998 when, after sustained campaigns by a range of excluded groups, the EU Treaty was amended to give the EU legislative competence in relation to a wider group of grounds. The new legislative competence was swiftly used to pass two new EU directives. The first, 'implementing the principle of equal treatment between persons irrespective of racial or ethnic origin' was adopted in June 2000.[18] The second extended the principle of equal treatment to prevent discrimination on grounds of age, disability, religion, and sexual orientation in relation to employment and vocational training, and was adopted five months later.[19]

A different way of expanding the coverage of grounds in a fixed list is to accept that discrimination on a particular ground is not limited to people who themselves have that characteristic. Particularly important has been the recognition by the CJEU in *Coleman* that the prohibition on grounds of disability not only applies to the person with the disability herself but also to carers and others who suffer discrimination because of their association with a person with a disability.[20] In that case, the Court distinguished between the person with the disability, on the one hand, and the ground of discrimination, or the reason for the detrimental treatment, on the other. The result was that an employee who was the primary carer of her disabled child could

---

[15] *P v S and Cornwall County Council* (n 6).
[16] At para 18. See also Case C-555/07 *Kücükdeveci v Swedex GmbH & Co KG* [2010] 2 CMLR 33 (ECJ); Case C-144/04 *Mangold* [2005] ECR I-9981.
[17] Case C-249/96 *Grant v South-West Trains Ltd* [1998] ECR I-621.
[18] Council Directive 2000/43/EC of 29 June 2000 [2000] OJ L180/22.
[19] Council Directive 2000/78/EC of 27 November 2000 [2000] OJ L303/16.
[20] Case C-303/06 *Coleman v Attridge Law* [2008] ECR I-5603, [2008] IRLR 722 (ECJ).

successfully claim that she had been discriminated against by her employer on grounds of disability. This takes an important step away from a highly individualist view of discrimination and instead situates the person with a disability in the context of her caring relations and surrounding social responsibilities and recognizes that discrimination on grounds of disability can also extend to those relationships.

Similarly, in *Chez*,[21] the CJEU held that discrimination against Roma people could be experienced by a non-Roma person who lived in the same district. In this case, the detrimental policy applied to all inhabitants of the district, regardless of whether they were themselves of Roma origin. The claimant herself did not identify as a Roma. Did this mean that the policy was not 'discrimination on the grounds of ethnic origin'? The Court held that it was not necessary to show that the claimant was discriminated against on grounds of *her* ethnic origin to establish discrimination contrary to the directive. The directive applies to a collective measure irrespective of whether it only affects persons of a certain ethnic origin or also subjects others not of that ethnic origin to the less favourable treatment or particular disadvantage resulting from that measure.[22]

On the other hand, the assumption that there are fixed boundaries between categories within an exhaustive list will continue to raise demarcation disputes. In particular, the attempt to create a bright-line distinction between ethnicity and religion continues to create serious anomalies. This is accentuated by the EU because the Race Directive, which prohibits discrimination on grounds of race and ethnicity, applies not just to employment but also to social protection, including social security and healthcare, social advantages, education, and access to goods and services.[23] Discrimination on grounds of religion or belief, by contrast, is only prohibited in relation to employment-related matters, vocational training, and membership of trade unions or professional organizations.[24] The difficulty in creating clear boundaries between ethnicity and religion has already been starkly demonstrated in the UK in relation to designated 'faith' schools. Such schools are legally permitted to reserve entry, in case of oversubscription, to pupils of the designated faith

---

[21] Case C-83/14 *CHEZ Razpredelenie Bulgaria AD v Komisia za zashtita ot diskriminatsia* [2016] 1 CMLR 14 (CJEU (Grand Chamber)).

[22] ibid para 60.

[23] Council Directive 2000/43/EC implementing the principle of equal treatment between persons irrespective of racial or ethnic origin, Art 3.

[24] Council Directive 2000/78/EC establishing a general framework for equal treatment in employment and occupation, Art 3.

without being guilty of a breach of the prohibition on religious discrimination. However, in the *JFS* case, a designated Jewish faith school was found to have discriminated on grounds of race (which includes ethnic origin) when it refused to admit a pupil who was not regarded as Jewish by Jewish orthodox rules. This was because the UK Supreme Court held that the ancient Jewish rule that a person is Jewish if their mother is Jewish or has converted to Judaism is not a religious but an ethnic rule. By a five to four majority, the Court held that because Jewish law as to who is Jewish is based on descent rather than practise of the faith, this was not a distinction on grounds of religion but of ethnic origin. It therefore constituted unlawful race discrimination.[25] As Lord Brown stated in his dissent: 'The difficulty in the case arises because of the obvious overlap here between the concepts respectively of religious and racial discrimination.'[26] Indeed, he continued:

> the Court of Appeal's judgment insists on a non-Jewish definition of who is Jewish . . . The root question for the court is simply this: can a Jewish faith school ever give preference to those who are members of the Jewish religion under Jewish law. I would answer: yes, it can. To hold the contrary would be to stigmatise Judaism as a directly racially discriminating religion. I would respectfully disagree with that conclusion. Indeed I would greatly regret it.[27]

In fact, the real concern of the case was a dispute as between Orthodox and other sects of Judaism in relation to what kinds of conversion were acceptable. The complainant and his mother had been converted to Judaism under the non-Orthodox Mazorti tradition, which was not recognized under Orthodox Judaism. Therefore, as Lord Brown recognized, 'the differential treatment between Jews recognised by the [Chief Rabbi] of Orthodox Jewry and those not so recognised within the wider group of ethnic Jews . . . is plainly on the ground of religion rather than race.'[28] The result of the decision has been that the Jewish Free School and other schools designated as Orthodox Jewish faith schools now require evidence of outward manifestations of the Jewish faith, which goes against the essence of the Jewish understanding of Jewish identity.

While legislative developments in the UK and the EU have somewhat relieved the pressure on the courts to expand existing categories, this has not

---

[25] *R (E) v Governing Body of JFS* [2009] UKSC 15.
[26] ibid [243].
[27] ibid [248].
[28] ibid [245].

been the case in other jurisdictions with fixed lists, particularly under Title VII of the Civil Rights Act in the US, and Article 15 of the Indian Constitution. In both these jurisdictions, the contestation has centred on sexual orientation and gender identity. Title VII prohibits employment-related discrimination in relation to 'race, color, religion, sex, or national origin'. Sexual orientation and gender identity are notably absent. Can 'sex', then, be construed to include claims of employment discrimination by gay or transgender people? In the 2020 case of *Bostock v Clayton County*, the US Supreme Court held that it could.[29] Gorsuch J, giving the judgment of the Court, was unequivocal: 'An employer who fires an individual for being homosexual or transgender fires that person for traits or actions it would not have questioned in members of a different sex. Sex plays a necessary and undisguisable role in the decision, exactly what Title VII forbids'.[30] Notably, his decision was not based on an understanding of sexuality as biological. Instead, the role of sex lay in the comparison between the treatment of a man and a woman: a man who was sexually attracted to men was treated differently from a woman who was sexually attracted to men. 'Homosexuality and transgender status are inextricably bound up with sex. Not because homosexuality or transgender status are related to sex in some vague sense or because discrimination on these bases has some disparate impact on one sex or another, but because to discriminate on these grounds requires an employer to intentionally treat individual employees differently because of their sex'.[31]

Three key elements contributed to this important outcome. First, Gorsuch J held that as long as sex is one causative factor, discrimination on grounds of sex is established. It makes no difference if other factors besides the plaintiff's sex, such as their sexual orientation, contribute to the decision. 'When an employer fires an employee because she is homosexual or transgender, two causal factors may be in play—*both* the individual's sex *and* something else (the sex to which the individual is attracted or with which the individual identifies). But Title VII doesn't care. If an employer would not have discharged an employee but for that individual's sex, the statute's causation standard is met, and liability may attach'.[32] A different result might have been reached if Congress had specified that the discrimination must be 'solely' on ground of sex, or even 'primarily because of' the plaintiff's sex. But Congress

---

[29] *Bostock v Clayton County* 140 S Ct 1731 (2020) (US Sup Ct).
[30] ibid 1737.
[31] ibid 1742.
[32] ibid 1742.

did not do so. Secondly, Gorsuch J held that Title VII's emphasis is on the individual not the group. It is therefore irrelevant to the particular claim that the employer treats women as a group in the same way as men as a group. The statute is violated when the employer intentionally relies on the individual employee's sex when deciding to dismiss them. The third striking element is Gorsuch J's finding that his conclusion was based on an interpretation of the terms of Title VII 'in accord with their ordinary public meaning at the time of their enactment'.[33] He conceded that those who adopted the Act might not have anticipated this result. 'But the limits of the drafters' imagination supply no reason to ignore the law's demands. . . . Only the written word is the law, and all persons are entitled to its benefit'.[34]

The result is a crucial breakthrough in the protection for LGBTQI+ people against discrimination in employment. In January 2021, President Biden issued an Executive Order[35] declaring that the reasoning in *Bostock* applies to other federal laws prohibiting discrimination 'because of sex' including in relation to education, housing, and immigration and nationality.[36] Notably, although the judgment in *Bostock* itself is seemingly predicated on an assumption of gender binaries, referring to gay and trans people, the Executive Order uses the terminology of gender identity. 'It is the policy of my Administration,' states the Order, 'to prevent and combat discrimination on the basis of gender identity or sexual orientation, and to fully enforce Title VII and other laws that prohibit discrimination on the basis of gender identity or sexual orientation'.[37] Similarly, despite the fact that Gorsuch J was keen to stress that the judgment says nothing about sex-segregated bathrooms and locker rooms, the Executive Order is clear that children should be able to learn 'without worrying about whether they will be denied access to the restroom, the locker room, or school sports'.[38]

The hope is that this puts the judgment in *Bostock* on a steadier footing than in other jurisdictions where the outcome depended not on the fact that sex was one of several causative factors, but on how the comparator was characterized. In the ECJ case of *Grant v South-West Trains*,[39] the employer

---

[33] ibid 1738.

[34] ibid 1737.

[35] Executive Order 13988 of 20 January 2021 <www.federalregister.gov/documents/2021/01/25/2021-01761/preventing-and-combating-discrimination-on-the-basis-of-gender-identity-or-sexual-orientation> accessed 27 July 2022.

[36] Education Amendments of 1972, Title IX; Fair Housing Act; and Immigration and Nationality Act, s 412.

[37] Executive Order 13988 of 20 January 2021.

[38] ibid. See also Chapter 3.

[39] Case C-249/96 *Grant v South-West Trains Ltd* [1998] IRLR 206 (ECJ).

refused to grant the same travel benefits to its employees' same-sex partners that it granted to opposite-sex couples. Ms Grant argued that as a woman living with a woman, she had been treated less favourably than a comparable man living with a woman. Looked at from the perspective of this comparison, this could clearly be regarded as discrimination based on sex. However, the Court chose a different comparison; namely, between male same-sex couples and female same-sex couples. 'Thus travel concessions are refused to a male worker if he is living with a person of the same sex, just as they are to a female worker if she is living with a person of the same sex.'[40] This led it to conclude that 'since the condition imposed by the undertaking's regulations applies in the same way to female and male workers, it cannot be regarded as constituting discrimination directly based on sex'.[41] This suggests that a better route is to include an express reference to sexual orientation and gender identity through an amendment to the legislation, as happened in the EU (see earlier).

This raises the question of how much further the closed list in Title VII can be expanded. The finding in *Bostock* entails that wherever a discriminatory criterion imposed by an employer is in part based on sex, it will be capable of inclusion in Title VII. In *Bostock*, Gorsuch J referred to other possibilities, some of which have already been established in case law. In *Phillips v Martin Marietta*,[42] the Court found that an employer had violated Title VII by refusing to hire women with young children, although it did hire women without children as well as men with children of the same age. On one view, the policy did not depend on sex per se but on motherhood, a non-protected trait. However, it was no defence to Title VII to argue that an employer intentionally discriminated against an individual only in part because of sex. Similarly, in *Oncale*,[43] the Court held that workplace harassment could violate Title VII's prohibition against 'discrimination because of sex' when both the harasser and the harassed employee are of the same sex. Taking the same approach to statutory interpretation as Gorsuch J two decades later, Scalia J stated: 'Male-on-male sexual harassment in the workplace was assuredly not the principal evil Congress was concerned with when it enacted Title VII. But statutory prohibitions often go beyond the principal evil to cover reasonably comparable evils, and it is ultimately the provisions of our laws rather than

---

[40] ibid para 27.
[41] ibid para 28.
[42] *Phillips v Martin Marietta* 400 US 542 (1971) (US Sup Ct).
[43] *Oncale v Sundowner Offshore Services* 523 US 75 (1998) (US Sup Ct).

the principal concerns of our legislators by which we are governed.'[44] It has been suggested that a similar analysis might be applied to other grounds protected against discrimination by Title VII. In particular, it has been argued that caste discrimination, which is increasingly visible in the US, might now be characterized as 'because of' race, religion or national origin.[45] This possibility has also been raised in the UK, where an Employment Appeal Tribunal (EAT) held that caste fell within the concept of 'ethnic origins' under the EA 2010.[46] Here, too, a preferable option would be an express legislative amendment to include caste.[47]

There have been similar contestations over the boundaries of prohibited grounds in relation to the closed list of grounds found in Articles 15 and 16 of the Indian Constitution. Article 15(1) provides that 'the State shall not discriminate against any citizen on grounds only of religion, race, caste, sex, place of birth or any of them'. Article 15(2) protects against discrimination in relation to public places using the same set of grounds. Article 16(2), which prohibits discrimination in respect of State employment, extends the list somewhat to include descent and residence. Notably absent are sexual orientation, disability, and age, as well as pregnancy and marital status. On the other hand, the list is distinctive in including caste.

On the face of it, these lists of prohibited grounds appear to be emphatically closed. The phrase 'on the grounds only of' the listed characteristics seems to preclude judicial expansion. In the 1981 case of *Air India v Nergesh Meerza*, the Indian Supreme Court construed this phrase even more narrowly. Taking a different direction from that of Gorsuch J in *Bostock*, the Court stated: 'What Article 15(1) and 16(2) lay down is that discrimination should not be made only and only on the ground of sex. These Articles do not prohibit the State from making discrimination on the ground of sex coupled with other considerations.'[48] On this basis, the Court held that to dismiss airhostesses if they married within the first four years of service was not discrimination on grounds only of sex, even though it applied only to women, but rather of sex and time of marriage.

---

[44] ibid 79.

[45] C Krishnaswami and G Krishnamurthi, 'Title VII and Caste Discrimination' (2021) 134 Harv L Rev 456.

[46] *Chandhok v Tirkey* [2015] ICR 527 (UK EAT).

[47] Krishnaswami and Krishnamurthi (n 45); Michael Ford, 'The Long and Winding Road of Caste Legislation in the UK' (*Oxford Human Rights Hub Blog*, 5 September 2018) <https://ohrh. law.ox.ac.uk/the-long-and-winding-road-of-caste-legislation-in-the-uk> accessed 27 July 2022.

[48] *Air India v Nergesh Meerza* (1981) 4 SCC 335. See I Jaising, 'Gender Justice and the Supreme Court' in B Kirpal and others (eds), *Supreme but not Infallible* (OUP 2000) 296.

However, as in the other jurisdictions, these boundaries have been contested by excluded groups, particularly in relation to sexual orientation and gender identity. An important step forward was taken by the Indian Supreme Court in 2014 in *NALSA*, where it held that discrimination on grounds of 'sex' in Articles 15 and 16 includes discrimination on grounds of gender identity. Radhakrishnan J held that 'gender identity refers to each person's deeply felt internal and individual experience of gender, which may or may not correspond with the sex assigned at birth'.[49] Recognizing that 'both gender and biological attributes constitute distinct components of sex,' he held that the expression 'sex' in Articles 15 and 16 is therefore not 'limited to biological sex of male or female, but intended to include people who consider themselves to be neither male nor female'.[50]

Much more contested has been the question of whether sexual orientation is also included. Central to this contestation has been section 377 of the Indian Penal Code, which criminalized 'carnal intercourse against the order of nature'. In the groundbreaking case of *Naz Foundation*,[51] the Delhi High Court held that section 377 breached Article 15(1) insofar as it criminalized consensual sexual acts of adults in private. The court used a purposive construction to hold that sexual orientation was analogous to sex as a ground of discrimination. However, four years later in *Koushal*, a two-judge bench of the Indian Supreme Court reversed this decision and reinstated section 377. The Court's reasoning on Article 15 was scanty, relying primarily on the fact that LGBTQI+ persons constitute a 'miniscule fraction of the country's population, and therefore this could not be a sound basis for declaring section 377 ultra vires'.[52]

It took several more Supreme Court decisions to lay a pathway to reinstating the *Naz* decision. Finally, in *Navtej Singh Johar*, a five-judge bench of the Supreme Court unanimously decided that section 377 should be read down to exclude consensual sexual relationships between adults in private. Chandrachud J held that discrimination based on sexual orientation is discrimination based on sex and therefore falls within section 15. But the route to this conclusion was very different to that of Gorsuch J in *Bostock*. Instead, Chandrachud J focused on stereotypes associated with gender roles. Any

---

[49] *National Legal Services Authority v Union of India* (2014) 5 SCC 438, para 19 (Indian Sup Ct).
[50] ibid para 59.
[51] *Naz Foundation v Government of NCT of Delhi*, WP(C) No 7455/2001, 2 July 2009 (High Ct of Delhi).
[52] *Suresh Kumar Koushal v Naz Foundation* (2014) 1 SCC 1, para 43 (Indian Sup Ct).

distinction founded on a stereotypical understanding of the role of sex, he held, will constitute discrimination on the grounds only of sex as prohibited by Article 15(1).[53] He thus decisively overruled *Nergesh Meerza* which, by purporting to exclude distinctions in which sex was only one factor, failed to grasp the stereotypes embedded in the marriage bar applicable only to women.[54] Stereotypical assumptions about gender roles were also at the root of section 377, which criminalized 'behaviour which does not conform to the heterosexual expectations of society'.[55] This led Chandrachud J to the clear conclusion that 'one cannot simply separate discrimination based on sexual orientation and discrimination based on sex because discrimination based on sexual orientation inherently promulgates ideas about stereotypical notions of sex and gender roles'.[56] The US Supreme Court has in fact recognized the corrosive role of stereotypes in its jurisprudence on discrimination against women.[57] However, it declined to follow this route in *Bostock*.

(b) An open-textured model: leaving it to the judiciary

The second model is at the opposite end of the spectrum. Instead of an exhaustive list of categories, this approach is based on an open-ended constitutional equality guarantee. This is epitomized by the Fourteenth Amendment of the US Constitution, which simply states that no State may 'deny to any person within its jurisdiction the equal protection of the laws'. In principle, then, any classification whatsoever may be challenged, be it a welfare law providing specific protection to vulnerable members of society or one that unduly burdens a group for reasons of pure prejudice. The only way in which the breadth of this provision can be handled is by adjusting the intensity of judicial scrutiny. In practice, then, the question of which classifications are illegitimate is determined by the judiciary through its power to decide how closely to scrutinize a legislative or other classification.

It is in this sense that the US Supreme Court has taken on itself the full responsibility of determining protected groups. To do this, it has developed the well-known double standard of scrutiny. In relation to most classifications, the Court will defer to the legislature, expecting the State to show only that the classification is 'rationally related' to a legitimate State interest. However, 'strict scrutiny' will be applied to legislative classifications which

---

[53] *Navtej Singh Johar v Union of India* (2018) 10 SCC 1, para 438 (Indian Sup Ct).
[54] ibid paras 437, 439.
[55] ibid para 447.
[56] ibid para 450.
[57] *Price Waterhouse v Hopkins* 490 US 228 (1989) (US Sup Ct).

impermissibly interfere with the exercise of a fundamental right or operate to the particular disadvantage of a particular group, or 'suspect class'. Strict scrutiny differs from rational review in that the classification must further not just a legitimate but a compelling State interest. Moreover, rather than being rationally related to that interest, the classification must be 'narrowly tailored' to achieve it, in the sense that no other alternatives are available. Classifications attracting the deferent rationality standard of scrutiny almost invariably pass muster, whereas strict scrutiny almost invariably leads to the measure being struck down. In determining which groups count as suspect classes, the Court has therefore been at the forefront of the development of protected grounds of discrimination law under the US Constitution.

It was in relation to racism that the most dramatic developments occurred in the jurisprudence of the Court. Early cases applied a mere rationality standard to blatantly racist classifications. In the notorious case of *Plessy v Ferguson*,[58] the Court held that laws segregating Black people and white people did not breach the equality guarantee. The leading judgment held that the State had every right to use classifications, as long as the classification was not capricious, arbitrary, or unreasonable. Although the segregation (in this case of train carriages) was clearly part of a widespread set of laws aimed at reinforcing the power structure which elevated white people and stigmatized Black people, the Court held that the government had done its duty by securing equal rights for all of its citizens. 'If one race be inferior to the other socially, the Constitution of the United States cannot put them upon the same plane.'[59]

It was thus of enormous historical significance when the Court eventually recognized the perniciousness of racial classifications. In a seminal case concerning the internship of Japanese citizens during the Second World War, the Court held: 'Legal restrictions which curtail the civil rights of a single racial group are immediately suspect . . . Courts must subject them to the most rigid scrutiny.'[60] Although this, in principle, leaves open the possibility of justification of a racial classification, in practice the strict scrutiny test has almost invariably led to the Court striking down racial classifications operating to the detriment of African Americans.[61] This was reiterated in the more recent case of *Johnson v California*,[62] where the Court was invited to make an

---

[58] *Plessy v Ferguson* 163 US 537, 16 S Ct 1138 (1896).

[59] 163 US 537, 552.

[60] *Korematsu v United States* 323 US 214, 65 S Ct 193, 216 (1944).

[61] See eg *McLaughlin v Florida* 379 US 184, 85 S Ct 283 (1964); *Loving v Virginia* 388 US 1, 87 S Ct 1817 (1967).

[62] *Johnson v California* 125 S Ct 1141 (2005) (US Sup Ct).

exception to the rule that strict scrutiny applies to all racial classifications on the grounds that deference to the particular expertise of prison officials requires a more relaxed standard of review. In this case, an African American inmate of a Californian prison challenged the California Department of Correction's unwritten policy of racially segregating prisoners. The respondent argued that this was necessary to prevent violence caused by racial gangs. The Supreme Court refused to relax the standard of review. All racial classifications, whether in prison or not, should be subject to strict scrutiny.

In the result, however, only alienage, race, and national origin have qualified for strict scrutiny. Indeed, the Court has been deeply resistant to attempts to expand strict scrutiny beyond these grounds. For most other grounds, rational basis has been deemed sufficient. Thus, when a classification based on age was challenged before the Supreme Court, its decision to subject it merely to rational scrutiny meant that age discrimination would go largely untouched by Fourteenth Amendment protection. In *Massachusetts v Murgia*,[63] the Court upheld a Massachusetts law which required uniformed State police officers to retire at the age of fifty. Protection of the public by assuring the physical preparedness of its uniformed police was a legitimate State interest, and a maximum age of fifty was a rational means of doing so. This is, in practice, a very deferent standard. States may rely on age as a proxy for other qualities, even where this proves inaccurate in any individual case.[64] In *Murgia*, the Court acknowledged that the complainant himself was in good physical health and could still perform his duties. But the age bar was still held to meet the rational-basis standard. 'That the State chooses not to determine fitness more precisely through individualized testing after age 50 [does not prove] that the objective of assuring physical fitness is not rationally furthered by a maximum-age limitation.'[65] Similarly, a provision in the Missouri Constitution that judges should retire at seventy was upheld even though the Court acknowledged that the generalization about the effect of old age on judges' abilities was 'far from true' and 'may not be true at all'.[66]

The rigid classification of grounds into those attracting strict scrutiny and those which are only subject to a rationality analysis has been criticized by Marshall J in a series of dissenting judgments. Because strict scrutiny invariably results in the Court striking down the classification, he argued, it has:

---

[63] *Massachusetts Board of Retirement v Murgia* 427 US 307 (1976) (US Sup Ct).
[64] *Kimel v Florida Board of Regents* 528 US 62, 84 (2000) (US Sup Ct).
[65] *Massachusetts Board of Retirement v Murgia* (n 63) 316.
[66] *Gregory v Ashcroft* 501 US 452, 453 (1991) (US Sup Ct).

lost interest in recognizing further 'fundamental' rights and 'suspect' classes . . . It should be no surprise . . . that the Court is hesitant to expand the number of categories of rights and classes subject to strict scrutiny, when each expansion involves the invalidation of virtually every classification bearing upon a newly covered category.[67]

This is particularly problematic in the context of affirmative action, or race-based preferences instituted to counteract previous disadvantage. As we shall see in Chapter 7, the Court takes a strictly symmetrical approach to discrimination on grounds of race, holding that both invidious discrimination and discrimination designed to compensate for past disadvantage should be subject to strict scrutiny.

Meanwhile, the Court has created some flexibility for itself by varying the intensity of review within the rationality standard. In particular, there is some evidence of what has been called a heightened rationality review in some contexts. In *Cleburne*,[68] the Court held that disability discrimination should be subject only to rationality review. Nevertheless, the discriminatory provision was struck down because it evidenced prejudice against people with learning difficulties. Similarly, in *Plyler v Doe*,[69] the Court invalidated a provision denying education to children of undocumented immigrants as falling below its standard of rational review.

This pattern has been particularly evident in relation to gender discrimination. In earlier cases, such as the exclusion of women from compulsory jury service, it was held that there was no parallel between sex and race discrimination. This meant that strict scrutiny did not apply. As long as any 'basis in reason' could be conceived for the discrimination, there was no violation of equal protection.[70] The reasons given for this conclusion simply show up the continuing prejudices of the judiciary. Thus, it was stated that sex discrimination differed from race discrimination because there was no history of prejudice against women. A good enough reason for differentiating, according to Harlan J, was that:

> Despite the enlightened emancipation of women from the restrictions and protections of bygone years, and their entry into many parts of community life

[67] ibid 318–19, there citing *San Antonio School District v Rodriguez* 411 US 1, 98–110, 93 S Ct 1278, 1330 (1973); and *Frontiero v Richardson* 411 US 677, 93 S Ct 1764 (1973).
[68] *Cleburne v Cleburne Living Center* 473 US 432 (1985) (US Sup Ct).
[69] *Plyler v Doe* 457 US 202 (1982) (US Sup Ct).
[70] See eg *Goesart v Cleary* 335 US 464, 69 S Ct 198 (1948).

formerly considered to be reserved to men, woman is still regarded as the centre of home and family life.[71]

In 1971, for the first time, the US Supreme Court ruled in favour of a woman who complained that her State had denied her the equal protection of its laws.[72] Nevertheless, the Court has consistently refused to regard gender classifications as suspect. Instead of requiring the most intense scrutiny, as applied to race, an 'intermediate' test is applied.[73] As reformulated in *US v Virginia* in 1996, this test requires the State to produce a justification which is 'exceedingly persuasive'.[74] This means that the State must show that the discriminatory classification is substantially related to the achievement of important governmental objectives. Ginsburg J in the *Virginia* case took care to draw a bright line between the rational-review standard and the heightened scrutiny appropriate for gender. Thus, whereas under rational-basis review, the defender of the classification is under no obligation to produce evidence to support its rationality, heightened review places a demanding burden of justification on the defender. In addition, the justification must be genuine, not invented post hoc in response to litigation. Particularly importantly, it cannot rely on 'over-broad generalisations about the different talents, capacities or preferences of males and females'.[75] Finally, under heightened scrutiny, the discriminatory means must be 'substantially related' to an actual and important governmental interest. In other words, whereas the availability of other suitable means is irrelevant in relation to rational-basis review, the availability of sex-neutral alternatives to a sex-based classification is of key importance in determining the validity of the classification.

On one level, the more flexible standard in relation to women is defensible. This is because it makes it possible to accommodate the more asymmetric understanding of equality law set out in Chapter 1. This was articulated by Ginsburg J, who saw the lesser standard as providing an opportunity to frame legislation which positively promoted equal opportunities for women, while striking down legislation based on overbroad generalizations about different talents, capacities, or preferences of men and women. Ginsburg J made it clear that sex classifications can be used to compensate women for particular

---

[71] *Hoyt v Florida* 368 US 57, 61–2, 82 S Ct 159 (1961).
[72] *Reed v Reed* 404 US 71, 92 S Ct 251 (1971).
[73] *Craig v Boren* 429 US 190, 97 S Ct 451 (1976); *Orr v Orr* 440 US 268, 99 S Ct 1102 (1979); *Michael M v Superior Court, Sonoma Cty* 450 US 464, 101 S Ct 1200 (1981).
[74] *United States v Virginia* 116 S Ct 2264 (1996).
[75] ibid 533.

economic disabilities or to develop their talents and capacities fully. But they cannot be used to perpetuate the legal, social, and economic inferiority of women.[76]

However, it has been difficult to maintain an intermediate position which does not subtly slide into mere rational review. In the 2001 case of *Nguyen*, a majority of the US Supreme Court rejected a challenge to immigration rules which permitted unmarried mothers giving citizenship to their children without further proof, while requiring unmarried fathers to prove patrimony before the child was eighteen. Nguyen had lived with his American father for most his life, but the latter had not taken the requisite steps before he turned eighteen. By a five to four majority, and over a blistering dissent by O'Connor J, the Court held that the additional requirements were substantially related to the important government objectives of ensuring reliable proof of the biological relationship between the father and child, and ensuring that the child and parent had the opportunity to develop real, everyday ties.[77] As O'Connor J argued, the majority recited the standard of heightened review but applied a standard much closer to that of rational-basis review. Thus, instead of taking seriously the possibility of a sex-neutral alternative, the majority simply declared that the requirement was a reasonable choice among several mechanisms and that there was no requirement that Congress choose one rather than the other. This relies on a stereotype; namely, that mothers are significantly more likely than fathers to develop relationships with their children; and by doing so, perpetuate it. Application of the stereotype carries with it a particular pathos in this case, where the father had indeed been the primary carer of his son for almost all his life.

In *Sessions v Morales-Santana*, Justice Ginsburg took the opportunity to reassert the more exacting standard she had established in *Virginia* while at the same time piercing the stereotypes at the foundation of much of US law on the acquisition of citizenship. This case concerned the transmission of US citizenship to a child born abroad, where one parent is a US citizen and the other is not. Here, too, the law drew a distinction between unmarried US citizen mothers and fathers. Unmarried US citizen mothers could transmit citizenship to a child born abroad if they had lived continuously in the US for one year prior to the child's birth. On the other hand, unmarried US citizenship fathers could only transmit citizenship if they had had ten years'

---

[76]   ibid text to nn 6 and 7.
[77]   Note that the case was decided under the Equal Protection Clause of the Fifth Amendment, which relies on substantially similar precedents to the Fourteenth Amendment.

physical presence in the US prior to the child's birth. Justice Ginsburg had no hesitation in recognizing the stereotypes and 'overbroad generalizations about the different talents, capacities or preferences of males and females' in the legislation.[78] Successful defence of such legislation requires 'exceedingly persuasive justification', a standard the government failed to meet. The government's rationale, she held, 'conforms to the long-held view that unwed fathers care little about, indeed are strangers, to their children'.[79] It may be true that overbroad generalizations are descriptive of the ways in which many people order their lives. However, to afford or deny benefits on the basis of such generalization 'may create a self-fulfilling cycle of discrimination that forces women to continue to assume the role of primary family caregiver. Correspondingly, such laws may disserve men who exercise responsibility for raising their children.'[80] Thus, the Court 'did something it had never done before, in an opinion that develops a progressive vision of gender equality for the non-marital family',[81] a step of crucial importance given the deference the Court usually grants to immigration laws. However, there remains some doubt about the extent to which the 'exceedingly persuasive' justification standard will endure. Rather than overruling *Nguyen*, the Court distinguished it, on the basis that the paternal acknowledgement requirement in that case could be described as minimal.[82] Moreover, the Court opted for a levelling-down remedy, by removing the exception for unmarried mothers rather than extending it to unmarried fathers.

It is against this background that campaigners have long argued for an amendment to the US Constitution which expressly provides for equality on grounds of sex. Known as the Equal Rights Amendment, or ERA, the proposed amendment states: 'Equality of rights under the law shall not be denied or abridged by the United States or any State on account of sex.' Such an amendment would also give Congress the power to pass legislation to enforce the constitutional guarantee. The ERA started on the long and tortuous road to ratification as long ago as 1972.[83] Having been passed by Congress, it required ratification by thirty-eight States within ten years. Although it came

---

[78] *Sessions v Morales-Santana* 137 S Ct 1678, 1692 (2017) (US Sup Ct), citing *US v Virginia* 518 US 515, 533 (1996) (US Sup Ct).

[79] *Sessions v Morales-Santana* ibid 1696.

[80] ibid 1693.

[81] K Collins, 'Equality, Sovereignty, and the Family in *Morales-Santana*' (2017) 131 Harv L Rev 170, 171.

[82] *Sessions v Morales-Santana* (n 78) 1694.

[83] Article V of the US Constitution provides that amendments become law when Congress votes to propose an amendment and it is ratified by three-fourths of the States.

tantalizingly close to achieving its goal, the period expired in 1982 with the total falling short by three States. Nevertheless, the campaign has continued. In January 2020, Virginia became the thirty-eighth State to ratify the ERA, following Nevada in 2017 and Illinois in 2018. Meanwhile, the US House of Representatives has passed a resolution to remove the original time limit but a similar resolution in the Senate was still pending at time of writing. However, this does not mean that the Amendment will succeed. Five States have now voted to rescind their earlier ratifications, although there is authority to the effect that rescissions are not valid. Litigation continues on various issues. There is clearly still a distance to traverse before the Amendment finally makes it into the Constitution.

Other grounds of discrimination remain contested. This is particularly true of sexual orientation. Indeed, the US Supreme Court refused, until very recently, to insist even on formal equality before the law. In the notorious case of *Bowers v Hardwick*[84] in 1986, by a narrow majority of five to four, the Court refused to strike down sodomy laws, which effectively made homosexuality a criminal offence. Strict scrutiny, the majority held, was only applicable in relation to a suspect class or for breach of a fundamental right. Because it held that the Constitution did not confer a fundamental right upon homosexuals to engage in sodomy, strict scrutiny was not appropriate and the sodomy laws were not struck down.

It was not until 2003 that this decision was reversed. In *Lawrence v Texas*,[85] a Texan statute prohibiting same-sex sexual activity was struck down. Giving the judgment of the Court, Kennedy J stated:

> To say that the issue in *Bowers* was simply the right to engage in certain sexual conduct demeans the claim the individual put forward . . . Although the laws involved in *Bowers* and here purport to do no more than prohibit a particular sexual act, their penalties and purposes have more far-reaching consequences, touching upon the most private human conduct, sexual behaviour, and in the most private of places, the home.[86]

Notably, however, the majority rejected the invitation to decide the case under the equal protection clause of the Fourteenth Amendment. This was because, taking a formal view of equality as requiring no more than

---

[84] *Bowers v Hardwick* 478 US 186 (1986).
[85] *Lawrence v Texas* 539 US 558, 123 S Ct 247 (2003).
[86] ibid 567.

consistent treatment, it did not regard equality as sufficiently robust to over-turn the *Bowers* precedent:

> Were we to hold the statute invalid under the Equal Protection Clause some might question whether a prohibition would be valid if drawn differently, say, to prohibit the conduct both between same-sex and different-sex participants.[87]

Instead, it relied on the guarantee of liberty from State intervention, found in the due process clause which is coupled with equal protection in the Fourteenth Amendment. Only O'Connor J held the sodomy laws to be un-constitutional because of a breach of the equality guarantee, on the grounds that the statute only prohibited homosexual and not opposite-sex sodomy. Nevertheless, Kennedy J regarded a decision on the liberty right as advancing both liberty and equality:

> When homosexual conduct is made criminal by the law of the State, that declaration in and of itself is an invitation to subject homosexual persons to discrimination both in the public and the private spheres.[88]

The route to equality via liberty was further developed by Kennedy J in the groundbreaking case of *Obergefell*,[89] where the US Supreme Court, by a narrow majority of five to four, struck down laws prohibiting same-sex mar-riage. Rather than locating the issue in the jurisprudence of suspect classes, Kennedy J focused on the exercise of a fundamental right, here the right to marry. The dynamic between liberty and equality, he held, was reflected in the Court's cases on the right to marry, from *Loving v Virginia*,[90] which struck down the prohibition on interracial marriage, to cases invalidating in-vidious sex-based classifications in marriage. 'The reasons why marriage is a fundamental right,' he stated, 'became more clear and compelling from a full awareness and understanding of the hurt that resulted from laws bar-ring interracial unions. Indeed, in interpreting the Equal Protection Clause, the Court has recognized that new insights and societal understandings can reveal unjustified inequality within our most fundamental institutions that once passed unnoticed and unchallenged.'[91] The exclusion of same-sex couples from the institution of marriage not only results in denial of the ma-terial benefits linked to marriage. It also demeans same-sex couples[92] and

---

[87] ibid 575.
[88] ibid 575.
[89] *Obergefell v Hodges* 576 US 644 (2015) (US Sup Ct).
[90] *Loving v Virginia* 388 US 1 (1967) (US Sup Ct).
[91] *Obergefell v Hodges* (n 89).
[92] The judgment uses the terminology of 'same sex couples' and not LGBTQI+.

'serves to disrespect and subordinate them'. Thus, rather than being an ad-
junct to the liberty right, *Obergefell* establishes that the exclusion of same-sex
couples from the right to marry—a fundamental right 'inherent in the liberty of the person'—breaches both the liberty right and the equal protection
clause in the Fourteenth Amendment of the US Constitution.

The *Obergefell* case, therefore, continued the trajectory whereby judicial intervention in relation to sexual orientation has occurred outside the
framework of strict scrutiny, rational review, or the intermediate standard.[93]
However, a different path, via gender equality, may well have been opened up
by *Sessions v Morales*. By holding that 'distinctions based on a parent's marital
status . . . are subject to the same heightened scrutiny as distinctions based
on gender,'[94] the *Morales* case makes it possible to challenge laws that privilege biological parenthood. This is of particular significance for same-sex
couples.[95]

A different trajectory can be seen in relation to the open-ended equality
guarantee in Article 14 of the Indian Constitution. Traditionally, Article
14 has been formulated as merely a rationality check on distinctions introduced by government. As the Court put it in a case in 1955: 'It is now well-
established that while Article 14 forbids class legislation, it does not forbid
reasonable classification for the purposes of legislation.'[96] To pass muster,
therefore, the classification should be based on 'intelligible differentia' and it
should have a rational relationship with the statute's objective.[97] Courts were,
however, aware that 'overemphasis on the doctrine of classification or an
anxious and sustained attempt to discover some basis for classification may
gradually and imperceptibly deprive the Article of its glorious content'.[98] This
led to the evolution of the test of arbitrariness. As Baghwati J put it: 'Equality
and arbitrariness are sworn enemies . . . Where an act is arbitrary it is implicit
in it that it is unequal both according to political logic and constitutional
law . . . Articles 14 and 16 strike at arbitrariness in state action and ensure
fairness and equality of treatment.'[99]

---

[93] *Romer v Evans* 517 US 620, 116 S Ct 1620, 1623 (1996).

[94] *Sessions v Morales-Santana* (n 78) 1700.

[95] Collins (n 81) 202.

[96] *Budhan Choudhry v The State of Bihar* 1955 SCR (1) 1045, 1049; see also *State of West
Bengal v Anwar Ali* (1952) SCR 284; *RK Dalmia v Justice Tendulkar* (1959) SCR 279; *Chiranjit Lal
Chowduri v Union of India* AIR 1951 SC 41; *DD Joshi v Union of India* AIR 1983 SC 420.

[97] ibid.

[98] *Lachhman Das v State of Punjab* (1963) 2 SCR 353, 395 (Indian Sup Ct).

[99] *EP Royappa v State of Tamil Nadu* 1974 SCR (2) 348, 386 (Indian Sup Ct).

Manifest arbitrariness, however, at least on the face of it, does not appear to constitute a particularly searching standard. To achieve the high ideals various judges have attached to equality, therefore, Article 14 would need to be infused with some more substantial value commitments. Chandrachud J recognized this in *Navtej Singh Johar*: 'The problem with the classification test [in Article 14] is that what constitutes a reasonable classification is reduced to a mere formula: the quest for an intelligible differentia and the rational nexus to the object sought to be achieved. In doing so, the test of classification risks elevating form over substance. The danger inherent in legal formalism lies in its inability to lay threadbare the values which guide the process of judging constitutional rights.'[100]

What, then, should these values be? Foremost among the values endorsed by all the judges in these cases has been those inherent in the recognition dimension; namely, dignity, humanity, and equal respect. These were made explicit in *Navtej Singh Johar*, where the Court finally read down the notorious section 377 of the Indian Penal Code, which criminalized sodomy or 'carnal intercourse', to exclude sex between consenting adults. For Chandrachud J, the law was arbitrary because its explicit intent was to demean and dehumanize LGBTQI people. Malhotra J held that 'legislation [which] discriminates on the basis of an intrinsic and core trait of an individual . . . cannot form a reasonable classification based on an intelligible differentia'. Similarly, Misra J held that Article 14 was violated because a 'certain class of people (LGBTs) owning to some inherent characteristics defined by their identity and individuality, have been woefully targeted.'[101] For the same reasons, the provision was held to be manifestly arbitrary. As in the US cases, the Court also drew on the relationship between equality and liberty, characterizing intimate relations as a matter of complete personal choice between consenting adults.

Like the Indian Court, the South African Constitutional Court (SACC) has more recently used the open-ended guarantee in section 9(1) of the Constitution rather than expanding the list of grounds in section 9(3). As in other jurisdictions, the Court has framed the section 9(1) test as one of rationality, contrasting with the fairness scrutiny used for the grounds-based approach in section 9(3). 'In regard to mere differentiation the constitutional state is expected to act in a rational manner. It should not regulate in an arbitrary manner or manifest "naked preferences" that serve no legitimate

---

[100] *Navtej Singh Johar v Union of India* (n 53) para 409.
[101] ibid paras 237, 252.

government purpose for that would be inconsistent with the rule of law and the fundamental premises of the constitutional state. The purpose of this aspect of equality is, therefore, to ensure that the state is bound to function in a rational manner.'[102] This has been used to invalidate a series of provisions, many of them left over from the apartheid regime.[103] This was particularly true of apartheid laws which entrenched patriarchy and the multiple disempowerment of African women.[104] In several cases, the government did not identify a legitimate purpose, raising the question why such cases have had to go to court rather than being repealed in Parliament. Most recently, in the important case of *Mahlangu*, the Court held that a provision excluding domestic workers from the protection of occupational insurance available to other workers was arbitrary and inconsistent with the right to equal protection and benefit of the law under section 9(1).[105]

Putting itself in the position of identifying illegitimate distinctions rather than being guided by the grounds in section 9(3) has, however, taken the Court into some turbulent waters. In *Herbert v Senqu*,[106] the use of section 9(1) rather than section 9(3) was salient in that the applicant, Teba, was by no means a disadvantaged minority. On the contrary, Teba had previously been a recruiting agency for Black mineworkers, perpetuating some of the worst excesses of apartheid. In the case, Teba challenged a statutory prohibition on full ownership of the property they occupied. The municipality, Senqu, opposed Teba's claim on the basis that it required the land for use by the people in its constituency, especially informal traders. In any event, it argued, Teba was far from a disadvantaged minority. In reality, however, the contested provision also barred millions of disadvantaged South Africans from full ownership, being a relic of the apartheid regime of prohibiting property ownership among Black South Africans. By striking down the provision under section 9(1), the Court benefited dispossessed South Africans even though the applicant could not be brought within the enumerated or analogous grounds in section 9(3), which are guided by the principle of redressing disadvantage. The High Court was left to grapple with the anomaly, deciding ultimately that

---

[102] *Prinsloo v Van der Linde* 1997 (6) BCLR 759 (CC), para 25 (SACC); see also *Mahlangu v Minister of Labour* [2020] ZACC 24, para 72 (SACC).

[103] See eg *Graham Roberg Herbert NO v Senqu Municipality* [2019] ZACC 31 (SACC); *Van der Merwe v Road Accident Fund and Another* (CCT48/05) [2006] ZACC 4 (SACC).

[104] *Rahube v Rahube* [2018] ZACC 22 (SACC).

[105] *Mahlangu v Minister of Labour* (n 102) para 73.

[106] *Herbert v Senqu* [2019] ZACC 31 (SACC).

the legislation in question, as amended by the SACC, was intended to benefit only disadvantaged South Africans, thereby excluding Teba.

The opposite scenario was presented to the Court in *Sarrahwitz v Maritz*,[107] where the applicant was a vulnerable person although the majority of other people in her category were not. The case concerned legislation enacted to protect vulnerable purchasers of residential property when the seller became insolvent. Under South African law, a seller's insolvency extinguishes the buyer's entitlement to transfer. This meant that many vulnerable purchasers lost their property and the money they had invested. The legislation facilitated transfer in such circumstances to vulnerable purchasers, but only those who paid by instalment. This was based on the assumption that purchasers who could afford to pay the full price in cash were not vulnerable. However, this excluded the applicant in the case, who was in fact a poor and unemployed person but who had been in a position to raise the purchase price in the form of a loan from her former employer.

The Court acknowledged that:

> None of the grounds for discrimination listed in section 9(3) seems to apply to this case. And the ground for the differentiation between the two categories of purchasers, namely the method of payment, does not appear to be based on attributes or characteristics which have the inherent potential to impair the fundamental dignity of persons as 'human beings'. . . . For this reason it will not be necessary to explore the possibility of developing 'one or more grounds' envisaged by subsection (3). Subsection (1) will instead be used as a platform for reflection on the equality of treatment of various categories of purchasers.[108]

The Court concluded that the concept of equal protection and benefit of the law meant that purchasers who are equally vulnerable should be equally protected regardless of their method of payment.[109] The concurring judgments, however, were concerned with the potential judicial overreach of reading a new category into existing legislation. Rewriting legislation was a complex task which should instead be left to the legislature.

(c) The non-exhaustive list

The third approach is a non-exhaustive list, which enumerates grounds but leaves it to judges to extend the list where appropriate. This is the approach

---

[107] *Sarrahwitz v Maritz* [2015] ZACC 14 (SACC).
[108] ibid para 48.
[109] ibid para 49.

adopted in the ECHR, the Canadian Charter of Rights, and section 9(3) of the South African Constitution. Article 14 ECHR states that the enjoyment of the rights and freedoms in the Convention shall be secured without discrimination 'on grounds *such as* sex, race, colour, language, religion, political or other opinion, national or social origin, association with a national minority, property, birth *or other status* . . .'. The Canadian Charter of Rights and Freedoms states:

> Every citizen is equal before and under the law and has the right to the equal protection and benefit of the law without discrimination and in particular without discrimination based on race, national or ethnic origin, colour, religion, sex, age or mental or physical disability.[110]

Section 9(3) of the South African Constitution prohibits unfair discrimination on grounds 'including' the listed grounds.[111]

The non-exhaustive list has made it possible for courts to 'update' the protected grounds in response to changing circumstances. This can clearly be seen by considering Article 14 ECHR. The list of grounds in Article 14 looks somewhat strange to modern eyes. Discrimination on grounds of property, birth, and association with a national minority are prohibited. But there is no mention of disability, sexual orientation, or age, let alone pregnancy or civil partnership. However, the non-exhaustive nature of Article 14 has made it possible for the European Court of Human Rights (ECtHR) to fill these gaps. Indeed, it expressly regards the Convention as 'a living instrument, to be interpreted in the light of present-day conditions'.[112] The process of updating the list has been further facilitated by the Court's reluctance to use a fixed, categorical approach. As the Court frequently reiterates, the list in Article 14 is 'illustrative and not exhaustive, as is shown by the words "any grounds such as"'.[113] This does not mean that the Court has collapsed Article 14 into an open-ended equality guarantee. It consistently emphasizes that Article 14 does not prohibit all differences of treatment, only those based on an 'identifiable, objective or personal characteristic, or "status", by which persons or groups of persons are distinguishable from one another'.[114] Nevertheless, the words 'other status' have generally been given a wide

---

[110] Canadian Charter of Rights and Freedoms, s 15(1); emphasis added.
[111] See s 9.
[112] *EB v France* (2008) 47 EHRR 21, para 92.
[113] *Salgueiro da Silva Mouta v Portugal* [2001] 31 EHRR 1055 (ECtHR).
[114] *Carson v United Kingdom* (2010) 51 EHRR 13, paras 61, 70; *Kjeldsen, Busk Madsen and Pederson v Denmark* (1976) 1 EHRR 711, para 56 (ECtHR).

meaning,[115] and personal characteristics are not confined to those that are innate or inherent.[116]

This has made it relatively easy to extend the scope of Article 14 to include some of the major missing grounds. In *Salgueiro da Silva Mouta*, the Court was able to conclude that sexual orientation was 'undoubtedly covered by Article 14'.[117] The inclusion of disability has been accepted with equally little fuss;[118] and in *Kiyutin v Russia*, the Court held that a distinction on account of an individual's health status should be covered, either as a disability or as a form thereof. This meant that discrimination on grounds of HIV status could fall within the Article.[119] This expansive approach has become so well accepted in the jurisprudence of the Court that when Protocol 12 was drafted it was decided against expressly including the additional grounds that were so blatantly missing from Article 14. As the explanatory notes state, this was not because of a lack of awareness that such grounds have become particularly important in today's societies. Instead, it was considered unnecessary since the list of grounds is not exhaustive and inclusion of any particular additional ground might give rise to unwarranted *a contrario* interpretations in relation to grounds not so included.[120]

Importantly, too, 'other status' is not limited to personal characteristics which are innate or inherent, as is evident by the inclusion of property, language, and political or other opinion.[121] This has allowed the Court to include cases in which an individual is treated less favourably on the basis of another person's status or protected characteristic. In *Guberina v Croatia*, the ECtHR held that discriminatory treatment of an applicant on the grounds not of his own disability but that of his child, was a form of disability-based discrimination covered by Article 14.[122] The striking similarity to the CJEU case of *Coleman*[123] demonstrates how similar destinations can be reached by very different routes.

The expansion of discrimination protection to include non-enumerated grounds, however, is counterbalanced by a sense that not all protected

---

[115] *Carson v United Kingdom* ibid para 70.
[116] ibid.
[117] *Salgueiro da Silva Mouta v Portugal* (n 113). See also *SL v Austria* (Application No 45330/99), Merits, 9 January 2003 and many other ECtHR cases.
[118] *Glor v Switzerland* (Application No 13444/04), Merits, 30 April 2009, para 80.
[119] *Kiyutin v Russia* (2011) 53 EHRR 26, para 58 (ECtHR).
[120] Protocol No 12 to the European Convention on Human Rights: Explanatory Report, available at <http://conventions.coe.int/Treaty/EN/Reports/Html/177.htm> accessed 27 July 2022.
[121] *Clift v UK* [2010] 7 WLUK 387 (ECtHR).
[122] *Guberina v Croatia* (2018) 66 EHRR 11, para 79 (ECtHR).
[123] *Coleman v Attridge Law* (n 20).

grounds should be regarded as equally invidious. This, in turn, triggers the impetus to create hierarchies, or differing levels of scrutiny, similar to that found in the US Supreme Court. The ECtHR does not use the terminology of 'suspect classes'. Nevertheless, the Court has identified specific grounds for which 'particularly convincing and weighty reasons' are required to justify differential treatment. This set of grounds is wider than the US Supreme Court's suspect classes and continues to evolve. It includes not just race and ethnic origin[124] but also gender,[125] sexual orientation,[126] and disability.[127] Similarly, birth or adopted status,[128] nationality,[129] and religion[130] have been held to fall into this category. On the other hand, a lighter touch justification is attached to grounds considered to be less weighty, such as age or residence.[131] Socio-economic distinctions have been regarded as requiring particular deference[132] on the grounds that these are part of a broader social policy which is better dealt with at the domestic level. Here the Court will only intervene if the classification is 'manifestly without reasonable foundation'.[133] However, the Court has not always been consistent in its application of these different standards of scrutiny. This is particularly true at the intersection of different grounds, as in gender and religion. Thus, in a series of cases, the Court has allowed the State a wide margin of appreciation in justifying the discriminatory effect on Muslim women of the ban on wearing a full-face veil in public.[134]

With the incorporation of the Convention into UK domestic law through the Human Rights Act 1998 (HRA), UK courts had their first experience of dealing with a non-exhaustive list. The transition from the fixed, categorical approach in the EA 2010, to the fluidity of the ECtHR has not been straightforward. Instead, the UK courts have sought a definition of the residual category 'other status' which would guide them in new and challenging situations.

---

[124] *DH v Czech Republic* (Application No 57325/00) (2008) 47 EHRR 3 (ECtHR (Grand Chamber)).

[125] *Abdulaziz, Cabales and Balkandali v UK* (Application nos 9214/80, 9473/81, 9474/81) [1985] 7 EHRR 471, Merits, 28 May 1985 (ECtHR).

[126] *EB v France* (2008) 47 EHRR 21 (ECtHR); *X v Austria* (2013) 57 EHRR 14 (ECtHR).

[127] *Kiss v Hungary* (2013) 56 EHRR 38 (ECtHR).

[128] *Inze v Austria* (1987) 10 EHRR 394, para 41.

[129] *Gaygusuz v Austria* (1996) 23 EHRR 364, para 42.

[130] *Hoffmann v Austria* (1993) 17 EHRR 293, 316, para 36.

[131] *R (Carson) v Secretary of State for Work and Pensions* [2005] UKHL 37 (HL).

[132] *Stec v United Kingdom* (2006) 43 EHRR 47 (ECtHR).

[133] ibid; *Connors v United Kingdom* (2005) 40 EHRR 9 (Application no 66746/01), Merits, 27 May 2004 (ECtHR).

[134] *SAS v France* (2015) 60 EHRR 11 (ECtHR (Grand Chamber)).

For this they have relied on the reference in ECHR jurisprudence to 'personal characteristics' as the defining feature.[135] Using this as a guideline, the UK Supreme Court has found 'homelessness' to be a personal characteristic.[136] Similarly, being a single, young adult was a category potentially protected by Article 14[137] as was habitual residence.[138] More recently, the Supreme Court has included lone mothers with children under two,[139] prisoners with extended determinate sentences,[140] and immigration status.[141]

However, like the US Supreme Court and the ECtHR, the UK Supreme Court has been inclined to create differential levels of scrutiny, creating a hierarchy of grounds. As Lord Hoffmann explained in *Carson's* case:

> Characteristics such as race, caste, noble birth, membership of a political party and . . . gender, are seldom, if ever, acceptable grounds for differences in treatment. In some constitutions, the prohibition on discrimination is confined to grounds of this kind and I rather suspect that Article 14 was also intended to be so limited. But the Strasbourg court has given it a wide interpretation, approaching that of the Fourteenth Amendment, and it is therefore necessary, as in the United States, to distinguish between those grounds of discrimination which prima facie appear to offend our notions of the respect due to the individual and those which merely require some rational justification.[142]

The result is that although place of residence,[143] being a single, young adult,[144] and homelessness[145] have all been found to be within the 'other status' category, a very minimal standard of scrutiny has been applied. This is particularly so where the challenge concerns inequalities in welfare measures. In these circumstances, it has been held, the courts should only intervene where they find that a measure is 'manifestly without reasonable foundation'. The UK Supreme Court has defended this highly deferent approach on the basis that issues of social policy should be left to governments rather than courts.[146] Yet this might abrogate judicial responsibility in precisely the

---

[135] *Kjeldsen, Busk Madsen and Pederson v Denmark* (n 114) para 56.
[136] *R (RJM) v Secretary of State for Work and Pensions* [2008] UKHL 63.
[137] *AL (Serbia) v Secretary of State for the Home Department* [2008] UKHL 42.
[138] *Carson v United Kingdom* (2009) 48 EHRR 41 (ECtHR).
[139] *R (On the application of DA) v Secretary of State for Work and Pensions* [2019] UKSC 21.
[140] *R v Stott* [2018] UKSC 59.
[141] *R (On the application of Tigere) v Secretary of State for Business, Innovation and Skills* [2015] UKSC 57.
[142] *R (Carson) v Secretary of State for Work and Pensions* (n 131) [15].
[143] ibid.
[144] *AL (Serbia) v Secretary of State for the Home Department* (n 137) [35].
[145] *R (RJM) v Secretary of State for Work and Pensions* (n 136) [56].
[146] *R (MA) v Secretary of State for Work and Pensions* [2016] UKSC 58 [32].

contexts in which a greater level of accountability is required. As Lord Hope put it in *In re G*: 'Cases about discrimination in an area of social policy . . . will always be appropriate for judicial scrutiny. The constitutional responsibility in this area of our law resides with the courts. The more contentious the issue is, the greater the risk that some people will be discriminated against in ways that engage their Convention rights. It is for the courts to see that this does not happen. It is with them that the ultimate safeguard against discrimination rests.'[147]

This has not, however, been the dominant view. Far more frequently, judges have seen the contentiousness of an issue as a reason for deferring rather than for scrutiny. According to Lord Reed: 'The question of proportionality involves controversial issues of social and economic policy, with major implications for public expenditure. The determination of those issues is pre-eminently the function of democratically elected institutions.'[148] Therefore, 'Unless manifestly without reasonable foundation, their assessment should be respected.'[149] It is this approach that has now been endorsed as the appropriate interpretation. In *DA*,[150] Lord Wilson was categorical: 'in relation to the government's need to justify what would otherwise be a discriminatory effect of a rule governing entitlement to welfare benefits, the sole question is whether it is manifestly without reasonable foundation. Let there be no future doubt about it.'[151] This was despite strong dissents from Lady Hale and Lord Kerr.

The difficulty with imposing different levels of scrutiny is that it requires the court to determine which category is relevant in a particular case, an exercise which is especially problematic where there is a combination of grounds with differing levels of scrutiny. This was particularly prominent in the decade of austerity after 2010, where cuts in social benefits frequently disproportionately burdened women, ethnic minorities, and disabled people. This led to a stream of cases in the UK courts, challenging such policies on grounds of breach of Article 14, as incorporated through the HRA. In such cases, the courts have had to choose between the deferential standard attached to socio-economic distinctions and the more piercing standard of

---

[147] *In re G (Adoption: Unmarried Couple)* [2008] UKHL 38 [48].
[148] *R (SG and others) v Secretary of State for Work and Pensions* [2015] UKSC 15 [93] (the first Benefit Cap case).
[149] ibid [93].
[150] *R (On the application of DA) v Secretary of State for Work and Pensions* (n 139) [59] (the second Benefit Cap case).
[151] ibid [65].

justification required for race, disability, or gender-related distinctions.[152] In an unfortunate turn, the Supreme Court has preferred the former. In the context of welfare benefits potentially discriminating on grounds of sex or disability, the normally strict justification has given way to the 'manifestly without reasonable foundation' test.[153] For example, *RJM* concerned a policy which excluded homeless disabled people from entitlement to a disability benefit available to all other disabled people. Although the Supreme Court held that homelessness was a characteristic protected under Article 14, and therefore the policy prima facie discriminated against homeless people, there was no breach of that Article in this case. This was because, the Court held, it should be slow to substitute its opinion for that of the State in a policy area such as this.[154]

This was taken even further in cases challenging the 'benefit cap', a statutory provision which places a limit on the total benefits a household is entitled to receive. The cap was imposed by the government as part of its austerity policies, ostensibly to save public funds and to incentivize households on benefits to undertake paid work. Evidence showed that 65 per cent of households which suffered a reduction in their benefits because of the cap were female, lone-parent households, and one-quarter of the total were female, lone-parent households with a child under two.[155] In principle, a household could escape the cap by moving into paid work, but this was something lone parents with young children clearly struggled to do. The cap was challenged on the grounds that it infringed Article 14.[156]

The UK Supreme Court accepted that the group of lone parents with a child under two constituted a 'status' for the purpose of Article 14.[157] However, it held that the relevant standard of scrutiny was merely whether the policy was 'manifestly without reasonable foundation'. Applying this test, the Court upheld the policy. As in *RJM*, this test yielded a light touch indeed. The government stated that its aims were to incentivize those on benefits to undertake paid work and to make fiscal savings. Yet government statistics could only posit that about 5 per cent of all capped households were likely to move

---

[152] *Stec v United Kingdom* (n 132).

[153] *Humphreys v Commissioners for Her Majesty's Revenue and Customs* [2012] UKSC 18.

[154] ibid [56].

[155] *R (On the application of DA) v Secretary of State for Work and Pensions* (n 139); *R (SG and others) v Secretary of State for Work and Pensions* (n 148).

[156] Together with Art 8 and Art 1 of Protocol 1. *R (On the application of DA) v Secretary of State for Work and Pensions* (n 139).

[157] Those not subject to the benefit cap, and specifically dual-care parents with a child under two or under five, and lone parents without a child under two or under five; ibid [47], [160].

into work to escape the cap. There was undoubted evidence of the financial advantages of being in work but this raised the question of how practicable it was for a lone parent of a child under two to work and whether it was reasonable to divert the lone parent from caring for her children. So far as fiscal savings were concerned, it turned out that the net savings were only 0.03 per cent of the State's overall annual expenditure on welfare benefits for those of working age (£68 million in the year in question). On the other side of the scales, the impact on the vulnerable class was serious. Lord Wilson accepted that the benefit cap could reduce a family's income well below the poverty line.[158] There was also striking evidence of the consequences of living in poverty on children's lives, including their educational attainment, health, and happiness in the long term.[159] Nevertheless, Lord Wilson held that the appellants had not entered any substantial challenge to the belief that there are better long-term outcomes for children who live in households in which an adult works. He conceded that this was not the 'surest foundation' but it was a 'reasonable foundation'.[160]

This contrasts with the approach of the dissenters. For Lord Kerr, the 'manifestly without reasonable foundation' test was not appropriate for the domestic courts to apply to the final balancing stage of the proportionality assessment. Instead, the proper test was 'whether the government has established that there is a reasonable foundation for its conclusion that a fair balance has been struck'.[161] For him, the aim of incentivizing parents to obtain paid work puts such parents in an impossible dilemma: they are unlikely to obtain employment which would remunerate them sufficiently to cover the costs of childcare and, even if they could afford it, childcare may not be available.[162] Similarly, Lady Hale held that the mass of evidence showed that the revised benefit cap was not suitable for achieving any of its aims. 'Striking a fair balance would have set the very limited benefits to the public interest against the damage done to the family lives of young children and their lone parents if either of their parents are forced to work outside the home in order to have enough for themselves and their children to live on or they are unable or unwilling to work outside the home and are thus forced to attempt to live on less than the state has decided that they need.'[163] On this basis, she

---

158 ibid [33].
159 ibid [34].
160 ibid [88].
161 ibid [177].
162 ibid [189]–[190].
163 ibid [156].

found that the weight of the evidence showed that a fair balance had not been struck between the public interest on the one hand, and the children and their parents on the other. Thus, she held, the regulations at issue constituted unjustified discrimination against lone parents of children under the age of five, and against those children.

While the UK courts interpreting the ECHR have focused on the meaning of 'other status', the Canadian courts have concentrated on whether a ground is 'analogous' to the grounds enumerated in section 15 of the Charter. However, rather than calibrating the standard of review to permit an increasingly wide range of grounds, the Supreme Court of Canada has closely guarded the gateway to recognition as an analogous ground. All the enumerated grounds (race, national or ethnic origin, colour, religion, sex, age, or mental or physical disability[164]), the Court has held, refer to a personal characteristic which is 'immutable or changeable only at an unacceptable cost to personal identity' and which the 'the government has no legitimate interest in expecting us to change to receive equal treatment under the law'.[165]

Only a handful of grounds have been recognized as analogous under this test, a stark contrast to the wide range of grounds admitted to the category of 'other status' under the ECHR. In *Andrews*,[166] the Court recognized non-citizenship as an analogous ground and, since *Miron v Trudel*[167] in 1995, marital status has been acknowledged. Particularly important was the recognition of sexual orientation as an analogous ground in *Egan v Canada*.[168] In *Corbiere*, the Court added the complex ground of 'aboriginality-residence as it pertains to a member of an Indian Band living off the reserve'.[169] However, 'residence on a reserve' has not been included as an analogous ground.[170] Indeed, the Court has consistently declined to find that place or province of residence is an analogous ground.[171] Similarly, professional or occupational

---

[164] The term 'colour' is used here because it is used in s 15 of the Canadian Charter and in international and regional human rights documents (CERD, Art 1; ICCPR, Art 2(1); ICESCR, Art 2(1); ECHR, Art 14) and national human rights instruments (eg South African Constitution, s 9; UK EA 2010, s 9(1)).

[165] *Corbiere v Canada (Minister of Indian and Northern Affairs)* [1999] 2 SCR 203, para 13 (Can Sup Ct).

[166] *Andrews v Law Society of British Columbia* [1989] 1 SCR 143 (Can Sup Ct).

[167] *Miron v Trudel* [1995] 2 SCR 418 (Can Sup Ct).

[168] *Egan v Canada* [1995] 2 SCR 513 (Can Sup Ct).

[169] *Corbiere v Canada (Minister of Indian and Northern Affairs)* (n 165).

[170] ibid. *Kahkewistahaw First Nation v Taypotat* 2015 SCC 30 (Can Sup Ct).

[171] *Siemens v Manitoba* [2003] 1 SCR 6 (Can Sup Ct); *R v Turpin* [1989] 1 SCR 1296 (Can Sup Ct). Similarly, 'substance orientation' has been rejected as an analogous ground: *R v Malmo-Levine; R v Caine* [2003] 3 SCR 571.

status has been rejected as a ground protected under section 15.[172] The question of whether poverty can be an analogous ground has not reached the Supreme Court but the lower courts have rejected the possibility. The same is true for homelessness.[173]

There have, however, been suggestions from some Supreme Court Justices that a more expansive approach should be taken. This has crystallized in relation to agricultural workers who have been excluded or marginalized from key trade union and collective-bargaining rights in Ontario. In *Dunmore*,[174] while the majority decision focused on a breach of the right to freedom of association, Justice L'Heureux-Dubé, in her concurring judgment,[175] held that in the right circumstances an occupational status could identify a protected group. Agricultural workers are subject to low pay and poor working conditions, and have limited employment mobility meaning that they cannot change their occupational status except at great cost. Although she (and the majority) made no findings in relation to occupational status generally, she held that agricultural workers' occupational status constitutes an analogous ground. This approach was taken a step further by Deschamps J in her concurring opinion in *Fraser*,[176] which, like *Dunmore*, addressed the exclusion of agricultural workers from certain labour law protections. Deschamps J was keen to stress that economic equality is not an 'equality right' for the purposes of section 15 and that employment status is not 'at least not at this time, regarded as an analogous ground'.[177] However, she suggested that 'to redress economic inequality, it would be more faithful to the design of the *Charter* to open the door to the recognition of more analogous grounds under s. 15, as L'Heureux-Dubé J proposed in *Dunmore*'.[178] She did, however, acknowledge that this would involve a 'sea change' in the interpretation of section 15.[179]

The South African Constitution has a different solution. The Constitution itself expressly distinguishes between enumerated and non-enumerated grounds in relation to the standard of scrutiny to be applied. All distinctions need to satisfy a basic rationality test.[180] But grounds which are enumerated

---

[172] *Baer v Alberta* [2007] 2 SCR 673, para 64.
[173] *Tanudjaja v Canada (Attorney General)* 2011 ONSC 5410 (Ont Sup Ct).
[174] *Dunmore v Ontario* [2001] 3 SCR 1016 (Can Sup Ct).
[175] Note that the majority regarded it as unnecessary to consider the status of occupational groups under s 15(1).
[176] *Ontario v Fraser* 2011 SCC 20 (Can Sup Ct).
[177] ibid para 315.
[178] ibid para 319.
[179] ibid para 319.
[180] South African Constitution, s 9(1).

raise a presumption of unfairness, whereas in the case of grounds which are not specified, unfairness must be proved by the applicant.[181] On the other hand, as in Canada, the Court does not adjust the standard of scrutiny depending on the ground. As Jaftha J noted in *Sali*,[182] an age discrimination case: 'It is significant to note that the Constitution lists a number of grounds on which the state is precluded from discriminating unfairly against anyone. And those grounds include age. Notably the Constitution does not rank discrimination on the basis of race or gender higher than discrimination on any of the other listed grounds. This means that discrimination on any of the listed grounds must be treated seriously.'[183] As far as unspecified grounds are concerned, the South African Court has regarded dignity as the guiding principle to determine whether an unspecified ground is included.[184] In practice, only a limited number of grounds have been recognized by the Court, the most important being citizenship and HIV status.[185] More recently, this principle was applied to a change in parole conditions which differentiated between prisoners depending on the date of sentencing rather than the date of conviction.[186]

(ii) A Unifying Principle?

Underlying all these approaches is the question of whether the choice of grounds, be it political or judicial, is based on a unifying principle. Judges have frequently articulated guiding principles. The US Court has focused on political powerlessness and a history of purposeful unequal treatment. This is summed up in *San Antonio v Rodriguez*, where the Court held that:

> A 'suspect class' requiring application of the strict scrutiny standard of equal protection analysis is one saddled with such disabilities, or subjected to such a history of purposeful unequal treatment, or relegated to such a position of

---

[181] *Harksen v Lane NO and Others* [1997] ZACC 12, 1997 (11) BCLR 1489 (CC), 1998 (1) SA 300 (CC).

[182] *Sali v National Commissioner of the South African Police Service* [2014] ZACC 19 (SACC).

[183] ibid para 7.

[184] *Harksen v Lane NO and Others* (n 181).

[185] *Hoffmann v South African Airways* (CCT17/00) [2000] ZACC 17, 2001 (1) SA 1, 2000 (11) BCLR 1235, [2000] 12 BLLR 1365 (CC). Marital status was an analogous ground in the interim Constitution but later incorporated into s 9 of the final Constitution.

[186] *Phaahla v Minister of Justice* [2019] ZACC 18, para 53 (SACC).

political powerlessness as to command extraordinary protection from the majoritarian political process.[187]

By contrast, the Supreme Court of Canada, although recognizing these factors, regards immutability or constrained choice as the central concept. Thus, the Court held in *Corbiere* that:

> S. 15 targets the denial of equal treatment on grounds that are actually immutable, like race, or constructively immutable, like religion. Other factors identified in the cases as associated with the enumerated and analogous grounds, like the fact that the decision adversely impacts on a discrete and insular minority or a group that has been historically discriminated against, may be seen to flow from the central concept of immutable or constructively immutable personal characteristics, which too often have served as illegitimate and demeaning proxies for merit-based decision making.[188]

The South African Court, while similarly emphasizing a history of disadvantage, regards dignity as a powerful motivating value, requiring equal protection for those burdened with demeaning and stereotypical attributions. For the Supreme Court of India, dignity and autonomy play a central role.

In practice, while emphasizing one particular value, all these courts tend to draw on a constellation of factors, which include immutability or lack of autonomy, political exclusion, denial of dignity, and a history of disadvantage. This section critically evaluates judicial use of each of these factors in turn, bearing in mind that these are analytic tools, which help to signal an analogous ground; but that no one indicator is required to be present.[189] It also considers the ways in which the choice of factors reflects background assumptions about the meaning of equality itself, and the extent to which they are used to exclude people or groups as much as to protect them.

(a) Immutability, choice, and autonomy

To subject an individual to detriment on the basis of a characteristic which she is powerless to change appears to liberal thinkers to be particularly

---

[187] *San Antonio Independent School District v Rodriguez* 411 US 959, paras 40–41 (1973).
[188] *Corbiere v Canada (Minister of Indian and Northern Affairs)* (n 165) para 13.
[189] ibid.

invidious. The first factor therefore focuses on whether the exclusion is a result of an immutable characteristic or whether there are choices available to an individual which might make her eligible for the opportunity or benefit at stake. This places autonomy at centre stage.

Immutability or absence of choice as a basis for delineating grounds of discrimination has appealed to judges across all the jurisdictions examined here. As Baroness Hale put it:

> It is not so very long ago in this country that people might be refused access to a so-called 'public' bar because of their sex or the colour of their skin; that a woman might automatically be paid three quarters of what a man was paid for doing exactly the same job; that a landlady offering rooms to let might lawfully put a 'no blacks' notice in her window. We now realise that this was wrong. It was wrong because the sex or colour of the person was simply irrelevant to the choice which was being made . . . it was wrong because it was based on an irrelevant characteristic which the woman or the black did not choose and could do nothing about.[190]

Similarly, for the Supreme Court of Canada, the factor common to all the enumerated and analogous grounds is that 'they often serve as the basis for stereotypical decisions made not on the basis of merit but on the basis of a personal characteristic that is immutable or changeable only at an unacceptable cost to personal identity' and which 'the government has no legitimate interest in expecting us to change to receive equal treatment under the law'.[191] It was on this basis that the Court held sexual orientation to be an analogous ground: it is 'unchangeable or changeable only at unacceptable personal costs'.[192] A similar approach led it to conclude that citizenship is an analogous ground. In *Andrews*, it was held that citizenship is typically not within the control of the individual and is, at least temporarily, a characteristic of personhood which is not alterable by conscious action and which in some cases is not alterable except on the basis of unacceptable costs.[193] A parallel approach has been followed by the SACC. Here, too, the Court has held that:

---

[190] *Ghaidan v Godin-Mendoza* [2004] UKHL 30 [130].
[191] *Corbiere v Canada (Minister of Indian and Northern Affairs)* (n 165) para 13.
[192] *Egan v Canada* (n 168) para 5.
[193] *Andrews v Law Society of British Columbia* (n 166) para 75 (La Forest J).

citizenship is typically not within the control of the individual and is, at least temporarily, a characteristic of personhood not alterable by conscious action and in some cases not alterable except on the basis of unacceptable costs.[194]

On this basis, it has held that citizenship is unquestionably an analogous ground.[195] This approach has also resonated with the UK Supreme Court. In *AL (Serbia)*, Lady Hale restated the role of choice:

> In general, the list concentrates on personal characteristics which the complainant did not choose and either cannot or should not be expected to change.[196]

Although intuitively appealing, a reliance on immutability raises a host of further problems. The fact that some aspects of our identity are indeed a matter of personal choice, or can in principle be changed or suppressed, should not be a reason for denying such characteristics the protection of discrimination law. Thus, for some, religion is a matter of personal choice; while for others, it is inherited through family or ethnic origin. Does that mean that whether a person is protected against religious discrimination should depend on whether or not she has chosen her religion? Similarly, pregnancy may or may not be a personal choice. But, either way, choice seems irrelevant to the question of whether pregnancy should be a protected characteristic. Indeed, even the apparent immutability of sex itself is not unassailable. Many recent cases have concerned discrimination against transsexuals: here it is the very mutability of their sex that has triggered the discrimination.

This difficulty is partially met by the concept of 'constructive immutability', which would include characteristics that can only be changed at an unacceptable personal cost. However, even in this nuanced form, the concept of immutability or absence of unconstrained personal choice does not always yield straightforward or appropriate answers to the question of whether a ground should be protected under an equality guarantee. How constrained does an individual choice need to be to fall within the principle of constructive immutability? When the Supreme Court of Canada held in *Corbiere* that off-reserve residence could be an analogous ground for First Nations people, it relied at least in part on the finding that for many First Nations people the

---

[194] *Khosa and Mahlaule v Minister for Social Development* 2004 (6) BCLR 569, para 71 (SACC).
[195] *Larbi-Odam v MEC for Education* [1997] ZACC 16 (SACC).
[196] *AL (Serbia) v Secretary of State for the Home Department* (n 137) [26].

decision to live off reserve was either forced or heavily constrained. On the other hand, the Court declined to make the same finding for First Nations people living on reserve.[197] Yet it is well documented that, especially for rural people living in the north of Canada, the possibility of moving to other areas is severely constrained by economic and social conditions.[198] The limits of the concept were further tested in the UK case of *AL (Serbia)*, where young, adult asylum seekers without families were excluded from an amnesty extended to asylum seekers with young families. Is 'being without a family' an immutable characteristic? To answer this required a particularly complex understanding of immutability: 'being without a family may not be immutable, like sex and race, but it is something over which the young person has no control'.[199] And what if a court decides that a person could have exercised their personal choice to avoid detrimental treatment on the basis of a characteristic recognized in anti-discrimination legislation? In *Stewart v Elk Valley*,[200] the Supreme Court of Canada held that although addiction is a recognized ground of discrimination under the Alberta Human Rights Act, the fact that a person with an addiction has the capacity to control his addiction could mean that the reason for detrimental action was not the addiction but his choice not to stop his drug use. However, as Gascon J put it in his dissenting opinion, 'stigmas surrounding drug dependence—like the belief that individuals suffering from it are the authors of their own misfortune or that their concerns are less credible than those of people suffering from other forms of disability—sometimes impair the ability of courts and society to objectively assess the merits of their discrimination claims'.[201]

It is for these reasons that the UK courts have moved away from the concept of personal choice in determining whether a ground is protected. This can be demonstrated in relation to residence. As we have seen, the Canadian courts have been reluctant to recognize residence in itself as an analogous ground. In the UK case of *Carson*, however, Lord Walker recognized that: 'Where an individual lives is in principle a matter of choice. So although it can be regarded as a personal characteristic it is not immutable.'[202] Nevertheless, he did not regard the role of choice as central to the question,

---

[197] *Kahkewistahaw First Nation v Taypotat* (n 170).
[198] Meghan Campbell, 'A New Ground of Discrimination: Rural Remoteness?' (*Oxford Human Rights Hub Blog*, 5 June 2017) <https://ohrh.law.ox.ac.uk/a-new-ground-of-discrimination-rural-remoteness> accessed 10 August 2022.
[199] *Kahkewistahaw First Nation v Taypotat* (n 170) para 32.
[200] *Stewart v Elk Valley Coal Corp* 2017 SCC 30 (Can Sup Ct).
[201] ibid para 58.
[202] *R (Carson) v Secretary of State for Work and Pensions* (n 131) [58].

accepting that residence fell within the category of 'other status'. A similar pattern can be seen in relation to homelessness. Courts in Canada have regarded homelessness as a matter of choice and therefore out of the scope of analogous grounds.[203] This was echoed by the UK Court of Appeal in *RJM*, which held that, because being homeless was a voluntary choice, homelessness was not protected as a ground under Article 14 ECHR. However, in the Supreme Court in *RJM*, Lord Neuberger acknowledged the limitations of too great a reliance on the question of choice:

> I do not accept that the fact that a condition has been adopted by choice is of much, if any, significance in determining whether that condition is a status for the purposes of Article 14. Of the specified grounds in the Article, 'language, religion, political or other opinion . . . association with a national minority [or] property' are all frequently a matter of choice, and even 'sex' can be.[204]

The difficulty in applying immutability as the litmus test for a protected ground opens up the more fundamental question of what role a principle of autonomy or choice should play in discrimination law. The initial instinct that an individual should not be subjected to detriment on the basis of a characteristic over which she has no choice may appear plausible at first sight. But this also assumes the converse; namely, that where she has a choice, she should pay the cost. Yet, individual choices may be constrained by a range of factors, not all of which are visible to the courts. Moreover, individual choices should be respected and accommodated rather than being burdened with the cost of rejection or exclusion. The choice to have a child should not bring with it the cost of exclusion from the workforce. The choice to follow a particular religion, or engage in an occupation, or live in a particular region, should not automatically trigger unjustifiable detriment. As argued in Chapter 1, discrimination law should not insist on conformity as a price of equal treatment.

(b) Access to the political process: discrete and insular minorities

A second factor frequently used by the courts to determine whether a group should be protected relates to the extent to which the group at issue is marginalized from the political process. Here the underlying assumption is that equality law should aim to redress imbalances in majoritarian democracy. This factor originated in one of the most famous footnotes in legal history,

---

[203] *Tanudjaja v Canada (Attorney General)* (n 173).

[204] *R (RJM) v Secretary of State for Work and Pensions* (n 136) [47]. Compare *Tanudjaja*, where the Ontario Court of Appeal refused to hold that homelessness was a ground.

footnote 4 of the *Carolene Products* case.[205] According to Stone J, 'more searching judicial inquiry' may be required for statutes directed at particular religious or national or racial minorities, or where 'prejudice against discrete and insular minorities . . . tends seriously to curtail the operation of those political processes ordinarily to be relied upon to protect minorities'.[206] John Hart Ely builds on this approach to develop his 'representation-reinforcing' theory of judicial review. In his view, judicial review is particularly appropriate when:

> (1) the ins are choking off the channels of political change to ensure that they will stay in and the outs will stay out or (2) though no-one is actually denied a voice or a vote, representatives beholden to an effective majority are systematically disadvantaging some minority out of simple hostility or a prejudiced refusal to recognize commonalities of interest and thereby denying that minority the protection afforded other groups by a representative system.[207]

It was on this basis, as we have seen, that the US Supreme Court identified African Americans as a suspect class, attracting strict scrutiny under the Fourteenth Amendment.

More recently, in *Romer v Evans*,[208] the US Court relied on the principle of political exclusion to protect LGBT rights. *Romer v Evans* concerned an amendment to the Constitution of the State of Colorado which prohibited any branch of the State from legislating to prohibit discrimination based on sexual orientation. Enacted as a response to local ordinances making it unlawful to discriminate against gay citizens, the amendment repealed all of these ordinances and forbade the adoption of any future similar ordinances. The US Supreme Court invalidated the amendment. Kennedy J, delivering the opinion of the Court, found that the amendment uniquely burdened LGBT people, in that, short of a constitutional amendment, they could not seek protection from discrimination. This breached the principle, 'central both to the idea of the rule of law and to our own Constitution's guarantee of equal protection . . . that government and each of its parts remain open on impartial terms to all who seek its assistance'.[209] Notably, rather than

---

[205] *United States v Carolene Products Co* 304 US 144, 58 S Ct 778 (1938).
[206] ibid 152.
[207] John Hart Ely, *Democracy and Distrust: A Theory of Judicial Review* (Harvard UP 1980) 103.
[208] *Romer v Evans* 517 US 620, 634, 116 S Ct 1620, 134 LE2d 855 (1996) (US Sup Ct).
[209] ibid 633.

determining whether this group constituted a discrete and insular minority, triggering strict scrutiny, Kennedy J found that the amendment did not satisfy even the lower standard of rational review.

The 'representation-reinforcing' theory has had a seminal influence on the courts in Canada and South Africa, as well as in the US. Thus, in the Canadian case of *Andrews*,[210] in affirming that non-citizens permanently resident in Canada were protected by the equality guarantee, Wilson J held that the test to be applied was whether this group was a 'discrete and insular minority' as specified in the *Carolene Products* case. Specifically citing John Hart Ely's representation-reinforcing theory, she held that non-citizens were one of 'those groups in society to whose needs and wishes elected officials have no apparent interest in attending'.[211] In that sense, they were held to be analogous to the groups specifically enumerated in the Charter.[212] The SACC has drawn expressly on *Andrews* and on the reference to Ely's theory embedded in it, to come to a similar conclusion about non-citizens permanently resident in South Africa. Thus, regulations excluding non-citizens from being employed as educators was held to be discriminatory, in part because of the recognition that non-citizens had little political muscle.[213] This was reinforced in *Khosa*, where it was held that citizenship is clearly a ground analogous to those listed in section 9(3).[214]

At the same time, the representation-reinforcing theory suffers from its continuing alliance with the notion of 'discrete and insular minorities', which it inherited from the paradigm case of race discrimination in the US. In particular, it is difficult to see how women could be regarded as constituting a discrete and insular minority: yet they have certainly been under-represented in the political process. Moreover, as Ackermann shows, those who are in fact least likely to succeed in the political process are those who are neither discrete nor insular. It is precisely because they are diffuse that certain groups find it difficult or impossible to organize themselves sufficiently to compete. Those who have the least access to resources are possibly the most diffuse, and it is they who should have the greatest claim to judicial concern with the fairness of the political process.[215]

---

[210] *Andrews v Law Society of British Columbia* (n 166).

[211] Ely (n 207) 151.

[212] *Andrews v Law Society of British Columbia* (n 166) 51.

[213] *Larbi-Odam and Others v Member of the Executive Council for Education (North-West Province) and Another* (CCT2/97) [1997] ZACC 16, 1997 (12) BCLR 1655, 1998 (1) SA 745, para 19.

[214] *Khosa and Mahlaule v Minister for Social Development* 2004 (6) BCLR 569 (SACC).

[215] B Ackerman, 'Beyond Carolene Products' [1985] 98 Harv L Rev 713, 718.

This is particularly evident in relation to poverty. In the *San Antonio* case, the US Supreme Court was asked to determine whether it was discriminatory against the poor to require communities to fund local schools through local taxes. The result was inevitably that poorer districts had fewer resources with which to fund their schools, leading to inferior education for poor children. Nevertheless, the Court held that this was not a breach of the Fourteenth Amendment. Poor people, in its view, did not constitute a discrete and insular minority; the boundaries of the group were shifting and definitions of poverty varied. Yet poor people are unlikely to have the resources to mobilize the political process in their favour and therefore could well be one of 'those groups in society to whose needs and wishes elected officials have no apparent interest in attending'.[216] A policy which locks poorer people into a cycle of disadvantage through the provision of inferior education appears particularly invidious. The representation-reinforcing theory, cut free from the requirement of a discrete and insular minority, should lead to the conclusion that classifications which burden the poor should be subject to particularly strict scrutiny.

The emphasis on discrete and insular minorities has in fact functioned more often to exclude groups from heightened scrutiny under the Equal Protection Clause than to include them. This can be seen in relation to both age and disability discrimination. As O'Connor J put in *Kimmel v Florida*: 'Older persons, . . ., unlike those who suffer discrimination on the basis of race or gender, have not been subjected to a history of purposeful unequal treatment. Old age also does not define a discrete and insular minority because all persons, if they live out their normal life spans, will experience it. Accordingly, . . . age is not a suspect classification under the Equal Protection Clause.'[217] Similarly, in *Cleburne*, the Court rejected the argument that people with learning difficulties are a suspect or quasi-suspect class on the ground that they constituted a 'large and amorphous class' which might invite other similar groups to claim such status. In addition, the Court held that they were not any more politically powerless than any other minority, and indeed had attracted the attention of legislators in several important areas.[218]

On the other hand, in its approach to race itself in recent cases, the Court has tended to depart from the principle that heightened scrutiny should only attach to discrete and insular minorities, defined by their political

---

[216] See *San Antonio v Rodriguez* (n 187); Ely (n 207).
[217] *Kimel v Florida Board of Regents* (n 64) 83.
[218] *Cleburne v Cleburne Living Center* (n 68).

powerlessness. Instead, all classifications based on race are subjected to strict scrutiny, even when the avowed objective is to benefit racial groups who have faced a history of intentional marginalization from the political process. As will be seen in Chapter 7, the result has been that strict scrutiny has primarily benefited white applicants who have challenged affirmative action policies in higher education, regardless of the absence of any evidence of political powerlessness. Indeed, in applying strict scrutiny to all racial classifications, the Court has questioned the very basis of the notion that Black people constitute a discrete and insular minority. Thus, in the 2014 case of *Schuette*,[219] Kennedy J, giving the judgment of the Court stated: 'It cannot be entertained as a serious proposition that all individuals of the same race think alike.'[220] Indeed, he held, the enterprise of defining individuals according to race would raise serious questions, risking 'inquiries and categories dependent upon demeaning stereotypes, classifications of questionable constitutionality on their own terms.'[221] By contrast, Sotomayor J, dissenting, emphasized the key principle of political exclusion: 'While our Constitution does not guarantee minority groups victory in the political process, it does guarantee them meaningful and equal access to that process. It guarantees that the majority may not win by stacking the political process against minority groups permanently, forcing the minority alone to surmount unique obstacles in pursuit of its goals.'[222]

(c) Dignity: treating individuals as less valuable members of society

Dignity constitutes a third factor frequently used by the courts to delineate protected groups. It can be seen across all the jurisdictions addressed here. In *Egan v Canada*, Cory J stated that 'the fundamental consideration underlying the analogous grounds analysis is whether the basis of distinction may serve to deny the essential human dignity of the Charter claimant.'[223] This has been even more emphatically affirmed by the SACC, which has held that under the South African Constitution:

> there will be discrimination on an unspecified ground if it is based on attributes
> or characteristics which have the potential to impair the fundamental dignity of

---

[219] *Schuette v Coalition to Defend Affirmative Action* 134 SC 1623 (2014) (US Sup Ct).
[220] ibid 1634.
[221] ibid 1635.
[222] ibid 1655.
[223] *Egan v Canada* (n 168) para 171. Although Cory J dissented in the outcome of the case, this part of his judgment is endorsed in later cases. See eg *Corbiere v Canada (Minister of Indian and Northern Affairs)* (n 165) para 59.

persons as human beings, or to affect them adversely in a comparably serious manner.[224]

More recently, the principle was applied to a change in parole conditions which differentiated between prisoners depending on the date of sentencing, rather than the date of conviction. Dlodlo AJ held that: 'Although not a listed ground, their status [as convicted persons] is an attribute or characteristic that undoubtedly has the potential to impair the fundamental dignity of [these] persons as human beings or affect them adversely in a comparably serious manner.'[225] Although less prominent, dignity has also appeared in the jurisprudence of the ECJ and the UK Supreme Court. In *P v S*,[226] the ECJ relied upon the principle of dignity to find that discrimination against a transsexual person was prohibited by the Treaty provisions making it unlawful to discriminate on grounds of sex.

> To tolerate such discrimination would be tantamount, as regards such a person, to a failure to respect the dignity and freedom to which he or she is entitled, and which the Court has a duty to safeguard.[227]

Similarly, in the UK Supreme Court, Lord Walker in *Carson* stated that grounds of discrimination requiring particularly severe scrutiny are those personal characteristics which, 'if used as a ground for discrimination, are recognised as particularly demeaning for the victim'.[228] Likewise, in giving meaning to the open-ended guarantee of equality in section 14 of the Indian Constitution, the Indian Supreme Court has relied on the concept of dignity. Chandrachud J has been at the forefront of these developments, regarding dignity as constituting the core of the rights guaranteed to the individual under the Indian Constitution.[229] In particular, he has stressed, discrimination against individuals on the basis of their sexual orientation is deeply offensive to their dignity and self-worth.[230]

Particularly notable has been the recent interest of the US Supreme Court in the role of dignity in determining the reach of the Fourteenth Amendment. As we have seen, the US Supreme Court, led by Kennedy J,

---

[224] *Harksen v Lane NO and Others* (n 181) para 46.
[225] *Phaahla v Minister of Justice* (n 186) para 53.
[226] Case C-13/94 *P v S and Cornwall County Council* [1996] ECR I-2143 (ECJ).
[227] ibid para 22.
[228] *R (Carson) v Secretary of State for Work and Pensions* (n 131) [55].
[229] *Puttaswamy v Union of India* (2019) 10 SCC 996, para 119 (Indian Sup Ct).
[230] ibid para 144.

has situated equality claims by LGBTQI+ people in the substantive values of liberty and dignity rather than the traditional discourse of political exclusion. Tribe has characterized this development as 'bringing maturity to the US Constitution's elusive but unquestionably central protections of liberty, equality, and—underlying both—respect for human dignity'.[231] Yoshino takes this one step further and argues that this 'liberty-based dignity' is the 'New Equal Protection'. By appealing to universal rights rather than creating a 'group-based slippery slope, in which it seems that an endless queue of groups clamour for our attention',[232] this approach functions as an antidote to the 'pluralism anxiety' triggered by group-based identity politics.[233]

This raises the question of what dignity adds to the interpretation of the Fourteenth Amendment's twofold protection of both liberty and equality. For Tribe, the central insight of *Lawrence* is that 'liberty is centred in equal respect and dignity for both conventional and unconventional human relationships . . . the network of human connection over time that makes genuine freedom possible'.[234] The emphasis on relationships rather than an individualistic view of dignity is a welcome recognition. However, Tribe continues to foreground equality as an essential prerequisite of dignity, as signified by his focus on equal respect and dignity rather than dignity per se. Dignity is thereby a label for prior substantive concepts rather than being a self-executing conception in itself. Yoshino, by contrast, argues that dignity is essentially an individual right. However, a rejection of group-based approaches in favour of an individualistic solution can have problematic consequences. This is clear from *Schuette*, where dignity was used as an exclusionary rather than inclusionary factor. As we have seen, Kennedy J held that it was demeaning to African Americans to assume that all African Americans have the same political beliefs. On this basis, he rejected the claim that African Americans were particularly burdened by a constitutional ban on affirmative action. As argued in Chapter 1, it is more helpful to focus on specific meanings of dignity, such as stigma, stereotyping, prejudice, and violence, which are likely to yield more specific resolutions. This is expanded upon in more detail when considering the meaning of discrimination and equality in Chapter 5.

---

[231] L Tribe, '*Lawrence v Texas*: The "Fundamental Right" That Dare not Speak Its Name' (2004) 116 Harv L Rev 1893, 1895.
[232] K Yoshino, 'The New Equal Protection' (2011) 124 Harv L Rev 747, 800.
[233] ibid.
[234] Tribe (n 231) 1955.

(d) History of disadvantage

A fourth factor assisting the courts to determine whether a group should be protected relates to whether the group has been subject to a history of disadvantage or prejudice. In the US Supreme Court, as we have seen, the list of factors in *San Antonio* includes 'a history of purposeful unequal treatment'.[235] In South Africa, this has also played a prominent role, although it goes to the issue of fairness rather than the delineation of analogous grounds. *Harksen* laid down the principle, oft-repeated in later cases, that in determining fairness under the equality guarantee, regardless of whether or not the discrimination is on a specified ground, a relevant factor is the position of the complainants in society and whether they have suffered in the past from patterns of disadvantage.[236] Similarly, a history of disadvantage has been a key factor in the Canadian jurisprudence.[237]

This is a powerful indicator of analogous grounds and fits well with the understanding of equality set out in Chapter 1. However, a focus on a history of disadvantage might create blind spots in the jurisprudence in relation to current and emerging forms of disadvantage. In *R v Turpin*,[238] prisoners in Ontario claimed that they were discriminated against in breach of section 15 because they did not have the same access to a jury trial as prisoners in other provinces. The Supreme Court of Canada held that because prisoners in Ontario did not have a history of disadvantage compared to prisoners outside that province, they were not within the contemplation of section 15.

This factor also depends on the openness of the courts in recognizing such a history. The rejection by the US Supreme Court of claims for suspect status on grounds of age, disability, and poverty rests in part on its refusal to recognize that these groups have been subjected to a history of disadvantage. It is also crucial to take a wide-angled view of what constitutes disadvantage. Importantly, in the Supreme Court of Canada in *Egan*, the Court rejected the contention that disadvantage was limited to economic disadvantage. Instead, it recognized that disadvantage must be read in the full social, political, and economical context.[239] Thus, while a history of disadvantage is clearly a factor, it should not be seen as the exclusive determinant of whether a characteristic should be protected under the equality guarantee.

---

[235] *San Antonio Independent School Dist v Rodriguez* 411 US 1, 93 S Ct 1278 (1973) (Powell J).
[236] *Harksen v Lane NO and Others* (n 181) para 50.
[237] *Corbiere v Canada (Minister of Indian and Northern Affairs)* (n 165).
[238] *R v Turpin* [1989] SCR 1296 (Can Sup Ct).
[239] *Egan v Canada* (n 168) para 172.

Thus, ultimately, there is no single element that can give a definitive answer to whether a characteristic should be within the inner circle of specially protected characteristics. Instead, the courts have tended to use a constellation of factors. Although perhaps leaving too much discretion in the hands of judges, this approach has in practice proved to be an important vehicle for the law to develop dynamically in response to changing circumstances.

(iii) Intersectional Discrimination

One consequence of the focus on group identity of current equality law is the assumption that each individual belongs to a single, well-demarcated identity group. In reality, however, we all have multiple intersecting identities, constituted by our gender, sexual orientation, age, ethnicity, capabilities, and religion or lack of religion. While this can enrich our life experience and create community cohesion born from interlocking interests and concerns, it can also intensify disadvantage for those who belong to more than one disadvantaged group. For example, Black women are subject to both sexism and racism, as well as bearing a 'third burden'; namely, discrimination against Black men. Women from marginalized ethnicities, Black women, indigenous women,[240] older women, and disabled women are among the most disadvantaged groups in many countries in the world. Similar intersectional discrimination is experienced by LGBTQI+ members of marginalized ethnicities, disabled Black people, younger indigenous people, or older disabled people.

Recognition of intersectional discrimination has been pioneered in the US by African American women, who have powerfully demonstrated the ways in which anti-discrimination laws render invisible those who are at the

---

[240] As in previous chapters, this book acknowledges that the terminology used to describe people subjected to discrimination is sensitive and contested. In the different jurisdictions covered here (UK, Europe, India, South Africa, Canada, and the US), outgroups, or groups that are 'othered' in their own societies or globally, prefer to refer to themselves in different and sometimes opposing ways. This can also change, reflecting changes in social forces and perceptions. Acknowledging these complexities, I have chosen to use 'Black people', 'marginalized ethnicities', and 'indigenous people', following the approach of the UN Special Rapporteur on the right to health, Tlaleng Mofokeng, in her report to the United Nations on sexual and reproductive health rights on 16 July 2021 (A/76/172) <https://undocs.org/A/76/172> accessed 31 May 2022. The reference to 'gender identity, gender expression and sex characteristics' follows her report on gender-based violence submitted to the UN on 14 April 2022 (A/HRC/50/28) <www.ohchr.org/en/documents/thematic-reports/ahrc5028-violence-and-its-impact-right-health-report-special-rapporteur> accessed 31 May 2022.

intersection of several grounds.[241] This invisibility is partly because of the structure of discrimination law, which requires a comparison only on the basis of a single ground. But it is also due to a more fundamental problem; namely, that the categories on which grounds are based focus on the more privileged of that group. As Kimberlé Crenshaw, the foremost thinker on this subject, has argued: 'The paradigm of sex discrimination tends to be based on the experiences of white women; the model of race discrimination tends to be based on the experiences of the most privileged blacks. Notions of what constitutes race and sex discrimination are, as a result, narrowly tailored to embrace only a small set of circumstances, none of which include discrimination against black women.'[242]

An intersectionality perspective highlights several key weaknesses in the focus of anti-discrimination law on a single ground. As a start, it assumes that groups are rigidly delineated by race, gender, disability, sexual orientation, or other status. This makes it impossible to traverse these boundaries and recognize those who are disadvantaged through a combination of grounds. Correspondingly, such an approach regards identity groups as internally homogeneous, obscuring the very real differences within such groups. This has been a major source of contention within the feminist movement. White, middle-class women have been rightly criticized by Black women for assuming that their own experience is a universal characteristic of gender oppression.[243] Atrey similarly shows how in India 'even if gender and caste impacted all women, they impacted women in qualitatively different ways'.[244] For upper-caste (or Brahmin) women, caste oppression manifests as strict regulation of their reproductive and sexual rights and choice in marriage.[245] For Dalit and Adivasi women, who fall at the very bottom of the hierarchy, caste oppression takes the form, inter alia, of sexual exploitation, by both upper-caste and Dalit men.[246] The categories of religion and belief, disability, and age are similarly fractured.

Even more fundamentally, the 'single ground' approach to discrimination law ignores the role of power in structuring relationships. Discrimination is not symmetrical; it operates to create or entrench domination by some over

---

[241] K Crenshaw, 'Demarginalising the Intersection of Race and Sex' (1989) University of Chicago Legal Forum 139.
[242] ibid 151.
[243] E Spellman, *Inessential Woman* (Beacon Press 1988) esp 114–15.
[244] S Atrey, *Intersectional Discrimination* (OUP 2019) 67.
[245] ibid.
[246] ibid.

others. But such power relations can operate both vertically and diagonally. For example, Black men may be in a position of power in relation to their gender but not in relation to their colour.[247] Conversely, white women may be in a position of power in relation to their colour but not their gender. At the foundational level, power operates to construct identity categories themselves. Race is a social construct, a marker for oppression rather than a biological reality. Ethnicity, too, is framed by power relations, with minorities in some countries being majorities in others. These structures of domination work in complex ways which cannot easily be captured through a single-identity model.

How, then, to address this issue? Crucially, Crenshaw argues, intersectional discrimination does not simply consist of the addition of two sources of discrimination. The impact is qualitatively different, or synergistic. In particular, the disadvantage experienced by Black women is not the same as that experienced by white women or Black men.[248] For example, in *DeGraffenreid*, a US redundancy case,[249] Black women, being the most recent entries to the company, were made redundant first. Since both white women and Black men were among those who escaped redundancy, these women could not claim that they had been less favourably treated on grounds of either gender alone or race alone. It was only the synergistic situation, of being both female and Black, that was the source of the discrimination.

In the UK and EU, this is illustrated by considering the position of migrant women. Migrants of both genders tend to be concentrated in specific segments of the labour market, but opportunities for immigrant women are particularly restricted. Immigrant women are ten times more likely to work as domestic workers than local women, and as many as 25 per cent of immigrant women in the EU work in menial jobs, compared to 15 per cent of immigrant men.[250] Women who come to the EU to join their husbands under family reunification schemes face long delays before they are permitted to work, leaving them financially dependent on their husbands. Because they

---

[247] The term 'colour' is used here because it is used in international and regional human rights documents (CERD, Art 1; ICCPR, Art 2(1); ICESCR, Art 2(1); ECHR, Art 14) and national human rights instruments (eg South African Constitution, s 9; UK EA 2010, s 9(1), Canadian Charter, s 15).

[248] See n 240.

[249] *DeGraffenreid v General Motors Assembly Division* 413 F Supp 142 (1976) (US Federal Ct of Appeals).

[250] European Union Agency for Fundamental Rights, 'Second European Union Minorities and Discrimination Survey: Migrant Women—Selected Findings' (2019) <https://ec.europa.eu/migrant-integration/library-document/findings-migrant-women-2nd-eu-minorities-and-discrimination-survey_en> accessed 27 July 2022.

are only given status as spouses, they are legally bound to their husbands.[251] Migrant women in an abusive marriage are particularly vulnerable if their status depends on marriage, since they face deportation if they leave their husbands, a vulnerability compounded by language difficulties, lack of knowledge of sources of protection, and difficulties in finding work or other sources of income to support themselves and their children.[252]

Domestic violence in the context of the synergistic impact of gender combined with racial or religious discrimination similarly raises specifically intersectional issues. For example, women might find it difficult to speak out against domestic violence, through fear of direct racism by the police or because they are concerned that reporting violence might reinforce negative stereotypes and expose their own communities to racist treatment, including deportation or injury. As we saw in Chapter 2, these intersectional concerns have been heightened by the Covid pandemic which raged across the world in 2020 and 2021.

The synergistic nature of intersectional discrimination also makes it difficult to monitor. Many national statistics do not include data disaggregated by both sex and race, still less by other sources of intersectional discrimination such as ethnicity and disability. For example, an Irish study demonstrates the invisibility of ethnic minority people with disabilities, underlined by the total absence of this group in national statistics.[253] Yet this group suffers in complex and often subtle ways from both race and disability discrimination. Service and healthcare providers tend to ignore their ethnicity in framing structures for accommodating disability, with the result that their culture and identity is devalued and they face greater difficulty accessing appropriate services. At the same time, they might face discrimination from their own ethnic community on grounds of disability. The central problem identified by the notion of intersectional discrimination, then, is how to render them visible and properly remedy the wrongs of those who are disadvantaged in multiple ways.

It has been argued, therefore, that intersectionality theory aims to disrupt the established group demarcations used in anti-discrimination law. The path to a solution is, however, challenging. The instinctive response is to create better delineated subgroups. This would grant 'greater inclusion to

---

[251] ibid.

[252] ibid. S Fredman, *The Future of Equality in Great Britain* (Equal Opportunities Commission 2002) 25–26.

[253] M Pierce, *Minority Ethnic People with Disabilities in Northern Ireland* (Equality Authority 2003).

differently defined subjects such as Black women plaintiffs or battered immigrant women'.[254] But does this mean that subgroups should be permitted to infinitely multiply and reconfigure?[255] And how can the law manage a proliferation of subgroups? This anxiety has been reflected by judges and lawmakers, who have been wary of opening a 'Pandora's box' to claims by multiple subgroups. For example, in *DeGraffenreid*, the US Federal Court of Appeals categorically refused to accept that Black women formed a separate category, arguing that this gave them a 'super remedy' or 'greater standing' than Black men or white women.[256] Subsequent US cases have been more promising. In *Jefferies*, the Fifth Circuit Federal Court of Appeal recognized that discrimination against Black women can exist even in the absence of discrimination against Black men or white women.[257] It is now accepted that Black women constitute a distinct subgroup.[258] However, later courts took fright at the possibility that this would turn 'employment discrimination into a many-headed Hydra, impossible to contain . . . Following the *Jeffries* rationale to its extreme, protected subgroups would exist for every possible combination of race, color, sex, national origin and religion.'[259]

To prevent the spectre that the benefits of the anti-discrimination legislation would be 'splintered beyond use and recognition,'[260] it was held that cumulative discrimination should be restricted to a combination of only two of the grounds (the 'sex plus' approach).[261] The result is both artificial and paradoxical. The more a person differs from the dominant norm, and the more likely she is to experience multiple discrimination, the less likely she is to gain protection. A similar pattern can be seen in the UK. Section 14 of the EA 2010 makes provision for discrimination on more than one ground. However, the legislation follows the US principle of confining the comparison to two protected characteristics. It therefore remains the case that the more a person differs from the norm, the less likely she is to gain protection. Even in this limited form, however, this provision has been regarded as problematic and section 14 has never been brought into effect.

---

[254] S Cho, K Crenshaw, and L McCall, 'Toward a Field of Intersectionality Studies: Theory, Applications and Praxis' (2013) 38 Signs 792.

[255] ibid 787.

[256] *DeGraffenreid v General Motors Assembly Division* (n 249).

[257] *Jefferies v Harris County Community Action Assn* 615 F 2d 1025 (5th Cir 1980) (US Federal Ct of Appeals).

[258] ibid 1034.

[259] *Judge v Marsh* 649 F Supp 770, 779 (1986) (US District Ct, District of Columbia).

[260] ibid.

[261] See *Jeffries* (n 257) 1033–34.

Anxiety about the management of multiple subgroups raises questions about whether the focus of intersectionality theorists on groups and identities is appropriate. In particular, the assumption that all members of the subgroup are the same and that identity is fixed and static falls into the very trap that intersectionality theory has aimed to avoid. Conaghan argues that intersectionality has become too bound up with notions of identity and especially subjective experiences of identity formation. This risks obscuring economic and distributive issues which relate to objective social structures rather than subjective experiences of social location.[262]

It has become clear, then, that intersectionality theory, at least in some of its manifestations, took a wrong turn in focusing on groups and identities. In their more recent work, Cho, Crenshaw, and McCall demonstrate that these seemingly intractable difficulties arise from a misconception of intersectionality as being preoccupied with groups and identities or 'fascinated with the infinite combinations and implications of overlapping identities'.[263] Instead, theorists have reformulated intersectionality in terms of structures of power and exclusion or 'structural intersectionality'. Rather than assuming that groups or categories have rigid boundaries, structural intersectionality reveals how power works through the creation and deployment of identities. In this sense, intersectionality concerns 'the way things work rather than who people are'.[264] Analysing power relationships, moreover, makes it possible to discern which kinds of differentiation warrant attention. As Tomlinson notes: 'If critics think intersectionality is a matter of identity rather than power, they cannot see which differences make a difference. Yet it is exactly our analyses of power that reveal which differences carry significance.'[265] This does not mean that identities are not important; more that they should be seen both as a manifestation of the intersection of multiple hierarchies and a way of maintaining such hierarchies.[266]

Integrating these insights into anti-discrimination law requires a closer look at the role of 'grounds', and whether they should necessarily be linked to 'groups'. Rather than regarding grounds as demarcating separate groups,

---

[262] J Conaghan, 'Intersectionality and the Feminist Project in Law' in E Grabham and others (eds), *Intersectionality and Beyond: Law, Power and the Politics of Location* (Routledge-Cavendish 2009) 21, 30–31.

[263] Cho, Crenshaw, and McCall (n 254).

[264] J Chun, G Lipsitz, and Y Shin, 'Intersectionality as a Social Movement Strategy: Asian Immigrant Women Advocates' (2013) 38 Signs 917, 923.

[265] B Tomlinson, 'To Tell the Truth and Not Get Trapped: Desire, Distance, and Intersectionality at the Scene of Argument' (2013) 38 Signs 993, 1012.

[266] C MacKinnon, 'Intersectionality as Method: A Note' (2013) 38 Signs 1019, 1023.

the significance of grounds should lie in the way specific characteristics pattern relationships with others. Everyone has a gender, a race or ethnicity, a sexual orientation, an age. Some have a religion or belief and some are secular. Taking a relational view, it can be seen that some of these characteristics might signal privilege, while others are relationships of further disadvantage. This means that power relationships not only operate vertically; they also operate diagonally and in layers. Ethnic minority men may be relatively disadvantaged in relation to women in their communities, but relatively disadvantaged in relation to both ethnic majority women and ethnic majority men. Similarly, white women may be relatively advantaged in relation to ethnic minority women while relatively disadvantaged in relation to white men.[267] For example, in the EU, the vast majority of domestic workers in Europe are women, many of them migrant women in irregular employment. Brigitte Anderson concludes from her research into this area that most employers of domestic workers in Europe are also women and that 'the power relations among these women are very complex, to the point where even acts of kindness work to reproduce an employer's status and self-image'.[268] Her research also points to the 'racialisation of paid domestic labour' in Europe.[269]

Intersectionality should, therefore, be seen in terms of relationships of power rather than in terms of identities per se. Whereas a focus on fixed identities renders invisible the most disadvantaged, a consideration of relationships of power has the opposite effect, requiring specific attention to be paid to those who are detrimentally affected by multiple interacting relationships. Since we all have multiple identities, a particular characteristic or ground should be interpreted as including everyone with that characteristic, rather than just the 'privileged' among them. For example, discrimination on grounds of gender is itself variegated depending on the ways in which power relations in the society as a whole are patterned. Women experience discrimination on grounds of gender because of the relationships of power constructed through gender, but these relationships differ for different women in material ways. In a society where power is also constructed along the axes of race or ethnicity, her race changes the nature of the power relationship without changing the fact that she has been discriminated against

[267] J Cock, *Maids and Madams* (Women's Press 1990).

[268] B Anderson, 'Just Another Job: The Commodification of Domestic Labour' in B Ehrenreich and A Hochschild (eds), *Global Woman: Nannies, Maids and Sex-workers in the New Economy* (Sage 2004) 113.

[269] B Anderson, *Doing the Dirty Work: The Global Politics of Domestic Labour* (Zed Books 2000).

on grounds of gender. This, in turn, means that a reference to a 'ground' does not necessarily mean that the ground demarcates a group with set boundaries.[270] If that were the case, it would indeed be impossible to deal with those who fall at the intersection of groups, without creating a proliferation of further groups. The focus should instead be on relationships of disadvantage, rather than on the configuration of the group itself. A structural approach to intersectionality therefore understands particular grounds in a relational way; that is, as a conduit to describe different power relationships rather than as delineating a group. This means that rather than constructing further subgroups, it is possible to construe existing grounds sufficiently capaciously to address the confluence of power relationships which compounds disadvantage.

How, then, can intersectional experiences be addressed within anti-discrimination law? Three possible ways forward can be identified. First, new subgroups could be created to reflect intersectional experiences. Secondly, grounds within the existing list could be combined. Thirdly, existing grounds can be interpreted expansively, so that intersectional experiences can be addressed by acknowledging that even within a single ground, multiple intersecting power relations can be addressed.

The first approach, delineating groups at the intersection, is based on the premise that to recognize the synergistic nature of discrimination, new, intersectional groups should be recognized in their own right. For example, rather than having to choose between litigating on grounds of race or gender, Black women can claim to be subjected to discrimination as Black women. Similarly, disabled older people do not have to choose between disability and age as a ground but can litigate as disabled older people. The Canadian Supreme Court has adopted an approach along these lines in some of its case law. In *Law v Canada*, the Court held that it was open to a claimant to articulate a discrimination claim under more than one of the enumerated and analogous grounds.[271] The Court made it clear that there was no reason in principle why an intersection of grounds could not be understood as analogous to the grounds listed in the constitutional equality guarantee, provided it could be shown to advance the fundamental purpose of that provision.[272] In particular, it should be asked whether discrimination on the proposed

---

[270] S Atrey, 'Realising Intersectionality in Discrimination Law' (D Phil thesis, Oxford University 2016).

[271] *Law v Canada* [1999] 1 SCR 497 (Can Sup Ct).

[272] ibid 554–55.

intersectional ground brings into play a potential violation of human dignity. This was applied in *Corbiere v Canada*,[273] in which, as we have seen, the Supreme Court of Canada recognized a new analogous ground of discrimination which combined ethnicity (in this case being a member of a First Nation band) and residence. Indigenous people who were members of a band but did not live on the reserve allocated to the band were not permitted to vote in band elections. The discrimination was therefore neither solely on the grounds of ethnic origin (membership of a First Nation band) nor of residence, but on the basis of an intersection of these two grounds. The judgment of L'Heureux-Dubé J also emphasized a third axis of intersectionality; namely, the adverse effect on indigenous women, or descendants of indigenous women, who lost their band status if they married a man without band status.

This approach is clearly only available in jurisdictions with a non-exhaustive list of grounds, or an open-textured approach, such as in Canada, South Africa, and the US. In other jurisdictions, such as the EU, UK, and India, the courts are not empowered to create new grounds to reflect the specific experience of discrimination experienced by groups such as Black women or Dalit women. Even where it is possible to extend the list, there are limits to the extent to which new grounds can be created to cater for the specific intersectional group. For example, if we have a category for Black women, do we also need one for Black women with a disability, and then for older Black women with a disability, or for older lesbian, Black women with a disability? As we have seen, not only have judges and lawmakers been wary of opening a 'Pandora's box' to claims by multiple intersecting groups. In addition, intersectionality theorists themselves have recognized these difficulties.

A second possibility is to combine grounds within an existing list without regarding this as a new subgroup. This is a more fluid approach, capable of being responsive to particular contexts rather than setting in stone a particular subgroup. Several jurisdictions already make provision for such an approach. For example, under the South African Constitution, the State may not unfairly discriminate against anyone on 'one or more grounds' including those listed.[274] The possibility of combining grounds in this way has allowed the SACC to be responsive to intersectional discrimination in very specific contexts. This has been particularly important for Muslim women

[273] *Corbiere v Canada (Minister of Indian and Northern Affairs)* (n 165).
[274] South African Constitution, s 9(3).

in polygamous marriages, who have argued that they have been treated less favourably than women in polygamous marriage governed by customary law in South Africa. This is particularly acute in relation to the recognition of a spouse for the purposes of testate or intestate succession. Women in customary law, polygamous marriages are recognized as surviving spouses both in relation to intestate succession and under the Wills Act. However, in polygamous marriages solemnized under Islamic law, only one wife was recognized as an heir.[275] In *Hassam v Jacobs*, the Court unanimously held that they were discriminated against on the triple grounds of religion, gender, and marital status.[276] Far from a Hydra-headed monster, this permitted the law to respond with appropriate sensitivity to a situation of multiple disadvantage. In *Moosa*, the Court underpinned this with the underlying right to dignity, which makes it possible to address the experience of discrimination of the individual person at the intersection, here the discrimination against her as a Muslim woman.[277] As Cachalia AJ put it: 'Its effect is to stigmatise her marriage, diminish her self-worth and increase her feeling of vulnerability as a Muslim woman.'[278]

The *Mahlangu* case gave the Court the opportunity to fully integrate an intersectional analysis into its jurisprudence.[279] The case, as we have seen, concerned the exclusion of domestic workers from the occupational insurance scheme available to other workers. Ms Mahlangu, a domestic worker, tragically drowned in her employer's swimming pool and her family was left without compensation. The uncontested evidence before the Court showed that the overwhelming majority of domestic workers are Black women. The Court held that this exclusion discriminated against them on grounds of sex, gender, and race. But this was more than the sum of these characteristics. By excluding them from the protection, they were rendered invisible not just because they were women, but because of the specific social history of racist and patriarchal oppression under apartheid, which limited their choice of work and their ability to demand decent working conditions. 'If the equality breach is analysed through an intersectional lens with all the multi axes of indirect discrimination taken into account, this can have an impact on achieving structural systemic transformation.'[280] The ECtHR is feeling its

---

[275] Intestate Succession Act 81 of 1987, s 1(4)(f).
[276] *Hassam v Jacobs NO and Others* (CCT83/08) [2009] ZACC 19, 2009 (11) BCLR 1148 (SACC).
[277] *Moosa v Minister of Justice and Correctional Services* [2018] ZACC 19 (SACC).
[278] ibid para 16.
[279] *Mahlangu v Minister of Labour* (n 102) para 75.
[280] ibid para 106.

way towards a similar analysis although without expressly incorporating the terminology of intersectionality. In *BS v Spain*, the Court held that the authorities failed to take into account the applicant's 'particular vulnerability inherent in her position as an African woman working as a [sex worker]' and therefore violated Article 14 in conjunction with Article 3 (right not to be subjected to cruel and inhuman treatment).[281]

The second approach has the great advantage of being capable of capturing synergistic discrimination without creating fixed subgroups. However, it is not available to all jurisdictions, particularly those with fixed lists where some of the intersectional grounds are not expressly enumerated. In some jurisdictions, such as the EU, this difficulty is compounded by the fact that specific grounds have differing scope and justification defences.[282] In EU law, race and gender are protected in the context of discrimination in social protection and housing, whereas age is not. It would therefore be difficult to challenge discrimination against older ethnic minority women in social protection or housing. Similarly, there is a wider defence of justification in relation to age in UK law than in relation to race or gender. This, again, makes it difficult in practice to bring a claim on intersectional grounds relating to age, race, and gender.

It is for this reason that it is worth exploring a third approach, the 'capacious' approach.[283] On this view, multiple intersecting relationships can be reflected within a capacious notion of each ground, making it possible to address intersectionality even in the absence of new groups or combined grounds. As we have seen, Crenshaw forcefully demonstrated how current discrimination law functions to protect only the more privileged of a group, for example Black men and white women. A 'capacious' approach would correct this by insisting that all aspects of an individual's identity should be brought under the spotlight. The category 'woman' covers all women, not just white women: it is only because of existing structures of vertical, diagonal, and layered power imbalances that the category 'woman' can be captured by the most privileged women. A capacious approach instead lays bare these axes of privilege and disadvantage among women. In this way, it reflects the move among intersectionality theorists from a focus on creating multiple subgroups to a structural approach, based on power differentials. Taking a

---

[281] *BS v Spain* (Application no 47159/08) (ECtHR).

[282] S Fredman, *Intersectional Discrimination in EU Gender Equality and Non-Discrimination Law* (European Commission: European Network of Legal Experts in Gender Equality and Non-Discrimination 2016).

[283] ibid.

capacious approach to the meaning of single grounds makes it possible to capture the diagonal, vertical, and layered structures of power which constitute discriminatory relationships. A woman who suffers intersectional disadvantage because she is an older ethnic minority woman is still subject to discrimination on the grounds that she is a woman. The category 'woman' covers all women and the more disadvantaged, the more she should attract protection. Similarly, all members of an ethnic minority, including ethnic minority women, should be protected against discrimination on grounds of ethnic origin, and the fact that a woman suffers specific discrimination as an ethnic minority woman should enhance her claim rather than preclude it.

This approach chimes with Atrey's development of the concept of integrity to counter the splintering of identities created by rigid conceptions of grounds:

> The dynamic of sameness and difference in patterns of group disadvantage may give the impression of a highly variegated and fragmented reality of intersectional discrimination. As if an individual or a group lives through multiple realities where some experiences of discrimination are similar to, whilst others are different from, disadvantage associated with each ground individually. But, in fact, the ontological reality that intersectionality seeks to convey is exactly the opposite: that sameness and difference in patterns of group disadvantage make sense only when they are considered *as a whole* or with *integrity*.[284]

The capacious approach can be seen in both CEDAW and the Convention on the Rights of Persons with Disabilities (CRPD). These conventions appear to be 'single axis' because of their focus on women and disabled people, respectively. Nevertheless, they expressly regard 'women' and 'people with disabilities' as including intersections of disadvantage. Thus, CEDAW does not regard 'women' as an undifferentiated category, but recognizes the ways in which different aspects of different women's identities interact to produce disadvantage. Campbell has convincingly argued that because CEDAW uses the category 'women' rather than a grounds-based approach, there is an implicit commitment to address all forms of disadvantage that women experience, including intersectional disadvantage.[285] There are multiple instances

---

[284] Atrey (n 270) 45.
[285] M Campbell, 'CEDAW and Women's Intersecting Identities: A Pioneering Approach to Intersectional Discrimination' (2015) Revista Direito GV 479.

of this in CEDAW. The preamble expresses its concern that women in situations of poverty have the 'least access to food, health, education, training and opportunities for employment and other needs'.[286] It also emphasizes that 'the eradication . . . racial discrimination, . . . is essential to the full enjoyment of the rights of men and women'.[287] Similarly, specific attention is given to rural women.[288] This can also be seen in General Recommendations produced by the CEDAW Committee. According to General Recommendation No 28, discrimination against women based on sex and gender 'is inextricably linked with other factors that affect women, such as race, ethnicity, religion or belief, health, status, age, class, caste and sexual orientation and gender identity'. Emphasizing that 'discrimination on the basis of sex or gender may affect women belonging to such groups to a different degree or in different ways than men', it requires States parties to legally recognize and prohibit such intersecting forms of discrimination, and to adopt and pursue policies to eliminate them.[289] Other General Recommendations deal with issues facing women in relation to migrant status, statelessness, and age.[290] It is further recognized that these specific contexts are not themselves unidimensional: for example, General Recommendation No 27 on older women refers to the discrimination experienced by older women as 'multidimensional', compounded by poverty, migrant status, family status, and ethnicity.[291] Campbell demonstrates further—through a close investigation of the CEDAW Committee's approach in its Concluding Observations, Inquiry Procedure, and Individual Communications—that 'there is overwhelming evidence that CEDAW Committee is applying the fluid and expansive concept of intersectional discrimination that it is pioneering in the General Recommendations'.[292]

A similar approach can be detected in the CRPD. Like CEDAW, the CRPD appears to be a 'single axis' convention, focusing specifically on people with disabilities. However, this has not meant that it ignores or neutralizes other disadvantaging aspects of an individual's social location. The preamble expresses concern about the 'difficult conditions faced by persons with

---

[286] CEDAW, Preamble.
[287] ibid.
[288] ibid Art 14(1).
[289] Committee on the Elimination of Discrimination Against Women General Recommendation No 28 on the Core Obligations of States Parties under Article 2 of CEDAW, CEDAW/C/2010/47/GC.2, para 18.
[290] CEDAW General Recommendation Nos 26, 32, and 27.
[291] CEDAW General Recommendation No 27, para 13.
[292] Campbell (n 285).

disabilities who are subject to multiple or aggravated forms of discrimination on the basis of race, colour, sex, language, religion, political or other opinion, national, ethnic, indigenous or social origin, property, birth, age or other status'.[293] It goes on to emphasize the need to incorporate a gender perspective in all efforts to promote the full enjoyment of human rights by persons with disabilities and to recognize that women and girls with disabilities are often at greater risk of violence, abuse, neglect, and exploitation, both within and outside the home.[294] It also makes specific mention of children with disabilities and highlights that the majority of persons with disabilities live in poverty.[295] This is echoed in the convention itself, with Article 6 referring to women with disabilities and Article 7 to children with disabilities. Moreover, Article 8b enjoins signatory States to take measures to combat stereotypes, prejudices, and harmful practices relating to persons with disabilities 'including those based on sex and age'. This can be seen, too, in the definition of disability in the convention, which recognizes that it is the interaction between impairments and social or other barriers which hinders full participation.[296] 'Other barriers' could include barriers due to other grounds, such as age, sexual orientation, or racial and ethnic origin.

The capacious approach, when applied to individual jurisdictions, has several benefits. Not only does it properly express the principle of intersectionality. It also frees us from the 'Pandora's box' scenario of infinitely reconfiguring groups. There is therefore no need, as in the US and UK, to attempt to restrict the analysis to only two groups or categories.[297] The perennial problem of the comparator, seemingly so intractable with a single-axis approach, is similarly avoided. Under a single-axis approach, the detriment experienced by a Black woman, a woman from a marginalized ethnicity, or an indigenous woman is not regarded as less favourable treatment on grounds of gender if white women do not suffer a similar detriment. Nor is it regarded as race discrimination if Black men, men from marginalized ethnicities, or indigenous women[298] are not subjected to similar detriment. A capacious approach accepts that a detriment can be gender or race discrimination even if not all others within the group experience the same detriment. This is already visible in relation to pregnancy. Even though not all women are pregnant,

---

[293] CRPD, Preamble, para p.
[294] ibid paras s and q.
[295] ibid paras r and t.
[296] ibid Art 1.
[297] Fredman (n 282).
[298] See n 240.

it has now been recognized that discrimination on grounds of pregnancy is gender discrimination.[299] The capacious approach also has some practical difficulties. Most of all, it depends on litigators to present cases in the holistic manner described in a way which is persuasive to the courts.

II SCOPE OF DISCRIMINATION LAW

It is not always the case that discrimination is prohibited in all walks of life. Nor is it the case that everyone is prohibited from discriminating. The reach of equality law is delineated in different ways in different jurisdictions, but this depends on specific legal, historical, and cultural factors, rather than on overriding principles.

At the constitutional level, coverage generally extends to all governmental actions.[300] This is more complex in federal systems where the limitations of federal power need to be borne in mind. In the US, the federal government only has the power delegated to it by the Constitution, with all other powers reserved to the States.[301] In the case of the Fourteenth Amendment, the Constitution does specifically give power to Congress to enforce its provisions by appropriate legislation.[302] However, Congress is not given carte blanche. Legislation passed at the federal level to enforce the Fourteenth Amendment must be congruent and proportionate to the Fourteenth Amendment breach. In addition, States have immunity against money suits in federal courts brought by citizens of other States and, increasingly, their own.[303] Congress can only abrogate this immunity by federal anti-discrimination statutes if this is an appropriate means of enforcing the equal protection clause.[304]

In recent years, the US Supreme Court has been progressively more restrictive in its interpretation of these limits on federal power. In *Kimel v Florida*, the Court struck down a provision in the Age Discrimination in Employment Act (ADEA) which permitted public employees to sue their State employers for breach of the ADEA.[305] The Court held that the Act

[299] See further Chapter 6.
[300] South African Constitution, s 8; Canadian Charter, s 32; *Retail, Wholesale & Department Store Union, Local 580 v Dolphin Delivery* (1987) 33 DLR (4th) 174 (Can Sup Ct).
[301] Tenth Amendment, US Constitution.
[302] Fourteenth Amendment, s 5.
[303] Eleventh Amendment; *Kimel v Florida Board of Regents* (n 64).
[304] *Board of Trustees of the University of Alabama v Garrett* 531 US 356, 364 (2001) (US Sup Ct).
[305] *Kimel v Florida Bd of Regents*, 528 US 62 (2000) (US Sup Ct).

went beyond the Fourteenth Amendment which, as we have seen, requires only rational-basis scrutiny. Because the Act prohibited substantially more State employment decisions and practices than the rational-basis standard under the Constitution, it was not a proportionate use of federal power.[306] The Court held that States therefore retain their immunity from suit for pecuniary damages for breach of the ADEA.[307] In *Garrett*, a provision in the Disability Discrimination Act (DDA) which gave individuals the right to seek damages against States in employment cases was similarly struck down.[308] In a far-reaching judgment, the Court held that Congress had not identified a sufficient pattern of past discrimination on grounds of disability to warrant intrusion on State immunity. Nor was the duty of reasonable accommodation, found in the DDA, a proportionate response to any discrimination that did exist. According to Rehnquist CJ, it would be entirely rational, and therefore constitutional, for a State employer to 'conserve scarce financial resources' by hiring employees who could use existing facilities.[309] Similarly, it held that the disparate impact provision in the DDA far exceeded the constitutional requirement. 'To uphold the Act's application to the States would allow Congress to rewrite the Fourteenth Amendment law laid down by this Court in *Cleburne*.'[310] In a powerful dissent, Breyer J found that 'by its very terms [the Fourteenth] Amendment prohibits *States* from denying their citizens equal protection of the laws'.[311] Removing the remedy of private damages actions against States, he held, means that enforcement can only take place through injunctions or federal standards to cure important national problems such as disability discrimination.

EU law, too, has resonances of the tension between federal and State law. Here the reach of discrimination law is determined by the extent of the powers afforded to the Union by the Member States through successive EU Treaties. As the spirit of the EU has evolved from aiming specifically to create a common market, to one underpinned by the constitutional values of the Member States, so the scope of the power afforded to the Union to regulate discrimination law has broadened. As we have seen, from the inception of the Community equality as a principle was only relevant insofar

---

[306] ibid.
[307] ibid.
[308] *Board of Trustees of the University of Alabama v Garrett* (n 304).
[309] ibid 372.
[310] ibid 375.
[311] ibid 388, italics in original.

as it was needed in the creation of a European-wide labour market.[312] For this reason, discrimination law at the EU level applied only to employment, vocational training, and membership of employers', workers', or professional organizations.

Restriction to the labour market, however, inevitably curtails the effectiveness of anti-discrimination protection. This is because inequalities in the labour market are frequently a result of discrimination outside the labour market: in education, in housing, in the division of labour within the home, and in an individual's ability to access services such as health, banking, and transport. In a belated recognition of these issues, these boundaries were breached for the first time by the Race Directive in 2000, which ventured beyond the employment field to incorporate discrimination in relation to four new areas: social protection, including social security and healthcare; social advantages; education; and access to and supply of goods and services which are available to the public, including housing.[313] The preamble to the Race Directive highlights the link between protection against discrimination outside the market and labour market efficiency. Discrimination based on racial or ethnic origin, it is declared, may undermine the achievement of the objectives of the EC Treaty, in particular the attainment of a high level of employment and of social protection. At the same time, the preamble stresses equity and justice as goals.

> To ensure the development of democratic and tolerant societies which allow the participation of all persons irrespective of racial or ethnic origin, . . . [it is necessary to] go beyond access to employed and self-employed activities and cover areas such as education, social protection, social advantages and access to and supply of goods and services.[314]

Equal treatment for men and women outside the labour market was addressed for the first time in 2004, with a directive implementing the principle of equal treatment between women and men in access to and supply of goods and services.[315]

Despite this recognition in relation to race and gender, the other grounds of discrimination continue to be protected by EU law only in relation to the traditional labour market arena. The Employment Directive, also passed in

---

[312] See eg W Streeck, 'From Market Making to State Building' in S Liebfried and P Pierson (eds), *European Social Policy* (Brookings Institution 1995) 397.
[313] Directive 2000/43, Art 3(1).
[314] ibid recital 12.
[315] Council Directive 2004/113/EC.

2000, which applies to sexual orientation, disability, religion or belief, and age restricted the reach of protection to employment, vocational training, and membership of professional associations. This is problematic in that it creates a hierarchy of grounds. Race and ethnicity, so long in the wilderness, were suddenly the best protected. This, in turn, creates pressure on the definition of the grounds, as seen earlier. Since ethnicity falls within the wider zone of protection and religion within the narrower, it becomes necessary to draw bright-line distinctions between ethnicity and religion. This is also problematic for intersectional claims, as we have seen. It was hoped that this awkward patchwork of protection, with some grounds better protected than others, would be remedied by a draft directive extending the protection provided against discrimination on grounds of disability, religion or belief, age, and sexual orientation, to areas outside the labour market (social protection, including social security and healthcare, social advantages, education, and access to goods and services, including housing).[316] Although the directive was adopted by the European Commission in 2008, and approved by the European Parliament in 2009, it has never received the required unanimous approval by the Council of Ministers. It has therefore been withdrawn for the present.

Constitutional protection, binding on the State, is generally complemented by statutes which address discrimination by private parties. Different jurisdictions tend to delimit the scope of statutory protection in different ways. Title VII of the Civil Rights Act in the US prohibits discrimination by employers (public or private) of fifteen or more employees.[317] Title VII also prohibits discrimination based on 'race, color, religion' , or 'national origin' (but not sex) by private and public entities in access to public accommodations (eg hotels, restaurants, and theatres).[318] Also important is Title IX of the Civil Rights Act 1964, which prohibits discrimination on 'race, color, national origin, and sex' by publicly funded educational institutions and by public entities that receive funds from federal government.[319] In addition, Title VI prohibits discrimination based on 'race, color, or national origin' in any 'program or activity' receiving 'federal financial assistance'.[320] Other statutes contain their own limitations. The ADEA applies only to employment,

---

[316] COM(2008) 426.
[317] 42 USC § 2000e-2 (2006) and 42 USC § 2000e(b) (2006); amended in 1972 to prohibit employment discrimination by public as well as private employers (92 PS 261).
[318] 42 USC § 2000a(a)–(b) (2006).
[319] 42 USC § 2000d (2006).
[320] Codified at 42 USC § 2000d (2010).

while the Americans with Disabilities Act 1990 prohibits discrimination in employment and requires access to public accommodation for persons with disabilities. The Individuals with Disability Education Act requires public schools to provide equal access to students with disabilities.

The Canadian Human Rights Act[321] proscribes discrimination only in relation to employment and in the delivery of goods and services. It applies to anyone working for either the federal government or a private company regulated by the federal government, as well as anyone who receives goods and services from any of those sectors. All federal government departments and Crown corporations, as well as private companies such as railroads, airlines, banks, telephone companies, and radio or TV stations, are bound by the Act. At the provincial level, there are further statutory provisions which are not dealt with here.

The South African legislation divides jurisdiction between employment- and non-employment-related issues. The Employment Equity Act of 1998 (EEA) provides protection against discrimination in the workplace while the Promotion of Equality and Prevention of Unfair Discrimination Act 2000 (Equality Act) provides comprehensive protection against unfair discrimination in the public and private spheres, except where the EEA is applicable.

India concentrates its efforts on reservations, which apply primarily in public employment and education.[322] There is no comprehensive statute giving individuals a right to complain of discrimination, but there are piecemeal interventions in various fields, many of which have been updated in recent years. The Rights of Persons with Disabilities Act 2016, replacing earlier legislation, prohibits discrimination on grounds of disability and requires the appropriate government to ensure reasonable accommodation for persons with disabilities. It also requires public institutions for higher education to reserve seats for persons with specified disabilities and government establishments to reserve a proportion of vacancies for such persons. The Code on Social Security 2020, replacing the Maternity Benefits Act 1961, provides for payment of maternity benefits, leave for miscarriage, breaks for nursing, and dismissal for absence during pregnancy as well as other duties of employers.[323] The Code on Wages 2019, which replaced the Equal Remuneration Act 1976, prohibits wage discrimination on grounds of gender within an establishment. Sexual harassment is prohibited by the

---

[321] RSC, 1985, c H-6.
[322] See Chapter 7.
[323] Code on Social Security 2020, Ch VI, ss 60–71.

Sexual Harassment of Women at Workplace (Prevention, Prohibition and Redressal) Act 2013. Notably, the definition of 'workplace' is wide, including both the public and private sectors, large and small enterprises, houses or dwelling places, and places visited by the employee arising out of or during the course of employment including transportation by the employer for undertaking such journeys.

In the UK where there is no entrenched written constitution, the boundaries of discrimination law have always been determined by statute. Outside these demarcated areas, discrimination remains lawful. Under the EA 2010, which aimed to harmonize the tangled web of provisions which had grown up incrementally in the UK, the coverage is now largely the same for all grounds. Discrimination is prohibited in relation to work, education, the provision of goods, facilities, and services to the public, and the disposal or management of premises. Discrimination in relation to membership of associations is also covered, as is transport in relation to disabled persons. However, outside the core area of employment, coverage is still somewhat uneven. Marriage and civil partnership are excluded from protection in relation to most areas, except for aspects of discrimination at work. Discrimination on grounds of age is not prohibited in relation to schools, premises, and, for those under eighteen, provision of goods and services and public functions. Harassment on grounds of religion or sexual orientation is not prohibited in relation to the provision of goods and services.

The ECHR has a different approach to demarcating the scope of protection. Article 14 ECHR is structured as a parasitic or dependent right.[324] It guarantees only that 'the enjoyment of the rights in this Convention shall be secured without discrimination' on the mentioned grounds. The early case law of the Court assumed that before Article 14 could come into play, a breach of one of the substantive rights had to be proved. It was not surprising, therefore, that Article 14 often appeared redundant. If the right had been breached, no further energy needed to be expended on considering Article 14; if the right had not been breached, Article 14 was not applicable in any event.[325] However, as a closer look at the wording of Article 14 reveals, the Convention requires that the 'enjoyment' of Convention rights 'shall be secured without discrimination' rather than that there should be a breach as a

---

[324] See further S Fredman, 'Emerging from the Shadows: Substantive Equality and Article 14 of the European Convention on Human Rights' (2016) 16 Human Rights L Rev 273.
[325] For a recent example, see *Mileusnic and Mileusnic-Espenheim v Croatia* (Application no 66953/09), Merits, 19 February 2015, para 74; *Oliari v Italy* (Application nos 18766/11 and 36030/11), Merits, 21 July 2015.

precondition to the operation of Article 14. It was thus of critical importance for the development of Article 14 that the Court began to move from 'breach' to 'ambit'. According to the formula regularly used by the Court: 'For Article 14 to become applicable it suffices that the facts of a case fall within the ambit of another substantive provision of the Convention or its Protocols.'[326]

One of the most important implications of the 'ambit' principle is that Article 14 can extend 'beyond the enjoyment of the rights which the Convention requires each State to guarantee. It applies also to those additional rights, falling within the general scope of any Convention Article, for which the State has voluntarily decided to provide.'[327] This is epitomized in *EB v France* which concerned discrimination against a gay woman who wished to adopt a child.[328] The Court made it clear that Article 8 did not expressly give a right to a single person to adopt a child. Nevertheless, adoption clearly fell within the ambit of Article 8. The result was that 'the State, which has gone beyond its obligations under Article 8 in creating such a right cannot in the application of that right, take discriminatory measures within the meaning of Article 14.'[329]

The result has been far-reaching. While not establishing socio-economic rights as such, it has had the effect of extending existing social provisions in social democratic European States to excluded groups. In *Belgian Linguistics*, the Court held that the education provision in Article 2 of Protocol 1 does not give individuals the right to a particular kind of educational establishment. However, a State that does set up such an establishment cannot do so in a discriminatory manner.[330] A similar result for the right to housing can be seen in Baroness Hale's statement in the UK case of *Ghaidan*: 'Everyone has the right to respect for their home. This does not mean that the state—or anyone else—has to supply everyone with a home. . . . But if it does grant that right to some, it must not withhold it from others in the same or an analogous situation.'[331] This has extended, too, to welfare benefits. In *Stec*,[332] the Court reiterated that the right to peaceful enjoyment of property in Article 1 of Protocol 1 'does not create a right to acquire property. It places no restriction on the Contracting State's freedom to decide whether or not to have in

---

[326] *Thlimmenos v Greece* (2001) 31 EHRR 4 (ECtHR), most recently see *Hamalainen v Finland* (2015) 1 FCR 379 (ECtHR (Grand Chamber)).

[327] *EB v France* (2008) 47 EHRR 21, paras 47–48 (ECtHR (Grand Chamber)).

[328] ibid.

[329] ibid para 49.

[330] *Belgian Linguistics (No 2)* (1968) 1 EHRR 252, para 9 (ECtHR).

[331] *Ghaidan v Godin-Mendoza* [2004] UKHL 30, [2004] 2 AC 557 (HL).

[332] *Stec v United Kingdom* (n 132).

place any form of social security scheme, or to choose the type or amount of benefits to provide.' Nevertheless, it held: 'If, however, a Contracting State has in force legislation providing for the payment as of right of a welfare benefit contributions . . . that legislation must be regarded as generating a proprietary interest falling within the ambit of [Article 1] for persons satisfying its requirements.'[333] This means that benefits which it does provide must comply with Article 14.

Article 14, however, has no purchase where the State has not chosen to take any steps falling within the ambit of a right, or if there is no right which covers the situation at all. Some of these limitations have now been more directly addressed in Protocol 12, which was opened for signature in November 2000. Article 1(1) of Protocol 12 to the ECHR provides that 'the enjoyment of *any right set forth by law* shall be secured without discrimination' on any of the specified grounds.[334] This means that protection against discrimination is provided in relation to the enjoyment of any right specifically granted to an individual under national law, not just in the enjoyment of Convention rights. The importance of this extension was seen in *Sejdić and Finci v Bosnia and Herzegovina*.[335] In this case, the applicants, of Roma and Jewish origin respectively, challenged the constitutional settlement barring them from standing for election to the House of Peoples (the second chamber of the State Parliament) and the presidency (the collective head of State). Only Bosniacs, Croats, and Serbs were eligible for these positions. The ECHR includes a guarantee of free periodic elections, but this does not in terms give the right to stand for election to the presidency.[336] Nevertheless, the Court held, the complaint concerned a 'right set forth by law' for the purposes of Protocol 12 and the provision was indeed discriminatory under the protocol.

Article 1(1) only covers rights which have been specifically granted by the State. Article 1(2) of the protocol is even wider, stating that 'no-one shall be discriminated against by any public authority' on one of the specified grounds. Thus, the non-discrimination guarantee applies in the exercise of public functions, regardless of whether a right has been specifically granted. The duty also arises in the exercise by a public authority of discretionary powers, for example the granting of certain subsidies, as well as in respect of any other act or omission of a public authority. Protocol 12 would cover,

[333] ibid.
[334] Emphasis added.
[335] *Sejdić and Finci v Bosnia and Herzegovina* (Application no 27996/06) 28 BHRC 201 (ECtHR).
[336] Article 3 of Protocol No 1.

for example, the behaviour of law enforcement officers when controlling a riot.[337] The UK has not, however, ratified Protocol 12 and there do not appear to be any moves in train to do so. The scope of influence of the ECHR on UK domestic law is therefore confined to the reach of Article 14.

III WHO IS BOUND?

Closely linked to the question of the scope of discrimination law is that of who should be bound. In jurisdictions with a constitutional guarantee, it is generally assumed that the State, and not private actors, should be bound. It is then the responsibility of the State to produce legislation which binds private individuals. This is true for the constitutional guarantees in the US, Canada, and India. Under US law, the Constitution only applies to discrimination by the States and their subdivisions and agents. As the US Supreme Court put it, since 1883 'the principle has become firmly embedded in our constitutional law that the action inhibited by the first section of the Fourteenth Amendment is only such action as may fairly be said to be that of the States. That Amendment erects no shield against merely private conduct, however discriminatory or wrongful.'[338]

However, private transactions are not entirely immune. In the well-known case of *Shelley v Kraemer*,[339] the US Supreme Court held that the courts were bound by the Fourteenth Amendment when applying the common law to individual contracts. In this case, landowners had entered into restrictive covenants with the aim of excluding Black people from the ownership or occupancy of real property, thus preventing Black families from moving into white neighbourhoods. The Court made it clear that, being a transaction between two private bodies, the restrictive covenant was not in itself in breach of the Constitution. However, it also held that the action of the courts and legal enforcement officers were actions of States within the meaning of the Fourteenth Amendment. 'In granting judicial enforcement of the restrictive agreements in these cases, the States have denied petitioners the equal protection of the laws.'[340]

---

[337] See para 22 of the explanatory report appended to Draft Protocol No 12 as transmitted by the Steering Committee for Human Rights, CCDH 99(10), 25 June 1999.
[338] *Shelley v Kraemer* 334 US 1, 13 (1948) (US Sup Ct).
[339] ibid.
[340] ibid 21.

The Canadian Charter similarly applies to Parliament, legislatures, and government action, but not to private acts of discrimination. The Supreme Court of Canada regards the Charter as 'essentially an instrument for checking the powers of government over the individual . . . To open up all private and public action to judicial review could strangle the operation of society and . . . could seriously interfere with freedom of contract.'[341] It is up to legislation to control the acts of private parties. As in other jurisdictions, the precise delineation of the 'government' has been the subject of some litigation. The Court has held, in a series of cases, that the 'test for determining whether entities such as hospitals, public broadcasters or the post office are "government" for the purposes of the Charter turns on the degree to which there is significant control by government ministers or their officials in their day-to-day operations and on the extent to which the entity acts on the government's behalf or furthers some specific governmental policy or program.'[342] However, the Charter has indirect effect: where legislation is ambiguous, it must be interpreted in a manner compatible with the Charter and human rights legislation.

Again, in India constitutional guarantees apply to State and public institutions. The main provision that binds both the public and the private sector is Article 17, which outlaws untouchability and forbids its practice in any form. In a significant new development, the prohibition on untouchability has been held to encompass the imposition of any form of social exclusion driven by the ideology of purity or impurity. This includes religious practices leading to the exclusion of menstruating women from Temple worship. According to Chandrachud J, 'Article 17 cannot be read to exclude women against whom social exclusion of the worst kind has been practiced and legitimized on notions of purity and pollution.'[343] He also suggested that the guarantee against social exclusion could emanate from Article 15(2), the equality guarantee.[344] This was expressed more directly in the earlier *Naz Foundation* case, where the Delhi High Court found that 'Article 15(2) incorporates the notion of horizontal application of rights. In other words, it even prohibits discrimination of one citizen by another in matters of access to public spaces. In our view, discrimination on the ground of sexual orientation is impermissible even on the horizontal application of the right enshrined under Article 15.'[345]

---

[341] *McKinney v University of Guelph* [1990] 3 SCR 229 (Can Sup Ct).
[342] R Sharpe and K Roach, *The Charter of Rights and Freedoms* (3rd edn, Irwin Law 2005) 102.
[343] *Indian Young Lawyers Association v State of Kerala* 2018 SCC OnLine SC 1690, para 357 (Indian Sup Ct).
[344] ibid.
[345] *Naz Foundation v Government of NCT of Delhi* (n 51) para 104.

The right to privacy was also held to have horizontal application by at least one judgment in the watershed *Puttaswamy* case.[346]

Only in South Africa is there an express commitment to the horizontal application of the Constitution. Section 8(3) of the Constitution states that the Bill of Rights binds individuals 'if, and to the extent that, it is applicable, taking into account the nature of the right and the nature of any duty imposed by the right.[347] In addition, in a development similar to that in *Shelley v Kraemer* discussed earlier, the Constitution provides that courts 'must apply, or if necessary develop, the common law to the extent that legislation does not give effect to that right.[348] In relation to equality, there is an express horizontality provision. Section 9(4) states: 'No person may unfairly discriminate directly or indirectly against anyone on one or more grounds. . . . National legislation must be enacted to prevent or prohibit unfair discrimination.' However, the Constitutional Court has held that since the South African government has in fact enacted legislation to prohibit unfair discrimination by private bodies, there should be no right of challenge directly under the constitutional provision.[349]

As far as European instruments are concerned, most closely tied to the vertical model is the ECHR which, as a treaty, binds only the State. Its major effect on private individuals comes through the obligation on the State to protect individuals against other individuals who breach their Convention rights.[350] In the UK, the strictness of this model is softened in important ways by the HRA, which widens the range of actors bound by the Convention to include private bodies when performing public functions. Recognizing that many State functions are now delegated to private bodies, the HRA provides that human rights duties should apply to private or voluntary sector bodies when performing functions 'of a public nature'.[351] Domestic courts have, however, been reluctant to give this concept the breadth of interpretation originally intended,[352] resting the definition on the relationship of the body to

---

[346] *Puttaswamy v Union of India* (n 229) para 79.

[347] South African Constitution, s 8(3).

[348] ibid s 8(4).

[349] *MEC for Education: Kwazulu-Natal and Others v Pillay* (CCT 51/06) [2007] ZACC 21, 2008 (1) SA 474 (CC), 2008 (2) BCLR 99 (SACC).

[350] *Costello-Roberts v United Kingdom* (Application no 13134/87) (1993) 19 EHRR 112, [1993] ECHR 16.

[351] HRA, s 6(5).

[352] See eg HC Deb, 16 February 1998, col 773 (Home Secretary); HC Deb, 17 June 1998, cols 409–10, 433 (Home Secretary), HL Deb, 24 November 1997, cols 800, 811 (Lord Chancellor).

the government, rather than the function itself.[353] The result has been to exclude important providers of public functions, such as housing providers or care homes. Instead, as the Joint Committee on Human Rights has proposed, the key test for 'public function' should be whether the relevant 'function' is one for which the government has assumed responsibility in the public interest.[354]

EU law has developed more sophisticated attempts to extend its reach from a purely vertical model to one which binds private individuals in some situations. It was initially envisaged that only the State would be bound, on the assumption that domestic legislation would be enacted to bind private individuals. However, a reluctance on the part of Member States fully to comply with EU law led the ECJ to develop a doctrine of horizontal direct effect. This has been particularly true in the equality field. Article 119 of the Treaty of Rome, which provided for equal pay for equal work for men and women, lay dormant for decades until, in the seminal case of *Defrenne v Sabena*,[355] the ECJ held that Article 119 was both vertically and horizontally directly effective. This meant that an individual could claim equal pay directly under Article 119, in the domestic courts, against both her employer and the State, even in the absence of domestic legislation. Article 119 became Article 141 under the Treaty of Amsterdam, and has now been transferred to Article 157 of the Lisbon Treaty.

The ECJ has stopped short of holding that directives can have horizontal direct effect. The Equal Treatment Directive,[356] which provides for equal treatment of men and women in access to employment, promotion, vocational training, and working conditions, has been held to be directly binding on the State but not private employers.[357] This principle continues to hold true for the newer version of the Equal Treatment Directive, the Recast Directive,[358] as well as the Race Directive and the Employment Directive. In *Kücükdeveci*, the Court stated as follows:

> In this respect, where proceedings between individuals are concerned, the Court has consistently held that a directive cannot of itself impose obligations

---

[353] *YL (By her litigation friend the Official Solicitor) v Birmingham CC* [2007] UKHL 27, [2007] 3 WLR 112.

[354] Joint Committee on Human Rights, 'The Meaning of Public Authority under the Human Rights Act', Ninth Report of Session 2006–07 (HL Paper 77, HC 410, 28 March 2007), para 7.

[355] Case 43/75 *Defrenne v Sabena* [1976] ECR 455 (ECJ).

[356] Council Directive 76/207/EEC.

[357] Case C-152/84 *Marshall v Southampton Area Health Authority* [1986] ECR 723 (ECJ).

[358] 2006/54/EC.

on an individual and cannot therefore be relied on as such against an individual.[359]

This has led to some problematic anomalies, with State employees better protected against discrimination than their counterparts in the private sector.

The impact of this limitation has, however, been softened in two important respects. First, the ECJ has interpreted the notion of the State widely,[360] including, for example, a nationalized industry which provides a public service under the control of the State.[361] Secondly, it has developed a principle of 'indirect effect', which means that, in applying national law, the national court is required to interpret it, as far as possible, in the light of the wording and the purpose of the directive in question, in order to achieve the result pursued by the directive.[362] This is true even when the case concerns a private body, with the effect that the latter is in practice bound.[363] Most recently, the ECJ has taken this still further, to have a similar effect even if national law is clear and cannot be interpreted consistently with the directive. In *Kücükdeveci*, the Court held that the Employment Directive (2000/78):

> merely gives expression to, but does not lay down, the principle of equal treatment in employment and occupation, and that the principle of non-discrimination on grounds of age is a general principle of European Union law in that it constitutes a specific application of the general principle of equal treatment.[364]

This meant that it is for the national court:

> hearing a dispute involving the principle of non-discrimination on grounds of age as given expression in Directive 2000/78, to provide, within the limits of its jurisdiction, the legal protection which individuals derive from European

---

[359] *Kücükdeveci v Swedex GmbH & Co KG* (n 16) para 46.

[360] Case C-409/95 *Marshall v Southampton and South West Hampshire Area Health Authority (Teaching) No 1* [1986] ECR 723 (ECJ).

[361] Case C-188/89 *Foster v British Gas plc* [1990] ECR I-3313.

[362] *Kücükdeveci v Swedex GmbH & Co KG* (n 16) para 48.

[363] Case 14/83 *Von Colson and Kamann v Land Nordrhein-Westfalen* [1984] ECR 1891 (ECJ); Case C-106/89 *Marleasing* [1990] ECR I-4135.

[364] *Kücükdeveci v Swedex GmbH & Co KG* (n 16), paras 20, 50; *Mangold* (n 16) paras 74–77.

Union law and to ensure the full effectiveness of that law, disapplying if need be any provision of national legislation contrary to that principle.[365]

The development of UK law has been in the opposite direction. Anti-discrimination law in the UK has always applied to private bodies, albeit only in their capacities as employers, service providers, and education providers. Public bodies were not bound in respect of all their functions but only insofar as they were employers, or service or education providers. It was not until 2000 that the race legislation was amended to make it unlawful for a public authority to discriminate against or victimize a person on racial grounds in carrying out any of its functions. Similar amendments were later made to sex and disability discrimination legislation.

The EA 2010 now consolidates this development by making it unlawful to discriminate in the exercise of all public functions. This means that so far as public bodies are concerned, the limitations of scope above do not apply: all public functions are covered, unless specifically excepted. This is true for all the protected grounds except for civil partnership, marital status, or age where this relates to a person under eighteen.[366] Moreover, the EA 2010 carries forward the trend already established by the HRA, by referring to all 'public functions' even if they are exercised by private bodies. At the same time, as we have seen, it has not been easy to define 'public functions' for the purposes of the HRA, a difficulty which the EA 2010 makes no attempt to resolve. Instead, it simply defines a public function as having the same meaning as that in the HRA.[367] This may, however, be less of a problem than under the HRA, given that a significant number of private functions, such as employment, the provision of services, and education, are also covered by the EA 2010.

IV CONCLUSION

This chapter has confronted a key challenge of discrimination law: how to fashion laws which are sensitive enough to outlaw invidious distinctions, while permitting and even supporting positive difference. It has also considered the reach of equality laws: what activities fall within such laws

---

[365] *Kücükdeveci v Swedex GmbH & Co KG* ibid para 50.
[366] EA 2010, s 29(6).
[367] ibid s 31(4).

in different jurisdictions, and who is bound. We now turn to the core principles of anti-discrimination laws. Chapter 5 examines the key concepts of direct discrimination or disparate treatment and indirect discrimination or disparate impact. In Chapter 6, these are applied to the central issues confronting discrimination law: equal pay, sexual harassment, reasonable accommodation, and pregnancy and parenting.

5

Legal Concepts

Direct, Indirect Discrimination, and Beyond

I INTRODUCTION

Anti-discrimination law has grown rapidly, in both scope and complexity. Yet true equality remains elusive. This prompts a closer examination of the different concepts of equality used in anti-discrimination law. Is the limited effect explained by flaws in the ways in which the equality principle is transposed into legal forms? Or are we expecting equality to achieve something of which it is incapable? It is to these difficult questions that we now turn.

The most basic principle is that of equality before the law, requiring the removal of specific legal impediments. Significant progress has been made towards achieving equality for some groups, although there remain groups for whom even juridical equality has not yet been achieved. At the same time, it quickly became evident that equality before the law is insufficient on its own. For women, equal voting and property rights did not eliminate pay structures in which women were explicitly paid less than men doing the same work; women were still dismissed from paid employment on marriage or pregnancy; and women remained segregated into low paid, low status jobs. Similarly, the right to vote for Black people, indigenous people, or people from marginalized ethnicities did not prevent racism, exclusion from jobs or housing, or institutionalized hostility from police forces and other service providers.[1]

---

[1] As mentioned in previous chapters, this book acknowledges that the terminology used to describe people subjected to discrimination is sensitive and contested. In the different jurisdictions covered here (UK, Europe, India, South Africa, Canada, and the US), outgroups, or groups that are 'othered' in their own societies or globally, prefer to refer to themselves in different and sometimes opposing ways. This can also change, reflecting changes in social forces and perceptions. Acknowledging these complexities, I have chosen to use 'Black people', 'marginalized ethnicities', and 'indigenous people', following the approach of the UN Special Rapporteur on the right to health, Tlaleng Mofokeng, in her report to the United Nations on sexual and reproductive health rights on 16 July 2021 (A/76/172) <https://undocs.org/A/76/172> accessed 31 May 2022. The reference to 'gender identity, gender expression and sex characteristics' follows her report on gender-based violence submitted to the UN on 14 April 2022 (A/HRC/50/28)

Discrimination Law. Third Edition. Sandra Fredman, Oxford University Press. © Sandra Fredman 2022. DOI: 10.1093/oso/9780198854081.003.0005

To tackle these phenomena, a more developed notion of equality was needed. Instead of simply removing juridical impediments, it was necessary to prohibit prejudiced behaviour and discrimination by public and private actors. The building block has been the basic conception that likes should be treated alike. In legal terms, this received its first major expression through women's right to equal pay for equal work. It is encapsulated more generally in the principle of direct discrimination or disparate treatment, which prohibits less favourable treatment of two similarly situated individuals on grounds of a protected characteristic. Importantly, it binds private employers and service providers, not just the State. However, as was seen in Chapter 1, the concept that likes should be treated alike is limited in important ways. Most importantly, equal treatment in the context of pre-existing disadvantage will simply perpetuate or even exacerbate inequality of outcome. Selection criteria based on educational qualifications, although equally applicable to all, will exclude those who have been deprived of proper schooling; jobs which require full-time working and mobility will exclude those with primary responsibility for childcare.

It was in recognition of this limitation that the US Supreme Court developed the concept of 'disparate impact'. Where equal treatment disproportionately disadvantages a group which already suffers from a history of discrimination, then it, too, can be unlawful, unless there is a good reason.[2] This concept was imported into UK law and gradually made its way into EU law. Known as indirect discrimination, it is formulated in different ways, but broadly speaking has three elements: equal treatment, a disproportionately exclusionary impact on those sharing a protected characteristic, and the absence of an acceptable justification. A similar concept, known as adverse effects discrimination, has been developed by the Supreme Court of Canada in relation to the equality guarantee in section 15 of the Canadian Charter.[3]

More recently, and primarily in the context of disability discrimination, a further concept has been introduced in the form of a duty of reasonable accommodation or adjustment. Whereas the equal treatment principle requires conformity to the dominant norm, the duty of reasonable accommodation or adjustment expressly requires a modification of the able-bodied

---

<www.ohchr.org/en/documents/thematic-reports/ahrc5028-violence-and-its-impact-right-health-report-special-rapporteur> accessed 31 May 2022.

[2] *Griggs v Duke Power Co* 401 US 424 (1971) (US Sup Ct).
[3] *Ontario Human Rights Commission v Simpsons-Sears Ltd* [1985] 2 SCR 53, 551.

norm to facilitate equal participation of people with disabilities. In jurisdictions such as Canada, this concept has also been used in the context of religious discrimination—requiring employers to provide exemptions or modifications of specific practices to accommodate individuals from minority religions.

Each of these differing legal formulations of equality invites a further question: how much weight should be given to equality in the face of competing priorities? If a finding of prima facie discrimination has been made, can it nevertheless be justified on the basis that the distinction serves other ends, such as the business interests of the employer, the social policies of the State, or the rights and interests of others?

In principle, these should provide powerful instruments to address the inequalities identified in Chapters 2 and 3. In many respects they do so. However, each concept has its own limitations, weaknesses which are only partially buttressed by strengths in alternative approaches. In addition, the interface between different concepts, such as direct and indirect discrimination, can be uncomfortably jagged. These complications have led courts in some jurisdictions, such as Canada, to reject a rigid distinction between these principles. Other formulations, such as Article 14 ECHR, use a more flexible notion of equality. The primary guiding principle behind Article 14 is that not all distinctions are discriminatory, only those for which there is no objective and proportionate justification. Dignity is also the express basis of the legal formulation in some contexts, such as sexual harassment. Finally, a more wide-ranging set of positive duties to promote equality of opportunity have been introduced since 2000. However, unlike the duty of reasonable accommodation, these do not give rise to individual rights. This chapter examines direct and indirect discrimination, while the next chapter considers how these concepts apply in the particular contexts of equal pay, pregnancy and parenting, reasonable accommodation, and sexual harassment. Positive duties are discussed in detail in Chapter 8.

The aim of this chapter is to develop an understanding of the concepts of direct and indirect discrimination and their relationship with each other. In particular, the chapter considers the extent to which they can achieve the four-dimensional understanding of equality posed in Chapter 1. It was argued there that substantive equality resists capture by a single principle, whether it be dignity, equality of results, or equality of opportunity. Instead, it should be seen as a multi-dimensional concept, consisting of four overlapping aims: to break the cycle of disadvantage associated with status or outgroups (the redistributive dimension); to redress stigma, stereotyping, humiliation, and violence thereby promoting respect for the equal dignity and worth of all (the recognition dimension); to facilitate full participation in society (the participative dimension); and to accommodate and positively affirm different identities and achieve structural change (the transformational dimension). To what extent can direct and indirect discrimination as understood in different jurisdictions simultaneously achieve all four dimensions of substantive equality? This chapter probes that question.

II DIRECT DISCRIMINATION OR DISPARATE TREATMENT

Judges on both sides of the Atlantic have described the concepts of direct discrimination or disparate treatment as relatively straightforward. As Lady Hale put it in the UK Supreme Court: 'Direct discrimination is comparatively simple: it is treating one person less favourably than you would treat another person, because of a particular protected characteristic that the former has.'[4] Similarly, for Stewart J in the US Supreme Court: 'Disparate treatment . . . is the most easily understood type of discrimination. The employer simply treats some people less favourably than others because of their race, colour, religion, sex, or national origin.'[5] Statutory prohibitions follow the same contours. For example, the EU Race Directive defines direct discrimination as occurring when 'one person is treated less favourably than another is, or would be treated in a comparable situation on grounds of racial or ethnic origin'[6] and equivalent definitions are found in relation to gender, disability, age, sexual orientation, and religion or belief.[7] In Britain, drawing together all the protected characteristics in one formulation, section 13 of the EA 2010 states that 'A person (A) discriminates against another (B) if, because of a protected characteristic, A treats B less favourably than A treats or would treat others'.[8]

This simplicity can, however, be deceptive. Courts in the different jurisdictions highlighted here have disagreed on some of its basic elements. Particularly contentious has been the role of motive or intention. For the US

---

[4] *Essop v Home Office* [2017] UKSC 27 (UK Sup Ct).
[5] *Teamsters v United States* (1977) 431 US 324, fn 15 (US Sup Ct).
[6] Council Directive 2000/43 on equal treatment between persons irrespective of racial or ethnic origin, Art 2(1)(a).
[7] Recast Directive 2006/54, Art 2(1)(a); Framework Directive 2000/78, Art 2(2)(a).
[8] EA 2010, s 13.

Supreme Court: 'Proof of discriminatory motive is critical, although it can in some situations be inferred from the mere fact of differences in treatment.'[9] The UK courts have, by contrast, firmly rejected any role for motive.[10] Also contentious is the question of whether direct discrimination can be justified, and if so, what factors would be acceptable justifications. Courts in both the EU and the UK have resisted any possibility of a general justification for direct discrimination, on the grounds that discriminatory motives or intentions could be reimported. Nevertheless, there are several particular issues where direct discrimination can be justified. Age discrimination is one of these. Other jurisdictions allow justification defences but calibrate the standard of scrutiny. As we saw in the previous chapter, for some grounds or protected characteristics, a very high bar is set before direct discrimination can be justified, while for others, mere rationality will suffice.

In whatever form direct discrimination is included in anti-discrimination law, it is invariably limited by its continued adherence to the principle that likes should be treated alike. As a start, direct discrimination aims only at consistent treatment. As long as both parties are treated in the same way, the principle is not violated, even if they are treated equally badly. Consistent treatment can also, therefore, be achieved by 'levelling down', or removing the advantage from the better-off party. Secondly, it is heavily reliant on a comparator, whether real or notional. As well as creating pressures to conform, this excludes situations in which a comparator cannot be identified. Thirdly, direct discrimination is a symmetric conception. It applies both to unequal treatment which furthers disadvantage, and unequal treatment which aims to compensate for past disadvantage. This means that affirmative action is presumptively forbidden. These three limitations are examined below, followed by an elaboration of the issues concerning justification and intention or motive.

(i) Consistency rather than Substance

Direct discrimination, with its emphasis on 'less favourable treatment' is primarily a relative concept. Equality is achieved if both parties have been equally well treated; but it is also achieved if they have been equally badly

---

[9] *Teamsters v United States* (n 5) fn 15.
[10] *James v Eastleigh BC* [1990] 2 AC 751 (HL); *R (On the application of E) v Governing Body of JFS and the Admissions Appeal Panel of JFS* [2009] UKSC 15.

treated. There is nothing to suggest that the first is more desirable than the second. This result can be seen clearly in surrogacy cases before the ECJ. In these cases, mothers of babies born through a surrogacy arrangement, known as commissioning mothers, claimed the right to paid maternity leave. In a series of cases, the Court of Justice held that a refusal to grant such leave to a commissioning mother did not constitute direct discrimination on grounds of sex. This was because a commissioning father was similarly denied such leave on the birth of the baby.[11] In other words, since both commissioning parents were treated equally badly, there was no direct discrimination.

Similarly, equality is fulfilled whether a benefit is removed from the advantaged group or extended to the disadvantaged group. This is clearly illustrated in the fraught area of protective legislation which provided for 'special' protection for women by, for example, prohibiting night work or underground work in mines. In recent decades, there has been a general consensus that such legislation breaches the equality principle. However, this led to two quite contradictory responses. The UK government, with few exceptions, simply repealed the protective legislation; thereby withdrawing protection from women without achieving any corresponding benefit to either men or women.[12] By contrast, the European Commission declared specifically that 'equality should not be made the occasion for a disimprovement of working conditions for one sex'.[13]

Even more problematic were the results of a series of cases in which men who were pensionable at age sixty-five claimed that they were being treated less favourably than women, who were pensionable at age sixty. The ECJ held that equality had, indeed, been breached. But it went on to find that it was not necessary to lower men's pensionable age to achieve equality. The breach could just as well be remedied by raising women's pensionable age to sixty-five, thus removing the extra benefits from women.[14] The result was stark. Equal treatment was achieved. But the position of women was worsened, while men were no better off. More recently, the ECJ mitigated this approach somewhat. In a series of cases, it has held that once a finding of direct discrimination has been made, disadvantaged persons should be placed in

---

[11] Case C-167/12 *CD v ST* [2014] 3 CMLR 15 (CJEU); Case C-363/12 *Z v A Government Department* [2014] 3 CMLR 20 (CJEU).

[12] S Fredman, *Women and the Law* (OUP 1997) 306 and see S Kenney, *For Whose Protection?* (University of Michigan Press 1992).

[13] Commission Communication, 'Protective Legislation for Women in the Member States of the EC', COM(87) 105 final.

[14] See Fredman (n 12) 350; see eg Case C-408/92 *Smith v Advel* [1994] IRLR 602 (ECJ).

the same position as those enjoying the advantage until measures reinstating equal treatment have been adopted. However, once such measures have been adopted, EU law does not prevent a solution which entails reducing the level of advantage of those previously favoured to the level of those in the disadvantaged category. EU law, the Court held, requires only that men and women should receive the same pay for the same work without imposing any specific level of pay.[15]

These consequences can be seen in other areas, too. *Cresco* constituted a challenge to Austrian legislation under which Good Friday was a paid holiday only for members of specified Churches.[16] This meant that members of those churches were entitled to fourteen public holidays, whereas everyone else was only entitled to thirteen. The ECJ held that this constituted direct discrimination on grounds of religion.[17] The Austrian government had several choices. It could level up by making Good Friday a public holiday for everyone or it could level down by abolishing Good Friday as a public holiday for everyone, including members of the specified Churches. It chose the latter option. Good Friday is now no longer a public holiday for members of the specified Churches. The outcome was somewhat softened by the introduction of a one-day 'personal holiday' which all employees can choose to use for religious festivals or other activities. However, this was not an additional day of leave, but came from the employees' existing quota.[18]

Particularly challenging for a notion of discrimination as consistency is the question of segregation. We have seen that in the foundational case of *Brown v Board of Education*,[19] the US Supreme Court held that segregation of African American and white pupils into separate schools constituted a breach of the equal protection clause of the Fourteenth Amendment. Although it was assumed that the facilities were equal, the stigma attached to the compulsion to attend a Black school meant that there could not be found to be equal treatment. More recently, this question has arisen in relation to segregation of girls and boys in mixed-sex schools. There is a specific exemption in UK law for single-sex schools. However, can a mixed-sex school operate a policy of segregating girls and boys? This question arose in *Al-Hijrah*,

---

[15] Case C-171/18 *Safeway v Newton* [2019] 10 WLUK 67 (ECJ).
[16] Case C-193/17 *Cresco Investigation GmbH v Achatzi* [2019] 2 CMLR 20 (ECJ).
[17] Contrary to Directive 2000/78.
[18] Diana Niksova, 'Religious Minorities Lose Good Friday as a Public Holiday in Austria' (*Oxford Human Rights Hub Blog*, 2019) <http://ohrh.law.ox.ac.uk/religious-minorities-lose-good-friday-as-a-public-holiday-in-austria> accessed 17 January 2021.
[19] *Brown v Board of Education* 347 US 483 (1954) (US Sup Ct).

which concerned a co-educational, voluntary-aided Muslim school which had a policy of segregating pupils by gender from age nine for all purposes, including lessons, breaks, school clubs, and trips. The school had an Islamic ethos and, for religious reasons, believed that the separation of boys and girls after the age of nine should be obligatory. Was this direct discrimination on grounds of sex? At first instance, the court held that since the treatment of each group was equivalent, and had equivalent consequences for both sexes, neither sex was treated less favourably than the other. The judge therefore held that the segregation of male and female pupils did not in itself constitute direct discrimination. In the Court of Appeal, however, this 'group' approach was rejected. Instead, it held that 'an individual girl pupil cannot socialise and intermix with a boy pupil because, and only because, of her sex; and an individual boy pupil cannot socialise and intermix with a girl pupil because, and only because, of his sex. Each is, therefore, treated less favourably than would be the case if their sex was different.'[20] Gloster LJ took a different view. For her, the facts that men have more influence and power in society than women, and that persistent gender inequalities in the workforce remain, meant that an educational system which promotes segregation within the school 'is bound to endorse traditional gender stereotypes that preserve male power, influence and economic dominance.'[21] This view is closer to the substantive understanding of the right to equality which requires account to be taken of the context of disadvantage and power imbalance and also of stigma and stereotyping.

(ii)   Equality as Conformity: The Role of the Comparator

Direct discrimination is fundamentally a comparative concept. It requires the claimant to establish that A treats B less favourably than A treats or would treat others because of a protected characteristic. Direct discrimination is somewhat more sophisticated than the equal pay concept which, as we will see in Chapter 6, requires an actual comparator. Instead, it permits a 'hypothetical comparison' or proof that A treats B less favourably than A *would treat* others. Nevertheless, the need for a comparator has been one of the most problematic aspects of direct discrimination. As a start, the choice of

---

[20] R (Interim Executive Board of Al-Hijrah School) v HM Chief Inspector of Education [2017] EWCA Civ 1426 [51] (UK Ct of Appeal).
[21] ibid [144].

comparator requires a value judgement as to which of the myriad similarities and differences among people should be treated as relevant and which
irrelevant. This has meant that the choice of comparator can profoundly influence the outcome of the case. Should the comparator be an exact mirror
of the claimant in all respects except for the protected characteristic? This
was the route chosen in earlier Canadian cases. According to Binnie J: 'The
appropriate comparator group is the one which mirrors the characteristics of
the claimant (or claimant group) relevant to the benefit or advantage sought
except . . . [for the protected] personal characteristic.'[22] The result was that
several claims were lost because the court rejected the claimant's choice of
comparator. Most striking was the case of *Auton*,[23] where the Supreme Court
of Canada fashioned a comparator which was 'so narrow and complex that
the claimants had no way of showing differential treatment based on the evidence they had led at trial'.[24]

Even more problematic is the way in which the choice of comparator
can obscure the social context which produces the disadvantage in the first
place. This is most graphically illustrated in relation to disability. To take a
commonly used example, assume that a restaurant which does not permit
dogs, refuses entry to a visually impaired person with a guide dog. On one
approach, the relevant difference is between a visually impaired and a sighted
person, both of whom have a dog. Since both would be excluded, there is no
breach of the equal treatment principle and no direct discrimination. But by
abstracting the comparison from the real social context, this choice of comparator empties discrimination law of any value. The reality is that the role
of the dog for the visually impaired person is wholly different from that of
a dog belonging to a non-blind person. It is the exclusion of the guide dog
which disables the visually impaired person not the visual impairment itself.
The comparison should therefore be between a blind person with a dog and
a sighted person. Nevertheless, the UK House of Lords in *Malcolm*[25] held
that it was much more 'natural' to regard the comparator as an able-bodied
person who was in all other respects similarly situated; that is, 'a person who
had a dog but no disability'.[26]

---

[22] *Hodge v Canada (Minister of Human Resources Development* 2004 SCC 28, para 23 (Can Sup Ct).
[23] *Auton v British Columbia (Attorney General)* [2004] 3 SCR 657, para 55 (Can Sup Ct).
[24] J Koshan and J Hamilton, 'The Continual Reinvention of Section 15 of the Charter' (2013) 64 University of New Brunswick LJ 19, 35.
[25] *Lewisham London Borough Council v Malcolm* [2008] UKHL 43 (HL).
[26] ibid [15].

Equally problematically, as was seen in Chapter 1, the need for a norm of comparison, be it male, white, able-bodied, or Christian, has created powerful conformist pressures. Most recently, this has manifested itself in relation to rules prohibiting the wearing of visible religious signs or clothing at work. In *Achbita*,[27] the employer had a rule prohibiting workers from wearing visible signs of their political, philosophical, or religious beliefs in the workplace. Ms Achbita, a Muslim woman, was dismissed for wearing a hijab or Islamic headscarf during working hours. The ECJ held that the rule treated all workers in the undertaking in the same way. All were required to dress 'neutrally', which precluded wearing visible signs of their beliefs. This ignores the fact that the rule favours the dominant Christian norm, which does not require signs of religion through dress or head coverings. By comparing her to employees from the dominant religion, the real detriment to which she was subjected was obscured. Strict comparison also raises almost intractable problems for intersectionality analysis. For example, a Black woman who claims sex discrimination might fail if white women are not less favourably treated than men. But her claim of race discrimination might also fail if Black men are not treated less favourably than white men.[28]

Recognizing these limitations, courts and legislatures in various jurisdictions have either softened the comparator requirement or abandoned it altogether. The Supreme Court of Canada in *Withler* firmly rejected the notion of a 'mirror comparator'.[29] Searching for a precisely corresponding comparator group, the Court held, 'becomes a search for sameness, rather than a search for disadvantage, . . . occluding the real issue—whether the law disadvantages the claimant or perpetuates a stigmatized view of the claimant'.[30] The mirror comparator approach also placed a heavy burden on the complainant, and made it difficult to establish intersectional discrimination. Instead, the Court held, what was needed was an approach that looked at the overall context, including whether the law perpetuated disadvantage or negative stereotypes.[31] This meant that claimants need only show that they had been denied a benefit granted to others, or carried a burden that others did not, by reason of a personal characteristic protected by section 15 of the Constitution. If they had established such a distinction, the claim should

---

[27] *Achbita v G4S Secure Solutions* (2017) 3 CMLR 21 (CJEU (Grand Chamber)).
[28] *DeGraffenreid v General Motors Assembly Division* 413 F Supp 142 (US District Ct). See Chapter 4.
[29] *Withler v Canada (Attorney General)* [2011] 1 SCR 396, para 40 (Can Sup Ct).
[30] ibid para 57.
[31] ibid para 40.

proceed to the next step, which was whether the distinction perpetuated disadvantage, prejudice, or stereotyping towards the claimant group.

The rejection of a strict comparator approach has been even more marked under Article 14 ECHR. As Lady Hale put it in *McLaughlin*: 'Unlike domestic anti-discrimination law, Article 14 does not require the identification of an exact comparator, real or hypothetical, with whom the complainant has been treated less favourably. Instead, it requires a difference in treatment between two persons in an analogous situation.'[32] There are very few ECtHR decisions based on a finding that the situations are not analogous. Indeed, Lady Hale has branded the search for a comparator as an 'an arid exercise'.[33]

Alternatively, courts and legislatures could discard the comparative element altogether. Rather than 'less favourable' treatment, the focus could be on 'unfavourable' or 'adverse' treatment. This has been the approach of the British EA 2010 in four specific areas: disability, victimization, harassment, and pregnancy discrimination. Pregnancy raises a set of complex challenges across all the jurisdictions and is dealt with in detail in Chapter 6. So far as disability is concerned, the EA 2010 has made some halting attempts to depart from a strict comparator approach, while resisting discarding it altogether. It does so by distinguishing between discrimination 'because of' disability[34] and discrimination 'arising from' disability.[35] The former retains the narrow basis of comparison. There must be no material differences between the circumstances of the disabled person and her comparator, where these circumstances 'include a person's abilities'.[36] Under this section, the relevant comparator for a visually impaired person with a dog is a sighted person with a dog, thereby obscuring most discrimination arising from the built environment. A very different approach is taken in relation to discrimination 'arising from' disability. Here, the Act moves away from the need for a comparator at all. Instead of 'less favourable' treatment, the statute simply requires showing that A has treated B *unfavourably* because of something arising in consequence of B's disability.[37] At the same time, the 'arising from' claim is deliberately weaker than the 'because of' claim. Whereas the 'because of' claim is available even if A did not know that B had the disability, the 'arising from' claim is not established if A did not know or could not be

---

[32] *In re McLaughlin* [2018] UKSC 48 [24].
[33] *AL (Serbia) v Secretary of State for the Home Department* [2008] UKHL 42 [28] (HL).
[34] EA 2010, s 13.
[35] ibid s 15.
[36] ibid s 23.
[37] ibid s 15.

expected to know that B had the disability. In addition, there is no possibility of a justification or excuse for the 'because of' claim. However, in the 'arising from' claim, A can defend her actions if the treatment is a proportionate means of achieving a legitimate aim.

A more decisive departure from the comparator approach can be seen in relation to victimization of employees for pursuing discrimination claims or supporting others. The requirement that such an employee show that she has been treated less favourably than one who had not pursued legal proceedings has led to some vexed litigation in the UK.[38] By contrast, EU law simply requires employees to be protected against adverse treatment as a reaction to complaints or legal proceedings.[39] The UK EA 2020, in compliance with EU law, now uses the language of detriment rather than adverse treatment. The Act now provides that victimization takes place where A subjects B to a detriment because B in good faith does a 'protected act'.[40] In other contexts, such as harassment, the principle that likes should be treated alike has expressly been replaced by a reliance on breach of dignity as the basis of the harm.

(iii) Motive and Intention

One of the key points of contrast between courts in different jurisdictions concerns the role of motive and intention in relation to direct discrimination or disparate treatment. From its early case law on direct discrimination, the UK courts firmly set their face against requiring proof of intention in a direct discrimination case. Thus, according to Lord Goff:

> The intention or motive of the defendant to discriminate . . . is not a necessary condition of liability . . . [Otherwise] it would be a good defence for an employer to show that he discriminated against women not because he intended to do so but (for example) because of customer preference, or to save money, or even to avoid controversy.[41]

For this reason, it is now settled law that the motive of the perpetrator is irrelevant. Rather, the UK courts have established a 'but for' test which founds

---

[38] *Chief Constable of the West Yorkshire Police v Khan* [2001] ICR 1065 (HL).

[39] Equal Treatment Directive, Art 7 (as amended by Directive 2002/73, Art 6); Race Directive (2000/43/EC), Art 9; Employment Directive (2000/78/EC), Art 11.

[40] EA 2010, s 27(1)(a).

[41] *R v Birmingham City Council, ex p Equal Opportunities Commission* [1989] AC 1155 [175] (HL).

liability on the simple causative assessment that 'but for' the applicant's protected characteristic, she would not have been treated less favourably.[42]

By contrast, the US Supreme Court has consistently held that to establish disparate treatment a plaintiff must prove that the defendant had a discriminatory intent or motive.[43] This distinguishes disparate treatment from disparate impact which focuses instead on adverse effect. As Kennedy J put it in *Ricci v DeStefano*: '[Title VII] prohibits both intentional discrimination (known as "disparate treatment") as well as, in some cases, practices that are not intended to discriminate but in fact have a disproportionately adverse effect on minorities (known as "disparate impact").'[44] The role of motive and intention is even more pivotal under the Fourteenth Amendment itself. In *Washington v Davis*,[45] the US Supreme Court held that only intentional action by the State could constitute a breach of the Fourteenth Amendment. As we will see later, this ruled out the possibility of a disparate-impact analysis at the constitutional level, leaving the latter to operate only under Title VII.

The role of motive and intention on both sides of the Atlantic has, however, been problematic. Under Title VII, as under equivalent UK provisions, the plaintiff must establish that the prohibited action was 'because of' her sex, race, or other protected standard. In both jurisdictions, this has been interpreted according to a traditional 'but for' test. But its functioning in the US is very different from that in the UK. Whereas in the US the 'but for' test aims to establish intention or motive, in the UK the emphasis is on the effect of the treatment. This has meant that the key issues before the courts in each jurisdiction have differed. In the US, the focus has been on how intention can be established. Recognizing that proving intention creates a heavy burden on a claimant, especially when the discrimination is not explicit, the US courts have allowed a shifting of the evidentiary burden (see later). An amendment to Title VII by the Civil Rights Act of 1991 provides that a claimant can also prove a breach by showing that an enumerated characteristic was a 'motivating factor for any employment practice, even though other factors also motivated the practice'.[46] This lesser standard of proof, however, is accompanied by a restricted range of remedies where the employer could prove that it would have taken the same action in the absence of the impermissible motive.

---

[42] *James v Eastleigh BC* (n 10) and *JFS* (n 10).
[43] *Watson v Fort Worth Bank & Trust* 487 US 977, 986, 108 S Ct 2777 (1988) (US Sup Ct).
[44] *Ricci v DeStefano* 129 S Ct 2658, 2672 (2009) (US Sup Ct).
[45] *Washington v Davis* 426 US 229, 96 S Ct 2040 (1976) (US Sup Ct).
[46] Civil Rights Act of 1991, amending Title VII to add § 2000e-2(m).

Importantly, too, the US Supreme Court has declined to stiffen the 'but for' test to require the protected trait to be the sole or only cause of the treatment. As long as the protected trait is a 'but for' cause, it need not be the only one. This allowed the Supreme Court, in the groundbreaking case of *Bostock v Clayton*, to find in favour of plaintiffs who had been dismissed for being homosexual or transgender.[47] Title VII does not refer to sexual orientation or identity. Nevertheless, Gorsuch J, giving the judgment of the Court, held that sex was a 'but for' cause of the action. 'It is impossible,' he stated, 'to discriminate against a person for being homosexual or transgender without discriminating against that individual based on sex.'[48] The result was that 'intentional discrimination based on sex violates Title VII, even if it is intended only as a means to achieving the employer's ultimate goal of discriminating against homosexual or transgender employees. There is simply no escaping the role intent plays here: Just as sex is necessarily a but-for *cause* when an employer discriminates against homosexual or transgender employees, an employer who discriminates on these grounds inescapably *intends* to rely on sex in its decision-making.'[49]

However, the Court has refused to distinguish between malevolent motives for taking race-based action and motives for race-based action which are benevolent or equality-advancing. This can be seen very clearly in *Ricci v DeStefano*.[50] In this case, selection tests for promotion to New Haven's fire force had a severely disparate impact. Indeed, none of the Black firefighters and only one Hispanic who took the examinations were in the group selected for promotion to lieutenant or captain. Faced with the possibility of a disparate action suit against it, New Haven decided not to certify the results but to adopt a new test and retest all the applicants. Disappointed white candidates, however, argued that the refusal to certify the results was directly discriminatory against them on grounds of their race. If the City had not discarded the test results, they maintained, they would have been promoted. In response, the City submitted that their intention was not to discriminate but to avoid an unlawful disparate impact. If they had certified the results, they could have faced liability under Title VII for adopting a practice that had a disparate impact on the minority firefighters. The Supreme Court, in a

---

[47] *Bostock v Clayton County* 140 S Ct 1731 (2020) (US Sup Ct). See Chapters 3 and 4.
[48] ibid 1741.
[49] ibid 1742.
[50] *Ricci v DeStefano* (n 44).

five-to-four judgment, held that the decision not to certify the results was it-self a race-based decision.[51] Kennedy J saw this as uncontroversial:

> Whatever the City's ultimate aim—however well-intentioned or benevolent it might have seemed—the City made its employment decision because of race. The City rejected the test results solely because the higher scoring candidates were white. The question is not whether that conduct was discriminatory but whether the City had a lawful justification for its race-based action.[52]

As Siegel points out, the finding of disparate treatment in *Ricci* is difficult to reconcile with the principle, clearly set out in *Washington v Davis*,[53] that only intentional action by the State can constitute a breach of the Fourteenth Amendment.[54] Neither the first selection test nor its withdrawal and re-placement by a new test involved express racial classifications. Nor was any individual applicant singled out for affirmative action for promotion.[55] Nevertheless, the Court regarded the withdrawal of the results as racially dis-criminatory against the white applicants.

As we will see later, Kennedy J's formulation of the test for disparate treat-ment is remarkably close to the evolving jurisprudence of the UK courts. Where it differs, however, is in leaving open the possibility of justification. Kennedy J rejected the petitioners' submission that avoiding disparate-impact liability should never excuse intentional disparate-treatment dis-crimination. On the other hand, he set a very high standard for justification. Good faith belief that race-conscious conduct is necessary to comply with the disparate-impact provisions would not be sufficient. The justification can only hold if there is a 'strong basis in evidence' that the remedial action is necessary to remedy past racial discrimination.[56] This contrasts with the standard which Ginsburg J, dissenting, would have preferred, namely, that the employer should merely have 'good cause to believe' that a test resulting in prima facie disparate-impact could not be justified as necessary for the business.[57] The result is that, while at least leaving some role for justification on the grounds of remedial purpose, the majority's formulation of the test of justification in practice establishes a very high barrier.[58]

---

[51] ibid 2673.
[52] ibid 2674.
[53] *Washington v Davis* (n 45).
[54] R Siegel, 'Equality Divided' (2013) 217 Harv L Rev 1.
[55] ibid 54.
[56] ibid 2675 citing *Richmond v JA Croson Co* 488 US 469, 500, 109 S Ct 706, 102 L Ed 2d 854 (1989) (quoting *Wygant* (n 19) at 277, 106 S Ct 1842 (plurality opinion)).
[57] *Ricci v DeStefano* (n 44) 2699.
[58] *Adarand Constructors v Pena* 515 US 200 (1995).

As Siegel vividly shows, this has the paradoxical effect that:

> when minorities challenge laws of general application and argue that government has segregated or profiled on the basis of race, plaintiffs must show that government acted for a discriminatory purpose, a standard that doctrine has made extraordinarily difficult to satisfy. . . . By contrast, when members of majority groups challenge state action that classifies by race—affirmative action has become the paradigmatic example—plaintiffs do not need to demonstrate, as a predicate for judicial intervention, that government has acted for an illegitimate purpose.[59]

Courts in the UK, by contrast, have eschewed any role for motive or intention. This stems from their concern that respondents might contend that they were not racist or sexist but responding to other factors, often beyond their control. For example, in the *Roma* case,[60] UK immigration officers operated a pre-clearance immigration control scheme at Prague airport aimed at stemming the flow of asylum seekers from the Czech Republic to the UK. The data showed that travellers who were of Roma origin were 400 times more likely to be refused the right to travel to the UK than non-Roma. While almost all Roma were rejected, this was only true of a tiny minority of non-Roma. The immigration officers argued that this was not because of the Roma's race or ethnic origin but because Roma, who were treated very badly in the Czech Republic, were more likely to claim asylum than others. Their contention was rejected. The underlying motive or intention was irrelevant. As Baroness Hale put it: 'If a person acts on racial grounds, the reason why he does so is irrelevant. The law reports are full of examples of obviously discriminatory treatment which was in no way motivated by racism or sexism and often brought about by pressures beyond the discriminators' control.'[61] Their actions were held to be directly discriminatory.

Because motive and intention are excluded in the UK formulation of direct discrimination, the 'but for' test is left to focus on the effect of the action rather than on why the perpetrator acted. This test was first formulated in *Birmingham City Council v Equal Opportunities Commission.*[62] In this case, because fewer places were available in girls' selective grammar schools

[59] ibid 3.
[60] *R (European Roma Rights Centre) v Immigration Officer at Prague Airport* [2004] UKHL 55, [2005] 2 AC 1.
[61] ibid [85].
[62] *R v Birmingham City Council, ex p Equal Opportunities Commission* (n 41).

than in selective schools for boys, the council required girls to obtain higher marks in the entry examination than boys.[63] The council argued that its motive was not to discriminate against girls but to ensure that the most meritorious pupils were given places. The House of Lords held that to establish direct discrimination, it was not necessary to prove that the council's motive was to put girl pupils at a disadvantage compared with boy pupils in the area. Instead, the causative factor was crucial.

> The question is whether, but for her sex, a qualified girl would have been given treatment and education opportunities equal to those given to a comparable boy. In the present case, there is no dispute that . . . were she male, she would have access to almost twice as many selective places.[64]

The difficulty with this approach is that it risks blurring the distinction between treatment and effects. Direct discrimination is distinctive in its focus on a perpetrator's actions and the reason for those actions. A discriminates against B if A treats B less favourably because of a protected characteristic. There is a necessary link between the treatment and the reason for it: if the 'less favourable' treatment is not 'because of' the protected characteristic, there is no discrimination. This underlies the demarcation between direct and indirect discrimination. Whereas direct discrimination is based on the ground of or reason for A's actions, indirect discrimination focuses on its impact. The distinction is important because in UK law in general, less favourable treatment cannot be justified, whereas disparate impact can do so. Advocate General Maduro has formulated this relationship particularly clearly:

> The distinguishing feature of direct discrimination . . . is that [it] bear[s] a necessary relationship to a particular suspect classification. The discriminator relies on a suspect classification in order to act in a certain way. The classification is not a mere contingency but serves as an essential premise of his reasoning. An employer's reliance on those suspect grounds is seen by the Community legal order as an evil which must be eradicated. Therefore, the Directive prohibits the use of those classifications as grounds upon which an employer's reasoning may be based. By contrast, in indirect discrimination cases, the intentions of the employer and the reasons he has to act or not to act are irrelevant. In fact, this is the whole point of the prohibition of indirect discrimination: even neutral, innocent or good faith measures and policies adopted with no discriminatory

---

[63] ibid.
[64] ibid 1184.

intent whatsoever will be caught if their impact on persons who have a particular characteristic is greater than their impact on other persons.[65]

It is clear that the fact that A is not hostile to B should not excuse A's actions. On the other hand, A's action must be *because of* the protected character-istic. If the treatment was for an entirely different reason but has the effect of discriminating, then it should fall under the indirect discrimination provi-sions and be capable of justification. Instead of ignoring the perpetrator's real reason, this would allow the courts to determine on proportionality grounds whether the real reason should be allowed to outweigh the differential im-pact. The fact that an employer was following customer preference, saving money, or avoiding controversy should not be sufficient to outweigh the fact that women have been excluded. On the other hand, if the reason for the treatment was to compensate for past disadvantage, this may well outweigh the exclusionary effect.

The court in the *Birmingham* case did not traverse the boundary between treatment on the grounds of sex and effect. This was because the council was itself responsible for maintaining selective schools with fewer places for girls. As Dillon LJ in the Court of Appeal put it (upheld by Lord Goff in the House of Lords):

> in truth the council's position really is that they are knowingly continuing their acts of maintaining the various boys' and girls' selective schools, which inevitably results in discrimination against girls in the light of the great disparity in the numbers of places available.[66]

In later cases, however, the distinction between treatment and effect became increasingly blurred. This was because the principle that the perpetrator's *motive* is irrelevant subtly transformed into an assertion of the irrelevance of the perpetrator's *reason* for the less favourable treatment. The courts have held that even if the reason is not on its face based on a protected charac-teristic, it might nevertheless be 'inherently' sex- or race-based. This severs the notion of direct discrimination from its moral anchor in fault and the responsibility of the perpetrator, and instead makes A responsible for putting in motion a series of steps which have a detrimental *effect* on B, thus crossing the border between direct and indirect discrimination.

---

[65] Case C-303/06 *Coleman v Attridge Law* [2008] ECR I-5603, [2008] IRLR 722 (ECJ).
[66] *R v Birmingham City Council, ex p Equal Opportunities Commission* (n 41) 1196.

The concept of an 'inherently' discriminatory criterion was first introduced in *James v Eastleigh BC*.[67] *James* concerned a challenge to Eastleigh Borough Council's policy of giving free access to swimming pools and other council facilities to anyone over pensionable age. The aim of the concessions was to compensate for the drop in income generally accompanying the end of one's working life. The problem arose because State pension ages were set at sixty for women and sixty-five for men. This meant that although both Mr James and Mrs James were sixty-one, she was entitled to free swimming but he was not. He argued that he had been discriminated against on grounds of his sex. The authority defended the policy by arguing that people living on pensions are almost always less well off than when in employment. The criterion of pensionable age, while somewhat broad brush, was the most practical way of identifying people living on pensions. The reason for the differentiation was not the sex of the complainant but the fact that he had not reached pensionable age.

However, the majority of the House of Lords found that the reason why the policy was adopted could not alter the fact that the man would have received the benefits 'but for' his sex. The reason for the difference—namely, to give concessions to pensioners to compensate for their loss of income—was irrelevant. Instead, it was held that the criterion of pensionable age '*itself* . . . treats women more favourably than men "on the ground of their sex",[68] and was 'inherently' discriminatory.[69] The result was paradoxical. As Lord Griffiths put it in his dissenting opinion:

> The result of your Lordships' decision will be that either free facilities must be withdrawn from those who can ill afford to pay for them or, alternatively, given free to those who can well afford to pay for them. I consider both alternatives regrettable. I cannot believe that Parliament intended such a result and I do not believe that the words 'on the grounds of sex' compel such a result.[70]

This difficulty arises because the court focused not on the reason for A's actions, but on its effect. In this case, the court assumed that pensionable age was simply a proxy for sex, whereas in reality the council regarded pensionable age as a proxy for relative disadvantage. It treated Mr James less favourably than Mrs James because he was not yet of pensionable age, not because

---

[67] *James v Eastleigh BC* (n 10).
[68] ibid 763.
[69] ibid 769.
[70] ibid 768.

he was a man. It is true that this had a differential impact on men and women but that was because the pensionable age was different for men and women. Although the council could foresee this effect, this was not the reason for its actions.[71] If pensionable ages were the same for men and women, it would still have used this criterion. Of course, it might be argued that pensionable age is too crude a mechanism for determining low income and, therefore, given its exclusionary effect on men, the choice of pensionable age was not appropriate or necessary to achieve the aim of ameliorating the loss of income post pensionable age. This, however, should be considered separately, in the form of a justification defence. This strongly suggests that if intention and motive are excluded from the original decision, a defence of justification should be permitted.

The paradoxical effect of ignoring the perpetrator's real reason for their action (as against the motive for so acting) is further underscored in the *JFS* case,[72] where the notion that a ground can be 'inherently' discriminatory was entrenched in the structure of direct discrimination. Here both Lord Mance and Lord Clarke expressly held that direct discrimination could arise in one of two ways: 'because a decision or action was taken on a ground which was, however worthy or benign the motive, inherently racial, or because it was taken or undertaken for a reason which was subjectively racial'.[73] In this case, as we saw in Chapter 4, a boy was refused admission to JFS, a Jewish faith school, because he was not recognized as Jewish according to the Orthodox religious rule. This rule, as set out by the Orthodox Chief Rabbi, requires Orthodox conversion or descent from a mother who is herself Jewish or has been converted according to the Orthodox faith. Although the boy's mother was a practising Jewish person, she had been converted to Judaism according to Masorti rather than Orthodox tenets. Designated faith schools are permitted to discriminate on grounds of religion but not on grounds of race or ethnicity. Was the school's decision, therefore, on grounds of his religion or his ethnicity?[74] Did the admissions policy 'religiously motivated as it was, involve grounds for admission or refusal of admission which were in their nature inherently ethnic'?[75]

---

[71] ibid 781.
[72] *JFS* (n 10).
[73] ibid [78]; and see Lord Clarke at [132].
[74] It has already been argued that this exception is problematic because it relies on a distinction between religion and ethnicity which only truly works from a Christian perspective. See Chapter 4.
[75] *JFS* (n 10) [78].

The majority of the court found that although the Chief Rabbi and the governors of the school were entirely free from moral blame, and acted on what must have seemed to them an entirely legitimate religious objective, the religious element was a mere motive and therefore irrelevant to the outcome. Instead, the ground was his ethnicity; any rule which relies on descent is an ethnic rule and, 'but for' the fact that his mother was not Jewish by Orthodox standards, he would have been admitted to the school.

The result was that the policy was held to be discriminatory on grounds of race. Yet the majority was at pains to stress that a breach of the prohibition of direct race discrimination did not connote that the school or the Chief Rabbi was racist. It was simply a technical application of the law. This disjuncture between a moral condemnation of racism and a breach of race discrimination legislation should itself give pause for thought. As Lord Rodger points out in his dissent:

> The majority's decision leads to such extraordinary results, and produces such manifest discrimination against Jewish schools in comparison with other faith schools, that one can't help feeling that something has gone wrong.[76]

What then might have gone wrong? First, the notion that a criterion is 'inherently' discriminatory ignores the structure of direct discrimination, which is to focus on why a person acted in the way they did. A decision or action is only 'inherently' discriminatory because of its effect; it is this which distinguishes it from an action which is, in the words of Lords Mance and Clark, 'subjectively racial'.[77] Focusing on the effect is the province of indirect discrimination. Direct discrimination, by contrast, requires a finding that the reason for the perpetrator's action was based on a protected characteristic.

Secondly, the 'but for' test gives the misleading impression that it is a value-free standard which can find a single and unequivocal cause for the less favourable treatment. In this case, however, it yields several different answers. 'But for' the fact that he was a Masorti rather than an Orthodox Jewish boy, he would have been admitted to the school. This would be a religious reason. Alternatively, 'but for' the fact that his mother was a Masorti rather than an Orthodox Jewish woman, he would have been admitted. This combines a religious and a descent-based reason. Or, 'but for' the fact that Judaism recognizes only the matrilineal and not the patrilineal line, the boy would have been admitted. This is a gender-based, religious, and

---

[76] ibid [226].
[77] ibid [78]; and see Lord Clarke at [132].

descent-based reason. The majority of the court took the view that as long as one of the reasons was descent-based, it did not matter that there were other non-descent-based reasons. But the freedom of the court to choose amongst different reasons undercuts the thrust of the 'but for' test. Only by referring back to the actual reason or set of reasons used by the perpetrator can a 'but for' test make sense.

Thirdly, the relegation of the real reason to a mere motive undercuts any moral rationale which might underpin direct discrimination. It will be recalled that Advocate General Maduro identified the 'evil' of direct discrimination as the fact that a suspect classification is an 'essential premise' of the discriminator's reasoning; or constitutes grounds on which the person's reasoning is based. It is the perpetrator's reasoning which is in issue. By contrast, in the context of indirect discrimination, the perpetrator's reasons are irrelevant.[78] As Lords Hope and Rodger pointed out in their dissenting opinions in *JFS*, to reduce the religious element to the status of a mere motive entirely misrepresents the position,[79] removing the link between A's actions and the reason for A's actions. The real reason for the Chief Rabbi's action was religious; he recognized some conversions to Judaism but not others. Indeed, the real dispute in the case was between the Orthodox and non-Orthodox understandings of who should be Jewish, a profoundly religious dispute. Yet the impact of the majority decision is not to require recognition of non-Orthodox conversions. It is to prevent the school from basing its selection policy on the Jewish definition of Judaism at all. Instead, it requires a practice-based definition, familiar to Anglicanism but alien to Judaism. Jewish faith schools have now changed their admissions policy to require evidence of practise of the Jewish faith through attendance at synagogue twice a month on the Sabbath as well as on all holy days. This is a result which profoundly undermines the stated mission of the school, which is to give a Jewish education to children with no knowledge of Judaism as much as to those who already have such knowledge. As Lord Brown put it, the result is:

> a test for admission to an Orthodox Jewish school which is not Judaism's own test and which requires a focus (as Christianity does) on outward acts of

---

[78] *Coleman v Attridge Law* (n 65).
[79] *JFS* (n 10) [201].

religious practice and declarations of faith, ignoring whether the child is or is not Jewish as defined by Orthodox Jewish law.[80]

In more recent cases, the 'but for' principle has been further elaborated to include a focus on 'indissociability'. Where the act or decision excludes everyone with the relevant protected characteristic, it might be thought that there is too much of a coincidence between the criterion applied and the exclusionary effect to regard the criterion as neutral.[81] This principle, first hinted at in *JFS*, was developed into a fully-fledged principle in *Hall v Bull*.[82] In this case, the owners of a private hotel believed that it was sinful for persons to have sexual relations outside marriage, and that they would be complicit in this sinful act if they permitted unmarried couples to share a double bed. They therefore restricted occupancy of the double-bedded rooms in their hotel to married couples. Under this policy, they refused to allow the claimants, a same-sex couple in a civil partnership, to occupy one of these rooms. The respondents argued that this was not direct discrimination on grounds of sexual orientation since they applied their rule to all unmarried couples, whether heterosexual or homosexual. They accepted that it could be indirect discrimination but claimed that it was justified by their religious beliefs.

Lady Hale reiterated that the distinction between direct and indirect discrimination is crucial, given that there is no general defence of justification for direct discrimination in the same way as there is for indirect discrimination. In this case, if, as argued by the respondents, this was a case of indirect discrimination, the Court would need to consider whether their claim for justification succeeded. On the other hand, if it was direct discrimination, then there would be no scope for introducing their religious justification.

Notably, the choice of direct or indirect discrimination did not affect the result, as the justification defence was ultimately rejected even on the alternative claim of indirect discrimination. Nevertheless, the majority of the Court held that this was a case of direct discrimination. In coming to this conclusion, Lady Hale expressly relied on the 'indissociability' principle. This holds that there is direct discrimination when there is an exact coincidence between an apparently neutral condition for receiving or being denied an advantage and a protected characteristic. In other words, even though the

---

[80] ibid [258].
[81] See ibid [71].
[82] *Bull v Hall* [2013] UKSC 73 (UK Sup Ct).

criterion is neutral on its face, everyone with the protected characteristic is excluded. An exact coincidence, Lady Hale held, suggests that the condition is necessarily linked to a characteristic indissociable from a protected characteristic. This contrasts with indirect discrimination which applies when a substantially higher proportion of a group with a protected characteristic is affected, rather than everyone in the group.[83] Lady Hale accepted that if the criterion was considered to be marriage, there was no such exact coincidence since unmarried heterosexual partners were also excluded. However, she reframed the criterion to be between married partners and those in a civil partnership. Since, as the law then stood, same-sex partners in a civil partnership could not, by law, enter into marriage, she held, 'I would therefore regard the criterion of marriage or civil partnership as indissociable from the sexual orientation of those who qualify to enter it. More importantly, there is an exact correspondence between the advantage conferred and the disadvantage imposed in allowing a double bed to the one [marriage] and denying it to the other [civil partnership].'[84] This contrasts with the opinion of Lord Neuberger who, while agreeing with the result, preferred to take the route of unjustified indirect discrimination.

As this case demonstrates, the criterion of indissociability, or exact correspondence, is an unsteady basis on which to distinguish between direct discrimination, which cannot be justified, and indirect discrimination, which can. By shifting from a comparison between unmarried and married couples to one between civil partners and married couples, the opportunity of justification can be permitted or removed. While Lord Neuberger saw the contrast as the former, and therefore a case of indirect discrimination, Lady Hale regarded it as the latter, and therefore direct discrimination. Nor does there seem to be a clear principled divide between a case in which a substantial proportion is affected as against everyone in the group. In both cases, the real focus is on effect rather than on treatment, apparently putting both in the camp of indirect discrimination The result was, as Lord Neuberger put it, to risk blurring the distinction between direct and indirect discrimination.[85] Given that Mr and Mrs Bull made it clear that their decision was based on their religious objections, it would seem more appropriate to follow an indirect discrimination route and expressly consider whether their actions

[83] ibid [19] citing AG Jacobs in Case C-79/99 *Schnorbus v Land Hessen* [2001] 1 CMLR 40, para 33 (ECJ).

[84] ibid [29].

[85] ibid [84].

could be justified on this basis. Lord Neuberger found that this was not a sufficient justification. It is submitted that this is a preferable route to the right outcome.

Indeed, in EU law such fact situations are generally regarded as cases of indirect discrimination. In *O'Flynn*,[86] the ECJ explicitly stated that a provision would be regarded as indirectly discriminatory if it were 'intrinsically liable' to affect migrant workers more than national workers, with the consequent risk that they would be placed at a particular disadvantage.[87] It has made no difference to the ECJ that the apparently neutral criterion in effect excludes all members of a particular group. In *Schnorbus*,[88] a legal training course was mandatory in order to qualify for the higher civil service or the judicial service. Priority for places on the course was given to individuals who had completed national service. Yet only men were eligible for national service. The ECJ held that regardless of statistics, the provisions at issue were themselves evidence of indirect discrimination since, under the relevant national legislation, women were not required to do military or civilian service and therefore could not benefit from the priority. This analysis closely resembles the 'intrinsically discriminatory' class identified by the UK courts as directly discriminatory. By classifying it as indirectly discriminatory, however, the ECJ was able to consider the justification for the rule. Since its aim was to compensate for the delay necessitated by military service, and the detriment to others lasted for only twelve months, it was held to be proportionate and justified.

(iv) Justifying Direct Discrimination?

One way forward is to permit direct discrimination to be justifiable. There has been a deep resistance in both UK and EU law to allow a general justification defence for direct discrimination although, as we will see, this is no longer true in relation to equal pay, age, and disability. One reason for this is that since direct discrimination is concerned with unequal treatment because of a personal characteristic, it is a central affront to individual dignity to permit it to be excused.[89] This argument certainly holds true in relation

---

[86] Case C-237/94 *O'Flynn v Adjudication Officer* [1996] 3 CMLR 103 (ECJ).
[87] ibid para 20.
[88] Case C-79/99 *Schnorbus v Land Hessen* [2001] 1 CMLR 40 (ECJ).
[89] T Gill and K Monaghan, 'Justification in Direct Sex Discrimination Law: Taboo Upheld' (2003) 32 ILJ 115.

to justifications based on cost. There is a danger that allowing cost to trump equality claims will mean that 'unlawfulness of any treatment will be determined by its "market value" or cost'.[90] There is also a danger that stereotypes will be reinforced by permitting less favourable treatment on a protected ground to be justified.[91]

The strength of the argument against permitting justification based on cost or stereotypes, however, should not obscure the possibility that there may be legitimate justifications, not least when called for by other conceptions of equality. Inequality of treatment might, in principle, be justifiable if it aims to redress previous disadvantage, as in affirmative action cases.[92] Moreover, the moral argument against allowing direct discrimination to be 'excused' loses its traction now that direct discrimination includes situations in which the protected characteristic is not the reason for A's actions, but instead the criterion used is 'intrinsically' discriminatory, or 'indissociable', from the protected characteristic. In such situations, permitting justification would make it possible to situate a policy, criterion, or practice within its context and test its purpose and function against the seriousness of its discriminatory consequences. For example, in *James* the council would have been required to show that there was no other less discriminatory means of achieving its aim of assisting pensioners. Similarly, in *JFS* the school would have had to prove that there was no less discriminatory manner of achieving its legitimate objective of providing a Jewish education for Jewish children. Permitting non-Orthodox conversions may have been such a means. By contrast, in *Bull v Hall*, the justification based on religious objections was rightly rejected. The key, therefore, is to provide for a justification defence which can differentiate between furthering a substantive understanding of equality, on the one hand, and subordinating equality to cost or perpetuating stereotypes, on the other. Moreover, the possibility of justification need not be a pretext for maintaining the status quo. In some contexts, justification may only be established if all reasonable adjustments have been made.

This is, indeed, the approach in other jurisdictions, where the issue is not whether a justification defence is permissible for direct discrimination but what the standard of scrutiny is. Under the Fourteenth Amendment in US law, as we saw in Chapter 4, the level of scrutiny depends on the ground at

---

[90] ibid 116.

[91] *R (European Roma Rights Centre) v Immigration Officer at Prague Airport* [2004] QB 811 [86] (CA). This approach was rejected in the House of Lords: see *R (European R (European Roma Rights Centre and Others) v Immigration Officer at Prague Airport* (n 60).

[92] See Chapter 7.

issue, with strict scrutiny applying to race and alienage, intermediate level scrutiny applying to gender, and rational basis to other grounds, including age and disability. Under Title VII, justification is permitted in the course of establishing intention through the framework of shifting the evidentiary burden. Once an employee has made a prima facie claim of discrimination, the burden shifts to the employer who can justify the action by providing evidence of a legitimate non-discriminatory reason for its actions. The burden then shifts back to the plaintiff to prove that those reasons were a pretext for discrimination.[93]

The ECtHR puts justification at the centre of its understanding of what amounts to discrimination. From its earliest jurisprudence, the Court has held that Article 14 does not forbid every difference in treatment. Instead, equality of treatment is violated if the distinction has no objective and reasonable justification. However, as in the US, the standard of justification can vary depending on the ground. Whereas 'very weighty' reasons would be needed to justify differences of treatment on grounds of ethnic origin,[94] gender,[95] sexual orientation,[96] or disability,[97] a much less exacting standard of justification is applied to other grounds. For example, in *Emel Boyraz v Turkey*[98] the applicant was denied a position as a security officer in the State-run electricity company because she was a woman. The State justified this exclusion on the grounds that the job required the incumbent to handle weapons, to work day and night, and to use physical force in case of an attack, for which women were not suitable. The Court took the high standard of justification for sex discrimination seriously, reiterating that since 'the advancement of gender equality is today a major goal in the member States of the Council of Europe . . . very weighty reasons would have to be put forward before such a difference of treatment could be regarded as compatible with the Convention.'[99] The Court concluded that 'the mere fact that security officers had to work night shifts and in rural areas and might be required to use physical force and firearms under certain conditions could not in itself justify the difference in treatment between men and women.'[100] The existence

---

[93] *Watson v Fort Worth Bank & Trust* 487 US 977, 986 (1988) (US Sup Ct).
[94] *DH v Czech Republic* (Application no 57325/00) (2008) 47 EHRR 3 (ECtHR (Grand Chamber)).
[95] *Abdulaziz, Cabales and Balkandali v UK* [1985] 7 EHRR 471 (ECtHR).
[96] *EB v France* (2008) 47 EHRR 21 (ECtHR).
[97] *Kiss v Hungary* (2013) 56 EHRR 38 (ECtHR).
[98] *Boyraz v Turkey* (Application no 61960/08) (2015) 60 EHRR 30.
[99] ibid para 51.
[100] ibid para 54.

of a possible justification defence is not, therefore, problematic. The real challenge is for it to be calibrated in a manner that can discern invidious discrimination and distinguish it from appropriate differentiation.

In fact, even in the UK and the EU, there are a growing number of ways in which direct discrimination can indeed be justified. As we will see, equal pay legislation has always permitted employers to justify differences of pay for equal work by reference to a material factor which is not itself the difference in sex. In addition, it has always been possible to justify direct race and sex discrimination where sex or race is a genuine occupational qualification. This has now been extended to most of the protected characteristics, subject to a proportionality requirement.[101] Similarly, direct discrimination in relation to age is expressly capable of justification, and there has been a long-standing equivocation in relation to disability. This makes it particularly important to be in a position to shape a justification defence which is context-sensitive without permitting cost arguments to trump equality or reintroducing the very stereotypes that direct discrimination aims to eliminate.

How, then, has the justification defence operated in the context of age discrimination? It has been argued that the availability of a justification for direct age discrimination should not be 'interpreted as putting age discrimination at the bottom of a perceived "hierarchy" of discrimination grounds' but instead a recognition of the fact that age discrimination is different and its scope needs more careful demarcation.[102] This suggests that there are contexts in which age differentiation is appropriate and even necessary. The challenge is to find a sufficiently incisive tool to distinguish between legitimate and illegitimate differentiation.

There are two quite different types of possible justification.[103] One is instrumental or cost-based. In the case of age discrimination, these would aim to address the demographic problems of an ageing population and its implications for the labour market and social security. A second is intrinsic, focusing on the recognition, redistributive, or transformative dimensions of equality (protection against stigma, stereotyping, and prejudice, redressing disadvantage, or accommodating difference and achieving structural change). Intrinsic justifications would make it lawful to use age-based classifications if the aim were to ameliorate the effects of old age or youth.

---

[101] EA 2010, sch 9 pt 1.

[102] *Boyraz v Turkey* (n 98) AG Mazák at para 76.

[103] See further S Fredman, 'The Age of Equality' in S Fredman and S Spencer (eds), *Age as an Equality Issue* (Hart Publishing 2003).

Examples might include concessions for older people, such as free bus passes or medical prescriptions.

The instrumental aim is clearly dominant in the EU Employment Directive. Direct age discrimination may be 'objectively and reasonably justified by a legitimate aim, including legitimate employment policy, labour market and vocational training objectives'.[104] More specifically, it may be justifiable to fix minimum conditions of age, professional experience or seniority for access to employment or advantages linked to employment. In addition, a maximum age for recruitment may be set if it is based on the training requirements of the employer or the need for a reasonable period of employment before retirement.[105] There are, however, gestures towards the intrinsic aim: differential treatment may be justified in relation to positive action (such as setting special conditions on access to employment or training, or in relation to such issues as dismissal and conditions of remuneration) if it is aimed at promoting the vocational integration of young people, older workers, or persons with caring responsibilities.

Given the predominantly instrumental nature of potentially legitimate aims of age differentiation, the weight of responsibility for achieving an appropriate role for a justification defence must be borne by the relationship between the age classification and these legitimate aims. The directive stipulates that the means for achieving the aim must be 'appropriate and necessary'.[106] Much therefore depends on the extent to which the courts are prepared to demand a high standard of proof that age discrimination is, indeed, necessary to achieve those ends. The ECJ will generally accept governments' stated aims, while requiring a reasonably strict standard of proof to demonstrate that age-related policies are in fact proportionate to those aims. Particularly important is the Court's demand for actual evidence. Mere generalizations will not suffice to show that a measure will contribute to one of the specified objectives. Nor do such generalizations constitute evidence that the specific measure is suitable for achieving the aim.[107]

This can be demonstrated by *Kücükdeveci*[108] which concerned a provision in the German Civil Code providing that periods of employment completed

[104] Council Directive 2000/78, Art 6(1).
[105] ibid Art 6.
[106] ibid, Art 6.
[107] Case C-388/07 R (*Incorporated Trustees of the National Council on Ageing (Age Concern England)) v Secretary of State for Business, Enterprise and Regulatory Reform* [2009] ICR 1080, para 51 (ECJ).
[108] Case C-555/07 *Kücükdeveci v Swedex GmbH & Co KG* [2010] 2 CMLR 33 (ECJ).

before the age of twenty-five were not to be taken into account in calculating a notice period. The German government claimed that a shorter notice period for younger workers facilitated their recruitment by increasing the flexibility of personnel management. Moreover, it claimed, young workers generally reacted more easily and more rapidly to the loss of their jobs and greater flexibility could be demanded of them. Despite the fact that such generalizations clearly stereotyped workers on grounds of their age, the ECJ held that these were acceptable employment and labour market objectives. However, the means were not acceptable because the exclusion of periods of employment completed before age of twenty-five was not an appropriate and necessary means of achieving that aim. It was overinclusive in that its effects were felt throughout a worker's life, not just when she was under twenty-five. This was because periods of employment under the age of twenty-five were discounted for the rest of a worker's working life and therefore did not only apply to young workers. Moreover, the impact was felt disproportionately severely by the most disadvantaged, namely, those who entered the labour market at a young age without further vocational qualifications. Germany was therefore held to be in breach of the directive.

In evaluating the application of justification in this respect, the four-dimensional understanding of substantive equality is helpful. The framework requires us to ask whether age-based measures cause socio-economic disadvantage, whether they are stigmatic, whether they are exclusionary, and whether they fail to accommodate difference and entrench structural inequality. Some clearly do not. Concessionary transport or prescription charges for older people are none of these, and therefore do not breach substantive equality. Other measures are more complex. One of the most challenging has been the mandatory retirement age which has been the subject of much case law before the CJEU. Mandatory retirement at a certain age is clearly prima facie discriminatory. But can it be justified? The substantive equality framework militates against an all-or-nothing approach. A focus on the first question—namely, the need to redress disadvantage—requires us to look at whether there is appropriate pension provision on retirement. This criterion would only be satisfied if any justification offered for a mandatory retirement age were required to show that adequate alternative income was available. The Court has recognized the importance of taking into account the financial consequences of a mandatory retirement age. In one of the earliest cases, *Palacios de la Villa*, the Court stated that compulsory retirement of workers at age sixty-five with the aim of encouraging recruitment would not unduly prejudice the legitimate claims of the workers concerned if they were entitled to a reasonable pension.[109] More specifically, in *Fuchs*, the Court took into account the fact that prosecutors subject to the mandatory retirement age were eligible for pensions at approximately 72 per cent of their final salary and were not precluded from continuing in other professional activities such as that of legal advisers, with no age limit.[110] This was one of the factors which led it to find that the mandatory retirement age did not go beyond what was necessary to achieve a balanced age structure, which it had already found to be a legitimate aim. Similarly, in *Georgiev*, the age limit applied to university professors was five years higher than the pensionable age. The Court stressed that the measure could not be regarded as unduly prejudicing the legitimate claims of workers subject to compulsory retirement because the relevant legislation took account of the fact that the persons concerned were entitled to retirement pensions.[111] The Court stated that the reason for the termination was not solely the worker's age. Instead 'the decisive factor is that the professor has an acquired a right to a retirement pension'.[112]

The second dimension—namely, the need to combat stigma and prejudice—is much more contested. The 'dignity' argument has been used on both sides of the debate. Those against mandatory retirement argue that it stereotypes retirement-age workers by assuming that they are no longer capable of doing the work. Instead, workers should be tested individually to determine their actual capacity. Those in favour of a mandatory retirement age argue that a fixed rule applying to everyone reaching a specified age prevents the indignity of individual performance assessments as workers get older. This latter position can be seen in *Fuchs*, where the Court accepted that establishing a retirement age which aimed at preventing possible disputes concerning employees' fitness to work beyond a certain age could constitute a legitimate aim of employment and labour market policy.[113]

The alternative to a fixed rule could be individual testing which would depart from age-based stereotyping. This possibility has received a mixed response from the Court, particularly in relation to airline pilots. In *Prigge*, German pilots contested a provision in a collective agreement requiring

---

[109] Case C-411/05 *Palacios de la Villa v Cortefiel Servicios SA* (2008) 1 CMLR 16, para 73 (CJEU); see also Case C-45/09 *Rosenbladt v Oellerking Gebäudereinigungsges mbH* [2011] 1 CMLR 1011, paras 73–76 (ECJ).

[110] Case C-159/10 *Fuchs v Land Hessen* [2102] ICR 93, para 67 (CJEU).

[111] Joined Cases C-250 and 268/09 *Georgiev v Tehnicheski Universitet—Sofia filial Plovdiv* [2011] 2 CMLR 179, para 54 (ECJ).

[112] ibid para 63.

[113] *Fuchs v Land Hessen* (n 110) para 50.

airline pilots to retire at the age of sixty.[114] The Court accepted that monitoring pilots' aptitudes and physical capabilities was essential and that it was undeniable that those capabilities diminished with age. However, it was not satisfied that it was necessary to assume that such capabilities automatically diminished at the age of sixty to such an extent as to require termination of employment. Given that national and international legislation considered that it was not necessary to prohibit pilots from continuing as pilots beyond the age of sixty, the Court held that the measure was not a proportionate means of achieving a legitimate aim.[115] By contrast, in the later case of *Fries v Lufthansa*,[116] the ECJ held that an EU provision establishing an age limit of sixty-five for commercial airline pilots transporting passengers, cargo, or mail was justified as proportionate to the aim of ensuring civil aviation safety in Europe. The ECJ held that individual examinations of the physical and mental capacity of licence-holders over the age of sixty-five were not a practical alternative. Pilots who had reached sixty-five could, however, continue to act as pilots of flights with no passengers, cargo, or mail.

The fourth dimension—namely, the need to look to structural change—is particularly complex. On the one hand, it suggests that reasonable accommodation should be provided for age-related incapacity. On the other hand, it requires a broader consideration of structures than simply the individual issue. Structural change might point towards making space for younger workers, an argument often made in favour of retirement ages. However, this would only be acceptable if there was clear evidence that in fact there was workforce turnover. In many modern situations, jobs are frozen or changed; or, alternatively, growing opportunities mean that there is not a fixed number of jobs. The structural dimension also requires consideration of intersectional issues. Mandatory retirement ages might detrimentally affect women or minorities who have not amassed sufficient pension. Alternatively, in some contexts the retirement of older, white, male workers might make space for previously disadvantaged women and other minorities. Here, too, the answer depends on detailed contextual evidence, bearing in mind the importance of the other dimensions. In this regard, the Court's approach has been hesitatingly in the direction of recognizing the need to look at the structural issues as a whole, while potentially being less vigilant about ensuring that statements concerning such structures are properly supported by evidence. In *Fuchs*, the

---

[114] Case C-447/09 *Prigge v Deutsche Lufthansa AG* [2011] IRLR 1052 (ECJ).
[115] ibid paras 58, 73.
[116] Case C-190/16 *Fries v Lufthansa CityLine GmbH* [2017] IRLR 1003 (ECJ).

Court accepted that establishing an age structure that balances younger and older civil servants to encourage the recruitment and promotion of younger people could constitute a legitimate aim.[117] But is a mandatory retirement age appropriate and necessary to achieve such an aim? In several cases, it has now accepted that if the number of posts available is limited, and incumbents tend to remain in post permanently with little or no turnover, mandatory retirement age may be the only means of ensuring that young people have a fair opportunity to enter the profession in question.[118] This has been held to be applicable to panel dentists,[119] university professors,[120] and prosecutors.[121]

(v) Conclusion: Direct Discrimination and Substantive Equality

Direct discrimination, because of its basis in the principle that likes should be treated alike, only weakly achieves any of the objectives of the four-dimensional conception of equality established in Chapter 1. At best, it can address stigma, stereotyping, and humiliation because of a protected characteristic. Enhanced judicial sensitivity to the dangers of stereotyping have in some cases made direct discrimination an effective instrument in this respect. As Baroness Hale put it in the *Roma* case, 'the object of the legislation is to ensure that each person is treated as an individual and not assumed to be like other members of the group'.[122] In that case, rather than judging each individual on her merits, the immigration officers assumed that all Roma applicants would be making false claims and therefore warranted particularly intensive questioning.[123] Racial profiling in the use of police stop and search powers might similarly breach the principle of discrimination.[124] However, even this dimension is undermined by the possibility that equality might be achieved by 'levelling down' rather than up. If everyone is treated in the same

---

[117] *Fuchs v Land Hessen* (n 110) para 50.

[118] ibid paras 58–59.

[119] Case C-341/09 *Petersen v Berufungsausschuss fur Zahnarzte fur den Bezirk Westfalen-Lippe* [2010] 2 CMLR 830, para 70.

[120] *Georgiev v Tehnicheski Universitet—Sofia filial Plovdiv* (n 111).

[121] *Fuchs v Land Hessen* (n 110) para 60.

[122] *R (European Roma Rights Centre) v Immigration Officer at Prague Airport* [2004] UKHL 55, [2005] 2 AC 1 [82].

[123] ibid [113].

[124] *R (Gillan) v Commr of Police of the Metropolis* [2006] UKHL 12, [2006] 2 AC 307 [45].

humiliating or stigmatic way, there would be no recourse under the direct discrimination provisions.

The remaining dimensions of equality are out of the range of direct discrimination. Its symmetry makes it difficult to advance the redistributive dimension. The rejection in UK law of both intention as an ingredient of direct discrimination and a defence of justification makes it even more difficult to rely on redressing disadvantage as a legitimate reason for discrimination. Nor can direct discrimination further the participative or transformational dimensions. Instead, the insistence on a comparator, hypothetical or otherwise, means that direct discrimination requires conformity to the dominant mode as a condition for equal treatment. Can these limitations be addressed by a complementary principle of indirect discrimination? It is to this that we now turn.

III INDIRECT DISCRIMINATION

(i) The Development of the Concept

We have seen that equal treatment is not in itself sufficient to address inequality in society. Equal treatment may well lead to unequal results. Selection criteria based on educational qualifications, although equally applicable to all, will exclude those who have been deprived of proper schooling; jobs which require full-time working and mobility will exclude those with primary responsibility for childcare. It is in recognition of this that the concept of indirect discrimination was shaped, initially by the US Supreme Court in the pioneering US case of *Griggs v Duke Power*.[125] The case was a clear demonstration of the way in which apparently neutral criteria sustain and reinforce the disadvantaged position of African Americans in the US. The employer, Duke Power, had followed a long-standing practice of excluding African Americans from the jobs in question. Following the passage of the Civil Rights Act 1964, which prohibited race discrimination, the employer removed the express exclusion but instead instituted requirements of a high school education and satisfactory scores in an aptitude test as conditions of employment or transfer. The same test was applied to all candidates. But because Black applicants had long received inferior education in segregated

---

[125] *Griggs v Duke Power Co* (n 2).

schools, both requirements operated to disqualify Black applicants at a sub-stantially higher rate than white people. Neither standard was shown to be significantly related to successful job performance. The Court responded by expanding the principle of equality. As Burger CJ, delivering the judgment of the Court, put it:

> The Act proscribes not only overt discrimination but also practices that are fair in form, but discriminatory in operation. The touchstone is business necessity. If an employment practice which operates to exclude [Black people] cannot be shown to be related to job performance, the practice is prohibited.[126]

Equal treatment was held to be discriminatory if the result was that fewer Black people could comply, unless the requirement was necessary for the proper execution of the job in hand.

The recognition that equal treatment can be discriminatory when it has a disparate impact opens up many new frontiers for the right to equality including, for example, striking down the criminalization of sodomy in India.[127] Particularly important has been the recognition that inferior terms and conditions of work for part-time workers can constitute indirect dis-crimination against women.[128] Thus, in a series of groundbreaking cases, the ECJ recognized that since the vast majority of part-time workers are women, inferior conditions of work for these workers constitute indirect discrimination on grounds of sex.[129] The power of the concept of indirect discrimination in addressing the consequences of women's interrupted work patterns due to their primary responsibility for childcare was most recently demonstrated by the Supreme Court of Canada in *Fraser*.[130] The case con-cerned a pension scheme which did not permit employees on job-sharing arrangements to be treated as eligible for full pension credits during the pe-riod in which their hours of work were reduced. This contrasted with full-time workers who were eligible for full pension credit for periods of unpaid leave or suspension. The Court found that, although the arrangement was seemingly neutral, it had a disproportionate effect on women, especially women with young children, who constituted the vast majority of workers in the job-sharing programme. Indeed, the fact that these pension plans were

---

[126] ibid 431.

[127] *Navtej Singh Johar v Union of India* (2018) 10 SCC 1 (Indian Sup Ct).

[128] Case 96/80 *JP Jenkins v Kingsgate* [1981] ECR 911; Case 1007/84 *Bilka-Kaufhaus* [1986] IRLR 317 (ECJ); *Fraser v Canada (Attorney General)* 2020 SCC 28 (Can Sup Ct).

[129] *JP Jenkins v Kingsgate* (n 128); *Bilka-Kaufhaus* (n 128).

[130] *Fraser v Canada (Attorney General)* (n 128).

historically designed for full-time employees with long service meant that they incorporated a structural disadvantage against women. Nor could the exclusion be justified: no pressing or substantial policy concern had been identified.

After its initial formulation in *Griggs*, the concept of disparate impact rapidly made its way across the Atlantic, first to the UK and later to the EU. In the UK, it was named indirect discrimination and incorporated into the earliest non-discrimination statutes, the SDA 1975 and the RRA 1976. In EU law, the major impetus came from the ECJ, primarily in the context of protection for discrimination against part-time workers.[131] Indirect discrimination was given its first statutory formulation in 1997, in a very similar form to that found in the UK.[132] Subsequently, however, drawing from the concept as developed in the context of free movement of workers,[133] it was reformulated and incorporated into the Racial Equality and Employment Equality Directives, passed in 2000, and the Recast Gender Directive in 2006. This concept is now central to the modern EU directives.[134] Meanwhile, it continued to evolve in UK law, largely under the influence of EU law, until it was consolidated in the EA 2010.

Similarly, the Supreme Court of Canada has recognized adverse impact discrimination both at the level of provincial human rights codes and under the Charter. In the landmark case of *Ontario Human Rights Commission v Simpson-Sears Ltd*, interpreting the equality guarantee in the Ontario Human Rights Code, McIntyre J stated that the main aim was 'not to punish the discriminator, but rather to provide relief for the victims of discrimination. It is the result or the effect of the action complained of which is significant . . . if its effect is to impose on one person or group of persons obligations, penalties, or restrictive conditions not imposed on other members of the community, it is discriminatory.'[135] This definition of adverse effects discrimination has been expressly adopted under the equality guarantee in section 15(1) of the Canadian Charter.[136] Thus in *Eldridge*, the Court held that the lack of sign-language interpreters in a healthcare situation had a disparate impact on people with hearing loss. The Court confirmed that section 15(1) of the

[131] *JP Jenkins v Kingsgate* (n 128); *Bilka-Kaufhaus* (n 128).
[132] Directive 97/80/EC on the burden of proof in cases of discrimination based on sex [1998] OJ L14/6. Subsequently, this directive was merged into Directive 2006/54.
[133] See in particular *O'Flynn v Adjudication Officer* (n 86).
[134] Council Directive 2000/43/EC, Art 2(2)(b); Council Directive 2000/78/EC, Art 2(2)(b); Directive 2006/54/EC (Recast), Art 2(1)(b).
[135] *Ontario Human Rights Commission v Simpsons-Sears Ltd* (n 3) para 12.
[136] *Egan v Canada* [1995] 2 SCR 513, para 138 (Can Sup Ct).

Charter could be violated through 'the adverse effects of rules of general application'.[137] Most vividly, in *Meiorin*, the Court held that an aerobic fitness test for forest firefighters in British Columbia was indirectly discriminatory against women and therefore breached the British Columbia Human Rights Code.[138] Evidence showed that due to physiological differences, most women have a lower aerobic capacity than most men. Nor could this be increased by training. Importantly, there was no evidence that the prescribed aerobic capacity was necessary to perform the job safely and efficiently.

Although the South African Constitution refers to direct and indirect discrimination, this was not clearly defined until the case of *Walker*.[139] According to the Court: 'The concept of indirect discrimination, . . . was developed precisely to deal with situations where discrimination lay disguised behind apparently neutral criteria or where persons already adversely hit by patterns of historic subordination had their disadvantage entrenched or intensified by the impact of measures not overtly intended to prejudice them.'[140] This was further endorsed in the 2020 case of *Mahlangu*,[141] which challenged the exclusion of domestic workers from the statutory occupational injury compensation scheme. As a result of the exclusion, when a domestic worker was injured or killed during the course of her work on her employer's premises (in this case by tragically drowning in her employer's swimming pool), her family was not entitled to the no-fault compensation they would have been had she been in another category of worker. In South Africa, as in many countries, domestic work is poorly paid and highly precarious, predominantly carried out by Black women. The Court held that the exclusion was indirectly discriminatory. Importantly, Victor AJ emphasized the centrality of an intersectional lens. Although the category of 'domestic worker' is not in itself a ground of discrimination, the exclusion disproportionately impacted Black women, and indirectly discriminated on grounds of sex, gender, and race. This made it presumptively unfair. Nor were any reasons advanced by the State to justify the discrimination. In particular, the State had not established that it was unable to include domestic workers through lack of available resources.

---

[137] *Eldridge v British Columbia* [1997] 3 SCR 624, para 77 (Can Sup Ct); see also *Kahkewistahaw First Nation v Taypotat* 2015 SCC 30, paras 15 and 22 (Can Sup Ct).
[138] *British Columbia (Public Service Employee Relations Commission) v BCGSEU* [1999] 3 SCR 3 (Can Sup Ct).
[139] *City Council of Pretoria v Walker* (CCT8/97) [1998] ZACC 1, 1998 (2) SA 363 (SACC).
[140] ibid para 115.
[141] *Mahlangu v Minister of Labour* [2020] ZACC 24 (SACC).

Indirect discrimination has been least well developed in India, but a recent string of cases, culminating in the Supreme Court decision in *Nitisha v Union of India* in 2021, have affirmed its role in Indian equality jurisprudence. In *Naz Foundation*,[142] the Delhi High Court struck down the criminalization of sodomy in part on the grounds of indirect discrimination against LGBTQI people. Although section 377 of the Indian Penal Code which criminalized sodomy was facially neutral, in that it applied regardless of sexual orientation, the fact was that 'these sexual acts which are criminalised are associated more closely with one class of persons, namely, the homosexuals as a class'.[143] This finding was eventually supported and developed by the Indian Supreme Court in *Navtej Singh*,[144] which came to similar conclusions. The Court subsequently took the opportunity to set out in more detail both the principles of indirect discrimination and its key components in the 2021 case of *Nitisha v Union of India*,[145] which concerned indirect discrimination against women seeking permanent commissions in the army. Importantly, the Court expressly tied its analysis of indirect discrimination to the four-dimensional understanding of substantive equality.[146]

Although this diffusion of the principle of indirect discrimination has manifested itself in a variety of formulations, each is built around three basic elements. First, there must be equal treatment. Secondly, despite being equal, the treatment must have disparate results. Thirdly, the disparate impact can be justified if there are good reasons for the treatment in question. For example, in the US, disparate-impact liability was codified twenty years after *Griggs* in the Civil Rights Act 1991.[147] Under this statute, a plaintiff can establish a prima facie violation by showing that an employer uses 'a particular employment practice that causes a disparate impact on the basis of race, colour, religion, sex, or national origin'.[148] An employer may defend against liability by demonstrating that the practice is 'job related for the position in question and consistent with business necessity'.[149] However, even if the employer establishes this defence, a plaintiff may still succeed by showing that the employer has refused to adopt an available alternative employment

---

[142] *Naz Foundation v Government of NCT of Delhi*, WP(C) No 7455/2001, 2 July 2009 (High Ct of Delhi).
[143] ibid para 94.
[144] *Navtej Singh Johar v Union of India* (n 127).
[145] *Nitisha v Union of India* 2021 (2) SCT 209 (Indian Sup Ct).
[146] ibid para 44.
[147] 105 Stat 1071.
[148] 42 USC § 2000e-2(k)(1)(A)(i).
[149] ibid.

practice that has a less disparate impact and serves the employer's legitimate needs.[150] Similarly, the EU Race Directive states that 'indirect discrimination shall be taken to occur where an apparently neutral provision, criterion or practice would put persons of a racial or ethnic origin at a particular disadvantage compared with other persons, unless that provision, criterion or practice is objectively justified by a legitimate aim and the means of achieving that aim are appropriate and necessary'.[151] The equivalent definition is found in other EU directives.[152] In a consolidated version of previous iterations, the British EA 2010 states that:

(2) ... a provision, criterion or practice [applied by A to B] is discriminatory in relation to a relevant protected characteristic of B's if—

(a) A applies, or would apply, it to persons with whom B does not share the characteristic,

(b) it puts, or would put, persons with whom B shares the characteristic at a particular disadvantage when compared with persons with whom B does not share it,

(c) it puts, or would put, B at that disadvantage, and

(d) A cannot show it to be a proportionate means of achieving a legitimate aim.

While all three elements clearly appear in these definitions, the legal formulation of the concept of disparate impact or indirect discrimination in different jurisdictions has left numerous opportunities for contestation and complexity. First, what, if any, is the role of intention? And is it necessary to show the reason why the apparently neutral requirement is associated with disparate results? Secondly, how do we measure disparate results? Do we need statistics and what are the appropriate pools of comparison? Thirdly, what standard of scrutiny should be applied to the justification defence? What aims are legitimate and how close should the fit be between the apparently neutral criterion and the aims deemed to be legitimate? Behind such questions lurks the overarching question: what are the aims of indirect discrimination and how are these reflected in the different answers to these questions? Is the aim to achieve equality of results, or to smoke out concealed

---

[150] § 2000e-2(k)(1)(A)(ii) and (C).

[151] EU Race Directive 2000/43, Art 2(2)(b).

[152] EU Directive 2006/54 (Recast Gender Directive), Art 2(1)(b); EU Directive 2000/78 (Employment Directive), Art 2(2)(b).

prejudice, or to achieve substantive equality? These questions are considered in more detail in the following.

(ii)   The Role of Intention and the 'Reason Why'

A key distinguishing feature of indirect discrimination or disparate impact is that it focuses on effects rather than intent or purpose. In *Griggs*, the District Court found no showing of a discriminatory purpose by the employer in adopting the criteria for selection based on high school qualification and aptitude tests. On that basis, it concluded that there was no violation. Crucially, however, the Supreme Court in *Griggs* held that 'good intent or absence of discriminatory intent does not redeem employment procedures or testing mechanisms that operate as "built-in headwinds" for minority groups and are unrelated to measuring job capability'.[153] That meant that 'unnecessary barriers to employment' must fall, even if 'neutral on their face' and 'neutral in terms of intent'.[154]

The lack of a requirement for discriminatory intent almost immediately led a different configuration of the US Supreme Court to refuse to extend the disparate impact from the statutory context of Title VII to the constitutional context of the Fourteenth Amendment. *Washington v Davis*,[155] like *Griggs*, constituted a challenge to selection criteria with a disparate impact, here on the representation of minorities in the Washington DC police force. The claim was, however, brought under the Fourteenth Amendment rather than Title VII. Distancing itself from the statutory standard, the Court held: 'We have not held that a law, neutral on its face and serving ends otherwise within the power of government to pursue, is invalid under the Equal Protection Clause simply because it may affect a greater proportion of one race than of another'.[156] The result is that whereas intention is not required in a Title VII claim, plaintiffs are required to prove that the government intended to discriminate to establish a breach of the Equal Protection Clause of the Fourteenth Amendment. Recent dicta suggest that the US Supreme Court might be taking an even more restrictive approach. In *Ricci v De Stefano*,[157] Scalia J in his dissenting opinion cast doubt on whether the disparate-impact

---

[153] *Griggs v Duke Power Co* (n 2) 432.
[154] ibid.
[155] *Washington v Davis* 426 US 229, 96 S Ct 2040 (1976).
[156] ibid 242.
[157] *Ricci v DeStefano* (n 44).

principle in Title VII is capable of reconciliation with the constitutional guarantee of equal treatment.[158]

Nevertheless, the US Supreme Court has continued to develop a non-intentional disparate-impact liability under statute. Disparate impact was read into the Age Discrimination in Employment Act 1967 (ADEA)[159] in *Smith v City of Jackson* in 2005.[160] In *Smith*, a plurality of the Court interpreted statutory language referring to actions which 'otherwise adversely affect' an employee as requiring an effects-based interpretation. According to the majority, this wording 'focuses on the *effects* of the action on the employee rather than the motivation for the action of the employer' and therefore entails recognition of disparate-impact liability.[161] Similarly, in 2015 in *Texas Department of Housing*, the Court drew on both *Griggs* and *Smith* to read the Fair Housing Act as likewise including disparate impact. Here, too, the Court situated the boundary clearly in the distinction between intention and effects: 'Together, *Griggs* holds and the plurality in *Smith* instructs that antidiscrimination laws must be construed to encompass disparate-impact claims when their text refers to the consequences of actions and not just to the mindset of actors, and where that interpretation is consistent with statutory purpose.'[162] Indeed, Kennedy J reaffirmed the 'Fair Housing Act's continuing role in moving the Nation towards a more integrated society'.[163]

Other jurisdictions have similarly steered away from the mindset of actors to the consequences of actions. As the Supreme Court of Canada put it in *Simpson Sears* in 2020: 'Whether the legislature *intended* to create a disparate impact is irrelevant.' Requiring proof of intent would put 'an insuperable barrier in the way of a complainant seeking a remedy'.[164] Similarly, in the South African case of *Walker*, Langa J was unequivocal: 'The purpose of the anti-discrimination clause . . . is to protect persons against treatment which amounts to unfair discrimination; it is not to punish those responsible for such treatment. In many cases, particularly those in which indirect discrimination is alleged, the protective purpose would be defeated if the persons complaining of discrimination had to prove not only that they were unfairly

---

[158]   ibid 2681–82 (Scalia J).
[159]   81 Stat 602 ff, as amended: see s 4(a).
[160]   *Smith v City of Jackson* 544 US 228 (2005).
[161]   ibid 236 (emphasis added).
[162]   *Texas Department of Housing and Community Affairs v The Inclusive Communities Project* 135 S. Ct. 2507 (2015) (US Sup Ct), 2547 (per Kennedy J).
[163]   ibid 2526.
[164]   *Ontario Human Rights Commission v Simpsons-Sears Ltd* (n 3) para 14.

discriminated against but also that the unfair discrimination was intentional.[165] Similarly, the Indian Supreme Court in *Nitisha* emphasized that 'as long as a court's focus is on the mental state underlying the impugned action that is allegedly discriminatory, we are in the territory of direct discrimination. However, when the focus switches to the effects of the concerned action, we enter the territory of indirect discrimination. An enquiry as to indirect discrimination looks, not at the form of the impugned conduct, but at its consequences.'[166]

Nevertheless, there has still been a temptation to find a reason why the apparently neutral practice or criterion has a disparate impact on those with a protected characteristic. While reaffirming the central importance of disparate-impact liability in combatting ongoing de facto racial segregation in housing in inner cities in *Texas Department of Housing*,[167] Kennedy J was still concerned to rein in what he considered could be an unacceptable intrusion on defendants' decision making and a temptation to use race-based quotas to deflect possible disparate-impact liability. He therefore held that a claim based on statistical disparity would fail if the plaintiff could not point to a policy causing that disparity. In a worrying reversion to a presumption that bodies should only be responsible for outcomes that they have created, he stated: 'A robust causality requirement ensures that "[r]acial imbalance . . . does not, without more, establish a prima facie case of disparate impact" and thus protects defendants from being held liable for racial disparities they did not create.'[168]

In recent years, UK jurisprudence has also appeared to be drifting in the direction of superimposing a requirement to demonstrate the reason why a policy, condition, or practice (PCP) has a disparate impact. This was the view of the Court of Appeal in two cases in 2017, *Essop*[169] and *Naeem*.[170] Like the US selection cases, *Essop* was concerned with the paradigmatic case of indirect discrimination: namely, the disparate impact of apparently neutral selection tests for recruitment, promotion, and training. The case was based on a statistical report commissioned by the government which showed that Black candidates, candidates from ethnic minorities, and candidates over the

---

[165] *City Council of Pretoria v Walker* (CCT8/97) (n 139) para 43.

[166] *Nitisha v Union of India* (n 145) para 53.

[167] *Texas Department of Housing and Community Affairs v The Inclusive Communities Project* (n 162).

[168] ibid citing *Wards Cove Packing Co v Atonio* 490 US 642 (1989) (US Sup Ct).

[169] *Essop and others v Home Office (UK Border Agency)* [2015] EWCA Civ 609.

[170] *Naeem v Secretary of State for Justice* [2015] EWCA Civ 1264, [2016] ICR 289.

age of thirty-five were systematically less likely to pass the Civil Service selection test for promotion than white or younger candidates. In the Court of
Appeal, Rimer LJ held that the statistical disparity was not sufficient. In addition, the claimant had to establish 'why the PCP [the selection test] disadvantages the group sharing the protected characteristic'.[171] This was despite the
fact that he himself acknowledged that no reason had been provided by the
expert report for that differential outcome and that it would in all likelihood
be impossible to prove the reason for the disparity. This focus on the 'reason
why' was taken even further by the Court of Appeal in *Naeem v Secretary
of State for Justice*,[172] which concerned pay disparities between Muslim and
Christian prison chaplains. These pay gaps arose because Muslim chaplains
had only relatively recently been introduced into the prison service, and pay
increases depended on seniority. Here the reason that the seniority system
disadvantaged Muslim chaplains was clear. The Court of Appeal, however,
held that it was not sufficient to show why the disparate impact occurred. In
addition, the applicant had to establish that this reason was something pecu-
liar to the protected characteristic in question.

However, to require the complainants to show the 'reason why' the PCP
disadvantages the group as a whole is to fundamentally misunderstand the
meaning of indirect discrimination. It is the disparate impact on the group
of a PCP itself which constitutes the prima facie discrimination. Any issues
which arise in relation to why this occurs should be dealt with at the justification stage, when the respondent must demonstrate that there is a legitimate
reason for the PCP and that it is necessary to achieve that purpose (see later).
In a welcome development, this was recognized by the Supreme Court in the
joined cases of *Essop* and *Naeem*.[173] As Baroness Hale reasserted, there can be
many and varied reasons why the PCP has such an impact. Indeed, she held,
the reason for the disadvantage need not be unlawful in itself or be under the
control of the employer or provider.[174] This was set out even more clearly by
the Supreme Court of Canada in *Fraser*: 'If there are clear and consistent statistical disparities in how a law affects a claimant's group, I see no reason for
requiring the claimant to bear the additional burden of explaining *why* the
law has such an effect. In such cases, the statistical evidence is itself a compelling sign that the law has not been structured in a way that takes into account

---

[171] *Essop and others v Home Office (UK Border Agency)* (n 168) [59].
[172] *Naeem v Secretary of State for Justice* (n 169).
[173] *Essop v Home Office (UK Border Agency)* (n 168).
[174] ibid [26].

the protected group's circumstances.'[175] Correspondingly, claimants' choices do not interrupt the chain of causation. It was therefore irrelevant whether or not the complainants in *Fraser* chose to job-share.

(iii) Measuring Disparate Impact

The second major challenge of indirect discrimination is to establish the criteria for determining disparate impact. What proportion of the protected group must be excluded to constitute disparate impact and what is the relevant pool of comparison? The use of statistics is clearly a potent tool for determining such questions. As was noted by Simon: 'the indirect discrimination concept . . . [is] intrinsically linked to statistics by their logic and objectives. . . . The group concept is the focus: treatment is no longer personalised, it is collective and only relates to individuals in terms of their real or assumed affiliation to a protected group. This shift from the individual to a group is strictly analogous to the operations carried out by statistics: impersonal aggregates that highlight a collective situation.'[176]

The importance of statistics is vividly demonstrated in the ECtHR case of *DH*,[177] where psychological tests were used to determine whether children should attend 'special' schools, which were in practice educationally undemanding and inferior. Statistics showed the disproportionate impact on Roma children who were over-represented in special schools. The Chamber of the ECtHR which initially heard the case refused to examine the statistics and insisted on considering only the individual case. This made it impossible for it to recognize that tests which it regarded as professionally administered with no intention to discriminate were, in practice, operating to consign dramatically more Roma children to special schools than their representation in the population.[178] By contrast, when the case was reheard by the Grand Chamber, statistical evidence was accepted, enabling the Court to uphold the claim of indirect discrimination.[179]

---

[175] *Fraser v Canada (Attorney General)* (n 128) para 63, citing S Fredman, 'Direct and Indirect Discrimination: Is There Still a Divide?' in Hugh Collins and Tarunabh Khaitan (eds), *Foundations of Indirect Discrimination Law* (Bloomsbury 2018) 46; see also S Fredman, 'The Reason Why: Unravelling Indirect Discrimination' (2016) 45 Industrial LJ 231.

[176] P Simon (coord), *Comparative Study on the Collection of Data to Measure the Extent and Impact of Discrimination Within the US, Canada, Australia, Great Britain and the Netherlands* (Medis Project (Measurement of Discriminations), INED—Economie and Humanisme), August 2004, 82.

[177] *DH v Czech Republic* (n 94).

[178] ibid para 41.

[179] See further later.

However, a statistical focus brings with it several problems. As a start, while data is often disaggregated in relation to men and women, data on other protected groups may not be available. This is in part because of an aversion to requiring individuals to reveal their identities, for the very reason that this might trigger discrimination against them. Even promises of confidentiality may not be enough to allay these anxieties. But even when data are available, it has been difficult to reach a consensus on how to analyse that data. How, initially, do we define the relevant comparator groups? For example, in determining disparate impact on grounds of gender in an employment context, should the comparison be drawn between all women and all men, or only between qualified women and qualified men, or between women and men who have actually applied for the job or promotion? The figures might differ substantially depending on which statistics are chosen and how the comparable groups are identified.[180] As Lord Walker pointed out in *Rutherford*,[181] 'the comparison of proportions (inherent in any assessment of indirect discrimination) produces startlingly different results depending on whether the comparison focuses on (i) proportions of advantaged men and women respectively ("advantage-led") or (ii) proportions of disadvantaged men and women respectively ("disadvantage-led")'. Most recently, in *Villar Laiz*, the ECJ suggested that where the national court has available statistical evidence, it will not be good enough to consider the actual number of persons affected, since that would be influenced, for example, by the number of women who are active in the workforce.[182] Instead, the best approach would be to compare the proportion of workers in the male workforce who are affected and are not affected by the rule with the proportions within the female workforce who are affected and not affected.[183] In the case in question, which concerned adverse pension entitlements for part-time work (less than two-thirds of full-time work), the workers affected would be those engaged in short part-time work. Spanish data for the relevant period revealed that approximately 75 per cent of part-time workers were women.[184]

Once agreement is reached as to which groups should be compared, when is the difference sufficient to constitute disparate impact? Here statistics do

---

[180] See eg *Wards Cove v Atonio* 490 US 642, 109 S Ct 2115 (1989).
[181] *Secretary of State for Trade and Industry v Rutherford (No 2)* [2006] UKHL 19.
[182] Case C-161/18 *Villar Laiz v Instituto Nacional de la Seguridad Social* [2019] 3 CMLR 28, para 39 (ECJ).
[183] ibid.
[184] ibid paras 42, 45.

provide a helpful approach. Statisticians weed out differences which are random or fortuitous by use of the concept of statistical significance.[185] It should be sufficient to show that the difference in impact between the groups is statistically significant in order for the burden of proof of justification to pass on to the respondent. However, this way forward has not been chosen in different jurisdictions. In the US, the formula chosen is what the Equal Employment Opportunity Commission calls a 'rule of thumb', known as the 'four-fifths' rule. On this approach:

> a selection rate for any race, sex, or ethnic group which is less than four-fifths (4/5) (or eighty percent) of the rate for the group with the highest rate will generally be regarded by the Federal enforcement agencies as evidence of adverse impact. Smaller differences in selection rate may nevertheless constitute adverse impact, where they are significant in both statistical and practical terms or where a user's actions have discouraged applicants disproportionately on grounds of race, sex, or ethnic group.[186]

For example, assume that there are eighty white applicants for a position and forty-eight are hired. The selection rate is 48/80 or 60 per cent. By contrast, out of forty Black applicants, applicants from marginalized ethnicities, or applicants from indigenous people,[187] only two are hired, so that the selection rate is 12/40 or 30 per cent, only half that of the white applicants. The rule of thumb suggests that this proportion should be at least 80 per cent or fourth-fifths. Adverse impact is therefore indicated.[188]

In the UK, this process has been much clumsier. Earlier sex discrimination statutes required showing that the proportion of women who could comply was 'considerably smaller' than the proportion of men who could comply. The vagueness of this approach led to much unproductive contestation. In *R v Secretary of State, ex p Seymour Smith and Perez*,[189] the application of the

---

[185] This was suggested by the European Commission in Case C-167/97 *R v Secretary of State for Employment, ex p Seymour-Smith* [1999] ECR I-623, [1999] 2 AC 554, para 57 (ECJ).

[186] Uniform Guidelines on Employee Selection Procedures, Code of Federal Regulations Title 29, vol 4, § 1607.4(D) (2018) <www.govinfo.gov/content/pkg/CFR-2018-title29-vol4/xml/CFR-2018-title29-vol4-part1607.xml> accessed 1 August 2022.

[187] See n 1.

[188] Equal Employment Opportunity Commission (EEOC), Uniform Employee Selection Guidelines: Interpretation and Clarification (Questions and Answers) para 12 <www.uniformguidelines.com/questionandanswers.html> accessed 1 August 2022.

[189] *R v Secretary of State, ex p Seymour Smith and Perez* [1997] IRLR 315 (HL); Case C-167/97 *R v Secretary of State for Employment, ex p Seymour-Smith* [1999] ECR I-623, [1999] 2 AC 554 (ECJ).

formula to the data at hand was aired before four different courts including the ECJ, over a period of six years, and all came to different conclusions. The result of these complexities has been that many indirect discrimination cases have become mired in the preliminary stages. Even if the applicants win these preliminary points, the case still has to return to the employment tribunal to make a finding on the merits.

Partly in response to these problems, and particularly the potential absence of relevant data, EU law has veered away from relying solely on statistics, using instead the terminology of 'particular disadvantage' derived from EU law on free movement of workers.[190] In the leading case of *O'Flynn*,[191] the Court held that:

> unless objectively justified and proportionate to its aim, a provision of national law must be regarded as indirectly discriminatory if it is intrinsically liable to affect migrant workers more than national workers and if there is a consequent risk that it will place the former at a particular disadvantage.[192]

It was not necessary to prove that the provision *in practice* affects a substantially higher proportion of migrant workers, as long as it was *liable* to have such an effect.[193] Statistics were not therefore required to prove that the impact had in fact occurred. This approach was transplanted into the EU non-discrimination directives[194] and has now been comprehensively introduced into British domestic law through the EA 2010. Thus, as we have seen, indirect discrimination is established where, subject to a justification defence, the provision or practice 'puts, or would put, persons with whom B shares the characteristic at a particular disadvantage when compared with persons with whom B does not share it'.[195]

On one level, this can be a more flexible test. While statistics may be used, courts might in principle take a common-sense view, based on judicial

---

[190] Directive 2004/38/EC of the European Parliament and of the Council on the right of citizens of the Union and their family members to move and reside freely within the territory of the Member States, amending Regulation (EEC) No 1612/68 on freedom of movement for workers within the Community, Art 39.

[191] Case C-237/94 *O'Flynn v Adjudication Officer* (n 86).

[192] ibid para 20.

[193] ibid para 21.

[194] Council Directive 2000/43/EC, Art 2(2)(b); Council Directive 2000/78/EC, Art 2(2)(b); Directive 2006/54/EC (Recast), Art 2(1)(b); Directive 79/7.

[195] Council Directive 2000/43/EC of 29 June 2000 implementing the principle of equal treatment between persons irrespective of racial or ethnic origin; Council Directive 2000/78/EC of 27 November 2000 establishing a general framework for equal treatment in employment and occupation; EA 2010, s 19(2)(b).

notice or on obvious facts.[196] This is helpful, particularly where statistics are not available or are contentious, or numbers are small. Provided the impact is obvious in this way, the case can quickly move to whether the policy or criterion can be justified, avoiding the lengthy threshold skirmishes as to whether disparate impact has been established. However, the role of statistics in establishing the group dimension should not be discarded simply because of technical difficulties. The notion of 'particular disadvantage' would not be sufficient to flush out measures which appear wholly neutral and not obviously suspect.[197] Aptitude tests, interviews, and selection processes, and other apparently scientific and neutral measures, might never invite scrutiny unless data is available to dislodge these assumptions. In *Homer*, Lady Hale acknowledged that the shift from the reliance on disparate impact to 'particular disadvantage' could obscure the foundational principle that certain protected characteristics are more likely to be associated with particular disadvantages. However, she emphasized that 'the new formulation was not intended to make it more difficult to establish direct discrimination: quite the reverse . . . It was intended to do away with the need for statistical comparisons where no statistics might exist. It was intended to do away with the complexities involved in identifying those who could comply and those who could not and how great the disparity had to be. Now all that is needed is a particular disadvantage when compared with other people who do not share the characteristic in question.'[198]

It is therefore crucial that statistics remain an alternative and complementary method of proving disparate impact. This was clearly recognized by the CJEU in *Villar Laiz* in 2019, which concerned the disparate impact on women of provisions reducing the pensions of part-time workers. 'The existence of such particular disadvantage,' the Court stated, 'might be established, for example if it were proved that [the challenged legislation] is to the disadvantage of a significantly greater proportion of individuals of one sex as compared with individuals of the other sex.'[199] At the same time, the Court stressed that indirect discrimination could be established by any means, and not only on the basis of statistical evidence.[200]

---

[196] C Tobler, *Limits and Potential of the Concept of Indirect Discrimination* (European Commission 2008) 40.

[197] O DeSchutter, 'Three Models of Equality and European Anti-Discrimination Law' (2006) 57 Northern Ireland Legal Quarterly 1, 18–20.

[198] *Chief Constable of West Yorkshire Police v Homer* [2012] UKSC 15 [14] (UK Sup Ct).

[199] *Villar Laiz v Instituto Nacional de la Seguridad Social* (n 181) para 38.

[200] ibid para 46.

(iv) Justification

If disparate impact has been established, on what basis can it nevertheless be excused or justified? The justification stage performs a crucial role, since a lower standard of justification could allow discrimination to be easily overridden by business or cost issues. Most jurisdictions use a proportionality principle. In EU law, it is a defence to indirect discrimination to show that the PCP in question is 'objectively justified by a legitimate aim and the means of achieving that aim are appropriate and necessary'.[201] The EA 2010 now imports this standard, albeit in truncated form; indirect discrimination can be justified if the respondent can show that the measure is 'a proportionate means of achieving a legitimate aim'.[202] In South Africa, a similar approach is followed, albeit in the context of the determination of fairness. Thus, to prove fairness the respondent must establish that the discrimination has a legitimate purpose, that it achieves its purpose, and that there are no less restrictive and disadvantageous means of achieving that purpose. In a notable addition, the court must also establish whether and to what extent the respondent has taken reasonable steps to address the disadvantage or accommodate diversity.[203] Under the Canadian Charter, the justification defence is carried out under the general limitations clause in section 1[204] which has, in turn, been interpreted as incorporating a proportionality analysis.[205] And in its most recent elaboration of the principle, the Indian Supreme Court has adopted a similar proportionality approach.[206]

Proportionality is not, however, self-executing. It depends on the judicial approach to each of its main elements: first, the legitimacy of the respondents' stated aims and, secondly, whether the means are appropriate for achieving those ends. Unpacking these two elements of a proportionality analysis requires us to pay closer attention to a further set of questions. What aims are legitimate? In particular, can discrimination be justified in order to save costs? And should the means be *necessary* to achieve the end or is it sufficient if there is a reasonable link? This raises the further question of how much attention should be paid to the possibility of alternative, less discriminatory,

---

[201] Council Directive 2000/43/EC, Art 2(2)(b); Council Directive 2000/78/EC, Art 2(2)(b); European Parliament and Council Directive 2006/54/EC, Art 2(1)(b).
[202] EA 2010, s 19(2)(d).
[203] The Promotion of Equality and Prevention of Unfair Discrimination Act 4 of 2000, s 14.
[204] *Fraser v Canada (Attorney General)* (n 128).
[205] *R v Oakes* [1986] 1 SCR 103 (Can Sup Ct).
[206] *Nitisha v Union of India* (n 145) para 70.

means of achieving the stated aims. A strict 'necessity' criterion requires a showing that the measure chosen is the only alternative. With this come questions of the burden of proof. It is generally accepted that the defendant has the burden of proving justification, but in some jurisdictions, such as the US, the burden of proving alternative measures shifts back to the plaintiff. There also remains contestation as to how much evidence is required. Is it sufficient for a respondent simply to assert that the indirectly discriminatory requirement was considered appropriate to achieve the stated aim, or should an evidential basis be required? Finally, should there be a difference between private and public respondents, in that a wider margin of discretion might be granted to the latter?

The key issue so far as legitimate objectives or ends are concerned relates to cost justifications. Can the State or private entities justify discriminatory outcomes simply on the grounds that the practice in question is necessary to save money? Only the ECJ, while generally deferent in relation to asserted aims, has taken a strong stand on this issue. In a series of cases on part-time workers, the Court has consistently held that an employer cannot justify indirect discrimination solely on the ground that avoidance of such discrimination would involve increased costs.[207] In other words, 'A discriminatory rule or practice can only be justified by reference to a legitimate aim other than the simple saving of cost.'[208] This is true, too, of State policy decisions. As the UK Supreme Court put it in *O'Brien v Ministry of Justice*: 'Sound management of the public finances may be a legitimate aim, but that is very different from deliberately discriminating against part-time workers in order to save money.'[209]

More attention has been paid to the second element; namely, the relationship of the means to the ends. *Griggs* set the value of equality high, requiring proof that the exclusionary practice was necessary for the business of the employer or that it was essential for effective job performance. Similarly, in the foundational case of *Bilka*,[210] the ECJ held that the respondent must show that the means chosen served a real business need, that they were appropriate for achieving that objective, and were necessary to that end.[211] Where State social policy is under challenge, there were some suggestions that this might

---

[207] Case C-243/95 *Hill v Revenue Commissioners* [1999] ICR 48, para 40 (ECJ).
[208] *Ministry of Justice v O'Brien* [2013] UKSC 6 [69].
[209] ibid [63].
[210] *Bilka-Kaufhaus* (n 128).
[211] ibid.

require a wider margin of appreciation.[212] However, the ECJ has arrested the drift away from a high standard of scrutiny of justification defences. This issue arises particularly frequently in the context of part-time workers, who are disadvantaged in relation to pay, State or occupational benefits, and pensions. As we have seen, since the vast majority of part-time workers in many European countries are women, this constitutes prima facie indirect discrimination unless it can be justified. For social policy measures which indirectly discriminate against women in this way, the Court has repeatedly held, the measures chosen must be appropriate and necessary to achieve a legitimate social policy objective of the Member State.[213] Importantly, mere generalizations should not suffice. An evidential basis is necessary to establish a defence of justification. 'Mere generalisations concerning the capacity of a specific measure to encourage recruitment are not enough to show that the aim of the disputed rule is unrelated to any discrimination based on sex nor to provide evidence on the basis of which it could reasonably be considered that the means chosen were suitable for achieving that aim.'[214]

The Court will also require the State to show that there are no less discriminatory alternatives. In particular, for part-time workers' benefits, the Court has required the reduction of benefits to be proportionate to the difference between full-time and part-time work. Although it accepts that a proportional reduction is objectively justifiable where it properly reflects the reduced time worked by a part-time worker as compared to a full-time worker, it is not acceptable to institute a reduction which goes beyond that necessary to achieve that objective.[215]

This approach has been endorsed by the Indian Supreme Court in the 2021 case of *Nitisha*. Here the Court held unequivocally that: 'The Court must resist the temptation to accept generalizations by defendants under the garb of deference and must closely scrutinize the proffered justification. Further, the Court must also examine if it is possible to substitute the measures with less discriminatory alternatives. Only by exercising such close scrutiny and exhibiting attentiveness to the possibility of alternatives can a Court ensure that the full potential of the doctrine of indirect discrimination is realized and not lost in its application.'[216]

---

[212] Case 371/93 *Nolte* [1995] ECR I-4625.
[213] *Villar Laiz v Instituto Nacional de la Seguridad Social* (n 181) and cases cited therein.
[214] *R v Secretary of State for Employment, ex p Seymour-Smith* (n 184) [71].
[215] *Villar Laiz v Instituto Nacional de la Seguridad Social* (n 181).
[216] *Nitisha v Union of India* (n 145) [70] citing S Fredman, *Discrimination Law* (2nd edn, OUP 2011) 194.

In the US, it has been more of a struggle to maintain the high standard of necessity set by *Griggs*. In *Ward's Cove*[217] in 1989, a majority of the Supreme Court reversed the precedents which had been followed since *Griggs* and substantially diluted the standard. In particular, the Court held that an employer should not have to demonstrate that the practice in question is essential or indispensable. Instead, the policy need only serve the 'legitimate employment goals of the employer'. It took the Civil Rights Act of 1991 to revert to a higher standard. Under the Civil Rights Act of 1991,[218] which codified the prohibition on disparate-impact discrimination, an employer can defend against liability by demonstrating that the practice is 'job related for the position in question and consistent with business necessity'. Even if the employer meets that burden, a plaintiff may still succeed by showing that the employer refuses to adopt an available alternative employment practice that has a less disparate impact and serves the employer's legitimate needs.[219]

However, the standard remains under challenge. In *Texas Department of Housing*,[220] as we have seen, Kennedy J reaffirmed the central importance of disparate-impact liability in combatting ongoing de facto racial segregation in housing in inner cities. Nevertheless, he was concerned to limit its reach, both in order to give housing authorities sufficient leeway to pursue their priorities and because of an anxiety that, to avoid liability, governmental or private entities might institute numerical quotas. As will be seen in Chapter 7, while quotas are embraced in some jurisdictions, such as India, the US Supreme Court regards quotas as an unacceptable response to redressing disparities which are not intentional. To ensure disparate impact is properly limited, therefore, Kennedy J held, housing authorities and private developers should be given leeway to explain the valid interest served by their policies and should be 'allowed to maintain a policy if they can prove it is necessary to achieve a valid interest'.[221] Moreover, where a breach is found, remedial orders should concentrate on the elimination of the offending practice or, at most, to use race-neutral means to eliminate racial disparities.

The US Housing Department quickly seized on the opportunity to amend its guidance rule to 'substantially weaken disparate liability by easing the

---

[217] *Wards Cove Packing Co v Atonio* (n 179).
[218] 105 Sta 1071.
[219] § 2000e-2(k)(1)(A)(ii) and (C).
[220] *Texas Department of Housing and Community Affairs v The Inclusive Communities Project* (n 162).
[221] ibid.

burden on the defendants of justifying a policy with discriminatory effect while at the same time rendering it more difficult for plaintiffs to rebut that justification.[222] For example, the new rule, issued in 2020,[223] allowed a defendant merely to 'advance a valid interest' rather than proving that the challenged practice was 'necessary to achieve one or more substantial, legitimate, non-discriminatory interests' as was set out in the earlier 2013 rule. In addition, the rule makes it more difficult for the plaintiff to rebut a justification defence. Rather than being required to show simply that there is a less discriminatory policy that would serve the defendant's identified interest, the rule adds the requirement that the alternative should serve the defendant's interest in an 'equally effective manner without imposing materially greater costs on . . . the defendant'. In a case brought in the US District Court in Massachusetts in 2020, the court held that these alterations to the rule would 'run the risk of effectively neutering' disparate liability under the Federal Housing Administration.[224] The court issued a preliminary injunction postponing the date of the rule pending conclusion of judicial review proceedings. The higher standard therefore remains, pending further proceedings.

In answering the questions posed, it is hoped that courts will continue to be vigilant in resisting the temptation to accept generalizations by respondents under the guise of deference and in lieu of close scrutiny of actual evidence. It is also particularly important to maintain the emphasis on possible alternatives which are less discriminatory. Otherwise, the justification defence risks allowing the status quo to be maintained without paying proper attention to whether the discriminatory practice can be adjusted to better accommodate the excluded group. This means that justification defences should be subject to a high level of scrutiny before being accepted. Most importantly, the respondent should be required to consider ways of modifying the discriminatory practice to better accommodate the excluded class.

Disparate impact has not, however, always been used to further substantive equality. It has also been relied on by privileged sections of society to challenge measures which aim to redress racial or gendered inequalities. As we will see in Chapter 7, indirect affirmative action has been deliberately used in some contexts instead of express affirmative action where neutral

---

[222] *Massachusetts Fair Housing Centre v US Dept of Housing and Urban Development* Civil Action No 20-11765-MGM (US District Ct of Massachusetts, 2020).

[223] *HUD's Implementation of the Fair Housing Act's Disparate Treatment Standard* 85 Fed Reg 60288 (24 September 2020).

[224] *Massachusetts Fair Housing Centre v US Dept of Housing and Urban Development* (n 221) 12. The appeal was withdrawn in 2021, leaving the injunction intact.

criteria, such as residence, are reliable proxies. For example, in Texas after express policies setting aside university places for African American and Hispanic students were struck down, legislation mandated universities to select students from the top 10 per cent of all high schools in their areas. Because there was a close correlation between disadvantaged schools and predominantly African American and Hispanic residential areas, this was an apparently race-neutral policy which led to a measure of diversity within universities.[225] However, such policies are vulnerable to disparate-impact claims. It is here that the justification defence should be sensitively applied to reflect all four dimensions of substantive equality, particularly the need to redress disadvantage. *Walker*, the case which established the principle of indirect discrimination in the South African Constitutional Court, was itself an example of such a situation.[226] The case arose because the city council of Pretoria levied different electricity and water charges on different parts of its constituency. The affluent, largely white, areas of old Pretoria were required to pay a higher metered rate (based on actual consumption) than residents of the overwhelmingly Black and poorly serviced townships of Mamelodi and Atteridgeville, who were required to pay a lower flat rate.[227] In addition, the council had a policy of deliberately forgiving payment defaults from the Black townships but not from the white suburbs. Walker, a white resident of old Pretoria, claimed that although the policy on its face differentiated on geographical rather than racial lines, it disproportionately disadvantaged white people. The Court held that because of the ongoing effect of apartheid rules compelling Black residents to live in poorly serviced townships, 'race and geography were inextricably linked and the application of a geographical standard, although seemingly neutral, may in fact be racially discriminatory. In this case, its impact was clearly one which differentiated in substance between black residents and white residents.'[228] This shifted the onus to the city council to rebut the presumption of unfair discrimination against the white residents of Pretoria. Langa CJ recognized that 'Courts should . . . always be astute to distinguish between genuine attempts to promote and protect equality on the one hand and actions calculated to protect pockets of privilege at a price which amounts to the perpetuation of inequality and disadvantage to others on the other.'[229] Reflecting the first two dimensions of

---

[225]   See eg *Fisher v University of Texas at Austin* 136 S Ct 2198 (2016) (US Sup Ct).
[226]   *City Council of Pretoria v Walker* (CCT8/97) (n 139).
[227]   ibid.
[228]   ibid para 32.
[229]   ibid para 48.

substantive equality, Langa CJ held that he was satisfied that the operation of the flat rate did not impact adversely on the respondent. Nor was there any invasion of his dignity. Residents of old Pretoria were not victims of past discrimination. More controversial, however, is the finding that the council's practice of failing to enforce payment of arrears only for those charged a flat rate in effect singled out white defaulters for legal action while deliberately exempting from suit defaulters from the overwhelmingly Black residents of Mamelodi and Atteridgeville. This breached the principle that no members of a racial group should be made to feel that they are not deserving of equal 'concern, respect and consideration'. The result was a finding of unfair discrimination.[230]

A similar pattern can be seen in the more recent case of *Fundza Lushaka*[231] concerning bursaries made available for students entering teacher training. The bursaries were aimed at training teachers in severely understaffed rural areas, and therefore were conditional on knowledge of a local language and willingness to teach in those areas. Although facially neutral, these conditions disproportionately excluded white applicants. The scheme was challenged as indirectly discriminatory on grounds of race. The High Court found that it was prima facie discriminatory, but justified as a proportionate means for achieving a legitimate State interest. It might be argued that even a finding of prima facie discrimination is inappropriate in these contexts. Instead, these schemes should be regarded as affirmative action which, as we will see in Chapter 7, are subject to a lower standard of scrutiny under the South African Constitution than claims of discrimination. The relationship between indirect discrimination and affirmative action is, however, complex and varies by jurisdiction. In *Fundza Lushaka*, for example, the respondents' claim that the bursary scheme was legitimate affirmative action was rejected because the beneficiaries of the bursaries, trainee teachers, were not the same as the beneficiaries of the policy, namely learners in rural areas. These issues area examined further in Chapter 6.

(v) Aims and Objectives

Despite the intuitive appeal of indirect discrimination, or disparate impact, its aims are not entirely clear. Indirect discrimination is often thought of as

---

[230] ibid para 81.
[231] *Solidariteit Helpende Hand v Minister of Basic Education* Case No 58189/2015 (High Ct of South Africa).

aiming to achieve equality of results. However, on closer examination of the principle as formulated in the jurisdictions discussed here, it can be seen that this is only partially true. Unequal results will not breach the principle of indirect discrimination if no exclusionary provision, criterion, or practice can be identified or if the inequality can be justified by reference to business needs or State social policy. This can be seen clearly in the *Texas Housing* case in the US Supreme Court. In this case, Kennedy J stressed that although disparate impact had an important role to play, its aim was not to achieve equality in distribution of housing opportunities. 'Racial imbalance does not, without more establish a prima facie case of disparate impact.'[232] Without such safeguards, he warned, 'disparate liability might cause race to be used and considered in a pervasive way', which in turn would 'almost inexorably lead' to the use of numerical quotas, in turn raising 'serious constitutional questions'. The result in *Ricci* reinforces this point. As Ginsburg J noted:

> By order of this Court, New Haven, a city in which African-Americans and Hispanics account for nearly 60 percent of the population, must today be served—as it was in the days of undisguised discrimination—by a fire department in which members of racial and ethnic minorities are rarely seen in command positions.[233]

Even if the aim were equality of results, the expansion of protected characteristics makes it increasingly difficult to identify what equality of results should entail. Should a workforce precisely reflect the demography of the population? This might make sense for race, gender, and disability. But is it the desired outcome in relation to age, religion, or sexual orientation?

A different approach could be to regard disparate impact as furthering equality of opportunities rather than equality of outcome per se. In her dissent in *Ricci*, Ginsburg J stated: 'Standing on an equal footing, these twin pillars of Title VII advance the same objectives: ending workplace discrimination and promoting genuinely equal opportunity.'[234] She pointed to the same underlying understanding of equality in *Griggs*: '[T]o achieve equality of employment opportunities,' the Court comprehended, Congress 'directed the thrust of the Act to the consequences of employment practices, not simply the motivation.'[235] Similarly, Baroness Hale in the UK Supreme

---

[232] *Wards Cove Packing Co v Atonio* (n 179).
[233] *Ricci v DeStefano* (n 44) 2690.
[234] ibid 2699.
[235] *Griggs v Duke Power Co* (n 2) 429, 432.

Court in *Chief Constable for West Yorkshire Police v Homer* stated: 'The law of indirect discrimination is an attempt to level the playing field by subjecting to scrutiny requirements which look neutral on their face but in reality work to the comparative disadvantage of people with a particular protected characteristic.'[236]

However, disparate impact liability or indirect discrimination on its own can only further equality of opportunities in a shallow sense. This is because business-related justifications are sufficient to displace the presumption of liability. Indirectly discriminatory barriers need not be dismantled if they can be justified. Criteria which are job-related therefore remain legitimate even though disadvantaged groups might find it impossible to comply. Certain qualifications may be necessary for a job, yet an individual may lack those qualifications precisely because of past or ongoing discrimination. For example, if it is shown that there are not enough women with the training necessary to be an airline pilot then, despite the inequality of results, the presumption of indirect discrimination is displaced. Nor does indirect discrimination on its own give rise to any obligation to ensure that applicants are equipped for a job or other benefit, for example by providing training for excluded groups or provision of childcare. As we saw in Chapter 1, genuine equality of opportunity requires measures to be taken to ensure not just that the gate is opened, but that disadvantaged and excluded groups can actually progress through it.

Could it be argued, then, that instead of constituting the aim of indirect discrimination, results are part of the diagnosis of discrimination, exposing the existence of obstacles to entry rather than the pattern of outcome? The assumption is that in a non-discriminatory environment there will be a fair distribution of men and women, ethnic and religious groups, different gender identities and age groups, able-bodied and disabled people. Under-representation of one of these groups is a sign that there might be a hidden obstacle to entry which, unless justifiable, should be removed. This is particularly useful where the practice is opaque and informal, such as a pay policy which is characterized by a total lack of transparency[237] or a recruitment policy based on unwritten and subjective criteria. It is also useful

---

[236] *Homer v Chief Constable of West Yorkshire Police* [2012] UKSC 15, [2012] 3 All ER 1287 [17].

[237] Case C-109/88 *Handels- og Kontorfunktionærernes Forbund I Danmark (Union of Clerical and Commercial Employees) v Dansk Arbejdsgiverforening (Danish Employers' Association)* [1991] 1 CMLR 8.

in situations in which the measure itself is not suspect and it is difficult to establish intention on the part of the perpetrator.[238] In *Texas Housing*, Kennedy J saw the purpose of disparate impact as playing an important role in uncovering discriminatory intent: it 'permits plaintiffs to counteract unconscious prejudices and disguised animus that escape easy classification as disparate treatment'.[239]

The difficulty with this approach is that it can quickly dissolve into a disparate treatment standard and undermine disparate impact entirely. Thomas J in his concurring opinion in *Seattle* demonstrated how easily this slippage can occur: 'Although a presently observed racial imbalance might result from past [discrimination], racial imbalance can also result from any number of innocent private decisions.'[240] He was even more stinging in his dissent in *Texas Housing*:

> As best I can tell, the reason for this wholesale inversion of our law's usual approach is the unstated—and unsubstantiated—assumption that, in the absence of discrimination, an institution's racial makeup would mirror that of society. But the absence of racial disparities in multi-ethnic societies has been the exception, rather than the rule.[241]

A better approach would be to consider the role of indirect discrimination in terms of all four dimensions of substantive equality simultaneously, revealing its strengths and limitations in the round. This requires us to consider the extent to which indirect discrimination can redress disadvantage; address stigma, prejudice, and stereotyping; facilitate voice and participation; and accommodate difference and achieve structural change. By focusing on redressing disadvantage as one dimension, this approach has the advantage of retaining the emphasis on impact while avoiding the difficult question of whether it aims to achieve specifically proportionate representation of each protected group. Substantive equality is also more demanding than both equality of results and equality of opportunity, in that it requires consideration to be given not just to disadvantage and prejudice, but also to including

---

[238] O DeSchutter, 'Three Models of Equality and European Anti-Discrimination Law' (2006) 57 Northern Ireland Legal Quarterly 1.

[239] *Texas Department of Housing and Community Affairs v The Inclusive Communities Project* (n 162).

[240] *Parents Involved in Community Schools v Seattle School District* 127 S Ct 2738 (2007).

[241] *Texas Department of Housing and Community Affairs v The Inclusive Communities Project* (n 162).

the voice of those affected and to changing the structures which perpetuate the outcome.

Applying this evaluative structure to the principle of indirect discrimination reveals that it can go some way towards achieving the first three dimensions, but it is seriously deficient in relation to the fourth, namely, structural change. Indirect discrimination can certainly redress disadvantage, provided, as we have seen, the PCP is not justifiable. Indirect discrimination can also play a role in redressing stigma and prejudice, for example by recognizing that apparently neutral rules, such as those prohibiting head coverings, could be indirectly discriminatory against Sikh men or Muslim women. In the landmark case of *Mandla v Lee*,[242] the court held that a school had unlawfully discriminated against a Sikh boy by excluding him from the school when he refused to take off his turban in order to comply with a school rule requiring boys to come to school bareheaded. An apparently neutral rule, applying equally to all pupils, was recognized as in practice requiring conformity to a Christian way of dressing and therefore creating unacceptable barriers to those of different cultures or religions.

Indirect discrimination could also have some effect on the third dimension—facilitating voice and participation—where it increases representation of outgroups in workplaces or representative bodies. But it has little purchase in relation to the fourth dimension which requires accommodation of difference and structural change. This is particularly so when the justification defence is used to rebut the presumption of discrimination raised by a disproportionate impact on an outgroup. Nor does indirect discrimination on its own give rise to any obligation to ensure that applicants are equipped for a job or other benefit, for example by training or provision of childcare. Furthermore, the remedy for indirect discrimination does not necessarily entail a requirement that the discriminatory barrier must be removed, although many employers may in fact do so to avoid further proceedings. Indeed, as we have seen, the weaknesses in the role indirect discrimination can play in relation to accommodation and structural change could undermine its strengths in relation to the other three dimensions.

The strengths and weakness of indirect discrimination when measured against the four-dimensional understanding of substantive equality are demonstrated well in relation to part-time workers. By recognizing inferior conditions for part-time workers as indirect discrimination against women, the

---

[242] [1983] 2 AC 548 (HL).

principle is capable of redressing disadvantage experienced by women in the labour force due to childcare and domestic obligations. Indirect discrimination can simultaneously address the stereotypes of women as available to work for lower pay. It similarly has the potential to increase women's voice in the workforce through facilitating their overall participation. Indeed, as we have seen, indirect discrimination provisions have made significant progress in the removal of specific detriments attached to part-time work in several jurisdictions. Policies or practices precluding part-time workers from access to pensions, protection against unfair dismissal, and equal hourly pay have been held to be indirectly discriminatory.[243] However, indirect discrimination does nothing to change the underlying division of power within the family which leaves women with the primary responsibility for childcare. The result is that women part-time workers might find their position at work improved as a result of the prohibition of indirect discrimination. But the fact that the vast majority of women are part-time workers remains unchanged. Thus, the structural dimension goes unaddressed.

IV REDRAWING THE BOUNDARIES

In principle, the divide between direct and indirect discrimination is vivid. Direct discrimination, or disparate treatment, deals with unequal treatment. Indirect discrimination or disparate impact deals with inequality of results. The powerful intuition behind *Griggs v Duke Power* remains unassailable.[244] Yet, it is becoming increasingly difficult to situate the divide. In some jurisdictions, such as the US, the distinction is based on intention. According to Kennedy J in *Ricci v DeStefano*: '[Title VII] prohibits both intentional discrimination (known as "disparate treatment") as well as, in some cases, practices that are not intended to discriminate but in fact have a disproportionately adverse effect on minorities (known as "disparate impact").'[245] In the UK, by contrast, intention or motive have been eschewed even for direct discrimination, replaced by a 'but for' causative test. Rather than intention, the key distinguishing factor has been justification. As Baroness Hale has put it: 'Direct and indirect discrimination are mutually exclusive. You cannot

---

[243] *Bilka-Kaufhaus* (n 128); *R v Secretary of State for Employment, ex p Equal Opportunities Commission* [1994] IRLR 176 (HL); *Fraser v Canada (Attorney General)* (n 128).
[244] *Griggs v Duke Power Co* (n 2).
[245] *Ricci v DeStefano* (n 44) 2672.

have both at once . . . The main difference between them is that direct discrimination cannot be justified. Indirect discrimination can be justified if it is a proportionate means of achieving a legitimate aim.'[246] However, as we have seen, relying on a 'but for' test without giving the respondents any opportunity to explain their reasons has meant that in practice direct discrimination depends largely on proof of impact on the individual, blurring the distinction with indirect discrimination. In addition, there are an increasing number of areas in which direct discrimination can in fact be justified, including genuine occupational qualifications, equal pay, age discrimination, and some kinds of disability discrimination.

Alternatively, it has been suggested that direct discrimination occurs when the criterion is 'indissociable' from the protected characteristic, in the sense that everyone with the protected characteristic is excluded. Indirect discrimination, by contrast, occurs when those with a protected characteristic are disproportionately excluded.[247] It has been demonstrated earlier that this yields an unsteady boundary between the two concepts, in that it depends heavily on how the criterion is defined in the first place. In any event, it is difficult to discern any clear principle explaining why indissociability should be the key to whether a criterion constitutes direct discrimination, which cannot be justified, as against indirect discrimination, which can. At best, we might surmise that a criterion which is indissociable from a protected characteristic is a proxy for expressly discriminating on that ground. This looks very much like disguised intention, which reinstates intention as the defining feature. Yet, without the possibility of justification there is no opportunity to establish whether the criterion is indeed a proxy for a disguised intention to discriminate.

The difficulty in delineating a clear boundary between the principles of liability means that it becomes important to ensure that, while both can be tools in detecting discrimination, the precise classification as one or the other should not significantly affect the defences available or the appropriate remedies. This was the conclusion reached in the Supreme Court of Canada. In a case in 1997 (the 'Firefighters' case),[248] McLachlan J took the opportunity of revisiting the conventional bifurcated approach which categorized discrimination as either 'direct', meaning discriminatory on its face,

---

[246] *JFS* (n 10) [57].
[247] *Hall and Preddy v Bull and Bull* [2013] UKSC 73 [189] (UK Sup Ct).
[248] *British Columbia (Public Service Employee Relations Commission) v British Columbia Government Service Employees' Union* [1999] 3 SCR 3.

or 'adverse effect', meaning discriminatory in effect. She recognized that 'the conventional analysis was helpful in the interpretation of the early human rights statutes, and indeed represented a significant step forward in that it recognized for the first time the harm of adverse effect discrimination'.[249] However, it no longer served the purpose of human rights legislation. There were a number of reasons for this. Most important was the fact that few cases could be neatly categorized as direct or adverse effect discrimination. The example given by McLachlan CJ is particularly instructive. She referred to a rule requiring all workers to appear at work on Fridays or face dismissal. This could be directly discriminatory, in that no workers whose religious beliefs preclude working on Fridays could be employed there. Or it could be characterized as a neutral rule that merely has an adverse effect on a few individuals (those same workers whose religious beliefs prevent them from working on Fridays).[250] The same analysis would work in UK law: the rule would be 'intrinsically' directly discriminatory under the *JFS* test; fulfil the 'indissociability' criterion under *Bull v Hall* because workers whose religious beliefs prevent them from working on Fridays would all be excluded; or be indirectly discriminatory on grounds of religion. She also recognized that the size of the 'affected group' is easily manipulable.

The difficulty in classification led McLachlan CJ to conclude that it was not appropriate for the distinction to constitute the basis for diverging remedial or other outcomes. Instead, she established a unified approach. Where a standard is prima facie discriminatory, it can only be justified if the employer can show that the purpose of the standard is rationally connected to the performance of the job, the standard was adopted in a bona fide belief that it was necessary to fulfil a legitimate work-related purpose, and the standard is reasonably necessary to the accomplishment of that purpose. The Supreme Court in *Fraser* confirmed that the same analysis applies to Charter cases.[251]

Other jurisdictions have relaxed the boundary in a different way. The ECtHR only adopted an indirect discrimination standard relatively recently, in the *DH* case. But the boundary between the two concepts is less rigid than that of the UK in that it leaves open the possibility of a justification defence in both equal treatment and indirect discrimination claims. Instead, the ECtHR has preferred to calibrate the strictness of the standard

---

[249] ibid para 25.
[250] ibid para 27.
[251] *Fraser v Canada (Attorney General)* (n 128).

of justification depending on the ground and context. The ECtHR has also been less concerned than both UK and US judges at the prospect of affirmative action. Indeed, it has held in some situations that the principle of equality requires different treatment in order to correct factual inequalities. In *Sejdić*, the applicants invited the Court to follow EU jurisprudence and hold that difference in treatment based expressly on race or ethnicity was not capable of justification and amounted to direct discrimination.[252] The Court rejected this approach, largely because of the danger that a blanket refusal to allow justification would also outlaw affirmative action.[253] Instead, it held that 'where a difference in treatment is based on race or ethnicity, the notion of objective and reasonable justification must be interpreted as strictly as possible'. Nevertheless, 'Article 14 does not prohibit Contracting Parties from treating groups differently in order to correct "factual inequalities" between them. Indeed, in certain circumstances a failure to attempt to correct inequality through different treatment may, without an objective and reasonable justification, give rise to a breach of that Article'.[254]

Even the EU, which has reserved justification for indirect discrimination, has shown signs of moving beyond a rigid boundary between direct and indirect discrimination. In *Chez v Nikolova*,[255] the Court found that the same facts could give rise to both direct and indirect discrimination. In this case, all the electricity meters in an urban district predominantly populated by Bulgarian citizens of Romani origin were placed in large silver locked boxes on pylons at a height of between six and seven metres. In other districts, the meters were placed in small boxes on the outer walls of houses. The company claimed that this was to avoid consumers from those areas manipulating meter readings. The Court held that a measure such as that at issue in this case would constitute direct discrimination if it proved to have been introduced and/or maintained for reasons relating to the ethnic origin common to most inhabitants of the district concerned. Importantly, the Court did not require the claimants to establish more than a prima facie case that the policy was on grounds of ethnic origin. Following its established jurisprudence, the

---

[252] *Sejdić and Finci v Bosnia and Herzegovina* [2009] 12 WLUK 713 (ECtHR).

[253] US jurisprudence has oscillated widely between accepting affirmative action as a means for achieving (substantive) equality and rejecting it as a breach of (formal) equality: *Ricci v DeStefano* (n 44). The EU permits affirmative action as an exception to the equal treatment principle only when it does not disrupt the merit principle, that is in 'tie-break' situations: Case C-450/93 *Kalanke v Freie Hansestadt Bremen* [1995] IRLR 660.

[254] *Sejdić and Finci v Bosnia and Herzegovina* (n 251) para 44.

[255] Case C-83/14 *CHEZ Razpredelenie Bulgaria AD v Komisia za zashtita ot diskriminatsia* [2016] 1 CMLR 14.

burden of proof shifts once facts have been adduced which give rise to a presumption of discrimination. This, in turn, required the respondent to rebut the presumption by showing that the practice and its retention were not in any way founded on the fact that it was instituted in predominantly Romani areas but was instead exclusively based on objective facts unrelated to any discrimination on grounds of racial or ethnic origin. Notably, the process of determining whether the discrimination is on grounds of racial or ethnic origin is not one of determining motive or intention. Instead, it is to establish facts from which a presumption of discrimination can be inferred. Notably, too, the process of rebutting the presumption is very similar to that of justification in indirect discrimination.

The ECJ went on to find that if direct discrimination was not established, then the practice could constitute a neutral criterion for the purposes of indirect discrimination. It was common ground that since the practice was only instituted in predominantly Roma areas, it was liable to affect persons of Roma origin in considerably greater proportions than others and therefore put them at a particular disadvantage compared with other persons.[256] This, in turn, leads to the difficult question of justification. Here the Court set a relatively high standard of scrutiny. The measure could, in the right factual situations, be appropriate. But to prove necessity required a demonstration that other appropriate and less restrictive measures would not resolve the problems. Even if no other measure could be identified, the referring court would need to decide whether the disadvantages it caused were disproportionate to the aim pursued and whether it would unduly prejudice the legitimate interests of the local inhabitants. In doing so, particular attention should be paid to three factors. First, the referring court would need to be mindful of the legitimate interest of consumers of electricity in having access to an electricity supply in conditions which would not have an offensive and stigmatizing effect. Secondly, it should take account of the fact that no individual unlawful acts had been proved to have been committed over the preceding twenty-five years. Thirdly, the inhabitants of the area have a legitimate interest in having access to meters to monitor their own electricity. On the basis of all these issues, the Court concluded, it seemed that the practice could not be justified because the disadvantages it caused seemed disproportionate to its objectives. Nevertheless, it was for the referring court to make the final decision on the issue.

---

[256] Council Directive 2000/43/EC of 29 June 2000 implementing the principle of equal treatment between persons irrespective of racial or ethnic origin [2000] OJ L180/22.

V CONCLUSION

As we have seen, in principle, the divide between direct and indirect dis-crimination is clear. Direct discrimination, or disparate treatment, deals with unequal treatment. Indirect discrimination or disparate impact deals with inequality of results. Yet, recent developments in the jurisprudence of the courts in the US and the UK make it increasingly difficult to situate the divide. At first glance, the reasons for this are widely divergent. In the US, those Supreme Court Justices who are hostile to disparate impact generally attempt to revert to intention and symmetry as the touchstone of the right to equality. They warn that a disparate-impact regime leads inexorably to af-firmative action or reverse discrimination, which they regard as anathema to their conception of equality as symmetrical, colour-blind,[257] and fault-based. The result has been to continually narrow down the principle of dis-parate impact. Dissenting Justices even argue that it is unconstitutional. In the UK, by contrast, there has been a strong sense that allowing intention or motive into even a direct discrimination analysis will open the door to legitimating discrimination on the grounds of ostensibly benign motives. This has had the consequence of turning direct discrimination into what is in practice an effects-based test, but one which leaves no scope for justifi-cation, on the grounds that this might reintroduce motive at the justifica-tion stage. This means that the divide is instead situated at whether or not a justification defence is available; or whether there is an exact fit between a criterion and members of the group. This leaves the background rationale for both direct and indirect discrimination unclear. In addition, little or no attention is paid to social context or implications. In the meantime, other jur-isdictions have been consciously remapping the territory to allow a fruitful interaction between the concepts. The Supreme Court of Canada has em-barked on a particularly careful analysis of the relationship between the two principles. Acknowledging that the divide is often unclear, it has been keen to streamline defences and remedies so that little hangs on the initial classifi-cation. The ECtHR and the ECJ, in their recent case law, are similarly flexible about the divide.

---

[257] The term 'colour-blind' Constitution has been used by Justices of the US Supreme Court who argue that skin colour should never be a relevant factor in determining access to university or jobs, and therefore affirmative action in favour of disadvantaged groups should not be per-mitted (see Chapter 7). For a critique, see R Kennedy, 'Colorblind Constitutionalism' (2013) 82 Fordham L Rev.

This raises the question of why, despite in principle having apparently clearly demarcated boundaries, the interaction between direct and indirect discrimination remains so tense and conflictual. Even more so, why has the UK addressed this tension by moving direct discrimination into an effects-based mould, while the US jurisprudence tends to push disparate impact into a treatment- or intention-based mould? A closer look at the case law in these two jurisdictions reveals some common closely intertwined themes. The first is a strong allegiance to a symmetrical notion of equality and an aversion to affirmative action. Majority judgments reveal a deep discomfort with the basis of an asymmetric approach, which is that we should be able to distinguish between legitimate and illegitimate uses of suspect or protected characteristics. A cause of action based on unequal results requires decision makers to pay attention to the gender- or colour-based[258] effects of their decisions even if the original decision is not expressly on grounds of race or gender. In adjudicating disparate impact, courts too are required to make colour- or gender-conscious decisions. The second is a continued attachment to an individualized notion of liability, both in terms of requiring individual liability on behalf of the respondent and individual harm on the part of the complainant. Thirdly, there is a problematic ambiguity about the aims of an effects-based test and its relationship to a treatment-based test. Is the aim to redress disparities in outcomes? Or to augment the equal treatment principle by flushing out illegitimate reasons for decision making which cannot otherwise be established or proved?

Nevertheless, the insights of disparate impact/indirect discrimination remain as compelling as they were when formulated in the *Griggs* case. To achieve coherence in the notion requires courts to recognize the asymmetric consequences of this test. This, in turn, entails differentiating between uses of protected characteristics which further equality against a background of antecedent disadvantage and those which deepen existing disadvantage. In addition, a genuine effects-based approach would place responsibility on those who are able to bring about change rather than insisting on finding a perpetrator who can be shown to be 'at fault'. Ultimately, an impact-based test needs to be capable of dealing with structural inequalities and this in turn requires greater attention both to pre-emptive action, whether or not

---

[258] This terminology reflects that used in international human rights law and relevant human rights instruments in other jurisdictions (see British EA 2010, s 9(1)(a); South African Constitution, s 9; Canadian Charter, s 15; International Convention on the Elimination of All Forms of Racial Discrimination, Art 1; ICCPR, Art 2(1); ICESCR, Art 2(2)), which all refer to 'colour' in the list of protected characteristics.

this involves quotas, and to remedies which are capable of addressing the underlying problem. All four dimensions of substantive equality need to be simultaneously addressed: an asymmetric approach focusing on redressing disadvantage rather than the achievement of a gender neutral, race- or 'colour-blind' society;[259] and a formulation of the basic concepts of discrimination which can address stigma, stereotyping, prejudice, and violence; facilitate participation and reduce social exclusion; and accommodate difference and ultimately achieve structural change.

This chapter has mapped the architecture of anti-discrimination law, drawing on comparative insights where appropriate to highlight different possible models and ways of addressing weaknesses. It can be seen that while important advances have been made, both in the depth and reach of anti-discrimination laws, these have brought with them new challenges and raised new questions about established understandings and demarcations. The following chapter examines four specifically challenging applications of these concepts—pregnancy and parenting, equal pay, sexual harassment, and the duty of accommodation. Chapter 7 turns to the even more controversial question of affirmative action.

[259] See n 256.

6

Challenges and Contestations

Pregnancy and Parenting, Equal Pay, Sexual
Harassment, and Duty of Accommodation

I INTRODUCTION

Chapter 5 set out the principles of direct and indirect discrimination and
their general application. This chapter dives deeper into four issues, all of
central social importance, which have challenged the application of these
principles: pregnancy and parenthood; equal pay; sexual harassment; and
reasonable accommodation. In each of these, the foundational principles
have had to evolve towards a more substantive understanding of equality in
order to fully address the social problem at hand.

II PREGNANCY AND PARENTHOOD: THE
SAMENESS-DIFFERENCE DICHOTOMY

Discrimination on grounds of pregnancy remains a key obstacle to women's
full and equal participation in the labour force. Yet the problem of equality
as conformity is at its most glaring in relation to pregnancy discrimination.[1]
Who is the relevant male comparator for a pregnant woman? Initially, courts
in the US, Canada, and the UK reacted in a strikingly similar way: detrimental
treatment of pregnant women did not breach the equality principle because
there was no relevant male comparator.[2] Most graphic was the approach of
the UK Employment Appeal Tribunal: 'When she is pregnant a woman is no
longer just a woman. She is a woman . . . with child and there is no masculine
equivalent.'[3] A similar approach can be found in the jurisprudence of the US

---

[1] For a more detailed discussion, see S Fredman, *Women and the Law* (OUP 1997) 184–92;
S Fredman, 'A Difference with Distinction: Pregnancy and Parenthood Reassessed' (1994) 110
LQR 106.
[2] See generally Fredman, 'A Difference with Distinction' ibid.
[3] *Turley v Allders Stores Ltd* [1980] ICR 66 (EAT).

Discrimination Law. Third Edition. Sandra Fredman, Oxford University Press. © Sandra Fredman 2022.
DOI: 10.1093/oso/9780198854081.003.0006

Supreme Court, where pregnancy was routinely excluded from occupational insurance schemes which provided benefits in respect of sickness or injury. This, however, was held not to constitute a breach of constitutional or statutory equality guarantees. In the words of Stewart J in *Geduldig v Aiello*: 'There is no risk from which men are protected and women are not. Likewise, there is no risk from which women are protected and men are not.'[4] In a similar vein, the Supreme Court of Canada in *Bliss* held that: 'Any inequality between the sexes in this area is not created by legislation but by nature.'[5]

One way out of this conundrum is to regard pregnancy as equivalent to illness for the purposes of the comparison.[6] Foreshadowed in the dissenting judgments of Brennan J in *Geduldig*[7] and *Gilbert*,[8] the 'ill male comparator' has become prevailing orthodoxy in the US. The Pregnancy Discrimination Act 1978 amended Title VII to provide: 'Women affected by pregnancy, childbirth, or related medical conditions shall be treated the same for all employment-related purposes ... as other persons not so affected but similar in their ability or inability to work.'[9] Courts in the UK briefly followed the same route.[10] The notion of the ill male comparator, however, comes at a cost. Pregnancy is not an illness and should not be stigmatized as 'unhealthy'. Moreover, it assumes that the main issue is a woman's inability to do her work. This ignores the positive reasons for leave, including breastfeeding and developing a relationship with the child. Particularly problematically, if there are no applicable protections in respect of illness, then pregnancy remains likewise unprotected. This raises the further question of which 'ill male comparator' will be acceptable. Complex litigation might be necessary to provide an answer to this question. This occurred as recently as 2015 when United Parcel Services (UPS), which employs over 480,000 workers in the US, refused to accede to a woman driver's requests for light-lifting duties during her pregnancy.[11] As a result, she was forced to take unpaid leave and eventually lost her employee medical coverage. She argued that UPS accommodated other drivers who were similar in their inability to work. UPS responded

---

[4] *Geduldig v Aiello* 417 US 484, 497 (1974) and see *General Electric Co v Gilbert* 429 US 125, 97 S Ct 401 (1976).

[5] *Bliss v Canada (AG)* [1976] 1 SCR 183 (Can Sup Ct).

[6] See eg *Webb v EMO Cargo Ltd* [1992] 2 All ER 43 (UK Ct of Appeal), cf Case C-32/93 *Webb* [1994] ECR I-3567 (ECJ).

[7] *Geduldig v Aiello* (n 4).

[8] *General Electric Co v Gilbert* (n 4).

[9] 42 USC § 2000e(k).

[10] *Webb v EMO Cargo Ltd* [1992] 2 All ER 43 (CA).

[11] *Young v United Parcel Service* 135 S Ct 1338 (2015) (US Sup Ct).

that these were not appropriate comparators since their policy specifically reserved these accommodations for specific categories, such as those classified as disabled under the Americans with Disabilities Act or those who had become disabled on the job. Since the applicant did not fall within these categories, it was argued, she was not discriminated against on grounds of her pregnancy, but simply treated as all other relevant persons who were unable to work. The US Supreme Court refused to hold that she could compare herself to any subset of drivers who were provided with an accommodation, calling it 'most favoured-nation status'. According to Breyer J, Congress could not have intended that as long an employer provides one or two workers with an accommodation, it must provide similar accommodation to all pregnant workers with comparable physical limitations. Instead, the Court resorted to the intent-based theory we saw in Chapter 5. 'Disparate-treatment law normally permits an employer to implement policies that are not intended to harm members of a protected class, even if their implementation sometimes harms those members, as long as the employer has a legitimate, non-discriminatory, non-pretextual reason for doing so.'[12] Pregnant women must therefore go through the tortuous route of proving that their employer's policies impose a significant burden on pregnant workers and that any 'legitimate, non-discriminatory' reason offered by the employer is not sufficient to justify the burden but rather gives rise to an inference of intentional discrimination.[13] Breyer J did emphasize that the employer cannot normally justify treating pregnant women differently from others similar in their ability to work simply by claiming that it is more expensive or less convenient to add pregnant women to the category of those whom the employer accommodates. Nevertheless, the case resoundingly proves the limits of a model based on an ill male comparator in protecting pregnant workers from detrimental treatment.

More constructive has been the move away from the need for a comparator in the first place. In a series of important cases, both the ECJ[14] and the Canadian Supreme Court[15] have held that there is no need for a comparator of any sort. As the ECJ stressed in *Dekker*, the fact that only women have the capacity to become pregnant means that discrimination on grounds of pregnancy is necessarily discrimination on grounds of sex. Similarly, in *Brooks*

---

[12] ibid 1350.

[13] ibid 1355.

[14] Case C-177/88 *Dekker* [1990] ECR I-394 (ECJ); Case C-32/93 *Webb* [1994] ECR I-3567 (ECJ).

[15] *Brookes v Canada Safeway Ltd* (1989) 1 SCR 1219 (Can Sup Ct).

v Canada Safeway in 1989, the Supreme Court of Canada, reversing *Bliss*, asserted: 'The capacity to become pregnant is unique to the female gender.'[16] This has culminated in the recognition of pregnancy as a ground of discrimination in itself, both in South Africa under section 9(3) of the Constitution, and in Britain, under the EA 2010.[17] Including pregnancy as a specific ground rather than searching for a 'male' comparator also has the potential to include trans men within the scope of pregnancy protection. Moreover, UK legislation now defines direct discrimination as occurring when a person is treated 'unfavourably because of the pregnancy'.[18] By using the words 'unfavourably' rather than 'less favourably', direct discrimination on grounds of pregnancy can be established independently of the need to find a comparator.

The Indian Supreme Court reached a similar conclusion by a different route. In *Air India v Nergesh Meerza*,[19] the Court held that distinctions on the ground of pregnancy were arbitrary and in breach of Article 14 of the Constitution. The Court made the welcome statement that pregnancy was not a disability. However, it allied its response to deeply gendered assumptions about women and maternity, holding that rather than being a disability, pregnancy was a natural consequence of marriage. These assumptions have permeated much Indian jurisprudence on this issue. More recently, however, the Delhi High Court took a bolder position, reaffirming that the violation of Article 14 stems from an interference with a woman's reproductive right and her right to employment by forcing her to choose between bearing a child and employment.[20] Importantly, the Court referred in detail to comparative case law, including from the EU and the US, as well as international human rights documents such as CEDAW.

An alternative approach is to eschew the quest for a comparator and instead aim to achieve equality through acknowledging difference. Such an approach takes the form of a demand for specific rights such as protection from dismissal for pregnancy and provision of maternity leave. ILO Convention No 3 of 1919[21] was well ahead of its time in insisting on a particular package of maternity rights for women aimed at ensuring that 'women's work does not pose risks to the health of the woman and her child and that women's reproductive roles do not compromise their economic and employment

---

[16] ibid.
[17] EA 2010, s 4.
[18] ibid ss 17, 18.
[19] *Air India v Nergesh Meerza* 1981 SC 1829 (Indian Sup Ct).
[20] *Neetu Bala v Union of India*, CWP No 6414 od 2014 (Punjab-Haryana High Ct).
[21] ILO Maternity Protection Convention, 1919 (No 3).

security'.[22] The key elements of this package, which have been broadly maintained in later iterations in 1952[23] and 2000,[24] include maternity leave, cash benefits, medical care, protection from workplace risks, protection from dismissal and discrimination, and the right to continue breastfeeding on return to work. Similarly, CEDAW requires States to introduce paid maternity leave, as well as to provide special protection to women during pregnancy in types of work proved to be harmful to them.[25]

The EU stands out for following both the non-discrimination and the specific rights approaches. Since the early 1990s, specific rights have been developed in parallel to the pioneering principle that pregnancy per se is a species of sex discrimination, even in the absence of a male comparator. Passed in 1992, the EU Pregnancy Directive provides protection for the health and safety of pregnant workers as well as maternity leave, of which a portion is compulsory. It also provides for protection against dismissal and detrimental treatment.[26]

However, the role of the comparator is not so easily banished. It re-emerges in several ways. First, the ECJ has held that where pregnancy-related illness continues after the expiry of maternity leave, however short, a woman will only be able to prove a breach of the equality principle if she can show that she was treated less favourably than an ill man would have been treated.[27] The ill male comparator even haunts the operation of statutory rights to maternity leave and pay. The Pregnant Workers Directive, despite appearing to move away from the need for a comparator, provides that pay during maternity leave is adequate if it is equivalent to sickness pay.[28] This, in turn, has created further opportunities to construe equality as sameness or conformity, rather than in the substantive sense of redressing disadvantage. Women claiming full pay while on maternity leave have been met with the argument that they are demanding preferential treatment and should be content with like treatment with men on sick pay. In *Gillespie*,[29] a claim by women that they should receive full pay while on maternity leave was dismissed on the grounds that

---

[22] ibid.

[23] ILO Maternity Protection Convention (Revised), 1952 (No 103).

[24] ILO Maternity Protection Convention, 2000 (No 183).

[25] CEDAW, Art 11(2).

[26] Council Directive 92/85/EEC of 19 October 1992 on the protection of the safety and health at work of pregnant and breastfeeding workers [1992] OJ L348/1.

[27] Case C-179/88 *Hertz* [1990] ECR I-3979. Illness during pregnancy or maternity leave still attracts protection without the need for a comparator; Case C-394/96 *Brown v Rentokill* [1998] ECR I-4185, [1998] IRLR 445.

[28] Council Directive 92/85/EEC, Art 11(3).

[29] Case C-342/93 *Gillespie* [1996] ECR I-475.

benefits received by ill employees were far less. Yet there are many countries in Europe which have recognized that maternity is not comparable to illness and have therefore been prepared to see maternity pay as a full substitute for earnings.[30]

The male comparator has played an even more vigorous role in the US. Despite the drag that it exercises on pregnant women's rights, as we saw earlier, many US feminists regard it as essential that women's protection is equivalent to that of ill men to prevent discrimination against pregnant women. 'Legislation solely protecting pregnant women,' it has been argued, 'gives employers an economic incentive to discriminate against women in hiring policies; legislation helping all workers equally does not have this effect.'[31] The ILO has two responses to this claim. First, there is a clear prohibition on discrimination on grounds of pregnancy and maternity, both in recruitment and dismissal. Secondly, the ILO Convention insists that the cost of maternity be borne neither by the mother nor by the employer, but the State. Cash benefits are payable to the mother for the duration of the leave, sufficient for the full and healthy maintenance of the mother and her child and a suitable standard of living. However, the employer should not be individually liable for payment of such benefits;[32] instead, they should be paid by the State or national insurance. The criticism is more apt for the EU which makes no provision for shifting the cost away from the employer.

More problematic is the second way in which the comparator continues to dog the pregnancy and parenting issue. This is when it is asserted that special rights for pregnancy and parenting actually discriminate against men. To pre-empt such claims, some jurisdictions have provided specific exceptions so that pregnancy is not regarded as direct discrimination. Article 4(2) of CEDAW states: 'Adoption by States Parties of special measures . . . aimed at protecting maternity shall not be considered discriminatory.' Similarly, at EU level, Article 28(1) of the Recast Equal Treatment Directive states: 'This Directive shall be without prejudice to provisions concerning the protection

---

[30] Women on maternity leave are paid in full in Austria, Belgium (for the first four weeks), Finland, Greece, Luxembourg, the Netherlands, Norway, Portugal, and Spain.

[31] S Rep No 101-77, 32 (1989) taken from Ginsburg in *Coleman v Court of Appeals of Maryland* 132 S Ct 1327 (2012) (US Sup Ct).

[32] ILO Maternity Protection Convention No 103 (1952), Art 4(2) and (8); ILO Maternity Protection Convention No 183 (2000), Art 6(8): the 2000 Convention allows this to be rebutted by individual agreement with the employer or by collective agreement (or by pre-existing law or practice).

of women, particularly as regards pregnancy and maternity.'[33] This repeats the identically worded provision in Article 2(3) of the earlier Equal Treatment Directive of 1976.[34]

However, ring-fencing women's rights in this way, while crucial in preventing challenges to maternity rights from employers, has also had the effect of stereotyping the 'special relationship' of mothers to their babies, and excluding claims by fathers. Particularly problematic is the extent to which pregnancy and maternity are regarded as a continuum and therefore unique to the mother. In the ECJ case *Hofmann v Barmer Ersatzkasse*,[35] a father claimed that he was being discriminated against because he was not eligible for a State payment during paternity leave, whereas the child's mother would have been eligible for such a payment during her maternity leave. The Court rejected his claim on the basis that maternity leave fell within the exception from the equal treatment principle in relation to pregnancy and maternity. In doing so, it held that maternity rights were necessary to protect not just the mother's health during pregnancy and childbirth, but also what it regarded as 'the special relationship between a woman and her child over the period which follows pregnancy and childbirth, by preventing that relationship from being disturbed by the multiple burdens which would result from the simultaneous pursuit of employment. . . . That being so, such leave may legitimately be reserved to the mother to the exclusion of any other person, in view of the fact that it is only the mother who may find herself subject to undesirable pressures to return to work prematurely.'[36] Of course, in the modern era, the pressure on fathers not to take leave is an equal cause for concern. The Court has consistently defended the exemption for maternity rights in these terms.

Aiming to achieve equality through different treatment, whether through specific rights or exemptions from a charge of direct discrimination, has been highly controversial in the US. When California preferred a specific rights model, by requiring employers to provide female employees with unpaid pregnancy disability leave of up to four months,[37] women's rights advocates were, in the words of Ginsburg J, 'sharply divided . . . "Equal-treatment"

---

[33] Directive 2006/54/EC of the European Parliament and of the Council of 5 July 2006 on the implementation of the principle of equal opportunities and equal treatment of men and women in matters of employment and occupation (recast), Art 28(1).

[34] EU Directive 76/207 (Equal Treatment Directive), Art 2(3).

[35] Case 184/83 [1984] ECR 3047, [1986] 1 CMLR 242.

[36] Case 184/83 *Hofmann v Barmer Ersatzkasse* [1986] 1 CMLR 242, paras 25 and 26 (ECJ).

[37] Fair Employment and Housing Act (FEHA).

feminists asserted it violated the PDA's [Pregnancy Discrimination Act] commitment to treating pregnancy the same as other disabilities. It did so by requiring leave only for disability caused by pregnancy and childbirth, thereby treating pregnancy as *sui generis*. . . . "Equal-opportunity" feminists disagreed, urging that the California law was consistent with the PDA because it remedied the discriminatory burden that inadequate leave policies placed on a woman's right to procreate.'[38]

A better approach to the demands of like treatment should be to level up fathers' rights to those of mothers. This possibility can be detected in the US Supreme Court decision in *Guerra*[39] in which an employer challenged the Californian statute mentioned above. The petitioners argued that the PDA, by requiring that pregnant workers be treated the same as other disabled workers, precluded any measure which afforded pregnant workers more favourable treatment. The District Court upheld the challenge. However, the Supreme Court deftly turned this argument back on itself. Thus, according to Marshall J, '[The impugned provision] does not compel California employers to treat pregnant workers better than other disabled employees; it merely establishes benefits that employers must, at a minimum, provide to pregnant workers. Employers are free to give comparable benefits to other disabled employees, thereby treating "women affected by pregnancy" no better than "other persons not so affected but similar in their ability or inability to work".[40] This opens up the possibility that the equality principle could take on a far more substantive hue since fathers could in principle lever up their rights by comparison with existing substantive rights of the mothers of their children.

Although the California statute was upheld by the US Supreme Court, equal treatment feminists began campaigning for gender-neutral legislation.[41] This eventually reached the statute books in the form of the Family and Medical Leave Act of 1993 (FMLA). Under the FMLA, eligible employees have the right to up to twelve weeks of unpaid leave per year for the birth, adoption, or fostering of a child; the care of spouse, son, daughter, or parent with a serious health condition; and for self-care in relation to a serious health condition.[42] This was supported in Congress on the grounds that it prevented discrimination against pregnant women: 'Because the bill

---

[38] Ginsburg in *Coleman v Court of Appeals of Maryland* (n 31).
[39] *California Federal Savings & Loan Association v Guerra* 479 US 272 (1987) (US Sup Ct).
[40] ibid.
[41] Ginsburg in *Coleman v Court of Appeals of Maryland* (n 31).
[42] 29 USC § 2612(a)(1).

treats all employees who are temporarily unable to work due to serious health conditions in the same fashion, it does not create the risk of discrimination against pregnant women posed by legislation which provides job protection only for pregnancy-related disability.'[43] Equal treatment has, however, been achieved at a very low level. FMLA leave is well below women's entitlement in the EU, providing only twelve weeks' unpaid entitlement. Despite the vigorous backing of the Biden administration, proposals in 2021 to provide twelve weeks of paid leave were first whittled down to four weeks and then dropped entirely due to opposition based on cost.[44]

Meanwhile, paradoxically, sustained challenges of the FMLA as an illegitimate intrusion on State sovereignty by the federal government could only be rebuffed by proof that the provision of maternity benefits without corresponding paternity benefits constituted discrimination against men.[45] 'Stereotype-based beliefs about the allocation of family duties remained firmly rooted, and employers' reliance on them in establishing discriminatory leave policies remained widespread.'[46] Faced with 'the States' record of unconstitutional participation in, and fostering of, gender-based discrimination in the administration of leave benefits',[47] Hibbs concluded that requiring State employers to give all employees the opportunity to take family-care leave was constitutional.

The low level of parental entitlements in the US can be compared to parental leave entitlements in the EU. The Parental Leave Directive[48] in 2010 signalled a breakthrough in giving both parents the right to four months' parental leave on top of women's right to maternity leave. However, while maternity leave is paid, parental leave is not, providing little incentive for fathers to avail themselves of the right. If the family income as a whole is likely to drop in this period, this is not surprising. A limited attempt was made to encourage fathers' uptake by providing that although most of the leave could be transferred from one parent to the other, one month was non-transferrable. Somewhat more progress has been made with the adoption in 2019 of the Work–Life Balance Directive,[49] which replaced the Parental Leave Directive.

---

[43] S Rep No 101-77, 32 (1989) taken from Ginsburg in *Coleman v Court of Appeals of Maryland* (n 31).
[44] <www.cnbc.com/2021/12/20/paid-leave-advocates-react-to-manchin-opposition-to-build-back-better.html> accessed 1 August 2022.
[45] *Nevada Dept of Human Resources v Hibbs* 538 US 721 (2003) (US Sup Ct).
[46] ibid 730.
[47] ibid 735.
[48] Council Directive 2010/18/EU.
[49] Directive 2019/1158/EU on work-life balance for parents and carers.

The directive provides individual rights to paternity leave, parental leave, and carers' leave, as well as the right to request flexible working arrangements for workers who are parents or carers. However, fathers' rights are still well below those of mothers, with only the right to ten working days' paternity leave on the birth of the child. This compares to leave of at least fourteen weeks under the Pregnant Workers Directive.[50] Moreover, the ill male comparator makes its reappearance here, in that paternity pay should be at least as high as the worker would receive for sick pay. More encouraging is the provision for paid parental leave of four months to be accorded equally to both parents, with a non-transferrable portion of two months. Moreover, the level of payment must be set in such a way as to facilitate take-up of parental leave by both parents.[51]

The best way out of the sameness–difference conundrum in this context is to distinguish between pregnancy and parenting. Pregnancy is genuinely unique to women and trans men. To achieve equality therefore requires different treatment, attaching specific rights to pregnancy and childbirth. However, to regard parenting as unique to those who have given birth is to reinforce stereotypes about women as primary childcarers and to entrench their resultant disadvantage in the labour market. Both parents should therefore be regarded as similarly situated in relation to parenting. However, the reintroduction of a male comparator should not be an opportunity for levelling down, either by settling for parenting rights at a low level or by removing women's existing rights. Substantive equality, in the four-dimensional sense, requires redressing disadvantage, unravelling stereotypes, greater participation, and structural change. Indeed, as practice has repeatedly shown, if fathers' rights are not equivalent to those of mothers, the former have no incentive to take up their entitlements. This simply reinforces stereotypes and maintains existing structures.

This possibility has been developed by both the ECJ and the ECtHR. The ECJ case of *Roca Alvarez*[52] breaks new ground on several fronts. The first lies in the nature of the comparator. The Court had no hesitation in declaring that 'the positions of a male and a female worker, father and mother of a young child, are comparable with regard to their possible need to reduce their daily working time in order to look after their child.' Secondly, it

---

[50] Directive 92/85, Art 8.

[51] Case C-463/19 *Syndicat CFTC du personnel de la Caisse primaire d'assurance maladie de la Moselle v Caisse primaire d'assurance maladie de la Moselle* EU:C:2020:932 (CJEU).

[52] Case C-104/09 *Roca Álvarez v Sesa Start España ETT SA* [2011] 1 CMLR 28.

rejected the Spanish government's submission that the aim of the measure was to compensate for the genuine disadvantages suffered by women in comparison to men.[53] Instead, the Court declared, to give this right only to an employed mother and not an employed father would be 'liable to perpetuate a traditional distribution of the roles of men and women by keeping men in a role subsidiary to that of women in relation to the exercise of their parental duties'.[54] Moreover, this could have the further effect of limiting the self-employed activities of the mother of the complainant's child, since the father had no rights to take time off work for childcare. As a result, she would have to 'bear the burden resulting from the birth of her child alone, without the child's father being able to ease that burden'.[55]

A similar positive turn can be discerned in the jurisprudence of the ECtHR. In the 2012 Grand Chamber case of *Konstantin Markin*,[56] a Russian serviceman claimed the right to three years of parental leave to look after his three children, for whom he was the sole carer after his divorce. The Russian Labour Code of 2001 had generous provisions for maternity and parental leave for civilian parents. However, whereas servicewomen were entitled to the full package of maternity and parental benefits available to their civilian counterparts, a serviceman was not entitled to any leave except if his wife had died in childbirth or he was bringing up a child left without maternal care. Even then, he was only entitled to three months' leave. The Russian Constitutional Court, in rejecting his challenge, reiterated the legitimacy of having regard to 'the special social role of women associated with motherhood'.[57] The ECtHR, however, rejected this approach. Instead, it drew a bright line between maternity leave, 'which is intended to enable the woman to recover from the childbirth and to breastfeed her baby if she so wishes', and parental leave and allowances which 'relate to the subsequent period and are intended to enable a parent concerned to stay at home to look after an infant personally'. This allowed the Court, like the ECJ in *Roca Alvarez*, to dispose of the comparator problem without much trouble. 'Whilst being aware of the differences which may exist between mother and father in their relationship with the child, the Court concludes that, as far as the role of

---

[53] See Equal Treatment Directive, Art 2(4).
[54] *Roca Álvarez v Sesa Start España ETT SA* (n 52) para 36.
[55] ibid para 37.
[56] *Markin v Russia* [2012] Eq LR 489, paras 132–33.
[57] ibid para 34.

taking care of the child during the period corresponding to parental leave is concerned, men and women are "similarly placed." It follows from the above that for the purposes of parental leave the applicant, a serviceman, was in an analogous situation to servicewomen.'[58] As in *Roca Alvarez*, the government in *Markin* claimed that the provision of maternity leave to servicewomen and not to servicemen was a measure of positive discrimination. The Grand Chamber gave short shrift to this argument. Instead, it agreed with the applicant 'that such difference has the effect of perpetuating gender stereotypes and is disadvantageous both to women's careers and to men's family life'.

The notion of the 'special relationship' of the mother and child has not, however, been entirely eclipsed. This can be seen in the case of *Moselle* in 2020, which concerned a collective agreement that provided leave to female workers who bring up children on their own but not to fathers in a similar position.[59] The Court was asked for a preliminary ruling as to whether this constituted direct discrimination on grounds of sex, or whether it fell within the exception for provisions as protecting pregnancy and maternity.[60] The Court held that leave can legitimately be reserved to the mother only if it is intended to protect her biological condition and 'the special relationship between her and her child in the period following childbirth'. However, it reiterated that so far as the status of a parent is concerned, the situation of male workers and female workers is comparable where it concerns the bringing up of children. The distinction between pregnancy and parenting is encouraging. However, the continued invocation of the 'special relationship' reflects an ongoing tension. On the one hand, the Court relies on this special relationship to justify leave which is exclusive to mothers. On the other hand, it stresses that protecting the special relationship of a woman and her child is not sufficient to exclude fathers from the benefit of the additional leave in question. It is therefore left to the referring court to determine whether the leave was intended to protect workers in connection with the effects of pregnancy, bearing in mind its length, conditions of entitlement, and the legal protections attached to that leave.

---

[58] ibid paras 132–33.

[59] *Syndicat CFTC du personnel de la Caisse primaire d'assurance maladie de la Moselle v Caisse primaire d'assurance maladie de la Moselle* (n 51).

[60] Directive 2006/54 Article 2(1)(a), Art 28.

III EQUAL PAY

The pay gap between men and women has been a stubborn and chronic feature of the labour force everywhere, proving impervious to straightforward legal solutions.[61] Equal pay legislation therefore needs to be crafted in ways which can respond to its root causes. As in other areas, the starting point has been limited to the principle that likes should be treated alike. The primary model has thus been legislation requiring equal pay for women doing the same or like work as men. This targets blatant discrimination, such as separate pay scales for men and women doing the same work.[62] In Canada, most jurisdictions[63] had introduced such legislation by the end of the 1950s.[64] In the US, Congress enacted the Equal Pay Act in 1963 guaranteeing equal pay for the same work for women and men, while in the UK the Equal Pay Act was enacted in 1970 but only came into force in 1975. In India, the Equal Remuneration Act 1976 required employers to provide equal pay to men and women performing the same work or work of a similar nature.[65] It has been replaced by the Code on Wages 2019 which extend this to all genders.

The removal of such flagrant pay discrimination is not, however, sufficient to resolve the pay gap between men and women. Equal pay legislation must go further and address the widespread undervaluation of women's work. Women are clustered in low paying and often precarious work, such as care, cleaning, and catering. Because of the assumption that this work can be done unpaid in the home, such work has been paid at significantly lower rates than predominantly male work. However, 'women's work' often includes similar levels of responsibility, skill, and effort. To make real progress requires a principle of 'work of equal value'. Rather than a focus on the content of the job, equal value insists on a comparison between the essential requirements (such as skill, effort, and responsibility), in the woman's job as compared to the man's. For example, the manual dexterity required for sewing has often been undervalued compared to heavy and dirty work. Equal value is particularly important when extensive job segregation makes it unlikely that there is a male comparator doing like work in the same establishment. Legislation

---

[61] See Chapter 2.

[62] ibid.

[63] Canada has fourteen jurisdictions with power to determine labour laws: one federal, ten provincial, and three territorial districts.

[64] P McDermott, 'Equal Pay in Canada' in F Eyraud (ed), *Equal Pay Protection in Industrialized Market Economies* (International Labour Office 1993) 43.

[65] Equal Remuneration Act, 1976 (India), ss 4 and 5.

should therefore go further than equal pay for like work, to entitle women to equal pay for work of equal value. This was recognized by the ILO as early as 1951, with the ILO Equal Remuneration Convention (No 100) which required Member States to provide equal pay for men and women for work of equal value. However, it was not until the 1970s that some countries began to adopt this concept.

The concept of equal value has radical potential. But it is not enough on its own. At least five further elements are required. First, widespread job segregation means that women often work in separate establishments from men doing work of equal value. For example, since nursery school-teachers are almost entirely female, a nursery teacher might have no male comparator doing work of equal value in her nursery school. Unless comparisons can be drawn between establishments, or even across industries, women in such segregated work will not benefit from equal pay legislation. Secondly, even where women work in mixed establishments, they frequently predominate in the lowest grades. Although they are not doing work of equal value, there are often disproportionately large differentials between their pay and those of the higher, predominantly male grades. This will not be captured by provisions which only concern equal pay for work of equal value, but requires provision for proportionate pay for proportionate value. Thirdly, where protection is limited to standard employment contracts, employers will have an incentive to classify workers as self-employed in order to avoid equal pay liability. Yet women predominate in precarious work, including part-time, agency, and informal work. The fourth element relates to the width of a justification defence, and whether employers can rely on costs or other indirectly discriminatory reasons to justify paying women less than men doing work of equal value. Finally, the adjudicative structure might itself prove an obstacle to successful equal pay litigation. Reliance on individuals to bring claims showing a one-to-one comparison with a male worker has been tortuously slow and complex, with the result that claimants might have left the employment or even died before the claim is resolved. Employers contest preliminary points wherever possible, drawing out the process and creating vast legal costs. These issues will be examined in more detail later.

It is because of the systematic undervaluation of women's work that women are the focus of ILO Convention No 100, but these patterns can also be found among other disadvantaged groups. This section will concentrate on the gender pay gap. However, attention will also be paid to other grounds, such as race, religion, and disability, and in particular to the intersection between these characteristics and gender. In the final section, alternate means of addressing the gender pay gap will be considered.

(i) Equal Value: A Radical Possibility

The concept of equal pay for work of equal value was introduced into EU law in 1975,[66] and thereby became binding on all EU Member States, including the UK. Article 157 of the EU Treaty now provides: 'Each Member State shall ensure that the principle of equal pay for male and female workers for equal work or work of equal value is applied.' Article 157 is a particularly powerful provision as it has direct effect in the Member States, both vertically and horizontally.[67] This means that, in proceedings in domestic courts in the Member States, parties can rely on Article 157 even in the absence of domestic legislation. Moreover, it binds both private and public employers. This has met resistance from some employers. As recently as 2021, Tesco, a large supermarket in the UK facing a wave of equal value claims, claimed that direct effect only applied to equal pay for like work, not to equal pay for work of equal value. This argument was resoundingly defeated by the ECJ. The provisions on equal value are clear and precise, the Court held, and there is no need for further implementing provisions.[68]

Equal value was incorporated into the British Equal Pay Act 1970 in response to the EU Equal Pay Directive of 1975. The British EA 2010 now provides for the right to equal pay for: (i) like work; (ii) work rated as equivalent under an employer-initiated job evaluation scheme; or (iii) work of equal value.[69] Like the ILO, it specifies that value must be determined by reference to factors such as effort, skill, and decision making. In Canada, provisions requiring equal pay for work of equal value were called for by the Commission on the Status of Women in 1970,[70] and incorporated into the Canadian Human Rights Act 1985.[71] Several provinces, including Quebec and Ontario, followed suit. Canadian pay equity legislation similarly states that the value of job classes should be based on factors such as skill, effort, responsibility, and working conditions.[72] In South Africa, it was not until 2014 that equal

---

[66] Equal Pay Directive 75/117/EEC.
[67] Case 43/75 *Defrenne v Sabena* [1976] ECR 455 (ECJ).
[68] Case C-624/19 *K v Tesco Stores Ltd* [2021] 6 WLUK (ECJ).
[69] UK EA 2010, ss 64–80.
[70] 'Report of the Royal Commission on the Status of Women in Canada' (1970) paras 236–37.
[71] s 11.
[72] Ontario Pay Equity Act, s 6; see also Canadian Human Rights Act 1985, s 11.

pay for work of equal value was introduced.[73] Legislation now states: 'A difference in terms and conditions of employment between employees of the same employer performing the same or substantially the same work or work of equal value that is directly or indirectly based on any one or more of the grounds listed in subsection (1), is unfair discrimination.'[74] By contrast, in the US as we saw in Chapter 2, the federal government is largely hostile to the possibility of comparable worth legislation. Only a small number of States have enacted such legislation, limited to public service employees.[75] Similarly, in India, when the Equal Remuneration Act 1976 was replaced by the Code on Wages in 2019, rather than using the opportunity to introduce the concept of equal value, the language of the 'same work or work of similar nature' was retained.[76]

The concept of equal pay for work of equal value has the potential to revolutionize women's role in the workforce. By penetrating job labels to examine the characteristics of women's work, the notion of equal value opens up dramatic possibilities for transcending evaluations of women's work which depend on deeply held stereotypes and entrenched inequalities in women's bargaining power. Properly handled, the concept of equal value reveals the extent to which women's work shares characteristics usually attributed only to men's work, such as heavy work and responsibility. It also requires recognition of chronically undervalued elements of women's work, such as manual dexterity and caring. As a result, a cook has been compared to a carpenter; a home help to a refuse collector; and learning support assistants to painters, drivers, and street cleaners.

The right to equal pay for work of equal value can therefore achieve a rare synthesis of the redistributive, recognition, and participative dimensions of equality identified in Chapter 1. The redistributive dimension is central to the mission of equal pay legislation: by correcting inequalities in pay, it clearly has the potential to redress disadvantage experienced by women because of their gender. Moreover, the concept of equal value acknowledges that many of these distributive consequences are a direct result of the underlying recognition harms, namely, the undervaluation of certain types of

---

[73] Employment Equity Amendment Act (EEAA) (47 of 2013), s 6(4) and (5).
[74] ibid s 6(4).
[75] J Bellace, 'Equal Pay in the United States' in Eyraud (n 64) 159.
[76] Rishika Sahgal, 'Equal Pay for Equal Work? Flaws in the Indian Law' (*Oxford Human Rights Hub Blog*, 6 December 2019) <https://ohrh.law.ox.ac.uk/equal-pay-for-equal-work-flaws-in-the-indian-law> accessed 1 August 2022.

work because it has traditionally been done by women.[77] Indeed, a central cause of unequal pay is the absence of full recognition of the value of women's work. The redistributive and recognition dimensions of equal value together enhance women's ability to participate as equal citizens in the labour market, thus furthering the participative dimension.

At the same time, care needs to be taken to ensure that the ways in which value is set do not replicate the assumptions that have always made male work appear more valuable. For example, responsibility for money or equipment is frequently given a higher value than the responsibility entailed in caring for others. This reflects the assumption that such work can be performed un-paid in the home and does not therefore attract a market value. Other char-acteristics of 'women's work' which might be ignored or undervalued include long periods of concentration on computers; training and orienting new staff; handling complaints; and cleaning offices or hospital wards.[78] It is thus important that legislation requires job evaluation to be non-discriminatory, and gives workers the opportunity to challenge systems which are potentially discriminatory. In the UK, it is possible to challenge an employer-initiated job evaluation study on the basis that it is discriminatory. If this complaint succeeds, the tribunal will allow an independent job evaluation. However, the UK definition of what counts as discriminatory is unnecessarily re-strictive, applying only to systems which openly set different values for men and women.[79] To properly achieve a synthesis of the redistributive and rec-ognition dimensions of substantive equality, more care needs to be taken in identifying these risks of in-built biases.

The concept of equal value is less adept at changing underlying struc-tures, and therefore addressing the transformative dimension. For example, a major achievement of equal pay legislation has been to give part-time workers the right to receive equal pay pro rata for their work. Since women predominate among part-time workers, this has been an important step for-ward. However, it has not changed the underlying structure whereby women are primarily responsible for childcare. Therefore, part-time work, while somewhat better paid, has remained predominantly female. More specific-ally, the radical potential of equal value has been drastically restricted by con-tinued adherence within equal pay legislation to more formal conceptions of

---

[77] S Fredman, 'Redistribution and Recognition: Reconciling Inequalities' (2007) 23 South African J Human Rights 214.

[78] M Oelz, S Olney, and M Tomei, *Equal Pay: An Introductory Guide* (ILO 2013).

[79] EA 2010, s 65(4) and (5).

equality, and especially the principle that the right to equality entails no more than treating likes alike. These limits are considered in more detail below.

(ii) Treat Likes Alike: The Male Comparator

Equal pay legislation has always been limited by a narrow understanding of the scope of comparison. Which man can a woman compare herself to? Under UK equal pay legislation, the notion that likes should be treated alike receives a particularly concrete formulation. A woman can only claim equal pay if she is paid less than a man doing equal work and employed contemporaneously for the same employer at the same or 'equivalent' establishment.[80] Not only must the comparator be employed by the same employer; he must also be at the same establishment. Nor is there any possibility of a 'hypothetical' comparator as is the case for direct discrimination claims. This severely curtails the reach of equal pay legislation. As we have seen, one of the chief causes of low pay among women is the fact that so many women work in segregated workplaces or in the lower grades of mixed professions. A woman working in a segregated workplace is unlikely to find a male comparator doing equal work for higher pay at the same establishment.

Under the EA 2010, this is somewhat mitigated by permitting A to compare herself with B if B is employed by the same employer at a different establishment in situations in which 'common terms apply at the establishments (either generally or as between A and B)'.[81] This opaque formulation has given employers multiple opportunities to contest claims at this threshold stage before the evaluation can take place. Indeed, there have been four cases in the UK Supreme Court and one in the ECJ determining the meaning of this formulation in preliminary proceedings. Several principles have emerged, although not without contestation. The first is that establishments can be compared where the woman and the male comparator are covered by the same collective agreement. Thus, in *Leverton*,[82] a nursery nurse worked at a nursery school, a paradigmatically segregated workplace, with no available male comparators. She was entitled to compare herself with a male clerical worker working for the same authority at the town hall because both job classes were covered by the same collective agreement.[83]

---

[80] ibid s 79.
[81] ibid.
[82] *Leverton v Clwyd County Council* [1984] IRLR 28 (HL).
[83] ibid.

This principle is helpful for segregated workplaces in those parts of the labour force where there are still collective agreements which span more than one workplace. However, these conditions are increasingly difficult to meet, due to the steep decline in collective bargaining, particularly in the private sector, and the technical approach of courts to the interpretation of the statutory provisions. Moreover, where several collective agreements cover different parts of the workforce, a woman's right to equal pay might depend on historical patterns of collective bargaining.[84] This was the case in *British Coal v Steel*,[85] where women canteen workers and cleaners, again a paradigmatically female and undervalued occupation, sought to compare themselves to surface mineworkers, an overwhelmingly male and better paid group of workers. Although they were employed by the same employer, many worked at different establishments and their terms and conditions were covered by a variety of collective agreements. As in most of these cases, the claim affected numerous women workers, working at forty-seven different British Coal establishments. For Lord Slynn, it was obvious why a woman was not limited to comparing herself with men employed in the same workplace: 'Otherwise an employer could arrange things to ensure that only women worked at a particular establishment or that no man who could reasonably be considered as a possible comparator could work there.'[86] The court therefore sought to provide an alternative pathway for cross-establishment comparisons even in the absence of a collective agreement covering both workplaces. If there are no male comparators at the claimant's place of work, it held, a cross-establishment comparison can be drawn where like terms and conditions would apply if men were employed at her establishment in the particular jobs concerned.[87]

However, this formulation was equally opaque, inviting further contestation from employers at the preliminary stages. In *North v Dumfries Council*,[88] 251 women classroom assistants and nursery nurses, employed at schools operated by Dumfries Council, sought equality of pay with male manual workers, including road workers and refuse collectors, employed by the same council and doing work of equal value. But the comparators were neither based at their schools, nor employed under the same collective agreement. Nor was there a real likelihood that the male workers might have been

---

[84] *South Tyneside Metropolitan Borough Council v Anderson* [2007] ICR 1581 (CA).
[85] *British Coal Corpn v Smith* [1996] ICR 515 (HL).
[86] ibid 525H.
[87] ibid 526.
[88] *Dumfries and Galloway Council v North* [2009] ICR 1363 (EAT).

employed at the schools. The employers again took a preliminary point all the way to the Supreme Court, arguing that the formula in *British Coal* did not apply where in practice the relevant male comparators would never be employed in their current jobs in the same place as women. Their argument was rejected by the Supreme Court. Instead, it held that the question was simply whether, if the comparators were transferred to do their present jobs in a different location, however unlikely, they would remain employed on the same or broadly similar terms and conditions to those applicable in their current place of work. Lady Hale reiterated that the object of the legislation is to allow comparisons between workers who would never work in the same workplace, for example a manufacturing company where (female) clerical workers worked in an office and (male) factory workers worked in a factory.[89] 'It is well known that those jobs which require physical strength have traditionally been better rewarded than those jobs which require dexterity. It is one of the objects of the equality legislation to iron out those traditional inequalities of reward where the work involved is of genuinely equal value.'[90] Importantly, too, she stressed that this was only the first hurdle the claimants needed to overcome. Claimants are still required to prove that the work is actually of equal value, and the employer has the opportunity to show that the difference was due to a material factor which was not the difference in sex. 'The "same employment" test should not be used as a proxy for those tests or as a way of avoiding the often difficult and complex issues which they raise (tempting though this may be for large employers faced with multiple claims such as these).'[91]

This must surely be the right approach. If it is believed that there might be good reasons why a woman is paid less than a man doing work of equal value at a different establishment of the same employer, this should be raised as part of a justification defence.[92] A regional differentiation, such as a London weighting, might well be justified in this way. Allowing complex skirmishes on the threshold question of cross-establishment comparison has simply protracted proceedings and allowed employers to delay implementation of the right to equal pay by many years. The *Dumfries* case, for example, began in 2006. But it was not until 2013 that the Supreme Court held that the first

---

[89] ibid [30].
[90] ibid [34].
[91] ibid [35].
[92] EA 2010, s 69.

hurdle had been surmounted. Job evaluation, justification, and other key steps still needed to be taken.

Despite Lady Hale's attempts to smooth the process of agreeing cross-establishment comparison, large employers continue to contest this point in an attempt to protract potentially very costly equal pay claims. Two large supermarkets, Tesco and Asda, took this approach when faced with multiple claims by low paid women workers. The *Asda* case, which reached the UK Supreme Court in 2021, was brought by 7,000 workers, overwhelmingly women, employed in Asda supermarkets.[93] They claimed that their work was of equal value to that of the male workforce at Asda's distribution depots, who were paid substantially more and worked at locations separate from the retail stores. The claim was part of a much larger claim, originally brought by 35,000 retail workers, and potentially affected many of the 133,000 workers at about 630 supermarkets owned by Asda.[94] The stakes were high for Asda: if the women were successful, Asda faced claims for backpay which could reach into the millions. But the stakes were even higher for the women workers, who were low paid, non-unionized workers, whose pay and conditions had lagged well behind their male counterparts doing work of equal value in the distribution centres. It is not surprising, then, that the employers protracted the procedure by taking preliminary points all the way to the Supreme Court, despite having been unsuccessful in the employment tribunal, the Employment Appeal Tribunal, and the Court of Appeal.

Asda argued that the retail workers and distribution workers were not employed on 'common terms' as required by the legislation, because they were at different locations and had different terms and conditions of employment. The Supreme Court roundly rejected their argument. Lady Arden held that there was a short and direct answer to the case, provided by the *North* case. The single aim, which emerged from the three preceding decisions, was to enable claimants to use comparators from a different establishment if the latter's terms and conditions could be transposed either in fact or in theory to the claimants' establishment. Crucially, this means that at this stage of the claim there is no need to establish, as the employment tribunal had attempted to do, whether the comparators' terms and conditions are equivalent to those of the claimant. This latter question belongs to a later stage in the proceedings. The need to address the 'common terms' requirement only arises because there may be differences due to geography. This should not

---

[93] *Asda Stores v Brierley* [2021] UKSC 10 (UK Sup Ct).
[94] ibid [7].

be allowed to stop claims *in limine* just because, as events turn out, there are different employment regimes—for example, as in this case, where the distribution workers were covered by a collective agreement but the retail workers were not. Thus, all the tribunal needed to do was ask whether, assuming the distribution depot was physically located at the same site as the retail stores, their terms and conditions would remain the same.

The case is of great importance for segregated establishments of the same employer. The result of the four cases combined means that an employer cannot avoid an equal pay claim merely by allocating groups of employees to separate sites. The case is also of great importance for the ability of future claimants to withstand protracted preliminary proceedings. As Lady Arden stressed, cases not meeting the threshold test are likely to be exceptional, making this issue relatively incidental to the principal stages in an equal pay claim. The employment tribunal should not allow a prolonged inquiry into the threshold test, she held, and appeals on this issue should be discouraged. Employers will have ample time, she stressed, to show that pay disparities are justified either at the job evaluation stage or at the justification defence stage. Lady Arden's conclusion should be heeded: 'The aim of the equal pay legislation is to remove pay disparities that are endemic in some pay awards and which do not properly reflect the value of the work for which they are paid. If in the absence of firm case-management, the threshold test is elevated into a major hurdle mirroring other elements of an equal pay claim, the purpose of equal pay legislation will be thwarted, and the pay disparities will not be investigated.'[95]

EU law contains some promise of a clearer pathway to cross-establishment comparisons. In the early case of *Defrenne*,[96] the ECJ held that inter-industry comparisons were too complex to give rise to directly enforceable rights without domestic legislation. Nevertheless, it left open the possibility of a comparison between employees in the 'same service'. This formula was refined in later cases to refer to a single source which was responsible for the inequality and could restore equal treatment. It was this avenue that the shopworkers in the *Tesco* case pursued in order to compare their work with better paid workers in Tesco's distribution centres. They were successful, but only after the case had proceeded all the way to the ECJ to decide the issue as a preliminary point.[97] Importantly, the Court held that Article 157 could

---

[95] ibid [71].
[96] Case 43/75 *Defrenne* [1976] ECR 455; see further *Scullard v Knowles* [1996] IRLR 344 (EAT).
[97] Case C-624/19 *K v Tesco Stores* [2021] 3 CMLR 33 (ECJ).

be relied on in relation to a comparator with the same employer but in a different establishment, provided the employer of both the claimant and the comparator could be regarded as a 'single source'. In other words, the employer should be responsible for the inequality and in a position to restore equal treatment. In this case, the Court held, Tesco Stores constituted such a single source to which the pay and conditions of shopworkers and distribution centres could be attributed, and which could be responsible for any discrimination. It is, however, for the referring tribunal to determine this issue on the facts of the case. The success of the workers at this stage is therefore only a threshold victory, with much of the hard work in establishing equal value still to be conducted.

The EU concept of a 'single source' is a much simpler formula than the one developed by the UK Supreme Court. By permitting cross-establishment comparisons in most cases where the employer has control over setting terms and conditions, it sidesteps the complex requirements of the 'common terms and conditions' formula and the technicalities of the 'North hypothetical'. However, its applicability in the UK after Brexit is still unclear. The case fell within the twelve-month window specified in the Withdrawal Agreement for the ECJ to retain jurisdiction, making it applicable to the facts of the Tesco case itself. Whether it can continue to apply, however, is still to be determined. UK courts have begun to develop criteria for continuing to apply EU law, which suggests, inter alia, that courts in the UK will not depart from EU law where there has been no change in domestic law.[98] However, this jurisprudence is still in the very early stages, and it remains to be seen how it will apply. No further guidance was available from Asda, where the Supreme Court held that since the case could be resolved on the basis of the North hypothetical, it was unnecessary to decide whether the claimants could succeed on the basis of a 'single source' where the common terms requirement is not met.[99]

These cases concern different establishments of the same employer. They do not address the even more challenging situation in which, due to intense job segregation, the only potential comparators are employed by a different employer. Since the 1980s, there has been an increasing tendency to cut costs in the public sector in many countries by contracting out services previously carried out in-house. This has led to the replacement of many public

[98] *Lipton v BA City Flyer* [2021] EWCA Civ 454 (UK Ct of Appeal); *Tunein Inc v Warner Music UK Ltd* [2021] EWCA Civ 441 (UK Ct of Appeal).
[99] *Asda Stores v Brierley* (n 93) [6].

sector jobs with services provided by private contractors, particularly in low paid, predominantly female-dominated areas such as cleaning and catering. Indeed, it is their ability to cut pay rates that gives private contractors the advantage in the tendering process. The result is that low paid female cleaning or catering staff who are employed by a private contractor may work in the same establishment and do work of equal value as workers employed directly by a public employer. Yet, because they are employed by a different employer, they would not be entitled to an equal pay claim under UK law.

Defrenne briefly signalled the promise of a wider scope of comparison in EU law by referring to a comparison between workers not just in the same employment but potentially in the same service. However, the ECJ very quickly withdrew the hope of a genuine broadening of the scope of comparison by substituting the need for the 'same employer' with a requirement that the respondent be responsible for the pay differential.[100] Thus in *Laurence*, the ECJ held that:

> where the differences identified in the pay and conditions of workers performing equal work or work of equal value cannot be attributed to a single source, there is no body which is responsible for the inequality and which could restore equal treatment . . . The work and the pay of those workers cannot therefore be compared on the basis of [Article 141(1) EC].[101]

The focus on responsibility makes it impossible to address institutional or structural discrimination which cannot be traced to the fault of any one individual. At the same time, it has the paradoxical effect of permitting deliberate avoidance by employers, who can minimize the scope for equal pay comparisons by contracting out and decentralizing pay structures. This was clearly demonstrated in *Allonby*,[102] where the employer transferred its part-time lecturers, who were predominantly female, to a separate employer in the form of an agency, thereby avoiding the possibility of comparison between full-time and part-time workers. The agency workers continued to do the same work at the same establishment but on considerably worse terms and conditions.

The challenges of job segregation for equal pay laws are addressed more clearly and explicitly in Canada. Crucially, rather than relying on individual claims, Canadian pay equity legislation puts the onus on the employer to establish a pay equity plan, based on the relative pay of the workforce as a

---

[100] Case C-256/01 *Allonby v Accrington & Rossendale College* [2004] IRLR 224 (ECJ).
[101] Case C-320/00 *Lawrence v Regent Office Care* [2002] ECR I-7325, paras 17–18.
[102] *Allonby v Accrington & Rossendale College* (n 100).

whole. The comparison is therefore not based on an individual complainant finding a male comparator doing work of equal value. Instead, pay equity plans compare female and male job classes. Under the Ontario Pay Equity Act 1990, a 'female job class' is one in which 60 per cent or more of the members are female, or has been denominated female by an order or a collective agreement.[103] The federal Pay Equity Act in Canada additionally regards a job class as female if it is one that is commonly associated with women due to gender-based occupational segregation.[104] Employers are required to establish a pay equity plan and to make relevant adjustments to achieve proportionate pay for proportionate value.

In segregated workplaces, such as nursing homes, where there is no possibility of a male comparator within the establishment, these Acts permit a 'proxy comparison'. Under the federal Pay Equity Act, this involves identifying a proxy employer. The proxy should be similar in that it is part of the same industry, operates in regions where the cost of living is similar, and has a similar number of employees, rates of unionization, and compensation practices. The proxy employer is asked to share information about three or more male job classes which are representative of the range of values of work not just those with similar values. The proxy employer should also share the highest salary rates for positions in the chosen job classes. These job classes are then used as 'proxy' male job classes which are treated as if the work were done at the segregated establishment.[105] The Ontario provisions, which apply to the public sector only, operate somewhat differently. They involve a 'seeking employer' finding a female job class at an establishment of another public sector employer where pay equity has already been achieved. This class becomes the 'proxy' class and is then deemed to be the appropriate 'male comparator' for the specified female job class at the original employer. For example, the workforce of a group in Ontario known as Participating Nursing Homes (PNH), operating up to 143 for-profit nursing homes in Ontario, was almost exclusively female. Nevertheless, pay equity was established by using a proxy drawn from Municipal Homes which had had some male job classes. This process was successfully followed, leading to

---

[103] Pay Equity Act (Ontario) RSO 1990, s 1 <www.ontario.ca/laws/statute/90p07> accessed 1 August 2022.
[104] Pay Equity Act SC 2018, c 27, ss 36 and 37, in force since 31 August 2021 <https://laws-lois.justice.gc.ca/eng/acts/P-4.2/page-1.html> accessed 1 August 2022.
[105] <www.canada.ca/en/services/jobs/workplace/human-rights/overview-pay-equity-act/consultation/discussion-paper.html> accessed 27 July 2022.

an increase in the compensation of all-female job classes and the establishment of pay equity at PNH by 2005.

The role of proxy comparisons has been regarded as crucial to facilitate pay equity for women in segregated public sector jobs. Indeed, when the government of Ontario attempted to repeal the proxy method, the Ontario court held that this discriminated against women in segregated public sector jobs:

> by denying them the opportunity of quantifying and correcting the systemic gender-based wage inequity from which they suffer, a benefit the [pay equity legislation] grants to other women working in the broader public sector.[106]

A further challenge confronted in Ontario, one which has also arisen in other equal value contexts, is when the gender pay gap re-emerges over time due to differential bonuses, wage increases, or other mechanisms. Indeed, this was what occurred in PNH, leading to a case before the Ontario Court of Appeal brought by unions representing registered nurses, personal support workers, and healthcare, dietary, housekeeping, and recreational aides. Notably, the Pay Equity Act requires employers subject to the Act not only to establish pay equity but also to maintain it in every establishment. The employers argued that the proxy method was no longer available in relation to maintaining pay equity. The Court of Appeal rejected this argument, finding that a proper interpretation of the Act required ongoing access to the proxy male comparators to maintain pay equity.[107] The result is once again to endorse the importance of proxy methods in segregated workplaces.

A small step towards a proxy method in the UK and EU might be to permit the use of a 'hypothetical' male comparator, as is found in the direct discrimination provisions. Instead of pointing to a male colleague, a claimant could argue that she has been less favourably treated than a man would be treated. This would facilitate equal pay claims in cases of severe job segregation. Equal pay in UK law has been traditionally separated from anti-discrimination law outside pay and conditions. This has meant that the direct discrimination provisions, which do include a hypothetical comparator, have not applied in the equal pay field. However, EU law now requires Member States to provide protection against direct discrimination in relation to pay, which would include a hypothetical comparator provision.[108] A tentative first step in this

---

[106] *SEIU, Local 204 v Ontario (Attorney General)* (1997) 151 DLR (4th) 273 (Ontario Ct of Justice).

[107] *Ontario Nurses' Association v Participating Nursing Homes*, 2021 ONCA 148 (Ontario Ct of Appeal).

[108] Recast Directive 2006/54/EC.

direction has also been taken by the EA 2010 which provides that although, as a rule, direct discrimination does not apply in relation to pay, it may do so if a sex equality clause (implying equal pay into the contract) 'has no effect'.[109] Arguably, then, direct discrimination, with its hypothetical comparator, would apply in a situation in which a sex equality clause has no effect due to the absence of an actual male comparator.

(iii) Consistency but not Substance

A second limitation of the reliance on the principle of treating likes alike in the context of equal pay is that it requires consistent treatment but does not dictate any substantive content. The principle will be satisfied even if both the man and the woman are equally badly paid. If the only appropriate male comparator is equally badly paid, equal pay laws are therefore of no assistance to a low paid woman. Yet this fails to address the structural causes of the gender pay gap. Men who work at a 'woman's' rate are most likely to be doing so in a transitory fashion, either as students or as a route to promotion.[110] Women, by contrast, tend to remain in such jobs throughout their working lives.

The adherence to consistency rather than substance also means that the requirement that likes be treated alike could be fulfilled by lowering men's pay to that of women's, rather than raising women's pay to that of men's. This issue became a major source of contention in local government in the UK.[111] A far-reaching job evaluation scheme was agreed, promising to bring about a radical change in relation to undervalued women's work. However, several local authorities, in the absence of appropriate government funding, threatened to reduce men's pay instead of increasing that of women. In other words, relatively low paid men would be footing the bill for achieving equality of pay with very low paid women. This solution, not surprisingly, proved deeply unpalatable to male workers. In response, instead of raising women's pay to that of men's, a number of local authority employers agreed to 'protect' the pay of the adversely affected (predominantly male) grades for periods of up to three years. The effect was simply to preserve the pay gap between men and women. This, in turn, led to further litigation by women, claiming equal

---

[109] EA 2010, ss 70–71.
[110] J Rubery, *The Economics of Equal Value*, Research Discussion Series No 3 (Equal Opportunities Commission 1992) 50.
[111] See further S Fredman, 'Reforming Equal Pay Laws' (2008) 37 ILJ 193.

pay with the men who were within the pay protection packages. In *Redcar v Bainbridge*,[112] the Court of Appeal agreed that the women would have been within the protected category had they not been the subject of past sex discrimination. However, the court did not require women's pay simply to be raised to that of men doing work of equal value. Instead, it left it open to employers to justify pay protection for male workers on the facts of the case. This was followed by a series of further cases against pay protection schemes in local authorities, where the question depended on what would amount to sufficient justification for excluding women from the protected pay grade.

In an important decision in 2017, the Court of Session in Scotland held that the question at issue was not simply whether it was reasonably necessary to offer transitional payments to those in detriment.[113] Instead, the employer should establish that it was necessary to exclude the claimants from that protection. Crucially, the court stated that consideration should have been given to extending the protection to the claimants. The court left open the possibility that the employer might argue that to extend pay protection to the claimants would have been unaffordable. However, importantly, it endorsed the decision in the earlier case of *Bury* that 'a local authority cannot prove unaffordability by mere assertion. A case of justification on this basis can only be proved by adducing sufficiently detailed evidence, both of the costs themselves, and of the financial context, to enable the Tribunal [to] reach an informed view'.[114]

(iv) Equal Treatment vs Proportionality

Equal pay legislation only requires that 'likes' should be treated 'alike'. There is no requirement that men and women be treated appropriately according to their difference. This leaves the law powerless to address the common situation in which a woman is doing work which is admittedly of less value than that of a man, but the difference in pay is disproportionately large relative to the difference in value. A claim lies only in extreme cases where the woman is doing work of greater value but is paid less. In such a case, the ECJ has recognized that to exclude the claim would be to go against the

---

[112] *Redcar and Cleveland Borough Council v Bainbridge; Middlesbrough Borough Council v Surtees* [2008] EWCA Civ 885.

[113] *Glasgow City Council v Unison* [2017] CSIH 34 (Scottish Ct of Session).

[114] *Bury MBC v Hamilton* [2011] ICR 655 (EAT); *Glasgow City Council v Unison* ibid [60].

spirit of the legislation.[115] The UK courts have therefore held that a woman could compare her pay to that of a man doing work of less value. In *Redcar v Bainbridge*,[116] in a highly segregated workforce, female catering employees and care workers were unable to find an appropriate male comparator doing equal work. Instead, they were permitted to compare themselves with refuse collectors, who were on lower grades but better paid. However, the remedy was to award the woman the same pay as the man on the lower grade, instead of the higher pay which was appropriate to her grade. Moreover, this is limited to extreme cases where women are doing work of greater value. It does not deal with disproportionate pay differentials in cases in which a woman is doing work of lower value.

This can be contrasted with pay equity regimes in Canada, which recognize the importance not just of equal pay, but of pay which is proportionate to the value assigned to the job. Proportional value schemes look at the relationship between the value of the work performed and the compensation received by male job classes. The same ratio should then be applied to the relationship between value and compensation for female job classes. The Ontario Pay Equity Act specifies that pay equity is achieved when the relationship between the value of the work performed and the compensation received is the same for both female and male job classes.[117] To take a very simplified example, assume that a predominantly male job class consisting of sales representatives receives 561 value points and the job rate is 26.00. The relationship of value to compensation is 0.046. Compare this with a customer service clerk in a predominantly female job class, where the job is given 391 value points and the job rate is 17.00. The relationship of value to compensation is 0.043, less than that of the sales representatives. While the work is clearly not of equal value, the compensation is disproportionately low. To achieve pay equity, the customer service clerk's compensation should be calculated by multiplying the value by 0.046 rather than 0.043. This brings their job rate up from 17.00 to 18.12.[118] While acknowledging that her work is of less value than that of the sales representatives, this approach nevertheless

---

[115] *Murphy v Bord Telecom Eireann* [1988] ICR 445 (ECJ).

[116] *Redcar and Cleveland Borough Council v Bainbridge; Middlesbrough Borough Council v Surtees* (n 112).

[117] Ontario Pay Equity Act, s 21.3(1). See <www.payequity.gov.on.ca/en/LearnMore/Tools/Pages/regression_plan.aspx> accessed 27 July 2022.

[118] This highly simplified example is drawn from figures given at <www.payequity.gov.on.ca/en/LearnMore/Tools/Pages/regression_males.aspx> accessed 1 August 2022.

leads to recognition of the appropriate compensation for the value of her work relative to others in the establishment.

(v) Competing Priorities: Justifying Unequal Pay for Equal Work

Even if a woman can show that she is being paid less than a relevant male comparator doing work of equal value, the employer is still entitled to justify the difference.[119] Under UK legislation, for example, if equal work has been established, the burden shifts to the employer to justify the inequality of pay on grounds which do not directly or indirectly involve sex.[120] In Canadian law, infringements of the equality guarantee in section 15 of the Charter can only be justified under section 1, which puts the burden on the State to show that the provision has a 'pressing and substantial objective' and that 'the means chosen to achieve that objective are proportionate to it'.[121] The presence of a justification defence for equal pay reflects a long-standing sense among policymakers that equality should not impose 'burdens on business'. Such an argument has been particularly salient in relation to equal pay, where decades of indolence in redressing the pay gap have run up a large and costly backlog. Indeed, women's right to equal pay for equal work is often represented as an unreasonable demand on resources, carrying with it an unsustainable cost. In this context, therefore, special vigilance must be exercised to ensure that the equality value is not simply subordinated to the competing self-interest of the employer. At the very least, respondents should be required to show that there is no other reasonable way to achieve a legitimate employment objective, or that the means chosen impairs the right to equal pay as little as reasonably possible.[122]

Particularly challenging are justifications which, while not explicitly based on sex, in effect reinforce existing patterns of discrimination. For example, there has been a widespread practice of paying part-timers less than full-timers for the same work. As we have seen, the fact that women remain primarily responsible for childcare has meant that the vast majority of part-time workers, in both the UK and elsewhere in the EU, are women. Can an

---

[119] EA 2010, s 69; Case 96/80 *Jenkins v Kingsgate* [1981] ECR 911 (ECJ).
[120] EA 2010, ss 64–80; Art 157 TFEU.
[121] *Quebec (AG) v APTS* [2018] 1 SCR 464, para 43 (Can Sup Ct).
[122] ibid paras 50–52.

employer justify paying a woman less than a man doing the same work on the grounds that she is part time while the male comparator works full time? This is a material factor which is not expressly based on gender but which in practice reinforces discriminatory structures.

The ECJ from early in its case law has been sensitive to this difficulty. In the seminal case of *Jenkins v Kingsgate*,[123] it was held that where a difference in pay is not directly based on sex, but in fact disproportionately affects women, it must be justified.[124] The standard of justification is searching: a difference can only be justified 'if the means chosen meet a genuine need of the enterprise, are suitable for attaining the objective pursued by the enterprise and are necessary for that purpose'.[125] Somewhat more latitude has been subsequently granted where the measure in question is a question of social policy, rather than one put in place by an individual employer. Here, rather than showing that the rule is necessary to attain a genuine need of the enterprise, the Member State must show that it could 'reasonably consider that the means chosen were suitable' for attaining 'a legitimate aim of its social policy' which is unrelated to any discrimination based on sex.[126] This descent from necessity to reasonableness has been somewhat mitigated by the ECJ's insistence that mere generalizations are not sufficient to show that the aim is unrelated to sex discrimination, and that evidence must be provided on the basis of which 'it could reasonably be considered that the means chosen were suitable for achieving that aim'.[127] Moreover, the ECJ has held that a State cannot rely on the aim of restricting public expenditure to justify a difference in treatment on grounds of sex. To hold otherwise might mean that 'the application and scope of a rule of Community law as fundamental as that of equal treatment between men and women might vary in time and place according to the state of the public finances of Member States'.[128] Properly applied, this standard can, therefore, be exacting. In *Schönheit* in 2006, it was held that while it is acceptable to pay part-timers a pro rata pension, a measure which reduces the pension by a proportion greater than warranted by her part-time work is disproportionate and cannot be objectively justified.[129]

---

[123] *Jenkins v Kingsgate* (n 119).
[124] ibid.
[125] Case 1007/84 *Bilka-Kaufhaus* [1986] IRLR 317, para 36 (ECJ).
[126] Case C-167/97 *R v Secretary of State for Employment, ex p Seymour-Smith* [1999] ECR I-623, [1999] 2 AC 554, para 77.
[127] ibid para 76.
[128] Joined Cases C-4 and 5/02 *Schönheit v Stadt Frankfurt am Main; Becker v Land Hessen* [2006] 1 CMLR 5, paras 84–5.
[129] ibid.

The courts in the UK have had more difficulty dealing with a justification defence which, while not expressly based on sex, has the effect of entrenching disadvantage. The EA 2010 has, however, moved towards resolving the problem. The statute distinguishes between two types of defence. The first is based on a material factor which is expressly based on sex. The second is one that, while not expressly treating a woman less favourably on grounds of her sex, nevertheless puts her at a particular disadvantage compared to a man doing equal work. In the second case, the burden of justification is not discharged unless the material factor cited in defence is a proportionate means of achieving a legitimate aim.[130] For example, if an employer seeks to justify paying part-time workers less on the grounds that they work part time, it would be relying on a material factor which puts women at a particular disadvantage when compared with men. In such circumstances, the defence cannot succeed unless the employer can show that paying part-time workers less is a proportionate means of achieving a legitimate aim.

The EA 2010 further introduced a provision stating that the long-term objective of reducing inequality between men's and women's terms of work is always to be regarded as a legitimate aim.[131] The means to achieve this aim must still be shown to be proportional to this long-term objective. This is an important means by which a programme of phasing in equal pay for a group as a whole can be defended against individual claims for immediate entitlements. However, it is important that the proportionality requirement is carefully observed. It would be unfortunate and regressive if this provision were used to justify long-term pay protection for men. There has, however, been little opportunity for the courts in the UK to deal with the justification defence because employers facing equal pay claims have consistently attempted to deflect cases by bringing preliminary challenges, as we have seen. In the *Asda* case in 2021, Lady Arden made it clear that cases should not be held up at these preliminary stages. The real issues, she recognized, concerned whether women were indeed doing work of equal value and, if so, whether the employer was able to justify the difference in pay. It is hoped that this will smooth the way for more substantive issues being dealt with by courts, including justification.

---

[130] EA 2010, s 69(1)(b), (2); this mirrors the proposals in ibid at 206. (This applies equally to men.)

[131] EA 2010, s 69(3).

(vi) Beyond Individual Complaints: Alternative Routes

The stubborn resistance of gender pay gaps in the face of equal pay legislation has led to calls for complementary measures, which take into account the collective nature of pay claims and harness the power of employers rather than depending on individual complaints. The most developed of these alternatives are found in Canada. Several provinces, responding to the ineffectiveness of reliance on individual complaints to achieve equal value, include proactive duties on the employer to develop and implement pay equity schemes. Thus, the purpose of the Ontario Pay Equity Act is to 'redress systemic gender discrimination in compensation for work performed by employees in female job classes'.[132] Like its Quebec equivalent, the Ontario Act imposes an obligation on employers to both establish and maintain compensation practices which provide for pay equity in all their establishments.[133] As we have seen, systemic pay discrimination is identified, not by requiring an individual to compare her pay with a male comparator, but by undertaking a comparison between female and male job classes to assess the relationship between the value of the work performed and compensation. In other words, employers are under a duty to measure pay equity, as well as correcting it.[134]

Pay equity has been held to be an integral part of the equality guarantee in section 15 of the Canadian Charter. In the 2018 case of *Quebec v AG*, the Supreme Court of Canada found that Quebec was in breach of section 15(1) when it amended the Quebec Pay Equity Act to remove the ongoing obligation to maintain pay equity. The amendments provided for five-yearly mandatory pay audits, permitting the employer to ignore retroactive pay adjustments and only requiring rectification going forward. According to Abella J:

> Although the scheme purports to address systemic discrimination, it in fact codifies the denial to women of benefits routinely enjoyed by men—namely, compensation tied to the value of their work. Men receive this compensation as a matter of course; women, under this scheme, are expected to endure five-year periods of pay inequity, and to receive equal compensation only where their employer voluntarily acts in a non-discriminatory manner, or where they can meet the heavy burden of proving the employer engaged in deliberate or improper conduct. . . . Absent such behaviour, working women are told that

---

[132] Ontario Pay Equity Act, s 4(1) and see Quebec Pay Equity Act 1996, s 1.
[133] Ontario Pay Equity Act, s 7(1).
[134] *Quebec (AG) v APTS* (n 121). For details of the scheme, see further paras 12 ff.

they must simply live with the reality that they have not been paid fairly, even where a statutorily mandated audit has made that fact clear. In this way, the scheme, by privileging employers, reinforces one of the key drivers of pay inequity: the power imbalance between employers and female workers.[135]

Despite calls for a similarly robust system of pay equity in the UK, the government instead chose to introduce a far weaker alternative, centring on pay transparency. The stated rationale is that the simple mechanisms of requiring employers to be transparent and create public reports of their gender pay gap will be sufficient impetus for change. Introduced in 2017, these provisions require large private sector employers (employing 250 or more workers) to report annually on the gender pay gaps in their institutions.[136] The same threshold applies to public sector employers in England, but it is much lower at twenty in Scotland. Notably, 'gender pay gap' is defined more widely than equal pay for work of equal value to encompass the spread of pay across the whole establishment. This casts light on occupational segregation and disproportionate pay, as well as unequal pay for work of equal value. Importantly, employers must publish information not only about pay differences but also about differences in bonuses, which are well known to contribute significantly but also invisibly to gender pay gaps. For example, in an inquiry into the gender pay gap in the financial services sector in 2009, the Equality and Human Rights Commission found that annual bonuses had a striking impact on earnings. Indeed, female full-time employees on average received only one-fifth of the annual bonuses of men working full time in the sector.[137] Transparency is also increased by requiring separate information about the proportions of male and female employees who were paid bonus pay. Finally, since much of the pay gap is due to segregation of women in lower paying grades, the regulations require employers to include the proportions of male and female employees in the lower, lower middle, upper middle, and upper quartile pay bands. The information should be published on the government portal and the organization's website. Failure to comply with the reporting requirement can lead to hefty fines. However, due to the Covid-19 pandemic, the government decided to suspend the reporting requirement in 2020, with a further extension of six months granted in 2021.

---

[135] ibid para 38.

[136] The Equality Act 2010 (Gender Pay Gap Information) Regulations 2017.

[137] Equality and Human Rights Commission, 'Financial Services Inquiry' (2009) 6 <www.equalityhumanrights.com/en/publication-download/financial-services-inquiry-sex-discrimination-and-gender-pay-gap-report> accessed 1 August 2022.

The reporting obligation depends for its efficacy entirely on the expected reputational risk to organizations with high gender pay gaps. There is no duty on private sector employers to take action to reduce the gap or indeed to even produce a plan to do so. Instead, the government encourages employers to publish a narrative explaining why the pay gap exists, and to voluntarily produce and publish an action plan for closing it. In fact, only 30 per cent of employers surveyed in 2018 had either published a specific Gender Pay Gap action plan or intended to do so, and only 16 per cent indicated that this would be published externally, for example, on their website.[138] Only in Wales is there a requirement on public sector employers to publish an action plan in cases in which the report reveals gender pay differences.

Initially, the 'name and shame' tactic appeared successful. The first two years of reporting attracted much negative publicity for companies and organizations whose published reports demonstrated striking inequalities. There was also initially a high level of compliance with the duty, with 100 per cent of eligible employers fulfilling the obligation in 2019.[139] However, a more comprehensive study of the first three years of reporting revealed a much gloomier picture. Analysis by the Equality Trust showed that despite increasing transparency, the same names have continued to appear every year on the list of those with the worst records. Even more worrying is the fact that while there has been a tiny narrowing of the gap in hourly pay (the average gender pay gap for reporting companies had decreased by a mere 0.5 per cent since 2018/19), the bonus gap has soared, increasing by as much as 178.7 per cent between the 2017/18 and the 2019/20 reporting years.[140] Indeed, in 2019/20, as many as eighty-two companies reported a gender bonus gap of 100 per cent, many of them in the public sector.[141] As the Equality Trust report puts it, this suggests that 'companies are paying men increasingly higher bonuses while placating women with minute pay rises'.[142] There are other weaknesses in the provisions. The 250 threshold is comparatively high, with many countries in Europe having a lower threshold, clustering at around fifty.[143] Similarly, the data requirements are relatively undemanding, with the

[138] James Murray, Paul Rieger, and Hannah Gorry, *Employers' Understanding of the Pay Gap and Actions to Tackle it* (Government Equalities Office, January 2019) 6.

[139] Fawcett Society, Global Institute for Women's Leadership, and Thomson Reuters Foundation, 'Gender Pay Gap Reporting: A Comparative Analysis' (2020) 17.

[140] The Equality Trust, 'UK Gender Pay Gap Reporting 2017–2020: Patterns and Progress' (September 2020).

[141] ibid.

[142] ibid 11.

[143] Fawcett Society, Global Institute for Women's Leadership, and Thomson Reuters Foundation (n 139) 17.

lack of detail making it difficult to diagnose the cause of the problem. By contrast, Australian private sector employers are required to report not just on wage levels, but also on the number of promotions and resignations, and on the gender composition of governing bodies.[144]

In the meantime, the European Commission has proposed a similar measure, in the form of a draft Pay Transparency Directive.[145] Like the UK provision, it requires employers with at least 250 employees to publish information on the pay gap between female and male workers in their organizations. The concept of pay is a wide one, including additional benefits, such as bonuses, overtime compensation, travel facilities (including cars provided by the employer), housing allowances, compensations for attending training, occupational pensions, and other complementary or variable components. Importantly, too, the draft directive requires an overall picture of gender differences in pay in the organization, such as the distribution of workers by gender in the quartile pay bands, which can demonstrate the proportion of women in the highest and the lowest paid positions. But it goes beyond the UK in proposing that, where there is a pay gap of at least 5 per cent, employers will be required to carry out a pay assessment in cooperation with workers' representatives. The aim of this joint pay assessment is to trigger mandatory action by employers to address any potential gender bias in pay. Where differences in average pay levels between male and female workers doing work of equal value cannot be objectively justified, the employer is required to take remedial measures. This is further backed up by remedies such as injunctions which can be issued by the courts or other competent bodies. Particularly important is the proposal that the courts should have the power to require the defendant to take structural or organizational measures to comply with its obligations. What is not clear, however, is whether these remedies are confined to achieving equal pay for work of equal value within the organization, or whether, as in the Canadian examples, the measures encompass a broader notion of pay equity which can address proportionate pay too.

Pay reporting for the purpose of pay equity in the US has been more contentious. Since 1966, the Equal Employment Opportunity Commission (EEOC) has required employers with 100 or more employees to file annual

---

[144] ibid 18.

[145] Proposal for a Directive of the European Parliament and of the Council to strengthen the application of the principle of equal pay for equal work or work of equal value between men and women through pay transparency and enforcement mechanisms, COM/2021/93 final <https://eur-lex.europa.eu/legal-content/EN/TXT/?uri=CELEX:52021PC0093> accessed 1 August 2022.

reports on the number of workers by job category, sex, race, and ethnicity. Federal contractors and subcontractors with more than fifty employees are also required to file reports, this time to the Office of Federal Contract Compliance Programmes (OFCCP). In 2010, the EEOC, together with other federal agencies, began seeking to identify ways to improve the enforcement of federal laws prohibiting pay discrimination. As part of this process, the value of collecting pay data from employers by sex, race, and ethnicity was recognized. This was eventually put into practice in 2016, as part of a joint programme with the OFCCP, after it had been approved by the Office of Management and Budget (OMB). However, barely a year later, once the Trump administration took office, the OMB suddenly rescinded its permission and stayed all data collection, asserting that the extra collection was unnecessarily burdensome on employers.[146] This was not, however, the end of the matter. The National Women's Law Center successfully challenged the OMB's decision before a federal court, which ordered that the EEOC should collect the data from 2017 and 2018.[147] By February 2020, the EEOC reported that more than 89 per cent of eligible employers had submitted the data. However, in a further set of twists, the EEOC issued a notice in March 2020 indicating that it would not continue to collect compensation data. The OFCCP, by contrast, decided that its own decision not to use the data was premature, and rescinded its notice to that effect. In a notice issued in September 2021, it stated that the analysis of compensation data could improve the OFCCP's ability to investigate potential pay discrimination efficiently and effectively. Such analysis could also be valuable in identifying criteria to select contractors in order to evaluate whether they were complying with their non-discrimination duties.[148]

IV SEXUAL HARASSMENT

Sexual harassment is problematic in a unique and corrosive way. Embedded in the power of the workplace, sexual harassment has been an insidious

---

[146] Narrative in the section is taken from *National Women's Law Centre v Office of Management and Budget* 358 F Supp 3d 66 (2019) (US District Ct, District of Columbia); and OFCCP, 'Rescission of Notice of Intention Not To Request, Accept or Use Employer Information Report (EEO-1) Component 2 Data, November 25, 2019' (2 November 2021) <www.federalregister.gov/documents/2021/09/02/2021-18924/rescission-of-notice-of-intention-not-to-request-accept-or-use-employer-information-report-eeo-1#citation-5-p49354> accessed 1 August 2022.

[147] ibid.

[148] OFCCP (n 146).

means of maintaining patriarchal structures in which women can only be included if they submit to unwanted sexual advances and other demeaning behaviours. As destructive as it is in ordinary relationships, sexual harassment is particularly so in the workplace, where it is imbued with the power of male supervisors or colleagues. Even if the harasser has no particular authority in the workplace, he has the power of patriarchy to make the workplace intolerable. At the same time, sexual harassment strips away a woman's identity as a participant in the enterprise, and instead reduces her to a mere sexual object.

For decades, sexual harassment has been legitimized by both law and culture. Empirical evidence has consistently revealed its scale. The risk of harassment is highest among groups which are already vulnerable in other ways: women with irregular or precarious employment contracts; women in non-traditional jobs; women with disabilities; and racialized women. LGBTQI+ and non-binary people, as well as young men, are also particularly vulnerable. But it was not until the 1970s that the pioneering work of feminists forced the issue into the public light.[149] Foremost amongst them was Catharine MacKinnon, who defines sexual harassment as 'the unwanted imposition of sexual requirements in the context of a relationship of unequal power'.[150] Legislative recognition was nevertheless slow in coming, leaving the initial battles to be fought in courts on the basis of existing definitions of sex discrimination. While some important progress has been made, this is limited by the inherent weaknesses of the equality principle, on the one hand, and judicial reluctance to transcend traditional assumptions, on the other. When statutory changes have been instituted, they too have generally relied on interpreting 'sex discrimination' to incorporate sexual harassment. Some, however, the EU in particular, have turned to dignity as the normative foundation and organizing principle of the legal prohibition of sexual harassment. Tackling the underlying power of patriarchy, which reinforces itself through sexual harassment, has proved much more elusive.

Recognition of sexual harassment as a species of sex discrimination was first articulated by the US federal Court of Appeals in 1977 in *Barnes v Castle*.[151] The lower court had rejected the plaintiff's suit on the grounds that it amounted to no more than a claim 'that she was discriminated against, not because she was a woman, but because she refused to engage in a sexual affair with her supervisor'.[152] The Court of Appeals recognized the centrality

---

[149] C MacKinnon, *Sexual Harassment of Working Women* (Yale UP 1979).
[150] ibid 1.
[151] *Barnes v Castle* 561 F 2d 983 (1977) (US Federal Ct of Appeals).
[152] ibid 990.

of her gender. 'Appellant's gender, just as much as her cooperation, was an indispensable factor in the job-retention condition of which she complains, absent a showing that the supervisor imposed a similar condition upon a male co-employee.'[153] This reliance on a direct comparison with a male comparator is, however, limited. Other courts have emphasized the uniquely demeaning nature of sexual harassment. In the UK, in the 1986 case of *Porcelli v Strathclyde*, Lord Elmslie found it to be 'a particularly degrading and unacceptable form of treatment which it must be taken to have been the intention of Parliament to restrain.'[154] Much more recently, the Indian Supreme Court similarly grounded the prohibition on sexual harassment in the value of dignity. In *Vishaka*, it held that gender equality includes protection from sexual harassment and the right to work with dignity, which is a universally recognized basic human right.[155] It is only the Supreme Court of Canada, however, which has expressly linked dignity to the imbalance of power. In *Janzen v Platy*, Dickson CJ stated: 'When sexual harassment occurs in the workplace, it is an abuse of both economic and sexual power. Sexual harassment is a demeaning practice, one that constitutes a profound affront to the dignity of the employees forced to endure it. By requiring an employee to contend with unwelcome sexual actions or explicit sexual demands, sexual harassment in the workplace attacks the dignity and self-respect of the victim both as an employee and as a human being.'[156]

Two further important steps have been taken by the courts to fashion the principle of discrimination to address sexual harassment. One is to recognize that sexual harassment is not limited to situations in which it is directly linked to the grant or denial of an economic quid pro quo. It can also occur when conduct has the purpose or effect of creating an intimidating, hostile, or offensive working environment.[157] As the US Supreme Court put it in *Harris v Forklift*: 'When the workplace is permeated with discriminatory intimidation, ridicule, and insult that is sufficiently severe or pervasive to alter the conditions of the victim's employment and create an abusive working environment, Title VII is violated.'[158] Nor is it necessary to show tangible psychological injury.[159] A second positive step is to extend the recognition of

---

[153] ibid 992.
[154] *Strathclyde Regional Council v Porcelli* [1986] IRLR 135, 137 (Scottish Ct of Session).
[155] *Vishaka v State of Rajasthan* (1997) 6 SCC 241 (Indian Sup Ct).
[156] *Janzen v Platy Enterprises Ltd* [1989] 1 SCR 1252, para 56 (Can Sup Ct).
[157] *Meritor Savings Bank, FSB v Vinson* 477 US 57 (1986) (US Sup Ct).
[158] *Harris v Forklift Systems* 510 US 17, 21 (1993).
[159] ibid.

sexual harassment as sex discrimination to same-sex harassment. In *Oncale v Sundowner*, Scalia J emphasized that 'nothing in Title VII necessarily bars a claim of discrimination "because of . . . sex" merely because the plaintiff and the defendant (or the person charged with acting on behalf of the defendant) are of the same sex'.[160]

These developments have been reflected in statutory form in several jurisdictions. The Supreme Court of Canada's affirmation of sexual harassment as a form of sex discrimination in *Janzen v Platy*[161] is now set out in the Canadian Human Rights Act[162] and the Canadian Labour Code.[163] EU law similarly includes an express reference to sexual harassment, relying, as we have seen, on dignity as its core principle. It also includes hostile environment in the definition of sexual harassment. Thus, the EU Gender Directive defines sexual harassment as occurring 'where any form of unwanted verbal, non-verbal or physical conduct of a sexual nature occurs, with the purpose or effect of violating the dignity of a person, in particular when creating an intimidating, hostile, degrading, humiliating or offensive environment'.[164] The British EA 2010 contains a similar provision. The US Supreme Court has endorsed guidelines issued by the EEOC specifying that 'sexual harassment', as there defined, is a form of sex discrimination prohibited by Title VII.[165] These likewise cover both 'quid pro quo' and 'hostile environment' discrimination. In *Vishaka*, the Indian Supreme Court framed guidelines on sexual harassment in the workplace and declared the guidelines as the law of the land until the legislature took further action.[166] It was not, however, until 2013—over sixteen years later—that legislation was passed setting up workplace procedures to address sexual harassment at work.[167] In South Africa, the Employment Equity Act states that harassment is a form of unfair discrimination and is prohibited on one or a combination of grounds listed,[168]

---

[160] *Oncale v Sundowner Offshore Services* 523 US 75, 79 (1998) (US Sup Ct).
[161] *Janzen v Platy Enterprises Ltd* (n 156).
[162] s 14(1).
[163] Canada Labour Code, 247.2 and 247.3.
[164] Directive 2006/54/EC on the implementation of the principle of equal opportunities and equal treatment of men and women in matters of employment and occupation (recast), Art 2(1)(c).
[165] *Meritor Savings Bank, FSB v Vinson* (n 157).
[166] See I Jaising, 'Gender Justice and the Supreme Court' in B Kirpal and others (eds), *Supreme but not Infallible* (OUP 2000) 296.
[167] The Sexual Harassment of Women at Workplace (Prevention, Prohibition and Redressal) Act, 2013.
[168] Employment Equity Act, s 6(3).

while the Equality Act simply states: 'No person may subject any person to harassment.'[169]

As the above demonstrates, some important gains have been made for women and sexual minorities in the legal recognition of sexual harassment as sex discrimination. However, there remain several challenging issues which have often served to narrow the operation of the law. The first is the familiar problem of the role of the comparator. The recognition of sexual harassment as a species of sex discrimination initially ran into the well-known problem of finding an appropriate comparator. Courts were tempted to conclude that if a heterosexual man would have harassed a man in the same way as he harassed the woman, no discrimination on grounds of sex had occurred. This potential trap was deftly avoided in EU law by grounding sexual harassment not in sex discrimination per se, but in a separate category entailing an infringement of dignity in the workplace. There is no need to find a comparator of any sort. This has also been extended beyond sexual harassment to any kind of harassment on the basis of a protected ground. The definition in the British EA 2010 is similar.

The second challenge is the role of consent. To what extent can it be claimed that because a woman apparently voluntarily submitted, sexual harassment did not take place? Fortunately, most jurisdictions have moved away from consent to a principle of 'unwelcomeness'. In *Meritor Savings Bank*, the US Supreme Court made it clear that 'the fact that sex-related conduct was "voluntary," in the sense that the complainant was not forced to participate against her will, is not a defence to a sexual harassment suit brought under Title VII. The gravamen of any sexual harassment claim is that the alleged sexual advances were "unwelcome".[170] EU law uses the concept of 'unwanted' conduct, and this is echoed in the British EA 2010. However, the courts are reluctant to allow a purely subjective standard, interposing a 'reasonableness' criterion on the basis that mere offence should not be sufficient.[171] As ever, reasonableness is frequently the purveyor of implicit assumptions by male judges as to what is acceptable. Particularly problematic is the fact that the US Supreme Court has held that evidence as to a respondent's 'sexually provocative' speech and dress can be admitted.[172]

---

[169] Equality Act, s 11.
[170] *Meritor Savings Bank, FSB v Vinson* (n 157).
[171] EA 2010, s 26(4); *Meritor Savings v Vinson* ibid: 'mere utterance of an . . . epithet which engenders offensive feelings in a employee', does not sufficiently affect the conditions of employment to implicate Title VII.
[172] *Meritor Savings Bank, FSB v Vinson* ibid.

A third challenge concerns the extent to which an employer can be held to be liable for acts of sexual harassment perpetrated against an employee in the workplace, whether by co-workers, supervisors, or even third parties such as customers or clients. Health and safety legislation already creates standards of strict liability on the part of employers for the safety of their workers, and indeed there have been well-supported proposals in the UK to introduce a mandatory duty on employers to protect workers from harassment and victimization in the workforce. Breach of the proposed duty should be an unlawful act with substantial financial penalties, enforced by the Equality and Human Rights Commission.[173] Such a duty would lighten the heavy burden on an individual claimant to bring a complaint in situations in which they are already vulnerable and exposed.

However, reflecting judges' preference for a fault-based, individualized understanding of sexual harassment, courts have limited employers' liability to the provision of internal procedures for the resolution of sexual harassment complaints. The US Supreme Court has held that an employer can be liable, not just for quid pro quo sexual harassment, but also for the hostile environment created by a supervisor. Nevertheless, the Court has made it relatively easy for an employer to mount a defence,[174] by focusing entirely on complaints procedures. An employer may defend against such a claim by showing both that it had installed a readily accessible and effective policy for reporting and resolving complaints of sexual harassment, and that the plaintiff unreasonably failed to avail herself of that employer-provided preventive or remedial apparatus.[175] Similarly under the British EA 2010, the employer is generally liable for the actions of its staff. However, employers can escape liability by showing they took all reasonable steps to prevent employees from harassing each other. This includes a well-drafted sexual harassment policy that all employees have been informed of and a clear procedure for bringing harassment complaints. The EA 2010 briefly included a heavily caveated liability on employers for third party harassment,[176] but this was repealed in 2013 on the basis that it imposed an unnecessary burden on employers. Attempts to argue that such liability was in any event implicit in the

---

[173] Equality and Human Rights Commission, 'Turning the Tables: Ending Sexual Harassment at Work' (March 2018); House of Commons Women and Equalities Committee, 'Sexual Harassment in the Workplace' (HC 725, 2018).

[174] *Burlington Industries, Inc v Ellerth* 524 US 742 (1998) (US Sup Ct).

[175] *Pennsylvania State Police v Suders* 542 US 129 (2004) (US Sup Ct).

[176] EA 2010, s 40(2)–(4) now repealed.

definition of sexual harassment at work were rejected by the UK Court of Appeal in 2019.[177]

More fundamentally, sexual harassment laws have failed to reflect the true foundations of sexual harassment in patriarchal power. As Reva Segal puts it: 'Legal recognition of sexual harassment as sex discrimination was at one and the same time a process of misrecognition.'[178] This is because 'as antidiscrimination law recognizes sexual harassment as sex discrimination, it never acknowledges the power dynamic that women over two centuries have described: the way that men extracting sex from economically dependent women reiterate a coercive relationship that organizes heterosexual relations in marriage and the market both'.[179] This, in turn, requires courts to acknowledge that sexual harassment is not an expression of sexual desire or sexuality but of power and coercion.[180] In *Oncale*, Scalia J stated that 'harassing conduct need not be motivated by sexual desire to support an inference of discrimination on the basis of sex'.[181] It would also include harassment 'motivated by general hostility to the presence of women in the workplace'.[182] However, this approach continues to focus on the attitudes of individuals, representing sexual harassment as concerned with individual victims and individual perpetrators. This is highlighted by the overwhelming focus on internal complaints procedures as the primary means to address sexual harassment in the workplace. As we will see in Chapter 8, procedures are readily used, both by employers and courts, to give the appearance of change without addressing underlying structures. Individual complainants face enormous risks in embarking on such procedures, especially in the need to prove fault by perpetrators who have significantly greater power in the workplace, whether it is through masculine culture, inequalities of power in the workplace, or absence of the scaffolding provided by collective voice.[183]

It is therefore not surprising that women have turned away from legally formulated sexual harassment procedures to social media—where they are able to find solidarity—to amplify their voices and overcome the inequality of power in the workplace necessary to achieve substantive equality. As Mackinnon puts it: 'Global #MeToo sprung from the law of sexual

---

[177] *Unite the Union v Nailard* [2018] EWCA Civ 1203 (UK Ct of Appeal).
[178] R Siegel, 'Introduction: A Short History of Sexual Harassment' in C MacKinnon and R Siegel (eds), *Directions in Sexual Harassment Law* (Yale UP 2004) 2.
[179] ibid 17.
[180] V Schultz, 'Reconceptualizing Sexual Harassment, Again' (2018–19) 128 Yale LJ 22.
[181] *Oncale v Sundowner Offshore Services* (n 160) 80.
[182] ibid.
[183] See Chapter 8.

harassment, quickly overtook it, and is shifting law, cultures, and politics everywhere . . . #MeToo is cultural, driven principally by forces other than litigation, and is surpassing the law in changing norms and providing relief for human rights violations that the law did not—in some ways in current form could not, although law is embedded in culture and can and will change with it.'[184]

There are some important ways in which the law can be changed to do so. At the very least, perpetrators should not be allowed to use the law to entrench their position. Both defamation laws and binding non-disclosure agreements have been mobilized by perpetrators to impede not just women's access to existing legal procedures, but also their use of social media. Freedom of speech and the right to gender equality should outweigh these legal possibilities. There are also more positive reforms which can be made. One approach, as we have seen, is to use dignity as the organizing principle. Dignity, however, only captures one dimension of substantive equality. Unless it is coupled with the other dimensions, it too risks creating the illusion that sexual harassment is simply about individual relationships of respect. It is also necessary to reflect the disadvantage, lack of voice, and patriarchal structures which continue to fuel sexual harassment. The ways in which stigma, stereotyping, prejudice, and violence feed off women's disadvantage in the workplace, while at the same time deepening it, need to be addressed. Equally importantly, it is necessary to depart decisively from an individualized model and aim for structural change. A mandatory proactive duty on employers to ensure that a workplace free of sexual harassment is one aspect of this. Equally important are measures tackling a workplace culture which legitimizes sexual harassment and silences victims. The #MeToo movement has amplified the voices of those who were otherwise silenced, especially when legal procedures function to stifle any real redress. But here, too, participation must be allied with redressing disadvantage. Particularly pressing is the need to recognize ways in which both the legal spheres and social media can replicate power imbalances, especially in relation to intersectional inequalities. As Tarana Burke powerfully emphasizes: 'What history has shown us time and again is that if marginalized voices—those of people of colour, queer people, disabled people, poor people—aren't centred in our movements then they tend to become no more than a footnote. I often say that sexual violence knows no race, class or gender, but the response to it does . . . . Ending sexual violence [and

[184] C MacKinnon, 'Global #MeToo' in A Noel and D Oppenheimer (eds), *The Global #MeToo Movement* (Full Court Press 2020) 1, 5.

harassment] will require every voice from every corner of the world and it will require those whose voices are most often heard to find ways to amplify those voices that often go unheard.'[185] The continuing power of patriarchy means that all possibilities, both in the law and in other social spaces, need to work together to achieve change.

V DUTY OF ACCOMMODATION

The duty of reasonable accommodation arises from the recognition that it is not sufficient to require individuals to conform to the dominant norm. The norm should be adapted to facilitate equal participation. This principle is particularly important in relation to persons with disabilities, endorsing a social model of disability, which emphasizes the disabling effect of society on people with impairments.[186] As Chandrachud J put it in *Vikash Kumar*, the introduction of a principle of reasonable accommodation 'travels beyond imposing restraints on discrimination against the disabled. . . . [It] imposes a positive obligation on the State to . . . create conditions in which the barriers posed by disability can be overcome.'[187] It is, however, a challenging duty. As a start, when does the duty arise? Both a proactive and an individualized duty are required. Ideally, there should be an ongoing duty to ensure that the built environment is inclusive of the whole spectrum of abilities, without putting the burden on an individual to claim accommodation as a right. At the same time, there is a very wide range of impairments, and there might be a need for individual tailoring of the work environment or working schedules, including the provision of auxiliary aids. The second major challenge concerns the extent to which an employer can claim that adjustments are too onerous. Is it enough for an employer to assert an inconvenience or minor cost; or should the standard be one of proportionality? Legislation uses the terms 'reasonable', 'proportionate', or 'undue burden', but it is up to courts to interpret the meaning of these terms. At the same time, the framing of the question as one entirely concerning costs on the employer is problematic. Any costs not borne by the employer do not simply vanish. Instead, they fall

---

[185] Tarana Burke, '#MeToo Was Started for Black and Brown Women and Girls. They're Still Being Ignored', *Washington Post* (9 November 2017) <www.washingtonpost.com/news/post-nat ion/wp/2017/11/09/the-waitress-who-works-in-the-diner-needs-to-know-that-the-issue-of-sexual-harassment-is-about-her-too> accessed 27 July 2022.

[186] See Chapter 3 on the social model of disability.

[187] *Vikash Kumar v UPSC* (2021) 5 SCC 370, para 43.

on the person with disabilities. Account should be taken of this in setting the balance. Moreover, it should be recognized that this is an issue which requires responsibility to be spread beyond the individual employer. There should also be a requirement that the State bear part of the costs.

The core definition of reasonable accommodation is found in the CRPD, which states: "'Reasonable accommodation' means necessary and appropriate modification and adjustments not imposing a disproportionate or undue burden, where needed in a particular case, to ensure to persons with disabilities the enjoyment or exercise on an equal basis with others of all human rights and fundamental freedoms."[188] This indicates that the modification should be geared to what is needed in the individual case, and should not impose a disproportionate or undue burden. A similar formulation is found in the Americans with Disabilities Act of 1990, which provides that it is discriminatory for an employer to fail to make 'reasonable accommodations to the known physical or mental limitations of an [employee] with a disability' unless the employer 'can demonstrate that the accommodation would impose an undue hardship on the operation of [its] business'.[189] Reasonable accommodation may include making existing facilities used by employees readily accessible to and usable by individuals with disabilities. It may also entail job restructuring; part-time or modified work schedules; reassignment to a vacant position; acquisition or modification of equipment or devices; appropriate adjustment or modifications of examinations, training materials, or policies; the provision of qualified readers or interpreters; and other similar accommodations.[190] The UK duty instead requires a comparative exercise. Known as the 'duty of reasonable adjustment', it applies to situations in which a disabled person is put at a substantial disadvantage in comparison with non-disabled persons by a provision, criterion, or practice, a physical feature, or the absence of an auxiliary aid. In such circumstances, the employer, service provider, or other relevant body must take such steps as are reasonable to avoid the disadvantage or to provide an auxiliary aid.[191] A similar duty applies in the EU.[192]

Much more recent is the inclusion of the duty in India, where it complements duties to set aside places in employment and education for people with disabilities, as well as the duty to provide free education for children

---

[188] CRPD, Art 2.
[189] 42 USC § 12112(b)(5)(A).
[190] 42 USC § 12111(9).
[191] EA 2010, s 20.
[192] Directive 2000/78/EC, Art 5.

with disabilities.[193] The Rights of Persons with Disabilities Act 2016 now requires 'necessary and appropriate modification and adjustments' as long as they do not impose a disproportionate or undue burden so that persons with disabilities can enjoy their rights equally with others. Its coexistence with the other specific positive measures for persons with disabilities, such as reservations, initially remained unclear, given the very strict definition of disability ('benchmark disabilities') for the purposes of these special provisions. However, in *Vikash Kumar*, a groundbreaking case in 2021, the Indian Supreme Court held that the duty should not be restricted in this way. Instead, it should apply to the wider definition of disability based on the CRPD formulation, which focuses on the disabling effect of impairments rather than the severity of the disability, as is the case for 'benchmark' disability.

Although in the UK this concept is confined to disability, in other jurisdictions it extends further. In the US, the duty of reasonable accommodation also applies for religious purposes. An employer is required to make 'reasonable accommodations' for the religious needs of its employees, short of 'undue hardship'.[194] Similarly, in Canada the duty has its origins in religious discrimination. In *Simpson-Sears*,[195] the applicant argued that a rule requiring employees to be available for work on Saturdays discriminated against those observing a Saturday Sabbath, thus contravening the Ontario Human Rights Code.[196] The Supreme Court of Canada held that the respondent had an obligation to take reasonable steps to accommodate the religious observance of the complainant, short of undue hardship in the operation of its business. This approach has been expressly adopted in relation to the constitutional guarantee of equality in the Canadian Charter.[197] Moreover, it is not confined to religion and disability in Canadian law. It has become an integral part of the broader understanding of adverse effects discrimination.

There are several important ways in which the duty of reasonable adjustment represents an advance towards substantive equality. The first is that it is explicitly asymmetric, aiming to redress disadvantage even if this entails different or more favourable treatment.[198] Indeed, the British EA 2010

---

[193] Rights of Persons with Disabilities Act, 2016, ss 31–37.

[194] 42 USC § 2000e(j) (1970 ed, Supp V). See also § 703(a)(1) of the Civil Rights Act of 1964, Title VII, 78 Stat 255, 42 USC § 2000e-2(a)(1) (prohibits religious discrimination in employment).

[195] *Ontario Human Rights Commission v Simpsons-Sears Ltd* [1975] 2 SCR 53.

[196] s 4(1)(g) of the Ontario Human Rights Code prohibiting discrimination on grounds of 'creed'; since superseded by the differently worded s 10 of the Human Rights Code, 1981.

[197] *Eldridge v British Columbia* [1997] 3 SCR 624, para 63.

[198] *Archibald v Fife Council* [2004] UKHL 32 [47], [57].

specifically protects such action against a challenge under the equal treatment principle.[199] The express endorsement of an asymmetric approach has been shown to be essential to protect the duty of reasonable accommodation or adjustment against challenges for breach of the basic equal treatment principle. In a case before the US Supreme Court, an employer argued that the duty of reasonable accommodation in effect constituted preferential treatment for employees with disabilities. By requiring an exception to rules which apply equally to all, it was argued, the duty was a breach of the principle of equal treatment specified in the US Disability Discrimination Act. The response of the US Supreme Court was emphatic:

> While linguistically logical, this argument fails to recognize what the Act specifies, namely, that preferences will sometimes prove necessary to achieve the Act's basic equal opportunity goal. The Act requires preferences in the form of 'reasonable accommodations' that are needed for those with disabilities to obtain the same workplace opportunities that those without disabilities automatically enjoy.... The simple fact that an accommodation would provide a 'preference'—in the sense that it would permit the worker with a disability to violate a rule that others must obey—cannot, in and of itself, automatically show that the accommodation is not 'reasonable'.[200]

Similarly, the Supreme Court of Canada has stressed that avoidance of discrimination on grounds of disability will frequently require distinctions to be made to take into account the actual personal characteristics of disabled persons.[201]

The second important way in which the duty of reasonable adjustment advances substantive equality is its focus on modifying the environment to facilitate the participation of those affected. In the context of disability, this endorses a social model of disability, highlighting the disabling effect of an environment adapted to able-bodied people. As Sopinka J put it in the Supreme Court of Canada:

> Exclusion from the mainstream of society results from the construction of a society based solely on 'mainstream' attributes to which disabled persons will never be able to gain access.... [I]t is the failure to make reasonable accommodation, to fine-tune society so that its structures and assumptions

---

[199] EA 2010, s 13(3).
[200] *US Airways v Barnett* 535 US 391, 397–98 (2002).
[201] *Eldridge v British Columbia* (n 197) para 65.

do not result in the relegation and banishment of disabled persons from participation, which results in discrimination against them.[202]

Thirdly, the duty of reasonable accommodation goes beyond other conceptions of equality in that it expressly imposes a positive duty to make changes. This applies not just to neutral rules or practices but also to a failure to provide specific aids. In the Canadian case of *Eldridge*,[203] the Court emphasized that the adverse effects suffered by disabled people need not stem only from the imposition of a burden not faced by the mainstream population, but also from a failure to ensure that they benefit equally from a service offered to everyone. In this case, the failure to provide sign language interpreters for deaf people in the health service was discriminatory and constituted a failure to accommodate their needs. In the British EA 2010, express provision is made for a duty of accommodation arising from the absence of an auxiliary aid.

It will be seen in Chapter 8 that there has been a more general development in UK anti-discrimination law towards the imposition of positive duties on public bodies in the context of equality ('the public sector duty'). The duty of reasonable adjustment is, however, more focused and specific. Whereas the public sector duty requires only that consideration be given to the need to take action, the duty of reasonable adjustment requires specific and focused action. It also differs from the public sector duty in that breach constitutes discrimination and therefore gives rise to an individually enforceable right. In addition, it is not confined to the public sector.

The duty therefore fulfils at least three of the dimensions of equality identified in Chapter 1: the distributive dimension of redressing disadvantage, the transformative dimension of accommodating difference, and the participative dimension of facilitating participation. At the same time, the duty confronts an ambiguity in the understanding of the need to accommodate difference. Does accommodating difference require general structural change or is it sufficient to create exceptions for individuals, while maintaining the general rule? An 'exceptionalist' approach has attracted criticism on the basis that, as Brodsky and Day have argued:

> The difficulty with this paradigm is that it does not challenge the imbalances of power, or the discourses of dominance, such as racism, able-bodyism

---

[202] *Eaton v Brant County Board of Education* [1997] 1 SCR 241, paras 66–67.
[203] *Eldridge v British Columbia* (n 197) para 66.

and sexism, which result in a society being designed well for some and not for others. It allows those who consider themselves 'normal' to continue to construct institutions and relations in their image, as long as others, when they challenge this construction are 'accommodated' . . . In short, accommodation is assimilationist. Its goal is to try to make 'different' people fit into existing systems.[204]

However, the dichotomy between exceptionalism and structural change might be overstated. There are clearly situations, particularly in the context of gender discrimination, in which the norm should be changed. However, in other situations it might be appropriate to retain the norm as a whole, but with specific exceptions to cater for religious differences. For example, if Sikhs are unable to wear a hard hat on a construction site because of their religious duty to wear a turban, the creation of an exception is preferable to the wholesale rejection of the rule.

An attempt to achieve an appropriate balance between creating an exception and structural change can be seen in the British EA 2010, where the duty of reasonable adjustment can be either anticipatory or reactive.[205] In some contexts it is reactive, only arising if the practice substantially disadvantages a particular disabled person or on request by a particular disabled person. For example, in relation to common parts of let residential premises, the duty is not owed to disabled persons generally but only to those where a request for an adjustment is made.[206] Similarly, employers need not take any action in relation to job applicants unless they have been notified by a person that she is applying for work, and they know or could be expected to know that she is disabled.[207] In such situations, the duty functions as a specific exception. In other contexts, however, it is 'anticipatory'. Service providers and those exercising public functions must anticipate the needs of disabled people and make appropriate reasonable adjustments. For example, the duty might require the installation of ramps, automatic doors, and hearing induction loops in national chain stores. A rail service provider might need to provide an alternative catering service for disabled people who cannot get to the buffet car.[208] In this way, the service is modified proactively, so that it is

---

[204] S Day and G Brodsky, 'The Duty to Accommodate: Who Will Benefit?' (1996) 75 Can Bar Rev 433, 447–57.
[205] B Hepple, *Equality: The New Legal Framework* (Hart Publishing 2011) ch 3.
[206] EA 2010, pt 4 'Premises', s 36 and Sch 4.
[207] ibid s 39; sch 8 pt 2.
[208] ibid Explanatory Notes, para 686.

as close as possible to that offered to the rest of the public.[209] In this sense, it signals structural change and can be transformative.

As with direct and indirect discrimination, the question arises as to how to balance competing priorities against the duty of accommodation. In the US and Canada, the standard is one of undue hardship, in the UK of reasonableness, while under EU law it is subjected to a proportionality measure. But regardless of the precise formulation, the background question is always who should bear the cost, both of providing the accommodation and of ensuring compliance. If addressing disability discrimination is regarded as a matter between the individual person with disabilities and the employer or service provider, it will always be difficult to achieve a fair balance of burdens. Any cost which is considered unduly onerous on the respondent will fall on the person with disabilities, who is the least able to bear it. However, accommodation and adjustments might be costly, especially for small employers and businesses. It is therefore crucial that the State shares some of the responsibility, for example through providing subsidies and incentives as well as supporting people with disabilities where accommodation is not achievable.

This is true, too, for compliance. Leaving individual plaintiffs to litigate to achieve compliance places an unfair burden on the person with disabilities, and is also inefficient and expensive. The aim of achieving a built environment with as few disabling features as possible is not well met by expensive lawsuits, where the ultimate benefit might be felt only by the lawyers. The US, for example, has witnessed highly controversial serial litigation by a handful of litigants and law firms. While such litigants have been accused of abusive litigation at the expense of small businesses, the reality is that compliance with legal standards of accommodation remains low. People with disabilities continue to be subjected to the humiliation and stigma of exclusion from many aspects of ordinary life. At the same time, the costs of making the requisite changes are frequently dwarfed by the extra costs of the litigation.[210] This is another example of the limits of an individual-centred discrimination model. As will be discussed further in Chapter 8, proactive duties to make adjustments, together with State regulatory enforcement, would be a more effective and efficient approach.

---

[209] Hepple (n 205) ch 3.
[210] E Clark, 'Enforcement of the Americans with Disabilities Act: Remedying "Abusive" Litigation While Strengthening Disability Rights ' (2020) 26 Washington and Lee J Civil Rights and Social Justice.

VI CONCLUSION

This chapter has critically assessed the ways in which discrimination law in different jurisdictions has been shaped to address four specifically challenging issues: pregnancy and parenting, equal pay, sexual harassment, and the duty of accommodation. Chapter 7 turns to the even more controversial question of 'reverse discrimination' or affirmative action.

7

Symmetry or Substance

Reversing Discrimination

> The way to stop discrimination on the basis of race is to stop dis-
> criminating on the basis of race.
>
> (Roberts J, *Parents Involved v Seattle*, US Supreme Court)[1]

> Remedial measures are not a derogation from, but a substantive
> and composite part of, the equality protection . . . Their primary
> object is to promote the achievement of equality.
>
> (*van Heerden*, South African Constitutional Court)[2]

Possibly the most controversial issue in anti-discrimination law is the question of whether it is legitimate to deliberately use gender, race, or other protected characteristic to benefit a group disadvantaged by discrimination. At
first glance, this appears to offend against basic principles of equality. Many
decades have been spent convincing judges and legislators that race and
gender are irrelevant, and their use in the allocation of benefits or rights is
invidious. How, then, can it be legitimate to permit their use for purportedly
remedial purposes?

The answer to this question depends on whether a formal or substantive
conception of equality is used. Using race, gender, or other protected characteristic to allocate benefits or rights is clearly a breach of formal equality,
regardless of the context. However, on a substantive view, deliberate preferences for a disadvantaged group could well be a means to achieve equality,
rather than a breach or exception. But this does not mean that deliberate
preferences automatically achieve substantive equality. Preference policies
may change the composition of those in power, so that more women, Black

---

[1] *Parents Involved in Community Schools v Seattle School District* 551 US 701, 127 S Ct 2738
(2007) (US Sup Ct).
[2] *Minister of Justice v Van Heerden* 2004 (6) SA 121 (CC), 2004 (11) BCLR 1125 (SACC).

Discrimination Law. Third Edition. Sandra Fredman, Oxford University Press. © Sandra Fredman 2022.
DOI: 10.1093/oso/9780198854081.003.0007

people, people from marginalized minorities, or indigenous people[3] will be represented at the higher levels. But the structure might remain intact. Inequalities between middle-class white people and Black people might diminish. But the gap between poor Black people and wealthy Black people might increase. Similarly, the gap might widen between poor people from marginalized minorities or indigenous people and wealthier members of those groups. 'Colour' consciousness might be necessary to redress racism.[4] But it might also entrench racial difference. Some check is necessary in order to ensure that preference policies genuinely further substantive equality before they are regarded as legitimate. It is here that the level of judicial scrutiny becomes important. How can judges maintain an appropriate supervisory role to ensure that preference policies further substantive equality? Judges have approached this through the principle of proportionality. What aims are legitimate and when are deliberate preference policies appropriate to achieve the stated aims?

The concept of affirmative action has several meanings. In this chapter, it is used to denote the deliberate use of gender, race, or other protected characteristic to benefit a disadvantaged group. Section I of this chapter briefly rehearses the main contours of the debate between formal and substantive equality and how this affects the legitimacy of affirmative action, sometimes referred to as reverse discrimination. Section II sets out the tools for assessing different jurisdictions' approaches to affirmative action. In particular, how do courts articulate the aims of affirmative action and what standard of scrutiny do they regard as appropriate for assessing whether affirmative action achieves those aims? Given that most cases are brought by excluded

---

[3] As in previous chapters, this book acknowledges that the terminology used to describe people subjected to discrimination is sensitive and contested. In the different jurisdictions covered here (UK, Europe, India, South Africa, Canada, and the US), outgroups, or groups that are 'othered' in their own societies or globally, prefer to refer to themselves in different and sometimes opposing ways. This can also change, reflecting changes in social forces and perceptions. Acknowledging these complexities, I have chosen to use 'Black people', 'marginalized ethnicities', and 'indigenous people', following the approach of the UN Special Rapporteur on the right to health, Tlaleng Mofokeng, in her report to the United Nations on sexual and reproductive health rights on 16 July 2021 (A/76/172) <https://undocs.org/A/76/172> accessed 31 May 2022. The reference to 'gender identity, gender expression and sex characteristics' follows her report on gender-based violence submitted to the UN on 14 April 2022 (A/HRC/50/28) <www.ohchr.org/en/documents/thematic-reports/ahrc5028-violence-and-its-impact-right-health-report-special-rapporteur> accessed 31 May 2022.

[4] This terminology reflects that used in international human rights law and relevant human rights instruments in other jurisdictions (see UK EA 2010, s 9(1)(a); South African Constitution, s 9; Canadian Charter, s 15; International Convention on the Elimination of All Forms of Racial Discrimination, Art 1; ICCPR, Art 2(1); ICESCR, Art 2(2)), which all refer to 'colour' in the list of protected characteristics.

third parties claiming to be victims of discrimination due to preference policies, how do courts fashion a conception of discrimination to respond to these claims? Are preference policies regarded as instances of discrimination, exceptions to discrimination, or ways of furthering equality? Even more complex are cases in which preference policies pit one type of disadvantage against another. How do courts assess the delineation of beneficiaries, particularly in the context of intersectionality? Section III takes a deeper dive into different jurisdictions' approaches to reverse discrimination. Three types of approach can be discerned. The first views reverse discrimination as a breach of equality. The second considers it as an exception to equality, to be narrowly construed. The third approaches reverse discrimination as a means to achieve substantive equality.

I CONCEPTS OF EQUALITY AND AFFIRMATIVE ACTION

Given its deliberate use of protected characteristics to allocate benefits, it is not surprising that the legitimacy of preference policies or affirmative action is highly problematic. Indeed, the arguments presented by opponents appear at first sight to be unassailable. If equality is the goal, how can it be possible to justify policies requiring unequal treatment on the grounds of sex or race?

This argument, however, only appears irrefutable because it is based on a particular formal conception of equality. There are three salient characteristics of formal equality which make it inevitable that preference policies or affirmative action will be regarded as constituting an illegitimate breach. First, formal equality presupposes that justice is an abstract, universal notion and cannot vary to reflect different patterns of benefit and disadvantage in a particular society. If discrimination on grounds of gender or race is unjust, on this view it must be unjust whether it creates extra burdens on a group already disadvantaged or whether it redistributes those burdens to a previously privileged group. Equality is therefore regarded as necessarily symmetrical, applying with equal strength regardless of whether it is directed against or in favour of a disadvantaged group. This position was clearly articulated by US Supreme Court Justice Powell in *Bakke*: 'The guarantee of equal protection cannot mean one thing when applied to one individual and something else when applied to an individual of another colour.'[5]

---

[5] *Regents of Univ of California v Bakke* 438 US 265, 288–90 (1978) (US Sup Ct).

For proponents of this view, there is a moral and constitutional equivalence between laws designed to subjugate a race and those that distribute benefits. Government-sponsored racial discrimination based on benign prejudice, according to Supreme Court Justice Thomas, should be considered to be just as noxious as discrimination motivated by malicious prejudice.[6] Other judicial statements have made it clear that the aim is not the alleviation of disadvantage: discrimination on grounds of race is considered to be odious even if directed against a group that has never been the subject of governmental discrimination.[7]

The second premise of formal equality which makes affirmative action or reverse discrimination appear internally contradictory is its individualism. On a formal equality approach, status such as sex or race should always be disregarded in distributing benefits or allocating jobs or promotion; instead, individuals must be rewarded only on the basis of individual merit. Reverse discrimination is not only regarded as unfair but also inefficient: it simply permits the appointment of people less well qualified and therefore less able to do the job properly.[8] Correspondingly, the individualistic premise of formal equality entails that burdens should only be allocated on the basis of individual responsibility. Individuals may be treated as responsible only for their own actions; they should not be held accountable for more general societal wrongs. This means, in particular, that an individual man or white person should not be required to compensate for historical or institutional sex or race discrimination by being excluded from a job or promotion for which they are well qualified. There can, on this view, be no 'creditor or debtor race'.[9]

Thirdly, formal equality entails equality before the law. This means that the State should be neutral as between its citizens, favouring no one above any other.

Without doing violence to the principles of equality before the law and neutral decision-making, we simply cannot interpret our laws to support both colour-blindness for some citizens and colour-consciousness for others.[10]

---

[6] *Adarand Constructors v Pena* 515 US 200, 241, 115 S Ct 2097, 2119 (Thomas J) (1995).

[7] *Wygant v Jackson Board of Education* 106 S Ct 1842 (1986) (US Sup Ct).

[8] M Abram, 'Affirmative Action: Fair Shakers and Social Engineers' (1986) 99 Harv L Rev 1312, 1322.

[9] *Adarand v Pena* (n 6) 239, 2118 (Scalia J).

[10] Abram (n 8) 1319.

The proposition that a group should be favoured on account of gender or race, even in a remedial sense, is therefore anathema. Moreover, argues Abram, any attempt to move from the individual to the group is bound to degenerate into a 'crude political struggle between groups seeking favoured status'.[11] State neutrality also entails a State which intervenes as little as possible in the 'free market'. In particular, the State should not use its contractual powers within the market to pursue public policies such as the elimination of discrimination. This necessarily outlaws the use of contract compliance or 'set-asides' of State funds for the purpose of aiding minorities or women.

Reliance on substantive rather than formal equality gives rise to a very different analysis of affirmative action or reverse discrimination. The substantive approach rejects an abstract view of justice and instead insists that justice is only meaningful in its interaction with society. The unfortunate reality is that it is women rather than men who have suffered cumulative disadvantage due to sex discrimination and Black people, people from marginalized ethnicities, and indigenous people rather than white people who have suffered from racism.[12] Once this is accepted, it becomes clear that to adopt a symmetrical approach—whereby unequal treatment of men is regarded as morally identical to discrimination against women—is to empty the equality principle of real social meaning. As Dworkin puts it: 'The difference between a general racial classification that causes further disadvantage to those who have suffered from prejudice, and a classification framed to help them, is morally significant.'[13]

Similarly, the substantive approach rejects as misleading the aspirations of individualism. It is true that the merit principle has played a valuable role in advancing equality of opportunity by displacing nepotism and class bias in the allocation of jobs or benefits. However, in the context of sex or race, the uncritical use of merit as a criterion for employment or promotion could perpetuate disadvantage. This is because, despite the appearance of scientific objectivity, the choice of criteria for deciding merit may well reinforce existing societal discrimination or incorporate implicit discriminatory assumptions. Equally misleading is the reliance on a notion of individual fault which generates an image of an 'innocent' third party who is deprived of a job or other opportunity because he is white or male. A substantive view of equality suggests that the responsibility for correcting disadvantage should not be seen

[11] ibid 1321.
[12] See n 3.
[13] R Dworkin, *A Matter of Principle* (Harvard UP 1985) 314.

to rest merely with those to whom 'fault' can be attributed. Instead, all who benefit from the existing structure of disadvantage should be expected to bear part of the cost of remedy. A community structured on racial or gender discrimination has conferred benefits on the dominant group as a whole. Each member of the community should, therefore, be required to bear part of the costs of correction, provided these costs are not disproportionate for the individual.

Finally, the substantive approach rejects the possibility of a neutral State which is separate from society with its current set of power relations. The State is no more than an emanation of the democratic process, the aim of which is to function as a conduit for or resolution of the cross-currents of social power. The modern State plays a central role in distributing benefits in society. It cannot therefore be truly neutral: if it refuses to take an active role in reducing disadvantage, it is in fact supporting the existing dominant groups in maintaining their position of superiority over groups which have suffered from discrimination and prejudice. A substantive view of equality would view the State as having a duty to act positively to correct the results of such discrimination. On all these counts, then, affirmative action or reverse discrimination could be entirely legitimate if a substantive view of equality is accepted.

Even then, important questions remain. The first concerns the definition of disadvantage. Does it cover both recognition and redistributive ills? Is it sufficient to be a Black person, a member of a marginalized ethnicity, an indigenous person,[14] a Dalit, or a woman? Or should it be necessary in addition to prove socio-economic disadvantage? A second question concerns how the demands of different disadvantaged groups should be balanced against each other. With the widening of the scope of anti-discrimination laws to include grounds such as religion or age, these issues loom larger. Thirdly, how should the burden be spread between those who benefit and those who bear the costs?

The four-dimensional conception of substantive equality is helpful in addressing these difficulties. As a start, it is expressly asymmetric. The right to equality aims to redress disadvantage, not simply to remove racial or gender ascriptions. This asymmetry means that equality is not necessarily breached by measures which specifically use race or gender as a means of distributing benefits and burdens. Indeed, provided that they aim to benefit

---

[14] See n 3.

the subordinated group, specific measures based on race or gender may be necessary to achieve substantive equality. Thus, whereas formal equality would regard affirmative action as a breach of equality, substantive equality sees such programmes as a means to achieve equality. At the same time, affirmative action should also aim to achieve the other dimensions of substantive equality. Affirmative-action measures can cause stigma and other recognition harms, either where beneficiaries are regarded as unmeritorious or where some groups, such as small intersectional minorities, are rendered invisible. For women, purported affirmative action might reinforce stereotypical roles, for example where women are regarded as primarily responsible for childcare. Programmes therefore need to be recalibrated to ensure that both these dimensions are optimized. This in turn points to the importance of paying attention to the voice of beneficiaries, to ensure that excluded groups' views are properly accounted for. The fourth dimension, structural change, might be hardest to achieve. Such measures might fail to reach underlying structures, merely altering the racial or gender composition of existing structures without transforming them. Paying attention to all four dimensions is therefore essential to ensure that the design and implementation of affirmative-action measures is in tune with substantive equality.

II ASSESSING AFFIRMATIVE ACTION: MEANS AND ENDS

The discussion above has demonstrated that the objections to affirmative action can be plausibly repudiated. From a principled perspective, affirmative action should not be regarded as a breach of or even an exception to equality. Instead, it is a means to achieve equality. But there remain important challenges facing affirmative-action measures. The line between invidious discrimination and appropriate steps to achieve equality may not always be clear. Before dealing with the detail of the comparative law on this issue, it is worth laying out some of the challenging questions to be answered by the jurisdictions, and setting out how the different responses match the aim of substantive equality set out above. This section considers the two main questions which need to be answered in determining which side of the line a measure falls. First, what aims are legitimate? And, secondly, how close should the fit be between the measure and the identified aims?

The aims articulated by the courts in various jurisdictions can be grouped under three main headings: (i) removing discriminatory barriers or redressing past disadvantage; (ii) fostering diversity and the creation of role models; and (iii) participation, or the representation of the interests, of the previously excluded group. The second question, the means–end fit, is widely performed by a proportionality test. But proportionality is an elastic measure which can be tighter or looser depending on whether affirmative action is regarded as an exception to equality or a means to achieve it. As we will see, jurisdictions which take the former view will tend towards a close fit; that is, that the measure must be a *necessary* means to achieve a legitimate aim. At its strongest, this means that there should be no alternative race- or gender-neutral means to achieve this end. Many US decisions are based on this approach. At the other end of the spectrum, jurisdictions which endorse a substantive understanding of equality require only a *reasonable* relationship, reflecting too a deference to decision makers as to how best to achieve equality. Canadian and South African jurisprudence reflects this approach.

Determining whether affirmative action is an acceptable means to achieve the selected aims requires answers to a further set of interrelated questions. One such question is how we delineate the beneficiary class. Should the criterion be solely based on membership of a group which has suffered prejudice, or should those who have succeeded in socio-economic terms be excluded, despite being a woman, Black, a member of a marginalized ethnicity, an indigenous person,[15] or other status? This, in turn, requires a deeper understanding of whether affirmative action is only intended to achieve the first dimension of substantive equality—to redress socio-economic disadvantage—or whether it goes further and addresses the other dimensions: prejudice, exclusion, and difference. A different question is whether a programme singling out one group for special protection may perpetuate stereotypes and freeze individuals into the very status identity which substantive equality aims to eliminate. At what point should it be accepted that the time has come to move beyond classifying individuals according to their status? Courts' responses to these questions are also influenced by their answers to other questions, such as the cost to affected third parties. Behind these issues is a further challenge; namely, the extent to which affirmative action can be genuinely transformative. Can it bring about structural change, rather than simply changing the 'colour'[16] or gender composition of classes within the existing structure?

[15] See n 3.
[16] See n 4.

These questions are considered in some detail in Section III in relation to different jurisdictions. But before doing so, this section provides a critical framework for analysing these legal frameworks in the light of the concepts of equality set out earlier from a comparative perspective.

(i)   Aims of Affirmative Action

(a) Remedying past discrimination and redressing disadvantage

The most familiar function of affirmative action is to remedy past discrimination, a function regarded as legitimate in many jurisdictions and which chimes with the first dimension of substantive equality. The major question before the courts has been whether affirmative action can extend to de facto, unintentional discrimination or whether it is confined to remedying intentional discrimination on the part of the respondent. This question is answered in different ways in different jurisdictions. As we will see, the use of reverse discrimination as a remedy for past intentional discrimination is well established in the US. The US Supreme Court has, however, refused to go beyond intentional discrimination. In *Bakke*, Powell J rejected an interest in 're-ducing the historic deficit of traditionally disfavoured minorities in medical schools and in the medical profession'.[17] He also refused to accept that race-conscious policies could be legitimated on the grounds that they remedy societal discrimination. This was because, he argued, such measures risk placing unnecessary burdens on innocent third parties 'who bear no responsibility for whatever harm the beneficiaries of the special admissions program are thought to have suffered'.[18] This was confirmed in the *Community Schools* case, in which the majority held that de facto discrimination did not constitute a compelling interest potentially justifying race-conscious desegregation measures in schools. This contrasts with the Canadian Charter which explicitly permits programmes that aim to 'ameliorate' the condition of disadvantaged groups identified by the enumerated or analogous grounds.[19]

This is an important question because affirmative-action measures may be particularly effective where intentional discrimination cannot be proved, but there remain hidden and structural barriers to advancement which can be more easily overcome by affirmative action than by individual claims for

[17]   *Regents of Univ of California v Bakke* (n 5) 306–07.
[18]   ibid 310.
[19]   s 15(2).

indirect discrimination. Despite apparently objective eligibility standards and ostensible equal opportunity policies, there remain many hidden obstacles to the advancement of disadvantaged groups. Given that, in the absence of barriers, there would be a random spread of men and women, white people, Black people, members of marginalized ethnicities, and indigenous people[20] across the labour force and government, the very fact that a group is seriously under-represented in a sphere or activity is evidence of the subtle operation of often invisible barriers.

A good demonstration of this phenomenon is found in the facts of *Kalanke* and *Marschall*, two major ECJ cases.[21] Because the formal assessment process in the German city of Bremen produced too many equally qualified candidates, informal selection criteria had come into being, including duration of service, age, and number of dependants. It is well established that all these criteria, despite being equally applicable to both men and women, in practice exclude substantially more women than men. As the ECJ acknowledged in *Marschall*, the 'mere fact that a male candidate and a female candidate are equally qualified does not mean that they have the same chances'.[22] It was to overcome these hidden barriers to women's advancement that the city of Bremen took the decision to institute a policy giving preference to women if they had equal formal qualifications as men.

Yet could this not be dealt with by the familiar principle of indirect discrimination? Indirect discrimination expressly aims to remove apparently neutral barriers which in fact function to exclude more women than men or more Black people, members of marginalized ethnicities, and indigenous people than white people unless they can be justified.[23] However, as we have seen, indirect discrimination has proved to be too clumsy a tool for achieving its aims. A complainant seeking to prove indirect discrimination must initiate court proceedings and show disparate impact, often on the basis of complex statistics. Even if she can surmount all these barriers, she may find that an employer successfully shows that the criteria, despite being exclusionary, are justifiable by reference to the needs of the business. Affirmative action resolves many of these difficulties. Instead of relying on litigation by individual victims, the employer takes the initiative. Nor is it necessary to prove

---

[20] See n 3.
[21] Case C-450/93 *Kalanke v Freie Hansestadt Bremen* [1995] IRLR 660 (ECJ); Case C-409/95 *Marschall v Land Nordrhein-Westfalen* [1998] IRLR 39 (ECJ); D Schiek, 'More Positive Action in Community Law' [1998] ILJ 155; D Schiek, 'Positive Action in Community Law' [1996] ILJ 239.
[22] *Marschall v Land Nordrhein-Westfalen*, ibid para 30.
[23] See n 3 and see Chapter 5.

that an exclusionary rule has had a disproportionate impact. Instead, it is sufficient to demonstrate a clear pattern of under-representation of women in particular grades or occupations. The complex questions discussed earlier are unnecessary. Moreover, discriminatory selection criteria are unequivocally removed: by creating a presumption in favour of women in conditions of equal merit, it makes it impossible for such criteria to be reintroduced surreptitiously through subjective decision making.

This approach was, until recently, well established in the jurisprudence of the US Supreme Court, where there has been a long tradition of encouraging employers to take voluntary affirmative action where their recruitment or promotion practices risk leading to an unlawful disparate impact. As Ginsburg J put it: 'This Court has repeatedly emphasized that the statute "should not be ready to thwart" efforts at voluntary compliance.'[24] There have also been a significant number of disparate impact settlements.[25] However, as we saw in Chapter 5, in *Ricci v DeStefano*[26] the US Supreme Court struck down an attempt by the city of Haven to take proactive action to prevent the severely disparate impact of its selection tests for firefighters by refusing to certify the results. Kennedy J, giving the judgment of the Court, stated:

> Without some other justification, this express, race-based decision-making violates Title VII's command that employers cannot take adverse employment actions because of an individual's race.[27]

Only if the respondent had a strong basis in evidence that it would lose a disparate impact case, would it be entitled to take race-based actions to prevent such disparate impact. This was not the situation on the facts of the case: the examinations were job-related and consistent with business necessity.

The aim of redressing past discrimination and removing hidden barriers, when fully realized, is clearly a good reason for taking affirmative action. It also moves away from the notion that individuals should only be responsible for discriminatory outcomes when they can be proved to be at fault. The redistributive dimension of substantive equality is therefore advanced. At the same time, it has a limited impact on the fourth dimension, the need to accommodate difference and achieve structural change. While preference policies may change the gender or racial composition of some higher paid

[24] *Ricci v DeStefano* 129 S Ct 2658, 2701 (2009).
[25] R Belton, 'Title VII at Forty: A Brief Look at the Birth, Death and Resurrection of the Disparate Impact Theory of Discrimination' (2005) 22 Hofstra Lab & Emp LJ 431, 470.
[26] *Ricci v DeStefano* (n 24).
[27] ibid 2673.

occupations, they do not challenge the underlying structural and institutional forces leading to the discrimination. As Iris Marion Young argues,[28] because affirmative action diagnoses the problem as one of maldistribution of privileged positions, its objective is limited to the redistribution of such positions among under-represented groups. However, this narrow distributive definition of racial and gender justice leaves out the equally important issues of institutional organization and decision-making power. For fundamental change to occur, the structural and institutional causes of exclusion need to be changed, including the division of labour in the home, the interaction between work in the family and work in the paid labour force, education, and other matters. This insight was recognized and articulated by Advocate General Tesauro in *Kalanke* when he said:

> Formal numerical equality is an objective which may salve some consciences, but it will remain illusory . . . unless it goes together with measures which are genuinely destined to achieve equality . . . In the final analysis, that which is necessary above all is a substantial change in the economic, social and cultural model which is at the root of the inequalities.[29]

(b) Diversity and role models

A second, increasingly popular justification for preference policies is that they provide diversity in an educational institution or workplace. In *Bakke*,[30] Powell J justified affirmative action in university admissions thus:

> An otherwise qualified medical student with a particular background—whether it be ethnic, geographic, culturally advantaged or disadvantaged—may bring to a professional school of medicine, experiences, outlook, and ideas that enrich the training of its student body and better equip its graduates to render with understanding their vital service to humanity.[31]

Diversity has now been recognized as one of two interests which could satisfy the requirements of the strict scrutiny test now prevailing in the US,[32] the other being that of remedying the effects of past intentional discrimination.[33] The most spirited defence of diversity is found in the Court's

---

[28] I Young, *Justice and the Politics of Difference* (Princeton UP 1990) 193.
[29] *Kalanke v Freie Hansestadt Bremen* (n 21) 665.
[30] *Regents of Univ of California v Bakke* (n 5).
[31] ibid 328.
[32] ibid 315.
[33] *Parents Involved in Community Schools v Seattle School District* (n 1) 2752.

decision in *Grutter*.[34] Here, the Court upheld a race-conscious policy of the University of Michigan Law School which, by enrolling a '"critical mass" of [under-represented] minority students', sought to 'ensur[e] their ability to make unique contributions to the character of the Law School'.[35] The Court accepted that the educational benefits that diversity is designed to produce were substantial. Such a policy can promote cross-racial understanding, help to break down racial stereotypes, and enable students to better understand persons of different races. It endorsed the District Court's finding that these benefits are 'important and laudable', because 'classroom discussion is livelier, more spirited, and simply more enlightening and interesting' when the students have 'the greatest possible variety of backgrounds'.[36]

While diversity operates to change the perspectives of the dominant group, the provision of role models operates on the self-perception of excluded groups, piercing stereotypes and giving them the self-confidence to move into positions they have previously been excluded from. This has not, however, been accepted in the US Supreme Court. In *Wygant*,[37] the defendant Board of Education argued that its policy of protecting newly hired minority teachers against lay-offs was justified by the State's duty to reduce racial discrimination by providing minority role models for minority students. This was roundly rejected by Powell J on the grounds that it would permit affirmative action long past the point of its remedial purpose.

By contrast, the provision of role models has been vigorously supported by the Supreme Court of Canada as a legitimate objective of affirmative action.[38] As Dickson CJ put it, the aim of an employment equity programme (in this case, setting a quota of one woman in four new hirings until a goal of 13 per cent of women in certain blue-collar occupations was reached) is not to compensate past victims; but 'an attempt to ensure that future applicants and workers from the affected group will not face the same insidious barriers that blocked their forebears'.[39] He identified at least two ways in which such a programme is likely to be more effective than one which simply relies on equal opportunities or the proscription of intentional prejudice. First, the insistence that women be placed in non-traditional jobs allows them to prove that

---

[34] *Grutter v Bollinger* 539 US 306 (2003) (US Sup Ct).
[35] ibid 316.
[36] ibid 330.
[37] *Wygant v Jackson Board of Education* (n 7).
[38] *Action Travail des Femmes v Canadian National Railway Co* [1987] 1 SCR 1114, 40 DLR (4th) 193.
[39] ibid 213.

they really can do the job, thereby dispelling stereotypes about women's abilities. This was particularly evident in the case at hand, in which the quotas ordered by the tribunal concerned traditionally male jobs such as a 'brakeman' or signaller at Canadian National Railways. Secondly, an employment equity programme helps to create a 'critical mass' of women in the workplace. Once a significant number of women are represented in a particular type of work, 'there is a significant chance for the continuing self-correction of the system'.[40] The critical mass overcomes the problem of tokenism, which would leave a few women isolated and vulnerable to sexual harassment or accusations of being imposters. It would also generate further employment of women, partly by means of the informal recruitment network and partly by reducing the stigma and anxiety associated with strange and unconventional work. Finally, a critical mass of women forces management to give women's concerns their due weight and compels personnel offices to take female applications seriously. As Dickson CJ concluded:

> It is readily apparent that, in attempting to combat systemic discrimination, it is essential to look to the past patterns of discrimination and to destroy those patterns in order to prevent the same type of discrimination in the future.[41]

Both diversity and the provision of role models can be criticized. As a start, they have a strongly instrumental flavour. Rather than redressing disadvantage, addressing stigma, and facilitating voice in the disadvantaged group, diversity is justified on the basis that it operates to the benefit of the majority, whose experience of higher education is improved by wider discussion or whose businesses are more likely to attract minority customers. The interests of the beneficiaries are sidelined. Moreover, diversity can lead to the imposition of maximum numbers of particular minorities, when it is thought that there is enough representation to fulfil the aims of the majority. This does not meet the first dimensional requirement of redressing disadvantage. It certainly falls into the trap of essentializing groups, thereby infringing on the second dimension (stereotyping) and the fourth dimension (changing underlying structures).

Role models are more in tune with the aims of the right to equality. However, they can create unfair burdens on beneficiaries of affirmative action to play a social role which they may not choose or feel comfortable with, and which are not expected of majorities. The concept of a critical mass, which

---

[40] ibid 214.
[41] ibid 215.

appears in both US and Canadian judgments, might overcome some of these limitations, in that the aim is to achieve sufficient numbers of the previously excluded group to create a momentum of its own in furthering their interests and attracting others to the student body or workforce. This does not place any particular extra burdens on beneficiaries. In practice, however, the ability of a critical mass to sustain further improvements has not always materialized. A clear example is at the University of California Berkeley School of Law where, as soon as its affirmative-action programme was removed in 1997, the number of minority students admitted plummeted, with only one minority student being admitted to the law school in the subsequent year.[42]

(c) Representation and perspective

A more dynamic way of justifying the use of affirmative-action policies is to argue that the very presence of women or other disadvantaged groups in higher status positions will lead to structural changes. Where a group has been excluded from a particular setting, be it a workforce or an educational institution, the likelihood is that the perspectives and experiences of members of the excluded group, particularly those relating to its exclusion, will be undervalued, misunderstood, or ignored by the dominant group, making it impossible for the excluded group to change its disadvantaged position. On this argument, members of excluded groups who are admitted to such positions will be able to represent the needs and interests of their groups in decision making, changing both the agenda of decision making and its outcomes. Women will, for example, be in a position to argue for maternity leave, childcare, and family-friendly policies, thus paving the way for more women to enter these positions. This representative function is important, on this view, for both formal decision-making institutions such as legislatures or trade union executive bodies, and for informal decision making. Managers, civil servants, judges, professionals, and chief administrators make a host of decisions, all of which require that the interests of women or minorities be properly represented.

However, more support is needed to underpin the assumption that the mere presence of women will guarantee that women's interests or those of other excluded groups will be articulated. As Phillips puts it, we generally reject a politics of presence in favour of a politics of ideas.

---

[42] J Williams, 'The Case for Affirmative Action' (*California Law Review Blog*, October 2020) <www.californialawreview.org/case-for-affirmative-action/> accessed 2 August 2022.

The shift from direct to representative democracy has shifted the emphasis from who the politicians are to what (policies, preferences, ideas), they represent, and in doing so has made accountability to the electorate the pre-eminent radical concern.[43]

Two possible arguments could be mounted to justify the renewed emphasis on presence, but both turn out to be problematic. The first is to argue that any woman or member of a disadvantaged group will inevitably articulate the needs, interests, and concerns of other women or members of the group. Their presence is therefore all that is needed. However, although some have argued that women may have a different moral sense to men,[44] modern feminists are acutely aware of the range of differing interests among women and, indeed, of the potential for conflict. Attempts to construct an 'essential woman' merely end up replicating the dominant ideology about women, obscuring crucial differences in class, race, sexual orientation, etc. This is equally true of other disadvantaged groups: for example, the assumption that Black people share common interests might veil deep differences based on religion, country of origin, or language.

A second way of justifying the representative function of affirmative action is to accept that the mere presence of women or members of other disadvantaged groups is not sufficient, but to argue instead that beneficiaries of affirmative action are there as genuine representatives of other members of their group. But this, in turn, requires some mechanism of accountability. The experience of the regime of British Prime Minister Margaret Thatcher demonstrated clearly that a woman in power is not necessarily a representative of women's interests. Indeed, she may have achieved power partly because she was able to conform to a male ethic and thereby suppress any belief in the importance of articulating women's concerns. There are no mechanisms for accountability in affirmative-action plans in public or private employment, and even on decision-making bodies, including the legislature. Women decision makers are not cast as accountable to women constituents. The same is true for a related justification, namely, that those who benefit from affirmative action will return to serve their communities. This goal, which has been rejected by the US Supreme Court,[45] places too great a burden on the

---

[43] A Phillips, *The Politics of Presence* (Clarendon Press 1995) 4.
[44] See C Gilligan, *In a Different Voice: Psychological Theory and Women's Development* (Harvard UP 1982) esp ch 5.
[45] *Regents of Univ of California v Bakke* (n 5).

beneficiaries of the measure, a burden which is not shared by those who are already privileged.

There is, however, a third and more promising way to justify the use of affirmative-action policies to improve the extent to which women's concerns and those of other excluded groups are addressed. This is to argue, as Young does, that decision-making is wrongly conceived of as a process of bargaining between interest groups, each of which represents a fixed set of interests, and whose representatives are mandated to further those interests and to compromise only as a quid pro quo.[46] Instead, it is argued, decision-making is a result of communication and discussion based on more than egotistical impulses, but on a desire to reach a fair and reasoned result.[47] Participants are prepared to recognize others' concerns and beliefs in their own right, not just in order to wrest return favours catering for their constituents' interests. In addition, this approach does not take an abstract, impartial view of rationality, but recognizes that the particular life experience of the decision maker is reflected in his or her view. Since gender and race remain such strong determinants of a person's life experience, the overwhelming predominance of one gender or race in decision-making fora make it unlikely that the experience and perspectives of the excluded group will be articulated.[48] Indeed, a study in Britain demonstrated that the biggest barrier to advancement for ethnic minorities, women, and disabled people within the senior Civil Service was believed to be a deeply embedded culture which acted to exclude those who were different from traditional Civil Service employees, who were generally middle-class, middle-aged white men.[49] On this view, it is possible to characterize the presence of historically disadvantaged groups as functioning to open up new perspectives on decision-making, to cast light on assumptions that the dominant group perceives as universal, and to enhance the store of 'social knowledge'.

On the face of it, this approach resonates with the third dimension, or the need for voice and participation. By highlighting the distinct perspectives of historically disadvantaged groups, which the very process of exclusion negates, it strongly supports the need for such groups to be guaranteed a place in deliberative decision-making. In addition, it demonstrates the necessity for

---

[46] I Young, 'Communication and the Other: Beyond Deliberative Democracy' in S Benhabib (ed), *Democracy and Difference: Contesting the Boundaries of the Political* (Princeton Paperbacks 1996) 118–19.

[47] ibid 92–94.

[48] Phillips (n 43) 52.

[49] (1999) 87 EOR 4.

a critical mass both to reflect differences in the interests in question and to make the common interests more audible. Such an approach was endorsed by O'Connor J in the US Supreme Court in *Grutter,* when she stated:

> Just as growing up in a particular region or having particular professional experiences is likely to affect an individual's views, so too is one's own, unique experience of being a racial minority in a society, like our own, in which race unfortunately still matters.[50]

This rationale might work better for schemes which set aside places for minorities or women on representative bodies, such as legislatures, on company boards, or in the judiciary than in employment or higher education. This is increasingly an approach which has been taken in different jurisdictions.

At the same time, such an approach risks essentializing a status group, assuming that all members share the same interests or perspectives, conflicting with the second dimension—redressing stigma and stereotyping. This makes us question the very definition of status groups, which is at the basis of a representation-based approach to affirmative action. Iris Marion Young argues that groups are better understood, not as fixed categories with impermeable boundaries, but as a set of relationships between different people. Such a relational understanding moves beyond the notion that a group consists of members who all share the same fixed attributes and have nothing in common with members of other groups. Instead, a group is characterized as a social process of interaction in which some people have an affinity with each other. Assertion of affinity with a group may change with social context and with life changes; and members may have interests which differ from other members of the group but are similar to members of other groups.[51]

A four-dimensional approach to substantive equality permits these issues to be taken into account, while at the same time optimizing the opportunity to include otherwise excluded perspectives. The way this can function is developed further later in relation to particular jurisdictions.

(ii) Standard of Scrutiny

The legitimacy of the aims of affirmative action is only the first question. Equally important is the question of whether the means fit the ends. This

---

[50] *Grutter v Bollinger* (n 34) 333.
[51] Young (n 46) 171–72.

question is overlaid by the need to take account of relative institutional competence. How much deference should judges be affording lawmakers and the executive in determining how best to further their legitimate aims? Courts vary widely in their response to this question. As we will see, the US courts have in recent years adopted the 'strict scrutiny' standard applicable to invidious racial discrimination,[52] framing the proportionality analysis in the narrowest terms. The State must demonstrate a 'pressing social need' and the measure must be 'narrowly tailored' to that end. The standard of strict scrutiny is premised on the notion that affirmative action is a narrow exception to the equal treatment principle. By contrast, under a substantive view of equality, affirmative action is a means to achieve equality, and therefore strict scrutiny should be unwarranted. Does this mean, however, that courts should entirely abdicate their supervisory function? The lightest touch review is found in the Supreme Court of Canada, which takes the view that review should be primarily directed to the genuineness of the government's stated ameliorative purpose, rather than to the results or effect of the programme.[53] To prevent the State from simply asserting an ameliorative purpose, the Court merely requires a showing that there is a correlation between the programme and the purpose. The South African Constitutional Court, while rejecting the strictness of 'narrow tailoring', has nevertheless retained for itself a role which goes beyond checking only for genuine ameliorative purpose. Instead, it requires a measure to meet the standard of reasonableness. This can be contrasted with the standard of scrutiny applied by the ECJ, which continues to regard affirmative action as a derogation from the principle of equality, and therefore to be construed strictly.

Ultimately, the role of the court should be to further substantive equality and therefore to support government measures which aim to achieve substantive equality. There is no equivalence between classification which perpetuates disadvantage or causes detriment, and measures which use status in order to achieve substantive equality. However, judicial support for affirmative action which furthers substantive equality should not be confused with deference to governmental decisions. Courts should still require governments to demonstrate that the aim of the measure is indeed to further substantive equality and to justify their choice of means. Justification need not amount to proof that there were no suitable alternatives, nor should the State have to demonstrate that the programme is effective. This preserves the

---

[52] *Adarand v Pena* (n 6).
[53] ibid para 47.

space for innovation, as emphasized by the Canadian Court. But justification does require that the State demonstrate that its measures are not based on assumptions, generalizations, or stereotypes. For example, in the ECJ case of *Lommers*,[54] the Dutch Ministry of Agriculture provided a workplace nursery catering for children of female but not male employees. According to Dutch law, the programme was legitimate because it was a 'distinction intended to place women in a privileged position in order to eliminate or reduce *de facto* inequalities' and was reasonable in relation to that aim.[55] The ECJ endorsed this approach. The Court pointed out that there was a significant under-representation of women in the Ministry of Agriculture, particularly in the higher grades. Similarly, there was a proven insufficiency of suitable and affordable nursery facilities, which the Court regarded as likely to induce women employees to give up their jobs. The Court was not oblivious to the danger that 'a measure such as that at issue . . ., whose purported aim is to abolish a *de facto* inequality, might nevertheless also help to perpetuate a traditional division of roles between men and women'.[56] However, it was not prepared to hold that the measure was disproportionate for failing to include working fathers.

The Court took into account the fact that the employer could grant requests from male officials in cases of emergency, to be determined by the employer, and the ministry assured the Court that male officials who brought up their children by themselves should, on that basis, have access to the nursery scheme. Nevertheless, it is submitted that the Court did not exercise sufficient scrutiny in the case. It is not sufficient to permit measures which exclude men from rights related to parenting on the ground that exceptions can be created for fathers who are primary carers. The scheme should be available to all fathers on the same terms as mothers. Genuinely transformative change can only occur when both parents are equally responsible for childcare.[57] Special measures for women, however well intentioned, run the risk of reinforcing their primary role as childcarers, and therefore perpetuating their disadvantage.

---

[54] Case C-476/99 *Lommers v Minister Van Landbouw, Natuurbeheer En Visserij* [2004] 2 CMLR 49 (ECJ).

[55] Dutch Law on Equal Treatment of Men and Women, art 5.

[56] *Lommers v Minister Van Landbouw, Natuurbeheer En Visserij* (n 54) para 41.

[57] See further S Fredman, *Women and the Law* (OUP 1997).

(iii)   Demarcating Beneficiaries: Recognition and Redistribution

A further challenging question concerns how the group of beneficiaries should be determined. Is it enough to define the beneficiary group according to their common experience of prejudice (recognition ills)? Or should it be necessary to show, in addition, that they have suffered socio-economic disadvantage (redistributive ills)? The relationship between redistribution and recognition need not require much attention when there is a substantial overlap. But what if status is no longer a fully reliable proxy for socio-economic disadvantage? As affirmative action measures become more effective, and some members of the status group begin to prosper, questions arise as to whether the latter should continue to benefit from the measure in question. One response is to overlay status with socio-economic disadvantage in demarcating the group of beneficiaries. To qualify for the benefit, the individual must show socio-economic disadvantage as well as membership of the status group. This can be seen in both India and the US.

The Indian Constitution permits special provision to be made for two categories of disadvantaged groups. The first are known as 'Scheduled Castes and Scheduled Tribes' (SC/ST) and are specified by the President.[58] The second are referred to as 'socially and educationally backward classes of citizens'[59] or other 'backward classes' (OBCs).[60] The latter are specified in a list drawn up by the National Commission for Backward Classes.[61] The equality guarantee in the Indian Constitution provides that special provisions, known as reservations, may be made for the advancement of any these categories.[62] Reservations are now widespread in higher education and public service jobs. But in recent decades, the question has arisen as to whether they should continue to be available to the 'creamy layer', or those members of the certified groups who are in fact no longer socially or educationally disadvantaged.

The Indian Supreme Court has held emphatically that, at least in the case of OBCs, the creamy layer should be excluded. Justice Jeevan Reddy stated in *Indra Sawhney*: 'In our opinion, it is not a question of permissibility or

---

[58]   Constitution of India, Arts 341(1), 342(2) <https://web.archive.org/web/20081022080607/http://www.commonlii.org/in/legis/const/2004/index.html> accessed 2 August 2022.

[59]   ibid Art 15(4).

[60]   See ibid Art 16(4).

[61]   See ibid Art 340(1); the list can be found at <http://ncbc.nic.in/backward-classes/index.html> accessed 2 August 2022.

[62]   ibid Art 15(4).

desirability of such test but one of proper and more appropriate identification of a class as a backward class.'[63] Similarly, the Chief Justice in *Ashoka Kumar* stated: 'To fulfil the conditions and to find out truly what is socially and educationally backward class, the exclusion of "creamy layer" is essential.'[64] In other words, the definition of the beneficiary class must correspond with the purpose of the provision, namely, to advance those who are disadvantaged. However, this objective is only imperfectly executed. As we will see later, the delineation of beneficiaries for reservation in India has been the subject of considerable struggle. On the one hand, there are now reservations on the basis of economic weakness on its own without the additional requirement of stigma or prejudice. On the other hand, Muslims and Christians who are subjected to stigma, segregation, and economic exploitation equivalent to their Hindu counterparts in the Scheduled Castes have not yet succeeded in their campaign for inclusion among the Scheduled Castes.[65]

A similar attempt to create a closer fit between status and socio-economic disadvantage is found in US affirmative action programmes, particularly in respect of programmes authorizing preferential treatment in the award of government contracts, which started life as expressly referring to racial and ethnic minorities. In order to comply with the strict scrutiny test, federal legislation mandating set-asides for status groups now also includes a requirement of evidence of socio-economic disadvantage. To participate in what has become known as a 'section 8(a) program',[66] a business must be 51 per cent owned by individuals who qualify as 'socially and economically disadvantaged'.[67] The relevant legislation defines 'socially disadvantaged individuals' as 'those who have been subjected to racial or ethnic prejudice or cultural bias because of their identity as a member of a group without regard to their individual qualities'.[68] There is a rebuttable presumption that members of certain groups are socially disadvantaged, including Black Americans, Hispanic Americans, Native Americans, Asian-Pacific Americans, and Subcontinent Asian Americans,[69] and members of other groups designated from time to time by the Small Business Administration (SBA).[70] The presumption of social disadvantage may be overcome with 'credible evidence to the contrary'.[71]

---

[63] *Indra Sawhney v Union of India*, AIR 1993 SC 447, 724.
[64] *Ashoka Kumar v Union of India and Others* [2008] 6 SCC 1, para 149.
[65] See Section II(iii).
[66] Small Business Act (SBA), 15 USC §§ 631 ff, sec 8(a).
[67] As defined in 13 CFR § 124.105.
[68] 15 USC § 637(a)(5); 13 CFR § 124.103(a).
[69] 13 CFR § 124.103(a). See also 15 USC § 637(a)(5).
[70] 13 CFR § 124.103(b).
[71] ibid § 124.103(b)(3).

On the other hand, an individual who is not a member of a listed group can be included if she or he can 'establish individual social disadvantage by a preponderance of the evidence'.[72]

In addition to their social disadvantage, individuals must be economically disadvantaged. The legislation defines 'economically disadvantaged individuals' as:

> those socially disadvantaged individuals whose ability to compete in the free enterprise system has been impaired due to diminished capital and credit opportunities as compared to others in the same business area who are not socially disadvantaged.[73]

Since 1989, objective monetary thresholds have been set to determine economic disadvantage. In 2020, this figure was set at personal net worth of less than $750,000, both at the time of entry into the programme and for continuing eligibility.[74] There is no presumption of economic disadvantage: each participant must prove such disadvantage.[75] The result is to exclude businesses which, regardless of race, are not in fact socially or economically disadvantaged, a similar effect to that achieved by the Indian 'creamy layer' provisions outlined earlier. Amendments adopted in 1994 specifically included 'small business concerns owned and controlled by women' in addition to 'socially and economically disadvantaged individuals'.

Also of importance has been the Transportation Equity Act for the 21st Century (known as TEA-21),[76] which authorizes the use of race- and sex-based preferences in federally funded transportation contracts. As in the SBA regulations, the TEA-21 regulations presume that Black Americans, Hispanic Americans, Native Americans, Asian-Pacific Americans, Subcontinent Asian Americans, and women are socially and economically disadvantaged.[77] However, this presumption is rebutted where the individual has a personal net worth of more than $750,000 or a preponderance of the evidence demonstrates that the individual is not in fact socially and economically disadvantaged.[78] Conversely, firms owned and controlled

---

[72] ibid § 124.103(c).

[73] ibid § 124.104(a). See also 15 USC § 637(a)(6)(A).

[74] Congressional Research Service, 'SBA's "8(a) Program": Overview, History and Current Issues' (November 2021) 7–8.

[75] 13 CFR § 124.104.

[76] TEA-21, extended through fiscal year 2009 by Public Law 109-59, signed into law during the 109th Congress.

[77] § 26.67(a).

[78] § 26.67(b).

by someone who is not presumed to be disadvantaged (ie a white male) can qualify for Disadvantaged Business Enterprise (DBE) status if the individual can demonstrate that he is in fact socially and economically disadvantaged.[79]

Behind the 'creamy layer' doctrine and its US counterpart is a powerful set of assumptions. By removing the socio-economically better off from the beneficiary class, it is assumed that affirmative action should only function to address the socio-economic dimension of status wrongs. On this view, ongoing status or recognition wrongs should be dealt with by anti-discrimination legislation, leaving affirmative action with a purely distributive function.[80] Indeed, to continue to use affirmative action for purely status wrongs could, on this view, simply reinforce stereotypes and therefore breach the recognition dimension. However, this unnecessarily narrows the role of affirmative action. Its aim should not be regarded as merely redistributive. Just as socio-economic disadvantage should not be hidden under an approach which focuses on status, so improvements in beneficiaries' socio-economic position should not obscure the ongoing effect of status. Indeed, it should go further. It is well known that beneficiaries of affirmative action can at times suffer from continued stigma, the assumption being that they have been selected regardless of merit. This perpetuates background stereotypes of individuals based on their race, caste, or gender. As Chandrachud J put it in *Pavitra*: 'Article 335 [efficiency of administration] cannot be construed on the basis of a stereotypical assumption that roster point promotees drawn from the SCs and STs are not efficient or that efficiency is reduced by appointing them. This is stereotypical because it masks deep rooted social prejudice. The benchmark for the efficiency of administration is not some disembodied, abstract ideal measured by the performance of a qualified open category candidate.'[81] Such prejudices last even when beneficiaries enter the 'creamy layer'. The answer is not to reduce the scope of affirmative action but to adjust its implementation so that ongoing stigma and stereotypes are also addressed. Affirmative action should take into account the other dimensions of affirmative action: facilitating voice and participation, and accommodating difference and achieving structural change.

---

[79] § 26.67(d).

[80] See further D Réaume, 'Dignity, Equality and Comparison' in D Hellman and S Moreau (eds), *Philosophical Foundations of Discrimination Law* (OUP 2013).

[81] *BK Pavitra v Union of India*, 10 May 2019, para 118.

III PREFERENTIAL POLICIES AND THE
LAW: CONTRASTING JURISDICTIONS

The arguments rehearsed here have been part of a lively debate in various jurisdictions about the legality of preferential policies or affirmative action. But the dominant model has differed widely between countries. Three broad approaches can be discerned. The first is to regard affirmative action as a breach of the right to equality (the 'formal' approach). The legislative framework in Britain broadly accepts this view. The second is to regard affirmative action as an exception to the prohibition against discrimination (the 'derogation' approach). As an exception, it is construed strictly but remains legitimate in defined circumstances. This has been the approach of the EU and the US. The final approach views affirmative action not as a derogation from the right to equality but as an aspect of equality. On this view, affirmative action is a legitimate means of fulfilling the non-discrimination principle, provided it is proportional (the 'substantive' approach). This approach can be seen in Canada, South Africa, and India, as well as in an increasing number of human rights instruments, both at the domestic and international levels, where express permission is given for affirmative action. The dispute has been at its fiercest in the US, where the battle between formal and substantive equality has yielded different victors at different stages of its development.

(i) Symmetry: The UK Approach

Traditionally, anti-discrimination legislation in Britain has left little room for reverse discrimination. The dominant characteristic is one of symmetry. The legislation explicitly provides that the provisions are applicable equally to the treatment of men and women;[82] and to all races or ethnic groups. Similarly, the legislation protects not just homosexual and bisexual but also heterosexual individuals.[83] The main exception to this symmetry, as we have seen, concerns disability: it is not discriminatory to treat a disabled person more favourably than a non-disabled person.[84] Similarly, no account is to be

---

[82] EA 2010, s 11. Northern Ireland has an established framework for positive action: see Chapter 8.
[83] ibid s 12.
[84] ibid s 13(3).

taken of special treatment of a woman in connection with pregnancy and childbirth.[85]

This symmetry is reinforced by judicial interpretation. As we saw in Chapter 5, in *James v Eastleigh Borough Council*,[86] the House of Lords held that the simple question to be considered was whether the complainant would have received the same treatment from the defendant 'but for' his or her sex. This line of reasoning is explicitly symmetrical, relying on a formal notion of justice which is abstracted from the social power relations within which it operates. As Lord Ackner declared, 'the reason why the policy was adopted can in no way affect or alter the fact that . . . men were to be treated less favourably than women, and were to be so treated on the ground of, because of their sex'.[87] This can be contrasted with the substantive notion of justice expressed in the dissenting judgment of Lord Griffiths. On his view, it could not be discriminatory to attempt to redress the result of an unfair act of discrimination by offering free facilities to those disadvantaged by the earlier act of discrimination.[88]

Some inroads have now been made into the overall symmetry of the legislative framework, inching the UK towards a 'derogation approach' and even demonstrating some signs of a substantive equality approach. However, these are narrowly confined by restrictive criteria, leaving the underlying commitment to a formal notion of equality largely undented and freezing out the possibility of the widespread affirmative-action measures seen in other jurisdictions. These opposing pressures are clearly seen in the two provisions in the EA 2010 which introduce the possibility of affirmative action, namely, sections 158 and 159. Particularly striking is the substantive manner in which the aims of the derogations are framed, closely tracking the four-dimensional approach to substantive equality. Section 158 of the Act applies to situations in which a person reasonably thinks that persons with a protected characteristic are at a disadvantage, or have different needs from others, or their participation in any activity is disproportionately low. In such circumstances, the Act 'does not prohibit' proportionate action to achieve the aim of encouraging persons with the protected characteristic to overcome or minimize that disadvantage; or to meet their needs or to participate in the activity in question. This reflects at least three of the four-dimensional

---

[85] ibid s 13(6)(b).
[86] [1990] 2 AC 751 (HL).
[87] ibid 769.
[88] ibid 768.

understandings of substantive equality. Section 159 of the Act expressly permits more favourable treatment in recruitment and promotion of those with a protected characteristic if their participation is disproportionately low, or they suffer disadvantage connected to that characteristic.[89] Charities are also permitted to provide benefits to persons with the same protected characteristic (apart from colour[90]) to prevent or compensate for disadvantage.[91]

This nod to substantive equality was recognized as such by the Scottish Court of Session in the 2021 case of *For Women Scotland v Lord Advocate*.[92] The case constituted a challenge of the Scottish Gender Representation on Public Boards Act 2018, which required public bodies to take steps towards achieving 50 per cent representation of women as non-executive members of public boards. It was argued, inter alia, that the Act breached the principle of equality of treatment. Taking an expressly substantive view, Lady Wise rejected this argument: 'It does not seem to me that the 2018 Act interferes with the principle of equal treatment once it is understood that measures designed to accelerate or achieve equality can be taken consistently with that principle. The 2018 Act is clearly designed to accelerate broad equality of representation on Scottish public boards.'[93]

An even more emphatic recognition of the substantive nature of the aims in section 158 is found in the 2020 Supreme Court case of *R (On the application of Z) v Hackney Borough Council*.[94] In that case, a charitable housing association's policy of giving first preference to disadvantaged Orthodox Jewish families in its allocation of housing was challenged as discriminatory on religious and racial grounds. It was argued that a policy which furthered equality of results was impermissible under EU law, which only permitted objectives furthering equality of opportunity. As we will see later, most of the cases before the ECJ were decided under the exception for positive action in Article 2(4) of the Equal Treatment Directive, which specified that such action should aim to achieve equality of opportunity. In rejecting the challenge, Lord Sales stressed that in section 158:

the range of permissible legitimate aims is wider than the legitimate aim specified in article 2(4) of the Equal Treatment Directive and includes seeking

[89] EA 2010, s 159.
[90] See n 4.
[91] Provided that this is permitted by their charitable instrument: ibid s 193.
[92] *For Women Scotland v Lord Advocate* [2021] CSOH 31 (Scottish Ct of Session (Outer House)).
[93] ibid [56].
[94] *R (On the application of Z) v Hackney Borough Council* [2020] UKSC 40 (UK Sup Ct).

to achieve particular outcomes, i.e. enabling persons who share the protected characteristic to overcome or minimise disadvantages they suffer which are connected to the characteristic or to meet needs particular to persons with the protected characteristic, . . . Accordingly, the correct question, . . ., is whether [the housing authority's] allocation policy is a measure which is proportionate to promoting such aims in relation to ameliorating the position of members of the Orthodox Jewish community. Those aims relate to improving outcomes for that community, not merely equality of opportunity of the more limited kind discussed in the cases on the Equal Treatment Directive.[95]

Given this recognition, the key issue is how the proportionality analysis is applied. As we will see, recent US decisions have insisted on 'strict scrutiny' for policies entailing a preference for Black or other minority people. The UK's response thus far has been, instead, to follow the standard proportionality approach found in EU law; in other words, that as a derogation from the right to equal treatment, such measures should 'remain within the limits of what is appropriate and necessary in order to achieve the aim in view and that the principle of equal treatment be reconciled as far as possible with the requirements of the aim thus pursued'.[96] Applying this test, the UK Supreme Court held that, given the evidence of the Orthodox Jewish community's religious needs, and the disadvantages to which they were subject on grounds of their religion, the first instance court had correctly found that 'the allocation policy was a legitimate and proportionate means of meeting those needs and of seeking to correct for those disadvantages'.[97]

These sparks of recognition of substantive equality signal a welcome move beyond Britain's strictly symmetrical approach. However, the deep ambivalence on this score is clearly in evidenced in relation to section 159 on recruitment and promotion, where the sparks of recognition of substantive equality are quickly extinguished by the remaining highly restrictive provisions. Positive action under section 159 only applies to those who are equally well qualified. Nor can it be part of a policy. Instead, individual assessments are required. In addition, it must be proportionate to the aim of enabling or encouraging persons who share the protected characteristic to overcome or minimize that disadvantage or participate in that activity. The Code of Practice interprets these requirements strictly.[98] As a start, it cautions against

---

[95] ibid [66].

[96] *Lommers v Minister Van Landbouw, Natuurbeheer En Visserij* (n 54) para 39.

[97] *R (On the application of Z) v Hackney Borough Council* (n 94) [73].

[98] <www.equalityhumanrights.com/en/publication-download/employment-statutory-code-practice> accessed 2 August 2022.

setting a low threshold for merit, which would in effect allow an employer to cherry-pick candidates on the basis of their protected characteristic even if not the most meritorious. This would constitute unlawful direct discrimination. Similarly, any suggestion that a policy was being pursued, for example making appointments or promotions to diversify the workforce, without determining individual merit, would open an employer to a charge of discrimination. In addition, employers are required to show clear evidence of disadvantage or disproportionate under-representation of groups with a protected characteristic. These, together with the need to show that a preference for the candidate with the protected characteristic was a proportionate means of achieving greater participation of that group in the workforce, make it very difficult to put in place any systematic process of affirmative action. Instead, the provision clearly reverts to a highly individualistic approach based on individual merit, individual fault, and an understanding of justice abstracted from the context.

A similar tension between symmetry and substance has accompanied the question of how to improve women's representation on public boards and legislative bodies. We have seen that the Scottish provision to achieve gender parity of non-executive members of public boards was immediately challenged as a breach of the equal treatment principle, but upheld by the Scottish court as a means of furthering substantive equality rather than a breach of the equal treatment principle. Similar controversy has surrounded positive action measures taken by political parties to increase their representation of women, ethnic minorities, or other groups with protected characteristics. The Labour Party introduced all-women shortlists in a limited number of constituencies[99] in 1993, a major factor in almost trebling the number of women Labour Party MPs returned to Parliament after the 1997 general election.[100] However, an employment tribunal struck down the policy as unlawful sex discrimination,[101] regarding the matter as conclusively decided by the 'simple' answer to the 'simple' test of whether the complainant would have received the same treatment but for his sex. 'It is obvious direct discrimination on grounds of sex.'[102] This led to a drop in the number of women elected to Parliament in the next general election.

---

[99] Fifty per cent of the constituencies were either: (i) marginal, (ii) new, or (iii) the sitting Labour MP was not standing at the next general election.

[100] See M Eagle and J Lovenduski, 'High Time or High Tide for Labour Women' (1998) Fabian Society Pamphlet 585.

[101] *Jepson v The Labour Party* [1996] IRLR 116 (IT).

[102] ibid 117.

In response, a provision was introduced in 2002 permitting political parties to use women-only shortlists in order to reduce the inequality in the numbers of men and women elected as candidates for the party.[103] The 2002 provision was originally introduced with a 'sunset clause', so that it would expire at the end of 2015. The EA 2010 extends the permission for single-sex shortlists until 2030. The EA 2010 also broadens this provision to cover all protected characteristics. Under this measure, political parties may make arrangements in relation to the selection of candidates to address the under-representation of any of those with protected characteristics in relevant elected bodies. However, arrangements in relation to protected characteristics other than gender cannot include shortlists restricted to that group. In addition, with the exception of gender, such arrangements must be proportionate to the aim of redressing inequality in representation.[104] For the Labour Party at least, the permission to use women-only shortlists has been highly successful. Indeed, in the 2019 general election, a milestone was passed when over half of all Labour Party MPs were women, many of them from constituencies with women-only shortlists. Paradoxically, this means that since the statutory purpose of reducing inequality has been achieved, women-only shortlists may no longer be permitted for future elections. Experience in the US, however, has shown that removing affirmative-action measures might lead to a drop in the number of under-represented people.

The measure has not, however, been without controversy, leading to further restrictive judicial decisions. Another political party, the Liberal Democrats (LibDems), found itself in court after withdrawing its policy of preferring female, Black, and ethnic minority candidates in the European parliamentary elections, which operate on a proportional representation or 'list' system. The party was sued for breach of contract by an ethnic minority candidate who would have been at the top of the list had the policy been in place. The court held that the policy, had it been left in place, would have been unlawful. Since the party only had one member of the European Parliament, and she was a woman, it could not be said that women were under-represented. Therefore, the criterion in section 104 of the EA 2010—namely, to 'reduce inequality in the party's representation in the body concerned'[105]—was not met. The court was also concerned that the effect of the paragraph preferring Black and ethnic minority candidates would be to dislodge candidates from other

---

[103] SDA, s 42A.
[104] EA 2010, s 104.
[105] *Dhamija v Liberal Democrats* [2019] EWHC 1398 (QB) (High Ct England).

under-represented groups, such as LGBTQI+ candidates. The judge took the view that given that the measure inevitably led to competition between disadvantaged groups, it could not be a proportionate means of achieving the statutory purpose of reducing inequality between under-represented groups.[106]

This raises the further question of what constitutes a disadvantaged group for the purposes of these provisions. This question was raised squarely before the Scottish court in relation to the Gender Representation on Public Boards (Scotland) Act 2018. The Act was challenged on the grounds that it included trans women in the definition of women for the purposes of achieving parity of representation. The court had no doubt that this was within the law, which permitted positive action both on grounds of gender and of gender reassignment for equal-opportunities measures relating to the inclusion of those with protected characteristics on Scottish public boards.[107] In Z, the housing authority case, there was also some contestation as to whether the housing allocation in favour of Orthodox Jewish people was proportionate to the disadvantages experienced by that group, given that the applicant was also a disadvantaged individual, namely, a single mother with four children in need of housing. The Supreme Court held that the allocation policy operated as a direct counter to discrimination faced by the Orthodox Jewish Community in finding housing in the private sector. Equally importantly, it endorsed a group-based application of the proportionality principle, holding that the first instance court was entitled to weigh up the disadvantage of this group as a whole against the minuscule disadvantage caused by the allocation policy to others in need of housing, given that the charity held less than 1 per cent of the total housing in the relevant borough, Hackney. The proportionality exercise would be distorted, Lord Sales held, by 'simply taking the worst affected individual who is not covered by the measure and comparing her with the most favourably affected individual who is covered by it', for example, by comparing the appellant with a member of the community who happened to be fortunate in having housing allocated to them.[108]

---

[106] ibid [43].
[107] *For Women Scotland v Lord Advocate* (n 92) [59].
[108] *R (On the application of Z) v Hackney Borough Council* (n 94) [82].

(ii) The Derogation Approach: EU Law

There is a much more established tradition in some EU countries than in the UK of using affirmative action to improve women's representation in the workforce and on public and elected bodies.[109] From early on in the development of gender discrimination law at the EU level, it was therefore accepted that it might be necessary to go beyond equality of treatment and take measures in favour of women to achieve equality in practice. Indeed, the EU Commission has promoted affirmative action. However, this has been formulated as a derogation from the principle of equality rather than as a means to achieve substantive equality. Since derogations must be strictly construed, it is through the principle of proportionality that the legitimacy of positive measures and their exceptionality has been determined. This, in turn, requires an explication both of the aims which are regarded as legitimate and of whether affirmative action achieves those aims, given the potential intrusion on the principle of equal treatment.

The guiding principle at the start was equality of opportunity. Thus Article 2(4) of the Equal Treatment Directive 1976[110] states that the principle of equal treatment 'shall be without prejudice to measures to promote equal opportunity for men and women, in particular by removing existing inequalities which affect women's opportunities'. The concept of equal opportunity has been contrasted with equality of results, considerably restricting the reach of affirmative-action policies. This was especially so in the *Kalanke* case, where the policy of a German public body to achieve parity of representation was struck down by the ECJ.[111] This led to a wider formulation in Article 141(4) with the Treaty of Amsterdam, later transcribed to its present position in Article 157(4) of the current treaty. While continuing to take the form of a derogation from equality, Article 157(4) no longer refers to equality of opportunity but instead to equality in practice. In addition, instead of the earlier reference to women's opportunities, this provision refers to the 'under-represented sex'. Thus Article 157(4) provides:

> With a view to ensuring full equality in practice between men and women in working life, the principle of equal treatment shall not prevent any Member

---

[109] Raphaële Xenidis and Hélène Masse-Dessen, 'Positive Action in Practice: Some Dos and Don'ts in the Field of EU Gender Equality Law' [2018] 2 European Equality L Rev 36 (revised 12 March 2020) <https://papers.ssrn.com/sol3/papers.cfm?abstract_id=3529537> last accessed 2 August 2022.

[110] Directive 76/207 EEC.

[111] *Kalanke v Freie Hansestadt Bremen* (n 21).

States from maintaining or adopting measures providing for specific advantages in order to make it easier for the under-represented sex to pursue a vocational activity or to prevent or compensate for disadvantages in professional careers.[112]

This approach is mirrored in the more recent directives. The Race Directive states as follows: 'With a view to ensuring full equality in practice, the principle of equal treatment shall not prevent any Member State from maintaining or adopting specific measures to prevent or compensate for disadvantages linked to racial or ethnic origin.'[113] The Employment Directive contains an identically worded provision in relation to religion or belief, disability, age, or sexual orientation.[114] The Gender Directive is the most encouraging of affirmative action, stating: 'Member states may maintain or adopt measures within the meaning of [Article 157(4)] with a view to ensuring full equality in practice between men and women in working life.'[115]

The 'derogation' approach reflects an underlying tension between a recognition of the limits of formal equality, on the one hand, and a firm adherence to individual merit, on the other. The ECJ has reiterated on numerous occasions that measures may be authorized which 'although discriminatory in appearance, are in fact intended to eliminate or reduce actual instances of inequality which may exist in the reality of social life.'[116] At the same time, as Advocate General Maduro put it in *Briheche*:

> The Court attempts to reconcile positive discrimination with the general principle of equality by allowing the former only to the extent that it does not lead to discrimination that favours a certain group at the expense of particular individuals: achieving a more equal representation of men and women in the workforce does not justify derogating from the right of each individual not to be discriminated against.[117]

---

[112] Treaty on European Union (2010). This was identically worded in Art 141(4) of the previous Treaty.

[113] Race Directive, Art 5.

[114] Framework Directive, Art 7(1).

[115] Directive 2006/54/EC of the European Parliament and of the Council on the implementation of the principle of equal opportunities and equal treatment of men and women in matters of employment and occupation (Recast Directive), Art 3.

[116] Case C-265/95 *Commission v France* [1997] ECR I-6959; *Kalanke v Freie Hansestadt Bremen* (n 21); Case C-409/95 *Marschall v Land Nordrhein-Westfalen* [1998] IRLR 39, para 26 (ECJ); P Alston, 'Strengths and Weaknesses of the ESC's Supervisory System' in G de Búrca and B de Witte (eds), *Social Rights in Europe* (OUP 2005) para 22.

[117] Case C-319/03 *Briheche v Ministre de L'Interieur* [2005] 1 CMLR 4, AG49.

The principle of equality of opportunity continues to be used by the Court to reconcile these apparently opposing imperatives.[118] Equality of opportunity goes beyond equal treatment in its recognition that, because of previous discrimination and disadvantage, affected groups are not in a position to compete on equal terms with others. Using the graphic metaphor of a running race, it is acknowledged that individuals who suffer from discrimination begin the race from different starting points. It is part of the function of equality to equalize the starting point, even if this might necessitate special measures for the disadvantaged group. However, equality of opportunity stops short of demanding equality of results. Once the starting point has been equalized, individuals enjoy equality of opportunity, and fairness demands that they be treated on the basis of their individual merit. As Advocate General Maduro explains:

> Equality of opportunities prevails over equality of results. The Court assumes that positive discriminatory measures can be accepted only if they are designed, in effect, to prevent discrimination in each individual case by forcing the employer to place women in a similar position to men.[119]

By embracing the principle of equality of opportunity, the Court has been able to recognize important limitations on women's ability to compete equally in the labour market. Thus, in *Marschall*,[120] the Court recognized that an apparently objective merit-based system could incorporate prejudicial assumptions:

> Even where male and female candidates are equally qualified, male candidates tend to be promoted in preference to female candidates particularly because of prejudices and stereotypes concerning the role and capacities of women in working life and the fear, for example, that women will interrupt their careers more frequently, that owing to household and family duties they will be less flexible in their working hours, or that they will be absent from work more frequently because of pregnancy, childbirth and breast-feeding.[121]

Thus, a measure giving preference to women candidates 'may counteract the prejudicial effects on female candidates of the attitudes and behaviour

---

[118] *Kalanke v Freie Hansestadt Bremen* (n 21) para 23.
[119] *Briheche v Ministre de L'Interieur* (n 117) AG42.
[120] *Marschall v Land Nordrhein-Westfalen* (n 21).
[121] ibid para 29.

described above and thus reduce actual instances of inequality which may exist in the real world'.[122]

At the same time, the Court's endorsement of equality of opportunity is tempered by its adherence to a principle of individual merit. This manifests itself in two ways. First, preference policies should not be automatic and unconditional. Meritorious individuals from outside the beneficiary class should have the possibility of individual assessment:

> National rules which guarantee women absolute and unconditional priority for appointment or promotion go beyond promoting equal opportunities and overstep the limits of the exception in Article 2(4) of the Directive.[123]

A measure giving priority to women in under-represented sectors of the public service would only be compatible with Community law if: (i) it does not automatically and unconditionally give priority to women when women and men are equally qualified; and (ii) the candidatures are the subject of an objective assessment which takes into account the specific personal situations of all candidates.[124]

For example, in *Kalanke*[125] a measure giving preference to equally qualified women was struck down. In *Marschall*,[126] by contrast, a similar measure was softened by a proviso allowing exceptions if 'reasons specific to another candidate predominate'. For this reason, the Court upheld the plan. The result was a highly circumscribed endorsement of such measures. A rule which gave priority to the promotion of female candidates was permitted where there were fewer women than men in the relevant post and both female and male candidates for the post were equally qualified, as long as the priority accorded to female candidates could, in principle, be overridden where an objectively assessed individual criterion tilted the balance in favour of the male candidate.[127]

It was this principle which the Norwegian government was found to have breached when, in an effort to remedy the under-representation of women in high-level academic positions, it provided funding for a small number of post-doctoral research grants and academic posts on the basis that they should be specifically earmarked for women. The European Free Trade

---

[122] ibid para 31.
[123] *Kalanke v Freie Hansestadt Bremen Kalanke* (n 21) para 22.
[124] Case C-158/97 *Badeck* [2000] IRLR 432, para 23 (ECJ).
[125] *Kalanke v Freie Hansestadt Bremen* (n 21).
[126] *Marschall v Land Nordrhein-Westfalen* (n 21).
[127] ibid para 35.

Association (EFTA) Court, which follows the jurisprudence of the ECJ, held that this measure was contrary to the principle of equal treatment and could not be regarded as falling within the exception defined in Article 2(4).[128] This was because it automatically excluded male applicants from the earmarked posts. Because the directive was based on the 'recognition of the right to equal treatment as a fundamental right of the individual', the EFTA Court explained, 'there must, as a matter of principle, be a possibility that the best qualified candidate obtains the post'.[129]

Secondly, the emphasis on individual merit has meant that preference measures can only be legitimate in the narrowly circumscribed situation in which all the candidates are equally qualified; that is, the preference policy can only operate as a 'tie-break'. It was for this reason that the ECJ struck down the measure in *Abrahamsson*.[130] In this case, the Swedish government was faced with a severe under-representation of women in professorial posts. It therefore promulgated a regulation requiring preference to be granted to a candidate of the under-represented sex provided she possessed sufficient qualifications, even if she were less qualified than a candidate from the opposite sex, unless the difference between the candidates' qualifications was so great as to give rise to a breach of the requirement of objectivity in the making of appointments. In the case in question, a woman had been appointed who, although sufficiently qualified, had been ranked below a male candidate for the job. Again, the ECJ held that individual merit should trump the demands of substantive equality. The measure was in breach of Article 2(4) because selection was 'ultimately based on the mere fact of belonging to the under-represented sex, and this is so even if the merits of the candidates so selected are inferior to those of a candidate of the opposite sex'. Nor were candidates subjected to an objective assessment which took account of their specific personal situations.

This was clearly articulated by Advocate General Saggio in *Badeck*,[131] whose opinion reiterates the dual emphasis on substantive equality and the primacy of the individual. The reconciliation of the two, he argued, lay in the development of a proportionality criterion. Equal treatment, or formal equality, comes into conflict with substantive equality only if the remedial measure, in this case positive action in favour of women, is disproportionate, either in that it demands excessive sacrifices from those who do not belong to

---

[128] Case E-1/02 *EFTA Surveillance Authority v Norway* [2003] 1 CMLR 23 (EFTA Court).
[129] ibid para 45.
[130] Case C-407/98 *Abrahamsson v Fogelqvist* [2000] IRLR 732 (ECJ).
[131] *Badeck* (n 124).

the group, or when the social reality does not justify it. Positive action could therefore be lawful if it was proportionate in that sense. Nevertheless, individual merit, provided it is purified of discriminatory assumptions, remains the governing principle. It is only permissible to institute automatic preferences for women to redress under-representation if there is an objective examination of the professional and personal profile of each candidate and there is no bar to the selection of a man if he is more suitable for the job.

Although the more recent formulations in Article 157(4) and the new directives might give Member States somewhat wider discretion in formulating positive measures than Article 2(4),[132] these foundational values remain. This was summed up well by Advocate General Maduro in *Briheche*.[133] He rejected an interpretation of Article 157(4) which would subordinate an individual's right not to be subjected to discrimination to the aim of achieving equality between groups. 'Such a reading is hardly compatible with the priority which the Court has given to equality of opportunities and to its traditional understanding of the general principle of equal treatment.' Instead, he favoured an interpretation according to which:

the purpose of compensatory measures of this type becomes that of reestablishing equality of opportunities by removing the effects of discrimination and promoting long-term maximisation of equality of opportunities . . . To base the acceptance of compensatory forms of positive discrimination on equality of opportunities and not on equality of results would still make equality among individuals prevail over equality among groups.[134]

Likewise, in *Abrahamsson*,[135] when dealing with Article 157(4), the ECJ held that the measure in question, which gave preference to women even if they were less well qualified than male competitors, was 'on any view . . . disproportionate to the aim pursued'.[136] The Court in *Briheche* was similarly of the view that Article 157(4) did not permit a measure which was disproportionate because it gave automatic and unconditional preference to women.[137]

While the Court has consistently emphasized the importance of protecting individuals from discrimination as a counter to positive action, it has paid less attention to the need to ensure that positive measures genuinely

---

[132] *Briheche v Ministre de L'Interieur* (n 117) para AG48.
[133] ibid.
[134] ibid AG49–51.
[135] Case C-407/98 *Abrahamsson and Anderson v Fogelqvist* [2000] IRLR 732 (ECJ).
[136] ibid para 55.
[137] *Briheche v Ministre de L'Interieur* (n 117) para 30.

further substantive equality, rather than reinforcing stereotypes. Protective legislation for women is an example of a provision which could be misinterpreted as remedying disadvantage for women when in fact it reinforces stereotypes. As we saw in the previous chapter, this danger is particularly evident in relation to pregnancy and parenting. While specific rights for women in relation to pregnancy and childbirth should not be regarded as a breach of the principle of equality, this is not the case for parenting rights. If the distribution of labour in the home is to be altered, parenting rights available to women should also be available to men. The ECJ in *Lommers* rejected a claim that it was discriminatory on grounds of sex to provide childcare facilities for working mothers and not for working fathers. Instead, it held, the aim of such provision was to reduce inequality for women.[138] However, genuinely transformative change requires both parents to be responsible for childcare. Rather than simply upholding the scheme, or striking it down as a breach of equality, the Court should have required that it be extended to both parents on the same terms.

(iii) Symmetry vs Substance: The US Supreme Court

Nowhere has the dichotomy between the formal and substantive approaches been more vividly demonstrated than in the US Supreme Court. The Court has been the arena of a fierce struggle between judicial proponents of a formal, symmetrical view of equality and those who advocate a more substantive position. Earlier case law witnessed the triumph of a vigorous substantive approach. This entailed an emphatic movement away from the core elements of formal equality, namely, adherence to a view of justice abstracted from its social context, individualism, and the principle of a neutral State. Thus, far from an abstract view of justice, a strong stream of Supreme Court jurisprudence recognized that although 'the enduring hope is that race should not matter; the reality is that too often it does'. Mandated by Title VII of the Civil Rights Act 1964, courts began to order affirmative action as a remedy in cases of proven past discrimination.[139] Having signalled a clear departure from an abstract, formal view of justice, the Court soon began to move beyond individualism, with its emphasis on individual merit and

---

[138] *Lommers v Minister Van Landbouw, Natuurbeheer En Visserij* (n 54) para 32; see Equal Treatment Directive, Art 2(4).
[139] *Franks v Bowman Transportation Co* 424 US 747, 96 S Ct 1251 (1975).

individual fault. As a start, it accepted that court-ordered reverse discrimination need not be restricted to the victim. Non-victims may also be beneficiaries provided they are members of a group previously suffering from invidious discrimination.[140] In addition, the emphasis on individual fault was replaced by a consideration of who would be in the best position to bring about change. This led the Court to move beyond recognizing affirmative action merely as a remedy for proven discrimination, to accepting voluntarily instituted affirmative action programmes. Instead of proof of fault, the Court only required sufficient evidence of imbalances and segregation for which the employer appeared responsible.[141]

With the departure from formal justice and individualism came a rejection of the principle that the State should remain neutral. Instead, the Court upheld both the right and the responsibility of the State to use its public and market powers in remedying discrimination. *Fullilove v Klutznick*[142] concerned a policy according to which 10 per cent of federal funds granted for the provision of public works were set aside to procure services from minority-owned businesses, even if they were not the lowest bidder. It was argued that this was in breach of the Fourteenth Amendment right to equality. The Court rejected the challenge. Chief Justice Burger stated specifically that in a remedial context, it was not necessary for Congress to act in a wholly 'colour-blind' way.[143] Indeed, substantive reverse discrimination was a necessary means to achieve equal economic opportunities.

However, recent cases have been marked by the ascendancy of a far more restrictive approach which centres on the question of whether 'strict scrutiny' should apply to affirmative-action measures in the same way as it applies to invidious discrimination. After much conflicting jurisprudence, the exacting standard of strict scrutiny won the day. In *Adarand v Pena*,[144] the Court decided by a majority of five to four that even in cases of 'benign' racial classification, or affirmative action, the standard of strict scrutiny should apply. Nevertheless, O'Connor J, giving the judgment of the Court, was at

---

[140] *United States v Paradise* 480 US 149, 107 S Ct 1053 (1988).

[141] *United Steelworkers v Weber* 443 US 193, 99 S Ct 2721 (1979); *Johnson v Santa Clara* 480 US 616, 107 S Ct 1442 (1987).

[142] 448 US 448, 100 S Ct 2758 (1980).

[143] The term 'colour-blind' has been used by Justices of the US Supreme Court who argue that skin colour should never be a relevant factor in determining access to university or jobs, and therefore affirmative action in favour of disadvantaged groups should not be permitted (see Chapter 7). For a critique, see R Kennedy, 'Colorblind Constitutionalism' (2013) 82 Fordham L Rev 1.

[144] *Adarand v Pena* (n 6).

pains to dispute the notion that strict scrutiny is strict in theory but fatal in fact.[145] Indeed, she held, the federal government might well have a compelling interest to act on the basis of race to overcome the 'persistence of both the practice and lingering effects of racial discrimination against minority groups'.[146]

The standard of strict scrutiny requires courts to decide the legitimacy of an affirmative action programme on two levels, similar to that of proportionality. First, what would constitute a compelling interest sufficient to legitimate an affirmative-action programme. Secondly, when is an affirmative action programme sufficiently 'narrowly tailored' to achieve those aims? Only two aims have been identified as legitimate: redressing unlawful discrimination and attaining diversity. The former has been increasingly narrowly interpreted, requiring an actual finding of discrimination and excluding discriminatory patterns, for example, those arising from de facto segregation or disadvantage. By contrast, the second aim, diversity, has left space for more liberal Justices to uphold carefully delimited race-conscious plans. This latter development has largely taken place in the context of higher education. Leading universities, acutely aware of large disparities in the representation of Black people, Hispanic people, and other minorities in student admissions, have regularly attempted to put in place appropriate policies to increase such representation. Time and again, however, disappointed students from the more privileged groups have challenged these policies as a breach of their own right to equal treatment. The result has been a stream of cases before the US Supreme Court, each constituting a more sophisticated attempt by universities to reach the standards set by the previous decisions, and each finding itself again in court. A key influence on the approach in US jurisprudence, as in the EU, has been the principle of individualized assessment so that race is considered only one factor. This is considered to achieve a balance whereby individuals outside the target group are not expected to bear too great a burden in redressing the disadvantage of the preferred group. Since cases are generally brought by or in the name of such parties, this has tended to be the focus of the judgments. By contrast, there is generally no scope for a disappointed beneficiary to bring a claim. This reinforces the underlying assumption that affirmative action is only a derogation of equal treatment rather than a means to achieve substantive equality. These trends are elaborated on later.

---

[145] ibid 2117.
[146] Rehnquist, Kennedy, and Thomas JJ all agreed.

The first case in which this issue arose was the famous *Bakke* case, in which Bakke, a white man who had been rejected by the University of California Medical School, challenged its admissions programme as a breach of the Equal Protection Clause.[147] Under the programme, sixteen of the one hundred places at the Medical School were set aside for economically or educationally disadvantaged minority-group applicants. Four Justices would have upheld the programme as a means to remedy disadvantage caused by past racial prejudice and four Justices would have found a pure violation of the Equal Protection Clause. The balance therefore lay with Justice Powell. In his famous judgment, he held that diversity was potentially a legitimate State interest which could fulfil the requirements of strict scrutiny. Diversity, however, could not be achieved by the use of an explicit racial criterion. Instead, diversity had to 'encompass [a broad] array of qualifications and characteristics of which racial or ethnic origin is but a single though important element'.[148] The programme was therefore struck down.

Universities in the US began to adjust their affirmative-action programmes to meet the Supreme Court's criteria, whereas litigants, frequently backed by strategic litigators, continued to contest such programmes as a breach of the equal treatment principle. Given the need for narrow tailoring, which entailed a demonstration that alternatives to racial preferences had been explored, particular attention was paid to potential race-neutral methods to achieve diversity. After the University of Texas had its racial preference policy struck down in *Hopwood v Texas*,[149] the State of Texas instituted a requirement that all students in the top 10 per cent of their high school class should be afforded a place at a State university. The rationale behind this rule was to ensure that students from disadvantaged schools, who were also predominantly African American and Hispanic, would have a pathway to admission. As the Court of Appeals put it in *Fisher*: 'The sad truth is that the Top Ten Percent Plan gains diversity from a fundamental weakness in the Texas secondary education system. The de facto segregation of schools in Texas enables the Top Ten Percent Plan to increase minorities in the mix, while ignoring contributions to diversity beyond race. . . . While the Top Ten Percent Plan boosts minority enrolment by skimming from the tops of Texas high schools, it does so against this backdrop of increasing resegregation in Texas public schools, where over half of Hispanic students and 40% of black

---

[147] *Regents of Univ of California v Bakke* (n 5).
[148] ibid 315.
[149] *Hopwood v Texas* 78 F 3d 932 (1996) (US Federal Ct of Appeals).

students attend a school with 90%–100% minority enrolment.'[150] Moreover, there was a stark discrepancy between attainment levels in these disadvantaged schools and those of mixed or white schools.

This ongoing contestation led to a pair of cases against the University of Michigan in 2003: *Grutter v Bollinger*,[151] in which the Court upheld the Law School's affirmative-action programme, and *Gratz v Bollinger*,[152] decided on the same day, in which the Court struck down the programme at the College of Literature, Science and Arts. The central issue was how to define and apply the concept of diversity without falling foul of the Court's prohibition of expressly race-conscious decision making. The Law School's aim of achieving a 'critical mass' of minority students, as distinct from a 'quota', was key to its success. O'Connor J accepted that this was part of the Law School's goal of 'assembling a class that is both exceptionally academically qualified and broadly diverse' rather than simply to ensure a specified percentage of a particular group because of its race or ethnic origin. The latter, she held, 'would amount to outright racial balancing, which is patently unconstitutional. Rather, the Law School's concept of critical mass is defined by reference to the educational benefits that diversity is designed to produce.'[153] Such benefits include improving racial understanding, advancing learning outcomes, and preparing students for a diverse workforce and society. Importantly, too, she accepted that a critical mass was important to break down stereotypes. The Law School did not assume that minority groups express a particular characteristic viewpoint; but that, nevertheless, a diverse range of perspectives would be achieved because of the different life experience of different racial groups.[154]

As well as accepting that its diversity aim was legitimate for the purposes of strict scrutiny, the Court held that Michigan Law School's programme was narrowly tailored to achieve this result. Crucial to this, as in the EU cases, was the use of individualized decision making which, the Court held, meant that applicants from minority groups were not insulated from the competition for admission. This, in turn, was part of ensuring that there was no undue impact on third parties. As O'Connor J put it:

---

[150] *Fisher v University of Texas at Austin* 758 F 3d 633, 650–51 (2014) (US Federal Ct of Appeals).

[151] *Grutter v Bollinger* (n 34).

[152] *Gratz v Bollinger* 539 US 244 (2003) (US Sup Ct).

[153] *Grutter v Bollinger* (n 34) 329–30.

[154] ibid 334.

> We acknowledge that there are serious problems of justice connected with the idea of preference. Narrow tailoring, therefore, requires that a race-conscious admissions program not unduly harm members of any racial group. The Law School's programme did not do so. As long as race is used as a 'plus' factor in the context of an individualized consideration, a rejected applicant will not have been foreclosed from all consideration for that seat simply because he was not the right colour or had the wrong surname. . . . His qualifications would have been weighed fairly and competitively, and he would have no basis to complain of unequal treatment under the Fourteenth Amendment.[155]

By contrast, the programme under scrutiny in *Gratz v Bollinger* awarded an additional twenty points to under-represented minority applicants, a significant contribution towards the seventy-five to one hundred points needed for admission. This was struck down for failing to provide the necessary individual consideration. Instead, the effect was to make 'the factor of race decisive for virtually every minimally qualified underrepresented minority applicant'.[156] The programme was therefore not narrowly tailored to achieve the diversity aim.

The decision in *Grutter* led other universities to reinstate an element of race-conscious decision making. In particular, the University of Texas decided that the Top Ten Percent rule was too rigid to achieve the true diversity that *Grutter* had upheld. While maintaining the Top Ten Percent Rule for the majority of is admissions, it set aside about 25 per cent of places for considering race as one factor among many in determining admission.[157] It was to these programmes that opponents of affirmative action next turned their attention. This time the litigant was not a white man but a white woman, Abigail Fisher, who claimed that she had been discriminated against on grounds of her race. The Court upheld the plan on the basis that it was narrowly tailored to achieve the constitutionally permissible goal of diversity. It reiterated the strong presumption against race-based decision making. 'Because racial characteristics so seldom provide a relevant basis for disparate treatment, [r]ace may not be considered [by a university] unless the admissions process can withstand strict scrutiny.'[158] Importantly, however, the Court was prepared to afford a measure of deference to the university to determine whether and how a diverse student body would serve its

---

[155] ibid 318.
[156] *Gratz v Bollinger* (n 152) 271–72.
[157] *Fisher v University of Texas at Austin* 570 US 297, 304–07, 133 S Ct 2411 (2013) (US Sup Ct).
[158] ibid 2418.

educational goals. A university cannot impose a fixed quota. But as long as it gives a reasoned, principled explanation for its decision, the Court should defer to the university's conclusion as to its goals. On the other hand, no deference is owed when determining whether the use of race is sufficiently narrowly tailored to achieve the university's permitted goals. 'Though narrow tailoring does not require exhaustion of every conceivable race-neutral alternative or require a university to choose between maintaining a reputation for excellence and fulfilling a commitment to provide educational opportunities to members of all racial groups, it does impose on the university the ultimate burden of demonstrating that race-neutral alternatives that are both available and workable do not suffice.'[159]

Applying these principles in *Fisher II*, the Supreme Court found that the university had provided a sufficiently reasoned articulation of the precise goals of its race-conscious admissions programme, including 'destroying racial stereotypes, promoting cross-racial understanding, preparing the student body for an increasingly diverse workforce and society, cultivating leaders with legitimacy in the eyes of the citizenry, providing an educational environment that fosters the robust exchange of ideas, exposure to different cultures, and the acquisition of the competencies required of future leaders'.[160] It had also discharged the heavy burden of showing that the programme was narrowly tailored to achieve those goals, including a good-faith attempt to use race-neutral policies, and concluding that these were not sufficient to achieve sufficient racial diversity.

The Court has been much less willing to exercise deference when it comes to addressing some of the roots of the problem of low representation in higher education; namely, de facto school segregation arising from residential segregation. In *Parents Involved in Community Schools v Seattle*,[161] a challenge was mounted against a school district student-assignment plan that relied on racial classification to allocate slots in oversubscribed high schools to address residential segregation. The Court struck down the plan by a majority of five to four. All the Justices in *Community Schools* agreed that the need to remedy intentional past discrimination constituted a compelling reason. However, the majority held that this did not extend to remedying de facto discrimination:

---

[159] *Fisher v University of Texas at Austin* 136 S Ct 2198, 2208 (2016) (US Sup Ct).
[160] ibid 2211.
[161] *Parents Involved in Community Schools v Seattle School District* (n 1).

This Court never has held that societal discrimination alone is sufficient to justify a racial classification. Rather, the Court has insisted upon some showing of prior discrimination by the governmental unit involved before allowing limited use of racial classifications in order to remedy such discrimination.[162]

Nor was a State permitted to voluntarily institute such measures. When de facto discrimination is at issue, States must 'seek alternatives to the classification and differential treatment of individuals by race'.[163]

Several of the majority Justices took the view that race should never feature in a government decision. However, Kennedy J, who held the swing vote, rejected this approach. To regard the Constitution as wholly colour blind[164] 'is too dismissive of the legitimate interest government has in ensuring all people have equal opportunity regardless of their race. The plurality's postulate that "[t]he way to stop discrimination on the basis of race is to stop discriminating on the basis of race," is not sufficient to decide these cases.'[165] Again, individual selection was regarded as the keystone of equal opportunity. Thus, Kennedy J held, if school authorities were concerned that the student-body compositions of certain schools interfered with the objective of offering an equal educational opportunity to all their students, they were free to devise race-conscious measures to address the problem in a general way, provided they did not treat each student on the basis of a systematic individual typing by race. Kennedy J also disagreed with the plurality finding that diversity could not constitute a compelling State interest outside higher education. Instead, he agreed with the dissent that 'diversity, depending on its meaning and definition, is a compelling educational goal a school district may pursue'.[166]

As we saw in Chapter 4, gender is not considered a suspect class that is subject to strict scrutiny. Affirmative-action programmes in favour of women, therefore, need not reach the standard of strict scrutiny required in race cases. In US v Virginia,[167] the Supreme Court reiterated that 'sex classifications may be used to compensate women for particular economic disabilities they have suffered, to promote equal employment opportunity, to advance the full development of talent and capacities of nation's people; but

---

[162] *Wygant v Jackson Board of Education* (n 7) 274.
[163] *Parents Involved in Community Schools v Seattle School District* (n 1) 796.
[164] See n 143.
[165] *Parents Involved in Community Schools v Seattle School District* (n 1) 788.
[166] ibid 784.
[167] *US v Virginia* 518 US 515 (1996) (US Sup Ct).

such classifications may not be used to create or perpetuate legal, social, and economic inferiority of women'.[168]

(iv) Substantive Equality: New Insights and New Challenges

India, Canada, and South Africa have had a much less anguished approach to affirmative action, largely regarding it as a means to achieve substantive equality rather than as a breach. This is assisted by the fact that affirmative action is expressly mandated in all three Constitutions. The Constitution of India was one of the earliest constitutions to expressly incorporate provisions for affirmative action, in the form of reservations of a proportion of university places or public sector jobs. The framers of the Constitution took note of the fact that certain communities in the country were suffering from extreme social, educational, and economic disadvantage, arising out of the age-old practice of 'untouchability' and caste discrimination, and needed special consideration to accelerate their socio-economic development. As discussed earlier, special provision is made in the Constitution for two categories of disadvantaged groups. The first are known as 'Scheduled Castes and Scheduled Tribes' and are specified by the president.[169] The second are referred to as 'socially and educationally backward classes of citizens',[170] or other 'backward classes'.[171] The latter are specified in a list drawn up by the National Commission for Backward Classes.[172] Article 15(4) permits special provision for the advancement of any 'socially and educationally backward' classes of citizens or for the Scheduled Castes and the Scheduled Tribes and, in particular, for their admission to educational institutions. Similarly, Article 16, which provides for equal opportunity in public employment, expressly permits the State to make provisions for reservations in recruitment or promotion in favour of the Scheduled Castes and Scheduled Tribes.[173] At the same time, Article 15(3) provides that the State may make special provision for women and children. To these are added the statutory provision requiring 5 per cent of university places to be set aside for people with 'benchmark'

---

[168] ibid 534.
[169] Constitution of India, Arts 341(1) and 342(1) (see n 58).
[170] ibid Art 15(4).
[171] ibid Art 16(4).
[172] ibid Art 340(1); see n 61 for the list.
[173] ibid Art 16(4A) and (4B).

disabilities which, as we saw in Chapter 3, are defined strictly.[174] Reservations are now widespread in higher education and public service jobs.

As in India, the Canadian Charter contains an explicit provision making it clear that measures will not be a breach of the equality guarantee in the Charter if the object is to ameliorate the conditions of disadvantaged individuals or groups. Section 15(2) states: 'Subsection (1) does not preclude any law, program or activity that has as its object the amelioration of conditions of disadvantaged individuals or groups including those that are disadvantaged because of race, national or ethnic origin, colour, religion, sex, age or mental or physical disability.'[175] It can be seen from this that, unlike US jurisprudence where an interest in diversity has been developed as a substitute for expressly focusing on de facto disadvantage, the Canadian Charter explicitly permits programmes that aim to ameliorate the condition of disadvantaged groups identified by the enumerated or analogous grounds.[176]

The South African Constitution contains the clearest endorsement of affirmative action as a means to achieve substantive equality. Section 9(2) of the South African Constitution provides: 'To promote the achievement of equality, legislative and other measures designed to protect or advance persons, or categories of persons, disadvantaged by unfair discrimination may be taken.' As in Canada, the aims are set out in the Constitution and avoid the challenge faced by the US Supreme Court of formulating such aims through its own jurisprudence. To escape the charge of discrimination, the measure must target persons, or categories of persons, who have been disadvantaged by unfair discrimination. This is taken forward by the Employment Equity Act (EEA), which requires designated employers to implement affirmative-action measures for people from designated groups (Black people,[177] women, and people with disabilities). The Act expressly provides that it is not unfair discrimination to take affirmative action measures in accordance with the Act.

The EEA is more specific in its aims than the Constitution. In particular, it draws on the concept of representativeness in section 195 of the Constitution, which provides that 'public administration must be broadly representative of the South African people, with employment and personnel

---

[174] Rights of Persons with Disabilities Act, s 32.

[175] Canadian Charter of Rights, s 15(2).

[176] s 15(2).

[177] The Act states: '"black people" is a generic term which means Africans, Coloureds and Indians' (Employment Equity Act No 55 of 1998, s 1).

management practices based on ability, objectivity, fairness, and the need to redress the imbalances of the past to achieve broad representation.[178] The preamble to the EEA declares that the disparities in the labour market resulting from apartheid and other discriminatory laws and practices 'create such pronounced disadvantages for certain categories of people that they cannot be redressed simply by repealing discriminatory laws'. It therefore aims, inter alia, to 'achieve a diverse workforce broadly representative of our people'. This is operationalized in section 15 of the Act, which states that affirmative action must include measures to 'ensure the equitable representation of suitably qualified people from designated groups in all occupational categories and levels in the workforce'.[179] The Act also refers to other aims, including: measures designed to further diversity in the workplace based on equal dignity and respect of all people; making reasonable accommodation for people from designated groups; and implementing training measures.[180] However, as we will see, it is the conception of representativeness which has dominated the case law. Affirmative action programmes are now a major part of the strategy of achieving equality, particularly in employment.

(a) From formal to substantive equality

In all three jurisdictions, the movement from formal to substantive equality has been clearly charted. The Supreme Court of India, having initially regarded reservations as an exception to the overriding principle of formal equality,[181] subsequently emphatically embraced them as a means of achieving substantive equality.[182] According to Justice Krishna Iyer: 'To my mind, this sub-article [16(4)] serves not as an exception but as an emphatic statement, one mode of reconciling the claims of backward people and the opportunity for free competition the forward sections are ordinarily entitled to. . . . It has not really carved out an exception but has preserved a power untrammelled by the other provisions of the Article.'[183] This perspective was reinforced in *Indra Sawhney*,[184] where Justice Reddy for the majority made it clear that Article 14 did not entail formal, symmetric equality in the form of aiming to remove all classifications. Instead, the concept of 'equality before

---

[178] South African Constitution, s 195(1)(i). See also Public Services Act, s 11(1), 11(2)(b); Correctional Services Act, s 96(3)(c).

[179] Employment Equity Act No 55 of 1998, s 15(2)(d)(i).

[180] ibid s 15(2).

[181] *MR Balaji v State of Mysore* 1963 AIR 649 (Indian Sup Ct).

[182] *State of Kerala v NM Thomas* AIR 1976 SC 490 (Indian Sup Ct).

[183] ibid 513.

[184] *Indra Sawhney v Union of India* (n 63).

the law contemplates minimising the inequalities in income and eliminating the inequalities in status, facilities and opportunities not only amongst individuals, but also among groups of people'.[185] Fifteen years later, in *Ashoka Kumar Thakur*,[186] the substantive approach was reiterated by the Chief Justice: 'Reservation,' he stated, 'is one of the many tools that are used to preserve and promote the essence of equality, so that disadvantaged groups can be brought to the forefront of civil life. It is also the duty of the State to promote positive measures to remove barriers of inequality and enable diverse communities to enjoy the freedoms and share the benefits guaranteed by the Constitution.'[187] Thus 'Article 15(4) and 16(4) are not exceptions to Article 15(1) and Article 16(1) but independent enabling provision[s]'.[188] In the same case, the Court was invited to hold that affirmative action decisions should be subject to 'strict scrutiny' in a similar fashion to the test used in the US. It rejected this view. Affirmative action was legitimated both by express constitutional provision for reservations and by the specific provision in the Directive Principles.

A similar trajectory can be seen in Canada. While there was some suggestion in earlier cases that section 15(2) should be read as an exception to the equality guarantee, the Supreme Court of Canada in its 2008 decision in *Kapp*[189] emphatically held that:

Sections 15(1) and 15(2) work together to promote the vision of substantive equality that underlies s. 15 as a whole. Section 15(1) is aimed at preventing discriminatory distinctions that impact adversely on members of groups identified by the grounds enumerated in s. 15 and analogous grounds. This is one way of combating discrimination. However, governments may also wish to combat discrimination by developing programs aimed at helping disadvantaged groups improve their situation. Through s. 15(2), the Charter preserves the right of governments to implement such programs, without fear of challenge under s. 15(1). . . . Thus s. 15(1) and s. 15(2) work together to confirm s. 15's purpose of furthering substantive equality.[190]

Moreover: 'Section 15(2) supports a full expression of equality, rather than derogating from it.'[191]

---

[185] ibid para 5.
[186] *Ashoka Kumar Thakur v Union of India* (n 64).
[187] ibid para 6.
[188] ibid para 100.
[189] *R v Kapp* 2008 SCC 41 (Can Sup Ct).
[190] ibid para 16.
[191] ibid para 37.

The same is true for South Africa. The meaning of this provision was elaborated in *Van Heerden*,[192] a claim of race discrimination brought by a white Afrikaner Member of Parliament aggrieved at a measure which enhanced the pension contributions of post-apartheid Members of Parliament but not pre-apartheid members. The High Court took a formal view of equality, holding that the affected white members had been less favourably treated on grounds of their race. The relatively advantaged position of the affected white members was regarded as irrelevant. The High Court therefore struck down the programme as unfair discrimination. The Constitutional Court resoundingly disagreed. Moseneke J stressed that instead of being an exception to equality, restitutionary measures are an essential part of it: 'What is clear is that our Constitution and in particular section 9 thereof, read as a whole, embraces for good reason a substantive conception of equality inclusive of measures to redress existing inequality . . . Such measures are not in themselves a deviation from, or invasive of, the right to equality guaranteed by the Constitution. . . . They are integral to the reach of our equality protection. In other words, the provisions of section 9(1) and section 9(2) are complementary; both contribute to the constitutional goal of achieving equality to ensure "full and equal enjoyment of all rights".'[193]

(b) Standard of scrutiny

The presumption against affirmative action inherent in a strict standard of judicial scrutiny is displaced by the recognition that affirmative action is a means of achieving substantive equality rather than a narrow derogation. This does not, however, mean that courts have no responsibility for ensuring that affirmative action programmes are indeed capable of furthering equality. How, then, have the courts in these three jurisdictions fashioned their role? In India, in *Ashoka Kumar Thakur*, the Court was invited to hold that affirmative action decisions should be subject to 'strict scrutiny' in a similar fashion to the test used in the US. It rejected this view. Affirmative action was legitimated both by an express constitutional provision for reservations and by the specific provision in the Directive Principles. The Court is less specific about the standard of review it does apply. In *Mukesh Kumar*, it was stated that: 'The Court should show due deference to the opinion of the State which does not, however, mean that the opinion formed is beyond judicial scrutiny altogether.'[194] It suggested that ordinary administrative law standards of

---

[192] *Minister of Justice v Van Heerden* (n 2).
[193] ibid para 30.
[194] *Mukesh Kumar v Uttarakhand* [2020] 3 SCC 1, para 13 (Indian Sup Ct).

review should apply, since it regarded the constitutional provision as leaving this matter to the subjective satisfaction of the executive. However, it is not clear that this level of deference is consistently applied, especially given that the Court rarely expressly sets out the standard it is using.

Similarly, given the commitment to affirmative action as a means to achieve equality, rather than a derogation from it, the Canadian Court has been clear that the standard of strict scrutiny is unwarranted. Instead, it has held that review should be primarily directed to the genuineness of the government's stated ameliorative purpose.[195] This draws directly on the wording of section 15(2) of the Canadian Charter, which states that a programme does not breach the equality guarantee if it has 'as its object the amelioration of conditions of disadvantaged individuals or groups'. Importantly, in *R v Kapp*, the Court held that the focus should be on the ameliorative *purpose* rather than on whether the programme is likely to achieve its ameliorative goal. Judicial examination of the actual effect of the programme was inappropriate, since results might be unpredictable or difficult to evaluate. Instead, governments should be actively encouraged to be innovative in their approach to affirmative action.[196]

A focus on purpose, however, runs the risk of giving governments carte blanche to characterize any programme as having an ameliorative objective, regardless of its actual effect. The Canadian Court dealt with this by holding that a bald declaration of ameliorative purpose would not be sufficient. To prevent programmes masquerading as ameliorative while at the same time preserving a significant degree of deference to the government, the Court requires a showing that there is a correlation between the programme and the purpose. By contrast with the US standard of strict scrutiny, this is not a searching standard. As the Court stated:

> Analysing the means employed by the government can easily turn into assessing the effect of the program. As a result, to preserve an intent-based analysis, courts could be encouraged to frame the analysis as follows: Was it rational for the state to conclude that the means chosen to reach its ameliorative goal would contribute to that purpose? For the distinction to be rational, there must be a correlation between the program and the disadvantage suffered by the target group. Such a standard permits significant deference to the legislature but allows judicial review where a program nominally seeks to serve the disadvantaged but in practice serves other, non-remedial objectives.[197]

---

[195] *R v Kapp* (n 189).
[196] ibid para 47.
[197] ibid para 49.

There is force in the Canadian Court's concern with the purpose of a programme rather than its effects. The *Kapp* case concerned the federal government's strategy to enhance indigenous involvement in commercial fishing. As part of the strategy, the government had issued a communal fishing licence to three indigenous bands permitting only fishers designated by the bands to fish for salmon in the mouth of the Fraser River for a period of twenty-four hours and to sell their catch. The appellants, commercial fishers who were mainly non-indigenous, were excluded from the fishery during that period. They argued that the communal fishing licence discriminated against them on the basis of race. In particular, they argued that the programme did not offer a benefit that effectively tackled the problems faced by these bands. The Court was rightly reluctant to adjudicate on the effectiveness of the programme in that sense. As it stated: 'If the sincere purpose is to promote equality by ameliorating the conditions of a disadvantaged group, the government should be given some leeway to adopt innovative programs, even though some may ultimately prove to be unsuccessful. The government may learn from such failures and revise equality enhancing programs to make them more effective.'[198]

Nevertheless, the Court was alive to the fact that courts had regarded a programme as ameliorative in surprising circumstances. Particularly worrying are measures which place restrictions on individuals which the government claims to be in their best interests.[199] Thus, the Court drew a careful line between deference to the judgement of the executive and appropriate judicial supervision: 'The meaning of "amelioration" deserves careful attention in evaluating programs under s. 15(2). We would suggest that laws designed to restrict or punish behaviour [of the target class] would not qualify for s. 15(2) protection. Nor, as already discussed, should the focus be on the effect of the law. This said, the fact that a law has no plausible or predictable ameliorative effect may render suspect the state's ameliorative purpose. Governments, as discussed above, are not permitted to protect discriminatory programs on colourable pretexts.'[200]

The South African Court has taken a middle ground between light-touch supervision and stricter scrutiny, stressing that the Court should be relatively deferent while retaining an important supervisory role. In *Van Heerden*, Moseneke J formulated this in terms of two questions: is the measure *designed*

---

[198] ibid para 47.
[199] ibid para 53.
[200] ibid para 54.

to protect and advance such people; and does it promote the *achievement* of equality? The remedial measures must be 'reasonably capable of attaining the desired outcome', namely, to protect or advance individuals or categories of persons who have been disadvantaged by unfair discrimination. This excludes measures which are arbitrary, capricious or display naked preference, or are not reasonably likely to achieve the end of advancing or benefiting the interests of those who have been disadvantaged by unfair discrimination.[201] Importantly, he emphasized that the Constitution did not 'postulate a standard of necessity between the legislative choice and the governmental objective. The text requires only that the means should be designed to protect or advance. It is sufficient if the measure carries a reasonable likelihood of meeting the end.'[202]

The standard of scrutiny has, however raised further controversies before the Court. This can be seen in the first main case under the EEA, *South African Police Service v Solidarity obo Barnard*.[203] *Barnard* concerned a challenge by a white woman who had been refused promotion by the National Commissioner of the Police Service although she scored higher than any other applicants. The reason given was that her appointment would worsen the representativity of the grade in question, Level 9, at which white women were already over-represented. Since failing to fill the post would not affect service delivery, it was decided not to fill the post, and in the interim a white man was transferred to fill the vacancy. She claimed that she had been discriminated against on grounds of race. The Police Service argued that it had acted lawfully in pursuit of a legitimate employment equity plan.

The Constitutional Court rejected her claim. Moseneke ACJ made it clear, as he had done in *van Heerden*, that both the Constitution itself and the EEA are quite explicit that affirmative-action measures are not unfair. Instead, the question is how strict the Court's scrutiny of the affirmative-action measure should be. Moseneke ACJ did not find it necessary to define the standard conclusively. What he did say was that at the very least a legitimate restitution measure must be rationally related to the terms and objects of the measure: 'It must be applied to advance its legitimate purpose and nothing else.'[204] This standard did not, however, attract agreement from all the judges on the SACC. Cameron, Froneman, and Masjiedt JJ took the view that the rationality standard posited

---

[201] *Minister of Justice v Van Heerden* (n 2) paras 38–40.

[202] ibid para 41.

[203] *South African Police Service v Solidarity obo Barnard* [2014] ZACC 23 (SACC).

[204] ibid para 39.

by Moseneke J was not fit for the task of setting an appropriate supervisory role for the court. Instead, they argued for a standard based on fairness. For his part, Van der Westhuizen J argued for a standard of proportionality. Both these approaches are, however, problematic. Proportionality could risk reimporting a necessity standard, which substantive equality aims to leave behind. Fairness, too, is risky in that it seems to import the standard of 'unfair discrimination' from section 9(3) into section 9(2).[205]

(v) Delineating the Beneficiaries

A particularly controversial issue in all these jurisdictions is how to delineate beneficiaries. A key strength of substantive equality is its move away from the individualism of formal equality or direct discrimination, which requires proof that an individual has suffered discrimination at the hands of an identified perpetrator before an individual remedy can be granted. Affirmative action does not require proof of individual detriment. Therefore, the category of beneficiaries need not consist only of proved victims. Nevertheless, there needs to be some correlation between the beneficiaries and the previous disadvantage. How, then, should the beneficiaries be determined?

In India, as we have seen, this question has primarily manifested itself in terms of whether more socio-economically advantaged individuals in a beneficiary group (graphically known as the 'creamy layer') should continue to benefit from reservations. In both *Indra Sawhney*[206] and *Ashoka Kumar*,[207] the Indian Supreme Court held emphatically that, at least in the case of OBCs (other backward classes), the creamy layer should be excluded. The difficulty with this approach, as suggested by the four-dimensional understanding of substantive equality, is that redressing socio-economic disadvantage (the first dimension) does not necessarily address stigma, stereotyping, prejudice, and violence (the second dimension). It is well known that Dalits and other lower caste Indians continue to face prejudice even if they advance economically. This was originally recognized by the Indian Supreme Court in excluding Scheduled Castes and Tribes from the creamy layer exception.[208] However, more recent cases have questioned this exclusion on the basis that

---

[205] For a valuable analysis of the differing emphases in the *Barnard* judgment, see C Albertyn, 'Adjudicating Affirmative Action' (2015) 132 South African LJ 711.

[206] *Indra Sawhney v Union of India* (n 63) 724.

[207] *Ashoka Kumar Thakur v Union of India* (n 64) para 149.

[208] *Indra Sawhney v Union of India* (n 63); *Ashoka Kumar Thakur v Union of India* (n 64).

the creamy layer principle is a facet of the wider equality principle and should therefore apply to all reservations.[209]

In the controversial case of *Nagaraj*, the Court went even further and required the State to collect quantifiable data showing the backwardness of the Scheduled Castes and Scheduled Tribes.[210] This was rejected in *Jarnail Singh* in 2018, which reinstated the principle that '[t]he test or requirement of social and educational backwardness cannot be applied to Scheduled Castes and Scheduled Tribes, who indubitably fall within the expression backward class of citizens' by virtue of being notified as such in the presidential list.[211] The result appears to be that while Scheduled Castes and Scheduled Tribes are identified by the presidential list and need not be proved by quantifiable data, the Court can now determine that some of this group should be excluded from reservations if they are deemed to be within the creamy layer. This conclusion, however, remains highly contested.

Paradoxically, the move to exclude the creamy layer in the groups of OBCs and SC/ST has come together with demands by upper castes for reservations on economic grounds. In 2019, a new amendment was passed incorporating provision for reservations for 'economically weaker sections of citizens' other than SC/ST or OBCs.[212] The amendment departs from the traditional approach to reservations in India. The earlier provisions refer to 'class' or 'caste', suggesting that there is a binding factor to the group which is more than economic weakness. By contrast, rather than focusing on the interaction between status misrecognition and disadvantage, as would be suggested by a four-dimensional approach to substantive equality, the amendment puts the spotlight only on economic deprivation. Economic weakness alone is usually dealt with through social security and good public services, such as education, healthcare, and housing. Reservations are inevitably inadequate to deal with economic deprivation not connected to status disadvantage, particularly because there are a limited number of jobs in public employment or places in higher education. The amendment has been challenged in the Court as contrary to the basic structure of the Constitution. Whether such a challenge succeeds depends on the Court's construction of the equality principle itself. Substantive equality would suggest that in determining a group

---

[209] *M Nagaraj v Union of India* [2006] 8 SCC 212 (Indian Sup Ct); *Jarnail Singh v Lacchmi Narain Gupta* (2018) 10 SCC 396, para 8 (Indian Sup Ct).
[210] *M Nagaraj v Union of India* ibid.
[211] *Jarnail Singh v Lacchmi Narain Gupta* (n 209) paras 14 and 15.
[212] Constitution of India, Arts 15(6) and 16(6).

for reservation, it would need to be demarcated on more than one dimension of substantive equality.

In the meantime, Christian and Muslim Dalits continue to struggle for inclusion in the Scheduled Caste category. In its earliest articulation in the Constitution (Scheduled Castes) Order 1950, the concept of 'scheduled caste' was expressly stated to refer only to followers of Hinduism,[213] later extended to Sikhs and Buddhists.[214] This exclusion was challenged as discriminatory against Christians in a case brought before the Supreme Court in 1985.[215] The petitioner had converted to Christianity but continued as a member of the Adi Dravida caste, which makes up about half of the Scheduled Caste population of Tamil Nadu. Dismissing the petition, the Court held that to prove the 1950 Order discriminated against Christian members of the enumerated castes, it was not sufficient to show that a person remained in the same caste after conversion. In addition, it was necessary to establish that 'the disabilities and handicaps suffered from such caste membership in the social order of its origin—Hinduism—continue in their oppressive severity in the new environment of a different religious community'.[216] The Court held that there was no evidence to that effect.

However, several subsequent reports have found extensive social and occupational segregation together with economic exploitation of Christian and Muslim Dalits. Most recently, the Report of the National Commission for Religious and Linguistic Minorities concluded on the basis of extensive evidence that the caste system was an 'all-pervading social phenomenon of India shared by almost all Indian communities irrespective of religious persuasions'. The insistence that the class of Scheduled Castes should remain religion-based was 'illogical and unreasonable'.[217] The Commission recommended that Scheduled Caste status be completely de-linked from religion and incorporate those groups of Muslims and Christians whose counterparts among Hindus, Sikhs, or Buddhists were included in Scheduled Caste lists.[218]

---

[213] Constitution (Scheduled Castes) Order No 19 of 1950.

[214] Scheduled Castes and Scheduled Tribes Orders (Amendment) Act, 1956; Constitution (Scheduled Castes) Order (Amendment) Act 1990, para 3.

[215] *Soosai v Union of India* AIR 1986 SC 733 (Indian Sup Ct).

[216] ibid para 250.

[217] Ministry of Minority Affairs, 'Report of the National Commission for Religious and Linguistic Minorities' (Ranganath Mishra Committee Report, 2007) 143 <www.minorityaffairs.gov.in/en/document/english-version/report-national-commission-religious-and-linguistic-minorities-ranganath> accessed 2 August 2022.

[218] ibid 154.

However, no change has taken place and a further challenge is pending be-fore the Indian Supreme Court.[219] Certain Muslim castes are recognized as OBCs, making them eligible for 27 per cent reservation in public sector employment and education. But reservation of electoral constituencies is only available to Scheduled Castes. Similarly, OBCs are not protected by the Scheduled Caste and Scheduled Tribe (Prevention of Atrocities) Act, 1989.

Delineating the affected group in Canada has been challenging in a dif-ferent way. While the Indian case law has focused on whether some individ-uals should be removed from the beneficiary class, in Canada the issues have centred on whether the beneficiary group is itself over- or under-inclusive. Under section 15(2), the programme must target a disadvantaged group identified by the enumerated or analogous grounds in the Charter.[220] In *Kapp*, the question arose as to whether the three First Nations bands denoted as beneficiaries of the exclusive fishing benefit were an 'identifiable disad-vantaged group' for the purposes of section 15(2) which, it will be recalled, permits measures the object of which is 'the amelioration of conditions of disadvantaged individuals or groups including those that are disadvan-taged because of race, national or ethnic origin, colour,[221] religion, sex, age or mental or physical disability'. The Court, having identified the distinction as being based on race, went on to examine whether, as required by section 15(2), the programme targeted a 'disadvantaged group identified by' race. For this, it referred to both status disadvantage—'the legacy of stereotyping and prejudice against [indigenous] peoples'—and socio-economic disad-vantage: 'the evidence shows in this case that the bands granted the benefit were in fact disadvantaged in terms of income, education and a host of other measures'. The Court drew a bright line between programmes targeting the conditions of a specific and identifiable disadvantaged group, which were protected by section 15(2), and broad societal legislation. However, it did not require the proof that each individual member suffered such disadvantage. 'The fact that some individual members of the bands may not experience

---

[219] <https://thewire.in/law/sc-agrees-to-examine-plea-seeking-scheduled-caste-status-for-dalit-christians> accessed 2 August 2022.

[220] *R v Kapp* 2008 SCC 41, para 41 (Can Sup Ct).

[221] This terminology quotes from the Canadian Charter and reflects that in relevant stat-utes and international conventions (see UK EA 2010, s 9(1)(a); South African Constitution, s 9; Canadian Charter of Rights and Freedoms, s 15; International Convention on the Elimination of All Forms of Racial Discrimination, Art 1; ICCPR, Art 2(1); ICESCR, Art 2(2)), which all refer to 'colour' in the list of protected characteristics.

personal disadvantage does not negate the group disadvantage suffered by band members.'[222]

This approach makes sense where the claimant is from a privileged or dominant group. But what if the claimants argue that they are equally or more disadvantaged than the beneficiary group, and should be included in the programme? Can they successfully claim that the beneficiary group is under-inclusive? This question arose in relation to provincial legislation enacted to preserve a land base for the Métis in Alberta, to enable self-governance, and to preserve Métis culture and identity. The legislation, however, excluded individuals who had registered under what is problematically still called the 'Indian Act' for 'Indian Status' (known as 'Status Indians').[223] The Cunningham family were members of a Métis settlement who had obtained 'Indian status' in the 1990s. The Act deprived them of their rights to reside in their community and participate in its governance.[224] They challenged their exclusion as discrimination based on their status, arguing that the statute thereby violated section 15(1) of the Charter. In *Alberta v Cunningham*, the Supreme Court of Canada rejected their claim, holding that the deferent standard adopted in *Kapp* applies even when the claimants share a similar history of marginalization and disadvantage as the beneficiary group.[225] As the Court put it: 'Ameliorative programs, by their nature, confer benefits on one group that are not conferred on others. These distinctions are generally protected if they serve or advance the object of the program, thus promoting substantive equality. This is so even where the included and excluded groups are [indigenous peoples] who share a similar history of disadvantage and marginalization.'[226]

Arguably, this is a special case, since the Court emphasized that what was at issue was a special type of ameliorative programme: 'one designed to enhance and preserve the identity, culture and self-governance of a constitutionally recognized group. . . . The object of enhancing the identity, culture

---

[222] *R v Kapp* (n 220) para 59.
[223] This book uses the term 'indigenous' people in Canada following the United Nations Declaration on the Rights of Indigenous People. The Canadian Constitution recognizes three groups: First Nations, Inuit, and Métis. These are three distinct peoples, each with their own histories, cultural practices, languages, and spiritual beliefs. See <www.national.ca/en/perspectives/detail/no-perfect-answer-first-nations-aboriginal-indigenous/>; <www.queensu.ca/indigenous/ways-knowing/terminology-guide>; <https://indigenousfoundations.arts.ubc.ca/terminology/#:~:text=%E2%80%9CFirst%20Nation%E2%80%9D%20is%20a%20term,not%20have%20a%20legal%20definition> accessed 3 June 2022.
[224] <www.leaf.ca/case_summary/cunningham-v-alberta/> accessed 3 August 2022.
[225] *Alberta v Cunningham* [2011] 2 SCR 670 (Can Sup Ct).
[226] ibid para 53.

and self-governance of the Métis as a [constitutionally recognized] . . . group, of necessity, must permit the exclusion of other [constitutionally recognized] . . . groups.'[227] The Court stressed that an 'essential part of their unique identity' was that they are not part of the First Nations peoples nor are they Inuit.[228]

Where protection of identity is not involved, it might be much more difficult to argue that exclusion of a similarly disadvantaged group will 'serve or advance' the promotion of substantive equality.[229]

In South Africa, delineation of beneficiary groups has been the flashpoint of much of the controversy over affirmative action before the SACC. The first question is whether individual beneficiaries must establish that they have been personally wronged. Moseneke DCJ in *van Heerden* made it clear that affirmative action under section 9(2) is a restitutionary remedy. It is emphatically not punitive nor retaliatory. This does not mean that individuals need to prove that they were individually wronged. Instead, according to Moseneke DCJ, the target should be a particular class of people who have been *susceptible* to unfair discrimination and the measure must be designed to protect or advance those classes of persons.[230] This reflects a key aspect of substantive equality, which moves away from the individualism of formal equality, requiring proof that an individual has suffered discrimination at the hands of an identified perpetrator before an individual remedy can be granted. Affirmative action, on a substantive reading, does not require proof of individual detriment, and the category of beneficiaries need not consist only of proven victims.

This raises the question of whether all the beneficiaries must be disadvantaged. Can the beneficiary category include some individuals who have never been disadvantaged by unfair discrimination? The Court in *Van Heerden* held that it could. In this case, although an overwhelming majority of the new Members of Parliament had been previously excluded from parliamentary participation by past apartheid laws, not all the new parliamentarians of 1994 belonged to the class of persons prejudiced by past disadvantage and unfair exclusion. Moseneke J recognized that it would often be 'difficult, impractical or undesirable to devise a legislative scheme with "pure" differentiation

---

[227] ibid para 54.
[228] ibid.
[229] <www.justice.gc.ca/eng/csj-sjc/rfc-dlc/ccrf-ccdl/check/art15.html> accessed 3 August 2022.
[230] *South African Police Service v Solidarity obo Barnard* (n 203) para 36.

demarcating precisely the affected classes. Within each class, favoured or otherwise, there may indeed be exceptional or "hard cases" or windfall beneficiaries. That however is not sufficient to undermine the legal efficacy of the scheme. The distinction must be measured against the majority and not the exceptional and difficult minority of people to which it applies'.[231] He thus held that the measure should be judged by 'whether an overwhelming majority of members of the favoured class are persons designated as disadvantaged by unfair exclusion'.[232] The validity of the remedial measures was unaffected by the existence of a tiny minority of Members of Parliament who were not unfairly discriminated against but who benefited from the measure. This can be contrasted with the decision of Mogkoro J, who held that a more exact fit was necessary. She regarded the measure as too loosely related to a proscribed group to fall within section 9(2), which relieves the State of the burden of proving unfairness. Instead, the measure should be subjected to the high standards of fairness required in relation to ordinary discrimination claims under section 9(3). On the facts, she held, it passed muster.

The *Van Heerden* case concerned whether non-members of the designated group can be included in the beneficiary class; in other words, whether the class can be over-inclusive. But can the class be under-inclusive—in other words, exclude equally disadvantaged individuals? As we have seen, in *Cunningham*, the Canadian Court was keen to preserve the preference policy for Métis, even though it excluded similarly disadvantaged 'status Indians'. The SACC took a different view in *SARIPA*, striking down the policy as a whole because, in the words of Jafta J: 'A section 9(2) measure may not discriminate against persons belonging to the disadvantaged group whose interests it seeks to advance.'[233] The difficulty with this approach is that the policy as a whole was struck down, meaning that even those who were included could not benefit, and the status quo, of widespread white privilege, was retained until a different policy could be devised.[234] This contrasts with the approach of the dissenting judge in the case, Madlanga J. For him, the overall purpose of the policy was clear, and therefore the appropriate remedy should be to uphold the policy, invalidating the provision excluding part of the disadvantaged class.

---

[231] *Minister of Justice v Van Heerden* (n 2) para 39.

[232] ibid para 40.

[233] *Minister of Justice and Constitutional Development and Another v South African Restructuring and Insolvency Practitioners Association* [2018] ZACC 20, para 42 (SACC).

[234] N Ramalekana, 'What's So Wrong with Quotas? An Argument for the Permissibility of Quotas under s 9(2) of the South African Constitution' [2020] Constitutional Court Rev 252.

The case concerned the attempt to transform the insolvency practitioners' industry from one which had been dominated by white practitioners, a pattern which showed no sign of changing with the advent of democracy in 1994. To address this, the Minister of Justice instituted a scheme affecting a small part of the industry, namely, the appointment by the master of insolvency practitioners as trustees at the provisional stage of insolvency. The policy did not affect the final stage of insolvency. The Act created a pecking order by which the master should assign the work among the insolvency practitioners who appeared on the list of those eligible. This required the list to be ordered in terms of four categories. Category A consisted of 'African', 'Coloured',[235] 'Indian',[236] and 'Chinese' women who became South African citizens before democracy was established on 27 April 1994. Category B consisted of 'African', 'Coloured', 'Indian', and 'Chinese' men who became citizens before 27 April 1994, while Category C consisted of white women. Category D was composed of all white male practitioners and all practitioners, regardless of colour, who became citizens on or after 27 April 1994. Insolvency practitioners were to be appointed consecutively in the ratio A4:B3:C2:D1. In other words, the master should assign the first four trustee assignments to members of category A, organized in alphabetical order; the next three to category B; the next two to category C; and the next one to category D; before starting again with category A. The assumption was that these categories reflected the extent of marginalization within the insolvency practitioner profession, and the aim was to ensure that the overriding dominance of white practitioners could be redressed, at least for provisional insolvency proceedings. Notably, all practitioners had to be suitably qualified to be on the list in the first place, and the master had the discretion to appoint a senior practitioner to partner with a practitioner who might be unsuitable for the task.

---

[235] Although these were the categories used by the apartheid government (see Chapter 2), the post-apartheid legislation continues to use these categories on the basis that the disadvantage of apartheid needs to be expressly redressed. This policy was one such measure. Many people in South Africa self-identify as 'Coloured'. In the 2011 Census, 8.9 per cent of the population of South Africa self-identified as 'Coloured' (Census 2011—Statistics South Africa: <www.statssa. gov.za> accessed 3 August 2022. Currently, while some identify as 'Black', others differentiate themselves politically from the 'Black' majority, self identifying as 'Coloured', or Khoisan. Most speak Afrikaans as their first language. See W Pirtle, '"Able to Identify with Anything": Racial Identity Choices Among "Coloureds" as Shaped by the South African Racial State' (2021) Identities: Global Studies in Culture and Power.

[236] As with the 'Coloured' category, the category 'Indian' was used by the apartheid government but retained post-apartheid to expressly redress the disadvantage suffered under apartheid. See Chapter 2.

The policy was challenged as unconstitutional by applicants largely representing the majority white practitioners. The Court upheld their claim. Both the majority and the dissents agreed that it was irrational to include 'African', 'Coloured',[237] 'Indian', and 'Chinese' practitioners who became citizens on or after 27 April 1994 in category D together with whites, given that the former were subjected to ongoing disadvantage. Jafta J, for the majority, re-emphasized that, according to the Constitution, simply guaranteeing equal rights would not lead to an egalitarian society. Nevertheless, he held that from the information on record, it did not appear likely that the policy would transform the insolvency industry. The main reason given was that the policy discriminated against younger practitioners and therefore could not fulfil section 9(2). However, while category D was clearly defective in including young 'African', 'Indian', 'Coloured', and 'Chinese'[238] practitioners, the policy as a whole, if this defect were remedied, could evidently be transformational as Madlanga J showed. As a start, although this policy only concerned the provisional stage, white people continued to dominate the final stages. 'Whatever perceived disadvantage white people may seem to suffer under the policy', he stated, 'is compensated for by their undeniable continued dominance at the final stage'.[239] Moreover, 'properly applied I do not see how that significant advantage cannot eventually uplift these beneficiaries to a point where the industry will be transformed'.[240] Notably, Jafta J was considerably more interventionist than Madlanga J, who reiterated that courts should 'exercise caution before knocking down measures calculated to redress the inequality of the past'.[241]

Even more complex is the question of how to resolve competition between disadvantaged individuals. As Moseneke ACJ pointed out in *Barnard*: 'We must be careful that the steps taken to promote substantive equality do not unwittingly infringe the dignity of other individuals—especially those who were themselves previously disadvantaged'.[242] In *Barnard*, the potential conflict between the claims of white women and those of Black[243] men and women, all of whom were designated groups, was not presented as the issue

[237] See n 235.

[238] ibid.

[239] *Minister of Justice and Constitutional Development and Another v South African Restructuring and Insolvency Practitioners Association* (n 233) para 81.

[240] ibid para 89.

[241] ibid para 90.

[242] *South African Police Service v Solidarity obo Barnard* (n 203) para 31.

[243] For the meaning of 'Black' under the Employment Equity Act, see n 177.

which the Court was required to address. This was because it was found that white women were already over-represented in her grade. However, in the subsequent case of *Solidarity v Department of Correctional Services*,[244] the conflict between status groups was more clearly in focus, in this case, between 'Coloured'[245] and Black African workers. The Employment Equity Plan drawn up by the Department of Correctional Services set numerical targets to be attained within its workforce within a five-year period. The targets aimed to achieve a workforce which reflected the population of the country, based on population estimates issued by Statistics South Africa. This meant that at the end of the five-year period, the workforce should consist of 9.3 per cent white men and women, 79.3 per cent African men and women, 8.8 per cent 'Coloured' men and women and 2.5 per cent 'Indian' men and women. The applicants, who were 'Coloured' men and women, were denied appointment to certain posts in the Western Cape despite being recommended for appointment by the respective interview panels. The reason given for this decision was that they were 'Coloured' persons, and 'Coloured' persons were already over-represented in the relevant occupational levels.

Zondo J's judgment put great emphasis on what he called the *Barnard* principle. In his view, the Court in *Barnard* upheld the principle that it was legitimate to refuse promotion to Miss Barnard on the basis that white people were already over-represented in the occupational level.[246] The question before the Court in the *Correctional Services* case was whether this principle only applied to white people or could also apply to designated groups. Can an employer refuse to appoint an 'African', 'Coloured', or 'Indian' person on the basis that 'African', 'Coloured', or 'Indian' people were already over-represented or adequately represented in the grade to which the person sought appointment? The same is true for gender or disability. In other words, is there a ceiling to the level of representation each group can achieve, and does that apply equally to disadvantaged groups as to advantaged groups?

For Zondo J, the answer was clear: 'The level of representation of each group must broadly accord with its representation among the people of South Africa.'[247] This meant that 'a designated employer is entitled, as a matter of law, to deny an African or Coloured person or Indian person appointment

---

[244] *Solidarity v Department of Correctional Services* [2016] ZACC 18 (SACC).

[245] See n 235.

[246] Moseneke ACJ in *Barnard* itself referred to the fact that white women were over-represented in Grade 9 to reject the argument that quotas were being imposed.

[247] *Solidarity v Department of Correctional Services* (n 244) para 40.

to a certain occupational level on the basis that African people, Coloured people or Indian people, as the case may be, are already overrepresented or adequately represented in that level.[248] This is true, too, for men and women. In the case in question, the employer was therefore in principle entitled to deny appointment to 'Coloured' applicants on the basis that they were already over-represented in a grade.

This, however, left open the question of how to determine representativeness. The applicants argued that it was wrong to use national population statistics for the Western Cape, where the 'Coloured'[249] population is largely concentrated. This demographic pattern was a result of the apartheid policy of excluding African workers from the Western Cape while giving workers designated as 'Coloured' preference. The EEA at that time specified that the equitable representation should be 'in relation to the demographic profile of the national and regional economically active population'.[250] Since the department used only national statistics, to the exclusion of regional population data, it was held to have acted in breach of its obligation. The result was that the determination of over-representation had been wrongly made. Because the basis relied on to justify refusing to employ 'Coloured' and female individual applicants was incorrect, the refusals amounted to acts of unfair discrimination.[251] The refusals to appoint should therefore be set aside. Where the relevant posts had remained unfilled, the individual applicant should now be appointed, with retrospective effect, including remuneration. If the posts had been subsequently filled, the applicants, who were all in lower positions in the service, should be accorded the difference in pay and benefits.

But can this principle of representation achieve substantive equality in the four-dimensional sense? Moseneke J, as we have seen, regarded the main aim of affirmative action as restitutionary. However, the class of beneficiaries in the current generation might not be identical to the victims of past discrimination under apartheid. Representation is therefore more than a restitutionary measure on an individual level. There are several further ways it could function. The first is to address hidden prejudice and other structural obstacles. In practice, despite apparently objective eligibility standards and ostensible equal opportunity policies, there remain many hidden obstacles to the advancement of historically disadvantaged South Africans. As we saw

---

[248] ibid para 49.
[249] See n 235.
[250] EEA, s 42(a).
[251] *Solidarity v Department of Correctional Services* (n 244) 81–82.

earlier, hidden prejudices can be more easily overcome by affirmative action than by individual claims for unfair discrimination. Rather than relying on litigation by individual victims, the employer is required to take the initiative. Nor is it necessary to prove unfair discrimination. Instead, it is sufficient to demonstrate a clear pattern of under-representation. In this way, implicit or hidden discriminatory selection criteria are unequivocally removed: requiring outcomes to be representative makes it impossible for such criteria to be reintroduced surreptitiously through subjective decision making.

Phrased in this way, affirmative action as representation can be legitimated as an effective means of redressing ongoing stereotyping and prejudice, bringing the second dimension into play. At the same time, this formulation reveals its limited role in relation to the other three dimensions: redressing disadvantage, facilitating voice, participation and structural change. While preference policies based on representation may change the racial composition of some higher paid occupations, they do not challenge the underlying structural and institutional forces leading to the discrimination. The underrepresentation of disadvantaged South Africans in higher positions on the employment ladder, both public and private, is only partially resolved by inserting some Black South Africans into those positions. It is not surprising that, in practice, affirmative action is often found to do no more than favour the relatively privileged of the disadvantaged group.[252] For fundamental change to occur, the structural and institutional causes of exclusion need to be changed. This requires more attention to be paid to the need for structural change, as required by the fourth dimension.

A different way of justifying the focus on representation maintains that the very presence of historically disadvantaged South Africans in higher status positions will fulfil the third dimension, namely, giving greater voice and enhancing the participation of excluded groups.[253] However, as we saw earlier, giving voice to a group as if all members have unitary interests could, without more, infringe on the second dimension, to redress stereotyping. A four-dimensional approach to substantive equality requires explicit attention to be paid to cross-currents of disadvantage within status groups. By regarding all members of a status class as identically positioned economically

---

[252] Rulof Burger, Rachel Jafta, and Dieter von Fintel, 'Affirmative Action Policies and the Evolution of Post-Apartheid South Africa's Racial Wage Gap', United Nations University World Institute for Economic Research (May 2016) 20; WF Menski, 'The Indian Experience and its Lessons for Britain' in B Hepple and E Szyszcak (eds), *Discrimination and the Limits of the Law* (Mansell 1992) 330.

[253] Phillips (n 43) 52.

and socially, an undiluted focus on representation can reinforce internal differences within groups and further marginalize the weakest in the group. This suggests that the sole use of population statistics to determine representativity, as in the *Correctional Services* case, is too rigid. To achieve voice and participation, while also avoiding stereotyping, would require more than simply a goal of representation based on broader population statistics. Moreover, very small minorities, such as Indian women, can be excluded for the very reason that they are such a small minority, as occurred in the case of *Naidoo v SAPS*.[254] Yet Indian women are subject to stereotyping and marginalization, specifically at the intersection of gender and race discrimination.[255] A four-dimensional approach requires a nuanced analysis of the power relations and the different aspects of an individual's social position, giving a more incisive account of the complex relationships which situate her than a reliance on pure population statistics. The focus of the recent Constitutional Court cases on representation also risks overshadowing the potential of the statutory requirements within the EEA to implement training measures.[256]

(vi) The Right to Affirmative Action

A further key issue which has recently arisen is whether there is a right to affirmative action. In other words, does the State have a duty to provide for reservations under the Indian Constitution? In *Mukesh Kumar*, the two-judge bench of the Supreme Court answered this question in the negative.[257] The case arose out of a decision by the State of Utarrakhand to fill all posts in public services without providing any reservations. The applicants, members of SC/ST working in the public works department, entered a writ petition to the Court seeking a direction that the State set aside a proportion of promotions for SC/ST. They argued that the right to equality included the right to reservations when data showed that there was an under-representation of SC/ST in specified positions. The Court held that Article 16 does not give

---

[254] *Naidoo v Minister of Safety and Security* 2013 5 BLLR 490 (LC).

[255] H Papacostantis and M Mushariwa, 'The Impact of Minority Status in the Application of affirmative action: *Naidoo v Minister of Safety and Security* 2013 5 BLLR 490 (LC)' PER/PELJ 2016(19), DOI <http://dx.doi.org/10.17159/1727-3781/2016/v19i0a1160> accessed 3 August 2022.

[256] EEA, s 15(2).

[257] *Mukesh Kumar v The State Of Uttarakhand* (2020) 3 SCC 1 (Indian Sup Ct).

a fundamental right to reservations in either appointment or promotion. Article 16 empowers the State to make reservations in favour of SC/ST 'if in the opinion of the State they are not adequately represented in the services of the State'. It was therefore up to the State to determine whether reservations were required, either on the basis of the material in its possession or by gathering new material. The Court would show due deference to the State, subject to the usual rules of judicial review.

Other jurisdictions have not confronted this question directly. However, under the South African EEA, an individual does not have a claim against their employer for failing to afford her preferential treatment.[258] Moreover, the Act draws a clear line between preferential treatment and numerical goals, on the one hand, and quotas, on the other. Nor are employers required to take any decision 'that would establish an absolute barrier to the prospective or continued employment or advancement of people who are not from designated groups'.[259] In addition, the Act requires people to be 'suitably qualified'.

IV   CONCLUSION

Because affirmative action measures tend to redistribute existing jobs or benefits, rather than widen the pool of benefits, they inevitably create competition between individuals. Such competition is not only between privileged and disadvantaged groups, but also between different disadvantaged groups. Moreover, notwithstanding the many statements re-emphasizing the need to use preference policies to achieve transformation in a society so deeply racially stratified, there remains a reluctance among some to depart too far from the background assumptions that individual 'merit' should not be displaced. Responding to this concern, like Chandrachud J in *Pavitra* in the Indian Supreme Court, Moseneke ACJ in *Barnard* was careful to dispel the notion that affirmative action opens the door to incompetence. As he put it: 'The [EEA] sets itself against the hurtful insinuation that affirmative action measures are a refuge for the mediocre or incompetent. Plainly, a core object of equity at the workplace is to employ and retain people who not only

---

[258] *Dudley v City of Cape Town and Another* (CA 1/05) [2008] ZALAC 10, [2008] 12 BLLR 1155 (LAC) (SA Labour Appeal Ct).
[259] EEA, s 15(3) and (4).

enhance diversity but who are also competent and effective in delivering goods and services to the public.'[260]

At the same time, it is important to stress the limitations of affirmative action as a strategy, particularly in achieving structural change. The introduction of new perspectives, while an important goal, can only have a limited impact on their own: entrenched structures are often resilient and, indeed, have powerful conformist pressures. Disadvantaged groups may find themselves forced to hide their views and ignore their own needs and interests in order to ensure that their continued participation is viable. Even if they do articulate their perspectives, the process of recognition and affirmation is halting and erratic. Thus, it is the fourth dimension, requiring transformation of institutional and structural barriers, that is the most difficult to achieve through affirmative action. Affirmative action should therefore be seen as only one part of a broad-based and radical strategy, which does more than redistribute privileged positions, but refashions the institutions which continue to perpetuate exclusion. As Moseneke concluded in *Barnard*: 'We must remind ourselves that restitution measures, important as they are, cannot do all the work to advance social equity.'[261]

---

[260] *South African Police Service v Solidarity obo Barnard* (n 203) para 41.
[261] ibid para 33.

8

Making Equality Effective

Refashioning Remedies

I INTRODUCTION

As we have seen, discrimination and equality law have become increasingly
sophisticated in recent decades. However, while initial successes fuelled early
optimism, deeper structures of discrimination have proved remarkably resilient. This raises doubts about the role of law in effecting social change. Is
law inevitably limited? Or can we refashion legal tools in such a way as to play
a major part in achieving substantive equality? In order to answer these questions, it is necessary to examine not just the conceptual apparatus of equality
law, but also the enforcement mechanisms.

The traditional approach has been to rely on an individual complaints
model of adjudication. But a range of new approaches is emerging, which
aim at institutional change through proactive measures to promote equality.
At the same time, more attention is being paid to strategic litigation, which
seeks to achieve social change rather than primarily focusing on the individual victim. This chapter examines the limitations of an individual complaints model and assesses these alternative or complementary approaches.
Section II assesses the strengths and limitations of the individual complaints model, drawing on the experience of different jurisdictions, with a
particular focus on the UK and the US. It is clear that this approach cannot
on its own be an engine for change. The complaints-led model places an inordinate burden on individuals to ensure their rights are not breached. The
result is that few victims pursue their claims through the courts and many
breaches go unremedied. Even more seriously, the complaints-led model has
little impact on systemic and structural discrimination, which reach far beyond the individual complaint. Section III therefore turns to ways in which
the complaints model might be strengthened, specifically by reducing the
burden on the individual and attempting to provide remedies for a wider
group of victims. This section examines class actions, strategic litigation, and

Discrimination Law. Third Edition. Sandra Fredman, Oxford University Press. © Sandra Fredman 2022.
DOI: 10.1093/oso/9780198854081.003.0008

agency enforcement, and touches on how the courts can be mobilized by social movements. Although these modifications are valuable in extending the reach of remedies for individual complainants, they are still largely rooted in an individualized understanding of discrimination. Section IV therefore turns to what have optimistically been labelled 'fourth generation' approaches. These approaches depart fundamentally from the dependency on individual initiative and instead require proactive action from those in the best position to bring about change. The section briefly surveys the range of measures which have been instituted, before turning to a deeper examination of several particular approaches, such as the public sector equality duty in the UK, Canadian employment equity legislation, and contract compliance in the US. Despite the great potential of proactive measures, in practice they easily slide into mere bureaucratic compliance. This section briefly attempts to explain these challenges in terms of different regulatory models, such as reflexive law, responsive law, and endogenous theories of law. The challenge remains to achieve the appropriate synthesis between harnessing the energy of responsible bodies to provide creative responses to systemic discrimination; and effective regulatory measures which can pierce the façade of compliance. Central to this is the need to involve those who are affected, as well as trade unions and civil society stakeholders, in defining the problem and in holding bodies to account.

II INDIVIDUAL COMPLAINTS MODELS

The complaints-led model places the responsibility of enforcement on individuals, requiring them to bring a complaint to a tribunal or agency to establish a breach of their right not to be discriminated against. In principle, this approach is an important avenue of redress for individuals. However, it is limited in two main ways. Crucially, it is based on a paradigm which regards discrimination as consisting of individual acts of wrongdoing causing harm to victims. This fault-based model puts the burden on victims to find an individual perpetrator and to prove that the latter's wrongful action caused them harm. In jurisdictions which require intent to be proved, this is a particularly difficult task. In addition, in a disparate treatment claim, the complainant must find a comparator who has been treated less favourably on grounds of a protected characteristic. Nor is the burden any less in a disparate impact claim, where relevant statistics or other evidence of particular disadvantage must be gathered. This paradigm takes little account of the central imbalance of power between perpetrator and victim, especially in the employment context.[1] Relevant information is inevitably in the hands of the employer and disclosure or discovery procedures might be difficult to access. This is especially challenging in equal pay claims where some employments prohibit disclosure of pay to colleagues for the purposes of equal pay. All this is made even more demanding by the widespread use of algorithms for both hiring and promotion. Algorithms purport to remove the influence of individual discretion, which could incorporate bias. In practice, however, because they are based on models of existing decision making, they might bake in or even amplify existing biases. For employees contesting the outcomes, the technical details of how algorithms function will inevitably be daunting. This adds to the difficulties they face in mounting individual complaints. Most importantly, the nature of an individual paradigm means that systemic or structural discrimination, which is often at the root of discrimination, cannot be proved.

The inherent limitations of an individual complaints model are compounded by the structure of adjudication. Court procedures are slow and costly. The cost is both personal and pecuniary. Employees who bring claims face the risk of retaliation. Indeed, the US Equal Employment Opportunities Commission (EEOC), reported that 55.8 per cent of the complaints it received in 2020 were of retaliation.[2] As well as the personal cost, complainants face the expense of bringing an application, including court charges and lawyers' fees. Here again the imbalance of power is replicated. Employers might well be able to afford lawyers, and they also have the advantage of being repeat players.[3] All this is set against the limited remedies available to a complainant. It is unlikely that the employer will be required to give the complainant the job or promotion originally sought. Compensation levels are frequently low, and it may not be worth a complainant's while to embark on the process at all. In this way, much discrimination goes unremedied.

Some modifications have been introduced to counter these limitations. These include shifting the burden of proof to the respondent once the applicant has made out a prima facie case of discrimination.[4] Most important

---

[1] R Yang and J Liu, 'Strengthening Accountability for Discrimination' (2021) Economic Policy Institute, Washington DC <https://epi.org/218473> accessed 2 November 2021.

[2] <www.eeoc.gov/statistics/charge-statistics-charges-filed-eeoc-fy-1997-through-fy-2020> accessed 4 August 2022.

[3] For the US perspective, see Yang and Liu (n 1) 20.

[4] EA 2010, s 136; Directive 97/80 [1997] OJ L14/6; Council Directive 2000/43/EC, Art 8; Council Directive 2000/78/EC, Art 10.

has been the introduction of cheaper and less formal means of adjudication, such as tribunals in the UK, Equality Courts in South Africa,[5] and the EEOC in the US for employment-related disputes. However, these continue to rely on the victim to take the initiative. They are also embedded within the ordinary court system, either through appeals on points of law, or through the ability to file a lawsuit if settlement is not possible. Outside employment, in both the UK and the US, ordinary courts remain the primary means of enforcement. As will be seen later, the UK, US, and South African individual complaints systems, although differing in detail, all demonstrate the limits of this paradigm.

(i) The Individual Complaints Model: Britain

In Britain, employment tribunals (ETs) have jurisdiction over employment-related anti-discrimination claims, with appeals on points of law to the Employment Appeal Tribunal (EAT) and then the Court of Appeal and the Supreme Court. The tribunal system was deliberately structured to provide an accessible, cheap, and speedy alternative to the existing court process. Tribunals are more informal and accessible than courts: there are no complicated pleadings and tribunals are not bound by strict rules of evidence. Representatives do not need to be lawyers and applicants can represent themselves. This means that tribunal cases are potentially less expensive than court cases. Tribunals are also intended to be more sensitive than ordinary courts to employment-related concerns. Hence, tribunals were designed to be tripartite in structure. Decisions are made by a legal chair and two lay members with industrial experience, one appointed after consultation with trade unions, the other after consultation with employers' organizations.

However, the record of tribunals in discrimination cases has been disappointing. Compared to the scale of discrimination in society, the number of complaints to tribunals is small. In 2019–20, there were only 4,472 complaints of sex discrimination and 2,812 of race discrimination. Disability discrimination received 6,285 complaints, while as few as 406 complaints of sexual orientation discrimination were made. Of these, only a tiny number reach the point of a tribunal hearing, with about 44 per cent withdrawn and a further 22 per cent reaching a conciliated settlement. Even then, the success

---

[5] Promotion of Equality and Prevention of Unfair Discrimination Act, 2000, ch 4 (ss 16–22).

rate is minuscule. In 2019–20, a mere seventy-one disability discrimination cases were awarded compensation; added to forty-six sex discrimination and twenty-eight race discrimination cases. This meant that 3 per cent of the sex discrimination cases disposed of during that year were successful at hearing, compared to 6 per cent which were unsuccessful.[6] In race discrimination cases, this figure was even starker, with 2 per cent of complaints successful at hearing and 13 per cent unsuccessful, while for disability, the figures were 3 per cent successful and 8 per cent unsuccessful. This success rate has not changed in the last decade, with success rates in 2009–10 similarly fluctuating between 2 and 3 per cent across all grounds.[7]

As well as the low success rate, tribunals have not lived up to the expectation of a quick and affordable procedure. Particularly disruptive was the introduction in 2013 of fees levied on complainants to ETs and the EAT.[8] Until then, claimants could bring proceedings in an ET and the EAT without paying any fees. This was central to the vision of tribunals as cheap and accessible in contrast to ordinary courts. However, in 2013, this changed. Citing the need to deter 'vexatious claimants', and to transfer part of the cost burden from taxpayers to users, the government introduced fees of as much as £1,200 for issuing the claim and for a hearing in discrimination, unfair dismissal, and equal pay claims. This rose to £1,600 for an appeal to the EAT. Costs of group payments were much higher, amounting to £7,200 in the ET for groups of over 200 claimants. This meant that ETs became more expensive than claims for an equivalent amount in the county court where fees are graded according to the amount claimed, starting at £50 for claims of less than £3,000 and rising to £745 for claims of between £5,000 and £10,000 in 2013. ET fees need to be considered in the context of the possibility of obtaining a remedy from the process. As we have seen, the vast majority of cases do not even reach the tribunal and even fewer are successful. Even for those who are, fees are likely to swallow up a significant proportion of any compensation. In the year before fees were imposed, about one-third of successful race discrimination cases resulted in awards of less than £3,000. Over half resulted in awards of less than £5,000.[9] Moreover, many ET awards go

---

[6] <www.gov.uk/government/statistics/tribunal-statistics-quarterly-july-to-september-2020> accessed 4 August 2022.

[7] Ministry of Justice Tribunals Service, *Employment Tribunal and EAT Statistics 2009–10*; Ministry of Justice Tribunals Service, *Employment Tribunal and EAT Statistics 2008–9* <www.tribunals.gov.uk/Tribunals/Publications/publications.htm> accessed 4 August 2022.

[8] Employment Tribunals and the Employment Appeal Tribunal Fees Order 2013 (SI 2013/1893).

[9] *R (On the application of Unison) v Lord Chancellor* [2017] UKSC 51 [30].

unmet: in 2013, only 49 per cent of successful claimants were paid in full even after taking enforcement action.[10]

The result, unsurprisingly, was a steep fall in claims to tribunals, with a long-term reduction in claims accepted by ETs of between 66 and 70 per cent. At the same time, the aim of deterring unmeritorious claims was not met. Instead, the proportion of successful claims was consistently lower after fees were introduced and the proportion of unsuccessful claims higher. Fortunately, the UK Supreme Court struck down the introduction of fees in 2017, holding that it effectively prevented access to justice.[11] A fee refund scheme was launched in 2017, which had paid out £18.2 million between October 2017 and June 2020.[12]

However, the total number of claims to tribunals has not rebounded to pre-fee levels.[13] Compensation levels have improved somewhat, pulled up by some high awards for sex discrimination and disability discrimination, while remaining flat or decreasing for the other grounds.[14] But there is no indication that the rate at which awards are actually recovered has improved. In the meanwhile, delays in tribunal hearings have been mounting, undermining the promise of a speedy and affordable procedure. This was aggravated by the Covid pandemic, meaning that waiting times for any case in the tribunal rose from a mean of thirty-five weeks in 2019/20 to forty-two weeks (over ten months) in 2020/21.[15] In the meantime, the tripartite structure of tribunals is being undermined. In a growing number of situations, employment judges are permitted to sit alone, breaching the fundamental principle of an adjudicative panel which includes lay expertise from both sides of the industry.

Several factors have contributed to the discouraging performance of tribunals in the discrimination arena. First, like the ordinary courts, the tribunals depend wholly on the individual plaintiff to initiate the case, bring the evidence, and make the legal arguments. Not only is such a procedure premised on the assumption that discrimination complaints are purely individual.It also places an excessive burden on an individual victim of discrimination, who must muster the courage to face an employer or ex-employer with a discrimination claim, and find personal and financial resources to

---

[10] ibid [36].
[11] ibid.
[12] <www.gov.uk/government/statistics/tribunal-statistics-quarterly-april-to-june-2020/tribunal-statistics-quarterly-april-to-june-2020> accessed 4 August 2022.
[13] <www.gov.uk/government/statistics/tribunal-statistics-quarterly-april-to-june-2021> accessed 4 August 2022.
[14] ibid.
[15] ibid.

pursue it. Moreover, each party bears their own expenses.[16] Compensation levels are low, so that even a successful applicant could well be out of pocket. This creates a powerful disincentive for individuals to enforce the law through tribunals. The second and related difficulty concerns the obstacles to obtaining evidence, since most relevant evidence is in the hands of the respondent. Until 2013, in a small gesture towards alleviating this difficulty, the statute permitted the complainant to serve a statutory questionnaire on the respondent prior to institution of proceedings.[17] However, even this was withdrawn in 2013.[18]

The third difficulty arises from the uneasy combination of a procedure which aims to be informal, simple, and accessible, with a set of legal provisions which are extremely complex, not least because of the interaction of anti-discrimination statutes with EU law and that of the Human Rights Act 1998 (HRA). This has prompted any party who can afford it to resort to legal representation. Research has repeatedly shown that parties who are legally represented in discrimination cases are more likely to be successful at a hearing than those who appear in person.[19] Yet the government's survey of ET applications published in 2020 found that fewer than half of all claimants to an ET are represented by a lawyer, with most of those who are unrepresented at hearings reporting that this was because they could not afford one.[20] Younger claimants, Black claimants, and those earning less that £20,000 were least likely to use a lawyer.[21] Although the tribunal is meant to assist an unrepresented party, this role creates an awkward tension with its adjudicative function. Yet legal aid is not available to cover the cost of legal representation in tribunals. The result is that many complainants have no option but to represent themselves. As a recent report by the Equality and Human Rights Commission (EHRC) demonstrated, this is particularly difficult in complex discrimination cases, when individuals, who are already stressed and often emotional in relation to their own cases, frequently find themselves appearing in tribunals up against a barrister. In sexual harassment cases, this

---

[16] Unless one party acts unreasonably: Industrial Tribunals (Constitution and Rules of Procedure) Regulations 1993, sch 1 para 12 (SI 1993/2687).

[17] EA 2010, s 138.

[18] Enterprise and Regulatory Reform Act 2013, ss 66(1), 103(3).

[19] B Hepple, M Coussey, and T Choudhury, *Equality: A New Framework Report of the Independent Review of the Enforcement of UK Anti-Discrimination Legislation* (Hart Publishing 2000) 4.34.

[20] <www.gov.uk/government/publications/survey-of-employment-tribunal-applications-2018> accessed 4 August 2022.

[21] ibid.

puts the claimant in the untenable position of having to cross-examine the perpetrator.[22] Moreover, the increasing role of lawyers in tribunal hearings has meant that some of the speed, informality, and inexpensiveness of the tribunal system are inevitably sacrificed.

The fourth factor contributing to the limited impact of the tribunal system is that, again like the courts, the procedure is essentially adversarial, processing the case as a bipolar dispute between two individuals, diametrically opposed, to be resolved on a winner-takes-all basis.[23] This all-or-nothing response leaves little room for compromise or synthesis. It is only outside the court process, in settlements, that compromise may be reached; indeed, parties are encouraged to do so by the statutory provision for conciliation on request or on the initiative of a conciliation officer from the Advisory, Conciliation and Arbitration Service (ACAS).[24] However, while the process of settlement may be more flexible than a full hearing, settlement is more intensely individualist. As Dickens shows, the primary aim of the ACAS conciliation process is to reach a compromise, rather than to eliminate discrimination or enforce individual entitlements. ACAS has consistently resisted the suggestion that it should prioritize legal results, preferring to characterize its role as one of problem-solving.[25] Settlements reached through ACAS conciliation are a matter for the parties themselves and are not publicized. No precedents are created, nor guiding principles for society as a whole.

Probably the most serious failing of the adjudication process has been in the nature of its remedies. As with the adversarial system as a whole, remedies are limited by their focus on the individual. Instead of engaging actively in forward-looking reform of the type essential to achieve comprehensive restructuring, the primary remedy available in complaints to tribunals takes the form of monetary compensation. When employment tribunals (then known as industrial tribunals) were created, it was not thought appropriate to entrust them with an injunctive remedy. Nor do they have the power of ordering reinstatement or re-engagement in discrimination cases, despite having such power in unfair dismissal cases. Instead, tribunals are armed with the timid weapon of a recommendation, which requests the employer to take specified steps to obviate or reduce the adverse effects of the

---

[22] Equality and Human Rights Commission, 'Access to Legal Aid in Discrimination Cases' (June 2019) 36.

[23] A Chayes, 'The Role of the Judge in Public Law Litigation' (1976) 89 Harv L Rev 1281.

[24] Employment Tribunals Act 1996, s 18.

[25] L Dickens, 'The Road is Long: Thirty Years of Employment Discrimination Legislation in Britain' (2007) 45 British J Industrial Relations 463, 480.

contravention.[26] An employer who fails to comply with the recommendation is treated gently in comparison with the vehemence of the sanction for contempt of an injunction. Failure to comply is not penalized if the respondent has a 'reasonable excuse'[27] and the standard of such justification is deliberately low.[28] If no such excuse is established, the sanction is mild: failure to comply with a recommendation is penalized merely by an increase in compensation,[29] in stark contrast with the hefty fine or even imprisonment which is the consequence of failure to comply with an injunction.

The EA 2010 made a small attempt to address more systemic issues by introducing the possibility that a recommendation could be fashioned to benefit persons other than the individual complainant. For example, the tribunal could recommend that the respondent should introduce an equal opportunities policy, retrain its staff, ensure its harassment policy was more effectively implemented, or set up a review panel to deal with equal opportunities and grievance procedures.[30] However, in 2015,[31] this power was withdrawn and replaced with the more limited power to make recommendations only in relation to the complainant.[32]

The law has similarly set itself against providing interim relief, which would keep the contract of employment alive in discrimination cases pending the final determination of the case. Such relief is available in a small handful of dismissal cases, such as dismissal on grounds of trade union membership, health and safety concerns, or in whistle-blowing cases. Interim relief is not the equivalent of an injunction or a requirement that the employer should permit the claimant to keep working. What it does provide, however, is for the claimant to continue to receive their salary and other benefits until the claim is determined. It is particularly valuable as it does not need to be paid back if the claim is ultimately lost. The employer therefore has an incentive to settle or expedite the process. In *Sabrina Steer v Stor*, the complainant alleged that the failure to make provision for interim relief in discrimination cases itself constituted discrimination against women in breach of Article 14 ECHR, read with Article 8 (right to respect for private life).[33] The Court of Appeal dismissed the claim. The reasons given epitomize the many ways in

---

[26] EA 2010, s 124(2)(c).
[27] ibid s 124(7).
[28] *Nelson v Tyne and Wear Passenger Transport Executive* [1978] ICR 183 (EAT).
[29] EA 2010, s 124(7).
[30] ibid s 124(3) Explanatory Notes, para 414.
[31] Deregulation Act 2015.
[32] EA 2010, s 124(3) as amended.
[33] *Steer v Stormsure* [2021] EWCA Civ 887 (UK Ct of Appeal).

which the courts and legislature refuse to see discrimination as embedded in systems, rather than as an individual claim. According to Bean LJ: 'Interim relief is a measure protecting employees who have done acts in a representative capacity, or on behalf of the workforce generally or in the public interest. This . . . distinguishes them from cases (or at any rate the great majority of cases) brought by individuals alleging that they have been subjected to discrimination or unfairly dismissed.'[34]

The substitute for dynamic and interactive remedies in Britain has been the almost exclusive reliance on compensation, which satisfies the law's neutrality and individualism by granting a one-off remedy to the individual alone. At the same time, there remains an ambivalence as to the function of compensation. Is it deterrent, or compensatory, or both? Reflecting the fault-based assumptions behind much of discrimination law, early anti-discrimination legislation did not permit compensation to be awarded for unintentional indirect discrimination.[35] This was removed but not fully abandoned by the EA 2010, which provides that, where indirect discrimination is unintentional, a tribunal should not award damages without first considering whether to make a declaration or recommendation instead.[36] Fortunately, the Court of Appeal, in a case in 2021, stressed that this should not be regarded as an obstacle to an award of compensation where compensation is due.[37] Indeed, the Court held, if loss and damage have been suffered due to indirect discrimination, it is to be expected that compensation will be awarded which is adequate and proportionate.[38] On the other hand, courts and tribunals have been unwilling to use damages in a punitive form. In principle, punitive damages are available for statutory tort cases if compensation is insufficient to punish a defendant for oppressive and arbitrary conduct.[39] However, the bar for exemplary damages is high: such damages should only be awarded if the respondent has been shown to be 'guilty of oppressive, arbitrary or unconstitutional action and if the award otherwise payable would not suffice by way of punishment and deterrence'.[40] There are no reported cases since the EA 2010 of such an award.[41] The primary aim of damages for unlawful discrimination therefore remains compensatory.

---

[34] ibid [60].

[35] RRA, s 57(3).

[36] EA 2010, ss 119(5) and 124(4), (5).

[37] *Wisbey v Commissioner of the City of London Police* [2021] EWCA Civ 650 (UK Ct of Appeal).

[38] ibid [40].

[39] *Kuddus v Chief Constable of Leicestershire Police* [2001] UKHL 29, [2002] AC 122.

[40] *Hackney v Sivanandan* 2011 WL 1152088 [32] (EAT).

[41] For an earlier case, see *City of Bradford v Arora* [1991] 2 QB 507 (CA).

The position of discrimination claimants has somewhat improved as a result of the input of EU law. Upper limits on compensation were removed from discrimination claims in 1993 after the ECJ held that such limits infringed the Equal Treatment Directive.[42] Most important was the ECJ's emphatic restatement of the principle that Member States must guarantee real and effective judicial protection of the right to equality of opportunity in a way that has a real deterrent effect on the employer. This sets discrimination claims apart from unfair dismissal claims, which still do have such a limit. Discrimination law claimants are also better off than those claiming unfair dismissal in that compensation for injury to feelings is payable. Nevertheless, the courts have been keen to provide their own upper limits for injury to feelings claims. Known as *Vento* bands,[43] the courts have established upper, middle, and lower bands for awards, depending on the seriousness of the discrimination. For claims presented on or after 6 April 2020, the lower band, for less serious cases or one-off occurrences, runs from £900 to £9,000, the middle band goes up to £27,000, and the maximum, for the most serious cases, such as a lengthy campaign of sexual harassment, is £45,000. The court in *Vento* stressed that the bottom band should rarely be used since it suggests that the injury is trivial. However, in practice, awards for injury to feelings are predominantly in this category. The result is that while there are some isolated cases in which high awards for a successful claim of discrimination are made, these are highly unusual.[44] Median awards for race discrimination, for example, were only £8,040 in 2019–20 over twenty-eight cases and the maximum award was £30,330.[45]

For non-employment cases, the picture is particularly bleak. In such cases, the victim must bring a claim in the ordinary courts. The county[46] and sheriff courts,[47] have jurisdiction over discrimination cases involving education, public functions, premises, associations, and the provision of goods, services, and facilities to the public.[48] There are no published data on discrimination claims in the county courts but anecdotal evidence suggests that only a

---

[42] Case C-271/91 *Marshall v Southampton and South West Hampshire Area Health Authority (No 2)* [1993] ECR I-4367.

[43] *Vento v Chief Constable of West Yorkshire Police* [2002] EWCA Civ 1871 (UK Ct of Appeal).

[44] The highest award was £416,015 (disability discrimination) in 2018–19; followed by £265,719 (disability discrimination) in 2019–20.

[45] <www.gov.uk/government/statistics/tribunal-statistics-quarterly-april-to-june-2020> accessed 4 August 2022.

[46] England and Wales.

[47] Scotland.

[48] EA 2010, s 114.

handful of discrimination cases come before these courts each year, a reflection of the formality, cost, and protracted nature of the county court process. Applicants have to pay court fees and may face an order for costs or expenses if unsuccessful. In addition, county court judges have little knowledge or experience of discrimination claims. A small gesture has been made in the direction of improving county court expertise in the field, by making provision requiring a judge or sheriff to appoint an assessor unless satisfied that there are good reasons for not doing so.[49] However, this procedure remains daunting for the ordinary applicant. This is especially problematic in relation to disability discrimination, since discrimination in the provision of goods and services, a key aspect of disability rights, must be litigated in the county courts.

Most serious is the difficulty in obtaining legal aid. Legal aid in the county courts is subject to strict financial eligibility requirements, which preclude most complainants. The result is that complainants must either represent themselves or find the resources to pay privately for lawyers. By contrast, respondents often have professional representation. Legislation which came into force in 2013 (known as LASPO[50]) made major changes to the scope and eligibility criteria for legal aid, leading to a dramatic fall in its availability. The report of an inquiry by the EHRC in 2019 found that as few as 0.5 per cent of discrimination cases receive funding for representation in court, a mere nine cases per year.[51] Applications for discrimination cases are more likely to be refused than applications for other areas of law, primarily because they do not meet the 'cost–benefit' test, due to their complexities and the failure of decision makers to recognize the broader public benefits of challenging discrimination.[52]

This has been somewhat mitigated by the power of the EHRC to give assistance to complainants, including the funding of legal representation.[53] The EHRC has followed the route of strategic litigation. Cases which qualify for support include those that clarify an important point of law or would have a significant impact on a particular sector. Support for a case might also be forthcoming if it challenges multiple discrimination, or a policy known to cause significant disadvantage.[54] However, the budgetary constraints on

---

[49] ibid s 114(7), (8).
[50] The Legal Aid, Sentencing and Punishment of Offenders Act 2012 (LASPO).
[51] Equality and Human Rights Commission (n 22).
[52] ibid 35.
[53] EA 2006, s 28.
[54] EHRC, 'Legal Strategy 2008–9', no longer available online.

the Commission make it inevitable that only a small number of complainants will receive financial assistance. Thus, most individual litigants must rely on their own resources or support from trade unions or other voluntary bodies.[55]

A further avenue of redress is the application for judicial review to the High Court. The HRA has opened up a new avenue for judicial review, leading, as we have seen, to a number of landmark cases. Breach of the 'public sector duty' to promote equality, which we discuss in detail later, is also subject to judicial review. Judicial review has some advantages over other methods of redress. A successful claim against a public body or challenging secondary legislation can lead to remedies which have effects well beyond the individual litigant. By striking down the discriminatory decision rather than focusing on the effect on an individual, judicial review can potentially change a discriminatory practice to the benefit of a whole class of present and future victims. For example, in *R v Secretary of State, ex p EOC*,[56] the requirement that part-time workers work continuously for five years in order to qualify for employment protection rights was struck down as indirectly discriminatory against women. In one fell swoop, all part-time workers were able to benefit. However, judicial review is itself limited in several ways. As a start, it is restricted to cases characterized as public by the courts.[57] In addition, it is expensive. Given the extensive cuts in legal aid, legal aid will not be accessible to any but the poorest complainant. The EHRC has the power to institute judicial review in matters of relevance to its functions, but its own limited resources have meant that it only brings cases which it regards as strategic. The result is that most judicial review proceedings are brought by NGOs, trade unions, or other civil society bodies.

(ii) The Individual Complaints Model: The US

As in the UK, the primary responsibility for enforcing anti-discrimination laws in the US lies with the individual. Again, as in the UK, this has meant that the right to equality, enshrined in both statute and the Constitution, has largely been unfulfilled. Berrey, Nelson, and Nielson estimate that only a tiny fraction of targets of discrimination in the workplace take formal action, and

---

[55] B Hepple, *Equality: The New Legal Framework* (Hart Publishing 2011) ch 7.
[56] [1995] 1 AC 1 (HL).
[57] *R v East Berkshire Health Authority, ex p Walsh* [1985] QB 152 (CA).

only 6 per cent of cases alleging discrimination in the workplace reach trial.[58] Those who do sue are likely to settle or lose.[59] This is borne out by a study of sexual harassment between 2012 and 2016 by McCann, Tomaskovic-Devey, and Badgett. Although an estimated five million employees are subjected to sexual harassment at work every year, they found that as many as 99.8 per cent never file formal charges. Of those who do, they estimate that fewer than 1,500 per year go to court.[60] This clearly demonstrates how individualization of claims reinforces the employers' overriding power in the workplace. As Berrey, Nelson, Nielson et al put it, civil rights law 'reinscribes' hierarchies, giving employers overwhelming power to control the process.[61]

This can be seen by tracing the trajectory of a discrimination complaint from its origins in the workplace. An ever-increasing role is played by internal complaints procedures. Although, in principle, these should facilitate dispute resolution in a cheap and speedy manner, in practice they frequently act as an obstacle to the vindication of rights. Such procedures are generally run by human resources departments. Yet, as Yang and Liu put it: 'Employers' human resources staffs and internal grievance processes often serve to protect employers from liability rather than address and prevent discrimination faced by employees. As a result, employees are often reluctant to report issues internally.'[62] Employees who do report discrimination face heightened risks of retaliation. Indeed, despite the fact that retaliation is unlawful, as many as 55.8 per cent of all charges filed with the Equal Employment Opportunity Commission (EEOC) in 2020 were of retaliation.[63] The study by McCann, Tomaskovic-Devey, and Badgett et al's study of sexual harassment complaints between 2012 and 2016 found similarly harsh reactions by employers, undeterred by the fact that retaliation is unlawful.[64] Almost two-thirds (64 per cent) of those filing sexual harassment charges reported losing their jobs as a result of the complaint.[65]

---

[58] E Berrey, R Nelson, and L Nielson, *Rights on Trial: How Workplace Discrimination Law Perpetuates Inequality* (University of Chicago Press 2017).

[59] ibid 13.

[60] C McCann, D Tomaskovic-Devey, and M Badgett, 'Employer's Responses to Sexual Harassment', Centre for Employment Equity, University of Massachusetts Amherst <www. umass.edu/employmentequity/employers-responses-sexual-harassment>   accessed   17 November 2021.

[61] Berrey, Nelson, and Nielson (n 58) 13.

[62] Yang and Liu (n 1) 15.

[63] <www.eeoc.gov/statistics/charge-statistics-charges-filed-eeoc-fy-1997-through-fy-2020> accessed 4 August 2022.

[64] McCann, Tomaskovic-Devey, and Badgett (n 60).

[65] Berrey, Nelson, and Nielson (n 58).

Nevertheless, such procedures are given increasing weight in the legal system. As Edelman puts it: 'Over time, organizational policies that symbolize diversity have become widely accepted indicia of compliance with civil rights laws, irrespective of their effectiveness.'[66] She argues that an important reason for the limited success of Title VII is that courts defer to organizations' anti-discrimination and anti-harassment policies, grievance procedures, and diversity programmes even when they are largely ineffective. These have become so common 'that they have been transformed in the public eye from a means of achieving civil rights to indicators of civil rights compliance.'[67] This was clearly in evidence in *Wal-Mart v Dukes*,[68] a class action alleging that women were systematically denied promotion and training, paid less than men for similar work, steered into lower paid jobs, and subject to retaliation and a hostile work environment over all Wal-Mart's 3,400 stores. Refusing to certify a class action on the basis that there could be no common experience of discrimination, the Court focused on Wal-Mart's announced policy forbidding sex discrimination rather than on the reality of women's experiences.[69]

On the face of it, the burden on the individual to enforce employment non-discrimination statutes is lightened by the role of the EEOC, the agency dedicated to resolving complaints of discrimination by workers against their employer in a more informal manner than the courts. The EEOC is responsible for enforcing Title VII of the Civil Rights Act 1964, together with other federal employment non-discrimination acts.[70] Cumulatively, these make

---

[66] L Edelman, *Working Law: Courts, Corporations and Symbolic Civil Rights* (University of Chicago Press 2016) 3.

[67] ibid 11.

[68] *Wal-Mart Stores v Dukes* 131 S Ct 2541 (2011) (US Sup Ct).

[69] ibid 2553; Edelman (n 66) 4.

[70] Civil Rights Act 1964, Title VII prohibiting employment discrimination based on 'race, color, religion, sex, and national origin'. (Note that Title VII uses the term 'colour', which is also widely used in international human rights law and relevant human rights instruments in other jurisdictions (see UK Equality Act 2010, s 9(1)(a); South African Constitution, s 9; Canadian Charter, s 15; International Convention on the Elimination of All Forms of Racial Discrimination. Art 1; ICCPR, Art 2(1); ICESCR, Art 2(2)), which all refer to 'colour' in the list of protected characteristics); Age Discrimination in Employment Act 1967 (ADEA), prohibiting employment discrimination against workers aged forty or over; the Pregnancy Discrimination Act of 1978 (PDA), amending Title VII to clarify that discrimination based on pregnancy, childbirth, or related medical conditions constitutes sex discrimination; the Equal Pay Act 1963 prohibiting sex discrimination in the payment of wages to men and women performing substantially equal work in the same establishment; the Americans with Disabilities Act of 1990 (ADA), Titles I and V, prohibiting employment discrimination based on disability by private and State and local government employers; and Genetic Information Non- Discrimination Act of 2008 (GINA), prohibiting employment discrimination based on an applicant's or employee's genetic information (including family medical history).)

it responsible for enforcing federal laws that make it illegal to discriminate against a job applicant or an employee because of the person's race, colour, religion, sex (including pregnancy, transgender status, and sexual orientation), national origin, age (forty or older), disability, or genetic information. It has jurisdiction over most employers with at least fifteen employees (twenty in the cases of age discrimination) as well as most trade unions and employment agencies. Aggrieved persons must file a Charge of Discrimination with the EEOC before filing a job discrimination lawsuit against the employer.[71] The EEOC has the authority to investigate charges of discrimination with the aim of assessing the allegations fairly and accurately and making a finding. Before investigating, the EEOC offers mediation to resolve a complaint and charges are sometimes settled during an investigation. If it finds that discrimination has occurred, it will attempt to settle the charge through a conciliation process. If conciliation fails, either the charging party or the EEOC may file a lawsuit in court. In determining whether to file a suit, the Commission considers factors such as the strength of the evidence and the wider impact the lawsuit could have on combatting workplace discrimination.[72] It only litigates a very small percentage of cases.

The EEOC clearly plays an important role in enforcing anti-discrimination laws in the workplace. It is cheaper and less daunting. Importantly, it has the power to subpoena the employer for information it regards as necessary to support the filing of a complaint. This sets it apart from individual complaints to ETs in Britain. However, this role is limited in several important ways. While potentially mitigating some of the difficulties of mounting a lawsuit from the start, this procedure continues to rely on individual initiative, despite asymmetries of power in the workplace.[73] As in tribunals in the UK, success rates are extremely low. Of 70,804 cases resolved by the EEOC in the fiscal year 2020, only 12,334 or 17.4 per cent were resolved with an outcome favourable to the charging party, or constituted a charge with merits. A favourable outcome is defined as including negotiated settlements, withdrawals with benefits, successful conciliations, and unsuccessful conciliations.[74]

In their study of the processing of 33,304 Title VII sexual harassment cases filed with the EEOC or state Fair Employment Practices Agencies (FEPAs)

---

[71] <www.eeoc.gov/filing-charge-discrimination> accessed 4 August 2022 (with the exception of the Equal Pay Act).
[72] <www.eeoc.gov/overview> accessed 4 August 2022.
[73] Yang and Liu (n 1).
[74] <www.eeoc.gov/statistics/all-statutes-charges-filed-eeoc-fy-1997-fy-2020> accessed 4 August 2022.

between 2012 and 2016, McCann, Tomaskovic-Devey, and Badgett et al found that most individuals derive little benefit from case-processing by the agency. Charges that proceed through mediation, conciliation, or court processes generally lead to no compensation or at best a small monetary award. Only 23 per cent of those who continued to pursue redress received some monetary compensation, with a median award of a mere $10,000. This means that, of the estimated annual average of approximately 1.3 to 2 million internal reports of sexual harassment between 2012 and 2016, only an average of 9,242 file charges with the EEOC or FEPA. Moreover, although a high number of these (8,147 on average) are judged to have potential legal merit, a mere 1,797 receive a benefit. Even more worrying is the fact that only 12 per cent of charges lead managers to agree to change workplace practices. In the meantime, the costs of filing a complaint are very high, as we have seen.

As well as its continued reliance on individuals to carry the burden of compliance, the EEOC is reliant on political will to ensure that it has the resources to fulfil its role. This has not always been forthcoming. Due to continued budget cuts, in fiscal year 2020 the EEOC's full-time staff numbers dropped to their lowest level in forty years, from 3,390 in 1980 to fewer than 2,000 in 2020. Staffing increased in 2021 due to greater investment from Congress but only by 450.[75]

Those complainants who do file a lawsuit find themselves facing an amplification of the imbalance of power inherent in the individual complaints model. As Berrey, Nelson, and Nielson et al demonstrate, employers are able to control the process in many ways, not least because they are often repeat players, while plaintiffs are 'one-shotters'. Whereas defendants always have legal representation, many plaintiffs do not hire lawyers. If they do, there are often advised to settle for small amounts.[76] When they settle, they typically sign confidentiality agreements, sealing off feedback and consequent change in the workplace.[77]

(iii)   Individual Complaints: South Africa

In South Africa, individual complainants under the Equality Act, which deals with non-labour-related matters, lie to specially created Equality Courts.[78]

---

[75] EEOC, 2022 Congressional Budget Justification Message from the Chair.

[76] Berrey, Nelson, and Nielson (n 58) 13.

[77] ibid 19.

[78] Promotion of Equality and Prevention of Unfair Discrimination Act, 2000 (PEPUDA), ch 4 (ss 16–22).

For employment discrimination, an employee is required to approach a labour court or the Commission for Conciliation, Mediation and Arbitration (CCMA) before approaching an Equality Court. Unlike tribunals in Britain, Equality Courts are not separate institutions. Instead, all High Courts and magistrate courts are designated Equality Courts, subject to the requirement that the presiding officer undertakes a training course for the purpose and is equipped with a specially trained clerk. However, when operating as Equality Courts, they are intended to be more accessible and less formal. No fees are payable for the institution of proceedings,[79] and the clerk is expected to provide assistance to complainants on the Act and the procedure. Although the ordinary rules of the High Court and magistrates' court apply, they should be applied in an informal manner with an emphasis on participation by the parties. As Moshidi J stated in the Equality Court proceedings in *Qwelane*, 'access to the Equality Court does not have the traditional and restrictive procedural red tape. The procedure thereat is also aimed to be informal as mirrored by sections such as s 21(1) of the Equality Act which refers to an "*inquiry*".[80]

There are wide locus standi provisions, which enable complaints to be brought by persons acting on behalf of or in the interests of a group or association, as well as the South African Human Rights Commission and the Commission for Gender Equality.[81] Remedies are also more far-reaching than those under the British provisions. The court can require the respondent to make an unconditional apology, or to do or not do something. It can restrain an unfair discriminatory practice. In addition, it can order payment of damages to the complainant which compensate not just for actual financial loss, but also for loss of dignity or pain and suffering. This means that the court can go much further than tribunals in Britain. For example, in a case in 2021, the Equality Court held that the decision of the minister not to appoint the complainant to the position of senior magistrate constituted unfair discrimination. It therefore ordered the minister to immediately appoint the complainant to that position.[82]

---

[79] Regulations Relating to the Promotion of Equality and Prevention of Unfair Discrimination Act, 2000, reg 12(1).

[80] *South African Human Rights Commission v Qwelane* EQ44/2009(EQ13/2012), para 6 (SA Equality Ct).

[81] PEPUDA, s 20(1).

[82] *Kroukamp v Minister of Justice* [2021] ZAEQC 1 (SA Equality Ct).

There is little recent research on the operation of Equality Courts. In her research published in 2011, Kruger pointed to the paucity of complaints to Equality Courts since their inception, concluding that this 'limits the opportunities of these courts to establish themselves as meaningful catalysts of social change'.[83] Little has changed in the past decade. Although complaints lodged in the Equality Courts are rising, the total remains miniscule compared to the scale of presumed unfair discrimination in South Africa. In 2017/18, a total of 236 complaints were lodged with Equality Courts, rising to 473 in 2018/19 and 621 in 2019/20.[84] Only thirty-eight decisions have been selected by the Equality Court for reporting between 2004 and 2021, with none reported in 2020, only seven in 2019, and only one in 2018.[85]

III MOVING FORWARD

The persistence of discrimination and breaches of the right to equality despite decades of anti-discrimination laws prompts more fundamental interrogation of the premise of individual enforcement, embedded in an adversarial structure. It is clear that a departure from the conventional adversarial framework is required, even in the more informal setting of a tribunal or agency enforcement. As Chayes demonstrates, legislation which explicitly modifies and regulates basic social and economic realities challenges the traditional adversarial model.[86] The bipolar structure is particularly inappropriate for public and private interactions which are not bilateral transactions between individuals, but have wide social implications. This, in turn, requires a transformation of the adjudicative structure, from what Fiss calls a 'dispute resolution' model, to a model of 'structural reform'.[87] In the dispute-resolution model, the victim, spokesperson, and beneficiary are automatically combined in one plaintiff. In the newer model, the victim is not an individual but a group; and the spokesperson is not necessarily a member of the group. In addition, because a beneficiary need not prove individual damage, the class of beneficiaries might extend to all members of a group in

---

[83] R Kruger, 'Small Steps to Equal Dignity: The Work of the South African Equality Courts' (2011) 7 Equal Rights Rev 27.

[84] Department of Justice and Constitutional Development, Annual Report 2018/19; Department of Justice and Constitutional Development, Annual Report 2019/20.

[85] <www.saflii.org/za/cases/ZAEQC> accessed 4 August 2022.

[86] A Chayes, 'The Role of the Judge in Public Law Litigation' (1976) 89 Harv L Rev 1281, 1288.

[87] O Fiss, 'The Forms of Justice' (1979) 93 Harv L Rev 1.

similar circumstances. A similar analysis applies to the defendant. Whereas in the dispute-resolution model, the defendant is both the wrongdoer and the provider of a remedy, in the model of structural reform, the wrongdoer disappears and instead the focus is on the body able to achieve reform. In the result, the individualism of the adversarial system is supplanted by a group-based model and the individual no longer bears the burden of enforcing their own equality rights. This section explores ways of reflecting the group nature of discrimination and lightening the burden on the individual to implement discrimination law.

(i) Class Actions

Class actions aim to assist plaintiffs in cases in which an injury simultaneously affects many individuals, and involves law so complex that for any one individual to sue entails disproportionate expense.[88] The class suit is a particularly flexible type of joint action because any member of the injured group may sue on behalf of the whole group. There is no need to organize all the victims before the trial or to prove that the spokesperson is representative. Instead, participation of all plaintiffs is deferred until after the trial: all members of the group are entitled to participate in the end result and, by the same token, all share the burden of expenses on a *quantum meruit* basis.

Trade unions and NGOs argued forcefully for the inclusion of class actions into the EA 2010, especially for equal pay claims, but without success. In the US, by contrast, it was the Supreme Court that effectively shut down the potential for class actions in discrimination claims. In *Wal-Mart v Dukes*,[89] the US Supreme Court refused to certify a class action brought by current or former employees on behalf of themselves and a nationwide class of as many as 1.5 million female employees of Wal-Mart, described as the US's largest private employer. The case concerned widespread and chronic gender inequalities in Wal-Mart's workforce. Although Wal-Mart delegated pay and promotion decisions to local managers' broad discretion, the claimants argued that a strong and uniform corporate culture of bias against women nevertheless permeated decision making. Local managers, they submitted, exercised their discretion over pay and promotions in a way which

---

[88] H Kalven and M Rosenfield, 'The Contemporary Function of the Class Suit' (1940) 8 University of Chicago L Rev 684.

[89] *Wal-Mart Stores v Dukes* (n 68).

disproportionately favoured men, constituting unlawful disparate impact on female employees. Moreover, they argued, Wal-Mart's refusal to curb these managers' authority constituted unlawful disparate treatment. The District Court found that Wal-Mart used many means to maintain a 'carefully constructed . . . corporate culture', including regular transfers of managers between stores and frequent meetings to ensure uniformity.[90] In the Supreme Court, it was argued that, in the light of this culture, it could not be mere chance that women filled 70 per cent of the hourly jobs in the retail stores but only 33 per cent of management employees, nor that women were paid less than men in every region, with the salary gap widening over years employed even for men and women hired into the same jobs at the same time. Nevertheless, Scalia J was not convinced that there was sufficient commonality in the claims of all the women to qualify as a class action. He refused to recognize the ways in which prejudice and stereotypes imbue themselves into the structure of an organization, which then perpetuates and reinforces itself by continuing to appoint and promote like-minded people for whom such bias appears natural and immovable. 'To the contrary, left to their own devices most managers in any corporation—and surely most managers in a corporation that forbids sex discrimination—would select sex-neutral, performance-based criteria for hiring and promotion that produce no actionable disparity at all.'[91] Although he conceded that some may be guilty of intentional discrimination, or might reward attributes that produce disparate impact, 'demonstrating the invalidity of one manager's use of discretion will do nothing to demonstrate the invalidity of another's.'[92] Each individual woman would therefore need to prove her own cause of action against her own individual manager.

Class actions have been more successfully pursued in South Africa, although not strictly in the equality field. There is express provision for such actions in the Constitution, which entitles 'anyone acting as a member of, or in the interest of, a group or class of persons' among those entitled to claim a breach of the Bill of Rights in court.[93] In a case in 2013, the Supreme Court of Appeal recognized the importance of class actions where a large group of people have small claims against a respondent, but which would not be worth litigating separately, not least because they would not find lawyers to act for

---

[90] ibid 2563.
[91] ibid 2554.
[92] ibid 2554.
[93] SA Constitution, s 38(c).

them on a contingency basis.[94] If such claims could not be pursued by way of a class action, they would not be pursued at all.[95] Class actions led to a remarkable victory in 2019 against twenty gold-mining companies operating in South Africa on behalf of mineworkers who had contracted silicosis and/ or tuberculosis over five decades.[96] However, it remains a difficult and protracted process and could span many years.

(ii) Strategic Litigation

Strategic or test case litigation is a second and complementary way to both relieve the burden on an individual and to address structural issues in discrimination law which extend beyond the individual. Strategic litigation aims to achieve a systematic development of the law by finding test cases which require courts to expand on a legal concept in a way which furthers not just the individual case, but sets a precedent for other similar cases. This can be facilitated through broadening rules of standing to permit representative institutional litigators, NGOs, and trade unions to bring proceedings. In addition, courts could permit amicus curiae or third party interventions, and relieve such public interest litigators of some of the risks of incurring costs orders against them. The advantage of permitting collective actors is that they are repeat players, who can bring carefully chosen test cases to advance the meaning and application of the law, as well as enhancing the ability of vulnerable individuals to claim their own rights.[97] Some progress has been made in the UK by giving the EHRC the power to bring proceedings in its own right.[98] However, the Commission's limited resources mean that this power will only be used sparingly. Similarly, in the US, the EEOC has the power to file suits, but only litigates a very small percentage, depending, inter alia, on the wider impact the lawsuit could have in combatting workplace discrimination.[99] Other jurisdictions, such as South Africa and India, have wide standing rules. In India, in particular, public interest litigation is

---

[94] *Trustees for the time being of Children's Resource Centre Trust v Pioneer Food* [2013] 1 All SA 648 (SA Sup Ct of Appeal).

[95] ibid para 19.

[96] Jason Brickhill, 'Historic South African Silicosis Class Action Settlement Approve' (*Oxford Human Rights Hub Blog*, August 2019) <https://ohrh.law.ox.ac.uk/historic-south-african-silico sis-class-action-settlement-approved/> accessed 4 August 2022.

[97] L Vanhala, *Making Rights a Reality?* (CUP 2010) 40.

[98] EA 2006, s 30.

[99] <www.eeoc.gov/overview> accessed 4 August 2022.

permitted in a very broad range of cases and the court can even initiate its own proceedings.[100]

Amicus briefs are a further way to reflect the fact that many cases involve far more than the parties before the court. They are a regular feature of the US Supreme Court and the Supreme Court of Canada. In the Supreme Court of Canada, in fact, nearly 60 per cent of appeals have at least one intervenor who is not the government, and the Court grants leave in almost all of these.[101] It sees the purpose of an intervention as providing relevant submissions which would be useful to the court and differ from those of the other parties. As the Court put it in a case in 2019: 'Interveners play a vital role in our justice system by providing unique perspectives and specialized forms of expertise that assist the court in deciding complex issues that have effects transcending the interests of the particular parties before it.'[102]

There are several important examples of strategic litigation being used to advance the frontiers of discrimination law. Particularly successful were the advances in EU law brought about by the combination of social movements and specific test cases on gender equality. As we have seen, Article 119 of the Treaty of Rome on equal pay for equal work for men and women lay dormant for several decades, until a series of test cases were brought by Eliaine Vogel-Polsky, a Belgian lawyer and activist who saw the potential of the provision to develop into a real instrument for gender equality driven by the ECJ. These culminated in *Defrenne v Sabena*, in which the ECJ declared that Article 119 (now 157) was directly effective both horizontally and vertically in EU Member States.[103] Equally significant was the series of test cases litigated in South Africa to dismantle barriers to equality for LGBTQI people. Beginning with a case challenging the criminalization of sodomy, the National Coalition for Gay and Lesbian Equality systematically challenged a series of further restrictions and exclusions,[104] culminating in the establishment of a right to

---

[100] For more detail on public interest litigation in India, see S Fredman, *Human Rights Transformed: Positive Rights and Positive Duties* (OUP 2008) ch 5; A Bhuwania, *Courting the People* (CUP 2017) ch 3.
[101] G Callaghan, 'Intervenors at the Supreme Court of Canada' (2020) 43 Dalhousie LJ.
[102] *R v Barton* [2019] 2 SCR 579, para 207 (Can Sup Ct).
[103] Case 43/75 *Defrenne v Sabena* [1976] ECR 455 (ECJ).
[104] *National Coalition for Gay and Lesbian Equality v Minister of Justice* 1998 (12) BCLR 1517 (SACC); *National Coalition for Gay and Lesbian Equality and Others v Minister of Home Affairs and Others* 2000 (2) SA 1 (CC), 2000 (1) BCLR 39 (SACC).

marry.[105] In Canada, disability groups expanded the conceptions of disability through successful test cases before the Supreme Court of Canada.[106] In the US, a carefully organized litigation campaign aimed at challenging wage discrimination in employment as between men and women led to the landmark wage discrimination decision of *County of Washington v Gunther*.[107] In that case, the US Supreme Court held that claims of discriminatory undercompensation are not barred merely because the complainants (women jail guards) did not perform work equal to that of male jail guards.[108] This in turn led to many additional lawsuits being filed around the country in later years.

There remains a great deal of often well-founded scepticism as to whether strategic litigation and other legal suits bring about social change. McCann points to the fact that actual gains from the pay equity litigation following *Gunther* fell short of expectations, and were subjected to a substantial backlash by both politicians and employers.[109] This appears to confirm the many studies on judicial impact which demonstrate the chasm between the promise of landmark court decisions and real social change. Among these is Rosenberg's famous work, *The Hollow Hope*, which brought together a wealth of social evidence pointing to a lack of any real influence of *Brown v Board of Education* in achieving equality in education. This, he argues, is true too in other areas, such as same-sex marriage.[110] In addition, judicial development of restrictive principles, such as the need to prove intent, can act as a real brake on change. Behind this is an overall scepticism about the potential of law to offer anything more than symbolic gains. Thus, Delgado and Stefanjic argue that to secure real gains, dispossessed groups should explore other avenues, including literature and storytelling.[111]

While studies such as *The Hollow Hope* clearly ring true in many situations, they may also underestimate the role strategic litigation can play in catalysing change through social movements. In his work on pay equity in the US, McCann shows that litigation and other forms of legal advocacy played

---

[105] *Minister of Home Affairs v Fourie* (CCT 60/04) [2005] ZACC 19, 2006 (3) BCLR 355 (CC), 2006 (1) SA 524 (CC) (SACC).

[106] Vanhala (n 97) 45; *E (Mrs) v Eve* [1986] 2 SCR 388; *Eaton v Brant County Board of Education* [1997] 1 SCR 241; *R v Latimer* [1997] 1 SCR 217; *Rodriguez v British Columbia (Attorney General)* [1993] 3 SCR 519; *Council of Canadians with Disabilities v VIA Rail Canada Inc*, 2007 SCC 15, [2007] 1 SCR 650.

[107] *County of Washington v Gunther* 452 US 161 (1981) (US Sup Ct).

[108] M McCann, *Rights at Work: Pay Equity Reform and the Politics of Legal Mobilization* (University of Chicago Press 1994).

[109] ibid.

[110] G Rosenberg, *The Hollow Hope* (2nd edn, University of Chicago Press 2008).

[111] R Delgado and J Stefancic, *Critical Race Theory* (New York UP 2001).

a role in defining the rights-based discourse which could be used to advance the cause, even when cases before courts failed to correct wage discrimination. McCann examined pay equity struggles in twenty-eight sites in the US in the 1970s, of which twenty-three involved legal action in the form of either or both an EEOC complaint and a lawsuit, and four of which went on appeal. He concludes that, although federal courts generally lacked the will and capacity to correct discriminatory wage practices, 'Legal norms significantly shaped the terrain of struggle over wage equity; and concurrently, litigation and other legal tactics provided movement activists an important resource for advancing their cause.'[112] Nevertheless, McCann acknowledges that the main contribution of law is in the movement-building phase, giving direction and weight to working women already aware of their unfair treatment at work. In other situations, he recognizes that the logic of anti-discrimination law is not easily adapted to address structural wage inequality,[113] and that there are situations in which litigation led to disempowerment.[114] As negative court decisions mounted after 1985, the use of the law as a plausible threat declined.

Vanhala's more recent study on the role of discrimination law in achieving disability rights in Canada and the UK is particularly illuminating. She uses the concept of 'framing' to examine the ways in which social movements transform their vision into plausible rights claims. 'Framing' analysis aims to 'capture the process of the attribution of meaning that groups and individuals give to symbols, events, behaviour and/or discourse.'[115] Strategic litigation requires a civil society movement to frame its objectives in legal terms. The aim is to imbue existing legal frames with new meanings. The disability rights movement, for example, sought to infuse the legal conception of disability, based on a medical model, with one drawing on the insights of the social model.

We have seen other examples of reframing in earlier chapters. Women's organizations in several jurisdictions successfully reframed the concept of sex discrimination to include pregnancy discrimination.[116] Similarly, discrimination against part-time workers was reframed as indirect discrimination

---

[112] McCann (n 108) 4.
[113] ibid 295.
[114] ibid 285.
[115] Vanhala (n 97) 31.
[116] Case C-177/88 *Dekker* [1991] IRLR 27 (ECJ); Case C-32/93 *Webb v EMO Air Cargo Ltd* [1994] IRLR 482 (ECJ).

on grounds of sex.[117] *Brown v Board of Education* led to the reframing of race discrimination to include segregation.[118] However, this might also come at a cost to the social movement. Social objectives might have to be squeezed into a legal frame which distorts their full meaning. This is especially so when lawyers become spokespersons for those who do not identify with legal framings, or even recognize their own struggle within the legal discourse. Litigation is lengthy and can take the passion out of a movement. This can be particularly problematic if test cases are unsuccessful. On the other hand, we might question whether sceptics of the use of law for social change are not expecting too much of the law. While it is clearly true that test cases might not have a significant impact on deep-seated social and economic inequalities, they may have an important impact on the development of the law itself, not just for the case before the court, but for other similar cases. The recognition of pregnancy as a form of discrimination by the ECJ meant that all EU Member States were required to give protection to pregnant workers. Even though discrimination against pregnant workers continues, women can now assert their rights in this context, and there are many employers who have changed their practice in this regard. Such reframing may even lead to legislative change. We have seen that this stream of cases led the UK to include pregnancy as a protected ground under the EA 2010.

All the solutions canvassed thus far are premised on finding an individual victim. However, given the institutional nature of discrimination, it is important to be in a position to challenge a discriminatory rule even if it is not possible to identify a specific victim. For example, women and ethnic minorities may be deterred from applying for certain types of jobs because of indirect discrimination; yet such practices should still be open to challenge.[119] It is thus of great importance that the ECJ has recognized that discrimination can be committed even if no victim has been identified. In *Firma Feryn*,[120] an employer publicly let it be known that, under its recruitment policy, it would not recruit any employees of a certain ethnic or racial origin. The Court recognized that a public declaration of this type would dissuade members of these groups from applying in the first place, hindering their access to the labour market. A central aim of the Race Directive, namely, 'to foster

---

[117] Case 96/80 *Jenkins v Kingsgate* [1981] ECR 911 (ECJ); Case 170/84 *Bilka-Kaufhaus* [1986] IRLR 317 (ECJ).

[118] *Brown v Board of Education* 347 US 483 (1954) (US Sup Ct).

[119] See Hepple, Coussey, and Choudhury (n 19) para 4.24.

[120] Case C-54/07 *Centrum voor Gelijkheid van Kansen en voor Racismebestrijding v Firma Feryn NV* [2008] ICR 1390 (ECJ).

conditions for a socially inclusive labour market',[121] would be hard to achieve if the scope of the directive were to be limited to cases in which an unsuccessful candidate for a post brought legal proceedings against the employer. Reflecting this principle, the Equality Act (EA) 2010 has now extended the powers of the EHRC to use its enforcement powers whether or not it knows or suspects that a person has been or may be affected by an unlawful act. Significantly, an unlawful act includes both direct and indirect discrimination, and also applies to arrangements to act in a way which would be a contravention if applied to an individual.[122]

(iii)   Agency Enforcement: The Formal Investigation

In the UK, some of the weaknesses of an individual complaints model channelled through an adjudicative structure have been addressed by the powers given to the EHRC to initiate and conduct a 'formal investigation' into cases of suspected unlawful discrimination.[123] The formal investigation departs from adversarialism in several key respects. As a start, it is an active rather than passive process. The Commission has the power to initiate the investigation, thus inviting a strategic approach instead of an ad hoc series of actions. Moreover, it has strong information-gathering powers, including the ability to demand written or oral evidence and the production of documents. The formal investigation also deviates significantly from the individualism of the tribunal procedure. The power is specifically directed at a practice of discrimination rather than at a particular discriminatory act against an individual. Nor is the situation characterized as an all-or-nothing bipolar dispute. Instead, the investigation is intended to be an interactive process, during which the Commission aims to secure a change in discriminatory practices through discussion, negotiation, and conciliation. Its remedial powers are therefore essentially forward-looking. The Commission has the power to issue an 'unlawful act notice', which can include a requirement that the respondent prepare and act on an action plan to avoid a repetition of the unlawful act. Judicial remedies are harnessed as a last resort: during the subsequent five-year period, the Commission can apply to court for an

---

[121]   Directive 2000/43, Preamble, recital 8.
[122]   EA 2010, sch 26 para 13 inserting EA 2006, s 24A(4).
[123]   EA 2006, s 20.

order requiring a person to act in accordance with the action plan. Failure to comply without reasonable excuse may be punishable with a fine.[124]

The formal investigation has the potential to stimulate significant change in structures of discrimination. Indeed, the Commission for Racial Equality (CRE), one of the predecessors of the EHRC, used these powers energetically, initiating twenty-four investigations between 1977 and 1982 alone. Its aim was not simply to enforce the law, but to uncover structural discrimination and trigger wider policy and procedural change.[125] However, the novelty of the procedure and the challenge it posed to deeply entrenched attachments to adversarialism led to a reaction against it by the courts. In a series of judicial review cases against the CRE, the formal investigation was trammelled with a chain of restrictive procedural requirements intended to protect the respondent against what was considered to be a harsh and inquisitorial procedure.[126] Indeed, Lord Denning went so far as to characterize the formal investigation as akin to the Spanish Inquisition.[127] Most damaging was the prohibition on the use of the power to investigate general evidence of structural inequality, requiring instead a reasonable suspicion that the named person had committed unlawful acts.[128] The opportunity to lift some of these restrictions presented itself with the creation of the EHRC in 2006. However, the restrictive jurisprudence of the courts was merely enshrined in statute. The Commission may only conduct a formal investigation against a named person if it suspects that the latter may have committed an unlawful act.[129] In addition, the power is hedged about with procedural protections for the respondent.[130]

The result has been that the EHRC's use of its powers has been timid and remains tethered to the individual complaints model. Only one investigation, against the Metropolitan Police Service, was reported in the first ten years of the creation of the EHRC. The report, published in 2016, was prompted by complaints of victimization of ethnic minority, gay, and female police officers who raised complaints of discrimination. Only three further investigations have been conducted since then, one into equal pay at the BBC (the British

---

[124] ibid s 21.

[125] Dickens (n 25) 475.

[126] *CRE v Prestige Group plc* [1984] 1 WLR 335 (HL); *London Borough of Hillingdon v CRE* [1982] AC 779 (HL); *R v Commission for Racial Equality, ex p Amari Plastics* [1982] QB 1194; and see generally G Appleby and E Ellis, 'Formal Investigations' [1984] PL 236.

[127] *Science Research Council v Nassé* [1979] 1 QB 144, 172 (CA).

[128] *CRE v Prestige Group plc*; *London Borough of Hillingdon v CRE* (n 126).

[129] EA 2006, s 20(2).

[130] ibid sch 2 paras 3, 6–8, and s 20(4).

Broadcasting Corporation), one into anti-Semitism in the Labour Party, and a third into a private care agency. Notably, the investigations remain narrowly focused on individual decisions and individual complaints procedures, with less attention to the structural issues which such investigations could have revealed. The report into victimization of complainants in the Metropolitan Police concluded that it was not possible to establish a breach of equality legislation, but pointed to 'poor practice' in the handling of difficult situations and in dealing with race issues.[131] The investigation into pay discrimination against women at the BBC was prompted by a series of high-profile cases in which female journalists complained that they were paid less than their male colleagues in similar roles. However, it largely focused on a sample of formal and informal complaints by individual women. The investigation was unable to find unlawful pay discrimination in the ten pay complaints it examined in depth. It did go on to examine the broader systems used by the BBC to set pay and assess complaints, and made recommendations for improvements, such as enhancing the transparency of pay decisions, and conducting equal pay audits at least every five years.[132] However, the BBC women's group and those who had initially raised complaints of unequal pay were highly critical of the investigation for not addressing the systemic issue of unequal pay.[133]

The only investigation clearly establishing a breach of the EA 2010 was that into anti-Semitism in the Labour Party. In its report, published in 2020, it found specific evidence of unlawful acts, both in relation to particular agents of the Labour Party and the way it handled anti-Semitism complaints.[134] Pursuant to these findings, the Commission served an unlawful act notice on the Party and required it to draft an action plan to tackle the unlawful act findings, based on a detailed set of recommendations. The action plan should have specific timetables and measures of success to achieve compliance. The Commission has powers to take enforcement action if the Party fails to live up to its commitments. When robustly used, therefore, the formal investigation can be highly effective.

As well as the formal investigation, the EHRC has the power to undertake an inquiry, which is closer to a fact-finding exercise than an enforcement

---

[131] <www.equalityhumanrights.com/en/publication-download/section-20-investigation-metropolitan-police-service> accessed 4 August 2022.

[132] <www.equalityhumanrights.com/sites/default/files/investigation-into-unlawful-pay-discrimination-at-the-bbc.pdf> accessed 22 November 2021.

[133] <www.personneltoday.com/hr/bbc-equal-pay-findings-come-under-fire/> accessed 4 August 2022.

[134] <www.equalityhumanrights.com/sites/default/files/investigation-into-antisemitism-in-the-labour-party.pdf> accessed 4 August 2022.

mechanism. The resulting report and recommendations are not binding: at most, a court or tribunal may have regard to the finding of an inquiry.[135] Although the inquiry may relate to one or more named persons, the Commission cannot use the mechanism of an inquiry to investigate whether a named person has committed an unlawful act. Nor may it state in its report that a named person has committed such an act. As in the case of formal investigations, the Commission's power to obtain information, documents, and oral evidence is strictly circumscribed and subject to judicial control. Its terms of reference must be publicized, with notice to any person specified therein, and it must send a draft of its report to any person who is the subject of adverse findings and give them twenty-eight days to make representations.

The main power of the inquiry and the subsequent report is in their ability to publicize inequalities. If used strategically, an inquiry can uncover important areas of structural discrimination. The EHRC has indeed energetically pursued this possibility, conducting several well-targeted inquiries. The inquiry into financial services was particularly illuminating, revealing an average pay gap of a shocking 55 per cent between the gross average annual salary of men and women in the sector. Further investigation showed that this was primarily due to the role of bonuses, with men receiving five times the performance pay of women. Nor was there any change in sight, with women in new jobs still earning well below their male counterparts.[136] Other inquiries have examined the treatment of ethnic minority workers in lower paid roles in the health and social care sectors; whether the criminal justice system treats disabled people fairly; legal aid for victims of discrimination; and racial harassment in universities and higher education colleges.[137]

However, the ability of the inquiry to generate change is doubtful. The recommendations in inquiry reports are 'light touch' and general. Because no particular organization or person can be named, they lack focus. For example, the inquiry into the financial sector encouraged 'organizations within the financial sector' to institute training on diversity, incorporate equality into organizational objectives, conduct and publicize equal pay audits, and ensure that parental support schemes are in place and effective. In addition, it recommended the appointment of a board member to 'set the tone, mainstream issues and drive change'. There is little incentive for organizations in

---

[135] EA 2006, sch 2 paras 2–5, 9–14, 17, and s 16.

[136] <www.equalityhumanrights.com/en/publication-download/financial-services-inquiry-follow-report> accessed 4 August 2022.

[137] <www.equalityhumanrights.com/en/our-legal-action/inquiries-and-investigations> accessed 4 August 2022.

the financial sector to respond to such encouragement; and, even if they did, it is not certain that the pay gap would diminish as a result. The statute does permit the Commission to use evidence acquired in the course of an inquiry to launch a formal investigation;[138] and this might be a way of taking the findings forward in a more concrete way.

More effective is a 'partnership' approach, which aims to facilitate cooperation between the Commission and the employer or other relevant body, but with a background sanction acting as an incentive to agreement. This includes the power to enter into binding agreements with private or public sector bodies, according to which the latter undertake to formulate and implement an equality plan. A power of this sort was used systematically and strategically in Northern Ireland in order to achieve the statutory aim of fair participation of Protestants and Roman Catholics. Indeed, between 1997 and 1999 alone, the Fair Employment Commission entered into approximately sixty such agreements each year. While some of the agreements were binding, the majority were voluntary. McCrudden, Ford, and Heath et al demonstrated that the existence and careful monitoring of these affirmative action agreements coincided with a trend towards more integrated workforces. Their research suggests that the Commission enjoyed some success in its attempts to achieve fair participation through the negotiation and monitoring of affirmative action agreements in the public and private sectors in Northern Ireland.[139] Heath et al also showed that the Commission has been more effective for entering into agreements which aim at institutional change than for embarking on lawsuits.[140]

A similar power was used effectively by the EHRC in relation to breaches of the equal pay reporting duties introduced in 2017 (see Chapter 5). In 2019, the Commission initiated four investigations into companies for failing to publish, and in all four cases entered into formal agreements with the four employers to publish their gender pay gap information retrospectively and to report on time in the future. A fifth investigation was started into the accuracy of the published gender pay gap information of a private sector employer.[141] Following this enforcement action, the EHRC noted that all

[138] ibid sch 2 paras 2–5, 9–14, 17, and s 16.
[139] C McCrudden, R Ford, and A Heath, 'Legal Regulation of Affirmative Action in Northern Ireland: An Empirical Assessment' (2004) 24 OJLS 363.
[140] A Heath and others, 'The Impact of the Northern Ireland Affirmative Action Programme on Catholic and Protestant Employment' (Spring 2009) Dondena, Centre for Research on Social Dynamics.
[141] <www.equalityhumanrights.com/en/pay-gaps/gender-pay-gap-our-enforcement-action> accessed 4 August 2022.

employers had reported their gender pay gap by August 2019. However, the Commission cannot enter into such an agreement unless it thinks the person concerned has committed an unlawful act.[142] This leaves little scope for the Commission to uncover unlawful acts and is likely to act as a severe constraint on the Commission's powers to enter into such agreements.

IV 'FOURTH GENERATION' EQUALITY LAWS: PROACTIVE MEASURES AND POSITIVE DUTIES

(i) Proactive Measures

More recently, attention has shifted to the possibility of alternative and complementary means of addressing inequality on a protected ground. These focus on measures to promote or achieve equality. Positive duties are proactive rather than reactive. They aim to identify and redress unlawful discrimination even if there has been no complaint by an individual victim. But they go further. Proactive measures are also preventative. Duty-holders should consider the impact on equality of any new or established policies or legislation and adjust them accordingly. Equally importantly, proactive measures aim to promote equality, for example by introducing measures to facilitate the entry of under-represented groups or through family-friendly measures. This, in turn, requires a clearer idea of what 'equality' entails. Broad definitions of 'equality of opportunity' or 'equality of results' might be uncertain guides to behaviour. Moreover, without a clear understanding of goals, it might be difficult to determine violations.

Proactive measures have the potential to overcome the central weaknesses of the complaints-led model. First, rather than being initiated by individual victims against individual perpetrators, responsibility is placed on bodies who are in a position to bring about change, whether or not they have actually caused the problem. This relieves individual victims of the burden and expense of litigation. Secondly, instead of consisting in reactions to ad hoc claims, change is systematic. The institutional and structural causes of inequality can be diagnosed and addressed collectively and institutionally. Thirdly, in recognition of the institutional basis of discrimination, there is no need to prove discrimination or find a named perpetrator. Instead, the

---

[142] ibid s 2(2).

focus is on systemic discrimination and the creation of institutional mechanisms for its elimination. This also avoids the adversarial attitudes of the parties. Rather than viewing equality as a site of conflict and resistance, equality should be regarded as a common goal, to be achieved cooperatively.[143] Finally, proactive models broaden the participatory role of civil society, both in norm setting and in norm enforcing. In this sense, the citizen is characterized not as a passive recipient but an active participant.

Proactive measures operate in several ways. One is to provide a more effective means of ensuring that existing anti-discrimination laws are fulfilled. Responsibility lies with the employer, public body, or enforcement agency to take the initiative in seeking out instances of unlawful discrimination and rectifying them. This means that the right to equality is available to all, not just those who have the courage and resources to bring a complaint to court or a tribunal. Moreover, rather than redressing unlawful discrimination only for the benefit of a particular individual, such an approach seeks to find collective solutions, covering all affected individuals. One example of this, which we have already seen in Chapter 6, is to require employers to conduct pay equity surveys and correct unequal payment patterns. In addition to eliminating existing unlawful discrimination, proactive measures might aim to assess new policy or legislative measures to determine their impact on protected characteristics. Impact assessment is receiving increasing attention. However, it is crucial that further action is taken once a negative impact has been identified, and that changes once instituted be reviewed. A further function of proactive measures is to actively create policies and plans to further equality, for example through affirmative action, adaptation of the built environment, or training programmes.

In assessing proactive duties, there are four central ingredients to be examined: responsibility, participation, monitoring, and enforcement. Proactive measures entail a shift in responsibility away from the individual claimant to a body which is in a position to take action to eliminate unlawful discrimination, address structural inequalities, and assess new policies for their impact on gender equality. The question of who has such responsibility is therefore of central importance. Is the duty confined to public bodies or is it extended to private employers? How specific is the allocation of responsibility? There is always a risk that the apparatus of responsibility is set up, but has little effect

---

[143] Pay Equity Taskforce, *Pay Equity: A New Approach to a Fundamental Right* (2004) 98.

in practice. As in other respects, much depends on political commitment and goodwill.

A second element is participation. Given the potential bureaucratic and 'top-down' nature of proactive measures, it is of central importance to involve stakeholders, potential victims, trade unions, service users, relevant NGOs, equality bodies, and others in the process. It is also important to examine the method chosen to identify consultees: in the absence of a specified victim, questions arise as to the representativeness of consultees, their expertise, and their capacity to engage in the process. Also of importance is to ask what function such consultation should be performing. Consultation is generally aimed at giving and gaining information rather than being of binding effect. Decision makers are generally simply required to consider the views of consultees; at most, rejection of such views must be accompanied by reasons. The influence of consultation therefore depends largely on the political culture, the goodwill of decision makers, and the political or industrial strength and influence of consultees. An active and engaged civil society is essential to the success of participation mechanisms.

Monitoring is a third essential ingredient of a proactive approach. Unlike an individual complaints model, which is concerned with a self-contained incident, proactive measures are programmatic and ongoing. A process of monitoring and review is therefore necessary to assess whether a proactive measure is effective, to review its progress, and to readjust it if necessary. Closely related is the final element, compliance. Without the ultimate sanction of judicial procedures, there is a risk that proactive measures might become mere rhetorical gestures. A key challenge for proactive measures, therefore, is to devise appropriate means of enforcement. This has proved to be the most problematic aspect of proactive duties. Much depends on political goodwill and a sense of responsibility on the part of duty-bearers, and when these are lacking, there is no easy solution. The ideal model in this context would be a pyramid of enforcement.[144] Under this model, the initial response to non-compliance would be for the regulatory body to begin a process of discussion and negotiation. If this is not successful, the recalcitrant respondent could be subject to an order to comply issued by the regulatory body. Only if this further step fails, would fines or other judicially enforced sanctions come into play. This raises the question of whether there is a need to retain some initiative for individuals within a proactive model.

---

[144] J Braithwaite, *Restorative Justice and Responsive Regulation* (OUP 2002).

Without reverting to an individual complaints model, proactive measures might nevertheless better serve the objective of achieving real and substantive equality if tools were granted to the victims themselves, for example by allowing individuals, trade unions, or equality bodies to seek judicial review where proactive measures have not been fulfilled.

Proactive measures lie on the interface between law and politics. It is therefore useful to distinguish between them according to the extent to which they mobilize or interact with legal norms. The approach which is most policy-led is that of mainstreaming. Mainstreaming means that equality is not just an add-on or afterthought to policy, but is one of the factors taken into account in every policy and executive decision.[145] 'The reactive and negative approach of anti-discrimination is replaced by pro-active, anticipatory and integrative methods.'[146] It is a 'social justice-led approach to policy making in which equal opportunities principles, strategies and practices are integrated into the everyday work of government and other public bodies'.[147] Although these policies originate from equality norms, they are autonomous. At the EU level, mainstreaming strategies have given a powerful boost to the effectiveness of sex equality legislation. Proactive measures are also increasingly widespread in the EU, as a recent study of twenty-seven Member States, together with Norway, Iceland, and Finland has shown.[148]

At the other end of the spectrum are specific statutory duties to take steps to achieve equality. Northern Ireland has been at the forefront of this approach. Pioneering legislation introduced in 1989 imposed a positive duty on employers to take measures to achieve fair participation of Protestant and Roman Catholic employees in their workforces.[149] Under this legislation, employers must periodically review the composition of their workforce and its employment practices to determine whether members of each of these two main communities are 'enjoying fair participation in employment in the concern'.[150] If this is not the case, then the employer is required to

---

[145] Commission Communication, 'Incorporating Equal Opportunities for Women and Men into all Community Policies and Activities', COM(96) final; see generally T Rees, *Mainstreaming Equality in the European Union: Education, Training and Labour Market Policies* (Routledge 1998).
[146] Hepple, Coussey, and Choudhury (n 19) para 3.8.
[147] F MacKay and K Bilton, *Learning From Experience: Lessons in Mainstreaming Equal Opportunities* (Scottish Executive Social Research 2003) 1.
[148] S Fredman, 'Making Equality Effective: The Role of Proactive Measures' (2009) Oxford Legal Studies Research Paper No 53/2010.
[149] Fair Employment and Treatment (Northern Ireland) Order 1998 (FETO), pt VII; C McCrudden, 'Mainstreaming Equality in the Governance of Northern Ireland' (1999) 22(4) Fordham International LJ 1696.
[150] FETO, s 55.

institute positive action in order to make progress towards fair participation. Similarly, in Canada, the federal Employment Equity Act 1995 makes it mandatory for federally regulated employers of one hundred employees or more to produce employment equity plans, the aim being to produce a workforce which is representative of the labour market. Covering visible minorities, indigenous people, persons with disabilities, and women, the Act requires employers to identify workplace barriers and to develop and implement equity plans for the four designated groups. Employers are subject to penalties of up to $10,000 for failing to file an employment equity report or filing an incomplete report without reasonable excuse, or for knowingly providing false or misleading information.[151] In addition, as we saw in Chapter 6, legislation in six provinces places a proactive duty on employers to achieve pay equity between men and women, the most innovative being that of Ontario.[152] Most recently, at the federal level, the Pay Equity Act establishes a pay equity regime within the federal public and private sectors, with the aim of redressing systemic gender-based discrimination.[153] The Act requires most federally regulated employers with ten or more employees to develop a proactive Pay Equity Plan for its employees, which must compare the compensation between predominantly female and male job classes doing work of equal or comparable value and increase the compensation of any predominantly female job classes receiving less pay than their male counterparts.[154]

Between the policy-led notion of mainstreaming and specific duties on employers lies a third approach, which is to place a statutory duty on public bodies to promote equality of opportunity. This was, again, pioneered in Northern Ireland. Under section 75 of the Northern Ireland Act 1998, a wide range of public authorities have a duty in carrying out their functions to have due regard to the need to promote equality of opportunity between specified groups, including between men and women, between persons with dependants and those without, between persons with and without disabilities, and between persons of different religious belief, political opinion, racial group, age, marital status, or sexual orientation ('the section 75 duty').[155] A positive duty to promote equality was first introduced in Britain after the

---

[151] Canadian Employment Equity Act, ss 35–36.
[152] See eg Ontario Pay Equity Act, RSO 1990 c P7. This section also draws on the Canadian Taskforce Report (n 143), which sums up the strengths and weaknesses of the models currently in use and makes recommendations for federal pay equity legislation.
[153] The Pay Equity Act received Royal Assent on 13 of December 2018. The federal government brought the Pay Equity Act and the Pay Equity Regulations into force on 31 August 2021.
[154] ss 60 and 88.
[155] Northern Ireland Act 1998, s 75.

Macpherson inquiry, which investigated the London Metropolitan Police Service for its handling of the racist murder of Stephen Lawrence, a young Black man. In its damning report in 1999, the Macpherson inquiry found that the Metropolitan Police Service was riddled with 'institutional racism'.[156] An amendment to the Race Relations Act, introduced in 2000, placed a positive duty on public bodies to have due regard to the need to promote equality of opportunity and good relations between people of different racial groups ('the race equality duty').[157] This was followed by a similar duty in respect of disability in 2005[158] and a gender duty a year later.[159] Section 149 of the EA 2010 consolidates and extends these to include all the protected characteristics.[160] Known as the 'public sector equality duty' (PSED), the duty applies to public bodies and others carrying out public functions. Public bodies are required to have due regard to the need to: (i) eliminate unlawful discrimination; (ii) advance equality of opportunity between persons who share a relevant characteristic and persons who do not; and (iii) foster good relations between those who share a relevant protected characteristic and those who do not. Compliance mechanisms are intended to steer clear of an individually enforceable right. These duties do not give rise to an individual cause of action. Instead, the general duty is enforceable by judicial review proceedings.

In a particularly innovative provision, a new duty in relation to socio-economic disadvantage was also introduced.[161] Under this provision, relevant public authorities 'must, when making decisions of a strategic nature about how to exercise its functions, have due regard to the inequalities of outcome which result from socio-economic disadvantage'. However, in a move of doubtful constitutional validity, successive governments have refused to bring this last duty into effect across Britain. Nevertheless, it has been brought to life in Scotland as of 1 April 2018 in the form of the Fairer Scotland Duty. This duty places a legal responsibility on named public bodies in Scotland, when making strategic decisions, to pay active consideration ('due regard') to how they can reduce inequalities of outcome caused by socio-economic

---

[156] *The Stephen Lawrence Inquiry: Report of an Inquiry by Sir William MacPherson* (Cm 4262-I, February 1999) paras 6.44–6.45.
[157] RRA, s 71.
[158] DDA, ss 49A–D.
[159] SDA, ss 76A–C.
[160] EA 2010, s 149.
[161] ibid s 1.

disadvantage and to publish a written assessment showing how they have done this.[162]

How, then, can socio-economic disadvantage be defined? Interim guidance for the application of the Scottish duty sets out a range of indicators to determine socio-economic disadvantage.[163] Low income is recognized as a key driver of a range of negative outcomes; but public bodies should also pay regard to wealth inequality, which is much greater in Scotland than income inequality. Wealth includes financial products, equity from housing, and a decent pension. Also relevant is material deprivation, or the inability to access basic goods and services such as warm clothes and access to IT and broadband services at home. Although material deprivation usually flows from low income, it needs separate attention because, whereas some low-income families might get support from extended family or friends, households with slightly higher income may not, meaning that their income is further stretched. To these factors should be added area deprivation: living in a deprived area can exacerbate negative outcomes for individuals. Intersectional issues need to be recognized in relation to all these factors. Headline statistics on low income might disguise the gendered nature of poverty, given that statistics generally measure household poverty. Similarly, lone parent households have a very high risk of low wealth; and women, persons with disabilities, and ethnic minority families face a greater risk of material deprivation. The interim guidance also sets targets for reducing inequalities of outcome caused by socio-economic disadvantage. It focuses on equal access to the internet; enough income to be able to save; equal outcomes in relation to education, children's health, and life expectancy; and equal satisfaction with their neighbourhoods.[164]

Positive duties change the whole landscape of discrimination law. Because they place responsibility on bodies that are in a position to bring about change, whether or not they have actually caused the problem, the duty-bearer is not identifiable simply from the definition of discrimination. Legislation must explicitly define and justify the choice of bodies upon whom to place the obligation. Similarly, legislation must specify when the duty arises, what the content of the duty is, and how it is enforced. All of these only make sense if the objectives are clear: beyond compensating the individual

---

[162] <www.gov.scot/publications/fairer-scotland-duty-interim-guidance-public-bodies/pages/2/> accessed 4 August 2022.
[163] ibid.
[164] ibid.

victim, what are proactive measures aiming to achieve? The following section contains an in-depth analysis of the PSED in Britain, in an attempt to situate it in broader debates about how to frame new generations of equality laws to achieve higher levels of effectiveness.

(ii) Deference or Innovation: The Due Regard Standard

From the start, proactive models in UK law have had a distinctive format. Rather than requiring action to produce results, the duty is to 'have due regard' to specified equality goals; namely, the need to advance equality of opportunity, eliminate unlawful discrimination, and promote good relations. This can be contrasted with positive duties in other contexts. For example, the International Covenant on Social, Economic and Cultural Rights imposes a duty on the State to '*take steps*, . . . to the maximum of its available resources, with a view to achieving progressively the full realization of the rights'.[165] However, under the PSED, public bodies are not required to achieve these goals or even to take steps to do so. Instead, the essence of the PSED in Britain is to leave it to the decision maker to make the ultimate choices. Does this standard simply signal deference to decision makers' prerogatives to determine the priority to be given to equality? Or, more ambitiously, can it be understood as an example of 'reflexive' law?

Reflexive law steers away from imposing prescribed solutions which are likely to encounter resistance or merely token compliance. Instead, it aims to harness the energy and problem-solving expertise of those who are in the best position to bring about change. Reflexive law is based on a particular understanding of society, known as systems theory. Systems theory rejects the assumption that law is at the apex of society, able to 'command and control' other parts of society.[166] Rather, it characterizes society as structured non-hierarchically into multiple sub-systems. Moreover, systems theory posits, each sub-system has its own 'language' which is not capable of being understood or translated by other sub-systems.[167] Instead, each system

---

[165] ICESCR, Art 2 (emphasis added).

[166] The following paragraphs are taken from Fredman (n 100) ch 6.

[167] G Teubner, 'Substantive and Reflexive Elements in Modern Law' (1983) 17 Law and Society Rev 239; C Scott, 'Regulation in the Age of Governance: The Rise of the Post-Regulatory State' in J Jordana and D Levi-Faur (eds), *The Politics of Regulation* (Edward Elgar 2004); J Black, 'Constitutionalising Self Regulation' (1996) 59 Modern L Rev 24; J Black, 'Proceduralising Regulation, Part II' (2001) 21 OJLS 33.

translates external stimuli into its own language and reacts according to its own internal logic.[168] This means that it is a mistake to regard law as capable of directly regulating the behaviour of other sub-systems. Command and control through law merely results in what Teubner calls the 'regulatory trilemma'. First, legal intervention may be ignored by the targeted sub-system, although the latter might give the appearance of complying. For example, the sub-system might translate the legal duty to comply into terms consistent with its own usual method of operating, such as creating a committee or a policy, which appear to comply but in fact amount to 'business as usual'. Alternatively, the intervention might trigger the second limb of the trilemma, namely, causing damage to the targeted sub-system. For example, the targeted body might translate the legal duty to comply as requiring a detailed and rigid bureaucracy, which paralyses the body and prevents dynamic change. Or, as the third limb of the trilemma suggests, the legal intervention might damage the legal sub-system itself, in that the perceived ineffectiveness of the law results in a crisis of legitimacy.[169]

The only way to avoid the regulatory trilemma, according to systems theory, is to adopt a new model by which the law adjusts itself in the hope of inducing adjustment in other systems. This is known as reflexive law.[170] Reflexive law rejects authoritative prescription, seeking instead to recognize the inner logic of social systems and to find ways to steer them.[171] In principle, the due regard standard might be capable of being characterized as an instance of reflexive law.[172] Rather than a solution being imposed on a public body, the body is required to come up with its own set of solutions on the basis of a wider consideration of the issues than it would, in the absence of the statutory duty, have undertaken.

An alternative understanding of the 'due regard' standard might be to enhance 'responsive law'.[173] According to this model, law should be shaped

---

[168] J Habermas and W Rehg, *Between Facts and Norms: Contributions to a Discourse Theory of Law and Democracy* (Polity Press 1996) s 2.1.

[169] Gunther Teubner, 'After Privatization: The Many Autonomies of Private Law' (1998) 51 Current Legal Problems 406.

[170] Teubner (n 167) 254.

[171] Scott (n 167) 9.

[172] See further C McCrudden, 'Equality Legislation and Reflexive Regulation: a Response to the Discrimination Law Review's Consultative Paper' (2007) 36 ILJ 255; S Fredman, 'Breaking the Mold: Equality as a Proactive Duty' (2012) 60 American J Comparative Law 265.

[173] M Stephenson, 'Mainstreaming Equality in an Age of Austerity: What Impact has the Public Sector Equality Duty had on Work to Promote Gender Equality by English Local Authorities?' (DPhil thesis, University of Warwick 2016).

to facilitate responses to social needs and aspirations.[174] For Nonet and Selznick, the paradigm function of responsive law is regulation not adjudication. Such regulation should be conducted by agencies with the objective of 'testing alternative strategies for the implementation of mandates and reconstructing those mandates in the light of what is learned'.[175] Responsive theorists acknowledge that, by making law more political and flexible, responsive law can become too malleable, eroding its authority. It also runs the risk of being over-responsive to particular interests and ideologies.[176] Ultimately, therefore, external incentives and deterrents should be combined with deliberative problem-solving and peer review at the local level to achieve effective change.

A less optimistic approach would be to regard the 'due regard' standard as entrenching what Edelman calls endogenous law. Her theory of why equal employment opportunity laws in the US have had limited success is that judges defer to organizations' procedural compliance, even when these procedures are largely ineffective.[177] She defines 'legal endogeneity theory' as a process by which the meaning of law is shaped by widely accepted ideas within the social arena that law seeks to regulate. Organizations respond to legal interventions by creating policies and programmes designed to symbolize attention to law, but this is merely symbolic. This could also be seen as reflecting the first limb of Teubner's trilemma. However, she takes this a step further and posits that as these policies become commonplace, they are equated with compliance with the law, not just by employers and employees themselves, but also by courts and other compliance agencies. The meaning of law therefore devolves upwards from organizations to courts. Over time, the evolution of law is fundamentally influenced by the very institutions the same legal structures are meant to regulate.[178] Symbolic compliance is accepted by the courts and regulators as actual compliance. The risk with the PSED is that the process of 'having due regard', usually in the form of an impact assessment, is mistaken for the substance of addressing institutional discrimination. Elements of all of these theories can be detected in the application of the due regard standard in the courts in Britain.

---

[174] P Nonet and P Selznick, *Law and Society in Transition: Toward Responsive Law* (Harper & Row 1978) 14.
[175] ibid 108–09.
[176] ibid.
[177] Edelman (n 66) 11.
[178] ibid 12, 13.

More empirical work is needed to discover whether the due regard standard has triggered real organizational change. In her research into three local authorities in England, Stephenson found little evidence that the PSED has resulted in action to tackle structural inequalities.[179] Although there was activity within the organizations to comply, this depended on the commitment of 'critical actors' within and outside the authority. Notably, however, most activity was motivated by a fear of judicial review, rather than the value of equality in itself, leading to a focus on bureaucratic compliance. Indeed, she found that most of the equality work in the authorities she studied concentrated on carrying out Equality Impact Assessments (EIAs) of cuts to services, rather than steps to positively promote equality.

This suggests that, in many respects, the implementation of the due regard standard has reflected Teubner's regulatory trilemma rather than addressing it. A common response of bureaucratic organizations to externally imposed requirements is to focus on generating procedures. This allows the organization to appear to comply while at the same time causing as little change to its internal systems as possible. This is the first horn of the dilemma. On the other hand, the threat of judicial review has sometimes prompted an inordinate amount of energy to be used in setting up such procedures— particularly impact assessments—risking diverting resources from more substantive change. This risks paralysing those parts of the organization which would be conducive to change. This is the second horn of the dilemma. The third horn of the dilemma concerns the effect on the legal system itself. The risk here is that highlighted by Edelman: that the law equates procedures with compliance, without paying attention to whether there has been real change. The remainder of this section examines the case law. Have the courts been able to shape the 'due regard' standard in a way that surmounts the regulatory trilemma?

An examination of the case law suggests that, at least at the level of rhetoric, the courts have been aware of the risks that PSED might attract no more than 'tick box' compliance. This is reflected in the consistent call on public bodies to regard the PSED as central to their decision-making processes. In the influential case of *Bracking*, McCombe LJ emphasized that: 'The 2010 Act imposes a heavy burden upon public authorities in discharging the PSED and in ensuring that there is evidence available, if necessary, to demonstrate that discharge. It seems to have been the intention of Parliament that these

---

[179] Stephenson (n 173).

considerations of equality of opportunity (where they arise) are now to be placed at the centre of formulation of policy by all public authorities, side by side with all other pressing circumstances of whatever magnitude.'[180] This reinforces the earlier and much cited dictum of Lady Arden in the *Elias* case: 'It is the clear purpose of [the race equality duty] to require public bodies to whom that provision applies to give advance consideration to issues of race discrimination before making any policy decision that may be affected by them. This is a salutary requirement, and this provision must be seen as an integral and important part of the mechanisms for ensuring the fulfilment of the aims of anti-discrimination legislation.'[181]

Nevertheless, the response has been to set standards which have largely amplified the procedural requirements. Courts have been quick to stress that the due regard standard 'is not a duty to achieve a result, namely, to eliminate unlawful racial discrimination or to promote equality of opportunity and good relations between persons of different racial groups. It is a duty to *have due regard to the need* to achieve these goals.'[182] Indeed, 'no duty is imposed to take steps themselves, or to achieve results'.[183] Moreover, it is for the decision maker to determine how much weight to give to the duty, as long as there has been a rigorous consideration of the duty. Provided that there has been a 'proper and conscientious focus on the statutory criteria,' according to Elias LJ in *Hurley and Moore*, 'the court cannot interfere simply because it would have given greater weight to the equality implications of the decision'.[184] This leaves courts to determine only whether there has been 'rigorous consideration' of the duty. This inevitably entails focusing on the procedure used, increasing the very risk they are meant to avoid, namely bureaucratic box-ticking.

How, then, have the courts attempted to provide appropriate principles to embed considerations of equality into the formulation of public bodies' policies without simply enhancing the proceduralization of the duty? In *Bracking*, McCombe LJ set out a series of principles drawn from preceding

---

[180] *Bracking v Secretary of State for Work and Pensions* [2013] EWCA 1345 [59].

[181] *R (Elias) v Secretary of State for Defence* [2006] 1 WLR 3213 [274] (CA) see also *R (Brown) v Secretary of State for Work and Pensions* [2008] EWHC 3158 (Admin) [79] (High Ct). Both these dicta are regularly repeated by courts in PSED cases.

[182] *R (On the application of Baker & Others) v Secretary of State for Communities and Local Government, London Borough of Bromley* [2008] EWCA Civ 141 [31].

[183] *R (Brown) v Secretary of State for Work and Pensions* (n 181) [84].

[184] *R (On the application of Hurley) v Secretary of State for Business, Innovation and Skills* [2012] EWHC 201 (Admin) [77]–[78] and [89] endorsed by Lord Neuberger in *Hotak v London Borough of Southwark* [2015] UKSC 30 [75].

case law, which are regularly cited in subsequent cases. These were summarized in the 2020 case of *Bridges* as follows: '(1) The PSED must be fulfilled before and at the time when a particular policy is being considered. (2) The duty must be exercised in substance, with rigour, and with an open mind. It is not a question of ticking boxes. (3) The duty is non-delegable. (4) The duty is a continuing one. (5) If the relevant material is not available, there will be a duty to acquire it, and this will frequently mean that some further consultation with appropriate groups is required.' Nevertheless, 'provided the court is satisfied that there has been a rigorous consideration of the duty, so that there is a proper appreciation of the potential impact of the decision on equality objectives and the desirability of promoting them, then it is for the decision-maker to decide how much weight should be given to the various factors informing the decision'.[185]

The key issue is therefore whether the principles of compliance generated by courts could make a difference to the quality of decision making, regardless of the actual outcome. The importance of procedure to quality of decision making was stressed by the Court of Appeal in *Bridges* when it stated:

> We accept (as is common ground) that the PSED is a duty of process and not outcome. That does not, however, diminish its importance. Public law is often concerned with the process by which a decision is taken and not with the substance of that decision. This is for at least two reasons. First, good processes are more likely to lead to better informed, and therefore better, decisions. Secondly, whatever the outcome, good processes help to make public authorities accountable to the public. We would add, in the particular context of the PSED, that the duty helps to reassure members of the public, whatever their race or sex, that their interests have been properly taken into account before policies are formulated or brought into effect.'[186]

However, this depends on whether the court is willing to insist that the duty is followed regardless of its outcome. One way of doing so is to give a clearer idea of its aims and objectives, as already seen with the Scottish duty. Prior to the EA 2010, the positive duties referred only to promoting equality of opportunity, a goal which is vague and difficult to measure. In the consultation leading up to the Act, the current author and Sarah Spencer submitted that the objectives be elaborated to include the four dimensions of

---

[185] *R (On the application of Edward Bridges) v Chief Constable of South Wales Police* [2020] EWCA Civ 1058 [175] (UK Ct of Appeal).
[186] ibid [176].

equality advocated in Chapter 1.[187] These objectives were accepted by the Discrimination Law Review, established by the government to provide proposals for a consolidated Equality Bill.[188] Thus, in the proposals put out for consultation, the Discrimination Law Review stated as follows:

> If public authorities do not understand what promoting equality of opportunity actually means in practice, this reduces the effectiveness of the equality duties in achieving meaningful outcomes for disadvantaged groups. We therefore want a clearer articulation of the purpose of a single public sector equality duty. In developing our proposals, we have had particular regard to the work by Sarah Spencer and Sandra Fredman on this subject and the general duty of the Commission for Equality and Human Rights. We have adapted the four 'dimensions of equality' as identified by Spencer and Fredman . . . (i) Addressing disadvantage—taking steps to counter the effects of disadvantage experienced by groups protected by discrimination law, so as to place people on an equal footing with others; (ii) Promoting respect for the equal worth of different groups, and fostering good relations within and between groups—taking steps to treat people with dignity and respect and to promote understanding of diversity and mutual respect between groups, which is a pre-requisite for strong, cohesive communities; (iii) Meeting different needs while promoting shared values—taking steps to meet the particular needs of different groups, while at the same time delivering functions in ways which emphasise shared values rather than difference and which provide opportunities for sustained interactions within and between groups; (iv) Promoting equal participation—taking steps to involve excluded or under-represented groups in employment and decision-making structures and processes and to promote equal citizenship.[189]

When finally enacted, the EA 2010 contained a version of the four dimensions. Thus, section 149(3) of the EA 2010 provides as follows:

---

[187] S Fredman and S Spencer, 'Beyond Discrimination: It's Time for Enforceable Duties on Public Bodies to Promote Equality Outcomes' [2006] EHRLR 598; S Fredman and S Spencer, 'Equality: Towards an Outcome-Focused Duty' (2006) 156 EOR 14; S Fredman and S Spencer, 'Delivering Equality', Submission to the Cabinet Office Review (2006).

[188] *Discrimination Law Review—A Framework for Fairness: Proposals for a Single Equality Bill for Great Britain* (2007) paras 5.28–5.30; 'Equality Bill Government Response to the Consultation' (Cm 7454, July 2008) para 2.25.

[189] ibid paras 5.28–5.29.

Having due regard to the need to advance equality of opportunity . . . involves having due regard, in particular, to the need to—

(a) remove or minimise disadvantages suffered by persons who share a relevant protected characteristic that are connected to that characteristic;

(b) take steps to meet the needs of persons who share a relevant protected characteristic that are different from the needs of persons who do not share it;

(c) encourage persons who share a relevant protected characteristic to participate in public life or in any other activity in which participation by such persons is disproportionately low.[190]

This formulation clearly echoes the first dimension (redressing disadvantage), the third dimension (encouraging participation among those where participation is disproportionately low), and the fourth dimension (accommodating difference). The second dimension (addressing stigma and prejudice) is reflected in the elaboration of the duty to foster good relations. Section 149(5) provides that having due regard to the need to foster good relations involves having due regard to the need to tackle prejudice and promote understanding.[191] However, these provisions hold back from fully endorsing asymmetrical treatment. This tension is manifested in section 149(6), which states that compliance with the duties may involve treating some people more favourably than others, but that this does not permit conduct which is otherwise prohibited by the Act. In other words, these provisions do not go so far as to permit reverse discrimination.[192]

The potential for these statutory aims to enable the courts to insist on quality of decision making rather than simply endorsing tick-box responses can be seen in *Bracking*. In this case, it was argued that the minister had breached the PSED when she decided to terminate a national fund established to support independent living by disabled persons. McCombe LJ held that there was insufficient evidence that the minister had given focused regard to the potentially very grave impact on persons with disabilities of cuts to their care packages. In particular, given that the minister was not told in clear terms that the impact of the policy in question was to put independent

---

[190] EA 2010, s 149(3).
[191] ibid s 149(5).
[192] See Chapter 6.

living of persons with disabilities in peril, it was impossible to conclude that she could have paid due regard to the aims set out in section 149(3), namely, to meet the needs of disabled people which are different from those of able-bodied people, or to encourage them to participate in activities in which their participation is disproportionately low.[193] *Bracking* was one of the few cases in which the decision was struck down for breach of the PSED.

Lady Hale's dissenting opinion in the Supreme Court decision of *MA* is an even clearer example of the potential role of the statutory objectives in enabling courts to steer decision makers towards better quality decisions. The case concerned a challenge to the policy, known as the 'bedroom tax', which imposed a cap on housing benefit (a benefit assisting tenants to pay their rent) based on the number of bedrooms recipients were deemed to require. This drastically cut the amount of benefit payable to those who were living in social housing with more bedrooms than they were deemed to require. It was argued that the Secretary of State in imposing this policy had failed to have due regard to women who had been subjected to domestic violence and were therefore living in properties which had been adapted to provide a high level of security. Lady Hale reiterated that under section 149(3), the decision maker must have due regard to the need, inter alia, to remove or minimize the disadvantages connected to a protected characteristic, and to take steps to meet the needs of persons with a protected characteristic where those needs are different from those who do not share that characteristic. She pointed out that gender-based violence is:

> undoubtedly a disadvantage suffered by people, namely women, who share a relevant protected characteristic within the meaning of section 149(3)(a) and produces needs that are different from those of people who do not share it within the meaning of section 149(3)(b). This brings it within the need to enhance equality of opportunity to which due regard is to be had under section 149(1)(b). In my view, therefore, the public sector equality duty requires public authorities at least to consider the impact of their decisions and actions on the victims of gender-based violence. This is not much to ask. People in sanctuary schemes may be small in number but victims of gender-based violence are many. Public authorities should take their needs into account when developing their policies. They are likely to make better decisions as a result. And they will be able to explain them better.[194]

---

[193] *Bracking v Secretary of State for Work and Pensions* (n 180).
[194] *R (MA) v Secretary of State for Work and Pensions* [2016] UKSC 58 [80].

She would therefore have found a breach of the PSED, one reason to strike it down. The majority in *MA*, however, made no mention of the statutory aims, simply upholding the Court of Appeal's conclusion that the Secretary of State had, in broad terms, addressed the question of gender-based discrimination.[195]

Whether the PSED can improve the quality of decision making depends, too, on the robustness with which the procedural requirements generated by the courts are enforced. In particular, will a policy or decision be quashed for failure to follow these requirements? Or will a court be persuaded that the outcome would have been no different had the duty been followed (the 'futility' argument)? There are several prominent cases in which the decision has been quashed due to failure to follow the PSED. As we have seen, *Bracking* is one example. McCombe LJ was unequivocal: 'It seems to me that if a decision is reached without due regard to the PSED then it is an unlawful decision and, subject to any overarching discretionary features, the decision should be quashed. That is the course that I would adopt in this case.'[196] This follows a similarly emphatic statement by Elias LJ in *Hurley*: 'It will be a very rare case, I suspect, where a substantial breach of the PSED would not lead to the quashing of a relevant decision.'[197]

However, in practice, courts are reluctant to go this far. At best, they prefer to settle for a declaratory remedy, on the basis that courts assume that the public body will discharge the duty diligently.[198] More worrying is the resurgence of the futility argument. Courts have been quick to accept submissions by the respondent public authority that either the breach was repaired by a later impact assessment, or, even more problematically, that, had the procedure been followed correctly, it would have made no difference to the outcome. This was the approach of the Court of Appeal in the 2019 case of *Forward v Aldwyck*.[199] In that case, the respondent admitted that it had failed to comply with the PSED. The main question in the case was therefore whether the court should assess whether it would have made any difference if the public body had complied with the duty. In other words, should the futility argument succeed? Longmore LJ declined 'to accept the proposition

---

[195] ibid [70].

[196] *Bracking v Secretary of State for Work and Pensions* (n 180).

[197] *R (On the application of Hurley) v Secretary of State for Business, Innovation and Skills* (n 184) [99].

[198] *R (On the application of Edward Bridges) v Chief Constable of South Wales Police* (n 185); *Hussein v Secretary of State for the Home Department* [2018] EWHC 213 [44] (UK High Ct).

[199] *Forward v Aldwyck Housing Group Ltd* [2019] EWCA Civ 1334 (UK Ct of Appeal).

that, as a general rule, if there is a breach of the PSED, any decision taken after such breach must necessarily be quashed or set aside.'[200] Courts have even suggested that to give a remedy would be regarded as punitive and patronizing. 'For my part,' stated Longmore LJ, 'I would resist the notion that the court should act as some sort of mentor or nanny to decision-makers.'[201] Laws and Treacy LJJ took this even further: 'The court's approach should not ordinarily be that of a disciplinarian punishing for the sake of it.'[202] They were quick to add that 'nothing we say should be thought to diminish the importance of proper and timely compliance with the PSED'.[203] However, there is little incentive to discharge the duty in a rigorous and genuine manner if the court will excuse a breach if followed by a later impact assessment. Yet this has been frequently the case. In the *West Berkshire* case, the Court of Appeal went so far as to hold that although it was important to comply with the PSED in a timely manner, the court would not quash the decision if an equality assessment was carried out at a later date and would not have led to a different decision.[204] Several judges, including McCombe LJ himself, have held that it is possible for a reviewing officer to comply with the PSED even if ignorant of it.[205]

The power of the futility argument has been enhanced by statutory provisions, in effect since April 2015, which require the High Court to refuse to grant relief on an application for judicial review 'if it appears to the court to be highly likely that the outcome for the applicant would not have been substantially different if the conduct complained of had not occurred'.[206] Again, courts have been quick to warn, as Turner J did, that 'the court must exercise the requisite degree of care when concluding that compliance would have made no material difference. Otherwise, there is a risk that the importance of fulfilling the duty may be impermissibly demoted'.[207] However, they are equally quick to immediately find a reason to uphold the futility argument. As Turner J put it in the same case: 'Any contrary approach would . . . mark the triumph of form over substance and give rise to risk of serious injustice

---

[200] ibid [21].

[201] ibid [25].

[202] *Secretary of State for Communities and Local Government v West Berkshire District Council* [2016] EWCA Civ 441 [87] (UK Ct of Appeal).

[203] ibid [87].

[204] ibid.

[205] *Powell v Dacorum Borough Council* [2019] EWCA Civ 23 [45] (UK Ct of Appeal).

[206] Senior Courts Act 1981, s 31(2A).

[207] *London and Quadrant Housing Trust v Patrick* [2018] EWHC 1263 (QB) [55].

to those whose interests the original decision, although procedurally flawed, was rightly intended to protect.'[208]

A similar magnetic pull towards procedural solutions can be seen in Northern Ireland. In its review of the effectiveness of section 75 in 2008, the Northern Ireland Equality Commission concluded that, while section 75 had been effective in key areas, particularly consultation, there was less evidence that the legislation had had the intended impact. 'A shift in gear now needs to take place within public authorities, away from concentrating primarily on the process of implementing Section 75 towards achieving outcomes.'[209] To address this, the Commission recommended that public bodies should develop action plans based on an audit of inequalities which identify the range of key inequalities to be addressed. However, a review of the action plans undertaken in 2016 found a continuing tendency for action measures to be process-oriented, with very few targets. Where performance indicators were included, they could not easily be measured. The review therefore recommended that public authorities should develop clearer, measurable performance indicators and numerical targets. All action plan reports should provide statistical evidence of progress towards such measures, and to clearly link processes to the impact they are intended to have.[210]

This contrasts with England where specific details of how to carry out the PSED have been stripped away. Earlier formulations included specific duties underpinning the general duty to 'have due regard', including to monitor the workforce.[211] Although these were largely procedural for race and sex discrimination, the specific duty under the disability regulations required public bodies to produce an action plan for each three-year period and to demonstrate that they had taken the actions they committed themselves to and achieved the appropriate outcomes. Public authorities were also required to involve disabled people in the development and implementation of action plans. After 2010, the specific duties were drastically reduced. Instead, public bodies are simply required to publish relevant, proportionate information demonstrating their compliance with the PSED and to set themselves specific, measurable equality objectives, which need to be published at least

---

[208] ibid.

[209] Equality Commission for Northern Ireland, 'Section 75 Keeping it Effective, Final Report' (November 2008).

[210] <www.equalityni.org/ECNI/media/ECNI/Publications/Employers%20and%20Serv ice%20Providers/Public%20Authorities/ReviewofActionPlans-FullReportMar2017.pdf> accessed 4 August 2022.

[211] Race Relations Act 1976 (Statutory Duties) Order 2001 (SI 2001/3458); Race Relations Act 1976 (Statutory Duties) Order 2004 (SI 2004/3125), art 3.

every four years.[212] The underlying principle is that it should be left to the local electorate or civil society to call public authorities to account, rather than relying on legal procedures. This is reflected in the guide to the specific duties, where the Government Equalities Office states that publishing relevant equality information 'will give the public the information they need to hold public bodies to account for their performance on equality'.[213] Strikingly, however, the guidance gives a great deal of attention to what is not required. In particular, specific duties do not require public bodies to publish equality schemes, impact assessments, action plans, or annual reports on equality. It is for each public body to decide what equality objectives it should set and how many there should be. The information need not be published separately and can be part of another document, such as the public body's annual report or business plan.

This change of approach contrasts vividly with that of the Welsh government, which has chosen to retain the requirement that a public body produce an equality plan, conduct impact assessments, and identify measurable targets.[214] A report published in 2014 found that the Welsh specific duties were thought to support progress on equalities work in ways additional to the specific duties in England. In particular, the requirement to conduct equality impact assessments was regarded as integrating equality and diversity into service planning.[215]

(iii) The Compliance Pyramid

Other jurisdictions have paid more attention to ways of combining external regulation with internal problem-solving, incorporating the insights of the compliance pyramid described earlier. In Northern Ireland, as we have seen, the fair employment legislation, introduced in 1989, imposed positive duties on employers to take measures to achieve fair participation in their workforces of Protestant and Roman Catholic employees.[216] The Northern Ireland Equality Commission plays a central role in ensuring compliance. Registered employers are required to send a monitoring return each year to

---

[212] Equality Act 2010 (Specific Duties) Regulations 2011 (SI 2011/2260).

[213] <www.gov.uk/government/publications/public-sector-quick-start-guide-to-the-specific-duties> accessed 4 August 2022.

[214] Equality Act 2010 (Statutory Duties) (Wales) Regulations 2011 (SI 2011/1064).

[215] <www.equalityhumanrights.com/en/advice-and-guidance/public-sector-equality-duty-research> accessed 4 August 2022.

[216] Fair Employment and Treatment (Northern Ireland) Order 1998 (SI 1998/3162) (FETO).

the Commission including details of the number of existing employees who belong to each Community, the composition of applicants for employment, and, in relevant cases, those ceasing to be employed. Criminal sanctions are available to enforce the obligation to serve a return. But the Commission also has a range of other sanctions at its disposal. It may make recommendations as to the affirmative action to be taken, and it can serve directions on an employer who fails to give written undertakings where appropriate, and a notice about goals and timetables. Enforcement is complemented by recourse to a tribunal, for example to enforce a written undertaking. Particularly important is the Commission's power to have recourse to economic sanctions, such as the denial of government contracts.[217]

The enforcement structure has worked relatively well in Northern Ireland. We have already seen that the Commission (and its predecessors) used their powers to enter into binding agreements with great effect (see earlier). Every year, the Commission receives almost 4,000 monitoring return forms from private sector employer and public authorities, and audits them for compliance. In 2019–20, a total of 3,413 monitoring return forms received from employers were audited and as many as 99 per cent of these were in compliance with the legal requirements, a compliance rate which has remained at this high rate for over a decade.[218] Employers are also required to conduct a review every three years for the purposes of determining whether members of each community are enjoying 'fair participation' and the 'affirmative action (if any) which would be reasonable and appropriate'.[219] In 2019–20, the Commission received eighty-five reviews for audit, and of the fifty-one audited, forty-nine (96 per cent) were compliant by the year end, following engagement with compliance staff. Work was ongoing with the remaining two employers to achieve compliance.[220] It is difficult to determine causation, but the figures show a broad trend of increasing Roman Catholic appointment to the monitored workforce, with their share increasing from 44.8 per cent in 2001 to 53.3 per cent in 2019.[221]

The Commission also plays a greater role in achieving compliance of the 'due regard' standard in section 75 of the Northern Ireland Act than its British counterpart. Unlike in Britain, the Commission is required to approve public authorities' equality schemes and check progress. This, too, has

[217] ibid arts 55–68.
[218] Equality Commission for Northern Ireland, 'Annual Report and Accounts 2019–20'.
[219] FETO, art 55.
[220] Equality Commission for Northern Ireland (n 218).
[221] Equality Commission for Northern Ireland, 'Annual Report and Accounts 2020–21'.

demonstrated a high rate of compliance. In 2019–20, of the 144 public authorities required to produce a scheme, as many as 94 per cent (135) submitted an annual progress report. In that year, the Commission provided feedback to fifty-seven public authorities in response to the report, as well as to two public authorities on the five-year review of their equality schemes. (This decreased in the subsequent year to 81 per cent (117), probably because of the Covid-19 pandemic.) The Commission similarly has the power to consider and investigate complaints against public authorities alleging that they have failed to comply with their equality schemes.[222] Two investigations conducted in response to complaints were concluded that year, and in both, the public authority was found to have failed to comply with its equality scheme. A third investigation, undertaken on the Commission's own initiative, found that the Department of Finance had not complied with its equality scheme in relation to the 2019 budget and a number of recommendations were made to improve practices.[223] The Commission has similar powers in relation to the Public Sector Disability Duty, which requires public authorities to produce a disability action plan and here, too, the Commission actively engages with public bodies to improve the quality of their measures.

The scale and effectiveness of Commission-led compliance has, however, been difficult to replicate in other jurisdictions, especially where there are larger numbers of employers to monitor and a lower level of political commitment. This can be seen in Canada. Under the Federal Employment Equity Act, federally regulated employers are required to develop and implement an employment equity programme in consultation and collaboration with employee representatives. The Canadian Human Rights Commission (CHRC) has the power to conduct compliance audits, negotiate undertakings, and issue directions. An on-site visit may occur during the validation process, and interviews with employees at all levels of the organization are conducted. Once validation is complete, employers receive an audit report with a letter confirming closure of the audit. Reflecting elements of the compliance pyramid, the Act specifies that non-compliance is to be resolved by focusing on persuasion, with directions to be issued as a last resort. In cases of non-compliance, an officer will negotiate a written undertaking from the employer to take specific remedial steps, with a specific deadline. Employers must then provide the Commission with proof that they have met all requirements of the Act. Although the Commission states that it always strives to

---

[222] Northern Ireland Act 1998, sch 9.
[223] Equality Commission for Northern Ireland (n 221).

work collaboratively with employers, it can apply enforcement measures if an employer is not complying, through issuing a letter of direction and, as a last resort, by referring the matter to the chairperson of the Canadian Human Rights Tribunal for an order confirming the direction.[224] The CHRC focuses on employers that have never been audited or have persistent gaps in representation. Since 2018, the CHRC has also been using a horizontal, issue-based approach to detect and potentially correct systemic discrimination. This entails examining an issue relevant to a particular designated group which has persistently low representation across many employers in a sector. As well as investigating specific employers' compliance, it aims to gather best practices and share them across the sector.

This raises the question of whether regulation based on a compliance pyramid can be effective. Writing in 2009, Agócs and Osborne were doubtful. According to them, the 'low-pressure and employer-friendly compliance review process was ostensibly designed to forestall employer resistance and win cooperation. . . . However, many employers continue in their previous pattern of . . . taking few steps towards compliance until the last possible moment. Once audited, many employers do not attain the goals they set for themselves.'[225] They attributed these low levels of compliance to a lack of meaningful sanctions. Has anything changed in the fifteen years since they made these observations? Agócs remains unconvinced. In many ways, the structure of the Act itself triggers the regulatory trilemma highlighted earlier. Under the Act, employers are fined for failing to file accurate annual reports but not for failing to develop and implement employment equity plans.[226] The result has been a focus on collecting and reporting workforce data, which, in Agócs's words, 'too often becomes a numbers game with little impact on real change.'[227] While some employers have taken employment equity seriously, others have preferred to use the narratives of diversity to 'enhance corporate images without making corporations accountable for taking action.'[228]

Analyses of progress towards employment equity is not encouraging. Data from the annual employment equity reports submitted by 595 employers

---

[224] <www.employmentequitychrc.ca/en/about-employment-equity-act> accessed 4 August 2022.
[225] C Agócs and B Osborne, 'Comparing Equity Policies in Canada and Northern Ireland: Policy Learning in Two Directions?' (2009) 35 Canadian Public Policy 237.
[226] C Agócs (ed), *Employment Equity in Canada: The Legacy of the Abella Report* (University of Toronto Press 2014) 308.
[227] <www.caut.ca/content/december-15-25-years-employment-equity-act> accessed 4 August 2022.
[228] ibid.

to the Canadian Minister of Labour in 2019 showed that the representation of women, indigenous people, and persons with disabilities remained static as compared with 2018, and in any event remained well below their respective labour market availability. The only real sign of progress relates to representation of members of racialized minorities, which has been consistently above their labour market availability since 2007, reaching 24.4 per cent in 2019.[229] The figure for women remained static at just over 39 per cent as against a labour market availability of 48.2 per cent; indigenous people at 2.3 per cent compared to labour market availability of 4 per cent; and persons with disabilities at 3.4 or 3.5 per cent compared to a 9.1 per cent availability.[230] One of the key reasons for low levels of success, Agócs suggests, is that other measures recommended by the original report proposing employment equity (the Abella Report) have not been implemented. She points especially to the failure to implement the recommendations on providing a national publicly funded childcare programme as essential for employment equity for women.[231] In addition, and crucially, she points to the importance of the democratic participation of stakeholders, especially members of groups who have experienced discrimination and exclusion and advocates for these groups.[232]

Proactive schemes can therefore be effective provided clear obligations of result are imposed on employers, and compliance mechanisms are properly resourced with meaningful sanctions that can operate as both an incentive and a deterrent. A particularly effective approach is to tie compliance closely to opportunities to gain lucrative State contracts.[233] In Canada, the Federal Contractors Programme requires organizations with contracts with the Canadian government to implement employment equity in their workplaces. It only applies to large employers with workforces of one hundred or more which have a federal government goods and services contract worth $1 million or over.[234] Contractors must collect workforce information on representation of four designated groups: women, indigenous people, persons with disabilities, and members of visible minorities. They should establish numerical goals, commence actions to identify and remove employment barriers,

---

[229] <www.canada.ca/en/employment-social-development/corporate/portfolio/labour/progr ams/employment-equity/reports/2020-annual.html#h2.7> accessed 4 August 2022.

[230] ibid.

[231] Agócs (n 226) 312.

[232] ibid 310.

[233] C McCrudden, *Buying Social Justice* (OUP 2007).

[234] <www.canada.ca/en/employment-social-development/corporate/portfolio/labour/progr ams/employment-equity/federal-contractors.html> accessed 4 August 2022.

and make reasonable efforts towards having a workforce representative of the four groups. At the end of 2019, 350 employers were covered. Compliance assessments are conducted after the first year and every three years thereafter to verify progress. In 2019, a total of 105 compliance assessments were completed with all contractors found to be in compliance.[235]

In the US, too, the threat to the economic well-being of private contractors by the sanction of withdrawal of lucrative federal contracts and debarment from future contracts have been regarded as crucial in securing the effectiveness of anti-discrimination laws. Known as contract compliance, this approach has had particular traction in the US, where it was introduced in 1961 by President Kennedy. Contract compliance requires contractors and subcontractors of the federal government (approximately one-fifth of the entire US labour force) to increase the representation of protected groups in their workforces as a condition for the award and the continuation of the contract.[236] Originally confined to race, these requirements have been extended to cover sex and religion.[237] In 2014, the programme was further amended to include a prohibition on federal contractors and subcontractors from discriminating against lesbian, gay, bisexual, and transgender employees and applicants.[238] There are also schemes for persons with disabilities and disabled war veterans.

Enforcement lies with the Office of Federal Contract Compliance Programs (OFCCP).[239] The OFCCP has a range of enforcement procedures, reflecting aspects of the enforcement pyramid. At the first stage, it offers compliance assistance and forms linkage agreements between contractors and job-training programmes to help employers identify and recruit qualified workers. At the second stage, it conducts compliance evaluations of personnel policies and procedures, investigates complaints, and monitors the progress of contractors and subcontractors in fulfilling the terms of their agreements through periodic compliance reports. The third stage involves responses to violations of regulatory requirements. At this stage, the OFCCP obtains conciliation agreements from those who are in violation and, where necessary, recommends enforcement actions to the Solicitor of Labour. The ultimate sanction is the loss of the company's federal contracts,

---

[235] <www.canada.ca/en/employment-social-development/corporate/portfolio/labour/progr ams/employment-equity/reports/2020-annual.html#h2.6.4> accessed 4 August 2022.
[236] Executive Order 10925.
[237] Executive Order 11246.
[238] Executive Order 13672, amending Executive Order 1124.
[239] <www.dol.gov/agencies/ofccp/about> accessed 4 August 2022.

or debarments. Relief to victims of discrimination, such as back pay for lost wages, may also be available.[240] OFCCP officials regard debarments as a last resort; they prefer to obtain compliance through conciliation agreements because, once debarred, contractors are no longer subject to the OFCCP's jurisdiction and therefore the worker protection it oversees. The result is that between 2010 and 2016, there was an average of fewer than one debarment per year.[241]

In the decade from 2011 to 2021, the OFCCP conducted compliance reviews of facilities with over 12.8 million workers, and obtained over $211 million in monetary relief for employees and job seekers who were discriminated against.[242] However, a report by the US Government Accountability Office in 2016 found that the OFCCP had no process to ensure that the tens of thousands of establishments which have signed a qualifying federal contract have complied with the contractual requirement that they should develop an affirmative action programme (AAP) within 120 days of the commencement of the contract, or updated it annually. According to the report, the OFCCP relies significantly on voluntary compliance by contractors because it is unable to conduct compliance evaluations for the large number of establishments within its jurisdiction. However, 'such an approach cannot ensure that contractors are complying with basic requirements like developing and maintaining an AAP'.[243] OFCCP data shows that as many as 85 per cent of contractors did not submit an AAP within thirty days of receiving a request from the OFCCP.[244] In response, the OFCCP is establishing a web-based interface to verify AAPs.[245] Supply and service contractors and subcontractors within the scheme were required to verify compliance for each of their establishments or lines of business by 30 June 2022. New contractors, who are obliged to develop their AAP within 120 days, must certify compliance within ninety days of developing their plan. Given that they may be subject to subsequent audit, contractors must continue to maintain their AAPs. Failure to comply can ultimately lead to debarment; and false certification can lead to serious civil and criminal penalties. It remains to be seen whether this promising new approach can ultimately improve the record of

---

[240] ibid.
[241] US Government Accountability Office (GAO), 'Strengthening Oversight Could Improve Federal Contractor Non Discrimination Compliance' (GAO-16-750, September 2016) 26.
[242] <www.dol.gov/agencies/ofccp/about/data/accomplishments> accessed 4 August 2022.
[243] US Government Accountability Office (n 241) 18.
[244] ibid 17–18.
[245] <www.dol.gov/agencies/ofccp/faqs/contractorportal#Q1> accessed 3 August 2022.

compliance. Certainly, it will need to overcome some resistance from the US Chamber of Commerce.[246]

Also of great importance in the US have been measures which make the grant of federal or State funds or contracts available to minority or women-owned businesses. As we saw in Chapter 7, a major vehicle for present-day set-aside programmes is section 8(a) of the Small Business Act, which reserves a proportion of federal contracting opportunities for small businesses owned by 'one or more socially and economically disadvantaged individuals'. The Act defines 'socially disadvantaged' individuals as 'those who have been subjected to racial or ethnic prejudice or cultural bias because of their identity as a member of a group without regard to their individual qualities'. There is a rebuttable presumption that members of certain groups are socially disadvantaged,[247] although individuals who do not belong to these groups may also prove social disadvantage. To be economically disadvantaged, individuals must fall below the thresholds set for net worth, income, and total assets. Other programmes provide similar opportunities for women-owned businesses. The Small Business Act establishes as a goal that 5 per cent of the total value of all prime contract and subcontract awards each fiscal year should be awarded to small business concerns owned and controlled by socially and economically disadvantaged individuals, with a similar goal of 5 per cent for participation by similar concerns owned and controlled by women. In recent years, the goal of 5 per cent to small disadvantaged businesses has generally been met: in the decade from 2010 to 2020, firms eligible under these 8(a) criteria were awarded about $313.962 billion in federal contracts, about 5.46 per cent of all federal contracts.[248] However, the federal government has had difficulty meeting the goal of 5 per cent to women-owned small businesses.[249]

Oversight of the 8(a) programme lies with the Small Business Administration (SBA), which is required to conduct annual reviews of 8(a) firms' progress towards achieving the targets in the business development plan, as well as checking for continued eligibility. However, its record is poor. A recent audit of a sample of twenty-five firms reviewed showed that as many as twenty should have been removed from the programme, based on

---

[246] US Chamber of Commerce, 'Right Mission, Wrong Tactics' (2017).

[247] Black Americans, Hispanic Americans, Native Americans, Asian Pacific Americans, and Subcontinent Asian Americans.

[248] Congressional Research Service, 'SBA's "8(a) Program" Overview, History, and Current Issues' (November 2021) 34–35.

[249] Congressional Research Service, 'An Overview of Small Business Contracting' (updated 17 November 2021).

'such issues as excessive income and lack of good character'.[250] This is despite the fact that eligibility concerns for some of these firms had been identified through its annual reviews.

V CONCLUSION

The introduction of proactive models into the arena of discrimination law holds much promise, as well as many new challenges. The architecture of proactive measures is increasingly visible, but the greatest challenge remains that of creating appropriate incentives, sanctions, and mechanisms for accountability to ensure that elaborate structures do not simply conceal apathy or proceduralism. Political commitment and goodwill, together with the active involvement of stakeholders, particularly trade unions and other representatives of those affected, are essential for success. The danger remains that the location of proactive measures on the borderline between law and politics makes it appear that fulfilment of such measures is discretionary or optional. The ultimate challenge is therefore to ensure that proactive measures are based on a recognition that equality is a fundamental right, not an optional policy.

In surveying the limits of law through the prism of enforcement, we have come full circle conceptually. What does equality mean, and what are we hoping to achieve? The questions asked in Chapter 1 have received a range of different answers. Indeed, it is not just the answers, but also the questions, which have changed. As equality law faces new and increasingly complex challenges, so the conceptual apparatus has been adjusted and its legal manifestations re-examined. But the responses, although innovative, have often represented incomplete solutions; progress has been evident, but uneven. Those dedicated to equality still face an exacting, but ultimately deeply rewarding, task.

---

[250] SBA OIG, 'Improvements Needed in SBA's Oversight of 8(a) Continuing Eligibility Processes', 4, 9; and see Congressional Research Service (n 248) 41.

Bibliography

Abram M, 'Affirmative Action: Fair Shakers and Social Engineers' (1986) 99 Harv L Rev 1312

Agócs C (ed), *Employment Equity in Canada: The Legacy of the Abella Report* (University of Toronto Press 2014)

Alexy R, *A Theory of Constitutional Rights* (OUP 2004)

Agócs C and Osborne B, 'Comparing Equity Policies in Canada and Northern Ireland: Policy Learning in Two Directions?' (2009) 35 Canadian Public Policy 237

Ambedkar B, *Dr Babasaheb Ambedkar: Writings and Speeches* (Government of Maharashtra 1979–2003)

Ambedkar B, *What Congress and Gandhi Have Done to the Untouchables* (Gautam Book Centre 2009 [1945])

Ansari H, *The Infidel Within: British Muslims since 1800* (C Hurst & Co 2004)

Atrey S, *Intersectional Discrimination* (OUP 2019)

Barua A, 'Revisiting the Ghandi–Ambedkar Debates over Caste' (2018) 25 J Human Values 25

B-BBEE Commission, 'National Status and Trends on Broad-Based Black Economic Empowerment' (2020)

Bell D, *Silent Covenants* (OUP 2004)

Bellace J, 'Equal Pay in the United States' in F Eyraud (ed), *Equal Pay Protection in Industrialized Market Economies* (International Labour Office 1993)

Berlin I, *The Long Emancipation: The Demise of Slavery* (Harvard UP 2015)

Berrey E, Nelson R, and Nielson L, *Rights on Trial: How Workplace Discrimination Law Perpetuates Inequality* (University of Chicago Press 2017)

Bhuwania A, *Courting the People* (CUP 2017)

Black J, 'Constitutionalising Self Regulation' (1996) 59 Modern L Rev 24

Black J, 'Proceduralising Regulation, Part II' (2001) 21 OJLS 33

Braithwaite J, *Restorative Justice and Responsive Regulation* (OUP 2002)

Burger R and others, 'The Middle Class in Contemporary South Africa' (2014) Stellenbosch Economic Working Paper 11

Butler J, *Undoing Gender* (Routledge 2004)

Campbell M, 'CEDAW and Women's Intersecting Identities: A Pioneering Approach to Intersectional Discrimination' (2015) Revista Direito GV 479

Callaghan G, 'Intervenors at the Supreme Court of Canada' (2020) 43 Dalhousie LJ

Carpenter M, 'Intersex Human Rights, Sexual Orientation, Gender Identity, Sex Characteristics and the Yogyakarta Principles plus 10' [2020] Culture, Health and Sexuality 1

Chant S, "Rethinking the Feminisation of Poverty" (2006) 7 Journal of Development and Capabilities 201-220

Chant S, ' The 'Feminisation of Poverty' and the 'Feminisation' of Anti-Poverty Programmes: Room for Revision?' [2008] 43 Journal of Development Studies 165-197

Chayes A, 'The Role of the Judge in Public Law Litigation' (1976) 89 Harv L Rev 1281

E. Clark, 'Enforcement of the Americans with Disabilities Act: Remedying "Abusive" Litigation While Strengthening Disability Rights ' (2020) 26 Washington and Lee Journal of Civil Rights and Social Justice

Cock J, 'Trapped Workers: Constraints and Contradictions Experienced by Black Women in Contemporary South Africa' (1987) 10 Women's Studies Int Forum 133

Collins K, 'Equality, Sovereignty, and the Family in Morales-Santana' (2017) 131 Harv L Rev 170

Collins P, *Black Feminist Thought: Knowledge, Consciousness, and the Politics of Empowerment* (Routledge 2000)

Crenshaw K, "Demarginalising the intersection of race and sex" (1989) University of Chicago Legal Forum 139

Crenshaw K and others, 'Introduction' in K Crenshaw and others (eds), *Seeing Race Again: Countering Colourblindness across the Disciplines* (University of California Press 2019)

Darity W, Addo F, and Smith I, 'A Subaltern Middle Class: The Case of the Missing "Black Bourgeoisie" in America' (2020) 39 Contemporary Economic Policy 494

de Beauvoir S, *The Second Sex* (new edn, Vintage Digital 2014)

Degener T, 'Disability in a Human Rights Context' (2016) 5 Laws 35

Delgado R and Stefancic J, *Critical Race Theory* (New York UP 2001)

DeSchutter O, 'Three Models of Equality and European Anti-Discrimination Law' (2006) 57 Northern Ireland Legal Quarterly 1

Dickens L, 'The Road is Long: Thirty Years of Employment Discrimination Legislation in Britain' (2007) 45 British J Industrial Relations 463

Dutta D, 'No Work is Easy!: Notes from the Field on Unpaid Care Work for Women' in R Bhogal (ed), *Mind the Gap: The State of Employment in India* (Oxfam India 2019)

Edelman L, *Working Law: Courts, Corporations and Symbolic Civil Rights* (University of Chicago Press 2016)

Ely JH, *Democracy and Distrust: A Theory of Judicial Review* (Harvard UP 1980)

England P, Levine A, and Mishel E, 'Progress Toward Gender Equality in the United States has Slowed or Stalled' (2020) 117 PNAS 6990

Fauconnier A and Mathur-Helm B, 'Black Economic Empowerment in the South African Mining Industry' (2008) 39 South African J Business Management 1

Fiss O, 'The Forms of Justice' (1979) 93 Harv L Rev 1

Fredman S, *Women and the Law* (OUP 1997)

Fredman S, *Human Rights Transformed: Positive Rights and Positive Duties* (OUP 2008)

Fredman S, 'Making Equality Effective: The Role of Proactive Measures' (2009) Oxford Legal Studies Research Paper No 53/2010

Fredman S, 'Breaking the Mold: Equality as a Proactive Duty' (2012) 60 American J Comparative Law 265

Fredman S, 'Emerging from the Shadows: Substantive Equality and Article 14 of the European Convention on Human Rights' (2016) 16 Human Rights L Rev 273

Fredman S, *Intersectional Discrimination in EU Gender Equality and Non-Discrimination Law* (European Commission: European Network of Legal Experts in Gender Equality and Non-Discrimination 2016)

Fredman S, *Comparative Human Rights Law* (OUP 2018)

Fredman S, 'Tolerating the Intolerant: Religious Freedom, Complicity and the Right to Equality' [2020] Oxford J Law and Religion 1

Fredman S, 'Redistribution and Recognition: Reconciling Inequalities' (2007) 23 South African Journal on Human Rights 214 -234

Friedan B, *The Feminine Mystique* (Penguin 1963)

Fukuda-Parr S, 'Keeping out Extreme Inequality from the SDG Agenda - The Politics of Indicators' (2019) 10 Global Policy 61

Grammond S, *Identity Captured by Law* (McGill-Queen's UP 2009)

Greenstein J, 'Narratives of global convergence and the power of choosing a measure' (2020) 48 Oxford Development Studies 100

Habermas J and Rehg W, *Between Facts and Norms: Contributions to a Discourse Theory of Law and Democracy* (Polity Press 1996)

Hassim S, ' "A Conspiracy of Women": The Women's Movement in South Africa's Transition to Democracy' (2002) 69 Social Research 693

Hepple B, *Equality: The New Legal Framework* (Hart Publishing 2011)

Hepple B, Coussey M, and Choudhury T, *Equality: A New Framework Report of the Independent Review of the Enforcement of UK Anti-Discrimination Legislation* (Hart Publishing 2000)

Himanshu H, 'Widening Gaps: India Inequality Report 2018' (Oxfam India) <https://socialprotection-humanrights.org/resource/india-inequality-report-2018-widening-gaps/> accessed 15 October 2020

Irwin L, 'Freedom, Law, and Prophecy: A Brief History of Native American Religious Resistance' (1997) 21 American Indian Quarterly

Jaising I, 'Gender Justice and the Supreme Court' in B Kirpal and others (eds), *Supreme but not Infallible* (OUP 2000)

Kant I, 'Groundwork of the Metaphysics of Morals' in Gregor M and Wood A (eds), *Practical Philosophy: The Cambridge edition of the works of Immanuel Kant 1724 –1904* (Cambridge University Press 1996)

Khaitan T, *A Theory of Discrimination Law* (OUP 2015)

Koshan J and Hamilton J, 'The Continual Reinvention of Section 15 of the Charter' (2013) 64 University of New Brunswick LJ 19

Krishnaswami C and Krishnamurthi G, 'Title VII and Caste Discrimination' (2021) 134 Harv L Rev 456

Kruger R, 'Small Steps to Equal Dignity: The Work of the South African Equality Courts' (2011) 7 Equal Rights Rev 27

Lacey N, *Unspeakable Subjects: Feminist Essays in Legal and Social Theory* (Hart Publishing 1998)

MacKinnon C, Feminism Unmodified (Harvard UP 1987) 34

McCann M, *Rights at Work: Pay Equity Reform and the Politics of Legal Mobilization* (University of Chicago Press 1994)

McCann C, Tomaskovic-Devey D, and Badgett M, 'Employer's Responses to Sexual Harassment' (Centre for Employment Equity, University of Massachusetts

Amherst) <www.umass.edu/employmentequity/employers-responses-sexual-har assment> accessed 17 November 2021

McDermott P, 'Equal Pay in Canada' in F Eyraud (ed), *Equal Pay Protection in Industrialized Market Economies* (International Labour Office 1993)

McLaughlin J, 'Falling Between the Cracks: Discrimination Laws and Older Women' (2020) 34 Labour 215

Mehrotra I, 'Inequality and Rural Employment: Agrarian Distress and Dalit Women' in R Bhogal (ed), *Mind the Gap: The State of Employment in India* (Oxfam India 2019)

Minow M, *In Brown's Wake* (OUP 2010)

Mondal B and others, 'Women Workers in India ' (2018) CSE Working Papers 3

Moreau S, 'In Defense of a Liberty-based Account of Discrimination' in Hellman D and Moreau S (eds), *Philosophical Foundations of Discrimination Law* (OUP 2013)

Morris J, 'Impairment and Disability: Constructing an Ethics of Care Which Promotes Human Rights' (2001) 16 Hypatia: A Journal of Feminist Philosophy 1

Muslim Council of Britain, *British Muslims in Numbers* (2015) (<www.mcb.org.uk/wp-content/uploads/2015/02/MCBCensusReport_2015.pdf>)

Neumark D, 'Age Discrimination Legislation in the United States' (2003) 21 Contemporary Economic Policy 297

Nonet P and Selznick P, *Law and Society in Transition: Toward Responsive Law* (Harper & Row 1978)

Otto D, 'Queering Gender [Identity] in International Law' (2015) 33 Nordic J Human Rights 299

Pay Equity Taskforce, *Pay Equity: A New Approach to a Fundamental Right* (2004)

Parfit D, "Equality and Priority" (1997) 10 Ratio 202

Phillips A, *The Politics of Presence* (Clarendon Press 1995)

Piketty T, *Capital in the Twenty-first century* (Harvard University Press 2013)

Porter B, 'Expectations of Equality' (2006) 33 Supreme Court L Rev 23

Raz J, 'On the value of distributional equality' in De Wijze S, Kramer MH and Carter I (eds), *Hillel Steiner and the Anatomy of Justice: Themes and Challenges* (Routledge 2009)

Rogan M and Alfers L, 'Gender Inequalities in the South African Informal Economy' (2019) 33 Agenda 91

Rosenberg G, *The Hollow Hope* (2nd edn, University of Chicago Press 2008)

Roy S and Mukhopadhyay P, 'What Matters for Urban Women's Work' in R Bhogal (ed), *Mind the Gap: The State of Employment in India* (Oxfam India 2019)

Sachar R, 'Social, Economic and Educational Status of the Muslim Community of India', Prime Minister's High Level Committee (2006) <www.minorityaffairs.gov.in/sites/default/files/sachar_comm.pdf> accessed 18 October 2020

Scott C, 'Regulation in the Age of Governance: The Rise of the Post-Regulatory State' in J Jordana and D Levi-Faur (eds), *The Politics of Regulation* (Edward Elgar 2004)

Schultz V, 'Reconceptualizing Sexual Harassment, Again' (2018) 128 Yale Law Journal

Seljak D, 'Protecting Religious Freedom in a Multicultural Canada' (2012) 9 Diversity Magazine

Sen A, *Development as Freedom* (OUP 1999)

Serano J, *Whipping Girl: A Transexual Woman on Sexism and the Scapegoating of Femininity* (Seal Press 2016)

Shakespeare T and Watson N, 'The Social Model of Disability: An Outdated Ideology?' in S Barnartt and B Altman (eds), *Exploring Theories and Expanding Methodologies: Where We Are and Where We Need to Go* (Research in Social Science and Disability), vol 2 (Emerald Group 2001)

Sharpe R and Roach K, *The Charter of Rights and Freedoms* (3rd edn, Irwin Law 2005)

Shava E, 'Black Economic Empowerment in South Africa: Challenges and Prospects' (2016) 8 J Economics and Behavioural Studies 161

Stephenson M, 'Mainstreaming Equality in an Age of Austerity: What Impact has the Public Sector Equality Duty had on Work to Promote Gender Equality by English Local Authorities?' (DPhil thesis, University of Warwick 2016)

Streeck W, 'From Market Making to State Building' in S Liebfried and P Pierson (eds), *European Social Policy* (Brookings Institution 1995)

Teubner G, 'Substantive and Reflexive Elements in Modern Law' (1983) 17 Law and Society Rev 239

Teubner G, 'After Privatization: The Many Autonomies of Private Law' (1998) 51 Current Legal Problems

Tribe L, '*Lawrence v Texas*: The "Fundamental Right" That Dare not Speak Its Name' (2004) 116 Harv L Rev 1893

Vanhala L, *Making Rights a Reality?* (CUP 2010)

Yang R and Liu J, 'Strengthening Accountability for Discrimination' (2021) Economic Policy Institute, Washington DC <https://epi.org/218473> accessed 2 November 2021

Yoshino K, 'The New Equal Protection' (2011) 124 Harv L Rev 747

Young I, 'Communication and the Other: Beyond Deliberative Democracy' in S Benhabib (ed), *Democracy and Difference: Contesting the Boundaries of the Political* (Princeton Paperbacks 1996)

Young IM, Justice and the Politics of Difference (Princeton UP 1990)

Index

For the benefit of digital users, indexed terms that span two pages (e.g., 52–53) may, on occasion, appear on only one of those pages.

Please see main entries for entries on particular countries (eg India)